THE NEW EVOLUTIONARY SOCIOLOGY

For decades, evolutionary analysis was overlooked or altogether ignored by sociologists. Fears and biases persisted nearly a century after Auguste Comte gave the discipline its name, as did concerns that its effect would only reduce sociology to another discipline—whether biology, psychology, or economics. Worse, apprehension that the application of evolutionary theory would encourage heightened perceptions of racism, sexism, ethnocentrism, and reductionism pervaded.

Turner and Machalek argue instead for a new embrace of biology and evolutionary analysis. Sociology, from its very beginnings in the early 19th century, has always been concerned with the study of evolution, particularly the transformation of societies from simple to ever-more complex forms. By comprehensively reviewing the original ways that sociologists applied evolutionary theory and examining the recent renewal and expansion of these early approaches, the authors confront the challenges posed by biology, neuroscience, and psychology to distinct evolutionary approaches within sociology. They emerge with key theoretical and methodological discoveries that demonstrate the critical—and compelling—case for a dramatically enriched sociology that incorporates all forms of comparative evolutionary analysis to its canon and study of sociocultural phenomena.

Jonathan H. Turner is 38th University Professor, University of California System; Research Professor, University of California, Santa Barbara; and Distinguished Professor of the Graduate Division, University of California, Riverside. He is also Director of the Institute for Theoretical Social Science, Santa Barbara, CA, USA.

Richard S. Machalek is Professor Emeritus of Sociology at the University of Wyoming. His work addresses the evolution of social behavior among both human and non-human species. He analyzes phenomena such as the evolution of societal complexity among both humans and the eusocial insects, the evolution of expropriative social behaviors across species lines, emergent properties of both human and non-human societies, the evolved human psychology implicated in reciprocity and exchange, and theoretical points of convergence and divergence between sociology and sociobiology. His publications have appeared in venues such as *Sociological Theory*, the *American Journal of Sociology, Advances in Group Processes, Rationality and Society, Advances in Human Ecology* and various encyclopedias, handbooks, and other edited volumes. He is co-editor (with Jonathan H. Turner and Alexandra Maryanski) of *Handbook on Evolution and Society: Toward an Evolutionary Social Science* (Routledge).

The New Evolutionary Sociology is the most recent and comprehensive treatment of the bridge between evolutionary biology and the principles of sociology.
Edward O. Wilson, *University Research Professor Emeritus, Harvard University*

This volume is on the cutting edge in the effort to develop explanations of human sociocultural evolution within a comparative framework that includes biology, neuroscience, non-human sociology as well as anthropology, sociology and the comparative world-systems perspective. The chapters on the emergence of non-human social complexity are original contributions that should be of interest to all scholars and students in the comparative social sciences.
Christopher Chase-Dunn, *Distinguished Professor of Sociology, University of California-Riverside*

Turner and Machalek offer insightful assessments of several distinctive approaches to what they call the new evolutionary sociology. These perspectives are compatible only in varying degrees, and some of them certainly have generated more coherent explanations of human social behavior. All told the volume has great merit, especially if it encourages readers to shed the blinders of disciplinary chauvinism, to pursue a serious rapprochement with relevant aspects of evolutionary biology, and to begin to realize the promise of a genuinely scientific sociology.
Timothy Crippen, *Professor of Sociology, University of Mary Washington*

The New Evolutionary Sociology by Turner and Machalek is clearly the best treatment available about the important and exceedingly relevant topic of human sociocultural evolution. The authors discuss in detail how sociologists have used evolutionary paradigms in a variety of different investigations. In addition, they discuss many of the challenges posed by biology and sociobiology and other disciplines. They also introduce several examples of special utility they have used in their studies of evolutionary patterns and social phenomena. Turner and Machalek are clearly the experts in evolutionary sociology. Their new book is written lucidly and authoritatively. I recommend this important book with the greatest enthusiasm.
Dudley L. Poston, Jr., *Professor of Sociology, Texas A&M University*

Evolutionary Analysis in the Social Sciences
A series edited by Jonathan H. Turner and Kevin J. McCaffree

This new series is devoted to capturing the full range of scholarship and debate over how best to conduct evolutionary analyses on human behavior, interaction, and social organization. The series will range across social science disciplines and offer new cutting-edge theorizing in sociobiology, evolutionary psychology, stage-modeling, co-evolution, cliodynamics, and evolutionary biology.

Published:

The New Evolutionary Sociology: Recent and Revitalized Theoretical Approaches
by Jonathan H. Turner and Richard S. Machalek (2018)

The Emergence and Evolution of Religion: By Means of Natural Selection
by Jonathan H. Turner, Alexandra Maryanski, Anders Klostergaard Petersen, and Armin W. Geertz (2017)

Forthcoming:

The Evolution of World-Systems
by Christopher Chase-Dunn

The New Evolutionary Sociology

Recent and Revitalized Theoretical and Methodological Approaches

Jonathan H. Turner
University of California, Santa Barbara

Richard S. Machalek
University of Wyoming

NEW YORK AND LONDON

First published 2018
by Routledge
711 Third Avenue, New York, NY 10017

and by Routledge
2 Park Square, Milton Park, Abingdon, Oxon OX14 4RN

Routledge is an imprint of the Taylor & Francis Group, an informa business

© 2018 Taylor & Francis

The right of Jonathan H. Turner and Richard Machalek to be identified as the authors of this work has been asserted by them in accordance with sections 77 and 78 of the Copyright, Designs and Patents Act 1988.

All rights reserved. No part of this book may be reprinted or reproduced or utilised in any form or by any electronic, mechanical, or other means, now known or hereafter invented, including photocopying and recording, or in any information storage or retrieval system, without permission in writing from the publishers.

Trademark notice: Product or corporate names may be trademarks or registered trademarks, and are used only for identification and explanation without intent to infringe.

Library of Congress Cataloging-in-Publication Data
Names: Turner, Jonathan H., author. | Machalek, Richard, 1946– author.
Title: The new evolutionary sociology : recent and revitalized theoretical and methodological approaches / by Jonathan H. Turner, University of California, Santa Barbara, Richard Machalek, University of Wyoming.
Description: 1 Edition. | New York : Routledge, Taylor & Francis Group, [2018] | Series: Evolutionary analysis in the social sciences | Includes bibliographical references and index.
Identifiers: LCCN 2017051545 | ISBN 9780815386117 (hb) | ISBN 9780815387084 (pb) | ISBN 9781351173889 (e)
Subjects: LCSH: Social evolution—Philosophy. | Human evolution—Philosophy. | Human ecology. | Social ecology.
Classification: LCC HM626 .T87 2018 | DDC 303.4—dc23
LC record available at https://lccn.loc.gov/2017051545

ISBN: 978-0-8153-8611-7 (hbk)
ISBN: 978-0-8153-8708-4 (pbk)
ISBN: 978-1-3511-7388-9 (ebk)

Typeset in Minion
by Apex CoVantage, LLC

Contents

List of Figures	ix
List of Tables	xi
Acknowledgements	xii
1 A Brief History of Evolutionary Analysis in Sociology	1
PART I: THE CONTINUING SOCIOLOGICAL TRADITION	15
2 Can Functionalism Be Saved? Toward a More Viable Form of Evolutionary Theorizing	17
3 Stage-Model Theories of Societal Evolution	37
4 Intersocietal Models of Societal Evolution	72
5 New Forms of Ecological Theorizing in Evolutionary Sociology	99
PART II: DARWINIAN ANALYSIS AND ALTERNATIVES	119
6 The Evolution of Social Behavior by Natural Selection	121
7 The Rise of Sociobiology	144
8 Sociobiology and Human Behavior	164
9 Evolutionary Psychology and the Search for the Adapted Mind	214
10 The Limitations of Darwinian Analysis	246
11 New Models of Natural Selection in Sociocultural Evolution	260

PART III: NEW DARWINIAN APPROACHES WITHIN SOCIOLOGY — 291

12 New Forms of Comparative Sociology: What Primates Can Tell Sociology About Humans — 293

13 In Search of Human Nature: Using the Tools of Cross-Species Comparative Analysis — 309

14 The Evolution of the Human Brain: Applications of Neurosociology — 337

15 Cross-Species Comparative Sociology — 365

16 Cross-Species Analysis of Megasociality — 396

17 The Behavioral and Interpersonal Basis of Megasociality: Evidence From Primates — 412

Epilogue: Prospect for a New Evolutionary Sociology — 424

Bibliography — 431

Index — 457

Figures

2.1	Bronislaw Malinowski's Portrayal of Functional Requisites at Different System Levels	23
3.1	Auguste Comte's Implicit Model of Evolutionary Dynamics in Societies	38
3.2	Herbert Spencer's Model of Selection Pressures Driving Societal Evolution	42
3.3	Parsons' Image of Societal Evolution Up to Modernity	54
3.3a	Primitive Societies	54
3.3b	Intermediate Societies	56
3.3c	Transition to Modern Societies	57
3.4	Lenski's Early Model of Forces Driving Evolution of Societies and Their Stratification	61
3.5a	The Basic Biological Problem	63
3.5b	The Sociological Paradigm in Evolutionary Analysis	64
3.5c	Sociocultural Paradigm Over Time	65
4.1	Christopher Chase-Dunn's Iteration Model of Intersocietal Dynamics	79
4.2	Predictions of Demographic-Structural Theory	90
5.1	Somewhat Abstracted Version of Emile Durkheim's Ecological Model	101
5.2	Early Model of Urban Ecology	105
5.3	More Recent Abstracted Model of Urban Ecology	106
5.4	The Core Elements of Darwinian Theory in Organizational Ecology Models	108
5.5	Michael Hannan's and John Freeman's Organizational Ecology Model	109
5.6	J. Miller McPherson's Ecological Model Organizational Ecology in Blau-space	111
5.7	Core Elements of Amos Hawley's Ecological Model of Societies	113
5.8	Amos Hawley's Expanded Ecological Model of Societal Evolution	114

10.1	Limitations in the Models of Sociobiology and Evolutionary Psychology	247
10.2	Levels of Selection in the Sociocultural Universe	253
11.1	Darwinian Selection and the "Modern Synthesis" in Biology	262
11.2	Type-1 Spencerian Selection Pressures	268
11.3	Type-2 Spencerian Selection From Geopolitics (and Geoeconomics)	271
11.4	Durkheimian Selection Among Corporate Units Within Societies	275
11.5	Marxian Selection and Institutional Change	285
14.1	Key Areas of the Bralin During Hominin and Human Evolution	339

Tables

11.1	Darwinian Selection Among Organisms	261
11.2	Selection in the Absence of Fitness-Enhancing Variants: Spencerian Type-1 Selection	268
11.3	Spencerian Selection, Type-2, From Geopolitics and Geoeconomics	271
11.4	Durkheimian Selection on Corporate Units and Multi-Level Evolution	274
11.5	Generalized Symbolic Media of Institutional Domains	278
11.6	Marxian Selection and Institutional Change	284
12.1	A Cladistic Analysis of Extant Great Apes	298
12.2	Relative Numbers of Species of Primates in the Primate Order	302
14.1	Relative Size of Brain Components of Apes and Humans, Compared to *Tenrecidae*	348
14.2	Hard-Wired Pre-Adaptations and Behavioral Propensities of the Last Common Ancestor to Humans and Great Apes	353

Acknowledgements

I (RSM) am thankful for the innumerable conversations about evolution and social behavior that I have enjoyed with colleagues, coauthors, students, and friends over the years. I am especially grateful to Paul B. Robertson and Edward O. Wilson for their guidance and encouragement as I began my sojourn into evolutionary biology. They have been wise mentors, supportive colleagues, and good friends, but of course I would expect no less from my fellow Southerners. I am also grateful to the late Joseph Lopreato who eventually convinced me that I could pursue my interest in sociobiology without having to forego a career in sociology. Donna A. Barnes, also a sociologist and my wife, may not share the strength of my conviction about the value of "this view of life" for sociological analysis, but she has been mercifully tolerant of the many uninvited Darwinian lectures that I have inflicted on her over the years. More importantly, I am grateful for our collaboration which has yielded two fitness investments, our wonderful sons Travis Barnes Machalek and Max Cameron Machalek. Finally, in recent years I have learned not to take for granted a university administration that honors and supports the liberal arts in general and sociology in particular. Accordingly, I express my gratitude to Tom Buchanan, Myron Allen, and Ollie Walter for their support of liberal arts teaching and scholarship, even though, admittedly, such pursuits rarely offer much promise in yielding clean coal or safe fracking.

1
A Brief History of Evolutionary Analysis in Sociology

Evolutionary Analysis and the Emergence of Sociology

Sociology emerged as a distinctive discipline with Auguste Comte's reluctant use of the Latin-Greek hybrid, *sociology*, to describe the new science of society in his *Course in Positive Philosophy* (1830–1842). In Comte's analysis on the origins of this new positivistic science, evolutionary ideas were a central part of his vision for sociology. Even in the decades before Charles Darwin's (1859) epic statement on evolution by natural selection, the idea of evolution was in the intellectual air for the whole of the 19th Century. Comte had visualized thought and idea systems in societies as evolving through three stages—the theological, metaphysical, and positivist—and, for him, the positivistic stage required the application of science—its theoretical and methodological tenets—to the analysis of human societies. This science was to evolve out of biology in his famous hierarchy of the sciences, with sociology becoming the "queen science"—a rather bold statement that only makes sense if we view Comte as trying to justify and legitimate sociology's desire to be present at the table of science. Comte's model of science was, in fact, more in tune with Newtonian physics, which is why he wanted to name the new science of society *social physics*. His view was that social physicists could formulate abstract laws, like Newton equations on gravity, but most of his actual analysis was evolutionary and involved developing an organismic analogy in which the properties and dynamics of societies could be viewed as similar to those among individual organisms. This organismic analogy was later adopted by Herbert Spencer, who was to write a great multiple-volume treatise on biology just before his *The Principles of Sociology* (1984–1896), and with Spencer, the study of *superorganisms*—that is, the organization of organisms—began with the organismic analogy and moved to an evolutionary view of human-based superorganisms, or societies, as evolving from simple to ever-more complex forms in terms of laws and principles that reflected more the physics than the biology of his time. Evolution was, for Spencer, a movement from relative homogeneity to more complexity, and this basic law of evolution could be applied to not only the sociological realm but also the physical, psychological, biological, societal, and even ethical realms of the universe.

Also emerging with the organismic analogy and modeling of the stages of evolution from simple to more complex societies was sociology's first theoretical perspective: functionalism. As with the human body, the parts of societies as they evolved can be analyzed in terms of their functions or how they operate to sustain the "body social" or superorganism.

These lines of thinking are, to varying degrees, still with sociology today. The organismic analogy has receded, although some have sought to revive this idea (Dunn 2016: 216), and whether or not such efforts prove successful, a new kind of evolutionary sociology has emerged that encompasses the stage modeling and functionalism that were once so prominent in the discipline. Stage modeling of evolution died in sociology in the first decades of the 20th Century, and the functionalism that accompanies such modeling also appeared to die, but as we will see in Part I, both of these traditions made dramatic come backs in the middle decades of the 20th Century.

Within functionalist theorizing and stage modeling came another theoretical perspective that never disappeared: ecological analysis. Emile Durkheim explicitly included ideas of natural selection borrowed from Darwin in *The Division of Labor in Society* (1893), arguing that the driving forces of social differentiation (or social speciation) revolve around population growth, increasing niche density (material and moral), escalating competition, and more intense selection leading to specialization (or social speciation). This approach was adopted in the early 20th Century and has never left the discipline.

A final approach always evident in early sociology was implicit notions of "human nature." Virtually all sociologists hold at least implicit ideas about the biological nature of humans and what motivates and drives them. Indeed, much early sociology was concerned with the "pathologies" of modernity, and these pathologies were conceptualized as social conditions that violate human nature. This approach has also continued to the present, often under the guise of "critical sociology," which makes many of the same assumptions as early sociologists about the pathologies in modernism, capitalism, and post-modernisms from the perspective of how they go against implicit, sometimes explicit, conceptions of human nature.

Thus, the history of evolutionary thinking began with (1) functionalism, an approach derived from the organismic analogy; (2) stage modeling of societies as they grow and differentiate, another idea borrowed from the organismic analogy; (3) ecological analysis, which comes closest to Darwin's' great insight into natural selection; and (4) speculations on the nature of humans as biological entities that can either be supported or violated by the nature of societies. In this chapter, we will review these early approaches and, in Part I of this book, see how they "evolved" over the last half of the 20th Century and into the 21st Century. We will also outline more recent developments in evolutionary thinking in sociology that will be examined in Parts II and III of this book.

The Rise, Demise, Rebirth, and Then Apparent Demise, Once Again, of Functionalism

As noted above, the organismic analogies developed by Comte and Spencer naturally led to a kind of functional analysis in which, to use Spencer's term, *superorganisms* (i.e., the organization of organisms) can be analyzed by assessing how particular parts operate to meet their basic needs for survival. Spencer did not quite phrase the matter in this way, but this is how his ideas have been interpreted, and the result was functionalism in which social systems are seen to have requisites or functional needs that had to be met in order for a system organizing organisms to remain viable in its environment. Emile Durkheim (1893) continued Spencer's functional approach in more muted form, but by the end of 1895, Durkheim clearly had doubts about its utility.

Because functionalism was associated with models on the stages of societal evolution from simple to more complex forms, the ethnocentric biases of such models doomed them to banishment from most social science in the first two decades of the 20th Century. And, as stage modeling became taboo, so did functionalism. The result that, except among anthropologists, both functionalism and stage models disappeared from social science from the second to fifth and sixth decades of the 20th Century. Then, they both came back into sociology, just as they began to decline in anthropology. Stage modeling has continued to flourish, and functionalism seemingly disappeared, but in fact, it still exists but in a dramatically altered form that eliminates some of the problems inherent with traditional functional analysis. Chapter 2 will tell this story in much greater detail, documenting how a revised form of functionalism can still be an important part of the new evolutionary sociology.

The Rise, Demise, and Rebirth of Stage Models of Societal Evolution

Even scholars outside the functionalist tradition initiated by Comte, Spencer, and Durkheim adopted evolutionary thinking in this sense: Societies move through stages from relative simplicity to more complex forms. In Karl Marx's scheme, the stages of history move from "primitive communism" through slavery (horticulture and early agrarianism) and feudalism to capitalism and, then, to communism, with each revealing their own laws of organization. For Marx, evolution is driven by the inherent contradictions inhering in each stage after primitive communism except, of course, the final "end of history" argument about the collapse of capitalism and the emergence of Marx's communist utopia. Even Max Weber, who was highly suspicious of any model outlining an inevitable march of history, implicitly suggested evolutionary sequences from various forms of horticulture and agrarianism to capitalism where, in contrast to Marx, the "rationalization of social life" under rational-legal authority would be orderly but without much emotion and life-blood for humans.

Thus, as will be outlined in more detail in Chapter 2, early sociology was built around a sometimes explicit, but almost always implicit, view of stages of development of societies, especially as anthropological and other accounts of pre-literate societies poured into European scholarship. And thus, by the turn into the 20th Century, at least the metaphor of evolution from simple to complex was part of sociology. As so, as sociological analysis focused on the great transformations associated with industrialization and urbanization that were dramatically changing the social universe, it sought to explain these as evolving out of agrarianism. Even scholars such as Georg Simmel (1906) and George Herbert Mead (1934), who are not normally associated with evolutionary analysis, implicitly adopted the view of society as moving from simple to more complex forms and, thereby altering the historical pattern of group affiliations and the nature of self.

Within sociology, however, stage modeling of societal evolution in sociology suddenly came to an end by the end of the second decade of the 20th Century, for several reasons. One was the ethnocentrism and, indeed, outright racism of many models that saw pre-literate societies as "primitive" when compared to the "civilized" world of European societies. Moreover, all societal evolution was viewed as moving toward the "civilized" state of European society, which is somewhat ironic given the ravages of World War I that were about to explode such myths. Another was the emergence of Social Darwinism (really Social Spencerianism) and eugenics, which legitimated racism in the analysis of stage models but, even worse, the continued mistreatment of the disadvantaged in societies because they could be seen as "less fit" which captured the basic law of evolution in Spencer's (1851) view of "the survival of the fittest." For the next decades, evolutionary thinking was, in essence, banned from sociology; moreover, biological ideas were viewed with hostility about, not only their potential for racism but also reductionism of sociological models of human organization to those from biology. Thus, rather than emerging from biology in Comte's illusionary scheme, sociology was in danger of being ostracized by the application of any idea from biology.

Stage models continued in anthropology, as did functionalism, and both re-emerged in American and later European sociology around the midpoint of the 20th Century. Functionalism became the dominant theoretical approach for a brief period in the 1950s and early 1960s (e.g., Parsons 1951; Parsons et al. 1953), while stage modeling was re-established in the 1960s (e.g., Lenski 1964; Parsons 1964, 1965) and, as we will see in Chapter 3, has become more firmly institutionalized in the discipline over the last five decades. These later views of societal evolution have incorporated more Darwinian and ecological ideas compared to early stage models of evolution postulated by the founders of sociology.

Even though it was Herbert Spencer (1851) who coined the Darwinian-sounding phrase, "survival of the fittest," years before Darwin published *On the Origins of Species*, most early sociological analysis was not Darwinian. Yet, while Spencer's emphasis on competition and selection (out) of the unfit influenced not only later Social Darwinism, Emile Durkheim's adoption of Darwin's ideas created yet another form of evolutionary analysis in sociology: social ecology.

Models of Social Ecology

Spencer often used the phrase "survival of the fittest" to describe warfare among societies, with the larger, more productive, and organized society generally winning wars and, as a consequence, incorporating the less organized or "fit" society into its institutional structure. As a result, the general level of complexity of societies had been driven by war, as the more fit societies conquered the less fit (because they were better organized). Spencer's argument implies an ecological view of the social universe. Like organisms, superorganisms or societies compete with each other for resources, with the more fit prevailing and either vanquishing the less fit or, more often, dominating the loser of a war and, over time, ratcheting up of complexity as the defeated society is incorporated into the institutional systems of the more fit society. As we will see in Chapters 3 and 4, this idea has reappeared in variants of world systems analysis.

In *The Division of Labor in Society* (1893: 265–67), Emile Durkheim explicitly incorporated Darwinian ideas into his model on the differentiation of societies. Occupational and other forms of specialization are, in his view, the sociocultural equivalent of the biological process of *speciation*. When actors are concentrated into physical and moral space, the level of competition among them increases, and with competition comes selection leading to specialization, or increases in the division of labor. But unlike Spencer, no one seems to have died in Durkheim's model; rather, those who cannot secure adequate resources in one niche move to another or create a new niche in which they can secure the resources necessary to sustain themselves. Thus, the mechanisms driving the differentiation of societies are very Darwinian: Population growth leads to increased population density that, in turn, escalates competition for resources and, hence, selection on individuals and social units, which results in increases in the complexity of the division of labor in society (see Figures 5.1 and 5.2).

In the United States, these ideas were adopted by what became known as the Chicago School of Urban Ecology (e.g., Park 1936a, 1936b, McKenzie 1933), where differentiation of communities was analyzed in ecological terms. Patterns of growth and differentiation of urban areas were seen as the result of growth, increased density, competition (institutionalized by real estate and other markets), selection among actors by the price of real estate, and differentiation of a population into distinct areas, zones, and districts within urban communities like Chicago. Later ecological analysis was, as we will see in Chapter 5, extended to organizations and, eventually, back to whole societies in a mode reminiscent of the macro-level theories of Spencer and Durkheim. The key point here is that a much more Darwinian approach to evolutionary analysis was part of late 19th and early 20th Century sociology and continues to the present day. Such analysis is, it should be emphasized, not Darwinian in this sense: Selection is not always on the individual but, instead, often on corporate units like groups and organizations. Hence, sociocultural speciation is often driven by what became known as "group selection," although this label has aroused considerable hostility and controversy, as is outlined in Chapter 10.

Theorizing on Human Nature

Most sociological analyses of the 19th and early 20th Century carried implicit, sometimes more explicit, views of the fundamental nature of humans. For example, Marx argued that it was fundamental to the nature of humans to control their productive activities as well as the distribution of their products, and when this fundamental need of humans cannot be realized, as is the case in industrial capitalism where labor is made the appendage of machine-production, human pathologies such as alienation result. Emile Durkheim saw egoism as a pathology resulting from the lack of attachment of individuals to groups, thus signaling that a fundamental need of humans is to be part of collective organization. The same can be said for anomie or the lack of regulation of desires and passions, which, like egoism, could drive people to suicide (Durkheim 1897). George Herbert Mead (1934) and Charles Horton Cooley (1902) posited that development of self and its verification by others are fundamental needs of all humans. Vilfredo Pareto (1916) argued that humans possessed fundamental sentiments and derivations of these and that these sentiments and derivations drove not only behavior but also patterns of social organization.

These and other conceptions of the fundamental nature of humans were just sociological extensions of more philosophical arguments from the 18th through 19th Centuries where the fundamental needs of humans or their basic nature were the starting point for a wide variety of philosophical critiques of society. Similarly, modernization was often analyzed by early sociologists as revealing a variety of pathologies, many of which were seen to violate often rather vaguely formulated views of "human nature." These arguments were not couched in Darwinian terms as evolved traits and behavioral propensities that had evolved by natural selection; they were far more "essentialists" than this, but then most who postulated views of human nature did not have the benefit of training in biology to assess what the evolved traits of humans might be, given their evolutionary history as primates adapting to arboreal habitats and, then, as hominins increasingly having to adapt to more terrestrial habitats. Still, like most people in general, there were both folk and intellectual formulations on the fundamental nature of humans and how this nature had effects on, and was affected by, patterns of social organization.

Most of these more philosophical views of human nature were highly speculative, but they would become more implicit during the 20th Century as social science adopted the tenets of science. They have also been a part of "critical sociology" because particular types of social arrangements are always seen by critical theorists as harmful to humans, and if they are harmful, they must be violating something fundamental about humans' nature. It is not a very big leap to positing that this nature is biologically based; and if biologically based, it must have evolved like all other fundamental needs and behavioral propensities of animals. But, in contrast to early sociology, it is now possible to address this issue in a less speculative way by using biological theory to assess the selection pressures on humans and their ancestors during the evolution of the human clade—as we will see in Chapter 12. Indeed, as more explicit Darwinian approaches—themselves often highly controversial among sociologists—have entered social science, they have brought with them a host of what are still often speculative conclusions about what drives human behavior. And so, even with explicit biological models, the subject of human nature remains somewhat speculative and always controversial, especially if it violates some of the assumptions that philosophers and social scientists hold about human nature. Still, this topic of what is basic to humans as beings has always been part of sociological analysis; and, as we will see in Chapters 13–15, it now can provide more disciplined and rigorous insights into what, at the biological level, pushes humans to behave in particular ways and, in so doing, puts subtle but constant selection pressures on social structures and culture.

The Challenge of Darwinian Ideas in Sociology Today

Even as the once disgraced stage models of evolution worked their way back into sociology and as organizational ecology began extended ecology analysis in the second half of the 20th Century, the distrust of biology among sociologists has persisted but to a lesser degree than was evident for most of the 20th Century. The fears of a revival of Social Darwinism and eugenics, or a call for reduction of sociological ideas into biology, were enough to make most sociologists highly skeptical, if not hostile, to *any* revival of biological analysis in sociology, despite the fact that social ecology had gained new status and stage modeling had been sufficiently purged of its ethnocentrism to be acceptable to most sociologists.

The Challenge of Sociobiology

With the publication of Edward O. Wilson's *Sociobiology: The New Synthesis* (1975), and with its bold pronouncements that the social sciences can become subfields within biology, all of the intellectual paranoia among sociologists was rekindled. Even those somewhat sympathetic to understanding the biological nature of humans were often hostile to such pronouncements because of what were correctly perceived as simplistic assumptions that paid virtually *no* attention to 150 years of work in sociology—a charge which, some who are highly sympathetic to a biologically informed sociology, still think holds true. Interestingly, before Wilson's book, there had been a revival of speculation of the nature of humans by anthropologists (Ardrey 1961, 1966; Morris 1969; Tiger and Fox 1966, 1971); ethologists (Lorenz 1966); and by respected sociologists like Pierre van den Berghe (1973), but these works were often couched in the older and highly speculative human nature tradition of the 19th Century. Among the anthropologists, for example, Ardrey argues for a "killing instinct" in his *African Genesis* and *The Territorial Imperative*, Morris in his *The Naked Ape* for a view of humans as naturally aggressive, Tiger and Fox in their *The Imperial Animal* for a view of humans as both aggressive and territorial, while sociologists like van den Berghe were polemical but not nearly as bold in pronouncements in his *Age and Sex in Human Societies* for humans as innately prone to domination by age and sex classes. Less shrill was the ethologist, Konrad Lorez, who also posited an "aggression instinct" but argued that historically such aggression had been mitigated and channeled by rituals, thus concluding that aggression could be maladaptive when not constrained by ritual. Much of this speculation involved a kind of reverse engineering whereby existing patterns of social organization could be seen as being generated by biological propensities of humans to behave in certain ways, and so, if societies reveal (a) inequality and stratification by class, age, and gender; (b) individual- and group-level aggression; and (c) territoriality, these observable social arrangements *must* be the result of innate behavioral propensity. Such arguments tended to ignore the sociocultural dynamics creating inequality, stratification, and conquest of territory through warfare—in essence, short-circuiting more sociological explanations of how particular patterns of social organization had evolved.

Yet, despite considerable skepticism among most sociologists on these early attempts in the modern era of sociology to posit views of human nature, other respected sociologists also began to accept some of the premises of sociobiology (e.g., Lopreato 1984; Lopreato and Crippen 1999), which seemed "more scientific" than the kinds of pronouncements made by anthropologists, ethologists, and sociologists. As a consequence, a beachhead was established for sociobiology on the fringes of sociology. Moreover, the reaction to extreme statements of sociobiologists by those sociologists who remained interested in biology was to redouble their efforts to develop a biologically informed sociology that was not so reductionist and simplistic, and it is this group of scholars that continues to have influence in the discipline, even as others remain committed to the assumptions of sociobiology summarized in Chapters 6–8.

The basic argument of sociobiology that human bodies are, in essence, survival machines for genes seeking to remain in the gene pool (Dawkins 1976) was fascinating but led to some extreme arguments that most behaviors, as they lead to the development of social structures and culture, are the result of blind natural selection as it affected the human genome and programmed humans to exhibit certain fundamental behaviors. This all smacked of society as being driven by genes rather than the topics of most interest to sociologists, and to this day, only a relatively small portion of sociologists adhere to these assumptions. Yet, these sociologists have been essential in building the organizational infrastructure for what we are terming in this book *evolutionary sociology* (e.g., Mazur 2003; Lopreato and Crippen 1999; Machalek 1996; Hopcroft 2002). And so, even though the reaction to sociobiology was mixed, if not mostly negative, it did move a rather diverse group of biologically oriented scholars to institutionalize biological ideas into mainstream sociology.

Another consequence of sociobiology, as we will see in Chapters 12 and 13, has been to force scholars thinking about human nature to be more precise and less speculative. Indeed, much of sociobiology is highly speculative in its pronouncements of what human behaviors are biologically driven, and this fact alone has moved many sociologists engaged in evolutionary analysis to bring new tools for discovering how selection has worked on the hominin brain, as inherited from the last common ancestor of humans and extant great apes with whom humans share a large proportion—from 95% (with orangutans) to 98.5% (with chimpanzees)—of their genetic material (albeit on a different number of chromosomes). In essence, the challenge of sociobiology ended up being interpreted by many scholars as a mandate that "if we do not like the assumptions and conclusions of sociobiology," then it was incumbent on us to find alternative ways to determine the biology of human nature, with some alternative outlined in Part III of this book.

The Challenge of Evolutionary Psychology

In the late 1980s and early 1990s, psychologists (Cosmides and Tooby 1992) began to argue for an approach that adopted many of the assumptions of sociobiology but that emphasized the rewiring of the hominin and thus human brain with new modules that served special functions in response to selection pressures during the late Pleistocene. For some time, but less so today, evolutionary psychologists argued that the brain was highly modular, with discrete modules evolving through the forces of evolution increase fitness of hominins under selection pressures from their habitats and niches in these habitats. For example, behaviors like reciprocity in exchanges were seen as behaviors that promoted fitness by creating ties and interdependencies among conspecifics—an argument that is reasonable except for the failure to find discrete modules in the human brain responsible for such behaviors and except for the additional fact that both monkeys and apes monitor reciprocity in exchanges (thus making reciprocity a behavior that evolved millions of years before the Pleistocene). Yet, the general idea that the evidence for what natural selection was doing to hominins in terms of their behavioral propensities should appear in the wiring of the brain remains sound and encouraged others to address at least the issue raised by evolutionary psychology (see, for example, Chapters 13 and 14).

Evolutionary psychology endured much the same reaction as sociobiology in mainstream sociology because it too seemed reductionist: The social structures and cultures that most sociologists see as directing behaviors are reduced to modules in the brain rather than broader social forces inhering in emergent sociocultural formations. Still, as with sociobiology, some sociologists have been drawn to this approach (e.g., Hopcroft 2006, 2009a, 2009b; Kanazawa 2004; Kanazawa and Hellberg 2010; Kanazawa and Still 2000) and, as a result, helped institutionalized *evolutionary sociology* within the discipline, even as many remain highly skeptical of explanations by evolutionary psychologists. Moreover and perhaps more significantly, the same reaction to those willing to examine the brain led the feeling that if we are "not satisfied with the explanations generated by evolutionary psychologists," then it is imperative to develop a more sociological approach to understanding how the brain was wired and rewired during the course of primate and hominin evolution to produce uniquely human behavioral propensities. And so, evolutionary psychology like its cousin, sociobiology, has forced sociology to defend its turf and offer explanations that are more compatible with the sociological tradition, and the result of this response to the challenge issued by evolutionary psychology has been to expand *evolutionary sociology* in ways that bring back the older speculation about human nature in a more rigorous guise as *neurosociology* (Franks 2010; Franks and Turner 2013) that can inform all types of sociological analysis (see Chapter 14).

The Chapters to Follow

We have dedicated this book to increasing the level of awareness that a *new evolutionary sociology* has quietly evolved on the sidelines of the discipline. Our goal in this review is make the various approaches that have been emerging over the last two decades more relevant to the core of sociology. Still, it is important to emphasize that there are limitations to wholesale and uncritical importation of concepts and models from biology into sociology; the evolution of organisms is different than the evolution of superorganisms or sociocultural formations organizing human organisms. When we focus on the evolution of humans, per se, with an interest in their biological nature, we come closest to being able to use ideas from the Modern Synthesis of evolutionary theory in biology (the integration of Darwinian evolutionary theory and Mendelian genetics), whereas when we are examining the evolution of sociocultural formations or emergent social structures and their cultures, the limitations of biological ideas will all become quite evident, as will be emphasized in Chapters 10 and 11.

So, our goal is to lay out the approaches that are available and useful to sociologists, the strengths and limitations of these approaches, and the overall utility of a more biologically informed evolutionary sociology. Evolutionary analysis is where sociology began, and it is time to bring it back to the center of the discipline, using it selectively and strategically to address problems where it is relevant. Evolutionary analysis will not explain everything of interest to sociologists, but it can be surprisingly useful in making sociology a more mature explanatory science.

Part I of this book contains four chapters on the revitalization of the continuing traditions that were evident at the turn into the 20th Century. In Chapter 2, we will review functionalism, as sociology's first theoretical perspective, and as the vehicle by which many biologically oriented ideas were first incorporated into sociology. The issue will be: Is functionalism still useful in the new evolutionary sociology? Or, is it best to discard this orientation, forever?

In Chapter 3, representative descendants of early sociological stage models of societal evolution will be examined. These have made a remarkable recovery in sociology over the last five decades, and they have added greatly to our understanding of human societies. They cannot answer all questions, and they also reveal limitations, but these models can tell us a great deal about the social forces driving the social universe and how these forces have operated on sociocultural formations from the simplest hunting and gathering band to the global system that is evolving in front of our eyes in the 21st Century.

Chapter 4 outlines the new insights that have come with world systems analysis which has incorporated many ideas from stage-model theorizing, as well as ecological analysis, in trying to understand how systems of societies evolve. Societies may be conceptualized as superorganisms, or as systems organizing organisms into societies, but societies themselves are generally part of a larger system of societies. Hence, to understand the evolution of societies, it is useful to recognize that the unit of evolutionary analysis may not be societies but, instead, the system of societies in which a given society is embedded.

Chapter 5 will review the continuing tradition in urban ecology, the first application in American sociology of Durkheim's explicitly Darwinian view of societal-level differentiation. Then, we will examine organizational ecology that emerged as a new variant of ecological analysis in the 1970s and that continues to this day. Finally, we explore several different types of theorizing from somewhat varying traditions that have taken ecological analysis back up to the macro-level of social organization. Some of these approaches come from upsizing the meso-level analysis of urban spatial configurations and populations of organizations, but as we will see, other macro-level ecological approaches have their roots in early sociological traditions, such as functionalism and conflict theorizing.

Part II of the book turns to the challenges posed by sociobiology and evolutionary psychology, reviewing the basic arguments of these approaches and illustrating how sociologists have used either or both of these approaches. We begin in Chapters 6, 7, and 8 with a review of sociobiology, and in Chapter 9, we take up evolutionary psychology. Since these approaches are the most controversial within sociology, we offer in Chapters 10 and 11 an assessment of where they might be useful and where the limitations of these approaches hinder rather than expand sociological analysis.

Part III presents three chapters that, to some extent, offer alternatives to sociobiology and evolutionary psychology. Chapter 12 outlines a form of comparative analysis using primates as a data source for understanding human origins and the nature of early pre-human societies. Chapter 13 outlines a strategy for using Darwinian and ecological analysis to uncover the nature of humans, or the behavioral propensities that drive humans to act in certain ways and that, as a result, exert a constant pressure on all sociocultural formations. This approach will draw upon cladistic analysis from biology, comparative neuroanatomy, studies on primates, and ecological analysis of the habitats and niches within these habitats generating selection pressures on the evolution of primates and then the evolution of hominins on the human clade (Turner and Maryanski 2008).

Chapter 14 will examine the new science of neurosociology, emphasizing an approach that examines the evolution of the human brain. This evolutionary emphasis focuses on the selection pressures that were operating on hominins during their evolution and how, and why, a large neocortex and all that it would allow (spoken language and culture) to evolve along the human clade.

Chapters 15 and 16 will offer examples of two comparative approaches to interspecies analysis and how they can inform sociological analysis of macrosocial structures. Studies of insect societies and the design problems that they provide key theoretical leads on how humans, as the only mammal to create a macrosociety, have overcome these same design problems, while the cladistic analysis involving comparisons of humans with their closest primate relatives can suggest why it was possible for such a large animal as *Homo sapiens* to overcome these same design problems, even for an animal with a comparatively large body. Chapter 17 will pursue these themes further by demonstrating how the study of primates outlined in Chapters 12 and 13 can also explain why humans can create megasocieties.

Finally, in a short epilogue, we will close with an assessment of the promise and limitations of using biological ideas in the social sciences in general, and sociology in particular. There are large differences between the evolution of individual organisms through reproduction and the evolution of human societies over the long course of history. There are emergent dynamics in superorganisms that cannot be explained by biology, and so, we must remained attuned to what can be borrowed and used profitably in the new evolutionary sociology, and what cannot.

Finally, it should be emphasized that we cannot cover every aspect of the new, emerging evolutionary sociology. Nor, are we trying to offer a handbook or textbook of this emerging field of sociological inquiry. Rather, our goal is to lay out the key approaches and to evaluate them as to how they can contribute to mainstream sociological analysis. We have written this book to communicate mostly to sociologists who might be skeptical about evolutionary sociology, emphasizing the many theoretical problems that an evolutionary approach can help resolve. In the future, the goal is to make evolutionary sociology more central to *mainstream* sociological analysis; evolutionary analysis was once central to sociology, and it can be so again, once old biases and prejudices are mitigated and, eventually, eliminated. There is nothing reductionist, racist, or ethnocentric about using biology sociology; it can offer almost any approach to sociological analysis some very useful information.

Part I
The Continuing Sociological Tradition

2

Can Functionalism Be Saved?
Toward a More Viable Form of Evolutionary Theorizing

The Organismic Analogy and Functionalism

The organismic analogy that can be found in the work of Auguste Comte and Herbert Spencer where patterns of human social organization are viewed as a larger "body social" or, in Herbert Spencer's words, as a *superorganism*. The conception of the social universe led to sociology's first major theoretical perspective: functionalism (Turner and Maryanski 1979). Auguste Comte's functionalism followed from the organismic analogy by looking for analogies or even true isomorphisms between the organic elements in the biology of individual organisms to what he termed the "Social Organism." For example, Comte (1830) emphasized that:

> We have thus established a true correspondence between the Statistical Analysis of the Social Organism in Sociology, and that of the Individual Organism in Biology. . . . If we take the best ascertained points in Biology, we may decompose structure anatomically into elements, tissues, and organs. We have the same things in the Social Organism; and may even use the same names.

Once this conceptual step was taken, it is a short additional step to asking what biological structures *do for* the maintenance of the "social" organisms. It is from this logic that functionalism was born. Comte argued that, like the human body, societies have normal and abnormal forms; and if abnormalities appear in the patterns of social organization, the task is to isolate what elements of the larger system are causing these abnormalities. Indeed, Comte visualized the new science of sociology as being able to "diagnose" like medical physicians the "health" of societies and to offer remedies for social pathologies. Functional analysis can easily be found in medicine where the "functions" of a particular body system—say, the heart and lungs—for maintaining the health and viability of the body are outlined, although like in sociology, rarely are the evolutionary steps by which these organs evolved outlined. Thus, sociology was born as a discipline with this implied functionalism in which particular structures and cultural elements would be analyzed for what they do to maintain the viability of a social system in its environment.

Herbert Spencer's organismic analogy became even more famous than Comte's; and indeed, Spencer (1864) was quite defensive about criticisms that he was "just repeating" Comte's argument. Still, the analogy itself simply listed the ways that superorganisms or patterns of sociocultural organization reveal a "parallel" pattern of organization to organic systems, and where they do not. And, in our retrospective view of Spencer, this analogy is considered a major theoretical blunder that led him to an even bigger blunder in formulating a more explicit functional approach than Comte. Indeed, if there was a clear founder of functionalism, it was Spencer more than any other sociologist. Yet, we should not forget that in a multi-volume treatise of over 2,000 pages, the discussion of the organismic analogy is only a handful of pages, which are not particularly relevant to his general scheme and which may only have been intended to show the continuity of his sociology with his much more detailed arguments in *The Principles of Biology* (1864–1867) that he had finished just before he began writing three volumes of *The Principles of Sociology* (1874–1896). Indeed, Darwin in the preface to *On the Origin of Species* (1859) praised Spencer for his larger effort to develop the science of biology and, apparently, saw his ideas on natural selection as somewhat similar to Spencer's statements on "survival of the fittest," which had first appeared in a more philosophical work, *Social Statics* (1851), eight years before Darwin published *On The Origin of Species* (1859). Thus, Darwin's praise of Spencer was probably just a professional courtesy. Still, as we hope to demonstrate, Spencer's ideas of "survival of the fittest" are not far from Darwin's ideas on natural selection; and moreover, Spencer was the first to propose a new kind of selection on superorganic forms that is not evident in the evolution of organic forms of life.

Spencer's grand law of evolution argued that population growth forced populations to differentiate along three (really four) major axes: *operation* or (1) *production* of necessary goods and commodities to sustain members of a population and (2) *reproduction* of individuals and social units organizing individuals, (3) *regulation* or the consolidation of power and development of cultural symbols to regulate, control, and coordinate a population; and (4) *distribution* or the development of infrastructures and markets to distribute people, information, and resources among members of a population within a given territory. These axes of differentiation can readily be interpreted as functional need-states or requisites that all superorganisms *must meet* if they are to remain viable in their environment; and it is not too difficult to recognize these as corresponding to key organ systems in organisms, as Spencer had outlined in *The Principles of Biology* (1864–1867). Indeed, Spencer was clearly borrowing from his analysis of biological organisms that, like superorganisms, grew and differentiated over the long course of evolution; and as they do so, they differentiated along the four axes listed above.

Subsequent theorists who clearly borrowed these basic ideas from Spencer tended to argue in terms of functional needs and requisites necessary to sustain a social system, with the ability to find the need or requisite that a particular sociocultural formation met constituting an "explanation" of this formation. And this is where functional theorizing goes wrong because it sets up several fundamental criticisms that were to be leveled at functional analysis later in the 20th Century, causing its decline into relative obscurity by the turn into the 21st Century. One problem is that explanations of this sort can be seen as an *illegitimate teleology* in which an end state (meeting the functional need or requisite) somehow causes the sociocultural formation meeting this end state to miraculously arise and evolve. Without specifying how outcomes cause the very things that bring about these outcomes, explanation becomes an illegitimate teleology. Another logical problem in functional explanations is that they easily become *tautological*, trapped in circular reasoning. For example, functionalists often get caught in arguments that "a social system is surviving; how do we know the function of a particular sociocultural formation in this social system is meeting a functional need; answer: because the system is surviving." To avoid such tautologies, it is necessary to specify the mechanisms and processes by which a particular sociocultural formation operates, and the means by which it does so, to increase or decrease the fitness of a superorganism to survive in its environment. Most functional explanations, however, short-cut this necessary step in an evolutionary explanation. A third problem is that functionalism would seem to operate as a *legitimating ideology* for the *status* quo in a society. Functionalism implicitly argues that existing structures are functional or adaptive for a system because this system is surviving; and without some hard criteria for what would constitute health or disease in a social system, it would be always be difficult to see a particular sociocultural formation as dysfunctional. Instead, tautological reasoning will tend to generate arguments that bias analysis toward seeing existing elements as functional for a system, thereby providing implicit support for the status quo in societies.

Thus, it is not so difficult to see how functionalism came crashing down in the 1960s under an assault from the revival of Marxist theorizing and conflict theory more generally within sociology. Particularly in the United States during the 1940s and 1950s, where Marx and anything remotely sounding like intellectual support for the dreaded "communism," was suspect, conflict approaches in the social sciences had been repressed, particularly during the McCarthy era in American politics. And so, it is not surprising that something like functionalism took hold in the United States during the 1950s because it did not threaten American sensibilities during the Cold War with the Soviet Union; and indeed, it appeared to be looking for what was "right" or functional for social systems, even though the sociological practitioners of functionalism were anything but political conservatives. Yet, despite these problems with functional explanations, this chapter is devoted to answering the question: Can functionalism be saved with a new evolutionary sociology? Our answer is "yes," but before moving forward, let us review briefly, the history of functionalism in the 20th Century to put into context efforts to save functionalism from itself.

The Rise, Demise, and Surprising Rebirth of Functional Analysis

Functionalism in sociology and anthropology tended to take two somewhat different directions for the whole of the 20th Century. One was to posit multiple functional requisites, as Spencer appeared to do in his *The Principles of Sociology* (1874–1896), and the other was to posit one master requisite, as Emile Durkheim (1893) did in his *The Division of Labor in Society*. Spencer's approach to functional analysis was picked up by the anthropologist Bronislaw Malinowski and sociologists like Talcott Parsons, whereas Emile Durkheim's master requisite approach was adopted by A. R. Radcliffe Brown in anthropology and Niklas Luhmann in sociology. Let us begin with Emile Durkheim.

Durkheim's Functional Analysis

Durkheim posited one master functional requisite: the need to *integrate* social systems; and in *The Division of Labor in Society* (1893), he posited two basic types of societal integration: *mechanical* and *organic*. Mechanical solidarity was a mode of integration achieved by the likeness of system parts in simple societies, with each part revealing the same structure and culture, whereas organic solidarity was the new basis for integration as societies become increasingly differentiated. For differentiated societies, new mechanisms of integration are essential, including: (a) structural interdependencies and exchanges among differentiated social units, (b) value generalization of moral premises to accommodate the diverse structural locations and lived experiences of individual and units organizing their activities, (c) normative specification generalized values in the laws of a restitute legal system and in beliefs regulating individuals and social units at similar places in the division of labor, and (d) formation of political parties composed of actors at common locations in the division of labor in a democratic political system. Thus, in Durkheim's sociology, analysis of particular structures—from laws to rituals—was designed to assess the degree to which structures and their cultures promoted or worked against the integration of the more inclusive social system. The master requisite, then, in Durkheim's sociology was *the need for integration* of societies.

What is often not recognized, or even noted, by commentators on Durkheim is that he dropped the distinction between mechanical and organic solidarity (see Maryanski 1918) in favor of an emphasis on emotion-arousing rituals as the mechanism driving solidarity in *all types* of social systems of varying degrees of complexity. Durkheim was clearly dissatisfied with his analysis in *The Division of Labor*; and one response was to write *The Rules of the Sociological Method* (1895: 96), which did not clarify very much, but which did reveal Durkheim's concerns about problems in functional analysis. This is why he proposed two-fold analysis of sociocultural phenomena: One revolved around the historical and proximate causes of phenomena, such as the division of labor and the evolution of mechanisms for its integration, and the other was an analysis of the functions of these sociocultural phenomena in terms of how they met the master requisite for system integration. In this way, he thought that he had avoided the problems of illegitimate teleology and tautology, as noted earlier. Soon, after *The Rules of the Sociological Method* was published, Durkheim dropped the notion of "mechanical solidarity" completely and downplayed his views on the "collective conscience" in favor of "collective representations" as he was moving toward an emphasis on emotion-arousal rituals directed by beliefs (as representations in collectivities of individuals) as the key to integration in *both* undifferentiated *and* highly complex societies (see Maryanski, 2018). And, after 1895, Durkheim broke the key rule of the "sociological method" and engaged in more psychological and even biological analyses to help explain the origins of religion as the key to understanding the origin of societies. So, Durkheim after 1895 had pretty much dropped functionalism; and he was increasingly engaging in what we call in this volume *evolutionary sociology*. Even in *The Division of Labor*, as we will see, he had already adopted Darwin's notion of selection in explaining the "causes" of the division of labor, which he considered to be the equivalent of "speciation" in sociocultural systems.

The Apparent Death of Functionalism in Sociology

Because functionalism was closely associated in stage-model evolutionism (see Chapter 3), Durkheim's death in 1917, and the earlier death of Spencer in 1903, caused functional analysis in sociology to disappear. The somewhat justified criticisms of stage-model evolutionary explanations briefly outlined in Chapter 1 also led to the ouster of functionalism that had been associated with some of these models of evolution.

Yet, as functionalism died in sociology, it was reborn in anthropology as a means for making sense of the accumulating bodies of data on pre-literate societies. Since such societies do not have a written history (only, at best, an oral history), anthropologists had trouble explaining why particular aspects of a culture (conceptualized broadly as social structures, cultural beliefs, and practices) existed. They could not trace their history, and yet, they wanted to know *why* they existed, and so, many anthropologists turned to functionalism, analyzing cultural items in terms of their functions for sustaining a population in a given environment.

The Rise of Functionalism in Anthropology

Two of the most influential anthropologists in the history of anthropology—A. R. Radcliffe-Brown and Bronislaw Malinowski—adopted functionalism in the third and fourth decades of the 20th Century. And, given their prestige and influence, many others followed their lead and began to let functional arguments slip into their analysis of various pre-literate populations.

A. R. Radcliffe-Brown

It is perhaps obvious that the unilineal kinship systems of horticultural populations (e.g., settled communities using human power to cultivate gardens) that evolved from hunting and gathering provide a basis for integration of these larger populations. The elaboration of kinship by consolidating nuclear families into extended families or lineages, lineages into subclans, sublclans into full clans, and then clans into moieties that divided the society in half was clearly a way to provide structural and cultural (through kinship rules) integration of larger settled populations. Thus, the elements of such kinship system could be analyzed for how they fostered political, social, and cultural integration for a population that did not have the resources to generate alternative mechanisms of integration; and so, as Radcliffe-Brown (1935, 1952) turned to kinship analysis, he followed Durkheim's lead, positing an overall need for integration and then analyzing elements of kinship in terms of how they met this need.

Bronislaw Malinowski

A far more flamboyant but still highly respected anthropologist, Bronislaw Malinowski (1936, 1939, 1941, 1944) pursued a strategy closer to Herbert

Spencer's approach by positing multiple functional requisites for what he conceptualized as different system levels: organic, social, and cultural. Each of these system levels reveals its own unique functional needs that are essential to survival of a population; and in positing distinctive needs for different system levels, Malinowski went beyond Spencer. Figure 2.1

Cultural Requisites:

1. Systems of knowledge for dealing with the world that can be used and transmitted to others across generations
2. Systems of symbols that give individuals a sense that they have control of their destiny and chance events around them (i.e., beliefs in magic and religion)
3. Systems of symbols allowing individuals to share a sense of a communal rhythm in their activities and daily lives

---

Instrumental/Social Structural Requisites of Institutional Systems:

1. Economic needs to maintain systems of production
2. Social control through law and cultural prescriptions that are institutionalized
3. Political organization institutionalizing authority and enforcement
4. Education or transmission of knowledge needed to sustain institutional systems

---

Biological Requisites ("Vital Sequences"):

1. Drives to breathe
2. Drives to ingest food
3. Drives to satisfy thirst through ingestion of liquids
4. Drives for sexual activity
5. Drives for activity to satisfy restlessness
6. Drives for sleep
7. Drives to relieve colon and bladder pressures
8. Drives to escape from danger
9. Drives to avoid pain

Figure 2.1 Bronislaw Malinowski's Portrayal of Functional Requisites at Different System Levels

outlines the functional needs of the structural and cultural-systems levels in Malinowski's scheme but also includes his notion of the needs of the organismic systems (human bodies) and, in so doing, includes ideas that reappear in various forms in more contemporary evolutionary sociology.

Malinowski's approach inspired other anthropologists to pursue functional analysis, and perhaps more importantly, he is the more direct link to the functional analysis that would eventually re-emerge in sociology in the 1950s. By finding the system level of a particular sociocultural item or practice and then the functional requisite that is met, a sense of explanation could be achieved when historical analysis of how and why this item emerged and evolved in the first place was not possible in societies without a recorded history. Oral traditions might reveal some insights, but these are generally so conflated with religion and myths that they are not typically very useful in what Malinowski saw as the need to develop scientific explanations. But, his ideas were noted among a group of sociologists who, in the late 1940s, would bring back functionalism as a tool for scientific explanation.

It could be that, without the adoption of functionalism by anthropologists, who carried the tradition forward for several decades, the rebirth of functionalism as sociology's dominant theoretical approach for a brief period in the second half of the century may never had occurred. For, the connection to Spencer had been lost in most sociological circles; and indeed the modern day refounder of functionalism in sociology—Talcott Parsons—had asked the question originally posed by Crane Britton—"Who now reads Spencer?"—in his first major work (Parsons 1937) fourteen years before his shift to functionalist theorizing emerged (e.g., Parsons 1951). So, with Spencer's evolutionism and functionalism dead, coupled with Durkheim's "weak functionalist" arguments about integration, it is entirely possible that functionalism would not have become part of sociology again. Once functionalism was back, however, so came its 19th Century sidekick, stage models of societal evolution, as will be examined in Chapter 3.

The Rebirth of Functionalism in Sociology and Its Apparent Death, Once Again

Functionalism re-emerged in sociology from a famous seminar at Harvard University in the late 1940s in which students and faculty examined theoretical approaches to understanding systems, one of which was functionalism. And from this seminar, a still relatively young Talcott Parsons along with others who radiated out along the east coast of the United States began to bring the functionalist approach back into sociology. Parsons was the most prominent of these new functionalists, and so, we will focus on his scheme because, despite his 1937 proclamation, he clearly had read Spencer and followed much of his lead in extending his analysis to many different system levels in not only the social but in the biotic, physical, and even ethnical realms. Our focus will be more focused, however, and deal only with Parsons' approach to sociological explanations. As a side note, it can be noted that Parsons had been a biology major as an undergraduate student, and so, perhaps there was something about functionalism—as a derivative of the organismic analogy of Comte and Spencer—that appealed to him as he sought to explain ever more dimensions of the social universe.

The Basics of Parsonian Functionalism

Parsons' (1951) approach began with a distinction among system levels that could be analytically isolated for analysis. These were not all fully conceptualized in his early work leaning toward functionalism, but within a couple of years, the social world was conceptualized as composed of four action systems: the organic (later behavioral), the psychological, the social, and the cultural. These systems are, of course, only distinguishable analytically, but each was considered to have the same set of fundamental functional requisites (Parsons et al., 1953): (1) *adaptation* or the need to secure resources from the environment, to covert these through production into system-sustaining resources, and to distribute these to individuals and system units; (2) *goal attainment* or the need to establish system goals and to mobilize and coordinate resources for realizing these goals; (3) *integration* or the need to coordinate subsystems within each action system; and (4) *latency*, which consisted of two sub-needs for: (a) *pattern maintenance* or the reproduction of system units and (b) *tension management* within and between social units.

For elements operating within each of these four action systems, these can be analyzed in terms of how they meet one of these four (really five) functional requisites for the more inclusive system. And once the functional need of a particular element has been determined, a kind of explanation of this element has been achieved, or so Parsons thought. Thus, if at the societal level of social organization, the economy is seen as meeting the functional need for adaptation, this realization constitutes a kind of explanation because its place within the social system and the overall action system consisting of relations among the four actions systems—i.e., organic, psychological, social, and cultural. Further explanation is achieved with the analysis of relations among subparts within and between actions systems meeting different functional requisites. What emerged from this kind of modeling is a large complex of categories that placed elements of organic, psychological, social, and cultural action systems in a sector of elements devoted to each of the four functional requisites of all action systems—that is, adaptation, goal attainment, integration, and latency. Then, the relations among these sectors organizing the ways that particular functional requisites in an action system are met can have relations across action systems, with analysis emphasizing the output of goal attainments of an action system—say, energy from the organic system—becoming an input to the adaptive sector of another action system—say, the psychological action system. Another interchange that is more sociologically relevant might be that goal attainment outputs from the psychological action system (e.g., motivated behaviors) become inputs into the social system giving individuals energy and commitments to play roles in status within the social system; and as individuals play roles, these become outputs of the social system into the cultural system reinforcing or potentially changing the informational culture of the overall action system (encompassing the organic, psychological, social, and cultural action systems).

If this kind of input-output analysis seems complex, it was, but it allowed Parsons and his followers to have the sense that they were explaining the most important properties of the social universe composed of four intersecting action systems. As a descriptive tool, whereby these categories and output-input relations in particular empirical systems—for example, a school or business corporation—were described empirically, a certain level of insight was achieved into how this empirical system operated. Parsons' theoretical categories could thus be useful tools as a kind of conceptual framework that highlighted important empirical properties of a social system. Indeed, Parsons' essays on particular empirical topics were among his most interesting and useful contributions to sociology in the 20th Century. As an explanatory tool, however, the scheme encountered the same critiques mentioned earlier about illegitimate teleology, tautology, and political conservatism.

The result of these continued shortcoming in functional analysis was that the re-emergence of conflict theory in the late 1950s and 1960s generated a persistent line of critique (e.g., Dahrendorf 1959) that undermined functionalism and, by the turn into the 21st Century, functionalism had, once again, declined into obscurity.

Niklas Luhmann

We should offer a short note on the German sociologist Niklas Luhmann (1982, 1984), who pursued the simplifying strategy of Durkheim and

Radcliffe-Brown by positing only one functional requisite—the need to *reduce the complexity* inherent in the three basic dimensions of the environment: (1) temporal, (2) material, and (3) symbolic. All of these dimensions pose the problem of complexity (a) in the present, endless past or future (temporal); (b) in the infinite number of relations possible (material); and (c) in symbol systems and the media by which these systems are constructed (symbolic). Thus, the paramount requisite of all social systems is to develop "mechanisms" that reduce the relevant spans of time for a given line of action, that define and delimit the space and the types of social relations in this space, and that specify the kinds of symbolic media that are used to generate the symbols regulating social relations.

The social world is constructed of three types of social systems: (1) interaction systems, (2) organization systems, and (3) societal systems, with interaction systems being embedded in organization systems, and with organization systems building up institutional domains (economic, political, family, religious, etc.) that are embedded in societal systems. Interaction systems emerge with co-presence of actors, which sets into motion mechanisms for delimiting the range of relevant cognitions, time frames, symbols, and media to be employed, and use of space and the relations possible in this space and time frame. However, interaction systems create "bottlenecks" because talk is sequential and because only one person can speak at a time, thus making such systems very slow and vulnerable to disruption by people talking over each other, creating inequalities in talk, and otherwise escalating conflict-producing tensions. Hence, organization systems were invented to coordinate actions in interaction systems by ordering tasks for specified periods of time and places governed by "entrance and exit" rules. Without organization systems, larger-scale organization is not possible, and with organizational systems, key mechanisms for reducing the complexity along all dimensions typical of large societal systems are in place. Organization systems specify what generalized symbolic media are to be used (e.g., money, love-loyalty, piety, knowledge, truth, justice, etc.) to produce communication that becomes organized into ideologies that regulate social relations where labor is divided and organized in space for specified periods of time.

Societal systems encompass the differentiated institutional domains built up from different types of organization systems employing various generalized symbolic media in exchanges and developing communication codes from generalized symbolic that, in turn, delimit the complexity of the symbol systems (i.e., norms and ideologies) that are relevant at particular times and places. Like most functional theorists from Spencer through

Durkheim to Parsons, evolution is seen as a process of increasing differentiation and, hence, complexity.

Like Durkheim, Luhmann invokes Darwinian ideas in emphasizing that sociological analysis should focus on the processes in sociocultural systems that generate (a) variation, (b) selection on variants, and (c) stabilization of traits that facilitate adaptation to the temporal, material, and symbolic environments. In so doing, Luhmann provides a hint of how the notion of functional requisites might be converted into a more interesting and less problematic evolutionary argument, although he does not fully realize this goal, as we will see in Chapter 3 in outlining his stage model of societal evolution.

None of the functional schemes, even those by Parsons and Luhmann, have prospered in the 21st Century. Their students and adherents can be found scattered across the United States and Europe, but it appears that the rebirth of functionalism was short-lived, dying once again by the end of the 20th Century. Thus, the functional analysis was abandoned in sociology at both the beginning and end of the 20th Century, leaving us to wonder, once again: Can functionalism be saved by the new evolutionary sociology?

Converting Functionalism Into an Explanatory Theory on Evolutionary Dynamics

Why Functionalism Does Not Die

There has always been something about functionalism that is appealing. It asks a big and interesting question: What must societies do to sustain themselves in environments? And, it seem to get at something truly fundamental to understanding societal-level dynamics by trying to answer this question. And yet, it is a flawed mode of explanation producing illegitimate teleologies, tautologies, and biases toward the status quo. So, what can be done to save this approach from these difficulties? If we pay attention to Luhmann's hint about how to convert functionalisms into a more evolutionary approach, there is one possible avenue for bringing a chastened functionalism into the new evolutionary sociology. But, as we will outline in Chapters 10 and 11, making functionalism relevant to the new evolutionary sociology requires that we recognize the limits on how much we can import ideas from the Modern Synthesis in biology into analysis of sociocultural phenomena, or superorganisms composed of symbol-using individual organisms that have capacities for agency. Invoking notions of variation, selection, and stabilization of traits (presumably the equivalent of "fitness enhancement" for sociocultural systems) cannot fully resolve the problems of functionalism.

Still, there *is* a way to convert functionalism into a viable explanatory tool in the new evolutionary sociology if we go all of the way back to Spencer's views and see what they imply about evolutionary dynamics. It may be that Luhmann was trying to make evolutionary dynamics in sociocultural systems, especially at the macrosocietal level, *too* Darwinian and *too* ecological by simply positing the mantra of ecological analysis (see Chapter 5). But, the Modern Synthesis in evolutionary theory revolves around the notion of selection (on variations) produced by mutations, gene flow, and genetic drift, but is this the best way for talking about emergent phenomena, or superorganisms, like whole societies? Our answer is partly "yes" but with a fundamental shift in what selection means and how variations are created.

What Spencer Saw and Sociologists Ignored

As we briefly summarized in Chapter 1 and mentioned again in this chapter, Emile Durkheim posited a Darwinian dynamic in his explanation of how specialization within a society occurs through processes revolving around population growth, increased density, mounting competition for resources, escalating selection, survival of those fit in one niche, and movement of the less fit into new niches where they can survive or creation (invention) of a new niches where they can secure resources. Durkheim's argument, and just about every sociologist since, has emphasized one property of human societies that is not part of the Modern Synthesis: Sociocultural evolution is highly Lamarckian in that humans and societies evolve by "acquired characteristics." Variations in human systems are often created by innovation or just pure luck (which perhaps is somewhat equivalent to mutations in the biotic universe); and while diffusion of new cultural information might be the equivalent of gene flow, with contact among previously isolated societies and exchanges of cultural codes (including technologies) might be viewed as somewhat isomorphic with genetic drift, the processes by which these sources of variation are created and, then, incorporated into sociocultural systems *are very different than* in the biotic world.

And, this difference is related to an even more fundamental difference between sociocultural and biotic life of organisms: There is no equivalent in sociocultural systems for "generations" by which to measure fitness defined by the persistence of genes in the gene pool. Societies are not like organic life forms; they do not reproduce in the same way by having offspring—unless we want to count fast food franchising—that carry their genetic codes. Of course, human beings produce new generations of offspring, and so, analysis of human evolution at the individual level can remain heavily Darwinian, but collective units of social organization cannot adhere to the Modern Synthesis with such fidelity.

Indeed, without a clear equivalent of the human genome (and the cultural "meme" will not do) and to its persistence or decline across generations of offspring, the entire discussion of reproductive fitness in biology becomes dramatically less relevant to sociocultural systems. It is not that societies do no not die or at least collapse; it is just that we do not know precisely *when* they die, *when* they are born, and hence, *when* they produce a new generation. They exist for varying amounts of time, respond to internal and external pressures for change, and eventually collapse through internal crises or through changes in their external environments or are conquered by better-organized societies.

This is what Spencer clearly understood, even as he used the infamous phrase "survival of the fittest." Societies survive when they can defend themselves from external threats, and they grow when they have enough resources to support a larger population or can conquer other populations. Conversely they "die" from internal conflict and other disintegrative processes, from conquest by more powerful societies, or from inability to secure sufficient resources because of environmental changes and/or degradation. Their "fitness," then, is determined by *how long and how well they are able to sustain themselves* in an environment, which in turn is related to the very capacities outlined by Spencer: (1) Can they produce sufficient resources to sustain their members and the social units organizing their activities? (2) Can they reproduce themselves by regularizing the process of procreation and socialization of new members, and moreover, can they develop sufficient numbers and types of social units to organize people's activities in a society? (3) Can they regulate, coordinate, and control members of a population and the social units organizing their activities by the use of consolidated power and authority and by the development of common symbols, such as ideologies, belief systems, and legal tenets? And (4), can they develop infrastructures for moving information, people, and resources about a territory, while at the same time developing systems of exchanges of resources to sustain the members of a population and the social units organizing their activities?

These ideas were generally interpreted to denote functional requisites, but if we are to save functionalism from itself, the notion of requisites *needs to be abandoned*. What, then, replaces the notion of requisites? Spencer did not have a clear vision, but a careful reading of *The Principles of Sociology* reveals that he was developing a new version of what Darwin termed "natural selection," but for superorganisms. While superorganisms reveal some parallels to organic bodies, they differ in how variations are generated and how selection works. In his stage model of evolution (see Chapter 3), Spencer saw the four processes listed above as axes along which societies evolved as they differentiate from simple to ever-more complex forms, but he never really emphasized that these are requisites for survival but, instead, he tended to see these as the dimensions along which selection pressures develop on a population as it grows. Societies are fit *if* individuals and corporate units can respond to these pressures through their capacities for agency; and these responses do not come from some underlying genome and the shuffling of genes into new variants on which selection occurs but, instead, by goal-directed actions and/or luck of individual actors or collective/corporate actors seeking solutions to these selection pressures.

In fact, this shift in emphasis is what functional theories have generally left out of their explanations. It is also what goes unsaid in medical explanations for the functions of various organs of the body, but behind the medical explanation is a selectionist argument: As life forms grow in size, selection pressures mount and begin to work on variations—whether generated by existing distributions of traits, mutations that shake the distribution up, gene flow across space, or genetic drift of altered genes from demes (subpopulations) previously isolated from the main population. And, as Spencer outlined in *The Principles of Biology*, there are some fundamental axes along which these selection pressures mount for organic life forms that are increasing is size. They must, first of all, develop more differentiated structures to support the larger mass, while at the same time differentiating in ways to increase the production of resources taken from the environment and the conversion of these resources into usable substances that are then distributed to the growing mass of cells from new kinds of differentiated structures (e.g., hearts, lungs, circulatory systems in larger organic bodies). Then, organic life must develop new mechanisms of reproduction of differentiated cells and organs. And, they must increasingly develop, at least among organic bodies, new structures for regulating and coordinating differentiated cells, tissues, and organs making up a body (e.g., a more complex nervous system).

These axes of differentiation in growing bodies thus generate selection pressures, which may or may not been met. If they are not met, then organisms die, and if enough organisms die, so does the species. A species dies because existing variants in phenotypes generated by the underlying genome did not produce variants that would allow natural selection to enhanced fitness, as measured by the life and death of individual organisms. The same is true for superorganic bodies, except that the variations are generated by invention, diffusion, or more active borrowing of cultural systems from other populations. If a population cannot create new structures and cultures that meet selection pressures arising from escalating pressures for more production, new forms of reproduction, new infrastructures and exchange systems for distribution to a larger, more dispersed population, or for regulation by power and related cultural symbols of social control, the superorganism eventually disintegrates. Often de-evolution involves regression to a simpler type of superorganism, as is the case with the collapse of a geopolitical empire back to a societal rather than an intersocietal superorganism, or with the inability of a horticultural or agrarian population to produce sufficient food under conditions of environmental degradation that, in turn, causes a population to disperse and perhaps de-evolve back to hunting and gathering modes of subsistence. Spencer emphasized that evolution builds up social structures into ever-more complex forms in superorganisms (as has been, by fits and starts, the case for organic evolution as well), but disintegration of superorganisms occurs when selection pressures from production, reproduction, distribution, or regulations cannot be met, often leading to de-evolution back to a simpler form of superorganism.

In Figure 3.2 on page 42, the model implicit in Spencer's analysis of societal evolution is diagramed. Population growth immediately increases selection pressures for new forms of production, reproduction, regulation, and distribution. The pressures increase to the extent that actors see the potential for disintegration of the sociocultural system; and as population growth begins to change its internal sociocultural structures, the adaptive relationship to physical, organic, and sociocultural environments also changes—for the better or worse. And as these changes in the relation of a population to its environment occur, selection pressures escalate. As these pressures escalate, individual and corporate actors begin to seek solutions to these problems by invention, borrowing, taking, or otherwise creating new types of productive, reproductive, distributive, or regulatory structures and their cultures that can reduce selection pressures. As these efforts proceed, they inevitably lead to increased differentiation of corporate units organizing individual actions that eventually become integrated into differentiated institutional domains. And if these domains prove viable, they reduce selection pressures, at least for a time, but eventually differentiation creates new pressures, what J. Turner (1995) has termed "second-order" selection pressures, for regulation, distribution, reproduction, and production from the increased complexity and, moreover, potentially from the effects of the more complex social order on the relation of that population to its environment (as would be the case, for example, if the larger, more complex system with escalated production degraded the bio-ecology of a population's environment).

As is evident in the model presented in Figure 3.2, the problematic notion of functional requisites has been shifted to what J. H. Turner has termed "functional selection" or "Spencerian selection" (see Turner 1995, 2010; Turner and Maryanski 2008a; Turner and Abrutyn 2016; and Chapter 11). This modest shift in emphasis converts functionalism into a more explanatory form that eliminates the problems of illegitimate teleology, tautology, and conservative bias. Like organisms, superorganisms are under selection pressures, particularly as they grow, but anytime there is a shift in the relationship between the population and its physical, biotic, or sociocultural environments—an idea consistent with Darwinian evolutionary analysis. These pressures arise from the four (and perhaps a few more) fundamental dimensions of human social organization: production, reproduction, distribution, and regulation. If a population can create, borrow or take away, beg, or get lucky in trying to respond to these pressures, it can survive for a time, at least until the next disjuncture with its environment emerges. In many ways, this is what functional analysis always tried to communicate, but much like the short-hand way that functions are addressed in medical discussions of organs in the body, functionalism never adopted Spencer's more general view, except perhaps the hints provided by Luhmann's functionalism and by Durkheim's dissatisfaction with his early functionalism and his later view of integration as a constant source of pressure on populations and their organization into societies. But, in the end, the most Darwinian element of Durkheim's scheme is the ecological model that he offered to sociology whereby Darwinian ideas are applied to individual and collective actors under conditions of increasing population growth, rising density in resources niches, competition, selection, and specialization into a more complex division of labor. J. H. Turner has termed this *Durkheimian selection* to distinguish it from *Spencerian selection* (Turner 1995; Turner and Maryanski 2008a; Turner and Abrutyn 2016; and Chapter 11). In both, evolution is more Lamarckian than Darwinian, and reproduction is not discrete so that fitness can only be measured by persistence of a superorganic system—from a group, neighborhood, organization, or community to a society or intersocietal system—over time in its environment. Notions of genes or memes, and pools of these things, and their reproduction over time are meaningless without a corresponding way to mark generations of offspring that carry these codes in their genotypes. The result is that we need to shift the analysis away from the Modern Synthesis in biology all the way back to the not so modern implications of Spencer's analysis. And with Durkheim's ecological model to be examined in more detail in Chapter 5, we have good complement to Spencer's model by adding a new type of selection dynamic to evolutionary analysis of superorganic systems—thus representing one of the many differences between organic evolution and sociocultural evolution, to be analyzed in examined in Chapters 10 and 11.

Conclusion

Has functionalism really been saved? Perhaps not, but the underlying ideas in functionalism that have sustained it for well over a century have been altered in ways that allow us to view them as an important part of the new evolutionary sociology. The emphasis is not fully Darwinian, but the revision of functionalism represents a reasonable extension of the Modern Synthesis if biological dynamics are ever to be used to understand super-organic life forms, or patterns of social organization among human bodies through the elaboration of social structure and culture. Much changes, as Spencer argued, when analysis shifts to the organization of organisms, and one key change for human organisms is that they can alter the very nature of society in relatively short periods of time; hence, the nature of selection is no longer wholly Darwinian or Durkheimian; it is also Spencerian and, we can add, Lamarckian. Moreover, as will be further emphasized in other chapters, selection is not only both Durkheimian and Spencerian, but it is almost always *multi-level selection* on corporate units and their structure and culture more than selection on individual people, although this assertion about the prominence of what was once called "group selection" remains controversial, even among sociologists committed to evolutionary explanations. Moreover, Spencerian selection can work on sociocultural formations at the same time that Durkheim selection operates on corporate units and, even at the same time as Darwinian selection works on human phenotypes and the underlying genotype of individuals, but until we recognize the fundamental differences among these levels of organization and types of selection, glosses like "co-evolution of genes and culture" will not provide adequate sociological explanations of the social universe.

If we revisit other functional approaches, we can see that they all converge on a similar set of dimensions along which selection pushes on sociocultural systems, and these look very much like those originally emphasized by Herbert Spencer in his analysis of superorganisms. For example, Durkheim's, Radcliffe's, and Parsons' requisites for "integration" are similar to Spencer's emphasis on regulation through power, structural interdependencies, and cultural beliefs, although Durkheim does not develop a useful theory of power while Spencer's theorizing on culture is not nearly as good as his analysis of power dynamics. Indeed, it might be useful to unpack Spencer's notion of regulation, Durkheim's and Parsons' formulation of integration, and Malinowski's views on social control and organization and execution of authority. There may be several additional axes of selection operating under these rubrics that can be separated out in developing explanations in terms of Spencerian selection.

Parsons' requisites in social systems are close to Spencer's and Malinowski's view of production at the societal level. Malinowski's requisite for education and Parsons' view latency are close to Spencer's views on reproduction as a basic operative process. Parsons' goal attainment at the societal level and Malinowski's organization and execution of authority are the same as the power part of Spencer's regulation, which is what he emphasized in *The Principles of Sociology*. Malinowski's social control is much of what Spencer meant by regulation. And, if we look at other functional schemes developed in the heady days of functionalism's revival, we can see similar convergences. In any case, we should not accept any of the current lists of functional requisites as definitive as axes or dimensions of Spencerian selection; some additional conceptual and empirical work appears to be necessary, but we are not talking about a dramatically expanded view of dimensions of Spencerian selection, just some elaboration and/or fine tuning.

Why is there this convergence noted above in lists of requisites that can be reconceptualized as dimensions of Spencerian selection? The lists converge because there is a *limited number of dimensions by which selection operates on superorganisms*. And, these dimensions are what is essential for the maintenance of both organisms and superorganisms, which, of course, is why the organismic analogy was so appealing to early sociologists in the first place. But once we move to a model which emphasizes "Spencerian selection," we can adopt requisites to this more Darwinian view by a relatively small shift in emphasis and some conceptual elaboration. Human societies and, indeed, most meso- and macro-level systems of human organization are under pressure to adapt to their respective environments, including the environments created by their own organization along certain axes that are, in essence, necessary for sustaining the "life" of superorganisms. Indeed, by understanding the fundamental nature of what it means for a superorganism to be viable in an environment or, in other words to "live" and/or be "fit," we have a much better understanding of where selection must ultimately push on superorganisms if they are to adapt and sustain themselves in a given environment. Selection on superorganisms pushes them in particular directions that were originally conceptualized by functionalists as needs or requisites but which can be just as easily conceptualized as the axes or dimensions along which selection pressures arise.

Selection pressures, of course, say nothing about whether or not superorganisms can, through Lamarckian processes, adapt and be fit. Just like any organisms or even species, superorganisms are not immortal; all have disintegrated, died, or been absorbed by more fit superorganisms in the history of superorganic life on the planet. Yet, sociologists can theorize the conditions under which populations are more likely to respond successfully to selection pressures of varying types and, of course, the conditions under which it is less likely to respond effectively and thereby sustain themselves in an environment.

3
Stage-Model Theories of Societal Evolution

From the very beginnings of a discipline with an explicit name—sociology—the social universe was viewed as moving from simple to ever-more complex forms of social organization. As emphasized in Chapter 2, functionalism often accompanied these analyses of the stages of societal development; and so, when both functionalism and stage models of societal evolution from simple to complex went out of fashion in the first two decades of the 20th Century, two of the intellectual pillars of sociology's first hundred years—functional theory and stage models of societal development—were suddenly abandoned. Fortunately, as reviewed in Chapter 2, they were kept on life support in anthropology, and by the 1950s in the United States, functionalism was reborn and, then in the 1960s, its theoretical companion—stage models of evolution—were reintroduced into sociology and the social sciences more generally. Functionalism, as emphasized in Chapter 2, appeared to die once again but, in fact, the basic idea of functionalist theories has been translated into a more robust and theoretically useful conception of selection as a basic force in the evolution of sociocultural systems (see Chapter 11).

In this chapter, we will first outline the most useful stage models of societal evolution from sociology's first hundred years and then review two of the models that emerged when this form of theorizing reappeared in the latter half of the 20th Century. These and similar models now continue to provide explanatory power in the 21st Century; and while they are not the only reason for the revival of evolutionary theorizing in the social sciences more generally, they remain a mainstay of evolutionary thinking in sociology, even as new branches of evolutionary sociology continue to be pursued.

Evolutionary Theorizing in the Classical Period, 1820–1920

We are reviewing the classical stage models of societal evolution not so much for historical reasons as for their continuing power to explain an important set of dynamics in societies. Some of this explanatory power was lost to sociology during the hiatus of such forms of theorizing in the first half of the 20th Century. But, as we hope to demonstrate, there is still much to be taken from these models and used—just as we argued for functional analysis in Chapter 2.

Comte's Early Theory of Societal Evolution

Auguste Comte's general theoretical mode—when liberated by his law of the three stages of thought, the hierarchy of the sciences, organismic analogy, and view of society as all of humanity—is actually theoretically quite powerful. Figure 3.1 outlines the basic model which, as we will see, becomes part of both Spencerian and Durkheimian sociology. For Comte, as societies become larger, they begin to differentiate (or "speciate") into more complex sociocultural formations. Increasingly, problems of maintaining "coherence" of the social whole increases, and while Comte did not use these terms, a more modern representation of what he was arguing is this: Increasing complexity generates *selection pressures* for actors in societies to find new ways of integrating differentiating societies. There are, Comte implicitly argued, three basic responses to these selection pressures. One is to create relations of interdependence among the differentiated structures of a society (and idea he took from Adam Smith); another is to centralize power and authority in order to regulate relations of differentiated structures; and a third is to develop highly general symbol (cultural) systems—what today we term values, ideologies, beliefs, and institutional norms—that apply across differentiated domains of societies.

Comte did not develop these ideas to any degree, but Herbert Spencer did when he turned to sociology in the 1870s. And indeed, Spencer's

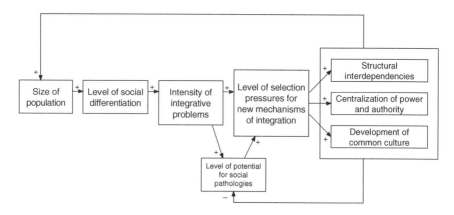

Figure 3.1 Auguste Comte's Implicit Model of Evolutionary Dynamics in Societies

general model of evolution of physical-chemical, biological, psychological, sociocultural, and even ethical domains of the universe retains Comte's emphasis that evolution is the process of movement of domains of the universe from simple, less coherent to more complex and coherent forms, with the concurrent evolution of mechanisms to integrate the larger, more complex mass of elements in each domain.

Herbert Spencer's Theory of Societal Evolution

In Herbert Spencer's (1874–1896) model of societal evolution, population growth initiates societal evolution—an idea also evident in Comte's work. As the population of a society grows, this population will begin to differentiate both their structures and cultures. Societal growth can be the result of simple reproduction of members at higher birth over death rates, or as he often argued, societies' growth by virtue of warfare, where one society conquers another, dominates those conquered in various ways from cooptation to coercive control and thereby increases the size and level of differentiation of the population to be integrated (see Chapter 4 on intersocietal evolution for more details). In either case, as emphasized in Chapter 2, societies differentiate along three (actually four) great axes that he labeled *operation* (production and reproduction), *regulation* (by power and cultural symbols), and *distribution* (by infrastructures and exchange dynamics). If we separate operation into its two components (i.e., production and reproduction), societies differentiate structures and attendant cultural systems (ideologies, beliefs, norms, texts) along four basic axes:

(1) Structures and cultures devoted to *production*, or gaining access to resources necessary to sustain the growing number of members in a society and the social units organizing their activities.
(2) Structure and cultures geared to *reproduction* of the growing numbers of members in a society and the social units needed to sustain the reproduction of not only members but the structures and cultures organizing their activities.
(3) Structures and their cultures devoted to *regulation* of the growing number of people in a society and the increasingly differentiated sociocultural formations organizing their activities.
(4) Structures and their cultures engaged in *distribution* of people, information, and resources among the growing numbers of people in a population and the growing number of differentiated structures organizing their activities across ever-larger territories.

These four axes of differentiation were often interpreted as functional needs or requisites, especially since Spencer had adopted an organismic analogy that saw similarities and differences between what he termed *organisms* (bodies) and *superorganisms* (organizing of bodies into societies). That is, as both organisms and superorganisms grow, they differentiate; and as they differentiate, they confront functional needs to increase production, reproduction, regulation, and distribution of resources. For human superorganisms, these requisites lead to institutional differentiation of economies (structures engaged in resource extraction and conversion to usable resources); reproductive structures (kin units, schools, investment banks, and other tools for building structures); regulatory structures (consolidations and centralizations of power and authority, new types of regulatory symbols such as laws, ideologies, beliefs, and norms); and distributive structures (infrastructures such as roads and ports and exchange structures like markets and widespread use of generalized media like money). Thus, the axes of differentiation are also functional requisites that must be met if a population is not to disintegrate to a state of reduced heterogeneity and coherence.

As we outlined in Chapter 2 and will further elaborate in Chapter 11, we can convert Spencer's argument into one of selection pressures. What he was, in essence, arguing is that population growth generates selection pressures along the fault lines of all superorganisms: production, reproduction, regulation, and distribution. Those populations that cannot innovate, borrow, steal, or otherwise generate new variants of sociocultural systems that increase production, reproduction, regulation, and distribution will be less fit than those that can. And he held out the distinct possibility that populations may not be able to respond to these selection pressures because of cultural or institutional rigidities, thereby causing the dissolution of the population and disintegration of its sociocultural formations. While long-term societal evolution involved increasing size and complexity along the four axes of differentiation, societies have evolved by fits and starts, moving toward more complexity but often disintegrating, only to begin evolutionary movement again toward more complexity and coherence.

Probably more than any other theorist of the 19th Century, Spencer documented his arguments with data that he had professional colleagues assemble in the massive volumes of his *Descriptive Sociology*, the precursor to, and inspiration for (via William Graham Sumner), George P. Murdock's (1949) creation of the Human Relations Area Files. *The Principles of Sociology* (1874–1896) is filled with data illustrating the principles articulated in this massive and not fully appreciated work (over 2,000 pages in three volumes). Thus, his laying out of the stages of societal evolution is not a theoretical exercise but, instead, an empirical one in which he sees different levels of differentiation along the four axes for societal types or forms that he labels in terms of their *compounding*, or level of differentiation; simple without head (e.g., nomadic hunting and gathering); simple with head (e.g., Big Men systems); compound (horticultural, pastoral, and fishing variants); doubly compound (agrarian); and trebly compound (industrial). The data in *Descriptive Sociology* describe all of the systems illustrating these five basic stages of societal evolution. If Spencer had lived beyond 1903, he would have added, no doubt, "quadrupedly compound" or something like this label, for post-industrial societal formations. Thus, by the early 1870s, Spencer had empirically illustrated the basic stages of societal evolution that would become those of later models of societal evolution (save for the post-industrial societies stage that he never saw).

But these were not simply descriptions; the movement from one stage to another was driven by (a) population growth (whether through warfare and conquest, increased rates of birth over deaths, or migrations); (b) increased differentiation along the four axes of societal growth; and (c) the selection pressures inherent in these axes for new levels and forms of production, reproduction, regulation, and distribution. Societies that can respond to (c) are likely to be fit; those that cannot do so will disintegrate and dissolve, or be conquered by a more fit society. There is, then, a very sophistical evolutionary theory contained in Spencer's sociology that, sadly, is often rejected because of his presumed organicism and functionalism. But, a more modern reading of Spencer (which is something that very few do) reveals by far the most sophistical theory of societal evolution before the 1960s in sociology, and even surpassing the theories in anthropology (e.g., White 1943, 1949; Steward 1953, 1955). There is still, as will become evident in Chapter 4, much we can learn from Spencer, once we take a more objective view of his work. Figure 3.2 anticipates some of the arguments that will be made in Chapter 11, where we outline new ways to conceptualize selection as a force in sociocultural evolution.

Additional Evolutionary Theorizing in the 19th Century in Sociology

Next to Spencer's work, other evolutionary theories pale, but each adds important elements to the new evolutionary theories of societal development that would emerge in the contemporary era. And so, we should touch upon some of these for their core ideas that become part of the newer stage models of societal evolution.

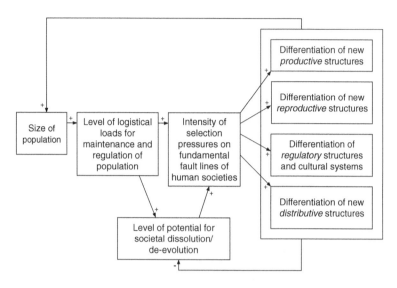

Figure 3.2 Herbert Spencer's Model of Selection Pressures Driving Societal Evolution

Emile Durkheim's Differentiation-Integration Theory

As outlined briefly in Chapter 1 and in more detail in Chapter 5, Emile Durkheim (1893: 211–12) developed a kind of ecological theory of societal evolution. Population growth increases both material (physical concentration) density and moral density (rates of interaction) among members of a population. This density increases the level of competition among actors, both individuals and corporate units, for resources; and from competition comes selection among individual and corporate units for various resource niches. And, from selection comes differentiation among individuals and collective units by their resource niches—as a kind of social speciation, or differentiation. He explicitly cites Darwin's views on natural selection, and in this sense, he may have been the first sociologist to begin borrowing from Darwin's theory in biology (in contrast, Spencer had produced his own biological theory based on his general theory of evolution as a movement from simple to complex; and, of course, he had coined the term "survival of the fittest" before Darwin's great work was published).

As became increasingly evident during Durkheim's career, he was more concerned with theorizing the basis of integration in complex societies. He had dropped by 1895 his distinction between *mechanical* and *organic* solidarity, and even the notion of "collective conscience," but even so, *The Division of Labor in Society* still proposes several key mechanisms of societal integration. One was structural interdependencies among differentiated units making up the more complex division of labor; another was normative regulation of interdependencies; still another was varying levels of what he then termed the *collective conscience*, or cultural beliefs that, he appeared to argue, could be couched at diverse levels of abstractness, ranging from specific units through sets of units in institutional domains to all units in an entire society, thereby providing a cultural basis integration among differentiated social units. Yet, the need for two different bases of societal integration—*mechanical* based upon likeness of all structural units and their cultures and *organic* based upon differentiation of units—led him to reconceptualize integration in both simple and complex societies as operating in a similar manner. This reconceptualization increasingly came to emphasize that both undifferentiated and differentiated societies can be integrated by the same mechanisms, revolving around common collective representations, totems or markers of these representations, and emotion-arousing rituals directed at totems that reaffirm the collective representations. And in this way, even with individuals located at different points in the division of labor and in different locations geographically where they never interact directly, they can nonetheless engage in ritual behaviors that integrate whole societies because their emotions are aroused by rituals directed at totems symbolizing society as a whole.

Implicitly, Durkheim was arguing that there are selection pressures in societies when they first evolved as small-scale populations and when they begin to grow and differentiate for creating abstract values and beliefs. These pressures also lead members of a growing society to formulate *collective representations* and thereby to symbolize these representations as totems toward which emotion-arousing rituals are enacted by actors at every different location in the division of labor. Societies that could not generate this system of collective representations, totems, and rituals would reveal many pathologies, such as his famous *anomie* as well as *lack of coordination, egoism* and *forced division of labor*. Thus, in Durkheim's two models, integration in evolving complex systems is generated by structural interdependencies regulated by law and norms, coupled with higher-order or more abstract collective representations that are reinforced by emotion-arousing rituals generating commitments to the whole society. Still, unlike Comte and Spencer, Durkheim gave little attention to power as an integrative force, but he did add layers of nuance to Spencer's views on the regulatory effects of cultural symbols and Comte's view of consensus over cultural beliefs.

But, in the end, Durkheim never did develop a coherent stage model of societal evolution beyond the mechanical-organic distinction, which simply notes that societies move from simple to complex forms. But, he did come to emphasize that integration of all social systems, no matter how simple or complex, requires a similar basis of integration by shared culture, totemic markers of this culture, and rituals directed to reaffirm this culture through the power of emotions to generate commitments to totems and the symbols systems that they represent.

Karl Marx's Stage Model of Societal Evolution

Karl Marx's (1846, 1847, 1867) evolutionary model emphasized five stages of societal evolution from primitive communism (nomadic hunting and gathering) to slavery (probably advanced horticulture slipping over into early agrarianism) to feudalism (advanced agrarianism) to capitalism (industrialization and market-driven economies) and, finally, to socialism (on the way) to communism. The sequence is rather loose, and only the capitalist stage is analyzed in any detail, and this looseness is typical of his analysis of communist stage where only the most general picture is offered. But, the analysis of capitalism is, of course, one of the great intellectual achievements of the 19th Century and, indeed, one that persists in evolutionary analysis into the 21st Century (Chapter 11 for Marx's implicit model of selection driving societal evolution).

The general Marxian model argues that the driving force of evolution is related to control of the *sub*structure of all societies—i.e., the means of production—which also leads to control by those who own the means of production of key *superstructural* systems, especially polity, law, and religion, and of cultural production of ideologies that legitimate elite control of the substructure and key superstructures. Increased control is necessary because exploitation dramatically increases inequalities that will, over time, lead to mobilization by the exploited against their exploiters and a revolution that ushers in a new phase of societal evolution. Marx's analysis of conflict, while flawed, still represents the basis for most analyses of conflict within societies, whether or not transformative in a fundamental way.

In many respects, Marx presents an important model of integration of societies by those who control the economy and are in a position to exploit labor (by taking profits from economic surplus produced by workers) and then to use that money to not only compound elite privilege but also to control the centers of power and ideological production in societies. With power and control of ideological production, including but not limited to law and religious beliefs, elites are able to control non-elites and justify exploitation and rising inequalities. The same forces as both Spencer and Durkheim articulated are invoked, but with a highly critical slant. Moreover, Marx's analysis of market dynamics as creating interdependencies among diverse sectors of a society (in Marx's case, exploitive interdependencies or what Durkheim called the "forced division of labor"). Both Durkheim and Marx thought, however, that exploitation would "wither away"—in Durkheim's case, with the full evolution of organic solidarity and, in Marx's case, with the eventual displacement of "the dictatorship by the proletariat" by installation of full-bodied communism. But unlike other theorists, Marx believed that just as other epochs of exploitation and inequality generated revolutionary conflict because of the inherent contradiction between collectively organized production of what is essential to life and well-being, on the one side, to limited ownership and control by elites of the very means for collective production, on the other side. This inherent conflict in all societies, save for primitive communism, would drive evolution, with capitalism providing for the first time since primitive communism the potential productive capacity for general welfare among all members of the society and, at the same time, with capitalism exposing in its labor and consumer markets the fundamental contradiction inhering in socially organized and collective production and individually controlled usurpation of economic surplus by capitalists. Moreover, capitalism would be forced by the very nature of competition in markets to sow the seeds of its own destruction by (a) exploiting labor in ways that allowed them to recognize the exploitation for what it was; (b) congregating labor in factories in urban areas where they could communicate their grievances; (c) forcing capitalists into cut-throat competition on prices that would lead to recessions, unemployment, and dislocation of workers' lives in ways that would make them aware of the unfairness of the system; (d) giving workers intellectual tools such as the ability to read political tracts; and (e) generally arousing alienation from, and anger toward, the system of exploitation and its capacity to disrupt and degrade workers' lives. For Marx, the transition to communism by conflict was inevitable, and the "end of history" would come with full-blown communism after the revolution and the temporary "dictatorship" of the proletariat.

Yet, for all of the thunder and bluster, Marx clearly underestimated the dynamics of markets to proliferate rather than polarize social classes; the ability of capitalists to compromise with their workers; the expansion of the state as a major source of employment in capitalist societies; the evolution of the state in most capitalist societies toward some degree of representative democracy (thereby diffusing, somewhat, power across classes); and mounting pressures on democratic states to make concessions to labor unions. These forces clearly worked against the inevitability of a capitalist collapse. Yet, the emphasis on production and the underlying technologies of production to drive evolution, on the emergence of markets as accelerating societal evolution, on conflict in general altering balances of power within societies and the distribution of resources as a driving force of evolution, and the power of ideology and culture to operate as both conservative forces legitimating inequalities and as also critical to mobilizing for conflict and social change (under the flag of counter-ideologies) are all part not only of contemporary social science in general but also of many types of evolutionary analysis in particular, at least within sociology. Thus, Marx's ideas still inform evolutionary sociology and particularly intersocietal evolution (see Chapter 4).

Max Weber's Stage Model

Like Marx, Max Weber (1922) saw conflict in societies arising from inequalities and stratification, but he also emphasized that the resources distributed unequally are not always highly correlated or consolidated in the same hands. When they are, he agreed, conflict is more likely. Indeed, his model of conflict is not that much different than Marx's, except for the less polemical tone. For Weber, class conflict is more likely to occur when (a) inequalities in the distribution of resources are consolidated (that is, high, medium, and low levels of power, money, prestige, honor, land, etc. are correlated with high-, medium-, and low-class locations); (b) social classes are homogeneous; (c) large distances in resources shares between classes exists; and (d) mobility up and down, but particularly up, the class system is low.

But, in contrast to Marx, Weber emphasized, first of all, that capitalism was not inevitable on the evolutionary march to communism, and secondly, when it did emerge, it reduced rather than increased conflict and revolutionary potential. Indeed, Weber posited an historical epoch increasingly dominated by "rationalism" in which virtually every institutional domain becomes bureaucratized, where money and calculation become the dominant ways to think about goals and means to goals, where tradition and affect are driven out of markets that pervade ever more transactions within and between individuals and bureaucratic units, and where what he termed a "steel enclosure" (often mistranslated as "iron cage") constrains individuals' options and perceptions of what is possible. Thus, what he termed "legitimated orders" (what can loosely be seen by what today is termed institutional systems or domains) are increasingly dominated by means-ends rationality and, as a result, are displacing older forms of domination such as tradition and emotional commitments. Institutional orders are legitimated by law and ideologies of rationality, particularly the centers of political power, but also other institutional systems, except perhaps kinship. In this form of what he termed "rational-legal domination," it becomes difficult to see the unequal distribution of resources as unfair and as a cause for conflict. There is stability in domination by means-ends and rational-legal rationality, even as such domination strips life's passions inside the "steel enclosure."

Thus, in contrast to Marx, societal evolution had allowed humans to return to something like the primitive communism (of the first human societies), but just the opposite. Weber posits a kind of "end of history" argument in which the last, and somewhat dreary, stage of societal evolution had arrived—a stage whereby rational-legal domination controlled the lives of individuals. For Marx, of course, the last stage of history had yet to arrive, but evolution to communism was now inevitable as the contradictions of capitalism led to revolution and eventually communism. Much of the 20th Century debate in sociology has been over these differing views of the "direction" in which societal evolution is moving. And this debate is still alive, as intersocietal theories of evolution examined in Chapter 4 reveal.

Georg Simmel's Stage Model of Evolution

Simmel is not normally seen as an evolutionary theorist, but he was implicitly so because he argued against both Marx's and Weber's views of societal evolution. In contrast to Weber, Simmel (1906 [1990]) argued that societies built around open markets open up new freedoms. Individuals now have more options to choose group affiliations, and they are no longer bound by old repressive traditions but by their own preferences that they can express in markets. Moreover, markets generate a sense of augmented value for individuals because when one gives up money to secure another valued good, a person does so because they have a preference for the good purchased; and the more this property of market exchange occurs, the greater will be a person's sense of value and well-being—thus countering Weber's view of the steel enclosure of rational-legal domination.

Moreover, markets encourage the spread or differentiation of new kinds of groups and organizations that open up memberships and possibilities for new types of group affiliations, thereby reducing the hold of traditional groups on choice. Markets encourage individualism over collectivism, thereby giving individuals choice and options to pursue their interests and preferences, thus creating just the opposite of Weber's "steel enclosure." Individuals may feel less embedded in supportive groups, but they are no longer constrained by them and have options to seek alternatives. Markets not only allow increased diversity of group affiliations (often for fees or dues), and hence the capacity to experience an enhanced sense of value, they also increase individuals' sense of efficacy and control over their lives. And while loneliness may increase to a degree, individuals have options and choices in how to reduce this psychological state.

Thus, while Simmel did not analyze in any detail the stages of societal evolution that had preceded market capitalism, and the dramatic increase in sociocultural differentiation that occurred, he took a much less critical stance than Marx and Weber, and perhaps even Durkheim. He actually was closer to Spencer, who saw capitalism and trade as reducing the need for war among societies because now there was an alternative mechanism—international markets for trade—that would allow for more peaceful relations among societies and for the capacity of individuals in societies to realize more of their preferences. Yet, Simmel does not appear to have relied very much on Spencer, but he added a less critical stance on the new capitalist order and perhaps even outlined the reasons that humans seem, despite all of the inequalities that capitalism generates, to prefer it to available alternatives. Such sentiments and the system of markets that have generated these sentiments will, no doubt, have large effects on the evolution of societies.

The Legacy of the Early Stage Models of Societal Evolution

We can list some of the key insights, mostly from Spencer's *The Principles of Sociology (1874–1896)* and volumes in *Descriptive Sociology* (1873–1935) but others as well. These early models anticipate the following features which appear in more recent models:

(1) Societies have, over the long run, evolved toward more complexity through differentiation of their structures and cultures.
(2) Societies have moved through a series of stages revealing particular patterns or configurations of structural and cultural differentiation. These include:

   a. *Nomadic hunting and gathering* composed of nuclear families in bands.
   b. *Communities of settled hunter-gatherers* with political leadership.
   c. *Simple horticultural communities* using wood, bone, and stone tools coupled with human power in gardening. Such systems typically are organized by extended kinship beyond nuclear families and by a system of communities, with power held by the heads of larger kinship units, often laced together by rules of descent and residence.
   d. *Fishing and pastoral, herding variants* of simple horticultural communities.

e. *Advanced horticultural societies* with more advanced tools and technology and with animals as sources of productive energy. Much activity is still organized by kinship, with political leadership still located in kinship but also with the beginnings of the first chiefdoms and early state-based polities. Communities are larger and often organized into more complex urban formations for governance as well as rituals toward the gods. Thus, higher rates of intersocietal warfare among societies begin to increase, and the first city-states and larger empires begin to evolve.
f. *Simple agrarian societies*, using the plow and animal and, at times, wind power, with a monarchy as the center of power and religion as a potential center of power. Markets and market communities begin to evolve, with dramatic increases in the differentiation of economy. Warfare among societies often leads to the consolidation of populations into larger societies after the fight has ceased.
g. *Advanced agrarian societies*, using animal, water, and wind power, governed by a monarchy and feudal system of organizing manorial states, and with religion an increasingly large and powerful institutional system legitimating the monarchy. Territories, population size, market towns, and cities and differentiation of economic actors—coupled with emerging new institutional systems, including education, arts, science, and medicine—begin to emerge, as kinship begins its de-evolution from unilineal kinship systems and patrimonial kin units to nuclear family units. Warfare and economic trade both increase, as does empire formations of potentially vast territories, large populations, extensive infrastructures for transportation, and ever-increasing military technologies.
h. *Industrial societies* using fossil fuels in economic activity and increasingly relying upon free market distribution systems within and between societies, governed by a bureaucratized state that is increasingly democratic in most societies, with some decline in religion (with exceptions) as a political force. Warfare remains chronic, internal conflicts from social movements increase, as all other institutional domains fully differentiate, with kinship completing its de-evolution to a nuclear family system.

(3) In addition to these general profiles and sequences, the classical tradition in sociology emphasizes several key forces during societal evolution:

a. Growth and differentiation at any stage set up selection pressures that, in turn, lead actors within existing institutional domains to seek new sociocultural variations that solve these adaptive problems, often by creating new institutional systems. These selection pressures revolve around:

  i. pressures to expand production
  ii. pressures to expand reproduction
  iii. pressures to increase integration among differentiated units
  vi. pressures to increase scale and scope of distribution of resources
  v. pressures to increase regulation and control
  vii. pressures to meet basic human needs for efficacy and needs generated by market systems

b. Kinship is the first institutional system to evolve and its elaboration into unilineal descent becomes the structural basis for supporting increased population growth through simple horticulture into advanced horticulture.
c. Religion is probably the second institutional system to evolve, emerging with hunting and gathering and becoming ever more elaborate through agrarianism.
d. Polity is the third institutional system to evolve, first emerging within kinship among settled hunter-gatherers, remaining in kinship through simple horticulture, and increasingly differentiating out of kinship with advanced horticulture and agrarianism.
e. Religious ideologies become the principle legitimating ideologies for polity and inequalities during simple horticulture, increasingly so through advanced horticulture and agrarianism, and even in few contemporary quasi-industrial societies.
f. Markets emerge even with hunting and gathering, based on barter, but markets increasingly expand with advanced horticulture and agrarianism and then accelerate as a force in industrial societies.
g. Intersocietal warfare has always existed between societies but increases with settled hunting and gathering, with its rate and degree of violence increasing with each new stage of societal evolution. Yet, at the same time, warfare has been a force in building up larger and more complex societies.
h. Inequalities increase through each societal stage after nomadic hunting and gathering up to industrial, where some decrease may occur relative to agrarian societies.
i. The permanence, size, connectedness, and specialization of communities begins to increase with simple horticulture.
j. Intersocietal trade has always existed but increases with evolution of markets and financial instruments for making exchanges (e.g., money, credit, holding houses, insurance, etc.).

k. The institutional system of law is evident in all societies but differentiates from kinship, religion, and even polity in advanced horticulture and then increasingly with advanced agrarianism and industrial societal forms.
l. Institutional domains—education, medicine, science, arts—begin to differentiate with advanced horticulture, early agrarianism, and fully differentiated with advanced agrarianism and industrialism.

These and other features of early evolutionary theorizing are often not examined by contemporary theories, but they were part of early evolutionary thrust of early social science and can still inform theorizing and research of human societies.

Stage Modeling of Societal Dynamics in the Contemporary Era

In the 1960s, after a long hiatus, stage models of societal evolution began to reappear in sociological theory. Functional theorists like Talcott Parsons (1966, 1971), who had been roundly criticized for a theory that could not explain social change, sought to quiet his critics by introducing a theory of long-term evolutionary change. A more conflict-oriented approach by Gerhard Lenski (1964) appears about the same time, and the differences in these approaches reflect their respective theoretical origins. Also stimulating a return to evolutionary theorizing about societies was a very large literature on "development" and "modernization" that had been accumulating, but this literature was very limited by its emphasis on stating the conditions necessary for movement from third and second world status to a modern society; and it was heavily influenced by the desire of governmental agencies, banks, and other non-governmental organizations to fund projects that would set the process of "modernization" into motion. In contrast, the more theoretical works of sociologists outside this modernization literature, which encompassed all of the social sciences, emphasis was on the long-term evolutionary change in societies from the simplest to most complex forms of organization—an emphasis that picked up where early evolutionary theorists had been shut down by negative reactions in the early 20th Century to stage models with their ethnocentrism and even somewhat racist connotations, often conflated with the eugenics movement built around Social Darwinism.

Talcott Parsons' Stage Model of Evolution

In his *Societies: Evolutionary and Comparative Perspectives* (1966), Talcott Parsons outlined a stage model that traced the history of human societies from the beginning to the period just before "modern" industrial and post-industrial societies evolved. In a second short volume, he outlined the *System of Modern Societies* (Parsons 1971) that is actually less interesting and important than the earlier effort. As is well known, Parsons conceptualized the social universe as a series of action systems: *cultural, social, personality,* and *organismic* (later termed, *behavioral*). Each of these systems exists because it resolves one of the four (really five) functional needs of all action systems for adaptation (organismic), goal attainment (personality), integration (social), and pattern maintenance/tensions management (cultural). The organismic system provides the energy for the entire set of systems. The personality system uses this energy to act and to set and seek goals; the social system coordinates relations among the social units created and sustained by action of personality systems; and the cultural system provides the information and symbols needed to regulate all of the other action systems in the form of values, beliefs, and norms for the social system, internalized moral codes and knowledge for the personality system, and as constraints on how energy is pulled into this set of action systems from the biotic and chemical-physical environment.

Parsons saw evolution as first an initial differentiation of personality, social, and cultural systems, on the one side, from the organismic system on the other (during the evolution of humans as a species). All subsequent evolution revolved around the increasing differentiation of the cultural, social, and personality systems from each other and also the internal differentiation of these three systems.

In some ways, Parsons was reproducing Spencer's grand theory of evolution in very different conceptual clothing. For example, evolution is differentiation from simple, homogeneous states to increasingly complex and differentiated states; and while Spencer wrote multi-volume treatises on the evolution of personality systems (*Principles of Psychology* 1855), organismic systems (*Principles of Biology* 1864–1867), social systems (*Principles of Sociology* 1874–1876), and at least part of cultural systems (*Principles of Ethnics* 1879–1892), Parsons simply wanted to emphasize that one way to analyze the organization of humans and societies is in terms of four action systems that, like all evolving systems, move from simple to ever-more complex forms internally and in their mutual effects on each other.

There is also a Durkheimian element in his theory because Parsons saw the cultural system (symbols and collective representations) as the regulatory force for all of the other three action systems in his functional scheme. He also drew from Durkheim in his emphasis that evolution is a process of differentiation which, in turn, generates problems of adaptation from increased complexity, thereby immediately setting into motion selection pressures for new mechanisms to integration of this complexity. Furthermore, stages of societal evolution can be viewed in terms of differentiation-integrative problems within and among the action systems. Each major stage of societal evolution always involves resolving the integrative problems—that is, coordination and control—of differentiated action systems and their relations; and until these integrative problems are resolved, further differentiation is not possible.

Thus, for Parsons, evolution is a process of differentiation, setting up selection pressures that allow for population growth, and vice versa, that generates selection pressures for integration of new levels of size and complexity; and when these integrative problems are solved, a society will have achieved *adaptive upgrading* that allows it to grow and differentiate more, until mounting integrative problems arise. In Figures 3.3a, 3.3b, and 3.3c, we have summarized Parsons' model from what he termed *primitive societies*, which were further divided into "low" and "high" primitive societies that were followed by two types of intermediate societies, (*archaic* and *advanced*) that take societal evolution to the transition to what he terms *modern societies*.

A general proposition is that, as each type of society evolves, it must reach a threshold point where the integrative problems generated by increased differentiation are resolved, hence *adaptively upgrading* the societal type. Once this threshold point is reached, societal growth, differentiation, integration, and adaptive upgrading can ensue for each basic type of society. It is important to recognize, however, that societal evolution can stall when growth and differentiation cannot be integrated; and indeed, societies can de-evolve when they cannot resolve their integrative problems. But, by fits and starts, just as Spencer emphasized, integrative problems are resolved, leading to adaptive upgrading that, in turn, makes it at least possible for further growth and differentiation. In these figures, we emphasize differentiation of cultural and structural ("social" and "cultural" as action systems) to the point of adaptive upgrading. Thus, by reading down the columns, it is possible to visualize what Parsons saw as the key points of differentiation within the cultural system and the social systems that had to occur before a society could evolve into a more complex form.

Low Primitive Stage

The basic components of this simplest form of society are means of (a) symbolic community, (b) kinship systems built around the nuclear family, (c) religion, and (d) economic technologies for hunting and gathering. Symbolic communication is the "constitutive symbolism" that enables individuals to denote and represent self, others, territories, and other key

Figure 3.3a Primitive Societies

Low	Advanced

Cultural System Differentiation:
 Symbolic communication/ religious beliefs about:
     magic
     supernatural forces
     powers of ancestors
     hunting-gathering technologies
 Conceptions of territories
 Normative regulation of:
     marriage
     economic roles
     kin roles
     relations between age/sex categories
	Cultural System Differentiation:
	 Religious beliefs begin to legitimate:
	     power and polity
	     property
	     inequality and stratification
	     control of territories
	 Normative systems elaborate and regulate:
	     systems of lineages
	     more complex divisions of labor
	     emerging administrative structures of polity
	     settlements and communities
	 Expanded technologies

Social System Differentiation: Kinship units (nuclear) Band Economic and kin divisions of labor	*Social System Differentiation:* Settlements and communities Lineages and linkages among nuclear kin units Hierarchies of power in emerging polity Emerging stratification system Expanded economic and kin divisions of labor Emerging religious structures

Figure 3.3 Parsons' Image of Societal Evolution Up to Modernity

dimensions of their environment and social organization. With this kind of symbolism, it becomes possible to develop rules and norms regulating and controlling social interactions; and with this level of regulation, it then becomes possible to create the first institutional system—nuclear kinship built around rules of incest and marriage—as well as activities within kinship that will eventually evolve into separate institutional systems—activities such as economic and religious practices. In turn, these fundamental human activities begin the process of differentiating new types of social structures and symbols of culture to regulate them; and as these initial processes of differentiation begin to unfold, individuals also begin to differentiate in terms of their personalities as action systems. Yet, only two basic categories of persons—age and sex/gender distinctions—are differentiated in these systems.

Advanced Primitive Stage

When the level of differentiation outlined above is integrated by rules and norms, further differentiation and population growth become possible. The social system begins to expand and differentiate kinship into new kinds of more complex systems built from lineages (of nuclear families) grouped into clans that can organize larger numbers of individuals and that, in turn, lead to differentiation of territories controlled and inhabited by clans. As territories are delimited, notions of property become more prevalent; and as properties are acquired and controlled, inequalities and stratification become new nodes of differentiation in human societies. Because both more complex kin systems and stratification generate new integrative problems, religion increasingly becomes institutionalized and operates as an ever-more important integrative mechanism; and as religion does so, it too becomes larger and more internally differentiated with distinctive religious personnel and beliefs about the supernatural realm and the forces in this realm.

Escalating inequalities along with increasing population size generate selection pressures for the evolution of polity, in which power is consolidated and centralized in chiefs who begin to develop military systems not only to sustain order but also to conquer the territories of other populations. With this level of political development, coupled with more complex kinship and religious systems, a society will have achieved sufficient adaptive upgrading to evolve to *archaic* and, then, to *advanced intermediate* societies.

The Archaic Stage

The invention of writing at this stage enables the cultural system to expand and differentiate because symbolism is now freed of the limits of human memory in face-to-face interaction, and indeed in time and space more generally. Knowledge, history, customs, traditions, and religious beliefs as well as other moral and even quasi-legal codes can now become written down and more systematic. It is now possible for all forms of knowledge, including technologies and other innovations to accumulate; and in Parsons' view, the cultural system can now become more differentiated from the other action systems (i.e., personality and social systems) and become more internally differentiated.

While literacy is typically confined to elites or representative of elites, primarily in the institutional domains of religion and polity, written records further differentiate these systems, while providing the means for them to become more internally differentiated and autonomous from other institutional systems like kinship and economy. And as the administrative system of polity expands, power becomes more consolidated, while the religious bureaucracy expands to legitimate polity and, in so doing, becomes politically and economically more central, if not more powerful, than polity. Even though the administrative bureaucracy of polity grows, it is still based on ascription, but it can still be used to expand the capacities of polity for coordination and control, war making, public works, taxation, and redistribution to other elites. And while inequalities increase, polity is sufficiently powerful, especially when legitimated by religion, to control the tensions that inequality always generates. Thus, with the expansion of polity as an autonomous institutional domain, archaic societies become *adaptively upgraded* to evolve to a more advanced stage of evolution.

Figure 3.3b Intermediate societies

Archaic	Advanced
Cultural System Differentiation: Written language system that:	*Cultural System Differentiation*: Expansion of writing, leading to:
expands symbol systems, including: technological, religious, political, historical, normative, and emerging laws	coherent set of quasi-codified religious beliefs
	accumulation of knowledge and technology
	histories and stable traditions
allows for increased differentiation between and within social and cultural systems	written contracts in expanded economy and emerging markets
allows for increased structural differentiation in social system	codified sets of more universalistic laws in emerging legal system
Social System Differentiation:	*Social System Differentiation*:
Larger, more permanent settlements	Increased differentiation among polity, kinship, religion, and legal system
Centralized polity and expanded administrative functions	Expansion of markets and market relations among social structures
Control of larger territories by polity and organized coercion	Increasing use of money and credit in markets
Expanded religious structures	Full institutionalization of contracts

Advanced Intermediate Societies

This stage of evolution is typified by increased differentiation among polity, religion, and kinship, with polity continuing to differentiate internally and thereby able to continue expanding its powers in order to tax and thus build up its military and administrative structures. As a result, inequality continues to increase, with the class system also becoming more differentiated.

A critical invention at this stage in Parsons' eyes is the emergence of universalistic law (equal application of the law), at least in principle. While ascription remains as the criterion for membership in groups and organizations across polity and religion, law encourages the development of another medium: money. With money, markets are freed from barter, thereby increasing the rate, velocity, and scope of economic exchanges to expand as trade and commerce within and between societies. With universalistic law, money, and market exchange using money, another critical invention occurs: credit. Credit allows exchanges to expand further, while those lending money are protected by contracts. And thus, as markets, money, contract law, and credit expand, they become differentiating forces in societies because they allow a diversity of preferences to be met by further differentiation of economic production, mediated by more differentiated forms of credit contacts. At this point, human societies now have in place the potential to begin the transition to fully modern societies. Indeed, for Parsons, the power of ascription and inequalities, coupled with power consolidated in polity and religion had worked against universalistic

Figure 3.3c Transition to Modern Societies

Key Cultural System Changes:
Universalistic and contract law
Beliefs about capitalism
New technologies using inanimate and fossil fuel sources of energy
Ideologies emphasizing rights of persons and political democracy
Sense of societal community, unified by common culture and sustained by commitments to this culture

Key Social System Changes:
Emergence of democratic polity
Expansion of positivistic and universalistic legal system
Expansion of free, profit-oriented markets using money and credit
Ascendance of polity over religion as agent of social control
Legitimation of polity by law and more secular legal codes
Expansion of educational system and access to citizenry in this system
Institutionalization of science and technological innovation

law; and without universalistic law, economic production and distribution in free markets using credit and contracts could not occur on a large scale. The result was blockage to further differentiation, and most importantly, to economic development. But, with universalistic law, the potential for further differentiation and integration to ever-higher levels of *adaptive upgrading* increases dramatically.

The Transition to Modernity

Modernity arises out of the cultural, social structural, and psychological base evident in advanced agrarian societies (in Parsons' terms advanced "intermediate" societies [Parsons 1971]). Economies are increasingly built around profit-seeking markets that generate incentives for increasing varieties of productive outputs; and these incentives continue to increase as differentiation accelerates across diverse institutional domains. Universalistic law is, in Parsons' eyes, the key ingredient to make markets more dynamic and to regulate exchanges; and universalistic law eventually paves the way for movement toward political democracy, which becomes one of the defining features of modernity, at least in Parsons' eyes. By the turn into the 19th Century, new sources of energy are harnessed to machines, generating the industrial revolution that only increases the volume, velocity, and scope of market exchanges involving money and credit for ever-increasing varieties of goods and eventually services. Parsons argues that during this process a "societal community" is created, which consists of territories revealing a common polity and culture that, in turn, leads to a sense of nationalism.

Parsons' theory was criticized when it first came out, but it does present some important theoretical points. Stages are defined by the particular configuration of social structures and cultural systems that solve adaptive problems; and once these are solved, growth and differentiation can continue until new integrative problems arise, forcing new cultural systems and social structures to evolve if societal evolution is to continue. Parsons' functionalism may have led him to this point of emphasis, but nonetheless, it is not entirely wrong; and it should be given a new hearing because even 19th Century stage models recognized that each stage has *involved similar configurations* of culture and social structure.

Gerhard Lenski's Theorizing on Societal Evolution

With the publication of his book, *Power and Privilege: A Theory of Stratification* (1964), Gerhard Lenski brought a more conflict-oriented model back into modern sociology; and for the subsequent decades before his recent death, Lenski continued to develop his theory in the many editions of *Societies: An Introduction to Macrosociology* (Nolan and Lenski 2015 is the 11th edition), and in his less well-known book, *Ecological-Evolutionary Theory: Principles and Applications* (2005), his descriptions and theorizing about societal evolution continued. Lenski's theorizing was based upon the extensive body of empirical research assembled in the Human Area Relations Files, first assembled in the late 1920s by George P. Murdock who, as noted earlier, had been a student of Albert Galloway Keller and, hence, exposed to Herbert Spencer's *Descriptive Sociology* (1873–1934 in 16 volumes, some of which were published after Spencer's death). The Human Area Relations Files continue to be developed and still provide the best database for doing comparative and evolutionary analysis on types of societies, although other evolutionary theorists are now consolidating new databases to test evolutionary theories (see discussion of Peter Turchin's work in Chapter 4). Thus, Lenski brought a more conflict-oriented approach, coupled with a new emphasis on ecology, which made his model much more influential than Parsons' scheme that was still embedded in functionalist reasoning of societies as evolving to meet needs and requisites. Lenski also brought Spencer's emphasis on using large amounts of data to build and assess theoretical generalizations with the result that his descriptions of the stages of societal evolution are very similar to Spencer's.

The Early Theory

Lenski argued, like many stage modelers, that there was a driving force in societal evolution, and this driving force is technology. Many other theories make a similar argument, phrasing the issue as the capacity of a society to "capture energy" (e.g., White 1943, 1959). The higher the *level of technology*, or knowledge base about how to manipulate the environment, particularly the knowledge needed to capture energy, the higher will be the *level of production*. And, the higher the level of production, the greater will be the *economic surplus*, above and beyond a population's subsistence needs. The greater the economic surplus, the more likely are those with power to usurp this surplus to further their hold on power, and prestige as well, and hence, the greater will be the *level of inequality* and *stratification* in a society. Although Lenski was not aware that his model expressed in modern terms much the same argument as Spencer did in his theory (1873–1996), Lenski outlined the elements and fundamental relationships in his theory in a manner similar to Figure 3.3 (note: Figure 3.2a models Spencer's theory). One factor that would take on greater importance in the theory over its development is environmental conditions, such as the level of resources available in geographical space, as well as the presence of others societies that can pose military threats or opportunities for trade. The level of technology, of course, determines to what extent resources are available because technology influences access to energy. Hunter-gatherers, for example, would not have knowledge or use for oil or coal if it were under their feet because they do not have the requisite level of technology.

Another factor in Lenski's early theorizing beyond resources available is demographic, revolving around the size of a population, its composition (by sex ratios, age, ethnicity) and characteristics (religion, class system, etc.). Still another factor is the nature of social organization generated from resources, with special emphasis on the form of polity and its degree of consolidation of power, but other institutional systems as well, especially the structure of kinship, religion, law, education, and science.

Yet another set of important factors is the geopolitical and geoeconomic situation of a society with respect to competition with other societies for economic resources and the potential for warfare with other societies. And, a final set of factors are cultural, revolving around values and ideologies that emerge and constrain patterns of social organization and, hence, possibilities for particular types of action by both individual and collective actors.

We have bold-faced those arrows that Lenski saw as the most important or "primary" in Figure 3.4. Thus, the relationships among technology, production, surplus, consolidation of power, inequality, and stratification are the primary variables in his theory. This line of emphasis removed the functionalism from stage modeling and was in tune with the rise of conflict theory in American sociology during the 1960s because, in the end, the theory sought to explain the evolution of inequality and stratification over the history of societal evolution. Without a surplus of resources, inequality is less likely because there is nothing to distribute unequally, and there would be little incentive to consolidate power, as is evident among nomadic hunter-gatherers. But, the history of human society since hunting and gathering is one where the level of technology, production, surplus, and usurpation of surplus by the powerful had all increased, and thus inequality and stratification should have increased through the various stages that Lenski outlines: nomadic hunter-gatherers without political leaders, settled hunter-gathers with political leaders (thereby initiating the dynamics outlined in Figure 3.3), simple and then advanced horticulture (with marine and pastoral variants), simple to advanced agriculture (with marine variants), and industrial to post-industrial. Each stage of societal evolution can be typified by technological advances: hunting, gathering, and fishing; gardening with human power; agriculture with animal, wind, and water power; and factory production using fossil fuels and nuclear, geothermal, and solar power.

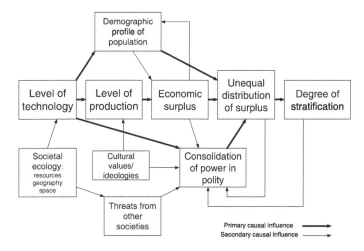

Figure 3.4 Lenski's Early Model of Forces Driving Evolution of Societies and Their Stratification

Like virtually all evolutionary stage models, each stage is also typified by a new level of complexity as technologies allow for population growth through increased production as these, in turn, cause institutional systems to differentiate and stratification to increase inequalities along many dimensions. The driving force is technology, compared to most functional theories' emphasis of population growth as generating the selection pressures that lead to more production, distribution, regulation, and reproduction. But, as the title of *Power and Privilege* makes clear: Lenski was trying to explain the evolution of stratification, but in so doing, he developed a model of the stages of societal evolution that closely parallel those of Spencer, at least up to the post-industrial period (which Spencer never saw).

Lenski "discovered" (but surely knew already) that the monotonic relationship among the variables in his theory cannot produce increases in inequality and stratification forever. The key "finding" in the data is that after the agrarian stage, inequalities decrease slightly in industrial and post-industrial societies—thus reversing to some degree the long evolutionary trend toward ever-more inequality and stratification. To explain this "reversal" of the evolutionary trend, Lenski introduced secondary variables, which incorporate some of the cultural and structural changes found in Parsons' model, including: democratization of power, extension of education to all members of a population and increasing use of education as a means for assessing skill, and changes in ideologies for more equality, or at least equalities of opportunities, in industrial societies.

This early theory did much more than Parsons' model to revitalize evolutionary thinking in sociology, not just of societal stages of development but even other forms of evolutionary thinking. In the ensuing five decades, he continued to develop his thinking, while turning more toward nature of societies at each stage of evolution. The focus on stratification shifted to an analysis of institutional systems in societies during societal evolution.

Lenski's Shift to an Ecological-Evolutionary Approach

In his last major work, Lenski continued his analysis of macrostructures, or the evolution of societies (see the next section for more details), but his *Ecological-Evolutionary Theory: Principles and Applications* (2005) places his approach in the context of the similarities and differences between evolution of humans and their societies, on the one side, and the evolution of life forms in general and those life forms that communicate and organize societies or collectivities, on the other.

(i) *The Unit of Analysis*. Human societies should be seen as a species-specific manifestation of a more general pattern of organization among conspecifics, including "colonies of insects, schools of fish, flocks of birds, herds of elephants, packs of wolves, and colonial invertebrates of various kinds (e.g., corals, sponges, the Portuguese man-of-war)" (2005: 17). Cooperation is thus a universal property of life forms, with human societies representing a unique form revolving around "*the degree to that an aggregation of people is politically autonomous and engaged in a broad range of cooperative activities, it can be considered a society*" (2005: 17, italics in original). The dependent variables of such societies to be explained by a theory include: mode and level of production; level of wealth and income inequalities; level of specialization (differentiation) of such forms as occupations, organizations, and communities; level of intersocietal connections; size of territories; and magnitude of resources controlled by a society. The interesting paradox for theory is to explain why, for most of human history, societies did not change dramatically from hunting and gathering, and then, about 10,000 years ago, societies began to change and grow larger and more complex. This raises the question of "*how has it been possible for the system as a whole to change so dramatically when the vast majority of its constituents parts were successfully resisting change* [for so long]?" (2005: 31, italics in original). To address this paradoxical question, it is important to compare humans and their forms of organization to earlier forms of human societies as well as to forms of organization among non-human animals.

(ii) *What Humans Share With All Other Species*. Lenski's list in this comparison represents a modern-day invocation of Spencer's early organismic analogy. Human cells are composed of the same basic materials; human metabolism is like that of larger life forms, particularly mammals; like all life forms, humans depend upon their environment for resources that can be converted into metabolic energy as well as other resources needed to build societies; humans are like other animals in genetic programming for self-preservation; and like other animals have means for reproducing themselves and the structures organizing their activities.

In Figure 3.5a, we lay out Lenski's model of the basic biological paradigm, but in somewhat modified form. For most life forms, the solid lines in Figure 3.5a outline the basic process of evolution where the phenotype of a population (behavior and organization) remain regulated by the information in the genome of a population and the biosocial environment as these have been affected by behaviors and organizational patterns of a species. Change occurs when population phenotypes have altered the distribution of genes and the biosocial environment to which a species must adapt. And, for most species there is virtually no information transmitted by learning via a system of signals and communication, although some species can do so (hence, the dotted line) in which change at Time-2 is directly affected by behaviors and organizational patterns, independently of any effects on

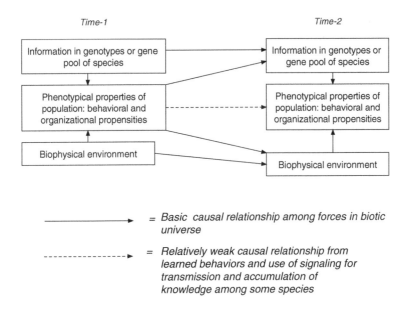

Figure 3.5a. The Basic Biological Problem

the genome or environment. Thus, for most life forms, when viewed from the perspective of genetics, evolution is directed by changes in heritable or transferable information in the genotype, as this is affected by members of a population's adaptation to biophysical environments by the behaviors of individuals and the organizational patterns (if any) that they evidence, or their "phenotypical properties."

Figure 3.5b emphasizes the effects of culture among humans, whereby new information can be added to the sociocultural phenotype of a population and passed on to subsequent generations, and while Lenski emphasized population-to-population phenotype transfer with the bold-face arrow, some additional arrows could be added, especially from phenotype Time-1 and Time-2 to the biophysical environment because human behaviors and patterns of social organization not only change the biophysical environment to which the population must adapt, they also change the sociocultural environment of any given population; and increasingly, adaptation is to sociocultural environments as much as biophysical environments. Symbolic culture thus gives human societies the capacity to change rapidly, thereby changing the basic nature of evolution. Still, Lenski emphasized, as we do in later chapters, that the biological propensities humans to act in certain ways cannot be ignored.

In Figure 3.5c, Lenski adds key forces in the phenotype of a population—population (size and characteristics), ideology (cultural

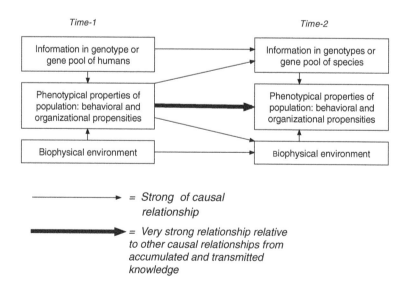

Figure 3.5b. The Sociological Paradigm in Evolutionary Analysis

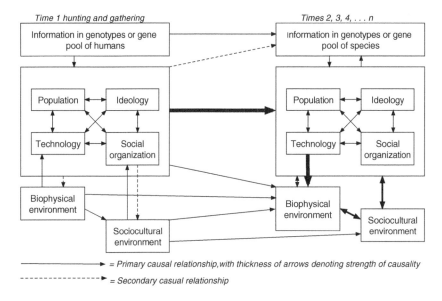

Figure 3.5c. Sociocultural Paradigm Over Time

prescriptions), technology, and social organization—and then denotes at the bottom the sociocultural environment as it is affected by the biophysical environment. In this first stage model outlining determinates of individual societies, Lenski adds a downward arrow on how a society can potentially change its biophysical and sociocultural environments (but the arrow is dotted because capacity of hunter-gathers to change their sociocultural environments is limited).

In this early conceptual setup for his theory, Lenski develops an equation on the forces affecting the level of economic surplus in a society, which initiates evolution, as he argued in *Power and Privilege* (1964). He begins with Malthus' famous "standard of living" arguments (as a function of level of resources relative to size of population), interestingly adds Sumner's and Keller's key ideas that population size is determined and limited by technologies, access to resources, and the standards of acceptable living by members of a population, and then ends with his own equation whereby economic surplus is a function of the multiplicative effects among level of (*resources*) × (*technology*) × (*capital*), divided by population size (recognizing that other forces can intervene in this basic relationship). The relations among these variables explain, to a high degree, the movement of societies during societal evolution from hunting and gathering through horticulture and agriculture (including fishing and pastoral variants) through industrial and post-industrial phases.

(iii) *The Nature of Human Nature.* Lenski emphasizes that *"what social theory should and cannot tolerate is the current widespread practice of leaving assumptions about human nature largely unstated and unexamined"* (2005: 48, italics in original). He offers a list of features of humans that have the most effects on behavior and social organization, including:

(1) Fundamental needs for (a) food, water, sleep, oxygen, etc., for sustaining life; (b) sexual needs that often go beyond what is necessary for procreation; (c) needs for play; (d) need for varied experiences; (e) needs for social experiences; (f) needs prefacing visual variety; (g) needs to explore; and (h) needs for physical contact.
(2) Capacities for spoken language using artificial symbols revealing phonemes, morphemes, and syntax communicating common meanings that can dramatically expand the stores of information available to members of a society.
(3) Motivations to maximize pleasurable experiences and minimize painful and unpleasant ones.
(4) Programmed capacities for learning from experience and for modifying behaviors in response to learning.
(5) Capacities to (a) develop derivative needs and desires from learning and experiences, including efficacy or control of others and circumstances, (b) possess material things, (c) obtain emotion gratifications, and even (d) discern the meaning of life.
(6) Propensities to see differences and to categorize self and others into distinctive types (by many criteria such as age, sex, gender, sexual preferences, ethnicity, class, religious affiliation, etc.).
(7) Preferences to economize most of the time and seek the greatest benefit for least expenditure of energy.
(8) Propensities to display emotions toward others, while reading the emotions of others.
(9) Develop a sense of self vis-à-vis others and to evaluate one's own and the sense of self of others.
(10) Revise definitions and conceptions of self and self-interests over the life course.

This list and the more complete explanations are still overly speculative, but Lenski is correct that it is necessary to begin to understand the nature of humans, as honed by natural selection, because so much of human behavior, and hence human social organization, is constrained by these needs and capacities. Much of sociobiology (examined in Chapters 6, 7, and 8 and evolutionary psychology in Chapter 9) has engaged in understanding how biologically hard-wired bioprogrammers affect human behavior. We will point out some of the limitations in these approaches in Chapters 10 and 11, but in Chapters 13, 14, 16, and 17, we use cladistic analysis from biology to provide more understanding of human nature as it evolved from the nature of humans' hominin ancestors and now affects human behavior and patterns of social organization. The goal is to bring a bit more precision into the search for human nature than is evident in Lenski's as well as others' analysis of human nature.

Lenski's and Nolan's Analysis of Societal Macrostructures

Over the decades in which editions of Lenski's *Societies: A Macrostructural Introduction* were published, societal development was increasingly seen in more Darwinian-sounding terms, using ideas from the Modern Synthesis in biology—an indicator of how much biological theorizing had already penetrated the social sciences. For example, over 20 years ago, the 6th edition of *Societies* (1995: 75) by Gerhard and Jean Lenski, along with Patrick Nolan, emphasized that both biological and social evolution are "based on records of experience that are preserved and transmitted from generation to generation in the form of coded systems of information" and "on processes that involve random variation and selection." There are, however, important differences between biological and social evolution, one of which is that genes are the preservers of informational codes in organic evolution, whereas cultural "symbol systems are the functional equivalent of the genetic alphabet in social evolution" (Lenski et al., 1995: 75). Another difference inheres in the way that information is transmitted. In biological evolution, genetic information can be transmitted only through reproduction of new generations of organism; and since diverse species cannot interbreed, transmission of information is confined to one species. Cultural information, in contrast, can be more readily and broadly transmitted, moving from one type of society to another, with the result that long-term evolution "is likely to eventuate in fewer and less dissimilar societies than exist today" (Lenski et al., 1995: 75–76), whereas transmission of genetic information leads to speciation and ever-more patterns of differentiation and diversification among species. Yet another, very important difference is that acquired traits can be transmitted across generations and societal types, whereas this is very much less the case with biological evolution. The result is that biological evolution is slow compared to societal evolution, which can be very rapid if new informational codes are invented, learned, diffused, and transmitted in one generation.

The upshot of these differences and similarities is that humans as organisms are like any other animal and are influenced by their genetic heritage, but humans are creators of their cultural heritage and its informational codes that guide behaviors and the formation of patterns of social organization. A society, then, is very different than an organism; and for analytical purposes, a society can be divided into (a) its population and the size and characteristics of this population; (b) its culture and systems of symbols, with special attention to technological information; (c) its material products generated by the application of technologies to productive processes; (d) its organizational formations that structure activities of individual and collective actors; and (e) its institutional systems that combine (a) through (d) into sociocultural systems addressing basic problems of survival and adaptation for individuals and the society as a whole. At the same time, (a) through (e) influence and, reciprocally, are influenced by the biophysical environment of a society, the social environment consisting of other societies and their cultures, the genetic heritage of humans as a species of evolved apes, and the prior social and cultural characteristics as these continue to influence the internal operation of society and its modes of adaptation to its biophysical and sociocultural environments. And, Lenski (1995: 23) increasingly began to emphasize that "it seems no exaggeration to say that advances in subsistence technology are functionally equivalent to adaptive changes in a population's gene pool; new energy resources and new materials enable populations to do things that could not be done before." Many of the above points will be part of our general assessment of how much, and how far, theoretical ideas from the biological sciences go in understanding the sociocultural universe (see Chapter 10).

For Lenski and Nolan, societal evolution is more rapid because of the capacities of humans to innovate new codes and, when needed, to extinguish old cultural codes and structural patterns that are no longer adaptive, as is outlined in Figures 3.5a, 3.5b, and 3.5c earlier. Humans have capacities for agency to create the very variations on which selection operate (see Chapters 10 and 11). Indeed, as listed earlier for Lenski's *Ecology-Evolution Theory* (2005), humans have needs, desires, and capacities that allow, indeed often push, them to create new cultural codes that can be used to build new sociocultural formations; and once built, these cultural systems can be copied and exported to other societies. Further, humans have been able to create entire institutional systems, such as science, that are devoted to generating new knowledge and information codes by which to organize societies.

There are, however, conservative forces built into the very nature of societies. One is *socialization* of individuals into culture, with the result that they may resist new cultural codes if they deviate too far from what they believe is important. A related conservative force is *ideology*, which biases perceptions and behavioral propensities and thereby preserves cultural systems and practices passed from generation to generation. The conservative power of ideology comes from its capacity to *moralize* existing cultural codes, although counter-ideologies can moralize efforts to change cultural codes. Another conservative force are the *interdependencies* that often make change difficult and highly disruptive, with the result that actors resist change. Still another force are *vested interests*, particularly of those with power, who can use this power to control changes that go against these interests. And finally, sociocultural *inertia* can limit change because current practices may be seen as satisfactory and as promoting sufficient well-being and adaptation to the environment.

Yet, the history of societal evolution has been one of change, fueled by technological innovations. And the direction of change has also been clear: toward ever-more complexity within societies and increasing similarity among even complex societies. Yet societies vary because of such forces as (a) the amount of information possessed in the present and its nature have large effects on how easy it is to develop new cultural codes or receive them from other societies; (b) the size of the population as this affects the ability to develop new ideas or incorporate ideas from other societies; (c) the stability or instability in both biophysical and sociocultural environments will affect a society's ability to innovate or to adopt information from other societies; (d) the nature of innovations with some stimulating further developments and others less so; and (e) the combination of conservative forces summarized that are in play in a given society affects its capacity to innovate or to adopt innovations of other societies.

In the end, however, societies are more fit when they can develop new productive technologies that can be used to build new kinds of sociocultural formations and that can be developed in response to changes in the sociocultural or biophysical environments—an idea similar to Talcott Parsons' notion of "adaptive upgrading." And this is why technology coupled with capital, as these affect production, has been the driving force of societal evolution. Higher levels of technology and capital generate surplus resources that can be used to build up new cultural codes and new institutional arrangements that can solve adaptive problems. And as more innovative societies engage in exchange, pursue warfare, and allow their ideas to diffuse to other societies, these innovative societies tend to push the larger system of societies in a given direction, thus leading to convergences with the culture and structure of fit societies.

There is, then, a kind of group selection, or multi-level selection, on sociocultural phenotypes more than on body phenotypes that drives the evolution of societies as they operate in systems of societies (see Chapter 4). Many of these point echo Spencer's views on evolution because, when he employed his famous phrase, "survival of the fittest," he emphasized that warfare leads to convergences of less fit societies to those that conquer them by being larger, more productive, and better organized; and as he emphasized near the end of his life, further societal and intersocietal evolution should be driven by exchange rather than warfare which can be destructive and which also biases technological development to military operations rather than more general production. Spencer thus hoped that, at the turn into the 20th Century, that warfare could be reduced (obviously his hopes did not come to fruition) and that a system of societies engaged in trade would be the force driving future societal and intersocial evolution (on this score he was more prophetic, as will be examined in Chapter 4). And so, as Lenski and Nolan have pushed their general theory (see Nolan & Lenski, 2014; Nolan 2014), they have not only converged, at least to some extent, with the Modern Synthesis (with qualifications to be examined in this book) but also with the often ignored insights of Herbert Spencer who was the dominant evolutionary theorist and researcher of the 19th Century.

Conclusion

Sociology began as a discipline oriented to explaining the evolution of societies. Such is clearly the case with Auguste Comte and Herbert Spencer, but also sociologically oriented theorist of the 19th Century—from Marx and Weber through Durkheim and Simmel and virtually all others—posited an evolutionary model. The obvious push behind this effort was the industrial revolution as it was transforming agrarian societies and, concurrently, new data on pre-literate societies that began to pour into Europe in the late 18th Century in the works of Alexander Humboldt, for example, but perhaps more importantly from missionaries and later field anthropologists in the 19th Century. It is important to recognize that thinkers like Spencer anticipated, rather than followed, evolutionary thinking in biology. For better or worse, Spencer introduced the world to the notion of "survival of the fittest" before Darwin introduced the idea of "natural selection," and his *The Principles of Biology* (1864–1867), followed by his more general treatise on the laws of evolution, *First Principles* (1862), developed a theory of evolution emphasizing movement of domains of the universe from simple to more complex systems, and in the case of the social universe, this movement is, to some extent like the biotic universe, because it is driven by a selection processes. All these ideas were developed either before and, mostly independently of Darwin's great work; and indeed, from the very beginnings of sociology as an explicit field of inquiry with Comte and even Saint-Simon, the notion of evolution was as paramount as it was in the development of biology in the 19th Century.

Where these early theories faltered was in seeing evolution in the context of social progress and the celebration of European advancement, eventually leading to theories that were rather ethnocentric. Yet, Spencer's theory and later those of Sumner and Keller in the early decades of the 20th Century are surprisingly sophisticated, if only contemporary scholars would be willing to read them. At any rate, the criticism about stage models is that they are too constraining in how evolution of societies is analyzed because they appear to lock societies into a step-by-step progression through discrete stages. Yet, they provide important information on what forces drive evolution and on what combinations of institutional system emerge under varying levels of technological-economic development. Whether Spencer, Parsons, or Lenski-Nolan, the models also inform sociology about what types of stratification systems develop from various configurations of institutional systems under varying technological-economic regimes.

Stage models have thus not only given sociology and other disciplines a sense for the longer-term development of human societies, but more importantly, of how this development occurs under ecological and sociological forces that, in turn, generate varying configurations of social and cultural organization. In fact, some such as J. H. Turner have taken these theories and eliminated the stage aspects of the theories and emphasized the explanatory power of the theories when seen as a series of abstract sociological laws (1995, Turner 2010a). Stage-model theories, then, are much more than simplistic or naïve presentations of how societies have evolved; they have been critical over the last 200 years in developing sociology as a scientific discipline. Indeed, there is as much of physics in many of these principles as biology, but the new evolutionary sociology should consider both the physics and bio-ecology of human social organization.

4
Intersocietal Models of Societal Evolution

Early Sociological Analyses of Intersocietal Systems

Evolutionary analysis in sociology has increasingly focused on intersocietal relations as a driving force of sociocultural evolution. Societies do not exist in isolation but, instead, are part of a system of societies, with the unit of evolution being this system as much as its constituent societies. Among early sociologists, Herbert Spencer (1894–1896) and Max Weber (1922) offered the most sophisticated analyses of intersocietal evolution. For Spencer, his famous phrase, "survival of the fittest," was used in his sociology to emphasize that one of the driving forces of societal evolution from simplicity to complexity has been war. Larger, more productive, politically centralized, and technologically advanced societies generally could win wars against societies that are smaller and not as productive, politically organized, or technologically advanced. While one society might vanquish the population of another, a much more typical pattern is to consolidate a conquered population into the institutional systems of the conquering society, thereby creating a larger and more complex society. Such complexity inevitably generates selection problems around production, reproduction, distribution, and regulation; and as these selection pressures are met, the resulting system was better adapted to its biophysical and sociocultural environments. Spencer did caution, however, that war and conquest could lead to too much centralization and reliance on the coercive base of power, resulting in internal tensions that lead to internal conflicts and societal disintegration. He also cautioned that such "militant" societies, where too much over-regulation occurred, also tended to bias production and the technologies of production toward military outputs, thus decreasing domestic productivity and, in the end, inviting problems of regulation. Near his death, Spencer came to realize that war and conquest leading to empire formations were, in the end, counter-productive because lowered domestic productivity, exploitative extraction of resources from those conquered, overcentralization of power, and increased inequality only make societies unstable. Instead, he increasingly argued that market forces rather than use of force are a better way to integrate societies into a larger system of societies—an idea that anticipates world systems theorizing over the last 50 years.

Less well known among all of his contributions to sociology is Max Weber's (1922) model of geopolitics, which builds upon his analysis of domination, stratification, and conflict. For Weber, high levels of internal domination by coercion or administration increase the dependence of productive actors on political authority, leading to two types of intersocietal relations: (1) cooptation by political authority of key sectors of neighboring societies and (2) conquest by warfare of neighboring societies. Success in either of these strategies increases the prestige and legitimation of polity in the dominant society in this new system of societies. However, as the size of these intersocietal systems increases and as the level of inequality among societies and often within the dominant society increase, revolts led by charismatic leaders can eventually occur. And, as the dominant polity mobilizes more resources for social control, inequalities escalate even more; and eventually, the central core polity of the system of societies will fail at either cooptation or coercive control of one or more of its neighboring societies. The result would be a loss of prestige in this "world system" and rapid de-legitimation of the central polity, often resulting in revolt by elites and/or non-elites, thereby assuring the breakdown of the intersocietal system.

Thus, early sociologists were obviously aware of the dynamics of intersocietal systems, but it was not until the second half of the 20th Century that sociologists began to emphasize that systems of societies are as important in understanding sociocultural evolution as are the internal dynamics of any one society. Societies have always had "neighbors," even in simple nomadic hunting and gathering societies, but as the size of (a) societies, (b) settlements within societies, and (c) borders demarking territories organizing populations have all grown, societal evolution is increasingly a process of *intersocietal evolution*. Even in early societal formations among pre-literate populations, the dynamics of intersocietal systems were evident, but they became increasingly obvious during the evolution of advanced horticultural and pastoral society through agrarian societies to the modern world system.

The Rise of World Systems Analysis in Sociology

In the 1970s, both Marx-inspired and Weber-inspired conflict approaches began to shift the unit of analysis in societal evolution to *relations among societies*. Capitalism was viewed as the dynamic engine of transformations that would eventually create a world-level economy and perhaps polity as well. The study of geopolitical empires had, of course, been prominent among historians, and early British economists like J. A. Hobson (1900,

1902a, 1902b, 1938) began to conceptualize economic empires at the turn of the 20th Century. But, it was the pioneering work of sociologists such as Immanuel Wallerstein (1974, 1979, 1984,1989) and a few others, such as Andre Gunder Frank (1969, 1978,1979, 1998), coupled historical analysis of capitalism by scholars like Fernand Braudel (1972, 1975, 1977, 1979), that led to a new conception of world systems built around capitalism.

These efforts began to emphasize two basic forms of interconnection among societies: (1) *world empires* created by military conquest, or threats thereof, and exploitive extraction of resources from dominated societies and (2) *world economies* consisting of asymmetrical exchange relations among multiple states, often revealing inequalities among societies in terms of their power in intersocietal markets. A *world empire* is created by military domination of other societies, but such domination can vary in terms of how much autonomy dominated societies can retain in exchange for tribute to the dominant polity. Whatever the exact nature and degree of domination or relative autonomy, world empires extract tribute, taxes, and other forms of direct appropriation of resources from other societies, which they then use to build up their military for control and perhaps further warfare, while lining the pockets of elites in the dominant society. Such empires eventually collapse from overextension and mounting logistical loads as is outlined by Randall Collins, whose work on empires will be examined shortly (see also Turner 1995, 2010a). World economies reveal a very different structure from world empires because, even though societies within a world economy may engage in warfare or threats of warfare, their relations are also regulated by market exchanges, and particularly if their respective military power is approximately equal. This distinction between world empires and world economies was, to a degree, viewed as an evolutionary sequence, with world empires being an earlier mode of intersocietal formation, while with the rise of capitalism, world systems were increasingly dominated by economic relations.

Immanuel Wallerstein's Conceptualization of World Systems

While there were many in the 1960s and 1970s who contributed to the recent conceptualization of world systems, Immanuel Wallerstein's (1974, 1979, 2004) work was foundational to the perspective. For Wallerstein, world empires are geopolitical formations that typified relations among societies before the 1400s, but with the rise of mercantilism and then capitalism, the fundamental nature of world systems increasingly evolved toward a world economy, although many have challenged this argument since world economies often have dominant political actors who extract resources to sustain their coercive powers and to reward elites. What Wallerstein added to the previous analysis of world systems was the idea this system is composed of three components: (1) the *core* states that have both political and economic power and that compete with each other militarily and economically; (2) *peripheral* states that are comparatively poor but resource rich and, hence, are viewed by core states as a lower-cost sources of raw resources and cheap labor; and (3) *semi-peripheral* states that are minor nations in the core or leading states in the periphery. As we will see shortly, these semi-peripheral states are often viewed by theorists as the engine of evolutionary change of world systems.

The core states have large consumer markets for both luxury and basic goods, well-paid labor forces, low rates of taxation allowing for the accumulation of private wealth, high levels of technology and innovation, coupled with markets encouraging innovations, and large-scale firms that engage in trade with peripheral states. The core can engage in exploitive trade because societies at the periphery are at a trading disadvantage because they do not have resources to fund infrastructural development, education, and other needs of their population and because they are often overpopulated which places a large welfare burden and potential source of revolt on peripheral states. Under these conditions, they must accept the tradeoffs offered by core states, which only increase peripheral states' problems while letting valued natural resources go to the core and, at times, to the semi-peripheral states mediating relations between core and periphery.

Core states reveal certain features in common with world empires. They have large military capacities and are often at war with each other over access to the resources of peripheral states. They also encounter the same problems of sustaining control of the periphery because they must incur large costs in coercive and administrative control over their own populations as well as those of the periphery. And, when core states engage in war, these fiscal problems only increase, thereby increasing the chances of either or both elite and mass revolts. Thus, as with geopolitical empires, the core states are often caught up in cyclical dynamics revolving around the high costs of social control that, over time, erode coercive and administrative power to control not only the periphery but the core as well.

Another political-economic dynamic emphasized by Wallerstein is what are termed *Kondratieff waves* or *oscillations*, lasting 45 to 50 years, in world systems. At the beginning of this long-term cycle, demand in core states for goods is high, leading to increased production and need for more raw materials that are secured from the periphery. Under these conditions, the world economy expands, but over time, the supply of raw materials exceeds demand in the core, leading core states to reduce geographical expansions and, especially important, causing core economic actors to cut back on production. These pull-backs by political and economic actors in the core set into motion the dynamics emphasized by Marx: lowered domestic demand, decreased production, layoffs of workers that further reduces domestic demand, increase competition by businesses and lowering of prices setting off "falling rates of profit," further reductions in demand, intensified competition, business failures, and increased rates of unemployment leading to decreased demand and accelerating failing rates of profit.

Eventually, oligopolies and monopolies are the only viable economic actors. The next stage in this oscillation is mobilization of workers, who become increasingly aware of their interests due to unemployment, leading (contrary to Marx's prediction) to the state's intervention to raise wages for workers and provide welfare and other opportunities to increase employment. These policies lead to increased economic demand, leading now concentrated capital producers to seek technologies that lower production costs. And, for a time, increased production, higher wages, and higher rates of employment increase demand for raw resources from the periphery, but in the end, this new round of prosperity falls victim to the forces emphasized by Marx: market saturation, increased layoffs due to reduced demand, increased unemployment that further reduces demand, decreased production, increases in business failures, and new financial crises—thereby closing out this 50-year wave.

Other economic cycles were increasingly conceptualized within Wallerstein's early world-economic analysis. The classical business cycle or *Juglar cycles* of 5 to 7 years is emphasized, not so much leading to a depression but as setting up demands for capital goods to replacing lower technologies and less efficient forms of capital, which increasingly becomes a larger proportion of demand in the economy. Another cycle is the *Kuznet cycle*, which lasts about 25 years in core and semi-peripheral states; and these appear related to generational turnover, as each new generation reaches full adulthood and begins to purchase consumer goods for new households.

Perhaps the most important contribution from world systems analysis is the notion of *hegemonic sequences*, an idea that others along with Wallerstein increasingly introduced into the analysis of intersocietal evolution. In world empires, these sequences revolved around the rise and fall of geopolitical empires as sequences of war, conquest, tribute, inequality, revolt, and collapse play themselves out (see later discussion of this form of evolution). With the rise of capitalism, however, these hegemonic sequences are altered. Hegemonic core states seek to control trade, particularly trade across oceans, thereby connecting core and periphery in exploitive trade arrangements. The core state, or states, of this system have the power to keep advancing empires from encroaching on this exploitive trade, and indeed, their power is so great that they can force world empires to act as capitalists in the system of world trade (e.g., the fate of China and Russia in the last half the 20th Century). This cycle thus revolves around the rise and fall of hegemonic core states that have controlled the terms of trade and exchange in the world economy. Shifts in dominance can come with wars, but unlike pre-capitalist empires, the domination that ensues is oriented to dictating the terms of trade as much as it is about outright conquest of territories or the extraction of tribute in response to military threats. The rise of the new hegemonic state allows for its increased access to the resources of peripheral and semi-peripheral, while allowing for some domination of other core states (e.g., the U.S. since the end of World War II).

Most world-systems theorists still accept an "end of history" argument about capitalism, free markets, and political democracy (e.g., Parsons 1966; Fukuyama 1999), and the current vision among many world-system theorists that the world capitalist economic system, when fully developed, will expose the inherent contradictions of capitalism, causing the rise of world-level socialism—although just how this is to occur is left vague. But the basic idea is that capitalism will continue to spread across the globe, and when this occurs, there will be no escape from the contradictions and revolutionary conflicts outlined by Marx that usher in world-level socialism (Wallerstein 1984; Arrighi 1994). This hypothesis is, we suspect, more of a hope driven by ideological commitments than an actual analysis of how the global system will evolve.

Christopher Chase-Dunn's Blending of World Systems Analysis With Evolutionary Theorizing

The sociologist who has been most interested in blending the ideas of Wallerstein with evolutionary analysis in sociology and, to a degree, with bio-ecology is Christopher Chase-Dunn (1998) who, along with various collaborators (e.g., Chase-Dunn and Willard 1993, 1994, 1998; Chase-Dunn and Hall 1991, 1997; Chase-Dunn et al., 1998), has extended Wallerstein's analysis. His work continues with the distinction among core, periphery, and semi-periphery but emphasizes the semi-peripheral as a prominent driving force in world systems evolution. Moreover, he has emphasized more than anyone the need to shift the unit of analysis from society to intersocietal system, even when engaging in stage-model evolutionary analysis (see Chase-Dunn and Lerro 2014). Another critical departure from much world systems analysis is Chase-Dunn's recognition that even pre-literate societies were often part of a world system, and thus, their evolution to more complex forms often occurs in the context of intersocietal dynamics (see Chase-Dunn and Mann 1998). Additionally, Chase-Dunn has been willing to explore the evolution of humans as a distinct kind of evolved great ape, the changes to the brain and other body systems during hominin evolution, the more complex and intense emotional systems that evolved, and the effects of the evolution of societies from simple foraging/hunting forms to more complex forms has affected the nature of self, thinking, emotions, and motives of humans. Virtually no other world-system theorists have treaded into these more biological subfields of inquiry (see Chase-Dunn and Lerro 2014: 1–72).

Thus, the evolution of the world system is ultimately a result of biological selection on the neuroanatomy of hominins and, then with the arrival of *Homo sapiens*, evolution of increasingly more complex societies from the original "stateless" nomadic hunting and gathering societies. The modern world system has been built up by smaller and simpler world systems of the past that, like the modern system, were driven by the dynamics of warfare and exchange.

Key Properties of World Systems

When the unit of analysis shifts to the world system, the evolution of any given society as well as the emergence of new stages or types of societies is an outcome of intersocietal dynamics. And while the stages look much the same as those outlined in Chapter 3 on stage models (see Chase-Dunn and Lerro 2014), and while analysis still focuses on transformations of institutional systems—e.g., economy, polity, kinship, religion, etc.—over time and space, the underlying dynamics are conceptualized somewhat differently when the unit of analysis is the system of societies rather than individual societies or types of societies.

The evolution of societies is now seen to be driven by longer-term time frames and larger tracts of the geographical space encompassing a world system. And, special attention is paid to the stratification of societies into a hierarchy of political domination and/or economic domination of a core or set of core societies over peripheral and semi-peripheral societies in this hierarchy. World systems can, as noted above, be rather small, and they do not always form hierarchies or even reveal the tri-part core, periphery, and semi-periphery, but ultimately the dynamics that change societies do reveal these properties conceptualized by Wallerstein. Moreover, Chase-Dunn has outlined in more detail the origins from simple to more advanced societies just how such hierarchies, revolving around core, periphery, and semi-periphery have evolved. Moreover, Chase-Dunn and collaborators

Intersocietal Models of Evolution • 79

have examined in more particular detail how semi-peripheral capitalist city-states have had important effects on the expansion and deepening of trade networks and the development of technologies that were important for profit-making as a form of accumulation of capitalism. The size of a world system is determined by the level of development of key technologies of transportation, production, communication, and distribution. The higher these technologies, the larger will a world system become across geographical space and the more likely will it come to evidence hierarchy among societies in a system of societies. Chase-Dunn (2001) argues that world systems have evolved because of demographic, ecological, economic, and political processes; and thus, focus is on the level of economic and political development of populations of varying size within the ecology of geographical space. He has consistently presented what he terms the "iteration model" to emphasize this emphasis. This model is outlined in Figure 4.1.

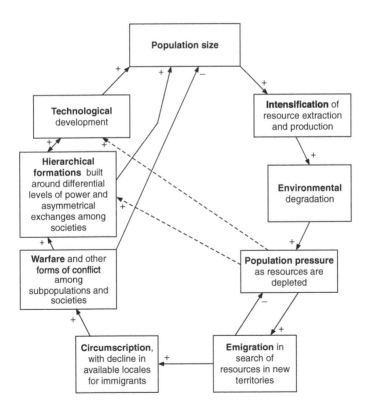

Figure 4.1 Christopher Chase-Dunn's Iteration Model of Intersocietal Dynamics

Population growth (at the top of the model) drives much of this system, but population growth is also a consequence of the dynamics outlined on the left side of the model. Population growth intensifies production (and often leads to fundamental changes in productive technologies), which in turn leads to intensification of production and, potentially, environmental degradation. Environmental degradation puts pressure on a population to find new sources of resources. Often the larger cycle is cut short by the population of one or more societies engaging in conflict to take the territories (and resources) of a less developed and powerful neighboring society, thereby setting up a pattern of domination or hierarchy among societies. The short cut around the cycle is denoted in Figure 4.1 by the dotted arrows. At other times, the cycle is fuller, with population pressure causing emigration to new territories, which only places more stress on resources, especially if there are no open territories to which to migrate because societies circumscribe the size of each other's territory. Under conditions of high circumscription, conflict becomes inevitable, leading to the formation of hierarchy by the dominant core society (or societies) over those that they have conquered or have come to dominate in exchange relations.

All of these dynamics, as they generate population growth and as they put pressures on the environment for resources, will typically cause technological innovations by core states, at least in the early phases of formation of a world system. The model emphasizes iteration, which means the short and long cycles outlined in the model occur again and again, and it is the dynamics outlined in these cycles that have caused societies to evolve from simpler to more complex forms. Thus, iterations are often much like spirals rather than cycles in that there is often evolution to higher levels of complexity as cycles play themselves out. But evolution is not smoothly linear; it occurs by fits and starts, and so often, a hierarchical world system will collapse, and societies may even devolve to simpler forms, only to be built up again as conflict among societies increases, leading to more hierarchy and technological development in response to population growth and pressures to secure more resources from the environment.

World system evolution occurs in somewhat the same manner outlined by early stage modelers like Herbert Spencer: Population growth generates selection pressures for new institutional systems—more productive economy; a polity capable of regulating and controlling the larger population; warfare with neighboring societies; and the formation of alliances, confederations, or hierarchies revolving around core, periphery, and semi-periphery. Once this basic pattern of world system is created, it tends to be reproduced; and by fits and starts, the system evolves, as do the individual societies in this system. Chase-Dunn and Bruce Lerro (2014) have outlined a stage model of the types of societies that have evolved from the original societal formation, nomadic hunting and gathering bands, but what they add to the models outlined in Chapter 3 is a view that these are the effect of world system dynamics, with the intersocietal system being the most appropriate unit of analysis in evolutionary theorizing about societies.

Dynamics of World System Growth

Chase-Dunn and various colleagues (e.g., Chase-Dunn and Hall 1997; Inoue, Chase-Dunn et al. 2016) have argued that societal and intersocietal evolution has occurred through what is termed "upsweeps" in which the size, complexity, and geographical reach of world systems suddenly increases. There are more normal changes in world systems where one dominant polity is replaced by another, but in these cases, the size and complexity of the system does not increase dramatically and, in fact, may even decrease. An upsweep is, therefore, much less frequent than the normal rise and fall of polities, and more importantly, it involves "a significant increase in the size of the largest polity relative to the previous peak" (Inoue, Chase-Dunn et al. 2016). Chase-Dunn and colleagues have counted twenty-one such upsweeps in the history of intersocietal systems in five world regions since the early Bronze Age. In this approach, Chase-Dunn and collaborators like Thomas Hall (2000) emphasize that semi-peripheral states have been a driving force in these upsweeps. Chase-Dunn with Hall and others report data revealing that about one-half of all the upsweeps can be attributed to non-core (peripheral or semi-peripheral marcher states), while they hypothesize that the other half have been caused by the secular cycle operating internally to core polities (see analysis of Turchin's work below).

Not all world systems have had the core, peripheral, and semi-peripheral structure of the modern world system, but they all reveal various kinds of networks of relations among societies that evidence varying "spatial scales." Chase-Dunn distinguishes among "place-centric" networks that reveal density near a focal polity and then fall off with greater geographical distance from this polity, "bulk goods" networks exchanging food and raw materials, "political-military networks" (PMNs) that are more extensive than bulk goods and place-centric networks, "prestige" networks that distribute and circulate symbols of honor, and "information" networks. Core-periphery-semi-periphery regions are typically evident with the presence of asymmetrical power inhering in political-military networks and unequal or exploitive exchanges of bulk goods, although information and prestige networks are almost always also involved in distinguishing societies in a hierarchy of relations.

The typical pattern in the normal rise and fall of societies in a world system revolves around a series of predicable events: (1) ever-higher levels of stratification within and between societies as new core powers rise; (2) higher degrees of political centralization evidencing more corruption and power-use to increase exploitive relations in all networks as core powers engage in one-sided extractive practices; (3) high-levels of sunk costs by the core in infrastructures and particular forms of institutional systems (e.g., economic, political, religious) generating high levels of institutional inertia that becomes increasingly difficult to change; and (4) high levels of conservatism and rigidity in cultural beliefs. The result is that core societies often become overpopulated, politically corrupt, and fiscally destitute from needs to sustain large coercive forces for social control and to provide domestic elites with privilege. As a result, during this decline, they become vulnerable to being supplanted by new core states which disproportionately come from the semi-periphery in the world system.

In Chase-Dunn's model, then, one of the most likely sources of challenge to core states is a society in the semi-periphery, in a number of ways: geographically on the edges and outside the territorial core of a world system, demographically less populated, organizationally small, with smaller settlement patterns, less complexity, and at time even surviving in a marginal set of ecological niches (which gives them incentives to take resources from other states). Such societies do not generally evidence the same level of inequality and stratification as core states, have fewer sunk costs in infrastructures, less differentiated institutional systems, and less conservatism in their cultures. And so, whether chiefdoms, city-states, or nation states, these semi-peripheral societies often become marcher states. They can ramp up their coercive capacities; often develop and deploy new military technologies (e.g., chariots, horse cavalry, new types of bows and arrows, etc.); and evidence high degrees of ethnic and societal solidarity (Turchin 2006). The result is that they can conquer or often force older core states into paying tribute and into making other political and economic concessions, thereby shifting the locus of the hierarchical structure of the more inclusive intersocietal system. Yet, not all semi-peripheral societies take over an intersocietal polity; instead, as noted above, they often force tribute from the core, come to dominate key markets that control the flow of both bulk and prestige goods, or become brokers among older but now weaker core states. Much of their preparation for war occurs as tensions along the borders of core and semi-periphery increase, causing them to ramp up their military, centralize polity, and develop new technologies for making war or gaining advantages in commercial exchanges.

Yet, like the core that they displace or force to accommodate, once semi-peripheral states become more dominant, successive generations become, themselves, increasingly as vulnerable as the core states that they supplanted, for many of the same reasons as the old core grew weaker: increased stratification, political centralization, commitment to existing institutional formations and thereby increasing institutional inertia, and cultural conservatism. And as the cycles in Figure 4.1 play themselves out, a new round of conflict and hierarchy becomes increasingly likely.

Is Intersocietal Evolution Directional?

Stage-model evolutionary theorizing tended to see societies as becoming larger and more complex, and in many ways, intersocietal theories make the same assumption, with the caveat that evolution is punctuated by rise and fall, or even de-evolution. World systems theories as they developed in the 1970s had a heavy dose of Marxist ideology in this sense: The evolution of world capitalism would, in the end, expose the inherent contradictions of capitalism and, as a consequence, usher in a world system organized around socialist principles. Theorists like Chase-Dunn see the modern world system as capitalist and, hence, as driven by the need to accumulate resources, increase production, and profit from sales of commodities. The interstate system that has been emerging for many decades, if not centuries, consists of a very large political-military network (PMN), but one revolving around sovereign nations that compete economically in global markets, even as they engage in military competition. The states that survive in, or enter, the core regions have strong polities (biased toward democracy), with economies that specialize in high-technology, high-wage production, while weaker peripheral states specialize in labor-intensive and low-wage production (often on behalf of core states). These features of the world system are constantly reproduced, even as some states move in and out of the core. And, they are subject to the cycles examined in the discussion of Wallerstein's work: Kondratieff waves (K-waves) over 50 years whereby production increases and then slowly declines and leads to stagnation, business or Juglar cycles of 5 to 7 or 8 years, and hegemonic sequences.

Chase-Dunn (2001) would add the severity of wars among nations in the world system, and the effects of these wars on K-waves, hegemonic sequences, and even the shorter business cycle. He also adds a list of trends, including: (a) the deepening and expansion of commodity relations in which land, labor, wealth, and technology are mediated by market systems within both the core and periphery; (b) the increasing power and control of states over their population, even with explicit efforts at deregulation; (c) international integration of economies, particularly the use of markets to facilitate the flow of capital across the globe; (d) the increasing levels of capital intensity and, hence, mechanization of production; (e) the proletarianization of work through the increased dependence of individuals as exchange commodities in labor markets; (f) the growing gap in income in core-periphery societies since the 19th Century, even with the mobility of societies like the United States, Japan, Korea, Taiwan, and China from semi-periphery to core; and (g) increasing political integration through stronger political and economic actors (e.g., World Bank, International Monetary Fund, European Union, United Nations, etc.).

The unresolved issue here is whether or not these trends, even in former state-communist societies, signal a march of capitalism to become fully global, at which point its inherent contradictions will force a new form of integration within and between nations. At this point, speculation about trends becomes somewhat ideological—i.e., what scholars *want* to happen—rather than an analysis of what will actually occur. One can argue for evolution into a world socialist system or, its converse, the collapse of world capitalism to regional confederations (e.g., the North American Free Trade Zone) and new rounds of intersocietal conflict. At this point, theoretical social science cannot offer definitive arguments one way or the other.

Randall Collins' Formative Theory of Geopolitics

In the 1980s, Randall Collins examined the Soviet Union and concluded that its viability was problematic—an assertion that contradicted the then current Cold War thinking. But, while his theory was not explicitly evolutionary, it was a theory that made predictions based upon historical data. Empires grow, with the largest reaching as much as 8 million square miles, and then they tend to decline and eventually lose key wars that push them back to their home base. We are examining Collins' theory here because it served as a source for even more sophisticated theories explaining how empires are built up and why they decline—a topic that had long been examined by historians but less so by sociologists.

Collins (1975: 408–11, 1986: 145–208) argued that warfare between two nation-states is related to (1) their relative *resource advantages* with respect to technology, productivity, population size, and wealth formation and (2) the marchland advantage of a nation-state, or the degree to which (a) a state is protected on its borders by natural buffers (e.g., mountains, oceans, deserts, etc.); (b) a state has a potential adversaries on only one border; and (c) a state is somewhat peripheral to systems of other states. Under these conditions, a nation can march outward and potentially conquer other states, especially if it can maintain its marchland resource advantages over other states. These conditions, however, become increasingly difficult to sustain as a state moves out from its home base. For, as a marcher state moves out and controls ever-more territory, it increasingly faces mounting challenges, including: (a) maintaining logistical loads (e.g., sufficient troops, administrative agencies, infrastructures for transportation and communication) necessary for controlling larger territories of potentially hostile and often ethnically or religiously diverse subjects increase exponentially; (b) potential adversaries along its expanded borders inevitably grow, thereby decreasing its marchland advantage; (c) coercive advantages with respect to sufficient numbers of standing military can decline with more enemies; (d) once superior military technologies are ever-more likely to be copied by potential adversaries, and (e) confronting another marcher state in a showdown war are likely to increase.

At some point, some or all of the conditions listed above cannot be avoided, with the result that an empire stops expanding and, over time, begins to lose the capacity to maintain its hold on territory. An empire will collapse, as did the Soviet Union in the early 1990s, because it is overextended beyond its logistical capacities to maintain full control over the territories of the empire, because it must engage in a showdown war with another expanding empire, or because it simply confronts other states with equal or superior military technologies. Collins' analysis of the Soviet Union emphasized, long before others had reached this conclusion, that the empire that had begun to expand from Moscow (1) was at the limits of its logistical capacities to control such a large territory; (2) was now in a "cold war" confrontation with a much wealthier, more productive, and more technological advanced empire (the United States and NATO); and (3) was potentially in a showdown war that it could not win (as became evident when the U.S. dramatically escalated its military and technological build up beyond the capacity of the Soviet Union to respond fiscally and, moreover, beyond the capacity of its weak economy to sustain the necessary production).

Collins' was one of the first sociological theories isolating particular forces that affect empire growth, size, and collapse that could make empirical predictions. His work was followed by others, who more explicitly began to conceptualize the growth of empires and the build-up of macrosociocultural formations in terms of the dynamics of war. The most prominent of these new theorists is Peter Turchin. Trained as a mathematical biologist, but with considerable knowledge of the history of societies, Turchin has increasingly used his formal theorizing skills, now incorporating social science dynamics, into a general theory of war-making as a driving force of societal evolution from simple to ever-more complex societies—much in the tradition of Herbert Spencer. Moreover, like Spencer, he has assembled large stores of data to test the plausibility of his and competing theories of societal evolution.

Peter Turchin's Intersocietal Analysis

Over that last two decades, Peter Turchin has been a strong advocate for a theory of "cultural evolution." His first major work in social science (as opposed to his home field of ecology) was titled *Historical Dynamics: Why States Rise and Fall* (2003), followed by a series of books that further developed a theory not only of the rise and fall of states but also of the evolution of more complex sociocultural formations, with the driving force of such evolution being warfare.

Ibn Khaldun's Theory of Political Cycles

Perhaps only someone entering sociology from the outside would invoke the ideas of a 14th Century Arab thinker as an inspiration for contemporary theorizing in sociology. Ibn Khaldun is a name that is known, but his work is rarely read by contemporary sociologists. Khaldun's *The Muquaddimah: An Introduction to History* was, at one time when sociologists still read Khaldun, often considered the first explicitly sociological treatment of populations and societies. And, ironically, it is a biologist who must remind sociology of this very early figure in sociology.

Turchin emphasizes in his first major book on social evolution, *Historical Dynamics* (2003), that Khaldun made very useful observations on the rise and fall of societies and their respective polities, emphasizing variables that become prominent in all of Turchin's theorizing. Khaldun developed a theory to explain the cyclical dynamics among the Medieval populations of the Middle East, but the theory is generalizable to many other regions. The theory emphasizes that solidarity built around ethnicity or other cultural characteristics that penetrates all social structures of a subpopulation is typically the key to their success in war, especially when they engage in conflict with seemingly more advanced or "civilized" populations. He termed this solidarity *asabiya*, which is a shared sense of solidarity and confidence among groups to realize their interests in opposition to others (Turchin 2003: 38). Two distinctive ethnic subpopulations were described by Ibn Khaldun: the Berbers and the Arabs who occupied different niches and, hence, were organized very differently. He stressed that the Berbers were a combination of nomads in the desert, coupled with more sedentary subpopulations, whereas the Arabs were urban and "civilized." The populations varied in their respective numbers, with the Arab population being much larger than the Berbers, as well as more politically organized into states and even empires, compared to the smaller-scale and less politically developed organization of the Berbers. The Berbers lived more on the edge of Arab territories in smaller communities and, in the case of nomads, in temporary communities.

The theory developed by Ibn Khaldun emphasizes that larger, urbanized populations tend to lose *asabiya*, whereas those living in more marginal habitats must constantly depend upon their capacity to cooperate in order to sustain themselves, and in so doing, they reveal more solidarity and confidence, or *asabiya*. Khaldun postulated that a new and viable polity will degenerate over four generations (around 100 years) from a combination of factors, including: overproduction and consumption of luxury goods, elite competition for luxuries and "conveniences," and corruption within the polity (which he saw as co-extensive with elites). This degeneration is accelerated with each generation by population growth that causes increased scarcity, increased oppression of non-elites by elites, and increased competition among elites. Eventually the state or polity is near collapse, and most importantly, the population will have lost *asabiya*. The more "civilized" society thus becomes vulnerable to better-organized populations on its margins that reveal high levels of *asabiya*; and as a consequence, these marginal populations sweep in and establish a new state, and set the process of initial growth and integration, eventually to be followed by degeneration, into motion once again. (In fact, Vilfredo Pareto [1916, 1935], the father of the neoclassical equilibrium model in economics, may have borrowed from Khaldun as he turned to sociology and began to view the circulation of elites and foxes in terms of a continuous cycle, as did Hebert Spencer in his distinction between the cycling of societies at all stages of evolutionary development from "militant" [politically centralized] to "industrial" [less centralized] profiles.)

Whatever the precise merits of Ibn Khaldun's analysis, several critical themes that now typify Turchin's more recent work emerge from this attention to Khaldun. First, many evolutionary dynamics are cyclical, often with phases within these cycles. Second, warfare is often the force behind the evolution of societies from smaller to larger sociocultural formations. Third, success in war is often related to the mobilization of populations at the margins of developed states and even empires that have developed institutional rigidities and degenerated from population growth and increased scarcity—a theme that can be seen in much world systems analysis like that developed by Chase-Dunn on the semi-periphery as a force of innovation. And so, Turchin's early work is a more sophisticated version of Herbert Spencer's argument that the driving force behind the evolution of societies from simple to more complex forms is competition and conflict between societies.

In this first major work, Turchin pursues all of these themes, developing mathematical models on the cyclical dynamics of geopolitics, collective solidarity, meta-ethnic frontiers, a demographic-structural theory, and secular cycles in population numbers. And, as becomes increasingly apparent in all of his work, these models are assessed against ever-increasing amounts of systemized data. In this chapter, we will only be able to examine Turchin's theoretical efforts selectively, but these are nonetheless the core of his evolutionary analysis.

Secular Cycles and the Demographic-Structural Theory

COMPONENTS OF THE MODEL

In *Secular Cycles* (Turchin and Nefadov 2009), a general theoretical model is presented, mostly in verbal terms in the opening chapter, and then illustrated with analyses in Europe and Russia during their agrarian eras. In more recent work (Turchin et al. 2013), Turchin and colleagues formalize the model and apply it to the analysis of instabilities of societies in both historical and contemporary settings. This theory often denoted by the label of a "demographic-structural" model and draws from Jack Goldstone's (1990) ground-breaking analysis of the long-term historical causes of state breakdown in agrarian societies.

Like Turchin, Goldstone (1990) sees population growth as setting into motion a series of related events over long periods of time: resource scarcity, price inflation, escalated costs to the state, state borrowing, elite expansion and demands for patronage, falling real wages, rural poverty, and migration of young age cohorts to urban areas. All of these cascading processes work to cause a polity to fail, whether from internal revolt by commoners and/or by elites or from external conquest by another polity. Turchin extends these ideas, viewing them as cycle that occurred in agrarian societies, but his goal is to generalize the model to apply to other historical epochs, thereby producing a more general theory of cultural evolution (Turchin 2013).

The model is constructed from several basic elements or "components." One is a demographic component emphasizing population density in relation to the carrying capacity of the environment, which is determined by "physiographic features" (availability of land, water, soil characteristics, etc.) for agricultural production; length of seasons; long-term changes in climate; and, of course, level of agricultural technology and its deployment.

As population density approaches the carrying capacity of the environment, shortages in land and food, coupled with oversupplies of agricultural labor, lead to a decline in per-capita consumption, particularly among the poor segments of a society. And, when the carrying capacity is reached or exceeded, economic distress leads to lower rates of reproduction and higher rates of mortality (due to such forces as simple undernourishment or disease and epidemics on the vulnerable population). Birth rates eventually appear to reach an equilibrium point between birth and death rates, but in fact, such is rarely the case because a new set of economic forces is unleashed that generally works against this equilibrium state.

In fact, when population growth exceeds the productive capacity of the economy, the economic component has further consequences for the demographic component. When the economy can no longer provide resources for the whole population, a number of significant changes in the distribution of the population and the structures organizing their activities are unleashed, including: high rents and prices for land, creating high profits and wealth for elites but, at the same time, "fragmenting" and loosening peasant land holdings, which in turn causes urbanization of many former peasants who are willing to work for lower wages in craft activities that expand and differentiate in urban areas. These changes encourage more manufacturing of goods and conspicuous consumption by elites, which in turn, expands regional and international trade. The gap in income and well-being between the poor and elite members of the society expands, creating increasing tensions over new levels of stratification. Periodic crop failures make the plight of the poor and common folk even worse, often creating widespread undernourishment that encourages epidemics. At some point, this economic misery leads to urban uprisings and peasant revolts that, if wealth is sufficient to maintain a strong state, are generally crushed.

Turchin and Nefadov's (2009) conceptualization of the social structural component is somewhat arbitrarily set apart from the demographic/economic components, but the general thrust of the argument is that worsening conditions for the poor create a "golden age" for elites, as depressed wages and chronic unemployment, coupled with rising prices and land rents, allow existing elites and aspiring elites to gain wealth rapidly, leading to an increase in the elite population and its capacity to support a strong state apparatus to protect their interests against the growing tensions with the poorer segments of the population.

Yet, this "golden age" cannot endure because as elite numbers grow, particularly when the state extends elite status in exchange for loans and

90 • The Continuing Sociological Tradition

other financial considerations to sustain its operations. The growth of the elites segment of the population, coupled with a leveling off of productivity, will lower per-capita elite income and wealth. In turn, as elite income and wealth stagnate and then decline, resources to support the state and its capacity for social control also decline, creating a legitimation crisis from not only the restless rural and urban poor but also from elites who see their patronage from the state and their incomes falling. The result is for the fiscal crisis of the state to fuel internal revolts or to encourage invasions and conquest by other societies in the environment of a society in crisis. There are many intervening forces that can affect the rate at which this state of affairs comes to pass, such as the ability of the state to secure resources from military conquests before its fiscal problems are exposed, the rate of competition among elites and their respective demands for patronage from the state, the number of hostile populations in the environment of a society, the effects of epidemics in reducing the size of the population and thereby increasing demand for labor, and other forces listed by Turchin and Nefedov (2009: 12–17).

Phases Within the Cycle

Figure 4.2 outlines the secular cycle discussed above into an "integrative" upward slope, followed by a "disintegrative" slope to complete the cycle,

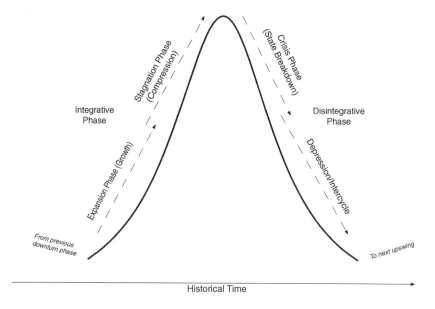

Figure 4.2 Predictions of Demographic-Structural Theory

with the integrative phase set in motion again when a new round of political control, increased production, and population growth occurs. Turchin and Nefedov (2009) also include in this larger cycle a set of sub-phases, which are denoted by the dotted lines. These lines overlap because the end and beginning of phases are, for a time, difficult to determine. On the integrative side, there is first an expansion phase, where the general population grows and elite membership declines somewhat, while the strength of the state and unity among elites increases, as does more general solidarity across the population. Turchin and Nefedov list for this phase a number of trends, including: low political instability, abundant free land (but declining), increased land cultivation, high land-to-peasant ratio (but declining), low land prices (but increasing), low grain prices, high real wages, low rents, high personal consumption, low levels of usury, high grain reserves, rural settlement growth, low levels of urbanization, few artisan and crafts workers, low levels of trade, reliance on local trading networks, low levels of economic inequality, taxes increasing, positive and optimistic ideology, and low levels of state intervention in the economy.

This phase of the cycle begins to set the conditions for the stagflation phase, however, causing a "compression" as the population grows but at a decreasing rate and as the carrying capacity of the environment is approached. Still, as noted, it is a "golden era" for elites, at least for a time, as high rents and prices create wealth and bring more individuals and families into the elites who now must compete against each other for patronage and, as a consequence, eventually see their per-capita income and wealth begin to decline. For all of the other features listed for the expansion phase, this phase sees the beginning of a reversal of the trends in the expansion phase: State strength is declining, and political instability is increasing; rural settlements stagnate as growth in their numbers declines, while cities are growing as rents, real wages, personal consumption, and grain reserves all decline, creating rural misery and setting off migrations to urban areas where low-cost labor begins to engage in craft and artistic production. For a time, elites enjoy privilege and engage in conspicuous consumption, as inequalities increase and begin to create tensions reflected in less optimistic cultural orientations. State revenue begins to decline, and the state initiates social reforms, infrastructure development, colonization of borderlands, and new territories. These can stave off, for a time, fiscal crises, but the logistical and administrative structures needed to sustain colonies incur new cost burdens on the state, all of which are accelerated by the costs of maintaining coercive forces across larger territories. As the stagflation phase comes to a close, the downward slide or disintegrative side of the cycle begins with a new "crisis" phase, or what Turchin and Nefedov (2009) label "state breakdown" as described by Goldstone (1990). The population begins to decline from its peak, as elites factionalize into conflict blocks, while sustaining high levels of corruption. Income and wealth inequalities increase, and service elites are increasingly impoverished along with rural peasants. Urbanization remains high, and craft and artistic production also remains high, as settlements in rural areas are abandoned. State is near collapse or has collapsed, and thus instability is at its peak, as the state goes bankrupt and loses control over its army and bureaucracy. The result is for trade to decline, often being interrupted by political unrest. Tax revenues decline, thereby escalating the fiscal crisis of the state. Wages, rents, and grain prices fluctuate, while personal consumption declines and creates a subsistence crisis for much of the population. Peasant uprisings, urban revolts, interelite conflict, and regional and national rebellions destroy internal peace and order; and increasingly cultural ideologies revolve around calls for social justice, debt forgiveness, and land redistribution.

This state breakdown phase of the downward side of the cycle moves into a "depression" phase. The size of the population is at a low from its peak, and the number of elites has declined as a result of civil war, downward mobility, and reduction in elite capacity to consume. Political instability remains high, and the state's financial problems continue and make it vulnerable to external invasion. Cultural ideologies are highly pessimistic. Trade continues to be disrupted, particularly longer trade routes; arts and crafts decline; and large tracks of land remain uncultivated. Level of urbanization remains high but is declining, while rural settlements do not increase, even as the land-to-peasant ratio increases, because the cultivation of land has declined. Inequalities remain high but are declining, while epidemics also remain high but also are declining. Land rents remain low, as do land and grain prices, with grain reserves and personal consumption variable (and depend upon the effects of political instability).

At the end of this disintegrative part of the secular cycle, the chances of invasion by another polity increase, especially a polity organizing more innovative populations on the margins of the older societal formations. At some point, whether from rebuilding from within after revolts and reform but, more likely, from conquest by another population, the integrative and expansion side of the secular cycle can begin again, but the time frames between the up- and down-slope side of the cycle can vary enormously but, in Europe, the cycle took several hundred years in agrarian societies. Applying the theory to more modern societies, it is likely that movement through the cycle would be accelerated and, hence, the time frame shortened. Interestingly, much of Turchin's emphasis on intersocietal dynamics is downplayed in this analysis of secular cycles, perhaps reflecting the use of Goldstone's (1990) basic ideas, which do not emphasize intersocietal relations.

War as the Driving Engine of Ultrasocieties

In *Ultrasociety* (2016), Turchin seeks to explain the evolution of societal complexity through the agrarian stage of societal development. In many ways, Turchin presents a theory very similar to the one developed by Herbert Spencer (1874–1896) because war is the driving force of evolution from small, simple societies to ever-larger and more complex societies. It is curious, however, that Turchin never mentions this aspect of Spencer's work, focusing instead on the long discredited influence of Spencer on the emergence of Social Darwinism 20 years after his death. Of course, Turchin's argument is more complex and up to date since, obviously, a great deal of theorizing and empirical work on history, and war in particular, has been done over the last 130 years.

Ultra Society stands out for how simply and elegantly his complex argument is written, even as it develops and illustrates his thesis across a wide time frame of societal evolution. Turchin argues against what he typifies as the "bottom-up" explanation for the evolution of larger, more complex societies, or ultrasocieties. In this bottom-up portrayal, population growth in response to a warming climate some 12,000 years ago sets into motion societal growth, as larger populations begin migrations and colonization into new territories, eventually filling up the Near East. At 10,000 years ago, formerly nomadic foraging populations began the domestication of plants and animals, which increased the level of productive output and thereby allowed for further population growth, larger settlements into cities, and hence, the evolution of "civilization."

Scaling Up Societies for War

Turchin's alternative to this scenario emphasizes that increased population growth and density in ecological space would likely lead to conflict with neighboring societies—as Spencer had stressed many decades earlier. Conflict would lead to the extinction of "weaker groups" in a process that Spencer had described as "survival of the fittest" societies in his sociology. Larger, better organized, and more cohesive groups will generally win wars, as Khaldun and Spencer had argued; and so over time successful populations would have formed alliances to scale up their coercive forces and organize them into more cohesive collective units. Eventually, they would have had to shift from foraging and move to agriculture, initially through simple to advanced horticulture; and as they did so, they would have to create new kinds of institutional systems that eventually could sustain larger, more complex, state-based societies. These systems would revolve around establishing property rights and new techniques for the domestication of animals. These techniques could increase animals as a food source, but more importantly, they led to the harnessing of animal power as an energy source for tilling larger tracts of land.

At first in this long-term process, settled foragers developed Big Man systems where political leaders needed to redistribute all of the resources nominally seen as his property in order to sustain his and his allies' legitimacy. As the first chiefdoms emerged in horticultural societies, much redistribution also occurred for the same reasons of achieving legitimacy through prestige to leaders that comes with redistribution of resources, but increasingly, as inequalities between political elites and commoners grew in accordance with the Matthew Principle (i.e., possession of wealth generates more wealth, and hence, inequality), political leaders sought to portray themselves as "priest-chiefs" who, as high priests, had special access to the gods. And, because of this access to the supernatural, political leaders have unique powers to win wars and the right to control a society.

Turchin portrays this consolidation of religious and political hierarchies as a necessary strategy and, indeed, as an easier and more efficient strategy than just being a king alone without special supernatural powers. As early "kingdoms" evolved from chiefdoms, they were highly vulnerable to disruption because they were created by alliances among politically motivated leaders and were constantly disrupted by "upstarts" who would seek to be king. Thus, existing kings needed to legitimate themselves by winning conflicts with neighboring societies and by arguing that their success was not just due to their special relationship to the gods as priests. Rather, the king was *a* god, deserving of the adoration and ritual homage in temples in cities developed for ritual observances that affirm the stature of the king. In addition, the king would still require a loyal retinue who would, of course, require patronage in exchange for remaining loyal as a coalition that could repress upstarts. In Turchin's words (2016: 178), "the king and his retinue are a coalition of upstarts, with the king as the alpha male."

In this process of consolidating power for warfare, Turchin introduces the mathematics of winning wars: The same number of fatalities to members of smaller and larger coercive forces represent a greater proportion of the total force in the smaller than larger force, with the result that a larger force will generally win conflicts as the smaller force runs out of fighters (an insight that Spencer emphasized as well, which is why he argued that larger and better organized societies generally won wars, thereby increasing the size of the societies as they incorporated conquered populations into their institutional systems). Thus, political leaders constantly needed to increase the size of their military forces, holding respective technologies constant, to assure winning key battles with other societies. And in so doing, the size of the state and society both increased. Yet, highly despotic societies are unstable in the long run because of growing inequalities.

A theme in all of Turchin's work is that much of the early and later impetus to warfare comes from smaller populations on the steppes of larger agricultural societies with centralized polities. Nomadic populations along the steppes are uniquely poised to be warriors because they must protect their herds which, in turn, leads to training in martial arts and to internal solidarities among members of these populations (Turchin 2016: 154). As was described earlier, flatland polities can go into a Khaldun decline, as illustrated in Figure 4.2, making them vulnerable to conquest by high-solidarity populations invading from the margins. Of course, once in power, these conquering populations can themselves go into a Khaldun decline over several generations and, thus, be conquered by another population from the steppes or another agrarian society. Moreover, as agrarian societies recognize the threat from their steppes or from other flatland agrarian societies, they learn to develop larger armies through alliances and recruitment, and they developed projectile weapons and defensive strategies against highly mobile invaders, particularly when horses became a key military technology. The end result in all of this warfare is that the size and level of cooperation in societies would increase, as societies "scaled up" their armies and consolidated power to coordinate offensive and defensive strategies.

Yet, there were limits to the capacity of god-kings, loyal retinue, and ritual worship of rulers in grand temples to integrate societies where systems relying on coercive control of populations was necessary and where inequalities were increasing, even as enemies at borders must be confronted. Turchin then turns to perhaps his most original interpretation of the Axial (pivotal) Age, especially the period between 800 to 200 BCE when the nature of religion and its effects on societies dramatically changed many institutional systems that allowed for further growth in the size and scale of societies.

Warfare and the Axial Age

Turchin argues that, in the Mediterranean, Near East, India, and China, political leaders were beginning to present themselves as "good" and concerned with the welfare of common people. Even if some of this was ideological hype, it represented a new way of incorporating religion into the process of legitimating polities geared to warfare. The nature of religion had begun to change during a relatively short time frame. Monotheism in the Middle East—as Islam and Christianity evolved from Zoroastrianism and Judaism—was evolving and rapidly spreading; the same was true in Northern India where Buddhism was spreading and in China where Confucianism and Taoism were diffusing across large expanses of territory. At some time in 500 BCE, the leaders of these religions were walking the earth spreading a new, egalitarian ethic in which anyone could belong to a religion. Why this change, and why did it spread across such as large swath of world geography?

Turchin's answer is, as might be expected, a new kind of warfare technology that originated in the Great Eurasian Steppe. For him, this was where the Axial Age began. Around 1000 BCE horses became a new military technology that changed the course of history and nature of warfare. Around 2000 BCE, Eurasian pastoralists in Kazakhstan learned how to harness horses to chariots, an innovation that rapidly spread to northern China, India, and Europe; and this invention became a platform for archers. But it took another century for the bridle, saddle, and stirrups to evolve; and when combined with iron and steel weapons ensured "the dominance of steppe horsemen for 2,500 years." Once horses were used as cavalry, they could strike in ways that made it difficult for the ground forces of agrarian empires to defend all of their territories. The end result of this vulnerability was for the size of states to increase, with larger populations that could be recruited for larger armies that could be housed in fortresses across larger swaths of territory. With a larger army spread across territories, and often with larger barriers (such as the Great Wall of China), nomadic invaders could be kept at bay. But, the important point in Turchin's argument is that the scale of societies had to grow dramatically, with a larger polity and with a more efficient tax collection system to support the army garrisoned across the entire territory of a society. The size of empires thus grew; and once they scaled up, they became threats to regions further away, with the result that these regions scaled up or were conquered. In either case, the degree of ultrasociality increased; and as these empires rose and collapsed, they became generally more organized. Moreover, as societies and their armies scaled up, leaders increasingly recognized if commoners are to be used in large armies to take and defend territories, they needed to be treated better than was the case with early archaic states.

Turchin argues that the extreme forms of inequality and despotism began to recede during the Axial Age, a contention that is likely to be disputed. The Axial religions, he further contends, introduced "innovations" that would allow for the increase in the scale of social cooperation in societies, including: (1) constraints on elites to act less despotically; (2) shifts from more closed tribal and ethnically based to universalistic and proselytizing religions that could integrate larger, more diverse populations; and (3) simplified pantheons of Big Gods possessing new capacities of social control (e.g., Norenzayan 2013), including the capacities to know (a) what people are thinking, (b) whether or not people are virtuous, and (c) who is bad and should be punished. These innovations dramatically increased social control of large, diverse populations, especially if political leaders are viewed as also under this control by the gods.

Thus, for Turchin, the dramatic shift in thinking among elites about being more "sincere" and "caring" of the commoners who would fight their battles emerged in the Axial Age at the very time that empires were expanding. Selection favored new mechanisms of social control and legitimation of polity, leading to the development of new world-level religions. And so, once again, it is warfare that ultimately drove the evolution of new forms of religion allowing for the growth of ultrasocieties and empires of advanced agrarianism.

Conclusion

Intersocietal evolutionary approaches emphasize the cyclical and episodic nature of societal and intersocietal evolution. Societies are seen as embedded in larger networks of relations with other societies that generally reveal some level of stratification, with dominant or core societies able to control the terms of exchange or to exert political control over other societies. World systems approaches increasingly emphasize the dynamics of economic exchange because they focus on contemporary capitalism, but the more evolutionary approaches of Chase-Dunn and Turchin emphasize conflict dynamics as drivers of long-term evolutionary cycles that gradually by fits and starts, and even episodes of de-evolution, have increased the size and scale of societies and the world systems in which they are embedded. Indeed, ultrasociality is often seen as moving to one world system, although this is typically more a hope than a clear reality. Yet, conflict—as Georg Simmel so ably emphasized—also tends to promote integration of the parties in conflict—whether economic competition or open warfare—will generally become better organized by consolidating power and pushing for cultural conformity in order to remain fit in systems of societies.

Still, the models developed to explain evolutionary dynamics are only works in progress, but they have all dramatically added to the legacy initiated by Spencer and Weber to view societies as part of larger systems of societies. And to the degree possible, much of this theorizing tries to sustain some continuity with more biological and ecological approaches to evolutionary analysis, even as the nature of the units under selection become teleological and the nature of selection itself differs from those seen as driving biological evolution. But, as is evident from the samples of world-system evolutionary analysis outline in this chapter, there has been a revitalization in the new evolutionary sociology of earlier forms of evolutionary analysis so evident during the very beginnings of sociology in the 19th Century.

5
New Forms of Ecological Theorizing in Evolutionary Sociology

The Origins of Ecological Theorizing in Sociology

Herbert Spencer's Geopolitical Approach

When Herbert Spencer coined the phrase "the survival of the fittest," these words would haunt his memory as the Social Darwinist and the eugenics movements began to take hold in the 1920s. This phrase—when first uttered in the early 1850s—had anticipated by almost a decade Charles Darwin's views on natural selection, but what is not commonly recognized is that, in Spencer's sociology, the phrase is hardly used at all; and when it is invoked, it is typically employed to describe the relations between societies rather than to the fate of individuals competing with each other in societies. To be sure, he also uses it to talk about intrasocietal competition, but it is conflict between societies that was of most interest to Spencer because, as emphasized in Chapters 1, 2, and 3, he viewed the evolution of societies from simple to complex forms to be, in today's vocabulary, an ecological process among societies competing for resources. As societies grow, they inevitably come into contact and, eventually, must compete for resources. Smaller societies often come into conflict with the larger, more productive, regulated, armed, and better able to use distributive infrastructures to move people, information, and resources across territory. These enhanced organizational capacities are generally decisive in determining which society will win a war. And, although societies can seek to exterminate their enemies, more typical is some form of consolidation of societies into a system of societies in a geoeconomic and/or geopolitical formation or an actual merger of societies in which the winner of a war forces incorporation of the loser into its institutional structure and culture. In either case, the size and complexity of societal formations has increased; and as these dynamics have proceeded over the last few thousand years, Spencer saw the overall level of societal complexity increasing—as emphasized again in Chapter 4.

This complexity is not lineal, however, because dissolution and disintegration of societies and intersocietal formations can occur, causing a decrease in complexity which, over time, will begin to increase once again. Thus, the long-term trend for increasing complexity occurs only by fits and starts as societies build up complexity, only to fall back, and then once again build up complexity. Not only can societies lose wars, but they can collapse from internal conflict; and as consolidated societies and intersocietal systems become larger, they often begin to disintegrate through internal conflict as inequalities and cultural diversities among subpopulations increase. Still, Spencer felt that the overall effect of warfare was a driving force of evolution, which he viewed as a process of moving from simple to ever-more more complex forms of organization. And yet, he had come to the conclusion that, with industrialization and growth of free markets, societal evolution need not, and should not, be driven by war. War, he emphasized, only increases the centralization of power that is then used to usurp resources for coercive control of populations which, in the end, only increases internal inequalities, tensions, and disintegrative pressures. The evolution of the distributive axes of societal evolution had now evolved, Spencer felt, to the point where free and open markets could institutionalize competition and drive future evolution of complexity, without the negative effects of centralized power and coercion on escalating inequalities and disintegrative processes. Obviously, he had underestimated the capacity of markets and those who control them to generate inequalities, but his vision was that competition could be institutionalized within a society by markets, and the same would, he felt, also be true for intersocietal relations. The result was the universe of societal and intersocietal evolution would work to institutionalize the competition in what could be seen as a Darwinian battle for the more fit, whether actors within a society or entire societies in an intersocietal system. It is hard to know just how much, if any, these views influenced the ultimate development of ecological theorizing in sociology, but clearly, Spencer had begun to think in ecological terms and to conceptualize markets as a more benign force driving evolution.

Moreover, it is clear also that Spencer anticipated by many decades world-systems analysis in the conclusion that geoeconomic systems would increasingly replace geopolitical intersocietal systems (see Chapter 4). Moreover, much as has been the case with at least some world systems models, Spencer anticipated the view of intersocietal systems in ecological terms during which, as societies grow and seek new resources, they often go to war. Yet, they eventually often begin to trade in markets, and over time, became ever-more complex, thereby creating regulatory or integrative problems for the larger, more complex sociocultural formations to emerge from these more ecological dynamics.

Emile Durkheim's More Explicit Ecological Approach

Emile Durkheim's analysis was decidedly more modest but truer to Darwin's vision of the ecology of evolution. Durkheim did not develop much in the way of a political sociology, nor did he ever address conflict within and between societies to any great extent. In *The Division of Labor in Society* (1893), he was concerned with the mechanisms by which human populations became differentiated and reintegrated. As briefly summarized in Chapter 1, Durkheim saw differentiation as occurring with population growth increasing material density (concentration in physical space) and moral density (concentration of social relations); and from increasing material and moral density, competition among actors for resources would ensue. This competition drove differentiation or "social speciation," with fit actors able to stay in a resource niche and the less fit having to move to a new resource niche or even having to invent and carve out an entirely new niche. As they did so, differentiation among actors in a population would increase, thus escalating the pressures to find new mechanisms for integration of the more differentiated population. His general model is outlined in Figure 5.1.

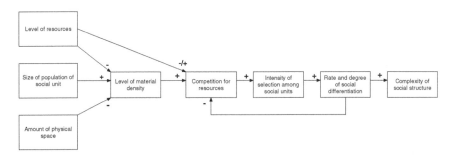

Figure 5.1 Somewhat Abstracted Version of Emile Durkheim's Ecological Model

Durkheim's model, in contrast to Spencer's, is designed to address the internal differentiation of a society. Of course, rates of immigration as influenced by transportation and communications technologies increase intersocietal relations and thus can have large effects on the internal ecological dynamics of a society. In this simple ecological model, there is a fundamental relationship among size of population, density, competition, selection and differentiation, but as noted in Chapter 1, Durkheim did not see this as a fight to the death. As he emphasized (Durkheim 1893: 267):

> Thus, as Darwin says that in a small area, opened to immigration, and where consequently, the conflict of individuals must be acute,

there is always to be seen a very great diversity in the species inability it. . . . [But,] in the same city, different occupations can coexist without being obliged to destroy one another, for they pursue different objects. The soldier seeks military glory, the priest moral authority, the statesman power, the businessman riches, the scholar scientific renown. Each of them can attain this end without preventing the others from attaining theirs.

This benign view of what differentiation is, of course, is rather Pollyannaish, but it captures Durkheim's view that there are diverse niches, already extant or yet to be discovered or invented, to which actors can move to secure sufficient resources to survive. Also of note, when giving this example, it is clear that Durkheim is emphasizing differentiation among individuals by professions; and hence, selection is pushing individuals to specialize. Those who would adopt and adapt Durkheim's ideas, however, were often willing to consider corporate units—groups, neighborhoods, communities, and organizations—as units of selection, with selection affecting individuals only through the fitness of the units organizing their activities within a given resource niche.

The Chicago School

The department of sociology at the University of Chicago was the very first to be founded in the world, which is perhaps surprising given the prominence of European sociologists in the 1890s. These early Chicago sociologists were interested in urban problems, and yet, scholars like Louis Wirth (1938) introduced theoretical ideas from Europe, especially the thinking of Spencer's and Durkheim's analyses of differentiation. But with Wirth, these differentiation dynamics were downsized to the more meso-level of social organization and applied to urban areas—particularly those in Chicago as a laboratory for studying urbanism—where clearly the proliferation of secondary groups and organizations increased the heterogeneity of Chicago as an urban system.

It is not clear how much Durkheim's and Spencer's work influenced the emergence of what became known as the Chicago School of Urban Ecology, but the first generation of thinkers—e.g., Robert Park and Ernest Burgess (1921), Louis Wirth (1938), Homer Hoyt (1939), Chauncy Harris (1945), and their students—began to conceptualize Chicago as an ecosystem and to borrow ideas from the emerging science of bio-ecology but again, it is not clear how much these determined their conception of urban space where humans could be seen as very much like a plant species distributing themselves over local areas where they can secure resources.

Recently, Michael D. Irwin (2015) has documented that the Chicago tradition, as it began to formulate what became known as "human ecology," looked to the emerging field of bio-ecology. But, it is important to remember that this new field of bio-ecology was itself rather ambiguous on its relevant unit of analysis. Bio-ecology actually borrowed ideas from sociology in its emphasis on community and "the web of life"—a turn of events that supports Comte's claim that sociology, as "the queen science," would begin to inform biology. Bio-ecology was treading lightly around Darwinian ideas in the later 19th and early 20th Century, seemingly de-emphasizing natural selection on communities of plants and animals and, instead, emphasizing the key properties of superorganisms as differentiation and integration through mutual interdependence. Early bio-ecology was not a micro-level approach emphasizing natural selection on individual life forms, but rather, it stressed the overall structure of the community as a "web of life." In many ways, early community-oriented ecology was very much like functionalism, stressing the goals of life forms as causing differentiation and interdependence of these forms into a superorganismic unit that, itself, had needs to survive as a whole. And so, bio-ecology was probably more influenced by sociological ideas than the reverse because Darwinian views on natural selection were used cautiously—a tendency that is associated with the decline of emphasis on natural selection in favor of mutations (as the driving force of evolution) in the first decades of the 20th Century before the Modern Synthesis took hold after R. A. Fisher's (1930) resurrection of natural selection as the driving force, with mutation only being one source of variation on which selection could work. Selection was considered to be one force that could shape communities but not the only force; and indeed, Darwin's metaphor of the "web of life" was far more influential than his views on natural selection. In fact, such is often the case today among ecologists. As Peter J. Richerson (1977: 4) notes:

> Ecologists are usually not directly interested in the process of natural selection operating on variable individuals within populations, but rather in the distribution and abundance of populations themselves and their interactions. Ecologists are thus primarily concerned with the phenomena of higher levels of organization ranging upward to ecosystem and the whole biosphere, and they tend to ignore individual variation and the evolution of populations.

Among the early human ecologists at Chicago, it is never completely clear if they were simply repackaging sociological ideas from Spencer and Durkheim into a more legitimating package using the language of bio-ecology or actually trying to develop a new approach in sociology. Yet, it is clear that they were committed to holistic notions of community, focusing on interdependence, and competition that was regulated by structure and culture, mutualism, and ecosystem equilibrium (Irwin 2015). As Robert Park emphasized in his 1936 Presidential Address to the American Sociological Society, ecology is a geographical science because it studies the distribution of plants and animals on Earth's surface; and this emphasis differs from that in sociology where concern is more human relations to each other. Use of bio-ecological terminology was more strategic than substantive (Gaziano 1996). And even when competition was noted, the metaphor was couched in an invasion and succession metaphor revolving around immigration, competition, and renewed equilibrium in the human community (Park 1936a). In many ways, there is an implicit stage model here of invasion and succession to a new state of equilibrium; and many of the dynamics of human communities appear to be more Spencerian and Durkheimian than Darwinian. Yet, selection does come in the back door, for as Park (1936b: 175) noted:

> the same biotic interdependence of individual species [among plants and animals] ... seems to exist likewise on the human level, except for the fact that in human society competition and the struggle for existence are limited by custom, convention, and law.

Thus, for Park, competition and selection drive change in human and biotic communities (Irwin 2015; Faught 1986); and in this respect Park comes even closer to Spencer and Durkheim who also viewed competition among nations (Spencer) and within societies (Durkheim) as the mechanism for change which, once completed, leads to a new stage of equilibrium or regulation (Spencer) and integration (Durkheim). Culture pre-empts competition; and as a result, the community order or equilibrium is achieved through cooperation (Gross 1999). The community thus moves to a new stage of functional interdependence among individuals and the corporate units organizing their activities.

This de-emphasis on competition in human ecology continued through the 20th Century, but at the midpoint of the century after World War II, bio-ecology was embracing ideas from the Modern Synthesis, with competition and natural selection seen as essential to an explanation of biotic communities. In contrast, scholars like Amos Hawley (1944) were distancing human ecology and the study of communities from a Darwinian perspective, eventually moving it back to the macro-level and rejecting much more explicitly notions of competition and selection in favor of functional processes (Hawley 1986), as we will see later in the chapter. There remains considerable bio-ecological terminology but not the substance of a biological approach. Even the rather minimalist emphasis on competition by Park is gone. Moreover, the unit of analysis has firmly shifted to community and/or society as the unit of adaptation, with group selection being far more important than selection on individuals—to the degree that any lingering notions of selection are to be found.

Darwinian Ideas in Contemporary Urban Ecology

Figure 5.2 outlines the underlying model that the Chicago School researchers appeared to use in their various works on the city of Chicago. Their emphasis was still on the web of community life as an organic whole, but there are threads of a more Darwinian approach also implied by the jostling of various types of actors engaged in different types of activities for the resources of urban space.

Urban growth was viewed by members of the Chicago School as related to production and population growth because production tended to aggregate people in various types of corporate units, such as families, neighborhoods, and businesses, that people use to survive in urban space—thus setting up a more *group*-selection model than was evident in either Durkheim's work or that of ecologists at the time. As aggregation increased, population density also increased; and as a result, competition for resources in urban space—governmental agencies, retail markets, or virtually any arena where resources could be secured—also increased. The real estate market was seen

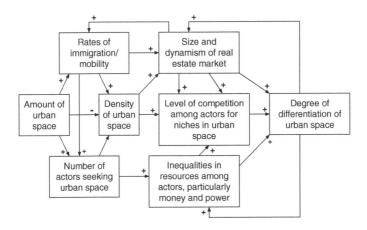

Figure 5.2 Early Model of Urban Ecology

to accelerate this competition for resources in space because it places prices on land and buildings and becomes, in essence, the mediator of which individuals and corporate units can secure resources in a particular locale of urban space. The result of this institutionalization of competition in markets is the differentiation of urban areas by actors and their activities as well as the evolution of the diverse cultural systems associated with varying types of actors—whether kinship actors, religious actors, educational actors, recreational actors, business actors, industry actors, or governmental actors. The models developed by the Chicago School were deeply flawed because they relied too much on one city as their model of what is now known as "urban ecology," but they did seemingly create a new field of inquiry that took the leads in Spencer's and Durkheim's works and applied them to a particular type of ecosystem: communities, particularly urban areas.

More recent analyses of urban areas have expanded upon the implicit model in Figure 5.2, but even here, there seems to be some ambiguity about the place of selection on community growth and differentiation. This more recent model is presented in Figure 5.3. This is an abstracted model of contemporary urban ecology, which draws from a number of sources, none of which examines all of the processes highlighted in the model. The model is biased to tracing out where selection can be fitted into the analysis of urban dynamics; and in this sense the model is probably not as representative of urban ecological analysis today.

As noted above, Amos Hawley, beginning in the later 1940s and through the 1960s, had pushed urban ecology away from Darwinian theory's emphasis on density, competition, and selection as forces in all ecosystems. Yet, perhaps to his dismay, it was two of Hawley's students who brought

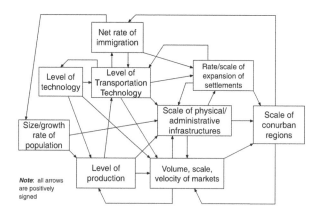

Figure 5.3 More Recent Abstracted Model of Urban Ecology

these notions from bio-ecology back into sociological models in their formation of the new science of organizational ecology.

Explicit Incorporation of Darwinian Ideas in Organizational Ecology

While urban ecological analysis remained somewhat ambivalent about the importance of selection, organizational ecology embraced the dynamics of selection from bio-ecology, as well as other elements in most biological approaches to evolution, with some changes to fit the nature of sociocultural phenomena. Organizations become the unit on which selection works, but it is the population of organizations in a given niche that evolves. Thus, selection works at the corporate unit level—the organization—but evolution occurs at the population level—a line of argument that, despite the "group selection" on organizations, resonates with modern biological theory. A population is conceptualized as organizations seeking resources of a given kind in a resource niche. The social universe can thus be viewed as a series of resource niches that organizations enter to secure resources needed to build up their structure and culture in order to survive. When initial organizations prove fit and are able to adapt to a given niche, other organizations will be attracted to the niche; and as more organizations enter the niche, population density among organizations increases. With increases in density, competition among organizations for resources will increase; and the more density reaches or surpasses the carrying capacity of a niche, the more likely will selection lead to the "death" of some organizations that are less fit. The result is that the number of organizations in a resource niche will decline, typically overshooting the carrying capacity on the downward slide, and thus creating some new space for other organizations to enter the niche, thus increasing density up to the carrying capacity of the niche. Organizations tend to copy the structure and culture of successful or fit organizations in a niche or adopt various strategies to compete successfully within a niche. The structure and culture of organizations in a society will thus reflect the nature of the niches in which they seek resources, the carrying capacity of these niches, the number of organizations in a niche and the density of these organizations, the intensity of the competition and selection, the death rates of organizations from selection over resources, and the adaptive strategies that organizations pursue in trying to survive within a niche. The basic model of organizational ecology is outlined in Figure 5.4 (Hannan and Freeman 1977, 1989; Carroll 1983, 1988, 1997; Dobrev et al. 2003).

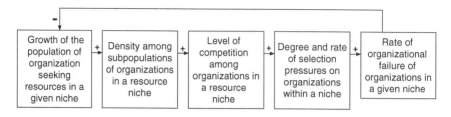

Figure 5.4 The Core Elements of Darwinian Theory in Organizational Ecology Models

The Hannan-Freeman Model of Organizational Ecology

Michael Hannan and John Freeman (1977) were the first to develop the model of organizational ecology. Their original model added a number of refinements, which are represented in Figure 5.5. First, the number of organizations is a joint function of the level of material and non-material resources available to organizations and the number of organizations seeking these resources. Obviously, when there are many resources, the carrying capacity of the niche is much higher, but this carrying capacity is reduced as more and more organizations enter a niche. Second, the scale and scope of markets distributing resources always affects the level of material and non-material resources and, eventually, the selection pressures on organizations. For, in the end, societies that have many organizations are integrated by markets that connect and regulate organizations through their exchanges of resources; and the more dynamic are markets, the greater is the number of resource niches that can be opened up and, hence, the greater is the number of organizations that can form around a particular market niche. Third, the rate of organizational founding in a society is not just related to size and number of niches, nor to the dynamism of markets alone; legitimization of particular types of organizations pursuing resources must also occur. When one form of organization has proven successful in a niche, then other organizations will copy its structure and culture as it enters the niche; and the more such isomorphic foundings occur, the greater will be the legitimacy for particular types of organizations seeking resources in a niche. There can be different types of legitimacy, including (Reuf and Scott 1998; Hannan 2005): (a) regulatory legitimacy bestowed by governmental agencies for organizations in a given niche; (b) normative legitimacy by values, ideologies, and normative systems in the institutional environments of a niche; (c) referential legitimacy where success by one organization justifies other organizations entering a niche to purse the same strategy and organizational forms; (d) certification legitimacy whereby organizations entering niches are required to display their competence through licenses and expertise; (e) niche overlap legitimacy where organizations are given legitimacy by virtue of the success in several, perhaps overlapping, niches with the presumption that success in one is likely to increase success in others; and (f), segmentation legitimacy in which the copying of existing organizational templates by new entrants to a niche increases the confidence in, and legitimacy of, those older players and their new competitors in a niche.

Fourth, these legitimating dynamics can lock organizations into a particular template of structural organization and its attending culture which, in turn, gives organizations inertial tendencies in their structures and cultures that can be difficult to change. These inertia tendencies become something more like the genome in an organism in that selection will now determine whether the structural form of an organization is fitness-enhancing or not. If not, often organizations cannot always change their structure or culture; they are like any other unit of selection that is trapped in a particular phenotype, or in the case of organizations, a sociocultural formation that cannot be altered. Thus, the more organizations reveal inertia tendencies, the greater will be the effects of selection on the population of organizations, whether fitness-enhancing or the reverse. In general, older organizations are likely to have to most inertial tendencies. Moreover, they are also more likely to reveal other liabilities, including: (a) technologies that have fallen behind the newer competition, (b) aging infrastructures that are too costly to replace, (c) out-of-date distribution systems, and (d) cultures that no longer match up well with the demands of the niche and markets in this niche.

The top portion of Figure 5.5 outlines these dynamics, indicating how they affect the core processes outlined at the bottom of the figure. As is

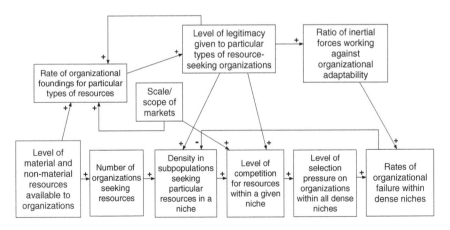

Figure 5.5 Michael Hannan's and John Freeman's Organizational Ecology Model

evident, the scale and scope of markets increase competition and selection pressures on organizations within a niche. Similarly, so does the ratio of inertial to adaptive tendencies in organizations; and when the ratio is high on the inertial side and/or when the other liabilities just listed are evident, the rate of organizational failings will increase. These inertial tendencies and other liabilities have been evident in many niches within industrial societies, including: automobile manufacturing (Dobrev et al. 2003), newspapers (Carrol 1994; Carroll and Delacroix 1982), hospitals (Reuf and Scott 2003), savings and loan banks (Rao and Nielsen 1992), credit unions (Baron 1995), labor unions (Hannan 1985; Hannan and Freeman 1989), and life insurance companies (Ranger-Moore 1997).

Some early ideas developed by Hannan and Freeman (1977) are not included in Figure 5.5. These are plausible but the data do not fully support the effects of these forces on the core ecological dynamics running across the figure. Yet, to mention some: When the rates of variability of resources in a niche are great—that is, resources come and go rapidly—competition for these variable resources increases, thus setting into motion selection against those organizations that cannot adapt. One strategy that organizations pursue when variability of resources is high is to specialize in a subset of resources within a niche. A more specialized organization can generally respond more rapidly to changes in resources available and thereby reduce the level of selection against them. When fluctuations in resource levels are of long duration, smaller and more specialized organizations often do not have the reservoir of resources to ride out longer-term decreases in the available resources. Under these conditions, being a generalist and also a large player in a niche with long durations in the cycle of resource availability is a more viable strategy.

Blau-Space and the Ecology of Organizations

As noted above, there are many kinds of quasi-markets that generate non-economic resource niches. Most organizational ecology studies profit-oriented companies seeking customers in markets and, hence, money for the sale of products and services, but within complex societies other types of resource niches can be found. Peter Blau (1977, 1993) conceptualized macrostructures as consisting of distributions of differentiated individuals marked by "parameters" such as ethnicity, gender, income level, educational level, occupation, profession, and virtually any difference that is relevant in a society. J. Miller McPherson and colleagues (McPherson 1983, 1988; McPherson and Ranger-Moore 1991; and McPherson and Rotolo 1996) have conceptualized these as constituting a *Blau-space* of characteristics, with each node or parameter marking differences potentially constituting a resource niche for organizations seeking members or perhaps donations. McPherson's work has been on service clubs that define particular demographic characteristics of people (in Blau-space) as the members that they prefer to recruit, with members (and their dues) being the resource sought in competition with other such clubs. Service clubs in the United States and elsewhere—e.g., Optimists, Lions, Shrine, Masons, Kiwanis, and the like—historically have competed within a delimited number of niches in Blau-space. These same dynamics can operate with other organizations seeking members or donations in quasi-markets seeking resources for political parties, philanthropy, or social movements. Figure 5.6 outlines the model in McPherson's analysis of service clubs in the United States.

In the United States, the overall level of resources in the niches of Blau-space where service clubs sought members has dramatically declined over the last 60 years, thus increasing density (relative to lower levels of resources), competition, and selection among service clubs. The result is that service clubs have had to search for members in new places in Blau-space. Thus, organizations of this type began to recruit women who were formerly under-represented, members of ethnic minorities, or members from lower social classes. By doing so, they expanded the resources available to them and thereby reduced the competition, selection, and rates

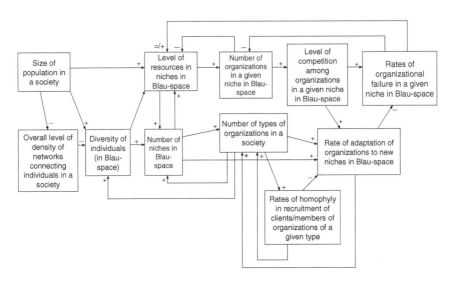

Figure 5.6 J. Miller McPherson's Ecological Model Organizational Ecology in Blau-space

of failure of various service clubs that had been increasing since the 1960s. Thus, once these organizations were able to reduce homophyly and adapt to new niches in Blau-space, they decreased their rates of failure to the point where the remaining clubs could survive—at least for a time. These same dynamics operate for other organizations that seek members to survive. For example, the U.S. armed forces found themselves in intense competition in Blau-space in the move to an all-volunteer military, thereby forcing them to adapt to this competition by seeking members in heretofore less exploited niches in Blau-space. Charities have had to do much the same thing by seeking donations from new categories of persons and, often, by changing their goals as was the case, for example, when the March of Dimes had to find a new cause when the polio vaccine removed this threat from children (in Blau space).

New Forms of Ecological Analysis at the Macro-Level of Social Organization

Amos Hawley's Return to Functionalism

At the end of his career took, Amos Hawley (1986), who was the last remaining member of the original Chicago School, took meso-level ecological analysis that he had helped develop back to the macro-level of social organization. This was not a great leap since early ecological theorizing was still very much influenced by the functionalism of Herbert Spencer and Emile Durkheim. Ecosystems were viewed as a community or even a superorganism composed of differentiated parts integrated into a whole composed of interdependencies. Hawley in this last important theoretical work began to conceptualize populations organized into societies as differentiated into diverse, but mutually interdependent, social units that could be typified by their functions. He distinguished between (1) *functions* or types of activities of mutual interdependencies among units that are engaged in necessary activities to sustain the system of interdependencies and (2) *key functions* which are units organized to deal with environmental inputs into a society and outputs of the society to its environment, including other societies. The more a set of units is connected to those engaged in key functions, the more the control of the latter over the former. Because key functions mediate the relations with the environment composed of information, energy, resources, and cultural symbols, they determine the kinds of inputs that can come into the system and thereby determine the size and complexity of the system. Thus, government, military, economy, and any other set of units engaged in key functions will disproportionately affect the dynamics of the ecosystem because they mediate the flow of environmental inputs as resources to be used by units engaged in non-key functions.

Environmental inputs, coupled with competition among members and the units organizing members, will increase the differentiation of functions, but there are limits imposed by other forces that are central to this kind of macro-level ecological analysis. One force is technology or knowledge that is used to lower what Hawley terms *mobility costs*, or the costs of moving information, people, and resources about the territory controlled by a population and the key function of government. If mobility costs are lowered, a population can grow and differentiate, whereas if mobility costs are high, there will be an upper limit on how much growth is possible. Figure 5.7 outlines this fundamental relationship in Hawley's ecological theory.

Another effect of technology is the capacity to increase production; and as production increases, so do markets for distributing the outputs of production. With markets comes another force causing differentiation of the population because markets institutionalize competition for resources and their distribution to individuals and the corporate units organizing their activities. This basic set of relations is outlined in Figure 5.8.

Taken together, the processes outlined in Figures 5.7 and 5.8 view *technology* as driving much of what occurs in a society because, in the end, technology determines the level of production and together technology and production determine mobility costs; and these together all determine the size of a population and its degree of differentiation into a variety of functional areas. As is evident in this analysis, Hawley has taken ecological analysis back to the level of Spencer's and Durkheim's theories, emphasizing the same key processes defining the evolution of a society—that is, growth of the population and its differentiation. And, the forces driving this growth are technology, production, mobility costs, and markets—all

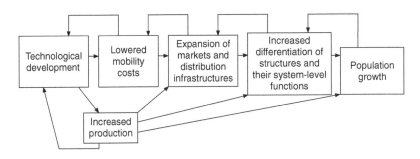

Figure 5.7 Core Elements of Amos Hawley's Ecological Model of Societies

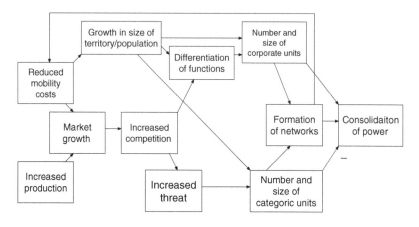

Figure 5.8 Amos Hawley's Expanded Ecological Model of Societal Evolution

of which resonate with the models of societal and intersocietal evolution examined in Chapters 3 and 4. Competition is part of this process, especially market competition that causes differentiation of functions and, hence, the size and number of *corporate units* (revealing divisions of labor in pursuit of functional goals) that are involved in functions and key functions. Competition, however, also causes threats which, in turn, leads to an increase in the number and size of *categoric units* (e.g., genders, ethnics, social classes) that have shared interests; and when such categoric units persist for a time, they can also become organized into *corporate units* with a division of labor organized around a political agenda.

Corporate units engaged in functions and key functions and those categoric units that become organized into a corporate unit(s) will both tend to become political, forming networks and coalitions designed to affect key functions revolving around the consolidation and use of power. These networks can reduce mobility costs, but they can also lead to the consolidation of power in highly centralized forms that, under certain conditions, can work against differentiation of functions. But, to the extent that consolidation of power leads to resource and informational inputs to the society and, hence, to increased production and market forms of distribution, while at the same time decreasing mobility costs, this pattern of consolidation will cause growth and differentiation of the members of a population and the units organizing their activities. In many ways, Hawley has come all the way back to Spencer, viewing the social universe as revolving around differentiation along a number of key axes: production, regulation, and distribution. Figure 5.8 tries to summarize the more general model implied by Hawley's theory.

Thus, ecological analysis in sociology has come full circle: Functionalism spawned an emphasis on competition and selection that remained locked into a web of life kind of view of ecosystem that was truly liberated by organizational ecology but, at the close of the 20th Century, had migrated back to its functionalist origins. Hawley was apparently grappling with what the early urban ecologists at Chicago confronted: a desire to embed sociology in a more respectable field—bio-ecology—but not lose the sense that the social world revolves around not just competition and social speciation (i.e., differentiation) but also integration of differentiated units into superorganisms. Urban ecology went part of the way in bringing a more Darwinian view into human ecology, and organizational ecology went all of the way in emphasizing Darwin's emphasis competition for resources and selection, but in the case of organizational ecology, selection is on a corporate unit. Still it is the population of corporate units that evolves—giving organizational ecology more commonality with biological models of evolution. As long as ecological analysis stays at this meso-level, a Darwinian approach can be very useful in understanding the dynamics of what are the building blocks of complex societies: populations of specialized organizations. But, when theorists wish to explain the more encompassing unit—the society or perhaps intersocietal system—then Darwinian analysis becomes less adequate. Concern shifts to how superorganisms operate as a whole; and once this shift in levels of analysis is made, something like Hawley's approach emerges and begins to look very much like where theoretical sociology began—that is, functionalism.

Making Functionalism Somewhat More Darwinian

As we emphasized in Chapter 2, it is possible to convert functionalist arguments into a form of ecological analysis where selection is at the forefront. Hawley's analysis brings back the vocabulary of functionalism but does not go all the way and specify lists of survival requisites or functional needs. What we have proposed is doing what Spencer and even Hawley implicitly did: specify basic axes along which selection pressures arise in superorganisms. This shift in emphasis retains the notion of selection, but it is a selection that is entirely different from what was proposed by Darwin. First, selection pressures often arise under very low density of structures that are capable of dealing with these selection pressures. There is, in essence, an absence of existing corporate units that can respond to selection pressures. The evolution of societies and other macroformations has always involved new adaptive problems generating selection pressures forcing the creation of new types of social structures and accompanying cultures to deal with selection pressures. Humans and the corporate units into which they are organized always have some capacity for agency, for innovation, for borrowing or stealing knowledge, and other means for creating new kinds of sociocultural formations that can reduce selection pressures. Thus, societal evolution is always Lamarckian, with individual and collective actors acquiring new characteristics that meet rising selection pressures.

Second, there is no guarantee that these Lamarckian efforts are sufficient to meet selection pressures; hence, societies disintegrate and de-evolve when agency proves inadequate; and given the cultural and structural rigidities that often become built into the institutional systems of societies, disintegration is almost inevitable in the long run. These institutional rigidities limit agency, and thus they are somewhat equivalent to a sociocultural phenotype that is resistant to change because of the underlying rigidities built into the structural and cultural forces generating this phenotype. The selection out of maladaptive sociocultural formations is, therefore, very much like Darwinian selection on organic phenotypes.

And third, by specifying the axes or dimensions along which selection pressures will generally increase, we can make better predictions about which institutional systems will be under pressure and their capacities to change and adapt to these pressures. What has always made functionalism interesting is that it seeks to specify where things can go wrong and where they must go right. Production, reproduction, regulation and integration, and distribution are at the core of any list of axes where selection pressures increase and, thus, must be resolved by agential efforts to create new sociocultural formations. Abandoning notions of requisites and then converting this flawed idea to dimensions along which selection pressures are most likely to arise, it becomes possible to engage in an evolutionary analysis that comes closer to retaining a Darwinian tone. These pressures can be met, to varying or lesser degrees, by creative efforts as sociocultural transformation, or they can go unmet by virtue of institutional rigidities that have locked a society or its key subsystems into an unfit phenotype. In this manner, analysis looks more in tune with bringing essence of Darwinian theorizing on evolutionary processes back into sociology in ways that can generate better explanations than the old functionalism of Spencer and all those in the 20th Century who followed his lead. And, when analyzing macro-level sociocultural formations, these explanations are better than a purely Darwinian approach that *cannot* adequately deal with the dynamics of superorganisms.

Conclusions

We could have added, perhaps, some of the more ecologically oriented approaches from intersocietal systems as having to deal with the same axes of potential disintegration as societies. For, by retaining a revised form of functionalism, we can gain a greater understanding where the selection pressures will be most likely to emerge in intersocietal systems—mostly, in the present, on the question of regulation by common cultural systems and acceptable political formations. These are the selection pressures currently on the capitalist world system, and it is not clear at all if it is possible to create sociocultural formations on a global scale that can deal with them. We will know within a decade or two. The spread of distributive infrastructural capacities and relatively unconstrained global markets was a selection pressure that must be met to build up the current world system, but the inherent instabilities of free markets, especially highly speculative metamarkets in money, equities, and derivatives, will inevitably increase selection pressures from distribution and regulation as a basic axis for selection pressures in all social systems. Thus, once we take what is useful from functionalism, it can be used to address the big questions of societal and world-societal viability in evolutionary terms that do not try to simply important ideas from biology but, instead, selectively to explain the realities of group selection and Lamarckian dynamics.

Still, we need to go back and see where a more purely ecological approach, inspired by present-day bio-ecology, is useful in evolutionary sociology. Certainly, the power of organizational ecology has demonstrated just how useful a Darwinian approach can be, with appropriate adjustments to the fact that the units of selection are the corporate units and that, despite inertial tendencies, selection generates pressures that are responded to by more Lamarckian processes of agency and innovation. Thus, while a Darwinian approach works best when we are addressing selection on individual human beings and seeing how the population evolves, Darwinian ideas still work rather well when analyzing corporate units, especially when markets institutionalize competition and selection. Similarly, urban ecology could also go this route, with a bit more emphasis on how markets and other sorting mechanisms in societies affect the differentiation and distribution of various categories of persons across geographical space but also the types of units organizing these persons. An analysis emphasizing competition among, and selection on, persons and organizations in urban areas could accomplish as much as organizational ecology has over the last 35 years, but in both urban and organizational ecology, we must remember what functional theorists and the Chicago School could not forget: These Darwinian-like dynamics are occurring within superorganisms that have emergent properties that cannot be adequately addressed by a rigid and orthodox adoption of ideas from the Modern Synthesis in biology.

Part II
Darwinian Analysis and Alternatives

6
The Evolution of Social Behavior by Natural Selection

Biology Turns to Explaining Social Life

A question rarely posed by sociologists is this: Why are humans social? For most sociologists, human sociality is a given, part and parcel of what Marx called our "species being." Human societies are said to exist because humans are "social by nature," and most sociologists see themselves as having much better ways to spend their time than puzzling about why humans are social rather than solitary.

The same is not true, however, of biologists. Whereas sociology is almost exclusively a "one species science," the range of biological inquiry extends to include many thousands of species. Most animal species are solitary, but biologists estimate that about 20,000 are highly social (Hölldobler and Wilson 2009: xvi). Among "large" species, those whose individual members can be seen without the aid of a microscope, the most highly social are invertebrates, ranging from colonial species, such as sponges and corals, to the "eusocial insects," which consist of ants, bees, wasps, and termites. Sociality also occurs in varying degrees and forms among all of the vertebrate taxa, including fish, amphibians, reptiles, birds, and of course, mammals. However, the incidence and nature of social behavior among these groups is highly variable, and many species in each taxon are solitary. Even when social behavior occurs among some species, it may be only transitory, even ephemeral, and it is often restricted to seasonal mating interactions. Consequently, while sociologists rarely wonder about why humans are social at all, behavioral biologists routinely ask that question. In fact, biologists have long wondered why *any* animal species is social rather than solitary. Stated casually, fundamental questions in behavioral biology are commonly posed as follows: What is society for? Why are some species social and others solitary? What makes social life even possible? What forces organize and regulate social life? Why is conflict ubiquitous in even the most highly cooperative species?

Evolutionary biologists routinely begin their inquiries with a default hypothesis about the traits of living things: They view them as possible *adaptations*, traits that increase the likelihood of survival *and* reproductive success of the individuals that possess them. This logic extends to behavioral traits, including social behavior. But why would any animal species be social rather than solitary? It was once common for biologists to interpret behavioral traits as having evolved for the "good of the group" or the "good of the population" or even for the "good of the species." For example, under conditions of extreme crowding and stressed food resources, it was observed that individuals seem to exercise reproductive restraint and produce fewer offspring than they might under more favorable conditions, or they might even refrain altogether from reproducing. This reproductive restraint was interpreted as a mechanism that reduces pressure on stressed resources such as food, thereby protecting affected groups, populations, or even an entire species from excessive competition and possibly succumbing to extinction. This kind of thinking was not uncommon in behavioral biology until the mid-1960s. In 1966, George C. Williams, now recognized as one of the most important evolutionary biologists of the 20th century, published a book with the title *Adaptation and Natural Selection: A Critique of Some Current Evolutionary Thought* (1966) which, along with a number of other developments in biology, revolutionized the study of animal social behavior.

Williams' book turned on its head the notion that natural selection produces traits for the "good of the group" or the "good of the species." Instead, Williams argued that natural selection operates on individuals, or even genes, and that evolved adaptations represent devices that increase the chances of the survival and reproductive success of individuals, not groups (much less populations or species). This idea was later made widely known by the evolutionary biologist Richard Dawkins who made a case for the position that, ultimately, the "unit of selection" is not even the individual, but rather, genes (or genotypes) that direct and control the development of individuals (Dawkins 1976). Alluding to Samuel Butler's famous quote that "A hen is only an egg's way of making another egg," Dawkins contended that a body is only a genotype's way of making another genotype. In this view, a trait that evolved for the "good of the individual" would, ultimately, be a trait that increased the reproductive success of that individual and thereby the persistence of genes that orchestrated the construction of that individual. Viewed at the level of the whole organism, reproduction is a process that produces another individual, but viewed at the level of the gene, reproduction is a process by means of which genes produce replicas of themselves. Extending the analogy that genes (or, more accurately, genotypes) are unconscious, "selfish" agents that build "survival machines" in which they live, the gene-centered thinking of evolutionary biologists illustrated the shift in focus from viewing evolution by natural selection as a process entailing differential reproduction of individuals to a process entailing differential replication of genes. As will become clear, this is important, because it means that genes can be thought of as agents that are distributed among multiple bodies and that they can influence relations among the bodies in which replicas of themselves are found. That is to say, it might be said that genes in any one body can "collude" with replicas of themselves that occupy other bodies, thereby causing those bodies to behave in concert and propel more copies of their genes into future generations than they would have by behaving only as individual bodies.

The difference between the "good of the group" and "good of the individual" arguments can be illustrated with the aforementioned example of individuals exercising reproductive restraint during periods when resources become scarce in stressed environments. Though it is intuitively appealing to believe that the exercise of reproductive restraint by individuals is an altruistic act that results in improved prospects for survival and a bright reproductive future for the group or the population as a whole, or perhaps an entire species, the alternative view whereby natural selection is seen as acting on genes (or the individuals that bear them) suggests otherwise. Under conditions of resource scarcity, the developmental health and even survival of offspring may be imperiled. Thus, if an individual "decides" (most commonly by means of unconscious biological processes) to forego reproductive effort during periods of environmental stress and then resumes reproductive effort when environmental conditions become more favorable, that individual has made a wise "Darwinian decision." That decision, however, is not driven by "good of the group" considerations. Rather, it is a decision made *purely on the behalf of the individual's prospects of reproductive success* and not the survival prospects of the group or population. Individuals that defer reproductive effort during periods of severe environmental success are more likely to achieve greater *lifetime reproductive success*, which is what matters by the logic of natural selection, than those who attempt to reproduce at every opportunity, regardless of environmental circumstances. Offspring produced under conditions of environmental duress still require the expenditure of *parental investment* (an important concept to be discussed later) which is wasted if those offspring fail to survive. Thus, reproductive restraint can evolve entirely in service of individual fitness or gene replication without being driven by group, population, or species survival considerations.

These types of considerations, rarely addressed in conventional sociological literature, provide an opportunity to pose questions such as "What is society for?"; "Why did social behavior evolve?"; and "Who, or what, is the fundamental beneficiary of social behavior and society itself?" It was in the wake of the work of evolutionary biologists such as Williams and others (e.g., Hamilton 1964; Trivers 1971) that an entirely new paradigm for analyzing animal social behavior developed and entirely new answers to questions such as "What is society for?" were posited by evolutionary biologists and animal behaviorists. This new paradigm for analyzing animal social behavior eventually acquired the label of "sociobiology," and the publication of a now-landmark book by Edward O. Wilson, *Sociobiology: The New Synthesis* (1975), helped consolidate and codify a cascade of empirical inquiries and theoretical developments which revolutionized the evolutionary analysis of animal social behavior. Expanding the scope of sociobiological analysis to include human social behavior marked the onset of what has been called a "quiet revolution," or a "second Darwinian revolution," a movement that led eventually to the revival of evolutionary thinking in the behavioral and social sciences, including psychology, anthropology, economics, political science, and even sociology (Wright 1994: 4–7). This chapter provides an overview of evolution by natural selection and the evolution of social behavior. It is succeeded by a chapter that addresses specifically the field of sociobiology and how it has revolutionized the evolutionary understanding of social behavior among more than 20,000 highly social species, including humans.

The material presented in both this chapter and the following will require some indulgence on the part of readers who are unfamiliar with some of the more technical aspects of organic evolutionary theory. Grasping evolutionary explanations of social behavior among animals, including both behavioral ecology and sociobiology, requires a basic foundation of knowledge in evolutionary biology. Toward that end, we strive to provide readers with a sufficiently detailed, but accessible to the non-biologist, treatment of key issues. We also ask for the reader's patience in our discussion of material that pertains to non-human species. It is not our goal to discuss other animal species for the sole purpose of familiarizing readers with non-human social systems (albeit many are at least as interesting as those found among humans) but, rather, to explain key concepts and explanatory principles used in evolutionary biology in efforts to explain the evolution of social behavior in *any* social species, including humans. In that regard, for example, ants provide an excellent "study organism" for explaining the "problem of altruism" as framed and analyzed by evolutionary biologists.

Evolution by Natural Selection: Basic Concepts and Principles

Conceptualized in perhaps its simplest form, evolution is a process comprising the organization, expression, and flow of information. *Organic* evolution entails the flow of genes, which are chemically encoded units of information. Genes "flow" from one generation to the next when organisms reproduce. *Alleles* are variants of a particular gene (e.g., a gene specifying eye color may come in three alleles: green, brown, and blue), and the flow of genetic information is enabled or inhibited by the products of the genes themselves, which biologists call *phenotypes*. In some environments, a phenotypic trait promotes the flow of the genes that produce it, but in other environments, that same trait can inhibit gene flow. Consider, for example, the instinctive behavior by which musk oxen defend themselves and their offspring. When threatened by predators such as wolves, musk oxen form a phalanx, a protective circle by standing nearly immobile, rear-to-rear with their formidable heads and horns facing outward, toward the threat. This constitutes a highly effective, nearly impregnable defense against predators such wolves, but when confronted by human hunters armed with high-powered rifles, the immobile phalanx becomes a slaughter-house. Thus, genetic information that produces a highly effective adaptation for protection in an environment populated by wolves produces fatally maladaptive behavior in an environment populated by heavily armed humans. The adaptive or maladaptive consequences of a phenotype are never determined by the features of the genotype alone, but rather, by the interaction of the genotype and features of the environments in which it is expressed.

This conception of organic evolution captures the three key elements of any evolutionary process: information, the products of that information, and the context in which that information exists and expresses itself. Restated in the vernacular of evolutionary biology, these three elements are familiar as genotypes, phenotypes, and environments. Organic evolution entails the expression of specific alleles as phenotypes which, in turn, are subjected to the influence of the environments in which alleles reside. The rate at which alleles spread or decline through populations over generational time is the consequence of various *selection forces* such as disease, climate, predation, or parasitism that act on the phenotypic traits produced by those alleles.

Phenotypic traits can be classified into three broad categories: morphological (anatomical) traits, physiological traits, and behavioral traits. In evolutionary biology, *adaptations* are conceptualized as phenotypic traits that increase the survival and reproductive success of the individuals that bear them. For example, cryptic coloration among snowshoe hares is a *morphological* adaptation that reduces their chances of being detected, killed, and eaten by carnivores that search for prey visually. Having pelage that is brown in the summer, white in the winter, and mottled during spring and fall helps camouflage snowshoe hares and makes it more difficult for predators to detect them. An example of a *physiological* adaptation is the complex of biochemical processes that modifies the metabolic rates of mammals that hibernate, thereby enabling them to survive prolonged periods of time without food. A *behavioral* adaptation is illustrated by migration patterns that transport waterfowl from habitats that become life-threatening in the winter to those that are less severe. The process by means of which a distribution of alleles varies over generational time in response to selection forces acting on the phenotypes produced by those alleles is *natural selection*. An even more economical way of defining natural selection is to say that it refers to changes in gene frequencies over generational time.

The study of how environmental selection forces shape the evolution of animal behaviors is called *behavioral ecology* (Krebs and Davies 1997). *Sociobiology*, then, is "that component of behavioral ecology that explores the effects of the *social* environment on behavioral evolution" (Alcock 2001: 9). The components of social environments that act as selection forces include social processes and structures such as population traits (size, composition, and density), competition, cooperation, conflict, mate selection and mating, dominance hierarchies and relations, coalition structures and dynamics, and so on. Sociobiologists attempt to identify social behaviors that constitute evolved adaptations produced by the selection forces that operated during the phylogeny (evolutionary history) of the species under investigation. It is important to be aware that a trait that was adaptive for individuals in the environment in which it evolved *may not remain adaptive in perpetuity* or in *future environments* in which descendants of those individuals will live. Strictly speaking, evolved adaptations are always responses to conditions presented by previous environments. Organic evolution, versus sociocultural evolution, lacks foresight, and all evolved adaptations are designed to solve "yesterday's survival and reproductive challenges."

Natural selection produces individuals that vary in their ability to survive and reproduce successfully, and evolutionary biologists use the concept *fitness* to refer to the ability of an individual to produce offspring which themselves reach reproductive age. Individual (or Darwinian) fitness refers specifically to the total number of offspring that an individual produces during its lifetime. Reproductive success means not only that an individual has cooperated with a partner (in a sexually reproducing species) to produce an offspring, but that it has replicated 50% of its own genes as well. Thus, recording the number of offspring an individual produces over its lifetime is a proxy for measuring the replicative success of that individual's genes. When Williams (1966) paved the way for thinking about organic evolution as a process that, fundamentally, entails variation in the distribution of alleles over generational time, he laid the foundation for an entirely new way of thinking about social behavior, a way that gives new meaning to the evolutionary significance of individuals, groups, and sociality itself. By reinterpreting the concept of adaptation from a "gene's eye point-of-view," evolutionary thinkers such as Hamilton (1964); Williams (1966); Trivers (1971, 1972); and Wilson (1975) helped launch a revolution in the way that biologists interpret social behavior.

In fact, a gene's eye point-of-view invites a fundamental reconsideration of the evolutionary significance of the *individual* as well. Every individual in a diploid (bearing *pairs* of chromosomes) species, including humans, represents a unique configuration of genes created by the fertilization of an egg. The body produced by that fertilized egg is, when considered from the perspective of evolutionary time, little more than ephemeral. However, the genes that directed the development of that body and its features are, in principle, near-immortal (Dawkins 1976: 22–48). Thus, it can be said that the forces of selection are operating *fundamentally*, though indirectly, on genes rather than individuals and their phenotypic traits. Stated differently, the gene (or complex of genes) is the *unit of heredity*, and the trait or traits produced by the gene is the *target of selection* (Wilson 2012: 162). Viewing organic evolution through a lens that makes genes rather than individuals—much less groups, populations, or species—the focus of analytical attention requires getting used to. However, it was precisely this shift of focus from groups to individuals to genes that made possible the paradigm shift in behavioral biology that eventually yielded entirely new explanations of certain types of animal social behavior that had been puzzling, in fact, even troubling, to Darwin himself.

If natural selection somehow favors certain types of individuals that are better at surviving and reproducing than are others, then the apparent "voluntary" restraint, or even total forfeiture, of reproductive effort by any individual presents a true "Darwinian puzzle" to the evolutionary thinker (Alcock 2001: 33). For this reason, Darwin openly admitted concern that the entire edifice of his theory of evolution by natural selection was threatened by some of the tiniest, most obscure animals on earth, the ants, bees, wasps, and termites. Specifically, the existence of "sterile castes" comprising entire categories of females that make up the populations of colonies of these insect taxa constitute a fundamental empirical anomaly for Darwin's theory of "modification by descent." In Darwin's words, the existence of sterile castes posed "one special difficulty, which first appeared to me insuperable, and actually fatal to my theory" (Hölldobler and Wilson 2009: 16). If, as Darwin argued, natural selection designs every individual of every species to compete for reproductive success, why, then, has natural selection produced entire subpopulations (castes) of female ants, wasps, bees, and termites that refrain altogether from personal reproductive effort? It was this very anomaly that provided the inspiration for William D. Hamilton, over a century after the publication of *On the Origin of Species*, to propose a "genetical" explanation of the evolution of sterile castes among the *eusocial* insects (ants, bees, wasps, and termites), an explanation that traced the causal chain from genes to social behavior and, thus, saved Darwin's theory from empirical disconfirmation (Hamilton 1964). And it was the shift of analytical focus from individuals (and groups) to genes that made this theoretical salvage operation possible.

By viewing evolution by natural selection as fundamentally entailing a process of the flow of units of information, sociobiology launched a revolution in the explanation of animal social behavior that has dominated behavioral biology now for over four decades. And by conceptualizing organic evolution as but one manifestation of a potentially broader set of processes by means of which self-replication units of information encoded in *any* medium can evolve by processes analogous to natural selection, the door was opened to explanations of patterns of social behavior that can evolve not only on the basis of genes, but on the creation and use of symbols and symbol systems as well. How did bringing a gene's point-of-view to Darwin's puzzle of sterile castes inspire a revolution in behavioral biology in the 1960s and 1970s?

Key Concepts and Explanatory Principles in Sociobiology

Until the mid-1950s and the early to mid-1960s, the predominant argument for explaining why some individuals would "willfully" refrain from reproductive effort entailed some version of the "good of the group" (or population, or species) logic. In this perspective, individuals were selected not only to maximize their prospects for personal survival and reproduction, but rather, on occasion, to behave so as to assure the best possible chances for the survival and reproduction of the group as well. Until Williams' publication of his benchmark analysis of the concept of adaptation, the logic of group selection was viewed as non-problematic by many biologists, and perhaps its most famous proponent was V. C. Wynne-Edwards (1962). The idea of what has come to be known as *group selection* goes all the way back to Darwin, and it was how he resolved his problem of sterile castes. Subsequently, the idea has assumed various forms of expression including *kin selection* and *interdemic* (or interpopulation) *selection* (Wilson 1975: 106–107). A deme is a breeding population, and the notion of interpopulation selection was considered as far back as 1945 by Sewall Wright. Wynne-Edwards used the notion of group selection to offer explanations of apparent fitness-reducing behaviors such as "voluntary" emigration from high-density populations, reduced fertility, abandonment or deliberate killing of offspring, or delayed growth and maturation (Wilson 1975: 109). Wynne-Edwards contended that group selection mechanisms often consisted of forms of communication by means of which animals would engage in "social conventions" (ritualized behaviors) that would activate behaviors which, in turn, would prevent populations from growing too large and crashing. These ritual behaviors are called "epideictic displays" by means of which members of a population become visible to each other and thus assess population density. In Wynne-Edwards' view, these displays provide the information that is necessary for animals to be able to determine if they need to exercise altruistic reproductive restraint for the good of group survival.

Within a couple of years of the publication of Wynne-Edwards' widely read and discussed book, Hamilton published a two-part article that was to become one of the most influential developments in the rise of sociobiology (1964). By taking a gene's-eye-view of "altruistic" behavior among the eusocial insects, Hamilton offered a way of explaining patterns of highly cooperative social behavior without having to resort to traditional group selection reasoning. It is important to note that the use of the term "altruism" by evolutionary biologists refers only to the fitness-consequences of behavior. Specifically, an individual's behavior is classified as altruistic if it reduces the fitness of that individual while simultaneously increasing the fitness of another, unrelated individual. Furthermore, the behavior does not have to be accompanied by selfless motives or intentions on the part of the altruist. Rather, altruism so conceived is determined exclusively in terms of its fitness consequences for the individuals affected by the behavior. Unfortunately, the use of the term "altruism" to denote behavior that is fitness-reducing for individual A but fitness-increasing for individual B sometimes created unnecessary confusion during the early years of the so-called "sociobiology debate."

Hamilton selected the eusocial insects as an optimal "study organism" for analyzing the problem of altruism and the forces that produce highly cooperative, even self-sacrificial, behaviors among members of some species. Like Williams, Hamilton gained new purchase on explaining the evolution of social behavior by redirecting his attention from individuals (much less groups) to genes as units of selection. Among the eusocial insects, the Hymenoptera (ants, bees, and wasps) feature an unusual type of genetics known as "haplodiploidy." A haploid sex cell is one that contains only one copy of each chromosome, and eggs and sperm are typically haploid (Wilson 1975: 585). Among ants, for example, males develop from unfertilized eggs and thus, contain only one complement of chromosomes that they inherit from their mother. All fertilized ant eggs are diploid and always develop into females. One complement of the daughter's chromosomes is provided by the mother, and the other is provided by the father.

Thus, the genetic system by means of which ants, bees, and wasps reproduce is said to be "haplodiploid." Hamilton linked the genetics of haplodiploidy to the highly social nature of eusocial insect colonies and the commonplace incidence of self-sacrificial behavior exhibited by the daughters of the "queen" (reproductive) caste of females in the colony. An ant queen's daughters are self-sacrificial in two senses. First, they refrain from personal reproductive effort. Second, their labor is devoted in its entirety to the survival and well-being of the entire colony rather than themselves. Metaphorically, it can be said that the daughters of the queen subordinate their individual genetic "interests" to the "interests" of the entire colony. The daughters are "genetic altruists." Again, it is important to understand that their behaviors are not to be understood as being motivated by conscious intentions or purposes. In fact, altruistic behavior as conceptualized by evolutionary biologists can evolve absent a nervous system, not to mention anything that resembles consciousness or self-awareness. As conceptualized in evolutionary biology, even plants can sometimes be understood to behave altruistically (Wu et al. 2013). By Wynne-Edward's logic, the altruism of female, non-reproductive worker castes (commonly labeled *major, media,* and *minor castes*) among ants, bees, and wasps is best explained as an instance of group selection. The system seems to be organized to assure the survival and the reproductive success of the colony as a whole, and the queen's daughters (divided into various worker castes, including "soldiers") appear superbly designed by natural selection to conduct themselves in a manner that puts colony well-being and survival above their own personal well-being and survival. However, by thinking carefully about the genetics of haplodiploidy, Hamilton concluded that the altruism of the worker (daughter) castes *is more apparent than real.* That is, despite refraining from personal reproductive effort, the sterile daughter-worker castes are behaving no less genetically "selfishly" than is the queen. Instead, the system of haplodiploidy can best be understood as one in which sterile daughters "reproduce by proxy" (Alcock 2001: 96). The role of the queen could be described as that of the "designated reproducer" for the entire colony. Hamilton explained that the system whereby the colony's population features a division of reproductive labor can produce higher fitness for all of its members than if each female in the population invested in personal reproductive effort. This is possible because the genetics of haplodiploidy produces genetic hyper-relatedness among daughters who have the same father. That is, while full siblings in diploid species, including humans, share on average 50% of their genes with each other, female ants who are full siblings share on average 75% of their genes with each other. How is this possible?

Ant colonies are established when virgin queens participate in "nuptial swarms" and are fertilized by males (Hölldobler and Wilson 1990, 2009). The queen then finds a nest site and lays fertilized eggs which become females, members of the worker castes of the queen's newly founded colony. Eventually, when the colony reaches maturity, the queen produces additional fertilized eggs which become the virgin females of the next colonies, and unfertilized eggs which become males. Members of both of the newly produced reproductive castes leave the colony to found new colonies. Daughters of the founding queen who share the same father all share the same paternal genes, because the father is haploid and has only one complement of chromosomes with which to fertilize eggs. Daughters of the queen can inherit genes from either of two complements of the queen's chromosomes since she is diploid, so they share on average, 50% of their mother's genes with each other. Thus, daughters who share the same father are 100% related to each other *through the identical genes they received from their haploid father*, but *are, on average, only 50% related to each other through genes they received from their diploid mother*. Consequently, ant daughters of the queen and same father share, on average, 75% of their genes with each other. Recall that full siblings in diploid species share, on average, 50% of their genes with each other. In comparison, full sisters that are ants, bees, or wasps are hyper-related to each other because of the unique genetic system of haplodiploidy.

Viewing the gene, rather than the individual, as the unit of selection, then, provided Hamilton with an opportunity to explain the high degree of sociality, including altruism, among the Hymenoptera. Simply put, the hyper-relatedness among workers promotes highly cooperative behavior among them due to the significantly overlapping genetic "interests" among members of the worker castes. In fact, by refraining from personal reproductive effort and supporting the reproductive success of the colony as a whole, the workers can propel more copies of their genes into the next generation than if each of them attempted to reproduce individually. Or, from the gene's point-of-view, more replicas of the colony's genes can be propelled into a newly founded colony by a form of social organization that divides reproductive labor among members of the colony than would be transmitted if the colony were a reproductive "democracy," in which every female member were free to reproduce rather than assisting the reproductive success of the queen, the designated reproducer.

Inclusive Fitness and Kin Selection

Despite the fact that current discussions of genetic processes in evolution are often "forbiddingly technical" (Wilson 2012: 162), the basic logic and explanatory principles pertaining to the role of genes in shaping social behavior are reasonably accessible. And adopting a gene's-eye-view of social behavior and how it evolves opens doors to entirely new research programs and promising ways of expanding the scope of traditional sociological analysis *without having to compromise over a century of hard-won insights* that have been produced by sociological inquiry. Nevertheless, giving serious consideration to the logic and methods of sociobiology and its application to the study of human social behavior requires a willingness to entertain ways of thinking that are novel and counterintuitive to those who have been well-schooled in the traditional "sociological imagination."

There are, however, at least two long-standing verities in mainstream sociological thought that receive support from a gene-focused approach to human social behavior: (1) The basic building block of human society is the family, and (2) societies' foundational institutions are based on kinship relations.[1] Efforts to discern how genes could be instrumental in explaining the evolution of social behavior led to the development of two closely related concepts that have become central to conventional sociobiological analysis: *inclusive fitness* (Hamilton 1964) and *kin selection* (Maynard Smith 1964). These two concepts mean that genes, or complexes of genes, are the unit of inheritance, but the targets of selection can be a higher level of organization than the individual, and the basic target beyond the level of the individual is the kin group. It is important to emphasize that, in this context, "kinship" refers to biological kinship independent of any conception of cultural kinship. Thus, individuals who are kin are individuals who share a common genetic lineage. The more recent that shared lineage, the closer the kinship.

Recall that individual (or Darwinian) selection refers to a situation where genes are transmitted by virtue of selection targeting the body in which the genes reside. That is, the individual is the *level (target) of selection*. Or, from the gene's point-of-view, its success at replication is a direct function of the reproductive success of the body whose development it directs and regulates. Thus, in a truly solitary species, an individual's lifetime fitness is determined exclusively by the number of offspring it produces. Imagine, however, that there might be a second pathway toward maximizing lifetime reproductive (or, gene replicative) success. As a distributed agent, replicas of a gene exist in bodies other than those in which it resides. The probability that a replica of a gene exists in the body of another member of that body's population is represented by the *coefficient of relatedness* (or r) defined as "the fraction of genes identical by descent between two individuals" (Hölldobler and Wilson 2009: 506). Thus, the coefficient of relatedness between a parent and its offspring in diploid species is 0.5, because each offspring receives half of its genes from each parent. For full siblings, r is 0.5 on average, due to the gene mixing effects of processes such as meiosis and recombination. The coefficient of genetic relatedness between a grandparent and a grandchild is 0.25, 0.125 between a great-grandparent and a great-grandchild, and so on.

Accordingly, there are two paths by means of which an individual can maximize its lifetime fitness: (1) by producing offspring (individual, or Darwinian, selection) and (2) by contributing to the survival and reproductive success of the offspring of its relatives with whom the individual shares genes by common descent (kin selection). From the gene's point-of-view, its replicative success is facilitated by its efficacy in producing a body that is good at surviving *and reproducing* (individual fitness) or by contributing to the survival and reproductive success of replicas of itself that reside in other bodies (inclusive fitness). Again, the probability of gene replicas existing in multiple bodies is a function of common descent. In both individual selection and kin selection, genes proliferate or decline in populations as a result of (1) their "handiwork," that is, their efficacy at building and influencing bodies that succeed in surviving and reproducing and (2) the ecological context in which the bodies live. Organic evolution is always a function of units of heredity, the forces of selection within an ecosystem, and the targets of those selection forces. Lifetime fitness (both individual and inclusive), then, is the result of an individual's success or failure both at producing offspring as well as the contribution made by that individual to the survival and reproductive success of its kin (by common descent). In Hamilton's view, selection targets and "rewards" not only individuals, but also *social relations and networks among individuals who are kin*. Thus, while individuals are the targets of Darwinian selection, kin networks are the target of kin selection.

Hamilton extended his analysis to identify the factors that determine the likelihood that an individual will behave altruistically toward another individual. The probability of altruistic action is a function of the relationship among three factors: (1) r, the coefficient of relatedness between the altruist and the recipient of the altruism; (2) b, the benefit of the altruism to the recipient of the altruism, measured as an increase in the number of offspring produced by the recipient; and (3) c, the cost of the altruistic act incurred by the altruist, measured in offspring not produced. The relationship among these three variables predicts the probability of altruism, and it has become known as "Hamilton's rule" and is stated as $rb > c$. Although Hamilton formalized the theory of inclusive fitness and Hamilton's rule for predicting altruism, the notion that prosocial behaviors that are more costly than beneficial to an actor can, nevertheless, evolve by natural selection (in the form of kin selection) preceded Hamilton's landmark 1964 paper. In 1932, J.B.S. Haldane contended that altruism can evolve by natural selection if the beneficiary of the altruistic act is a genetic relative of the altruist, thereby conferring indirect genetic "returns" to the altruist (Haldane 1932).

The theory of inclusive fitness and kin selection became the foundation of sociobiology's explanation of social evolution among animals, including humans. Recently, however, E. O. Wilson and D. S. Wilson (2007) have challenged the sociobiological orthodoxy that kin selection and inclusive fitness explain eusociality among ants, bees, and wasps, and they contend that kin selection cannot explain the highly evolved form of eusociality evident among termites, because termites are diploid. As an alternative to focusing on the genetics of haplodiploidy in order to explain insect eusociality, Wilson and Wilson offer an ecological explanation. Specifically, they attribute the "hyper-sociality" of these animals to the fact that they occupy a defensible residence (such as a nest), live in reasonably close proximity to a food source, and provision their young (Wilson 2012; Wilson and Wilson 2007). This approach does not require individuals to be close genetic kin in order to explain highly cooperative patterns of social life. Rather, it turns to ecological factors in explaining the evolution of large, complex societies comprising, in some cases, populations consisting of hundreds of millions of individuals.

The approach advocated by Wilson and Wilson (2007) reintroduces the topic of group selection, which Wilson (2012) and Wilson and Wilson (2007) characterize as "multi-level selection." This has provoked a lively debate among evolutionary biologists, and as of this writing, the matter appears far from settled. In a recent article about the evolution of cooperation among humans, the authors identify sixteen misconceptions about human social evolution, and almost one-third (five) of these misconceptions pertain to the topic of group selection (West et al. 2011). Efforts to determine if group selection actually occurs in organic evolution are complicated by the fact that the concept of group selection has at least four different meanings (West et al. 2011: 246–49). Furthermore, in addressing the question of whether "cultural group selection" occurs in the evolution of human societies, the authors conclude that "while it is often argued that the group is a fundamental unit of cultural evolution, or that cultural evolution is a group-level process (Boyd and Richerson 1985), there is no formal basis for this" (West et al. 2011: 248). And by "formal basis," they are referring to mathematical models of population genetics in terms of which evolutionary biologists routinely frame such inquiries.

There is, however, a sense in which almost all sociologists, including us, view group selection in human social systems as obvious and non-problematic (Turner and Maryanski 2015). For example, when describing and analyzing patterns of sociocultural evolution, sociologists view various sorts of collectivities as "superorganisms" that are "potential units subject to selection," and such superorganisms include groups, organizations, communities, institutional domains, entire societies, or even intersocietal systems (Turner and Maryanski 2015: 103). In this view, "sociocultural phenotypes" are seen as "survival machines" (Dawkins 1976) which, like physical phenotypes, facilitate the survival and reproduction of individuals whose behaviors are expressed in sociocultural patterns. However, in sociocultural evolution, the targets of selection are complex and multi-layered forms of culture and social structure, not merely the physical phenotypic traits of individual organisms. Over time, some sociocultural phenotypes exhibit variable "fitness," which is defined in terms of length of time that a sociocultural system exists or in terms of its ability to exist and endure in a range of environments (Turner and Maryanski 2015: 95). Thus, when sociocultural fitness is conceptualized in these terms, the history of human societies presents unassailable evidence of the existence of group selection, a complex set of processes by means of which diverse sociocultural phenotypes evolve among different groups and populations. And, as Turner and Maryanski contend, "it is so obvious that selection is working on social structures and their cultures organizing individual organisms that it is difficult to see what the controversy (about group selection) is all about in biology" (Turner and Maryanski 2015: 104). However, the question of why the issue of group selection is more hotly disputed among evolutionary biologists than among evolutionary sociologists becomes clear when differences in the way group selection is conceptualized by these "two cultures" of evolutionary thought are understood.

In order to understand why the idea of group selection is viewed as highly problematic among evolutionary biologists but less so, if at all, among evolutionary sociologists, it is necessary to understand that evolutionary biologists approach the levels of selection (including group selection) issue in terms of the *genetic*, not *cultural*, forces that underpin social evolution. According to mainstream, neo-Darwinian evolutionary theory, natural selection favors any genetically based trait that increases the survival and reproductive success of individuals that bear the trait, but not of other members of groups to which those individuals belong. In neo-Darwinian evolutionary theory, the idea of group selection means that natural selection would somehow favor genes that *reduce* the survival and reproductive chances of any individuals that bore them, and, simultaneously, *increase* the survival and reproductive success of other members of the group as a whole. One might say that genetically based group selection would mean that natural selection would favor genes that are "good for the group" *at the expense of* genes that are "good for the individual." And, of course, "good for" means contributing to survival and reproductive success. In neo-Darwinian discussions of group selection, the adaptive consequences of a trait are always measured using the metric of "gene-counting," not the persistence or demise of a collectivity organized and regulated by the "sociocultural phenotypes." Thus, for example, presenting the case of the variable success and failure of businesses in a competitive market economy as an example of group selection in sociocultural evolution fails to address the central issue around which the debate over group selection in organic evolution revolves. Unless, and *only* unless, the survival or demise of businesses could be shown to be linked somehow to genetic variability among individuals who comprise the populations of those companies, the issue of group selection as conceptualized in *organic evolution* is not addressed in such examples of *sociocultural forms* of group selection.

From Kin Selection to Reciprocal Altruism

Another question left unanswered by Hamilton's theory of kin selection was how cooperation, even altruism, could evolve among individuals who are genetically unrelated (lacking genes shared by descent from a common ancestor). And once it evolves, what forces could sustain patterns of cooperation in systems of social interaction comprising non-kin? The answer to this question was provided in a now-classic article published by Robert L. Trivers (1971), and interestingly, Trivers' explanation was as "sociological" as it was "biological." Specifically, Trivers addressed the role of *reciprocity* in assembling and sustaining cooperative social relations, and the key concept in his account was *reciprocal altruism*, a term that is, in fact, oxymoronic. The phenomenon designated by Trivers' concept of reciprocal altruism will be familiar to sociologists as delayed reciprocity (also called *unilateral reciprocity*) because "the timing of reciprocity can be delayed" (Molm et al. 2007: 211). In fact, in directing the attention of evolutionary biologists to the role of reciprocity in the evolution of social behavior, Trivers cited the work of a well-known sociologist, Alvin Gouldner, and his influential essay on the "norm of reciprocity" in human social life (Gouldner 1960). What, then, is reciprocal altruism, and how can it evolve by natural selection?

If close genetic kinship were the only factor enabling the evolution of social life, increases in population size, especially among diploid species, would inhibit the emergence and persistence of stable patterns of cooperative social relations. As population size increases, the coefficient of relatedness (r) among members of a population decreases. At a certain point, many of the members of a population come close to sharing no genes beyond *baseline relatedness*, which refers to the minimal number of genes required to make an individual a member of a species (Dawkins 1989: 288–89). Thus, as r declines to baseline relatedness, kin selection is no longer able to account for even simple forms of cooperation, much less altruism, among members of a population. And though the theory of kin selection has been very persuasive to many biologists as an account of the evolution of the extremely large, complex societies found among many Hymenoptera, it has no explanatory power in accounting for how the only other social species on earth, *Homo sapiens*, evolved "macrosociality" (Machalek 1992).

Macrosocieties (or megasocieties) are defined as

> societies with very large populations (hundreds to millions of individuals) whose members are organized into a complex division of labor that is executed by social categories (castes among ants, occupational groups among humans) comprising anonymous individuals engaged in impersonal patterns of cooperation.
> (Machalek 1992; Machalek and Martin 2015)

While the theory of kin selection has been invoked to explain the evolution of megasocieties among the Hymenoptera, kin selection can explain cooperation in human societies only at the scale of micro-corporate structures (relatively small kinship networks). Though numerous factors are responsible for producing megasocieties among humans, relations of reciprocity and exchange are among the most important, and Trivers' theory of reciprocal altruism represents a good starting point for exploring the evolutionary origins of these processes.

Ironically, relations of reciprocity and exchange are more easily (and intuitively) understood when considering a cognitively complex, culture-bearing species like humans than they are when considering species like ants whose mental processes are much simpler.[2] Consciousness and culture enable humans not only to enter into relations based on reciprocity and exchange, but also to *conceptualize* dynamics of reciprocity and exchange and assess their consequences for participants, including themselves. As a result, foresight enables humans to envision the possibility that participating in a system of give-and-take might be more beneficial to them than solitary existence. It also enables humans to monitor the cost-benefit consequences of reciprocity and exchange and deliberate about future opportunities for participating in such systems. In short, human consciousness is a powerful enabling mechanism of exchange relationships, and it is little surprise that economies have long-been among the most important and influential institutional complexes produced and enacted by humans.

Trivers contended that systems of cooperative social life can also emerge on the basis of reciprocity among even species with very limited mental capacities. His theory of "reciprocal altruism" has been prominent and influential in sociobiology, and it can be applied to groups consisting either of kin or non-kin, though its primary value has been to offer a possible explanation of how cooperation can evolve among "genetic strangers," that is, individuals who do not share genes beyond baseline relatedness. As explained earlier, if an individual behaves altruistically (in the sociobiological sense of incurring a fitness cost) toward another, closely genetically related individual, the behavior is *apparently* altruistic, because the "altruist" will actually receive indirect fitness gains from the fitness benefits conferred on the recipient of the behavior who is a relative. Stated differently, the "altruist" is being *phenotypically* altruistic, but *genotypically* selfish. For example, if you incur a fitness cost by paying for the college education of a niece or nephew whose parent is one of your full siblings, you will receive an indirect "fitness return" on your investment, because you share 25% of your genes with your niece or nephew. (The "return on investment" presupposes, of course, that your niece or nephew survives to reproduce, thereby transmitting 12.5% of your genes to each of their offspring.) Similarly, behavior that Trivers calls *reciprocal altruism* is only apparently altruistic. If individual A (whom we will call the *benefactor*) confers a fitness benefit on individual B (whom we will call the beneficiary), and the benefactor's behavior causes it to incur a fitness cost, the behavior is altruistic. However, if at some point in the future, the benefactor's action causes the beneficiary to "return the favor" and behave altruistically toward the benefactor, then the behavior constitutes reciprocal altruism, or, in the sociological vernacular, *delayed reciprocity*. As becomes evident with only slight reflection, the expression "reciprocal altruism" is an oxymoron, because by definition, a true altruist never receives return fitness benefits from an altruistic act. The concept of delayed reciprocity is arguably more felicitous, because it does not create the possible confusion that using the oxymoronic neologism "reciprocal altruism" might. Nevertheless, Trivers' paper on reciprocal altruism was very influential and, in fact, contributed significantly to the emergence and early development of sociobiology (Wilson 1975: 120–21).

Reciprocal altruism is a subset of *social mutualism*, one of the three basic types of *social symbioses* identified by behavioral biologists; the other two forms of symbioses are *social commensalism* and *social parasitism* (Wilson 1975: 353–77). These three concepts were developed for analyzing "prolonged and intimate" relationships among organisms belonging to different species (Wilson 1975: 353–54), but they can be used to analyze interactions among *conspecifics* (members of the same species) as well. Social symbioses can develop among actors ranging from individuals to entire societies. In social mutualism, both actors benefit from the interaction. In social commensalism, one actor benefits, but the other is unaffected by the interaction. In social parasitism, one actor benefits at the expense of the other for whom the consequences of the relationship are more or less costly. Many forms of social mutualism, including systems of cooperation within an ant colony, represent what sociologists would call *collective action*. That is, the members of a group (or any corporate structure) interact in the pursuit of a common goal(s). In the case of members of an ant colony, the individuals are all working toward the eventual founding of a new colony (Hölldobler and Wilson 1990, 2009). However, social mutualism is also common among organisms that are members of different species.

For example, aphids provide food for some species of ants which, in turn, provide the aphids with hygienic cleaning, shelters in which aphids take refuge, and protection from predators and parasitoids (Hölldobler and Wilson 1990: 525–26). Aphids and some other homopterans (e.g., scale insects, mealybugs, jumping plant lice, treehoppers, leafhoppers, froghoppers, and "lantern flies") secrete substances that are used as food by ants. Aphids consume the phloem of plants which passes through their guts and is expelled as droplets of "honeydew." Some species of ants eat the honeydew, which is rich in several types of sugars and other nutrients, as food. Evidence suggests that the relationship between aphids and ants is very old and specialized. For example, some aphids possess specific anatomical structures that present the droplet to the ant, and the abdomen of some species of aphids resembles the head of an ant. Ants exchange liquid food with each other by regurgitation, a process known as *trophallaxis*. It is possible that the anal region of aphids co-evolved with ants to resemble the head of an ant and thus stimulate the ant to solicit and receive the droplet from what resembles the mandible area of another ant (Hölldobler and Wilson 1990: 523). An analogy to food-sharing among humans would be visually troubling. No less interesting is the possibility that aphids have evolved to signal their "intention" to release food for nearby ants by elevating their hind legs, a behavior that invites (with caution) a close analogue to the process of "advertising" a commodity to a potential trade partner. The exchange relationship that has co-evolved between aphids and ants is a form of social mutualism of the sort that comprises an elementary form of reciprocal altruism, and biologists call it *trophobiosis* (Wilson 1975: 356–58).

A social relationship such as trophobiosis can become a target of selection and favor the spread of alleles, even among different species, that maintain this type of relationship because of its adaptive benefits to both of its participants. However, the stability of any form of reciprocal altruism can be threatened by several factors including: (1) the absence of iterated interaction, thereby denying participants the opportunity to maintain exchange interactions, (2) the failure of one party to somehow register and recall a "debt" incurred by its exchange partner and fail to reciprocate when the opportunity arises; (3) an inability to recognize an individual as an exchange partner; this creates the opportunity for another individual, even the member of another species, to insinuate itself into the relationship and misrepresent itself as a legitimate trade partner, thereby transforming social mutualism into social parasitism; and (4) overt "cheating," the process by which one party deliberately fails to reciprocate, thereby eroding and eventually destroying the exchange relationship.

The threat of failing to reciprocate in organisms with complex cognitive capabilities like humans was addressed by Trivers (1971, 2005). Trivers argued that emotions such as shame or guilt and other forms of affect associated with intimate relationships like friendship, often both the product and cause of reciprocity and exchange among humans, could have evolved to reduce the temptation of either exchange partner to cheat. He also posited the evolution of another emotional complex that he called "moralistic aggression" (sometimes characterized as "altruistic punishment") whereby the victim of cheating experiences a sense of moral indignation at having been victimized. The sentiment of moralistic aggression then activates retaliation, often with a degree of severity that is disproportionate to the harm incurred by the victim. Trivers contends that such retaliatory over-reaction may not be an over-reaction at all when considering its possible deterrent effect on future acts of cheating. However, because any act of retaliation could cause the victim to suffer risk of harm inflicted by the cheater, Trivers argues that selection would favor a system that activates retaliation by means of emotions rather than conscious cost-benefit deliberations (Trivers 1971, 2005). Moralistic aggression thus functions to deter future acts of cheating. Interestingly, Trivers and other sociobiologists have adopted the mathematical and social scientific perspective of game theory to frame and analyze the dynamics of cooperation and defection in relations of reciprocity and exchange. The incorporation of game-theoretic modeling into sociobiology has resulted in the development of "evolutionary game theory" (Maynard Smith 1982). Various social and behavioral scientists have also drawn upon evolutionary game theory for analyzing the evolution of cooperation and exchange in different domains of human social interaction (e.g., Axelrod 1984; Cohen and Machalek 1988; Cosmides and Tooby 1989; Machalek 1995).

Despite the early enthusiasm about reciprocal altruism as a process by means of which systems of cooperation among non-kin might evolve among non-human animals, a recent survey of studies conducted since the publication of Trivers' seminal article revealed that, with a few exceptions, the incidence of reciprocal altruism in animal societies is rare (Clutton-Brock 2009). Clutton-Brock concludes that most examples of putative reciprocal altruism among animals are better explained as incidents of other types of mutualism, kin selection, or manipulation. Still, behaviors that clearly represent reciprocal altruism have been identified among some animal species such as New World vampire bats (*Desmodus rotundus*). Work by Wilkinson (1984) and Carter and Wilkinson (2013) confirms that vampire bats often provide food regurgitations to roost-mates that fail to find food on their own. If a vampire bat fails to find food for three successive days, it is in danger of starving. In such situations, it will often solicit a blood regurgitation from another colony member that has fed successfully. In a 2-year, controlled experiment in which vampire bats were subjected to fasting, it was discovered that food sharing occurred among both kin and non-kin. However, 64% of dyads that shared food were unrelated, and having previously received food was 8.5 times more likely to predict the sharing of food than was close kinship (Carter and Wilkinson 2013). This finding is strongly suggestive of the incidence of reciprocity that is not based on close genetic relatedness among participants.

Clutton-Brock concludes, unsurprisingly to sociologists, that among all social species, humans are surely the premier practitioners of both reciprocal altruism (delayed reciprocity) and exchange. In fact, the existence of an entire school of sociological thought known as *exchange theory* (and more recently, *rational choice theory*) testifies to the importance of processes of reciprocity and exchange in human social life (e.g., Blau 1964; Coleman 1990; Ekeh 1974; Emerson 1972; Hechter 1987; Homans 1958, 1961; Lawler and Yoon 1996). Clutton-Brock attributes the pervasiveness of systems of reciprocity and exchange in human societies to human traits such as "language (and associated psychological capacities)" which permit humans "to establish the intentions and expectations . . . regarding the nature and timing of exchanges as well as social norms that discourage cheating" (2009: 55). In short, Clutton-Brock's conclusions converge on an already well-established point-of-view (and body of knowledge) provided by sociology and other social sciences such as economics, political science, and anthropology. It would be imprudent, however, to disparage Clutton-Brock for having concluded the "sociologically obvious." Rather, his conclusions are important because they provide empirically based insight about the fact that, while systems of reciprocal altruism can be found on occasion among species such as vampire bats, the constraints that must be overcome for any species to evolve even fairly simple systems of reciprocity and exchange are daunting. It is, of course, possible that systems of cooperation based on reciprocal altruism are common among as-yet-unstudied species. Hölldobler and Wilson (1990, 2009) estimate that about 14,000 species of ants have been identified, and the total number that now exist may exceed 20,000 species, so ample opportunity remains in this taxon alone for the discovery of new, improbable forms of sociality. More likely, however, only humans have evolved the complex cognitive capabilities to produce and sustain the types of social behaviors that comprise a foundation on the basis of which even fairly simple forms of reciprocity and exchange develop. Even in foraging (hunting-gathering) societies, the simplest form of social systems found among humans, relations of reciprocity and exchange are complex, subtle, and highly nuanced attributes that derive from human consciousness and culture.

As noted earlier, the evolution of social behavior has been a topic of inquiry at least since Darwin expressed concern about how the existence of "sterile castes" among ants, bees, wasps, and termites posed a serious threat to his theory of evolution by natural selection. But it was not until the onset of the "Modern Synthesis" in evolutionary biology, the integration of Darwin's theory of natural selection with Mendelian genetics, that a foundation was laid for the development of a theory of the evolution of social behavior by natural selection. Later, the work of Williams (1966) and Hamilton (1964) constituted a watershed that heralded the rise and development of both behavioral ecology and sociobiology, the two disciplines that now dominate the biological study of social behavior among animals. Chapter 7 provides a relatively detailed introductory overview to sociobiology which, in turn, will provide a foundation for a discussion of how contemporary thinking in evolutionary biology has led to the emergence of both human sociobiological analyses and the more recent, and derivative, field of evolutionary psychology.

Notes

1 Elsewhere, one of us (Jonathan H. Turner) has challenged the received wisdom that the nuclear family is the primordial unit of social organization in human society. Maryanski and Turner (1992), Turner (2000), and Turner and Maryanski (2008a) contend that the strong social ties on which the nuclear family and other primary groups are based are unlikely to have been inherited from the last common ancestor to humans and apes. Instead, the emotional capabilities that can produce and support strong social ties of the sort that are said to typify the nuclear family have evolved fairly recently in the hominin line. Thus, while the nuclear family may have become foundational to human societal life, that development is likely to have occurred much more recently than commonly believed by most sociologists.
2 The brain of an ant is about the size of a grain of salt, but the human brain weighs about 3.5 pounds.

7
The Rise of Sociobiology

One of the earliest, and perhaps among the broadest, definitions of sociobiology was provided by Wilson when he defined the field "as the systematic study of the biological basis of all social behavior" (1975: 4). In practice, however, the scope of most sociobiological research is somewhat narrower and more focused. Specifically, sociobiologists try to determine if actual patterns of social behavior observed among members of social species are evolved adaptations, and if so, what adaptive problems are they designed to solve (Alcock 2001: 10–16, 23–40). Sociobiologists are interested primarily in trying to identify the ultimate, rather than proximate, causes of a particular form of social behavior. In fact, sociobiologists often deliberately ignore the types of biological factors that many might think are the truly important causes of social behavior, such as variation in hormonal states, the activity of complex neural networks in the brain, and the presence of stimuli that activate physiological responses in multiple body systems, the final effect of which is to generate behavioral outputs such as fighting, caring for offspring, courting potential mates, competing for positions in a dominance hierarchy, or collaborating with other members of one's species. These are all questions of *proximate* causation, and answering them is important in identifying the detailed causal chains that convert the perception of stimuli eventually into overt behavior by a social organism. Nevertheless, the basic questions posed by sociobiologists do not require them to attend to this level of analysis.

While all sociobiologists would affirm the basic biological fact that behavior is the product of complex, and potentially identifiable and specifiable neural networks in the brain, basic sociobiological research questions can be posed and answered by empirical research, *without having to consider the neural, hormonal, or other proximate physiological causes that result in behavioral outputs by the organism.* That is, productive empirical research in sociobiology does not require attention to specific neural processes that actually activate behavior. Rather, the primary questions of concern to a sociobiologist include the following: (1) Is the social behavior under consideration adaptive, regardless of the proximate mechanisms that produce it, (2) what specific adaptive problem (or, "Darwinian problem" of survival and/or reproductive relevance) does the behavior solve, and (3) what sorts of selection forces are likely to have produced this evolved behavioral adaptation during the organism's phylogenetic history? If a pattern of behavior has evolved and occurs because it confers adaptive value to the individual that expresses it, then the adaptive consequences of that behavior constitute its *ultimate* causes.

Although any category of social behavior is, in principle, of potential interest to a sociobiologist, behaviors that are likely to have the greatest effect on the organism's reproductive prospects typically have been of greatest interest to sociobiologists. Consequently, our attention now turns to social behaviors that are candidates for the status of evolved adaptations for increasing reproductive success. And insofar as sociobiology emerged and developed as a field designed for the analysis of non-human social behavior, the social species discussed in this chapter are non-human.

Why devote an entire chapter to reviewing sociobiological studies of non-human animals in a book on evolutionary *sociology*? Why not simply "cut to the chase" and begin by focusing directly on humans, the only social animal in which most sociologists have a professional interest? In simplest terms, by adopting a comparative, cross-species analysis of social organisms and their behaviors, it becomes possible to isolate and understand the universal evolutionary *processes* by means of which natural selection can shape social behavior in *any social species*, human or non-human. And the generic, or universal processes that comprise evolution by natural selection can sometimes better be observed by studying certain species rather than others. As the physiologist Kroh once put it, "For many problems, there is an animal on which it can be most conveniently studied" (in Hölldobler and Wilson 1990: 335). If, for example, one is interested in the basic physiological processes by means of which animals exchange gases during respiration, a fish might be a better "study organism" than a mammal, since gills are much more accessible to direct observation than are lungs. By the same logic, an ant colony might present a better opportunity to isolate and analyze the forces that enable ants to assemble and execute complex patterns of societal organization at the macro-level than might a troop of chimpanzees. While it might be productive to study chimpanzee biology as an avenue of analysis for gaining insights about certain elementary human behavioral propensities, there is little compelling reason to study the biology of individual ants for insight into such propensities among humans. On the other hand, by identifying and specifying the elementary components of an ant *macro-* (or "mega-") society, it might be possible to make inferences about the "design problems" that are common to *any* megasociety, regardless of the species that constructs it.

This type of logic accounts for evolutionary biology's heavy reliance on cross-species analysis. By subordinating a preoccupation with any particular species, including humans, to a more basic commitment of trying to understand *universal processes* of evolution by natural selection, it becomes productive to range widely in one's search for appropriate study organisms. Toward that end, we will review a range of social behaviors among a variety of social species in order to illustrate how sociobiological analyses of non-human species may provide insight into the evolution of social behavior among many different species, including, on occasion, even humans.

But First, a Cautionary Preamble

Evolutionary biologists are fond of anthropomorphic communication, and a vigilant consumer of evolutionary thought might not be able to resist sounding an alarm about the dangers of biologists' habit of attributing "selfishness" to genes, "choice" to females that are "selecting" mates, discernment among parents that are "trying" to "invest" in offspring that will "pay the greatest fitness returns," "altruistic" sacrifices by individuals for the good of others, the expression of "moralistic aggression" toward cheaters, much less the practice of "slavery" among ants, and so on. Among those who are unfamiliar with biologists' use of such analogies, greatest offense might be taken to biologists' all-too-casual inclination to impute human-like *agency* to organisms that clearly fail to qualify for such an attribution. An example is available in myrmecologists' descriptions of "slavery" (technically called "dulosis") among ants. Describing patterns of social interaction among ants as constituting slavery may seem preposterous to some, in that it implies a purposiveness that is impossible to attribute to insects. Robin Stuart, however, defends the cautious use of such analogies by biologists as helpful for evolutionary analysis (1983).

Recently, Richard Dawkins, the very perpetrator of the now four decade-old characterization of genes as "selfish," has addressed this issue (2015: 53–55). Like the sociologist/economist Thorstein Veblen before him (1914), Dawkins sees in humans a strong propensity to personify nature, perhaps as a projection of humans' own experiences of deliberative action and its causal efficacy (2015: 53–54). Veblen, in fact, saw humans as unwittingly misled by their own agency in that, rather than attributing events in nature to the processes of "brute causation," humans have long projected onto nature an "animistic impulse" and thereby created obstacles to the development of a dispassionate, scientific understanding of relations of cause-effect (1914). In Veblen's view, a major force by means of which humans have been liberated from animistic thinking is what he called the "machine discipline." Technology in general, and machines in particular, act as unwitting "teachers" that "instruct," by vivid example, their users in elementary relations of cause and effect in the physical world, including friction, inertia, gravitation, leverage, momentum, mass, and so on. As machines become more complex, they provide increasingly sophisticated lessons about the natural forces that make them work. Thus, over time, humanity's growing experience of the machine discipline erodes superstitious, animistic thinking which is slowly replaced by science.

Though much less fully developed than Veblen's thesis, Dawkins' comments about how biologists' propensity to "personify" nature converge on Veblen's, and much thinking in organic evolutionary theory employs a metaphor of genes and individual organisms as "applied economists." According to Dawkins (2015: 53), whereas economists describe human behavior as entailing efforts to maximize various utility functions such as "gross national product; personal income; personal wealth; company profits; human happiness . . . [natural selection] maximizes only one 'utility': gene survival. If you personify a gene as a metaphorical 'agent' doing the maximizing, you'll get the right answer." Dawkins goes on to say that "We leave open the question of whether the organism is a conscious agent. We know the gene *isn't* [emphasis ours]. The organism makes decisions calculated (unconsciously is all we need to assume) to maximize the long-term survival of the genes that reside inside it . . . [and the] decisions give every appearance of being those of a shrewd economist, acting as if deploying (distributing, eking out) limited resources in the service of passing genes on to future generations" (Dawkins 2015: 54–55).

Simply put, evolutionary theorists (and researchers) employ a metaphorical short-hand to characterize organisms and the genes that direct their assembly and guide their behavior. They describe organisms as behaving *as if* they are in a quest to acquire traits and utilize them in order to achieve a life-long "goal" of producing as many offspring that attain reproductive age as they can. Ironically, the metaphor is *less* misleading when applied to life forms that are (apparently) utterly devoid of consciousness, lacking the capacity of purposiveness, or devoid of goal-oriented behavior than it is when applied to humans. Instead, when applied to humans, the metaphor of organisms as engaged in the pursuit of "fitness maximization" can lead to misunderstanding and confusion. Consequently, it is important to remain aware that, despite the eagerness with which sociobiologists describe the evolved behavioral propensities of humans, they never intend to say that humans have even minimal awareness of their "fitness interests," much less the slightest conscious motivation to try to "maximize" them. Contrary to the critics Tooby and Cosmides, contemporary sociobiologists are not guilty of promoting evolutionary explanations that are flawed by a variant of "fitness teleology" that compromises the scientific nature of their analyses (2016: 14). And what is true of humans in this regard applies even more appropriately to other animals. A simple example, often cited in sociobiological literature, is the "sweet tooth" preference exhibited by some animals, including humans. A taste preference for sweetness guides frugivorous (fruit-consuming) animals toward ripe fruit which, biochemically, is more nutritious than fruit that is not ripe. Accordingly, by indulging a preference for sweetness, frugivores are unwittingly making a "decision" to eat more nutritious food which then makes them healthier and, thus, more likely to reproduce successfully. Therefore, food preferences among frugivores cause them to behave *as if* they were *trying* to become more reproductively successful (and, by the way, increase their genetic representation in future gene pools). Such reasoning is not to be taken at all literally.

This example of taste preference also provides an opportunity to illustrate the relevance of the distinction between "proximate" and "ultimate" causes of behavior. In this case, the physiology of taste comprises a complex of biochemical processes and their reaction to the biochemistry of fruit that explains the immediate causal mechanisms that explain frugivores' taste preferences for sweetness in their consumption patterns. However, by having been directed toward sweeter fruits by their taste preferences, these animals are "making good choices" in eating food that is more nutritious and, will in turn, increase the consumer's long-term health, survival, and reproductive future. In the language of evolutionary theory, the adaptive (fitness-enhancing) value of a preference of sweet fruit is the *ultimate cause* of this behavioral tendency. This example illustrates how proximate and ultimate causes "collude" to produce particular patterns of behavior.

It is also important to understand what sociobiologists mean when they use the expression fitness "maximization." Simply put, this concept is used only to mean that, if a particular form of a heritable phenotypic trait, be it morphological, physiological, or behavioral, enhances an individual's chances of surviving *and reproducing* better than do alternative variants of that trait, it will increase in frequency over evolutionary time. The notion of "maximization" is *not* used to denote an "optimal" trait or what might be thought of as a "best possible" trait. The notion of fitness maximization means only that, among the range of phenotypes that can be produced by a range of genotypes in a survivable environment, those phenotypes that enhance their bearers' survival and reproductive prospects *better than do alternatives* are more likely to proliferate over generational time.

However, the characterization of evolved traits as strategic devices by means of which organisms compete successfully in the struggle for life (and reproduction) provides a very useful convention that enables the mind to think fluidly, creatively, and productively about evolution by natural selection, *if the metaphorical nature of this convention remains at the forefront of the analyst's consciousness*. That having been said, we will now review behaviors of a number of species to learn how they "play" mating (and parenting) "games." Though sociobiologists study a wide range of social behaviors, mating, sex, and reproduction are fundamental to processes comprising evolution by natural selection, so we have chosen these behaviors to illustrate basic aspects of reasoning and research in sociobiology.

Sex, Reproduction, and the Evolution of Social Behavior

The fundamental logic of sociobiological theory implies that, of all of the types of social behavior exhibited by members of a social species, those that pertain most directly to sex and reproduction can be expected to have been most strongly subjected to forces of selection. Accordingly, studies of social interactions among males and females, same-sex competitors, and parent-offspring relations constitute a large body of theory and research in sociobiology and behavioral ecology. The remainder of this chapter provides a review of several sociobiological analyses of these patterns of social behavior in order to convey the basic logic entailed in sociobiological thinking and research. This will provide readers with a fundamental understanding of sociobiology as it has been applied to non-human species and thus, a basis on which they can better assess efforts to apply sociobiology to humans, the topic of Chapter 8.

Parental Investment, Paternity Uncertainty, and Male-Female Cooperation and Conflict

Among sexually reproducing species, social relations of mating and reproduction constitute a fundamental form of cooperation, because they potentially increase the fitness of reproductive partners by producing offspring. Viewed in terms of an economic analogy, the fitness "interests" of female and male reproductive partners overlap, but they do not coincide. If a mated pair of diploid organisms produces an offspring, each mate derives a fitness "return" of 50% on its genetic "investment." (Notice the use of analogical reasoning and expression in this account, with reasoning and expression framed in terms of an economic metaphor.) However, the *costs* and *risks* incurred by the male and the female in this partnership are not equal; thus, despite the fundamentally cooperative nature of mating, biological dimensions of the reproductive division of labor create a foundation for the development of male-female conflict, even in the context of what is arguably the most basic type of cooperation of which two sexually reproducing organisms are capable.

Two biological asymmetries between males and females give rise to conflicts between reproductive partners. The first asymmetry entails the differential costs borne by one reproductive partner compared to the other in producing an offspring which attains reproductive age. In most cases, females incur greater costs in producing offspring than do males, but in at least a few species, the costs to the male may equal or exceed those incurred by the female.[1] The second asymmetry entails a risk created by the possibility of uncertain parentage. Maternity uncertainty is virtually never a concern experienced by a mother, but uncertainty about whether a male is, in fact, the father of an offspring produced by his mate is a chronic concern experienced by males in many species, including humans. Either, or both, of these asymmetries can trigger the development of male-female conflict in mating partnerships.

Conflicts between reproductive partners can also arise from the disproportionate share of metabolic and behavioral costs incurred by a female in bringing a pregnancy to term and caring for her offspring. Elaborating on the aforementioned economic analogy, the sociobiologist Robert Trivers has developed a theory of *parental investment* that has stimulated additional theoretical developments and inspired much research about male-female conflict in reproductive relationships (Trivers 1972). Sociobiologists contend that male-female asymmetry in parental investment is based ultimately in the cellular level phenomenon called *anisogamy* (gamete asymmetry), which refers to the fact that eggs are much larger and metabolically more "expensive" than are sperm, which are tiny and "inexpensive" to produce. In addition, sperm are abundant, but eggs are, literally, precious few.

This asymmetry in gamete quantity and quality is very important when one considers that, in evolutionary terms, females and males represent valuable resources *to each other* in their respective pursuits (almost certainly unconscious and unintentional) of "trying to maximize" their lifetime fitness. For example, the fertilization of a mammalian egg typically entails a significant metabolic commitment by females until at least birth of the offspring and, typically, long after. For males, however, the commitment to reproductive effort may entail nothing more than the time and energy expended to achieve a copulation. Furthermore, in comparison to males, females produce relatively few gametes available for reproductive investment over the course of their lifetimes, but the supply of gametes available to males is, for all practical purposes, almost limitless. As expressed rather colorfully by the sociobiologically minded sociologist Joseph Lopreato, comparing sperm to eggs is "another way of comparing dirt with gold" (1984: 324).

The asymmetry between eggs and sperm comprises the first element of the biological roots of conflict between males and females. The fact of anisogamy alone leads us to expect significant behavioral differences between males and females. Imagine, for example, a hypothetical species in which females (1) can produce only one offspring at a time, (2) have a relatively short reproductive life-span, and (3) produce offspring that require intense care for a prolonged period of time. Imagine also that males of the same species enjoy (metaphorically, of course) reproductive options that are limited only by the number of females that will consent to mate with them. After mating, males contribute nothing to the care of any offspring they sire. In such a scenario, sociobiological thinking would lead us to predict that males and females are likely to approach a reproductive opportunity quite differently. If, as the theory of evolution by natural selection predicts, organisms are designed to behave *as if* they were attempting to maximize their fitness, then males of this hypothetical species can be expected to be virtually indiscriminate in their choice of reproductive partners and to seize virtually every mating opportunity that comes their way. They can be expected to adopt what could be described as a highly promiscuous mating "strategy."[2] Females, on the other hand, could be expected to behave much more cautiously and judiciously in their "choice" of a reproductive partner. From the female's point-of-view, the value of the male as a reproductive partner in a scenario such as this is restricted to the quality of genes that are delivered by his sperm. And, of course, gene "quality" is operationalized in terms of its potential contribution to the survival and reproductive prospects of any offspring sired by the male with whom the females mates.

A helpful way to understand the biological dimensions of this situation and their consequences for the prospective mates is to consider the implications of either participant's having made a poor "Darwinian choice" in a reproductive partner. For the male, the negative consequences of his having made a poor choice are typically negligible, if not non-existent. Because "sperm are dirt," the only significant costs incurred by a male are those in pursuing and mating with a female. If, of course, the male had to engage in physical confrontations with other males in order to secure a mate, or if the female attempted to repel his mating efforts with physical force, he may run the risk of serious injury or even death, costs whose significance is not to be minimized. It is also possible that the male could make an imprudent "Darwinian choice" if he suffered an opportunity cost by mating with Female X rather than Female Y when Female Y turned out to be not only equally available, but more fecund and promising higher fertility by producing offspring that were equal or superior (as defined in fitness-enhancing terms) to those produced by Female X. Still, relative to the consequences likely to be incurred by a female who makes a bad Darwinian mate choice, the costs of a poor mate-choice exercised by a male are typically minimal. Thus, the incidence of sexually promiscuous males in this hypothetical species should come as no surprise to a mind informed by sociobiological theory.

On the other hand, the consequences of a bad mate choice exercised by a female are much more momentous and are likely to be more severely "penalized" by the forces of selection. For example, the opportunity costs suffered by a female who is impregnated by a male with "low-quality genes" are much greater than they would be for a male. Should a female make a poor choice in mates, then she typically is burdened by the consequences of her choice throughout her pregnancy (and an entire reproductive cycle) and, depending on the species, often well beyond. In a lifetime of limited reproductive opportunities for females, every mating decision "counts" disproportionately to that made by a male. Accordingly, a hypothetical mate-selection scenario such as the one described here would favor females that are very judicious, circumspect, and cautious in selecting males as reproductive partners. We would expect females, for example, to have evolved very sensitive capabilities for discerning males whose genes would confer the greatest survival and reproductive advantages on any offspring sired by those males. In discussing this dynamic of "female choice" whereby males actively exhibit their qualities to a prospective female mate during an "epigamic display," Wilson (1975: 320) provides the following characterization:

> Pure epigamic display can be envisioned as a contest between salesmanship and sales resistance. The sex that courts, ordinarily the male, plans to invest less reproductive effort in the offspring ... so, strong selective pressures exist for less fit (male) individuals to present a false image. The courted sex, usually the female, will therefore find it strongly advantageous to distinguish the really fit from the pretended fit. Consequently, there will be a strong tendency for the courted sex to develop coyness ... (the quality of being) hesitant and cautious in a way that evokes still more displays (by the male) and makes correct discrimination easier.

The phenomenon of anisogamy and the additional asymmetries to which it gives rise is foundational to understanding male-female conflict in sexually reproducing species. However, another consideration looms large in the dynamics of mate selection and mating that is independent of the qualities of the prospective male and female mates themselves, and it bears directly on the issue of parental investment constraints faced by members of both sexes. At birth, species vary widely in terms of the amount and nature of parental investment they must make in their offspring. Some offspring are entirely independent at birth (e.g., fish and many reptiles), while others require much more time and effort to raise young to the point of being capable of independent survival and reproductive success (e.g., many birds and mammals). Biologists describe species whose offspring are independent at birth as *precocial*, while those whose offspring are highly dependent at birth are said to be *altricial*. The precocial-altricial distinction constitutes a continuum along which species are variably distributed. Even some fairly complex vertebrates, such as sea turtles, are entirely precocial at birth. Though highly vulnerable to predation when emerging from the sandy nests from which they hatch and then racing with all possible dispatch to the sea, these newborn animals do not enjoy any protection from their mothers. At the other extreme, more than a few species of mammals, humans perhaps being foremost, produce highly altricial offspring that require years, if not decades, of protection and nurturance.

Among highly precocial species, then, the issue of choosing the best available mate becomes an additional consideration for individuals designed by natural selection to behave so as to maximize their fitness. Imagine, for example, the sorts of eligibility criteria that could be expected to guide the choices of females trying to select the best male with whom to mate. Regardless of the species, the female's standards should begin with identifying the male with the "best genes." The basic value of a male as a reproductive partner is the quality of genes he provides to any offspring he sires, not his contribution to the care and nurturing of offspring. However, if the species produces highly altricial offspring, then males with strong parenting predispositions gain added value for a female designed to maximize her lifetime fitness. In such situations, males vary both in terms of the quality of reproductive resources (genes) they have to offer, as well as the somatic resources (material resources pertaining to health and survival) that they can bring to the reproductive partnership. An optimal choice for females that give birth to altricial offspring would be a male with both "good genes" and devoted parenting skills and behaviors. Such males can provide a range of resources that will contribute to the female's health and well-being, but especially to the health and well-being of her offspring. Such somatic resources could include protection from predators and infanticidal males (African lions are a good example), "baby-sitting" services that would enable a female to forage while her mate cares for her young, food-provisioning to the female and her offspring, the provision of shelter/residence, and even socialization activity whereby the male behaves so as to transmit survival and reproductive skills to offspring.

From the male's point-of-view, prudent mate-selection practices are also very important among species with altricial young. For example, if the fate of offspring is linked closely to the health of the mother, then it pays males to choose as mates healthy females, and various cues detectable by males can help them make a prudent choice. Similarly, if the quality of maternal care is crucial to the survival and development of offspring, then natural selection should provide males with evolved adaptations that enable them to discern females that will be highly nurturing and solicitous of the offspring they produce. A negligent or indifferent mother would be a poor mate-choice for a male in terms of his prospects for maximizing his lifetime fitness. Nevertheless, in many cases, asymmetries in parental investment are less likely to be costly for a male that mates with a "sub-optimal" female than for a female that makes a "bad choice" in a reproductive partner.

A second asymmetry that can jeopardize the fitness prospects of either a male or female reproductive partner derives from *parental uncertainty*, a threat that most commonly confronts males but, as we shall see, confronts females of some species as well. A male that lacks "confidence" in the paternity of "his" offspring is said to suffer from *paternity uncertainty*, a phenomenon that can pose serious threats not only to the stability of the mating relationship, but possibly to the very survival of the female and her offspring as well. It should be emphasized that, while paternity uncertainty as a property of consciousness can be attributed with confidence to humans alone, behavioral adaptations even among species with dubious claims to consciousness can cause males to behave "suspiciously" toward mates that are possibly "guilty" of infidelity. Mate guarding refers to any behavior by means of which a member of one sex attempts to inhibit the efforts of her or his mate to copulate with other members of her or his sex, members that are reproductive competitors. For a male, unsuccessful mate guarding can result in cuckoldry, and the male could suffer not only a lost opportunity to gain an increment of fitness, but he could be deceived into providing parental investment in offspring that are not his. With the exception of members of some species such as birds, most females are not threatened typically by misdirecting maternal care toward offspring other than their own, but they may still engage in concerted efforts of mate guarding so as to reduce the possibility that a male will abandon them and form a mating relationship with a female competitor. In such a case, the most serious cost likely to be incurred by a female would be the loss of parental investment provided by her errant mate. Such females do not face a threat of investing in an offspring that does not carry her genes, but they can face the loss of valuable somatic resources denied them by male infidelity.

Though maternity uncertainty is rare in nature, an exception merits brief discussion. Some species of birds, most famously the cuckoo, will lay eggs in the nests of other species, such as warblers. The cuckoo deposits its eggs into the warbler's nest surreptitiously, when she is absent, typically foraging. Upon returning to her nest, the mother warbler may discover additional eggs but fail to recognize them as alien. When an alien egg hatches, the warbler mother typically begins to feed the chick as if it were her own, often at the expense of neglecting her own chicks or diverting food from them to the alien hatchling. Sociobiologists call this phenomenon "brood parasitism," and it represents a form of social parasitism that is enabled by maternal uncertainty.

Sexual Selection and the Evolution of Male-Female Behavioral Differences

The gene-centered view of sociobiology affords insight about how social relations between the sexes, as well same-sex interactions, function as selection forces that help shape the nature of females, the nature of males, and the differences between them. As noted earlier, Darwin (1871) realized the importance of *sexual selection* as a powerful force of organic evolution, and the rise of sociobiology in the 1960s and 1970s featured sexual selection as a primary focus of theoretical development and empirical research. Sexual selection assumes two forms: (1) intersexual selection and (2) intrasexual selection. Intersexual selection refers to interactions between males and females that affect the probability that they will mate. Intrasexual selection refers to interactions among members of the same sex that affect the probability that each will mate with a member of the opposite sex. The epigamic display discussed previously in relation to parental investment is an example of intersexual selection. Competition between males for reproductive privilege among "harem" species such as many ungulates (e.g., bighorn sheep, elk, and American bison) is an example intrasexual selection.

Evolutionary theorists distinguish between natural selection and sexual selection in terms of the adaptations produced by each. Natural selection produces adaptations that contribute to the general well-being (i.e., health, longevity) and survival prospects of an organism. Sexual selection yields traits that influence the reproductive opportunities of an organism. In some instances, these two types of selection can work at "cross-purposes." For an example, if natural selection predisposes a male to be overly cautious in physical contests for breeding opportunity, his survival prospects may increase at the expense of his reproductive opportunities. Conversely, a male predisposed to high levels of risk-taking in such physical contests may increase his reproductive opportunities, but he may also be severely injured or even killed and, therefore, fail to benefit from these opportunities. Another example of evolved traits that can be favored by one type of selection but penalized by the other is brightly colored plumage among males in some species of birds. Among some species of birds, such as the ring-necked pheasant (*Phasianus colchicus*), males display highly visible, brightly colored plumage. Their faces are bright red; their feathers are iridescent green, blue, and copper; and a highly visible white ring (or "collar") bedecks their necks. Females, by way of contrast, feature drab, brown plumage without any of the dramatic coloration found in males. Why would such dimorphism in plumage evolve among organisms such as these? The obvious (to a sociobiologist) answer would be "female choice" (Darwin 1871: 921–27; Trivers 1972). Male pheasants strut around in their gaudy outfits, because that is what females prefer. Why, however, would females express a preference for brightly colored males? Do the females possess some sort of innate aesthetic sense that attracts them to such males, or, does brightly colored plumage signify some sort of survival or reproductive quality that would benefit offspring sired by such males? Or, as always must be considered, is bright coloration in males simply a *by-product* of other traits which, in fact, have been selected because they confer survival or reproductive value to individuals that inherit them?[3]

Hamilton and Zuk have brought an interesting perspective to bear on the question of bright coloration in birds (Hamilton 2001: 199–220; Hamilton and Zuk 1982). In a now-classic publication (1982), they adduced data in support of the idea that bright plumage in North American passerine (perching) birds may be the product of female choice mechanisms in sexual selection. Among these birds, parasites and pathogens are a significant source of mortality. Any heritable trait that would protect them from succumbing to such threats should be favored by females discriminating among males competing for mates. In a survey of 109 passerine species comprising 7649 individual birds, Hamilton and Zuk found support for the hypothesis that parasite loads are positively correlated with less vivid plumage and that females prefer brightly colored males (1982: 225–27). Hamilton and Zuk, in fact, note that the process by means of which females inspect males as prospective mates is not unlike that of a physician inspecting a patient for eligibility for life insurance. Such a physical examination would entail the doctor's weighing the patient; listening to the heartbeat; taking samples of blood, urine, and fecal matter, and so on (Hamilton 2001: 223). In both cases, prudence (economic in the case of the insurance company, genetic in the case of the bird) calls for the exercise of due diligence before a commitment is made.

Intrasexual Selection: Male-Male Competition

Among males of many species, sexual selection takes the form of male-male competition by means of which males often forcibly repel or otherwise inhibit male competitors from mating with or impregnating females. In this form of sexual selection, males do not evolve traits to make them more likely to be chosen by females as mates. Rather, they evolve traits that enable them to thwart the reproductive efforts of other males. First identified and discussed by Darwin, the phenomenon of sexual selection, including male-male competition, has been the subject of extensive research by behavioral ecologists and sociobiologists. One of the most familiar forms of male-male competition can be found among ungulates such as pronghorn antelope, elk, and other "harem" species in which males attempt to assemble groups of females for reproductive partnerships and sequester them from other males. However, male-male competition is common among species ranging from invertebrates to humans, and a brief review of a few cases will illustrate this important force of evolution.[4]

At the risk of anthropomorphizing the creativity of biological processes, it could be said that natural selection exhibits considerable ingenuity in terms of the range of strategies it has produced in the context of male-male competition. A familiar example is variation in the forms of weaponry available to male competitors, among the most common of which are antlers, horns, tusks, and even "clubs" of the sort wielded by giraffes. More interesting still are structures that resemble the horn of a rhinoceros, and they are found among species as diverse as narwhals, chameleons, unicorn fish, dinosaurs, pigs, rodents, beetles, isopods, and trilobites (Alcock 2013: 182). Though much male-male competition entails overt fighting, the evolution of dominance hierarchies in many species obviates the need for actual physical combat in every competitive encounter. Though fighting is commonly involved in the production of a dominance hierarchy; once ranks are established, a dominant individual often needs only to signal the threat of aggression to produce submission in an opponent. This kind of arrangement confers benefits to both dominant and subordinate occupants of the hierarchy, because it enables both to avoid the risk of serious injury or even death if the likely outcome of a confrontation can be predicted by the respective rank of the prospective combatants.

Among some species such as baboons, males form coalitions that are sometimes described by primatologists as "friendships" (Smuts 1985).

When subordinates form such coalitions, they can sometimes overpower the dominant male in the troop and achieve mating success. In other species such as marine iguanas, large males often approach small males that have mounted a female and forcibly remove them from the female. Similar behavior has been reported among baboons, which will rush a male that is mounted on a female and attempt to dislodge him.

Though much male-male competition occurs at the level of competition among individuals, some males compete with each other at the cellular, "sub-individual" level, a process that is very common among animals and described as "sperm competition" (Baker and Bellis 1995). In this type of intrasexual selection, the challenge for males is not to prevent other males from mating with a female, but rather, to out-compete other males by out-competing their sperm. This can entail a strategy as simple as delivering more sperm per copulation than other males (which is often discernible by the size of males' testes), or it can entail more complex mechanisms such as inhibiting competitive sperm from actually reaching an egg and fertilizing it. Among some primates, males deposit a sperm morph that was originally mistaken as "lazy" sperm, because they failed to swim vigorously toward the egg and fertilize it. Subsequently, biologists produced an alternative interpretation in which these sperm were observed to cluster in a manner that inhibited any sperm subsequently deposited from swimming past them and fertilizing the egg. These "sperm blocking forces" are commonly described by biologists as "kamikaze sperm," because they sacrifice themselves for their "brothers," thereby enabling them to fertilize eggs by preventing competitors from reaching the egg.

Among members of some species, male-male competition persists beyond the actual act of mating, and that competition sometimes takes the form of mate guarding. In most cases, mate guarding refers to efforts to prevent a copulation by a competitor. However, in some cases, a male may continue to guard a female after he has mated with her. As Alcock reports, this presents a Darwinian puzzle, because the male incurs an opportunity cost by remaining with a female after copulation when he could spend that time seeking and mating with another female. As one might expect, males that remain with females after copulating with them are trying to prevent other males from engaging in activities like the sperm removal practiced by the male black-winged damselfly. The threat of post-copulatory mating and insemination by other males is sometimes met by depositing a "mating plug" in the female's genitalia (Dickinson and Rutowski 1989, Polak et al. 2001). Mating plugs are secretions produced by a male (and sometimes a female) that coagulate and clog the female's reproductive tract, thereby preventing the sperm of another male from reaching her egg.

In some species, males may compete for reproductive privilege by means of both intersexual and intrasexual selection strategies. A vivid example of the expression of such dual strategy systems is found among male satin bowerbirds in Australia. Males of this species construct elaborate, tunnel-like structures from twigs and other materials. The bowers are commonly decorated with brightly colored, shiny objects which help attract mates. Having attracted a female with the product of his handiwork, the male proceeds to enact a complex display that entails both vocalizations and ritualized behaviors. Females that find the display satisfactory exercise female-choice and reward the male with a mating. However, males do not restrict their mating efforts merely to constructing bowers, attracting females, and mating with any that are receptive to them. Instead, they will also engage in male-male competition by destroying any bowers constructed by their male neighbors.

Although it has been less studied than male-male competition, intrasexual selection also occurs among females (Drea 2005). As among males, the existence of dominance hierarchies among females creates the opportunity for intrasexual interactions that yield variation in fitness among occupants of different ranks. Some of this variation derives from differential access to resources, but the social dynamics of female-female competition also "can have profound fitness consequences independent of dominance or resource allocation" (Drea 2005: 918). Specifically, dominant females among callitrichid primates suppress ovulation among subordinate females, and among cercopithecine primates, the estradiol levels influence the incidence of female-female aggression (Drea 2005: 918). Female primates disrupt their competitors' reproductive efforts by attacking and harassing them, as well as killing their infants and evicting them from their groups (Drea 2005: 918). The effects of dominant status enable females to "mature earlier, live longer, have a longer reproductive life span, have a lower incidence of miscarriage, produce more offspring . . . and have shorter interbirth intervals with shorter periods of lactation" (Drea 2005: 918).

Parent-Offspring Conflict

As we have seen, though male-female cooperation is required for both sexes to maximize their fitness interests, conflict can, and does, develop routinely even between reproductive partners. When first considered within the framework of sociobiological theory, it would seem that the fitness interests of a parent and its offspring would coincide perfectly and that only in pathological circumstances would parent-offspring conflict develop. For example, in what conceivable Darwinian scenario could a mother and her daughter or son engage in a potentially lethal conflict of fitness interests that could result in the mortality of either, or even both, of them? Before reviewing how a sociobiologist might address this question, it is important to be reminded that evolutionary theory views individuals as behaving *as if* they behave in a deliberate, calculated manner toward a conscious goal of maximizing their inclusive fitness. As discussed earlier, sociobiologists' practice of thinking and talking about organisms as if they are in conscious pursuit of the goal of maximizing their genetic representation in subsequent generations is never meant literally. Rather, it is only a convenience that expedites discussion of how evolution by natural selection designs individuals and their behavior. Consequently, the following discussion about how a parent and its child may be "using" each other so as to enhance their respective fitness should not be taken literally but, rather, as an economical way of portraying social interaction within an evolutionary frame of analysis.

In a now-classic paper, Trivers developed a theoretical interpretation of parent-offspring conflict framed in evolutionary terms (1974). Essentially, Trivers contended that, while offspring are resources to their parents' (non-intentional) efforts to maximize their lifetime inclusive fitness, parents are also resources to their offspring in *their* efforts to maximize their lifetime inclusive fitness. Accordingly, since the fitness interests of parents and their offspring do not always coincide, a gene-centered view of social behavior can illuminate some circumstances in which parent-offspring conflict develops.

Among animals, evidence of the divergence between the fitness interests of parents and their offspring can be found in competition among siblings which, on occasion, can be lethal. Among diploid species such as birds, 50% of a parent's genes are present in each offspring it produces. Yet, under variable conditions, a parent may exhibit favoritism toward some of its offspring at the expense of others. Alcock provides interesting examples of parental favoritism in his discussion of various species of birds (2013: 284–90). Intense conflict for food is not uncommon among chicks in a number of species. In the case of species such as masked boobies, the conflict can result in siblicide. A masked booby mother provides fish for her chicks, but she does not intervene in their struggle for the food. It is possible that this strategy serves her fitness interests by a selection process that leaves her with only the healthiest chicks whose survival and reproductive futures are the brightest. Blue-footed booby mothers, on the other hand, actively intercede and inhibit sibling conflicts among their chicks. When viewed within an anthropocentric frame, the unwillingness of masked booby mothers to intervene in conflicts among their chicks that result in siblicide can seem heartless and cruel. The apparent "heartlessness" of masked boobies is amplified in the conduct of egrets and coots. Egrets actively promote siblicide among their chicks, thereby leaving parents with only those offspring that are likely to survive. Such a "culling" process prevents parents from making ill-advised investment in offspring that are unlikely to survive, much less reproduce successfully. As Alcock observes, the differential manner in which parents treat their own offspring demonstrates that natural selection is not acting so as to produce the *maximum possible number* of offspring, but rather, the number of offspring that are *likely to survive and reproduce*, thereby transmitting the genes of the parents that produced them (2013: 289).

Beyond Sex and Reproduction: Extending Sociobiological Analysis to Other Forms of Social Behavior, and to Humans

Our discussion of mate selection and mating, intra- and intersexual selection, mating cooperation and conflict, and parent-offspring conflict only scratches the surface of the types of social behaviors that have been subjected to sociobiological scrutiny. For example, sociobiologists also investigate behaviors such as cooperative foraging and defense, the construction and maintenance of collective residences such as nests and hives, variation in mating systems (monogamy, polygyny, polyandry), systems of communication used in both cooperation and conflict, relations of cooperation and conflict among kin as well as among non-kin, contests over rank within dominance hierarchies, and even the evolutionary foundations of symbolic communication and culture among humans. Each of these areas of inquiry is fascinating in its own right, but a comprehensive review of the literature generated by studies of these topics is not the purpose of this chapter. Instead, we seek to provide a basic understanding of how evolutionary theory and research has been developed and applied by sociobiologists toward a more complete understanding of social behavior and societies among the roughly 20,000 highly social species, and possibly many more, that biologists estimate currently populate the earth (Hölldobler and Wilson 2009: xvi).

Though sociobiology does not, cannot, and never was intended to *replace the social sciences, including sociology*, as disciplines that are specialized for explaining human sociality and societies, it does offer the prospect of locating human social life in the broader context of the evolution of sociality on earth, as well as providing valuable insights and information about the evolutionary origins and phylogeny of human social behaviors and societies. It also has opened up new avenues of inquiry into the connections between the evolution of the human mind and the ways in which evolved properties of human mental life contribute to and shape human social conduct. Social and behavioral scientists who have been influenced by evolutionary theory in general, and often sociobiology in particular, have pursued two basic evolutionary approaches to the study of human social behavior. Some of the earliest among such thinkers attempted to apply sociobiological principles such as kin selection in a straightforward manner to human social behavior (van den Berghe 1981; Lopreato 1984). As with sociobiologists who study non-human social species, this "first wave" of human sociobiologists attempted to determine if certain patterns of social behavior among humans could be interpreted as evolved adaptations that were fitness-enhancing in even contemporary societies.

Later, another group of evolutionary-minded behavioral and social scientists, many (but not all) of whom are psychologists adopted a different evolutionary approach to human social behavior. Rather than trying to assess the possible adaptive value of social behaviors in contemporary societal contexts, the new "evolutionary psychology" program was devoted to efforts to try to identify evolved mental (cognitive) adaptations in the human mind, the totality of which can be characterized as an evolved human nature that is species-typical and shared by all humans. Behavioral and social scientists engaged in this line of evolutionary analysis are not of one mind regarding many aspects of their orientations and research programs; however, they share one fundamental premise in common: None of them subscribe to the tabula rasa view of the human brain/mind, and all commit themselves to the search for evolved properties of the human brain/mind that are candidates for the status of specialized, evolved behavioral adaptations for social living. It is to the efforts of both of these communities of evolutionary thinkers that we turn our attention in Chapters 8 and 9.

Notes

1 A widely used example of a reversal in typical male-female patterns of parental investment is that of the emperor penguin. After female penguins lay an egg, the male incubates it in his brood pouch until it hatches about 2 months later. During this time, the male provides all of the parental investment by sitting on the egg, during which time the male fasts. The female, however, is free to forage and engage in other behaviors until the chick hatches at which time the female returns to share caring of the chick.
2 Biologists routinely characterize evolved traits, including behaviors, as "strategies" that are the product of natural selection and are designed to solve one or more survival or reproductive challenges. This does not mean that the traits are consciously conceived or held strategies; rather, they represent evolved devices that contribute to an organism's survival chances or its prospects for reproductive success. In this way of thinking, even organisms lacking nervous systems, such as plants, act strategically. For example, maple

trees have adopted the strategy of dispersing their seeds with propeller-like structures that cause the seed to rotate and drift as it descends. Similarly, cottonwood trees have adopted a "parachute" strategy for seed dispersal that enables the seeds to float suspended on wind currents and disperse successfully from their parent tree. Animals are also characterized as behaving strategically, even among species that are devoid of the cognitive capacities to think and act strategically as might humans in a game, business transaction, or military confrontation.

3   The distinction between traits that evolve because of the adaptive value they confer to their bearers versus traits that are simply the by-product of other traits that are truly adaptive was made famous by an essay written by Stephen Jay Gould and Richard C. Lewontin, "The Spandrels of San Marco and the Panglossian Paradigm: A Critique of the Adaptationist Programme" (1979). Gould and Lewontin, both severe critics of sociobiology from its inception, contended that sociobiologists are often all-too-eager to find an adaptive value in any trait that comes to their attention, hence, sociobiology's putative "adaptationist programme." Instead, Gould and Lewontin argued that certain traits may simply be incidental by-products of other traits, not evolved adaptations in and of themselves. Dawkins, however, regards Gould and Lewontin's critique of Panglossian thinking in sociobiology as misplaced (1982: 50–3).

4   This is not to say that males fail altogether to provide any sort of evidence of qualities that could increase their attractiveness to prospective mates. Among such traits are any that signal social status, and a considerable literature has developed that documents male preoccupation with status attainment, precisely because of the mating opportunities that it affords.

8
Sociobiology and Human Behavior

As noted in the beginning of Chapter 7, it is useful to define sociobiology in both broader and narrower terms, as do behavioral biologists. In broader terms, "Sociobiology is defined as the systematic study of the biological basis of all social behavior" (Wilson 1975: 4). Defined more narrowly, sociobiology is viewed as a branch of *behavioral ecology*, the study of how environmental selection forces shape the evolution of animal behaviors (Krebs and Davies 1997). So viewed, sociobiology then, is "that component of behavioral ecology that explores the effects of the *social* environment on behavioral evolution" (Alcock 2001: 9). Consequently, sociobiology can be understood as the branch of behavioral biology that studies patterns of social behavior as possible *adaptations* that evolved by natural selection (as well as sexual selection).[1]

It is extremely rare for most sociologists to try to determine if a pattern of social behavior constitutes an evolved adaptation. Among the last questions to come to the minds of most sociologists studying phenomena like competition and conflict over the control of the governing apparatus of a state-based society is whether the outcomes of the contest will affect the lifetime reproductive fates of the winners and losers. Accordingly, wondering whether such struggles are guided by evolved mental adaptations that are the product of evolution by natural selection is rarely a focus of inquiry among conventional sociologists.

Sociobiologists, however, have opened the door to a new kind of social analysis that may bear on the efforts of any social scientists to understand and explain human social behavior. This chapter reviews the ways in which sociobiology might be relevant and of possible value for sociological inquiry. It identifies and evaluates a number of common misconceptions about sociobiology and attempts to assuage fears concerning unsavory outcomes that could derive from a newly "Darwinized" sociology. It acknowledges and discusses key features of human nature and behavioral capabilities that require special consideration in pursuing sociobiological analyses of human social behavior. And it provides brief summaries of the work of a number of sociologists who have conducted analyses of human social behaviors in a sociobiological key.

The possibility that genes could somehow be relevant to understanding human social behavior does not come easy to many sociologists. In part, this is because the persistence of a number of common misconceptions about genes and behavior that still prevail not only in popular culture, but even in the scholarly and scientific literature of disciplines such as sociology. In order to alleviate this problem, we identify a number of such misconceptions, correct them, and explain how, in principle, sociobiological thinking might be fruitfully applied to the study of human social behavior. We also identify the limits of sociobiological analysis in explaining emergent features of human groups and societies, and we explain how conventional sociological analysis picks up where sociobiology, of necessity, leaves off.

Getting From Genes to Social Behavior

Despite the looming presence of evolutionary thinking in early sociology (e.g., Spencer, Durkheim, Sumner), biological explanations failed to meet with a warm reception in sociology for most of its 20th Century history. Sullied by the early and unfortunate rise of Social Darwinism, sociologists have long been understandably suspicious of and uncomfortable with efforts to bring biology to bear on explanations of human social behavior. In part, the resistance is rooted in the fear of ideological agendas masquerading as scientific explanations and thereby lending legitimation to unsavory political agendas (Segerstråle 2000). Despite alarms to this effect sounded by early critics of sociobiology, this threat has not materialized. A second, and potentially more defensible criticism of sociobiology, addresses perceived deficiencies in the logic of sociobiological explanation and its putative failure to accurately characterize human nature itself.

Three serious analytical charges have been leveled at sociobiology: (1) It falls prey to the fallacy of *genetic determinism* and fails to consider the myriad influences, most of which are environmental, that contribute to the development of human behavior, influences that extend far beyond whatever minimal contributions might be attributed to the human genome. (2) It promotes naïve *reductionism* and fails to acknowledge, much less grapple with, the *emergent* features of human social life. (3) It fails to represent accurately human nature itself and misattributes to "nature" behaviors that are said to be indisputably the product of "nurture." These, and other closely related concerns, have inhibited many sociologists from understanding sociobiology, the ways in which it is relevant to sociology, and its strengths and limitations for explaining human social behavior.

The discussion that follows represents an attempt to provide a more accurate and complete understanding of sociobiological explanations of how genes influence social behavior, an understanding which, in turn, can empower sociologists to assess, *for themselves*,[2] from a more fully informed point-of-view, the explanatory virtues and vices of sociobiology and its possible value for social scientific inquiry and explanation.

What Genes Do, and Do Not Do

Most academics are cautious, often to a fault, when addressing professional peers. When, however, their audience consists of undergraduate college students, caution is sometimes thrown to the wind, and the same speakers can become much bolder and more declarative. This propensity is sometimes evident in the textbooks that academics write for undergraduate readers, and thus, the narratives found in those textbooks often reveal a degree of candor that is absent in discourse conducted among professional peers. A study in which best-selling introductory sociology textbooks were inspected for their treatment of the topic of sociobiology illustrates these very sorts of patterns (Machalek and Martin 2004, 2010).

In order to get a sense of the sorts of misconceptions that some sociologists commonly attribute to sociobiology, consider the following claims extracted from best-selling introductory sociology textbooks: Humans are said to be "prisoners of their genes" and fated to enact "biologically fixed" and "inalterable" patterns of action and behavioral complexes; sociobiologists are said to have failed to conduct research that has identified even one "gene responsible for any particular aspect of social behavior"; sociobiologists are said to pit "social learning" against "instinct" in trying to explain social behavior; and, furthermore, that sociobiologists fail even to consider the role of "the uniquely human mind" in producing social behavior (in Machalek and Martin 2004). Additional claims erroneously attributed to sociobiology by the textbook authors include statements that sociobiologists assert that "biological principles can be used to explain *all human behavior* [emphasis ours]"; that sociobiology is but the "most recent version of biological reductionism"; that "in its extreme form, sociobiology suggests that *all* behavior is the result of genetic or biological factors and that social interactions play no role in shaping people's conduct"; that sociobiology "bypasses the essence of what sociologists focus on: humans developing their own cultures, their own unique ways of life"; and that "sociobiologists and sociologists stand on opposite sides, the one looking at human behavior *as determined by genetics* [emphasis ours], the other looking at human behavior as determined by social learning, by experiences in that social group" (in Machalek and Martin 2004: 458).

As will become clear, none of these claims accurately represent sociobiology. Unfortunately, students who read such passages are not only being misinformed about sociobiology, they are, on occasion, misinformed about basic facts of biology itself. Consider, for example, Henslin's assertion that "pigs act like pigs because they don't have a cerebral cortex, and instincts control their behavior. So it is for spiders, elephants, and so on" (2009: 60). Though the author is correct about spiders' cortical deficits, he is completely wrong about elephants because "reptiles and mammals are the two groups of vertebrates with well-developed cortices" (Ulinski 1990: 139). The learning capabilities and intelligence of pigs and elephants are well known to anyone even vaguely familiar with their biology.

However unfortunate the circumstances of students who fall victim to such uninformed and irresponsible claims about a branch of science, as well as misstatements about fundamental empirical facts of biology, these statements are very useful in shedding light on widespread misconceptions about sociobiology and its relevance to human social behavior. By identifying *four major misconceptions* about sociobiology, we are presented with an opportunity to identify and discuss *four key concepts* on which sociobiological reasoning is based and thereby help explain why this branch of evolutionary biology has developed rapidly over the past four decades. These four key concepts comprise the following: epigenesis, the interaction principle, the norm of reaction, and prepared learning. Each will be introduced in relation to the misconception(s) they help correct.

Misconception 1: Sociobiology Advocates Genetic Determinism and Ignores the Effect of Environments on Social Behavior

One of the earliest and most strident critics of sociobiology was the paleontologist and evolutionary biologist Stephen Jay Gould. In criticizing sociobiology for "genetic determinism," he stated: "If we are programmed to be what we are, then these traits are ineluctable. We may, at best, channel them, but we cannot change them either by will, education, or culture," to which the philosopher Daniel Dennett replied, "If this is genetic determinism, then we can all breathe a sigh of relief: There are no genetic determinists" (Dennett 2003: 156).

The misplaced charge that sociobiology advocates genetic determinism in explaining social behavior in *any* species, much less humans, can be made only in ignorance or willful neglect of two important concepts in evolutionary biology, *epigenesis* and the *interaction principle*. Genes encode information for the expression of phenotypic traits, including behavior. Epigenesis is the developmental process during which genetic information is expressed *under the influence of the environments in which the genes reside*. Phenotypes, then, are not strictly "genetically determined" absent environmental influences, but rather, they are the product of gene-environment interaction which is characterized in sociobiology as the "interaction principle" (Lopreato 2001: 412). The interaction principle applies to the development of all phenotypic traits, morphological, physiological, and behavioral.

Contrary to belief that the influence of genes on behavior is impervious to the environmental context, including social context, within which genes express themselves, the "gene by environment (G × E)" model of behavior draws upon epigenetics to explain genetic influences on behavior, including social behavior (Simons et al. 2012). Thus, if a particular allele can be shown to influence behavior, the G × E model enables researchers to assess how the expression of that allele is influenced by the environmental forces to which it is subjected.

An early example of how this kind of thinking has led to more sophisticated research on possible genetic influences on social behavior is provided by studies of the effects of the maltreatment of male children on the likelihood that they will grow into adults who themselves abuse children, thereby manifesting a "cycle of violence" (Caspi et al. 2002). This research showed that individuals who possess a low activity allele of the MAOA (monoamine oxidase A) gene are more susceptible to maltreatment than are individuals who possess a high-activity variant of this gene. Consequently, individuals with low-activity MAOA alleles are more likely to develop abusive behaviors themselves than are individuals with high-activity MAOA genes. This suggests that high-activity MAOA alleles act as a buffer that inhibits the development of abusive behavior among victims of abuse. Accordingly, this research found support for the "cycle of violence" thesis, but it qualified the thesis with a "differential susceptibility" component. In short, being subjected to an abusive social environment is more likely to contribute to the development of abusive behavior among individuals with low-activity variants of the MAOA gene. This is an empirically documented example of the "interaction principle" in action among humans.

More recent research on humans documents the existence of "risk alleles," later called "plasticity" or "sensitivity" alleles, in accounting for individual variation in how social influences shape the development of heritable social behavior (Simons et al. 2012). Plasticity alleles have been found among 40–50% of individuals in the populations studied, and these individuals are more sensitive to social environmental influences in direct proportion to the number of these alleles they possess. And while plasticity alleles predispose those who possess them to be more sensitive to social influences than are those lacking these alleles, the alleles themselves do not make those individuals more susceptible to adverse environmental forces than they do to favorable environments. Simply put, individuals with plasticity alleles, especially those with multiple copies, are more likely both to suffer from exposure to negative social environments (e.g., exposure to delinquent gangs) as well as to derive benefits from exposure to positive social environments (e.g., exposure to "positive role models"). Plasticity alleles are indifferent to the normative valence of the behaviors they predispose; rather, they simply increase the probability that individuals bearing those alleles will be more strongly influenced by the social forces to which they are subjected than are individuals who lack those alleles.

Similar examples of the interaction principle are available in research conducted on the possible effects of androgens such as testosterone on social behavior. Even in popular media, high levels of testosterone among humans have been portrayed as contributors to aggression (Machalek and Martin 2015: 18–19). However, research has shown that elevated testosterone levels can be both the cause and consequence of rank attainment in status hierarchies, but not a contributor to elevated levels of aggression *per se* (Mazur 2005; Booth et al. 2006). Furthermore, the influence of testosterone on behavior is mediated by various factors within social environments. For example, the effect of testosterone on one's position in a dominance order has been found to be related to factors such as anticipating a dominance contest, parent-child relations, relations among other family members, relations among peers, marital relations, and the presence of honor cultures (Booth et al. 2006; Mazur 2006). Sons who have elevated testosterone levels and poor relations with their parents are more likely to engage in antisocial behaviors, but they are more likely to experience depression if they have low levels of testosterone. Daughters experience similar effects though the influence of testosterone levels varies by the mother-daughter versus the father-daughter relationship. Boys with elevated testosterone levels who have good relations with their peers are more likely to exhibit assertive and dominance behaviors that are associated with effective leadership, but if they have poor relations with their peers, they are more likely to express non-aggressive character disorders (Booth et al. 2006: 179).

The interaction principle and empirical findings such as those discussed above make it clear that the influence of genes on behavior, including social behavior, is always mediated by the environments in which genes reside, ranging from their cellular environments to the societal-level, institutional social structures in which they are embedded. Accordingly, sociobiology does not advocate any variant of "genetic determinism" or the neglect of environmental forces in shaping and directing patterns of social behavior. Sociobiologists view environments as equal to genes in explaining social behavior and its evolution.

Misconception 2: Because Humans Share a Common Genome, Sociobiology Cannot Explain Cultural Variation Which Far Exceeds the Genetic Variation Expressed by Humans

Begun in 1990, the Human Genome Project has led to the discovery that humans share a common genome consisting of approximately 25,000 genes that code for the 100,000+ proteins that constitute the fabric of the human body (Simons et al. 2012: 145–46). Prior to the findings yielded by the Human Genome Project, it was often assumed that each protein must be coded by one gene, a view sometimes called the "one-gene, one protein assumption" (Simons et al. 2012: 146), an assumption that proved incorrect. Instead, the study of epigenetics and the development of the "gene by environment model" led to the understanding that the range of phenotypic variation made possible by any given genotype often far exceeds the number of genes responsible for generating that phenotype.

What is true of proteins is also true of behavior. Sharing a common genome of 25,000 genes does *not* impose narrow limits on the numbers of social behaviors that humans can exhibit, nor does it mean that sharing a common, species-typical genome limits humans to producing a single culture, or a narrow range of cultures. Rather, though humans the world-over share a common genome that makes them all members of the same species, that common genome is expressed in *variable environmental contexts*, and the result of gene-environment interaction is the production of a range of cultural forms that far exceeds what one might expect from a suite of 25,000 genes alone, a number that exceeds only slightly the total number of genes possessed by a barely visible roundworm, an acultural organism with 20,000 genes (Simons et al. 2012: 146). Were there a close correspondence between the number of genes in a species and the number of products generated by those genes, the world of roundworms would be appreciably more complex than it is. Or, the range of cultural variation exhibited by humans would be exceedingly narrow.

The *norm of reaction* is an important concept derived from evolutionary biology that refers to the "total variation in the trait in all survivable environments" in which an organism exists (Wilson 1998: 137). For some genotypes, such as the genes that prescribe the number of chambers in the human heart (four), the norm of reaction is very *narrow*. Selection would not tolerate a genotype that produces three chambers in some environmental settings, but five in others. However, the norm of reaction that specifies the amount of fat deposited on a human body is much broader, permitting the human body to vary significantly in terms of how much fat it can acquire and store in response to variable environmental circumstances such as diet, activity levels, and the thermal conditions to which the organism is exposed.

Some organisms exhibit heritable traits that manifest an astonishingly broad norm of reaction. Consider, for example, the common arrowleaf plant. The arrowleaf is an amphibious plant, and it can grow on dry land, in shallow water, or totally submerged. The shape of its leaf varies with each of these three environments. On dry land, the leaf resembles an arrowhead. When it takes root in shallow water, the leaf resembles that of a lily pad that floats on the surface. When totally submerged, the leaves resemble ribbons that sway underwater in response to currents and other types of water movement. According to Wilson, "No known genetic differences among the plants underlie this extraordinary variation. The three basic types are variations in the expression of the same group of genes caused by different environments," and each phenotypic leaf form represents an evolved adaptation to variation in the environments in which the plant grows (1998: 137).

Another example of a phenotype that can vary widely in response to environmental variation is the size of leafcutter ants, *Atta sexdens*. In this species of ant, the head-width among castes can vary "8-fold and the dry weight 200-fold from the smallest minor workers to the huge major workers" (Hölldobler and Wilson 2009: 426). According to Hölldobler and Wilson,

> all colony members have the same genotype for caste formation, from which differences in the environment launch a newborn individual on a developmental pathway that leads to its final destination as either a queen or a worker. The genes, in other words, determine not castes but caste plasticity: In response to environmental conditions, they either turn on or turn off growth along the development of immature individuals, and by this commitment or default they guide progress, step by step, toward one caste or another.
>
> (2009:136–37)

Six classes of environmental factors regulate gene expression to produce one or another caste: larval nutrition, temperature of the nest chambers, winter chilling of eggs, caste self-inhibition (the presence of members of a caste inhibit the development of particular caste members), egg size, and the age of the queen (Hölldobler and Wilson 2009: 136–37).

The dramatic differences in phenotype and the wide range of the norm of reaction that will enable the same ant egg to develop either into a minor worker or a soldier can be dramatized by considering this phenotypic variation in *Atta* at the human scale. If a minor worker is represented in comparison to a 200 pound human factory worker, that same factory worker, were a developmental biology similar to that of ants at play, could have developed into a soldier who would weigh 40,000 pounds. In such a case, the same human genotype would have been modified by some sort of environmental factors to produce a soldier whose enormously magnified phenotype would appear possible only as the stuff of science fiction.

The concept of the norm of reaction, along with epigenesis and the interaction principle, liberates critics from the unjustifiable concern that there is insufficient variation in the human genome to account for the full range of cultural variation that has been expressed in the human experience. Instead, behavior can feature a heritable component that, simultaneously, permits environmental forces to determine the particular form which that behavior will take. Thus, genes specify the general trajectory of the behavior's development, but environmental factors contribute to the realization of its final, completed form. Nor does entertaining the possibility that a behavior may be under the influence of a genotype mean that one must subscribe to the "one gene, one behavior" argument that Wilson compares to the "one gene, one disease" (OGOD) model of heritable pathologies sometimes found in medical science literature (1998: 146). Rather, Wilson contends that any heritable pattern of behavior is likely to be subject to the influences of entire "ensembles of genes" called "polygenes," and that, for example,

> there is no gene for playing the piano well, or even a "Rubenstein gene" for playing it extremely well. There is instead a large ensemble of genes whose effects enhance manual dexterity, creativity, emotive expression, focus, attention span, and control of pitch, rhythm, and timbre.
>
> (Wilson 1998: 137)

And when biologists talk about a "gene 'causing' a particular behavior ... they never mean it literally" (Wilson 1998: 137).

Misconception 3: Sociobiology Ignores Learning and Misattributes Complex Social Behavior to Instinct

This is one of the most egregious misconceptions on the basis of which ill-informed critics have rejected sociobiology and, of greater concern, often misrepresented it to their students. Highly successful textbook authors have all-too-often misled students with statements such as the claim that sociology and sociobiology are diametrically opposed ways of knowing in which "social learning" and "instinct" are incommensurable and that sociobiology not only fails to consider the relevance of culture in explaining human social behavior but ignores altogether the important role of "the uniquely human mind" in shaping human social behavior (Giddens 1996; Henslin 1997; Hess et al. 1996). Only 6 years after the publication of *Sociobiology: The New Synthesis* (Wilson 1975), Charles Lumsden and E. O. Wilson gave center-stage attention to the phenomenon of *prepared learning* (also called *biased learning* and *directed learning*) in their analysis of the co-evolution of genes, mind, and culture (1981: 35–98). Far from ignoring learning and human culture, Lumsden and Wilson helped establish a program of theoretical thought and empirical research that gave rise to a cascade of subsequent studies designed to discover how learning itself and the development of culture have evolved by natural selection.

The idea of prepared learning means that natural selection installs learning mechanisms in the brain/mind that increase the propensity to develop and retain patterns of behavior that were adaptive in the environments in which the mind evolved. For example, if an animal were to eat something toxic with a distinctive smell or taste and later experienced nausea, that animal would easily learn and retain an aversion to such a substance and avoid ingesting it in the future. During the 1960s, ethologists documented a number of "mammalian learning biases" of this sort (Shaw and Wong 1989: 63). Even humans display such patterns of prepared learning, one of which is famously known as the "*sauce béarnaise* effect," a food aversion developed by an experience of eating something that later induces nausea and violent illness (Seligman 1971). In a series of experiments, it was discovered that such food aversions would develop only if paired with stimuli in nature that could induce nausea and illness. For example, laboratory rats would develop the food aversion after having consumed saccharin-flavored water which was followed by a dose of nausea-inducing radiation (which they could not detect). However, when they were subjected to a bright light and a loud nose, followed by exposure to radiation, the rats did not develop an aversion to the light or noise. A moment's reflection makes clear that it is highly unlikely that loud noises or bright lights in a natural environment will induce nausea, so no selection forces would operate to make an animal associate such stimuli with the subsequent experience of nausea. However, if eating a contaminated food source would induce illness, then one or a very few such experiences could cause the development of an aversion to such food by means of mechanisms of prepared learning (Seligman 1971, 1993; Rachman and Seligman 1976).

The concept of prepared learning leads to a view of the human mind not as a "blank sheet for individual mental and cultural development, but [as] a sheet at least lightly scrawled with tentative outlines that assist survival and reproduction" (Shaw and Wong 1989: 66). Shaw and Wong's metaphor of a sheet that is "lightly scrawled" with "tentative outlines" for survival and reproduction is a far cry from the misrepresentations of genes as determinants of rigid, inalterable patterns of behavior that have been provided by ill-informed critics of sociobiology.

Prepared learning replaces classical and operant conditioning models with more sophisticated ways of analyzing how learning occurs among a wide range of animals, including humans. Instead of expecting that all animals learn by means of a few simple mechanisms that operate identically across species lines, the notion of prepared learning means that the ways in which animals learn varies among species, and that "learning is *tailored to the animal's needs*" (Shaw and Wong 1989: 69, emphasis ours). By this logic, we should expect natural selection to have installed in a species learning biases that are directed toward stimuli that were highly *adaptively relevant* within the environments in which members of the species evolved. Such learning biases are vividly evident in the phobias that develop among some humans. Human phobias develop in response to threats such as spiders, snakes, height, running water, and enclosed spaces. And though automobiles, firearms, and electricity pose greater threats to humans in contemporary society than do most of the phenomena previously mentioned, humans do not typically develop phobic reactions to cars, electricity, and guns.

The notion of prepared learning represents a process that entails the integration of instinct and learning. It means that experience is required to develop a pattern of behavior, but that some experiences are more highly conducive to creating particular patterns of behavior than are others, which reflects the instinctive component of this process. Alternatively, one might think of prepared learning as a suite of "aptitudes" with which humans are equipped at birth. An aptitude may *predispose* an individual to learn certain information and develop an overt behavioral pattern based on that information, but experience is required for that aptitude to become activated and guide the development of an overt behavior. And sociobiology suggests that the existence of such learning biases is likely the product of evolution by natural selection.

Prepared (biased, directed) learning is a phenomenon that has had a great influence on the development of the neo-Darwinian discipline of evolutionary psychology. It is important to realize that both learning (including symbolic learning) and culture are seen by sociobiologists as species-typical traits of humans, traits which, if ignored, would lead to the inevitable failure of any attempt by sociobiologists to explain *any* human behavior. Learning, symbolic language, and the capacity to produce and use culture are as *innate* to humans as is echolocation to bats. In the words of E. O. Wilson,

> We know that virtually all human behavior is transmitted by culture. We also know that biology has an important effect on the origin of culture and its transmission. The question remaining is how biology and culture *interact*, and in particular, how they interact across all societies *to create the commonalities of human nature*.
> (1998: 126, emphases ours)

Misconception 4: Sociobiological Explanations Entail Biological Reductionism and Fail to Acknowledge Emergent Properties of Human Social Systems

Ever since Durkheim, sociologists have waged a hard-fought battle, which they have won, against crude reductionist explanations of human social behavior. Durkheim and his successors argued persuasively that human society is not simply an additive phenomenon, the mere sum of all the individuals (and their behaviors) that comprise the population of a society. Rather, human society is a complex of *social facts*, and social facts are an *emergent* reality, a reality constituted of the *relationships* among the components that make up groups and societies. The sociological properties of groups derive from, but *cannot be reduced to, the individual properties, biological or psychological*, of the members of those groups.

A common, but entirely misplaced, criticism of sociobiology is that it advocates a crude form of reductionism of the sort to which Durkheim objected strenuously. This criticism commonly takes the form of statements of the following sort:

> Sociobiology tries to explain away complex, emergent social realities by reducing them to genes. Sociobiology ignores the definitive feature of society, which is that it is an emergent reality, and sociobiology tries to reduce social behavior and society to nothing more than genes and their effects.

Implicit in such a mischaracterization is an erroneous assumption that sociobiology's reductionism may work in explaining the social behavior of other (non-human) species, but it fails miserably when applied to the study of human social behavior and society.

Ironically, crude reductionism, typically in the form of genetic determinism, is as flawed an approach to the study of non-human societies as it is for studying human societies (Machalek 1999). In fact, among large organisms (those that can be seen by unaided human vision) such as ants, bees, wasps, and termites, social behavior and societal-level organization would remain *utterly unintelligible absent careful attention to emergent properties of social behavior in those societies*. Emergent properties of animal societies are discussed in detail in Chapter 15 ("Cross-Species Comparative Sociology") and Chapter 16 ("Cross-Species Analysis of Megasocieties").

Acknowledging and studying the importance of emergent properties of social systems does not, however, require the total abandonment of reductionism in scientific analysis and explanation. Rather, Wilson attributes to Newton's Cartesian reductionism an "unbroken string of successes" during the three centuries after which Newton lived (1998: 30–32). However, Wilson also cautions that reductionism, in the absence of holism, is destined to fail as a method of scientific inquiry:

> I have already described how an entire cell cannot be predicted from a knowledge of its scrambled molecules and organelles alone. Let me now indicate how bad the problem really is. It is not even possible to predict the three-dimensional structure of a protein from a complete knowledge of its constituent atoms.
>
> (1998: 83)

What is true for proteins is true of whole organisms and societies as well, including even societies of organisms as simple as ants. Ant behavior at the colony level cannot be explained by the genes alone that are possessed by individual members of the population. Instead, Wilson and Hölldobler explain that

> there can be little doubt that the target of selection molding caste systems are the *emergent properties of the colony* [emphasis ours]. The colony as a whole—superorganism—contains feedback loops of communication among nestmates that regulate both the proportions of castes and the tasks they undertake.
>
> (Hölldobler and Wilson 2009: 155)

Hölldobler and Wilson elaborate further to make clear that complex, dynamic, and emergent features of ant colonies are key determinants of the conduct of any individual ant, or subpopulation (caste) of ants, and furthermore, they insist that understanding how ants actually behave in their natural environments requires an explanatory *integration of reductionistic and holistic thinking*. Absent either perspective, all explanatory efforts are doomed to failure (2009: 156–59).

Finally, it should be emphasized that emergent properties of neither human societies nor those of social insect societies can be attributed to individual traits shared in common by members of both taxa. Ants and humans do not share common alleles that produce behaviors which give rise to the emergent features of the societies in which each live. The total repertoire of individual acts of which an ant is capable of executing is dwarfed by the range of distinct behaviors which any human is capable of manifesting. Human consciousness, powers of symbolization, language, and culture increase by orders of magnitude the full range of behavioral variation producible by humans when compared to any other social species, and accordingly, the range and variety of emergent features of human social organization are also comparably magnified. However, all such behavioral complexity derives ultimately from evolved features of the human brain and mind, and both reductionist analysis and holistic integrative efforts are required to yield a comprehensive, evolutionary account of the evolution of social behavior among humans.

The Evolved Actor

The notion that the human brain/mind is "lightly scrawled" with innate information that assists humans in surviving and reproducing constitutes, perhaps, the fundamental difference between traditional sociology and sociobiology. The tabula rasa view of human nature, long-favored by sociologists as foundational to their discipline, was directly challenged by the rise of sociobiology and later, evolutionary psychology. Instead of viewing the human brain/mind at birth as virtually "empty" of informational content that could contribute to the development of specific forms of social behavior, sociobiology proposes a view of human nature as richly supplied with evolved mental processes for developing and engaging in social interaction. Early in sociobiology's history, these mental processes were conceptualized by Charles Lumsden and E. O. Wilson as "epigenetic rules" (Lumsden and Wilson 1981: 11–25), which can be described casually as "rules of thumb" for behavior and more formally as the "genetic biases in the way our senses perceive the world, the symbolic coding by which we represent the world, and the responses we find easiest and most rewarding to make" (Wilson 2012: 193). In contrast to traditional sociologists, sociobiologists pursue their inquiries on the basis of the default assumption that the human mind is equipped with numerous evolved mental processes which are the product of natural (and sometimes sexual) selection and the generators of adaptive behaviors, including some social behaviors.

For example, numerous sociobiologists, evolutionary psychologists, and other evolutionary social and behavioral scientists claim to have identified species-typical trait preferences that humans have for prospective mates, including but not limited to phenotypic symmetry (Sugiyama 2016). Developmental, bilateral symmetry is said to be a cue signaling health and favorable reproductive prospects in a potential mate (Gangestad and Thornhill 1997). Upon initial encounter with such thinking, an understandable response to this way of thinking about human nature and behavior is likely to be expressed as follows:

> This kind of thinking is fraught with the peril in that analysts of human social behavior will isolate a particular pattern of social behavior found commonly in societies, assume that it is the product of natural selection, and then merely posit the existence of mental adaptations that have evolved for producing this behavior. Thus, this is but another instance of fallacious, teleological reasoning.

Caution about engaging in such fallacious reasoning is prudent counsel, but such thinking simply does not characterize the theoretical and empirical work currently undertaken by the vast majority of social scientists who are working in a sociobiological key. The image of the human brain/mind that has been adopted by sociobiologists is neither the tabula rasa model of long-standing in traditional sociology, nor its putative sole alternative, that of an instinct-driven, robotic being under the inalterable and deterministic influence of tyrannical genes. Instead, sociobiological thinkers have replaced both of these images of the human brain/mind with another image, one that is grounded in current evolutionary biology, especially sociobiology and behavioral ecology. Rosemary Hopcroft has provided a felicitous expression for this image, the "evolved actor," and this concept is a good candidate for characterizing the way that many practitioners of the new evolutionary sociology think about human nature and social behavior (2009b).

The very expression "evolved actor" connotes the integration of evolutionary biology and mainstream sociology in characterizing human nature. "Evolved" represents the position that the human brain/mind is not a tabula rasa information processor empty, at birth, of informational content that can be provided only by individual experience but rather, a complex, "adapted mind" that is rich supplied with "behavioral algorithms" that can go by various names, including neural subassemblies (Turner

2015); behavioral predispositions (Lopreato 1984; Lopreato and Crippen 1999); evolved predispositions (Hopcroft 2016); and evolved psychological programs/neurocomputational programs/behavior-regulatory programs/ adaptive specializations/"modules"/information processing mechanisms (Tooby and Cosmides 2016), as well as others. The second term, "actor," captures a critical trait commonly attributed to human beings by sociologists, that of "agency," the capacity of being able to act on the world and not be moved passively only by forces that are "external" (environmental) or "internal" (genetic). Using a literary metaphor, the image of agency exercised by actors is sometimes described as the ability to be the "author" of one's own conduct and biography. The notion of humans as "actors" also expresses another assumption that is fundamental to sociology itself, the idea that human behavior commonly takes the nature of a "performance" that is directed to the existence and conduct of "others," including "consociates" (those with whom one shares time and space); "mere contemporaries" (those with whom one shares time, as in historical period, but not space, as in geography proximity); and "predecessors" (those who lived before and, though now dead, lived lives that deposited a "residue" of culture, social structure, and institutional forms that both constrain and potentiate the behavioral possibilities of the living actor).

Thus, sociologists like Hopcroft who are receptive to sociobiology as a new, but by no means exclusive, way of studying human social behavior have embraced a view of human nature and social behavior that represents an attempt to integrate the best insights available in both evolutionary biology and the conventional social sciences, including sociology. Accordingly, social thinkers whose work is informed by the notion of the "evolved actor" do not find themselves having to choose between the Scylla of a "disembodied, asomatic" entity whose conduct is propelled only by extrinsic cultural information versus the Charybdis of a "genetically determined automaton" whose conduct is reducible entirely to the double helix instantiated in its cells. Instead, they can base both their theoretical thinking and empirical research on the best thinking and research available in the life sciences (including sociobiology) and the social and behavioral sciences (including sociology). A summary of three, basic principles to which *all practicing sociobiologists subscribe* makes clear that many of the concerns about sociobiology that still appear to trouble many social and behavioral scientists simply do not characterize today's sociobiological project and its application to the study of social behavior among both humans and other animals:

1. Any evolved features of the human brain/mind that contribute to the production of behavior, including social behavior, are the product

of previous, archaic environments in which hominin ancestors lived. Accordingly, all such evolved adaptations represent solutions to "yesterday's adaptive challenges," and they *may or may not* remain adaptive in contemporary environments. Consider, for example, a behavioral propensity toward aggression and physical violence often attributed disproportionately to human males by both evolutionary thinkers (e.g., Chagnon 1988) and sociologists (e.g., Collins 2008). Absent a third-party mediator, such as a body of tribal elders or a legal representative of a state apparatus such as a police officer, in the context of intense conflicts of interests between young males, a willingness and ability to pose a credible threat of physical force has often been a common means of conflict resolution in the human experience. Accordingly, some evolutionary-minded thinkers have explored the possibility that human males, even more than females, possess a strong propensity to behave aggressively toward threats posed by other males and that such threats often inhibited escalation, thereby resulting in resolutions without lethal consequences. Or, if physical conflict ensued, it rarely was executed with sufficient competence to inflict serious physical harm on the contestants (Collins 2008).

As a result, some evolutionary scientists have suggested that a male propensity to display a "credible threat of violence" could have been adaptive as a form of defense during much of human evolutionary history (Daly and Wilson 1988: 128). However, fast-forward to the contemporary era in which young men often have ready access to lethal technologies such as auto-loading firearms, and it is easy to conclude that expressions of even moderate aggression and threat that may have been adaptive in deterring violence 10,000–100,000 years ago are now much more lethal when enacted by individuals armed with weaponry of unprecedented destructive capability.

2. Any evolved features of the human brain/mind are the products of selection forces that were present in the ancestral social worlds in which the human brain and mind evolved; thus, it cannot be assumed that they remain adaptive in contemporary societies. Organic evolution by natural selection is devoid of foresight. Natural selection cannot anticipate the properties of future environments, so consequently, evolved actors cannot be equipped with specialized mental adaptations to cope with novel social environments produced by major transitions such as those from the hunting-gathering era to the horticultural era, or from the agrarian era to the industrial era, before those transitions occur. In sociobiology, this is often called the "novel environments" problem. If, in fact, it can be established that the machinery of the human brain/mind is equipped

with innate psychological capabilities for coping successfully with social life at the small, band-level scale of societal organization, there is no reason to expect that natural selection has installed innate capabilities enabling humans to cope with human social organization at the mega-scale that emerged even as early as the advanced horticultural era, much less during the agrarian, industrial, and post-industrial periods of societal evolution. In short, only the psychological resources comprising language, human learning, and the collective resource of culture have enabled humans to adjust to the novel environments that have arisen in the post-foraging era (10,000 years ago to present). Both sociobiologists (e.g., Wilson 1998, 2012) and traditional social scientists concur that symbolic learning, communication, and culture are *the* resources that enable humans to cope more or less successfully with rapid, large-scale changes in their physical, technological, and sociocultural environments.

3. Any evolved features of the human brain/mind do not prescribe *specific attributes of contemporary human societies and the range and complexity of their social structures and social institutions*. The "adapted mind" of the "evolved actor" is not equipped with specialized algorithms for constructing the specific, unique, and emergent features of contemporary societies and their institutions. The defining features of modern (and, of course, "post-modern") societies are novel, emergent structures and processes that were absent in the archaic environments in which the human brain/mind evolved its species-typical qualities. Thus, there are no genotypes that specify the properties of a state-based polity, a societal-scale system of class relations in an industrial society; a market (or, for that matter, industrial socialist) economy; or even a world religion. Rather, the unique cultural and structural features of contemporary societies and their institutions are the products of complex suites of evolved mental adaptations operating in unique historical eras and situated in unique environments.

However, the unique features of these contemporary societies, despite their being the product of evolved mental adaptations, were not *specified* by these adaptations. Rather, they represent forms, the exact features of which were "permissible," and sometimes even "predisposed" (but not specified) by the norms of reaction underpinning the evolved mental adaptations that produced them. In a manner of thinking that is entirely consistent with Emile Durkheim's sociological explanation of the origins and nature of religion, a sociobiologist might say that an evolved psychological propensity or predisposition to attribute agency to anything that moves might constitute the foundation of an entire sociocultural system comprising animism, but the *specific features* of any existing form of animistic belief and practice are unspecified by the mental adaptations from which it derives. One of the most challenging, and interesting, kinds of research projects that could develop from this view of human nature and society would be any attempt to identify specific evolved mental adaptations that are implicated in the production of emergent features of group life and then try to delineate the epigenetic processes by means of which such social structures emerge, and how such emergent processes are conditioned by the environmental contexts in which these dynamics unfold.

Relatedly, sociobiological reasoning invites the development and pursuit of inquiries into how humans' evolved mental adaptations for social living might operate in contemporary societal contexts. For example, within sociobiological thinking, it is reasonable to hypothesize, as does Trivers (1971, 2005), that the human mind may be equipped with evolved emotional resources that produce behaviors (like "moralistic aggression") which enable humans to cope with the challenges associated with participating in systems of simple reciprocity and exchange at the band level of social organization. Correlatively, however, there is no reason to speculate that the human brain and mind is instantiated with evolved mental adaptations *that specify and regulate the properties of complex societal institutions of production and exchange*, such as modern business organizations and market economies. Stated differently, complex institutional configurations such as market economies exhibit features *which themselves are not evolved adaptations or phenotypic expressions of specific genotypes "for" market-based economic structures and transactions.*

However, evolved mental adaptations for capabilities such as (1) monitoring and remembering specific episodes of reciprocity and exchange, (2) recognizing and remembering the participants in those episodes, (3) making rough estimates of the quantity of resources exchanged among the participants during such episodes, as well as basic assessments of the quality of resources provided and received, and (4) remembering the general number and frequency of such episodes experienced *are* among the categories of information that it is reasonable to expect natural selection to have installed specific evolved mental adaptations for recording and processing. In short, while it is reasonable for evolutionary-minded social and behavioral scientists to conduct inquiries in search of something like a "cheating-detection cognitive algorithm" (Cosmides and Tooby 1992), it is not tenable to search for evolved adaptations that prescribe the features of corporate business bureaucracies and the complex *sociological* process that generate and regulate such entities.

To paraphrase and qualify an expression favored by some contemporary evolutionary thinkers, humans may possess a "cave-man's mind" for engaging in face-to-face relations of reciprocity and exchange, but that cave-man's mind is not equipped with specific cognitive algorithms that are the product of evolution by natural selection and that have been designed specifically for producing and regulating even local, money-based economic institutions, much less global capitalism. Nevertheless, even in the context of global economies which may be prospering without precedent or teetering on the edge of catastrophic collapse, it should come as no surprise that an evolved actor will, on occasion, detect the pungent whiff of a cheater encountered in a micro-level, routine, day-to-day episode of social exchange and consequently react with an outburst of moralistic aggression, itself an evolved emotional reaction to being wronged. And though such an evolved psychological response may express itself in the context of a contemporary economic transaction, this response does not specify or explain the properties of a legal system that evolved as the product of *cultural processes* for addressing and resolving disputes in the context of a market-based economy with a unique history organized in the context of specific technological environments.

Sociobiological Analyses of Human Social Behavior

In the broad sense in which sociobiology is understood as the study of the biological basis of social behavior and how it evolves by natural selection, almost all practitioners of the new evolutionary sociology can be thought of as human sociobiologists. However, in the more restrictive sense of sociobiology as the science that analyzes certain human social behaviors as evolved adaptations that are fitness-enhancing and are products of processes such as kin selection and sexual selection, relatively few evolutionary sociologists can be said to be engaged in sociobiological research that is designed to identify specific evolved adaptations and actually determine if they produce adaptive behaviors in contemporary societal contexts. Simply put, while sociobiological thinking and explanatory principles are foundational to much of evolutionary sociology, most evolutionary sociologists are not engaged in sociobiological analysis in the same way as behavioral biologists who pursue sociobiological studies of non-human animals.

Even before Wilson published *Sociobiology: The New Synthesis* (1975), a few social scientists were developing biological approaches to the study of human social behavior. For example, the sociologist/anthropologist Lionel Tiger and the anthropologist Robin Fox advocated the adoption of a "zoological perspective" in social science research (Tiger and Fox 1966). Not long thereafter, the sociologist Pierre van den Berghe proposed the development of a "biosocial approach" for studying human social behavior (van den Berghe 1973, 1974). In 1984, the sociologist Joseph Lopreato published an entire volume on "human nature and biocultural evolution" in which he proposed reframing much of sociological theory and research in sociobiological terms (Lopreato 1984). In a manner not dissimilar to that of Marx when he wrote to Engels saying "Darwin's book is very important and serves me as a basis in natural science for the class struggle in history" (in Lopreato 1984:13), sociobiology has been viewed by some sociologists like van den Berghe and Lopreato as providing a basis in biology for explaining human sociality and society. Both van den Berghe and Lopreato were early pioneers of efforts to try to "reformulate the foundations of the social sciences," including sociology, so as to incorporate them into the Modern Synthesis (Wilson 1975: 4). The fundamental step in van den Berghe's and Lopreato's reformulation of sociology is to call for a fundamental reconsideration of the notion of human nature. Informed and guided by the logic of neo-Darwinian evolutionary theory in general and sociobiology in particular, van den Berghe and Lopreato vigorously criticized and rejected the tabula rasa view of human nature and insisted that it be replaced by a conception of the human mind as a complex of evolved, species-specific "behavioral predispositions" and that these behavioral predispositions constitute the raw material from which human social behavior and societies eventually arise (Lopreato 1984: 37–78).

More generally, both van den Berghe and Lopreato drew upon basic explanatory principles provided by sociobiology in order to reframe sociological theories and explanations of human behavior about fundamental patterns of social interaction found among humans the world over. For example, both sought to bring basic sociobiological concepts and explanatory principles like kin selection, inclusive fitness, epigenetic rules, altruism and reciprocal altruism, sexual selection, assortative mating, the maximization principle, anisogamy, and other basic sociobiological concepts to bear on the study of phenomena of routine interest to sociologists.

Highly critical of Wilson's sociobiology, a few biologists such as Stephen Jay Gould and Richard Lewontin have portrayed human sociobiologists as naïve reductionists and overzealous genetic determinists. In truth, sociologists like van den Berghe and Lopreato were much more cautious and restrained in their efforts than some of their more strident critics sometimes avowed. For example, Lopreato's self-declared interest in using sociobiology in an effort to identify possible evolved behavioral predispositions and how they might influence human social behavior is surprisingly understated:

> My aim is merely to buttress my inclination to accept as *heuristically useful* [emphasis ours] the *hypothesis* that to an unknown degree the circumstances of our phylogenetic history still have a causal bearing on our sociocultural behavior, just as the latter, in turn, influences our continually evolving genetic endowment.
>
> (1984: 37)

The very tone of Lopreato's statement illustrates two important elements of his sociobiological approach: (1) It is cautious and tentative. Lopreato does not treat the value of a sociobiological approach to the study of human social behavior as a foregone conclusion. Rather, his approach entails an exploration of the *possibility* that human phylogeny might be influential in understanding human sociality in contemporary contexts. (2) The arrow of causation in sociobiological explanation is two-directional. While genes may influence what Lopreato calls "sociocultural behavior," sociocultural behavior itself comprises a complex of selection forces that act on the human genome. In that regard, Lopreato's human sociobiology focuses consistently on the "*mutual influence* [emphasis ours] of culture and natural selection," a process that he describes as the "interplay of biology and culture" (1984: 80–103).

Accordingly, criticisms that charge human sociobiologists such as Lopreato with ignoring the dual influence of biology and culture on human behavior are simply ill-founded. In fact, Lopreato was careful to inform his readers that his approach to sociobiology was based on "hunch and curiosity" and did not, in any way, represent a conviction of "certainty" about sociobiology's relevance to human social behavior. Instead, Lopreato counsels the reader to understand that his adoption of a sociobiological perspective reflects only "an expression of enthusiasm for the hypothesis, and nothing more" (1984: 37). Thus, even in instances where the enthusiasm of early human sociobiologists like Lopreato seems to suggest an "extreme" overconfidence in their newly found, neo-Darwinian ruminations, it is clear that their adoption of a sociobiological perspective is more tentative and cautious than has often been acknowledged by their critics. More often than not, the alarm sounded by early critics of human sociobiology was directed toward what they feared human sociobiology *might be* or *might become*, rather than what it actually entailed. Still, the propensity of early critics to issue dire warnings has probably been very useful in the development of human sociobiology in that most sociologists who adopted a sociobiological approach to the study of human social behavior have heeded these critics and have avoided the sorts of explanatory pitfalls about which critics expressed concern, i.e., reductionism and genetic determinism.

Using Sociobiology to Identify the Basic Contours of Human Nature

Though Lopreato credits several classical social and behavioral scientists, including Veblen, Sumner, Mead, Malinowski, Durkheim, and of course, Freud, with having made "remarkable contributions to the emerging theory of human nature," he finds in the early 20th Century writings of economist-sociologist Vilfredo Pareto a theory of human nature that adumbrates most clearly the thinking of late-20th Century sociobiologists (Lopreato 1984: 35). Pareto characterized human nature as comprising three basic elements that he called "sentiments," "residues," and "derivations" (1935). *Sentiments* are the fundamental and universal subconscious psychological components of human nature. Sentiments give rise to a finite number of fundamental, overt behavioral tendencies that Pareto called residues. *Residues* are the product of sentiments, and they are evident in human social behavior in all human societies. Pareto's residues are the precursors of what Lopreato calls *behavioral predispositions*. And in a manner that is audacious by contemporary standards, Pareto proposed that human nature consists of six classes of residues comprising forty-four *specific* residues from which human behavior derives (1935: 516–19). Finally, what Pareto called *derivations* refer to properties of human consciousness, especially motivations, to which humans commonly attribute the causes of their own behaviors. Though his work was not framed explicitly in evolutionary terms, Pareto's theory of human nature and social behavior is remarkably consistent with contemporary evolutionary perspectives. A keen student of Pareto, it is hardly surprising that Lopreato was highly receptive to sociobiology and its possible applicability to human social behavior. In fact, it would not be inaccurate to observe that Lopreato's scholarly interest and receptivity to Pareto's theory of human nature may have "pre-adapted" him intellectually for in interest in sociobiological theory.

The most comprehensive statements in which Lopreato provides his sociobiologically based theory of human nature and social behavior are the monographs *Human Nature and Biocultural Evolution* (1984) and his more recent volume, co-authored with the sociologist Timothy Crippen, *Crisis in Sociology: The Need for Darwin* (1999). Both Lopreato and Crippen provide additional sociobiological analyses of human social behavior, but their basic approaches can discerned from these two volumes. Our following discussion of Lopreato's and Crippen's work is based largely on these two volumes. Like Pareto before him, Lopreato contended that underlying the kaleidoscopic, cross-cultural, and pan-historical variability of patterns of human social behavior is an array of species-typical behavioral "universals" (1984). Using inductive reasoning informed by a wide array of sources about human social behavior, Lopreato identifies twenty-three specific behavioral predispositions that he classifies into four major categories: predispositions of "self-enhancement," "sociality," "variation," and "selection" (1984: 105). Taken together, Lopreato regards these as the evolved components of a behavioral nature that is shared universally by humans. Lopreato divides the behavioral predispositions into two categories: (1) those produced by natural selection and shared by all members of a species and (2) those produced by sexual selection and sex-specific. Predispositions in the first category give rise to and support general behaviors like cooperation, exchange, competition, affiliation, conformity, and domination and deference, for example. Predispositions in the second category give rise to and support sex-specific behaviors like inter- and intrasexual competition, mate selection, and parenting strategies. Rooted in the biology of anisogamy and the biological division of labor in reproduction, different behavioral predispositions evolve among females and males as sex-specific adaptations.

The search for a species-typical human nature, inspired initially by sociobiology, has been taken up by social and behavioral scientists representing multiple disciplines. Among psychologists, the project has come to be known as "evolutionary psychology," but scholarship and research are by no means limited to psychologists alone. Instead, a number of evolutionary sociologists are also leading efforts to identify the suite of behavioral predispositions that comprise human nature. Included among this community of researchers are Jonathan H. Turner, Alexandra Maryanski, Rosemary Hopcroft, Satoshi Kanazawa, Stephen Sanderson, David Franks, and Michael Hammond, each of whom has, in his or her own way, pursued evolutionary thinking in order to advance our understanding of the evolved adaptations that can be said to comprise "human nature."

Evolutionary sociologists whose work is framed in sociobiological terms have pursued two lines of inquiry. The first is to select phenomena of long-standing interest to sociologists and then analyze and interpret them in sociobiological terms. The second entails the development and execution of empirical studies of select aspects of human social behavior and social organization. We will provide brief discussions that illustrate how a number of evolutionary sociologists have approached the study of various topics of long-standing interest to sociologists from a sociobiological point-of-view. Specifically, we will consider sociobiological analysis conducted by sociologists of ethnicity, mating, parenting, gender relations and demographic patterns, and change.

Ethnicity in Sociobiological Perspective

Ethnic groups and their identities and behaviors present interesting challenges for sociobiological research. In that sociologists typically conceptualize ethnicity as a cultural, not a biological attribute, ethnicity presents an opportunity for integrating biological and cultural perspectives in an effort to make intelligible an important and sociologically intriguing phenomenon that is, among all social species, almost certainly unique to humans. What can sociobiological thinking, when integrated with conventional sociological thought, offer efforts to explain this interesting and important dimension of human social behavior?

Sociologists routinely conceptualize "race" as a socially constructed category that is based on biological attributes such as skin color, hair color and texture, and facial features. They use the concept of "ethnicity" to denote groups sharing cultural attributes such as language, religion, styles of dress, a sense of place, customs, an awareness of common origins, dietary preferences, and sometimes physical features as well (Whitmeyer 1997: 163–64). Yet, a number of sociologists who approach the study of ethnicity in sociobiological key have explored the possibility that ethnicity develops on a platform of evolved, species-typical behavioral predispositions, and that ethnicity itself provides a good example of the "interplay," as Lopreato calls it (1984), between biology and culture. Pierre van den Berghe (1981), Joseph Lopreato (1984), Lopreato and Timothy Crippen (1999), and Joseph Whitmeyer (1997) are among those sociologists who have provided sociobiological analyses of ethnicity, ethnic groups, ethnic identity, and ethnic conflict.

One of the earliest, and well-developed, sociobiological analyses of ethnicity was provided by van den Berghe (1981). Drawing upon the sociobiological concepts of kin selection and inclusive fitness, nepotistic favoritism, and reciprocal altruism, van den Berghe provided an analysis of ethnicity as a phenomenon that represents an extension of the biologically natural phenomenon of kinship. In short, van den Berghe interprets ethnicity as having evolved on a platform of behavioral predispositions that are the product of kin selection. In van den Berghe's view, ethnicity is "kinship writ large." Unlike biological kin groups whose existence and solidarity are based largely, if not exclusively, on shared genetic "interests," ethnic groups typically share some degree of genetic relatedness, but their existence is also based on the phenomenon of reciprocity, or in the parlance of sociobiology, "reciprocal altruism." Thus, even when members of a group share no more genetic relatedness with each other than they do with members of the larger population to which they belong, they can identify with each other on the basis of "putative kinship" (van den Berghe 1981), "cultural kinship," or "fictive kinship" (Whitmeyer 1997). These forms of kinship, while often including some sense of common origin and shared biological traits, rest predominantly on shared cultural traits and interests. According to scholars like van den Berghe, Lopreato, Crippen, and Whitmeyer, however, the capacity to form ethnic groups derives from processes of organic evolution via natural selection.

As a social phenomenon that is manifested in contemporary societies, Lopreato (1984), Lopreato and Crippen (1999), and van den Berghe (1981) regard ethnic groups, or "ethnies" as van den Berghe calls them, as successors to clans, which were trans-familial forms of social organization during early human evolutionary history. In fact, Lopreato and Crippen regard ethnicity as a form of "post-clan" identity that has emerged among humans over the past 10,000 or so years (1999: 247–77). Clans were kin groups whose members shared a sense of common origins, and those origins may have been patrilineal or matrilineal. In addition to evolved mental capabilities for processes such as *kin recognition*, the ability to distinguish kin from non-kin and close kin from distant kin (Hames 2016; Hepper 1991; Fletcher and Michener 1987), behavioral capabilities for reciprocity and practices such as *assortative mating* and *homogamy* (preferring mates who resemble oneself) are said to have evolved by kin selection but then became "extended" to non-kin, thereby enabling the evolution of ethnic groups (ethnies). All organisms have kin, but it is unlikely that members of any species other than humans have a *concept* of kinship that can form the basis of collective identity and group life. The evolved capability for forming kin-*like* collectivities that are conceptualized by their members in kinship terms is, in the view of scholars like van den Berghe and others, foundational to the evolution of ethnicity, ethnic favoritism, ethnocentrism, and what Lopreato and Crippen call "ethnic parochialism" (1999: 260), a phenomenon of remarkable durability that has contributed to the persistence of ethnic conflict and discord, even in the era of megasocieties, or what Lopreato calls the "Leviathan nation" (1984: 182–83).

Possessed of a "clannish brain," as Lopreato and Crippen call it (1999: 247–77), the cohesiveness of recent, megasocietal forms is threatened "from within" by local attachments associated with ethnic group identity. Territoriality itself, a behavioral predisposition in Lopreato's characterization of human nature, supports ethnic group identity and cohesiveness in defense of space and the resources contained therein (1984: 120). Territoriality is commonly linked to an emotional attachment to *place*, a defining feature not only of clans but of ethnic groups as well (Lopreato 1984: 128). Echoing Max Weber's prior notion of "status groups" as collectivities within society, especially within social classes, that inhibit the formation and maintenance of more comprehensive levels of group consciousness and solidarity (such as working-class consciousness), Lopreato explains how ethnic groups can threaten societal-level cohesion, especially when they exist in large-scale societies (Lopreato 1984: 182–83). In large-scale, "Leviathan societies" such as contemporary urban-industrial societies, Lopreato and Crippen assert that both nepotism and ethnocentrism, defining properties of ethnic groups, contribute to the "mischief-making" activities of the "clannish brain," mischief-making that erodes and destabilizes societal level cohesion (Lopreato and Crippen 1999: 276–77). Thus, the very evolutionary processes such as kin selection that contribute to societal cohesiveness in archaic, smaller-scale societies can act as forces of societal dissolution in contemporary, megasocieties.

Though van den Berghe, Lopreato, and Crippen all attribute the existence of ethnic groups to the "extension" of kin-selected behavioral predispositions, an alternative sociobiological conceptualization of ethnicity provides a finer-grain evolutionary analysis of ethnicity and how biology and culture are intertwined in this social phenomenon. Building on previous sociobiological analyses of ethnicity, especially that of van den Berghe (1981), Whitmeyer interprets ethnicity as the product of endogamy (1997). Whitmeyer identifies three main perspectives in efforts to explain the "ethnic phenomenon": (1) ethnicity as an extension of normal kinship relations, (2) ethnicity as an instrumental strategy for material or political gain, and (3) ethnicity as a form of cultural expression (1997: 162–63). Although all three of these approaches enable scholars to gain some purchase in explaining ethnicity, each entails limitations. For example, the view of ethnic groups as extended kin groups cannot explain why most members of large ethnic groups do not share common descent and are not close kin, or why all *possible* ethnic groups do not form among population members who share common descent (Whitmeyer 1997: 163). Similarly, the instrumentalist approach cannot explain non-instrumental "passions" that commonly characterize membership in an ethnic group, nor can it explain why other forms of association, such as class mobilization, do not arise as instrumental strategies for advancing group interests, since phenomena like class actions are often more effective in achieving collective goals than are ethnic groups (Whitmeyer 1997: 163). Finally, though various cultural markers (e.g., language, dress, religion, customs, etc.) are commonly associated with ethnicity, no *particular* cultural traits are universal to all ethnic groups. Furthermore, while cultural traits are used commonly to describe ethnic groups, common cultural traits are not reliable in *predicting* and *explaining* why an ethnic group evolves (Whitmeyer 1997: 164).

While conceding that these three aforementioned types of explanations can shed some light on ethnic groups, Whitmeyer attributes the emergence of ethnic collectivities to endogamy, and he provides a novel explanation of how natural selection could favor traits that predispose the formation of ethnic groups. Whitmeyer contends that it can be adaptive for individuals to behave in a manner that confers benefits to other individuals who comprise a set of people to whom both the benefactor and beneficiaries belong. He calls this set an "endogamous set," which typically is the "minimum endogamous set" (MES) to which all the members belong. When many members of the MES direct beneficial behavior toward other set members, Whitmeyer conceptualizes the MES as an ethnic group, or "ethny" (1997: 164). Ethnic groups comprise both kin and non-kin, and kin of varying degrees of relatedness. And though kin selection can promote cooperation among some members of ethnic groups, most members of large ethnic groups are not close kin and thus, not eligible for kin selection. Yet, Whitmeyer contends that natural selection can favor the evolution of ethnic groups because of the genetic fitness benefits that ethnic groups can confer.

The foundation of Whitmeyer's argument rests on the notion of "co-progenitors" (1997: 164). Cooperation between two reproductive partners is not explained by genetic kinship between the partners. In fact, if the partners are too closely related, inbreeding depression may compromise the health and viability of any offspring they produce (Fox 2015). Mates derive Darwinian (individual) fitness benefits from mating and producing offspring and possibly, grand-offspring, great-grand offspring, etc. This is simple Darwinian fitness and the product of collaboration between a male and a female, not inclusive fitness, the product of kin selection. The fitness benefits that derive from reproductive cooperation with a co-progenitor (one's mate) to whom one is genetically unrelated can be extended to cooperation with *other possible co-progenitors*. For example, if one contributes to the well-being of other members of one's MES *to whom one is unrelated*, descendants of those other members could become co-progenitors of one's own descendants. Simply put, if one assists other members of one's MES, the descendants of those other members may become husbands or wives of one's own descendants, co-progenitors of one's offspring, grand offspring, great-grand offspring, etc. Thus, through a process of natural (versus kin) selection, social interactions comprising collaboration, reciprocity, exchange, and other forms of cooperative behavior among members of one's MES who are *not kin* can yield fitness benefits to cooperators by offering a future MES populated with potential co-progenitors for one's descendants.

Accordingly, an endogamous group (in Whitmeyer's terms, an MES) can become what is commonly regarded as an ethnic group, and the benefits of cooperation among ethnic group members can be explained by natural selection's producing possible future co-progenitors for one's own descendants. Whitmeyer coins what he calls the "HPCP principle" for explaining how and why an ethnic group could evolve by natural selection and how cooperation could evolve among members of the ethnic group. The HPCP principle means that pro-social behaviors directed toward members of one's MES entail "helping-possible-co-progenitors" in one's MES, as well as possible-co-progenitors among one's descendants. Thus, Whitmeyer offers a sociobiological explanation of the evolution of ethnic groups that doesn't require the explanatory principles of kin selection and inclusive fitness. This is not to say, however, that kin selection is inoperative among members of an MES. Rather, it explains how cooperation among MES (ethnic group) members can evolve and operate *absent* processes of kin selection.

Mating, Parenting, and Gender Relations

The logic of evolutionary theory in general and sociobiology in particular leads to the inference that behaviors that are most salient to survival *and to reproductive success* are likely to be subjected to the strongest selection forces. Consequently, social relations of mating and parenting are, arguably, among those most likely to be shaped by natural selection. Several sociologists have framed analysis of mating and parenting relations, and sex/gender relations in general, in sociobiological terms, and we will review a few such analyses to see how they purport to explain these types of social behaviors.

Reproductive cooperation between a female and a male is fundamental to efforts by any sexually reproducing species to achieve fitness. Collaboration between a female and a male to produce an offspring is requisite for the realization of each partner's fitness interests. Since each collaborator contributes 50% of its genes to its offspring, the fitness "returns" on reproduction are equivalent for each reproductive partner. However, because of the biology of mammalian reproduction, the *costs* of reproductive collaboration are asymmetrical. Two basic types of asymmetry are involved. The first pertains to variable *parental investment* and the second to variable *parental confidence*. Sociobiological theory suggests that these two types of asymmetry could lead to the evolution of psychologies that diverge between males and females, psychologies that could influence social relations of mating and parenting, and gender relations in general.

Variable parental investment in reproduction is rooted in the biology of anisogamy, which means that egg cells, in comparison to sperm, are large, relatively scarce, and physiologically "expensive," while sperm are small, abundant and "cheap." Or, as noted earlier, eggs are said to be "gold" and sperm are said to be "dirt" (Lopreato 1984). (Recall our earlier discussion of anisogamy in Chapter 7.) Since the lifetime fitness potential of a male far exceeds that of a female, the implications of male and female reproductive behaviors diverge significantly. In simplest terms, female fitness is enhanced by the judicious selection of a "good" mate, and this means a mate that provides both "good genes," and in the case of species like humans that produce highly altricial offspring, reliable paternal care of offspring as well. For a male, however, the selection of mate "quality" is less significant, and the "quantity" of matings can offset any injudicious behaviors that result in the selection of an "inferior" mate as a reproductive partner. In the extreme, few human females give birth to as many as twenty or more offspring over the course of their lives, but some males have sired hundreds, and probably more (Hopcroft 2016: 23). This asymmetry in the reproductive division of labor, which derives fundamentally from the biology of anisogamy, can provide direction for conducting research about differences between male-female behaviors. Two examples of the sort of thinking this has inspired sociologists are available in the work of Timothy Crippen on the male-female pair bond in human mating, and the work of Rosemary Hopcroft on female deference to males at different stages in the life-cycle of the human female, and we will discuss each in turn.

Pair bonding among mates is very rare among mammals, occurring among as few as 3–4% of species (Crippen 2015: 403). Among humans, however, pair bonds are ubiquitous, even in the absence of the formal institution of marriage (Chapais 2008: 160; Crippen 2015: 403). Though virtually species-typical among humans, the pair-bond among mates is also fragile and tenuous. Crippen turns to sociobiological theory in order to try to explain this ironic social relationship. Crippen reviews two basic hypotheses for explaining pair bonding as a reproductive strategy. The first characterizes pair-bonding as a *parenting strategy*, and the second as a *mating strategy* (Crippen 2015: 406). The parenting strategy, which Crippen calls the "parental collaboration hypothesis," proposes that mates form stable pair bonds because males can make significant contributions to the survival of offspring, especially highly altricial offspring, by provisioning and protection. In fact, Crippen concludes that the contributions human males have made to the provision of food in foraging societies have been underestimated, and the most important form of such provisioning occurs by means of big game hunting. In a critical review of the common claim that females, not males, provide most of the calories ingested by foragers, Chapais claims that big game hunting may be a more significant source of caloric intake in foraging societies than has been previously recognized (2008). Responding to the work and claim of Hawkes (1991) that big game hunting in foraging societies may better be understood as a means of status attainment by males (what she calls the "showing off hypothesis") and may contribute little to food provisioning, Chapais (and Crippen) reject the notion that such hunting is *exclusively* about male mating effort, and thus only a mating strategy, but rather is likely to represent a paternal role in provisioning, thus, a parenting strategy as well (Crippen 2015: 408–10).

In addition to striving to achieve mating success by "showing off," males also engage in mate guarding in their pursuit (albeit it typically unconscious) of Darwinian fitness. Though polygyny offers the prospect of opportunities for enhancing a male's fitness, it also increases the threat of cuckoldry in light of the challenges it poses to effective mate guarding. As male-male competition intensifies, selection is likely to produce an "equalization" effect among males whereby competitive skill becomes more equally distributed in the population, and the number of mates that can be guarded effectively by males dwindles. Over time, the polygynous structure of "multiharem groups" gives way to communities organized on the principle of monogamous pair bonds (Chapais 2008; Crippen 2015: 411). By entering into and maintaining membership in a stable, pair-bonded mating relationship, males can cope more successfully with the challenges associated with effective mate guarding.

However, though Crippen finds the view that the mating hypothesis better explains the pair bond than does the parenting hypothesis more compelling in light of available evidence, he views the matter as far from having been resolved. Instead, he concludes tentatively that both sociobiological reasoning and available evidence *currently* lend more credence to the mating than to the parenting hypothesis about the origins of the pair bond among humans. Finally, Crippen considers three aspects of human biology in their relation to the incidence of pair bonding. Each of these features of human biology is consistent with the view that humans have evolved to develop *relatively stable, pair-bonded mating relationships* that are, nevertheless, fraught with a degree of instability that is reflected in the propensity with which mated pair bonds among humans often dissolve.

The three features of human biology that Crippen views as implicated in pair bonding are: (1) modest sexual dimorphism, (2) sperm competition, and (3) select features of human neurobiology (Crippen 2015: 412–19). We will briefly review Crippen's analysis of each of these factors and their role in pair-bonding. Sexual dimorphism refers to average differences between males and females within a species, and size dimorphism is perhaps the most commonly analyzed of such forms. For example, on average, male orangutans may be as much as twice the size of females, male mountain gorillas 50% larger than females, common chimpanzee males as much as 30% larger than females, and bonobo ("pygmy" chimpanzees) males as much as 20% larger as females; among humans, males on average are about 10–15% larger than females (Crippen 2015: 413). Biologists view polygyny as the product of intrasexual selection, or male-male competition. The greater the intensity of male-male competition, the greater the sexual dimorphism, and the stronger the propensity toward polygyny (Crippen 2015: 413). When compared to mountain gorillas and orangutans, both of which are highly dimorphic, and to chimpanzees and bonobos, both of which are less dimorphic, humans are only modestly dimorphic and somewhat polygynous, but less so than the other "great apes." Only the gibbons, which feature minimal dimorphism, form relatively stable pair bonds. And as Crippen reports, even in societies where a relatively small number of high-ranking men acquire large numbers of mates, most other males in those societies have a pair bond with only one woman (2015: 414). Accordingly, the "modest" degree of sexual dimorphism among humans is consistent with an interpretation of humans as constituting, by nature, a pair-bonded species.

Most intrasexual selection among human males occurs before copulation. That is, most males achieve matings by repelling competitors (male-male competition) or by becoming selected by females as sexual partners (female choice). As a result, sexual selection occurs before mating itself, and the "victor" thereby monopolizes the privilege of fertilizing the female over which the competition occurs. However, one form of intrasexual selection occurs *after* two or more males copulate with the same female, and it occurs in the form of fertilization contests among sperm deposited by the two or more males with whom the female has copulated. In sociobiology, this is called "sperm competition," and the phenomenon was first discovered in insects (Parker 1970). Sperm competition typically occurs when mate guarding fails. Failing at inhibiting a mate from copulating with other males, males engaged in sperm competition try to secure fertilization by delivering the greatest quantity of sperm, thereby increasing their chances of fertilizing an ovum. Sperm competition occurs among species in which females routinely engage in matings with multiple males. The incidence of females mating with multiple males is associated with male testes size. Large testes are associated with the species that are highly promiscuous and in which females engage in matings with multiple partners.

Crippen reports that comparative analysis of testes size and mating patterns among mountain gorillas, chimpanzees, and humans provides suggestive evidence in relation to pair bonding. Male gorillas weigh about 400 pounds, and their testes weigh about an ounce. Male chimpanzees weigh about 100 pounds, and their testes weigh about 4 ounces. Male humans weigh, on average, about 150–175 pounds, and their testes weigh between 1 to 2 ounces. Female gorillas comprise harems, and they mate only every 3 to 4 years during short periods of estrus, and Crippen reports that matings are typically with the same male (2015: 404–406).[3] In contrast, chimpanzees comprise multiple male-female groups, and they are highly promiscuous, with females mating with multiple males. Weighing only about one-fourth of what a male gorilla weighs, but having testicles that weigh four times those of gorillas, male chimpanzees appear clearly designed for sperm competition, since mate guarding among chimpanzees is typically a futile enterprise. In both body weight and testes size, humans are intermediate between gorillas and chimpanzees. Accordingly, human reproductive morphology and physiology leads to an expectation that human pair bonds are more vulnerable to disruption by female extra-pair copulations than are those comprising gorilla society, but not as vulnerable as are chimpanzee pair bonds. Though challenged by other researchers, Baker and Bellis (1995) claim to have adduced evidence that sperm competition occurs among humans, and that human pair bonds for mating are far from impervious to "cheating" (Crippen 2015: 417).

Finally, Crippen contends that features of human neuroanatomy and neurophysiology support the view that natural selection has designed humans for pair bonding but that pair bonds feature an inherent instability, the consequences of which result in humans forming, with relative ease, a succession of pair bonds during their lifetimes. Maryanski and Turner (1992) contend that, like most apes, human society features weaker social ties than those among other species such as monkeys. Accordingly, it is not surprising that pair bonds among humans are "tenuous," to use Crippen's characterization (2015). Yet, the phylogenetic record of humans reveals a long-term trend toward enhanced emotional capabilities, and some of these emotions clearly support the formation and maintenance of pair bonds among human mates (Turner 2000). Informed by the work of Helen Fisher on love (1992, 2004), Crippen directs our attention to two areas of the human brain that probably contribute to the production of emotions that accompany pair bonding. The two areas are the caudate nucleus and the ventral tegmental area (Crippen 2015: 417). Both regions are implicated in the pursuit of rewards, and the preferential pursuit of one specific reward over another. Among individuals involved in the early stages of a romantic relationship, as well as those involved in relationships about 2 years old, these regions of the brain exhibited elevated levels of activity (Crippen 2015: 418). Fisher (2004) reports that three distinct neural networks are implicated in the experience of sexual desire, romantic love, and deep attachment. Other researchers have identified "attachment hormones," vasopressin among males and oxytocin among females, that are implicated in the formation of social bonds (Crippen 2015: 418–19). Yet, as Crippen observes, attachments once formed are not permanent. Rather, it appears that pair-bonded individuals often remain vigilant for opportunities to escape current pair bonds and form new pair bonds with new partners, thereby illustrating the fragile, tenuous nature of pair bonds among *Homo sapiens*.

Anisogamy, internal fertilization, and multiple-matings by females all give rise to a problem experienced commonly by males, the problem of paternity uncertainty. Paternity uncertainty can arouse emotions like sexual jealousy and activate behaviors like mate guarding by males. Unlike females, males confront a persistent threat of misplaced paternal investment if they are not the fathers of the offspring of their mates. For females who rely upon paternal investment in caring for their offspring, reducing paternity uncertainty in their mates is an adaptive problem. This is particularly important among species with highly altricial offspring, like humans, who require high levels of parental investment. Grounding her research in sexual selection and parental investment theory, the evolutionary sociologist Rosemary Hopcroft adopts a sociobiological approach to the study of mate guarding by human males, and she examines the possibility that young human females may have evolved an adaptation for reducing paternity uncertainty among their mates. Sociobiological research reveals male-female differences in mate preference (Hopcroft 2016: 31–55). Though female and male preferences for traits in mates overlap, distinct differences also exist (Hopcroft 2016: 35). Females prefer high status in males, because status is linked to resources from which a female and her offspring can benefit. Males prefer traits (such as youth) in females that signify high fertility *and* traits that signify high fidelity to a mate, thereby helping alleviate a male's experience of paternity anxiety. Hopcroft hypothesizes that certain empirical differences in behavior between young males and females may derive from these differences in evolved mate preferences and the threat of paternity uncertainty experienced by males. Specifically, divergence in deference patterns and self-esteem may reflect evolved differences between females and males in their mate preferences. For example, Hopcroft reports that experiments have provided evidence that males are less likely to defer to females, and females are more likely to defer to males (2002; 2016: 93). Anticipating criticisms that gender differences in evolved adaptations for mate preferences may serve ideological interests, Hopcroft is emphatic in asserting that ideologies of female inferiority are not derivative of evolutionary thought and analysis (2016: 93). However, Hopcroft suggests that patterns of female deference and low self-esteem exhibited by *young* females may be tractable to evolutionary interpretation, and these patterns may be expressions of evolved adaptations that are the product of sexual selection.

How might deference by young females toward males and their experience of low task-related self-esteem, in relation to males, have evolutionary significance? As discussed earlier, sexual selection theory suggests that paternity confidence is always problematic for males. It would be maladaptive for a male to direct paternal investment toward offspring that are not his own, and this is the basic fitness threat posed to a male by his mate's sexual infidelity. Accordingly, males have evolved to be vigilant to cues that signal female sexual fidelity as well as cues that signal female tractability to mate-guarding behavior. Such traits would be preferred by males in prospective mates and thus could be the product of intersexual selection. Furthermore, while high status is an asset for males in their competition to be chosen by females as mates, female high status can pose a threat to males, because it can signal independence of the female and imperviousness on her part to mate-guarding efforts by the male (Hopcroft 2006). As Hopcroft puts it, such females lack "controllability" and thus may present the threat of infidelity to their mates (2006, 2016). To the extent that such males are discriminating in their choice of mates, it is to the advantage of females to be "persuasive" about their fidelity to their mates. This dynamic is particularly important in systems that feature monogamous, or near-monogamous, mating.

Reviewing research on male-female differences in deference behavior and task related self-esteem, Hopcroft notes interesting patterns that invite sociobiological interpretation. As noted earlier, (1) females tend to defer to males but not to other females, and males tend not to defer to females (2002); (2) deference displays are greatest among young females, but they decline, and even disappear, as females age (2006); (3) females exhibit lower self-esteem during the ages 15–18, despite performing better in school, earning higher grades, and being more likely to attend college (2016: 210–11); (4) both self-esteem and status attainment rise among females as they age, especially during their post-reproductive years (2009a); and (5) by age 50, patterns of female deference to males virtually vanish (Hopcroft 2006: 368). In short, Hopcroft interprets these patterns as possible evidence of evolved psychological adaptations among females to enable them to secure high status mates by signaling both high fecundity (via youth) and sexual fidelity (via "controllability"), thereby reducing the threat of paternity uncertainty among prospective mates. It is worth noting, however, that such signals may not be "honest" in that they need not actually convey information about sexual fidelity, but rather, that they need only be persuasive in giving prospective mates confidence in their "controllability" and thereby reducing paternity anxiety among the males.

Furthermore, Hopcroft concludes that, since both female deference and low self-esteem patterns are age specific (i.e., most prevalent among young females during peak reproductive years) and then decline and even disappear among older women, especially those in their post-reproductive years, these patterns are unlikely to be the product of socialization alone. That is, while socialization by a patriarchal culture almost certainly contributes to the expression of female deference and lower self-esteem while women are young, either the effects of the socialization process must be fleeting, or these patterns may reflect features of an evolved female psychology that is adaptive during a female's peak reproductive years. In fact, Hopcroft suggests that these evolved adaptations could constitute a behavioral "platform" on the basis of which a patriarchal culture could evolve and amplify patterns of male dominance (2009a, b). It is very important to note, however, that Hopcroft's reasoning *cannot* be taken to mean that she has fallen victim to the naturalistic fallacy and has concluded that male dominance in any form is a "fixed and inalterable" feature of human societies. Rather, Hopcroft's analysis suggests that females may possess evolved psychological traits that were adaptive in ancestral environments but may very well feature a norm of reaction that is sufficiently broad so as to permit them to be "over-ridden" by a culture that promotes gender equality. In fact, the temporary, age-specific expression of both female deference to males and lower self-esteem among young females suggests that both of these behavioral patterns are likely to be sensitive to environmental forces that can either mute them or reduce their duration and intensity. Simply put, Hopcroft's work does not lead to the conclusion that female deference and lower self-esteem means that "biology is destiny."

Nor should Hopcroft's analysis be seen as monocausal and narrowly reductionistic. Hopcroft identifies only two phenomena, the expression of deference and low self-esteem among young females, which she says may be implicated in the evolution of more general patterns of gender inequality. She does not claim that gender inequality and the sociocultural complex of patriarchy can be reduced in their entirely to female deference and low self-esteem. Accordingly, it is best to think of Hopcroft's analysis as having revealed the existence of evolved psychological predispositions that function with an array of other factors to yield general patterns of gender inequality. For example, the work of Joan Huber, which is also informed by what she calls "biodata," but is *not* framed in sociobiological terms, identifies another set of biological factors that almost certainly have contributed to the evolution of gender inequality (2007). Unlike Hopcroft, Huber does not look for the origins of gender inequality as rooted in gender-specific, evolved features of female psychology. That is, Huber makes no mention of behavioral predispositions among females that could help explain patterns of female deference toward males, lower task-related self-esteem, or less status-striving and attainment. Instead, Huber develops an argument that is based on a concept that is familiar to economists, *opportunity costs*, the inability to pursue a given opportunity because of resources (time, energy, material goods) invested in the pursuit of another opportunity. In Huber's view, the near-universal pattern of female subordination to males derives from a simple but far-reaching biological fact (a "biodatum"): Females lactate and nurse their young, but males don't. What does lactation have to do with the origins of gender inequality? Human infants are highly altricial and require very high levels of parental investment to survive, much less thrive (2007: 93). For up to the first 4 years of their lives, the only source of nutrition available to human offspring is their mothers' milk. In addition, the frequency with which babies must nurse imposes serious constraints on a mother's activity regimen. The prolonged, intense requirements imposed on a mother for nursing and caring for her offspring severely limit her ability to engage fully in other types of activity within her community and society. Among such activities from which nursing mothers are largely excluded are opportunities to participate in economic, political, and military activity, all of which, according to Huber, are important pathways to societal power and influence (2007: 117). By having to nurse offspring and forego participation in non-reproductive related activities like business and politics, for most of human history, nursing mothers incurred "opportunity costs," that is, opportunities lost by virtue of having to provide maternal care. Over evolutionary time, the systematic exclusion of women from full participation in societal life because of the constraints imposed by pregnancy, nursing, and child care contributed to the evolution of gender inequality.

However, the origins and persistence of patterns of gender inequality can be reduced in their entirety neither to Hopcroft's analysis of how evolved features of female psychology nor to Huber's analysis of the female physiology of lactation. Instead, other factors contribute as well, including at least one additional feature of human biology: sexual dimorphism. As noted earlier, humans are "mildly" sexually dimorphic, with males, on average, being 10–15% larger than females. In addition, males feature greater upper body (chest, back, arm) strength on average than females. It is likely that greater male upper body strength is the product of male-male competition, particularly in the form of physical confrontation. Accordingly, and though size/strength distributions between women and men overlap considerably, it can be said that males typically benefit from a size/strength advantage over females in direct, interpersonal, one-to-one physical confrontations. This physical advantage, though not overwhelming, is very likely enough to contribute further to the evolution of male dominance over females and, eventually, contribute to the emergence of patriarchy.

It should be emphasized, however, that it is not sheer male size/strength that contributes to their frequent physical dominance of females at the interpersonal level. Instead, threats of severe injury and death are much more significant *in evolutionary terms* for females than they are for males. Specifically, the severe injury or incapacitation, much less death, of a mother typically imposes much greater fitness consequences on her than it does on a father. Following a logic of the sort developed by Huber, if a mother is incapable of nursing and caring for babies and very young offspring, the lives of those offspring are seriously imperiled. To the extent that the survival, health, and well-being of a human offspring depends asymmetrically on the ability of its mother to care for it, evolutionary reasoning would lead us to conclude that females should be much more risk-averse than should males. And female risk aversion should be greatest among mothers of infants and very young children, with the possible exception of the risks incurred by a mother by protecting her offspring from threats such as predation or male violence. Males, on the other hand, have much more to gain in potential fitness returns by winning male-male contests, even those that entail the risk of severe injury. Of course, death ends the reproductive futures of both females and males, but the potential lifetime fitness returns of winning a male-male contest are high, so elevated risk-taking by males is a behavior that can be expected to have evolved by natural selection. Thus, sexual dimorphism and differences in behavior typically associated with this dimorphism are also likely contributors to the evolution of gender inequality among humans.

Answers to the question of the origins of gender inequality are far from settled science, and our purpose here is not to advocate the explanatory power of one approach over others. Rather, our discussion of Hopcroft's analysis of behavior patterns exhibited by young females is meant only to illustrate how sociobiological thinking can yield novel explanatory approaches regarding phenomena of common interest to mainstream sociologists and other social scientists. It is important to recognize that Hopcroft does not intend her interpretation of patterns of female deference and self-esteem to constitute an exhaustive analysis of gender inequality and its origins. Instead, Hopcroft's work merely introduces another element into sociological analyses and discussions of this phenomenon. By looking for evidence of possible evolved behavioral predispositions that may be implicated in male-female interactions, Hopcroft has applied ideas derived from sociobiology (e.g., sexual selection, parental investment, mate guarding) to the study of a phenomenon of common interest to social scientists, patterns of gender inequality among humans. Consequently, sociobiological work of the sort provided by Hopcroft illustrates ways in which sociobiology can open new avenues of inquiry that can be pursued by evolutionary sociologists and, in fact, sociologists in general.

Demographic Patterns

Though Wilson states his position with unmistakable clarity in the first chapter of *Sociobiology: The New Synthesis* (1975: 4–6), it is unlikely that most social scientists are aware that sociobiology is, properly understood, a branch of population biology. In Wilson's words,

> Its [sociobiology's] central precept is that the evolution of social behavior can be fully comprehended only through an understanding, first, of demography, which yields the vital information concerning population growth and age structure, and second, of the genetic structure of populations.... The principal goal of a general theory of sociobiology should be an ability to predict features of social organization from a knowledge of these population parameters combined with information on the behavioral constraints imposed by the genetic constitution of the species.
>
> (1975: 5)

Accordingly, it is to be expected that sociobiology can provide direction for research by human demographers and other sociologists who study the relationship between basic population traits and social organization. We will discuss briefly the work of a few sociologists who, in fact, have pursued such courses of inquiry on topics such as the demographic transition, the effects of social status on fertility patterns, and sex ratios.

The emphasis on "fitness maximization" in evolutionary biology in general and sociobiology in particular can be misleading. Upon first consideration, to maximize fitness seems to imply that organisms should be striving for maximal reproductive output, that is to say, maximum fertility. But that is not the case. In fact, if reproductive partners produce more offspring than can be expected to survive to reproductive age, perhaps due to insufficient resource availability, they would have behaved in a maladaptive manner. What "counts," in evolutionary terms, is not the number of offspring maximized in any given reproductive cycle, but rather, an individual's *lifetime reproductive output of offspring that survive to reproductive age and viability*. If, however, reproductive output fails to achieve a level at which it can be supported by available resources and circumstances, then fitness will not have been "maximized." In short, for any reproductive pair in any range of environmental circumstances, there is, in principle, an optimal level of fertility (reproductive "success") that represents fitness "maximization," even if it falls below the maximum number of offspring that a mated pair could have produced.

Is there an optimal level of fitness (fertility rate) that is species-typical of humans? If so, what determines it? This question has been posed by several sociobiologically minded evolutionary sociologists, and we will review their thoughts about the matter. Several scholars have framed this question in terms of analyses of the *demographic transition*, the long-term historical trend whereby societies undergo transitions from a long period of high fertility and high mortality, to a period of high fertility and declining mortality, to a period of low fertility and low mortality. The demographic transition is a sequence seen as accompanying the modernization (industrialization, urbanization) of societies. What might sociobiological theory and research bring to efforts in trying to explain the demographic transition? The sociologists Arlen Carey and Joseph Lopreato have provided an analysis, framed in sociobiological terms, in an attempt to answer this question. In reviewing the Carey-Lopreato analysis, Stephen Sanderson, another evolutionary sociologist whose work is framed in sociobiological terms, identifies three evolutionary explanatory approaches for understanding the long-term decline in fertility associated with the demographic transition. Remember that, at first glance, *any* decline in fertility might seem to constitute evidence against the sociobiological claim that humans, like all organisms, have evolved to maximize fitness. Sanderson labels the three explanatory approaches as the "economic," the "female empowerment," and the "behavioral ecological" theories of the demographic transition (2014: 197–200). The economic approach contends that where children were an economic asset (as labor) in pre-industrial societies, especially in agrarian societies, they became liabilities and drained family resources in industrial societies, so the fertility level dropped (Sanderson 2014: 197). The female empowerment approach contends that women generally avoid having many children due both to the discomfort of pregnancy and the burden of caring for infants and young children (consistent with Huber's hypothesis about the opportunity costs imposed by child bearing and child care), but until they gained social status, they were unable to resist their husbands' pressure to have children. By gaining status in industrial societies, largely through educational attainment and consequent economic participation, they became more effective at resisting their husbands' pressure to bear children.

Both the economic and female empowerment hypotheses can be developed absent the adoption of an evolutionary perspective. The Carey-Lopreato approach, however, rests firmly on the foundation of sociobiological theory. Following the lead of Darwin himself, Carey and Lopreato posit that fertility tracks mortality, especially infant and child morality (Sanderson 2014: 199). Thus, when mortality increases, fertility increases, and when mortality declines, fertility declines. Essentially, Carey and Lopreato are arguing that infant and child mortality rates provide cues about environmental conditions and the availability of resources to support offspring. High infant and child mortality rates signal resource deficits of some sort, which mean that maximizing lifetime fitness might mean refraining from producing offspring under such stressed conditions. This reasoning closely parallels the earlier discussion in Chapter 6 of reproductive restraint and Wynne-Edwards' work (1962) in relation to the topic of group selection. Responding to epideictic displays, individuals who occupy environments in which resources are severely limited may refrain from reproducing, because stressed environments may not support new offspring, thereby increasing the risk of infant mortality. As environmental conditions improve, the threat of infant mortality declines, and fertility levels may rise accordingly.

Compared to many other species, humans historically have featured fairly low fertility rates. And, in fact, over the course of human history, human females have typically produced only about two surviving children over the course of their reproductive lives (Carey and Lopreato 1995). Carey and Lopreato contend that humans have evolved a "two-child psychology" that predisposes couples to produce, on average, two children over the course of their life history. This means that, on average, producing two children has been optimal in the full range of environments that have been inhabited by humans, because the resources in those environments have been able to support about two children per couple. Intuition might lead to the inference that, as societies became more abundant and stable in terms of the availability of resources, fertility levels would rise. However, the total fertility rate, or the average number of children a woman produces over the course of her reproductive years, of advanced industrial societies like Japan and Germany is only 1.4, and in the United States, it is 2.1 (Hopcroft 2015: 125). And, as we shall see shortly, total fertility varies by socioeconomic status of women. The relatively low total fertility rate found in industrial societies is influenced by a number of proximate causes including higher levels of education, greater female participation in the paid labor force, better prenatal care and health care in general, and especially increased resource availability within the family.

According to Carey and Lopreato, humans have evolved a "two-child psychology," because ancestral environmental conditions have favored fertility levels that track variable mortality levels which, over the course of the human species' history, has resulted in a total fertility rate of about two children per female. Though the proximate causes of total fertility vary among environments over time, the ultimate cause can be attributed to the "two-child psychology" that has optimized fitness for most humans over most of the course of human history. Thus, Carey and Lopreato conclude that, whatever the fertility and mortality rates that prevail in a population, humans possess an evolved psychology that predisposes females to calibrate their reproductive effort so as to produce, on average, two children over the course of their reproductive lives.

Social Conflict

Inspired by Malthus and his observation that population growth can surpass the capacity of an environment's resources to support it, Darwin came to view natural selection as a protracted "struggle for existence," a "complex battle of life" (in Lopreato 1984: 7). In recent decades, evolutionary biologists have placed new emphasis on how cooperation aids individuals in waging the battle, but alongside this insight, the ubiquity of social conflicts over survival and reproductive success has captured the attention of sociobiologists. Along with the other social sciences, sociology has devoted much attention to social conflict in its myriad forms, including class conflict, race/ethnic conflict, religious conflict, intersocietal conflict, sex/gender conflict, generational conflict, and so on. In this regard, multiple variants of "conflict theory" have developed within sociology alone. Such conflicts are typically seen as transpiring over various sorts of interests, both material and symbolic. Efforts to apply sociobiological thinking to the study of human social conflict has focused attention primarily on the "foundational" nature of *genetic* interests, as measured by the reproductive success or failure of individuals participating in social conflict. An organizing heuristic routinely employed by sociobiologists is found in the explanatory principles of *kin selection* and *inclusive fitness*. And though the roles of kin selection and inclusive fitness in explaining sociality have come under recent criticism by none other than E. O. Wilson and others (Nowak et al. 2010; Wilson and Wilson 2007), sociobiologists have long viewed the incidence of conflict or cooperation among individuals as strongly influenced by the degree to which those individuals share genetic kinship based on common descent.

Recently, the sociologist Stephen Sanderson has outlined a framework for integrating sociobiological thinking about social conflict with four major social science approaches to the study of social conflict among humans. Sanderson calls his proposed synthesis and the research program which it will support "Darwinian conflict theory" (DCT) (2001, 2015). We will review key elements of Sanderson's DCT as one example whereby sociobiology and sociology might achieve a degree of consilience on topics of common interest, like explaining social conflict among humans. Sanderson identifies four schools of social theory (derived primarily from sociology, anthropology, and economics) as potentially valuable contributors to his DCT project: rational choice theory, sociological conflict theory, the theory of cultural materialism, and social evolutionism (2015: 230). The DCT project entails finding ways of integrating each of these theoretical perspectives with sociobiology in order to derive testable (falsifiable) propositions for empirical research. Each theoretical perspective, including sociobiology, is characterized in terms of the following elements: axioms (statements whose truth is assumed), postulates (statements that are less general and abstract than axioms and that focus on a specific substantive content), and propositions (empirically falsifiable statements) (Sanderson 2015). The 5 theoretical perspectives comprising DCT have yielded, up to this point, a total of 51 axioms, 52 postulates, and 354 propositions (Sanderson 2015: 230).

For our purposes, it would be impractical to discuss all, or even a significant number, of this large array of statements. Instead, we will identify key ideas present in each of the four social scientific perspectives and explain how Sanderson attempts to synthesize these ideas with elements of sociobiological theory.

Rational Choice Theory

Consistent with traditional utilitarian schools of thought, both rational choice theory and sociobiology view individuals as goal-oriented beings that try to realize their interests by attaining specific goals in the most efficient, effective manner possible. For example, rational choice theory can predict that individuals will pursue status and prestige under the constraints exercised by specific cultural patterns and social structural arrangements. Status and prestige often yield material resources and thereby represent a means to an end. By incorporating sociobiological thinking into the study of the pursuit of status and prestige, it becomes possible to analyze status attainment as a goal that serves to enhance fitness, because status and prestige yield resources that can support reproductive effort. Put differently, if people express certain preferences (e.g., high status), those preferences can be explained more fully using sociobiology to identify the fitness consequences they yield. Choices and behaviors that have fitness consequences, however, are always circumscribed by environments, including the sociocultural environments in which humans identify, rank, and pursue goals.

An example of a proposition that illustrates the integration of sociobiological and rational choice thinking in DCT is the following: "Foragers adopt strategies of resource collection that will *optimize calories* produced and *minimize labor time and energy*, except when males seek to acquire resources that are *harder* to obtain and that impress women as potential mates" (Sanderson 2015: 241–42, our emphases). Rational choice theory invites the prediction that the rational pursuit of material resources favors the *maximization* of a resource's caloric value at *minimal* time and energy cost. Thus, pursuing resources that are more costly is inconsistent with rational choice theory. However, by drawing on the evolutionary theory of sexual selection, more specifically, the principle of "female choice" in the selection of a mate, it is possible to predict a female preference for males that can secure highly costly resources, thereby displaying their mate-value by displaying potential paternal investment in the female's offspring. From a sociobiological perspective, a female values a male as a potential mate on two grounds: (1) He possesses "good" (fitness maximizing) genes that can be inherited by her offspring, and (2) he can provide resources that can help support both the female and her offspring, thereby enhancing her fitness prospects. Thus, the expenditure of male effort in selectively pursuing resources that are difficult to acquire can help explain the "irrational" expenditure of male effort in failing to maximize caloric return via his efforts at "resource collection." While apparently "irrational" from the viewpoint of rational choice theory alone, viewed through the lens of sexual selection theory (female preferences in mate choice), a male's foregoing the pursuit of easily collected resources in favor of pursuing those that are harder to obtain serves both his and his prospective mate's fitness interests. Thus, an integration of sociobiology and rational choice theory provides greater explanatory purchase of a behavior than would either perspective taken alone.

Sociological Conflict Theory

Until the mid- to latter-part of the 20th Century, American sociology was dominated by the theoretical perspective known as "functionalism," or "structural-functionalism," and whose best-known proponents were Talcott Parsons and Robert K. Merton. By the 1960s, critics charged functionalism with an overemphasis on societies as largely cohesive, self-sustaining entities instantiated with mechanisms that inexorably tended to keep societies in equilibrium, or moved them toward the same when they became perturbed. Social conflict, even when acknowledged, was said to have been viewed as a "pathological" state of the overall social "system." Having been shaped disproportionately by the thought of Emile Durkheim, American sociology increasingly came under the influence of Karl Marx as early as the 1950s with the work of mid-20th Century thinkers such as Ralf Dahrendorf (1959), who sought to move sociology "out of utopia," and C. Wright Mills, who dissected America's "power elite" (1956). About the same time, and influenced by the 19th Century philosopher and sociologist Georg Simmel, Lewis Coser subjected social conflict to scrutiny in an effort to delineate its possible "functions" for society and its components (1956). By the 1960s, a new "conflict theory" was gaining ascendance in American sociology departments, and with it, a new emphasis on the nature and dynamics of social conflict. In that regard, the work of other "founding fathers" of sociology, especially Marx but also Max Weber, gained influence in the work of American sociologists determined to analyze the prevalence of social conflict in the human condition.

In 1975, Wilson published *Sociobiology: The New Synthesis*, and given the centrality of the "struggle for existence" and the importance of "competition" in evolutionary theory in evolutionary biology, one might have thought that a trend toward the integration of social conflict theory in sociology and sociobiology in behavioral biology might have begun. To the contrary, the most strident early critics of sociobiology sprouted from the Left, especially Marxist sociologists. Sanderson takes exception to this early development and sees, instead, a significant opportunity to synthesize elements of social conflict theory with sociobiology (2015: 232–34). Sanderson sees competition over resources, especially economic resources and social power, as the "essence of social life" according to conflict theorists (2015: 232). And, in fact, he describes sociobiology as the "deepest" form of conflict theory, by which he means a view of social conflict rooted in human biology. Social conflict derives from an organic foundation, from conflicts of interest at the genetic level. In fact, Sanderson contends that what the sociologist Randall Collins only labels descriptively as a "conflict-prone human nature" must be explained in evolutionary terms (2015: 233). Social conflict emerges from competition among humans for resources that are necessary for survival and the enhancement of fitness. To the degree that the realization of one actor's fitness interest comes at the expense of a competitor, the stage is set for social conflict.

Sanderson's effort to synthesize sociobiological thought with sociological conflict theory is illustrated by one of four axioms about "human interests" that he provides for his DCT project: "Humans' most important interests and concerns are reproductive, economic, and political. Political life is primarily a struggle to acquire and defend economic resources, and economic life is primarily a matter of using resources to promote reproductive success" (2015: 237). Evolutionary theory in general, and sociobiology in particular, provides an explanation of why humans value and pursue, respectively, power and material resources. Ultimately, power and material resources support reproductive effort, and the pursuit of reproductive success is the driving force of organic evolution. In a manner consistent with the conclusion that Marx and Engels drew from Darwin's *Origin of Species* as foundational to their own work on class struggle, Sanderson sees social conflict as reducible, in large part, to competition over genetic "interests," or fitness outcomes. While acquiring power and wealth may be intrinsically satisfying to humans, the capacity to experience such satisfaction itself evolved because power and wealth, and also status as would be noted by Max Weber, support reproductive success. Thus, Sanderson makes explicit elements of explanatory interconnectedness between basic ideas in sociological conflict theory and related notions in sociobiology, thereby advancing his program of developing a robust "Darwinian conflict theory."

Cultural Materialism

Closely related to strains of sociological conflict theory that are based on Marx's dialectical materialism is the anthropologist Marvin Harris' theory of cultural materialism (Harris 1979). Like sociological conflict theories based on Marx's materialist conception of history whereby basic patterns of human social interaction and the basic contours of human societies are regarded as deriving from the modes and means of production, cultural materialism sees human societies as grounded in an "infrastructure" that comprises both a "mode of production" (subsistence technology and basic features of the natural environment) and a "mode of reproduction" (population characteristics, and technologies of birth and population regulation) (Sanderson 2015: 234). Furthermore, the "structure" of society (primarily the political economy and the domestic economy) derives from the infrastructure, and the "superstructure" of society (e.g., ideology, art, music, literature, sports, science) derives from the structure. Thus, by incorporating the notion of the "mode of reproduction" into his conception of infrastructure, Harris accommodates the integration of sociobiological analysis into his cultural materialist theory of human society. In that regard, Sanderson's DCT project allows for the development of a type of societal analysis that is able to synthesize the *biological infrastructure* of human life with the societal structures and superstructures that constitute the primary foci of analysis in the social sciences, including sociology. As Sanderson puts it, Harris' contribution to DCT lies in "the postulate that evolutionary mental adaptations interact with socioecological context to produce behavioral outcomes" (2015: 236). Darwinism and Marxism are thus unified to provide a more comprehensive and complete analysis of human social behavior and societal life.

Social Evolutionism

The fourth broad school of theoretical thought in the social sciences that Sanderson seeks to synthesize with sociobiology is "social evolutionism." Social evolutionism is best known in the form of what Turner calls "stage-models" of societal evolution, and they date back to the earliest days of sociological thought (Turner 2013: 421–45, 2013). Represented by the work of founding sociologists like Herbert Spencer and Emile Durkheim as well as contemporary sociologists like Talcott Parsons, Gerhard and Jean Lenski, and Patrick Nolan, stage models of social evolution help shed light on societal dynamics, particularly on how changes in societal arrangements constitute adaptations (Sanderson 2015: 236). By integrating a focus on the evolved human propensity to pursue power with historical information about the evolution of major types of polities throughout human history, Sanderson offers no less than thirty-nine propositions that provide a broad overview of societal changes as macro-level adaptations evident in various stages of human societal evolution. He thereby adds another dimension to the development of DCT and its basic goal of explaining social conflict by means of a synthesis of sociobiological theory and theoretical thinking in the social sciences.

From Sociobiology to Evolutionary Psychology

The quest to try to identify and analyze evolved psychological processes in the human brain/mind that constitute evolved adaptations for social behavior has been taken up by behavioral and social scientists engaged in what has come to be known as *evolutionary psychology*. Many, but not all, of these researchers and scholars are professional psychologists, but others come from disciplines such as biology, anthropology, economics, political science, literary study, communication studies, management and business, law, and even sociology. Though their theoretical and empirical research approaches sometimes differ significantly, they all regard the human brain/mind as a product of organic evolution by natural selection, and they eschew the tabula rasa view that has dominated most of the behavioral and social sciences until relatively recently.

As we shall see, some of these evolutionary thinkers regard human sociobiology and evolutionary psychology as essentially the same enterprise, while others emphasize what they regard as significant differences between the two. Persuaded that the label of "evolutionary psychology" is little more than a strategy for evading the antipathy of some critics toward sociobiology, E. O. Wilson observes the following: "Given our growing understanding of gene-culture coevolution, however, and in the interest of simplicity, clarity, and—on occasion—intellectual courage in the face of ideological hostility, evolutionary psychology is best regarded as identical to human sociobiology" (1998: 150). In contrast, John Tooby (by training an anthropologist) and Leda Cosmides (by training a psychologist) who regard themselves as evolutionary psychologists distinguish between human sociobiology and evolutionary psychology: "Hence, one of the several reasons that evolutionary psychology is distinct from the fitness-teleological branch of human sociobiology and other similar approaches lies in its rejection of fitness maximization as an explanation for behavior" (Tooby and Cosmides 2016: 16, 18). Both sociobiology and evolutionary psychology entail, at a basic level, the unitary effort to analyze human behavior and the human brain/mind in terms of Darwin's theory of evolution by natural selection. Even in biology, this is a wide-ranging enterprise, and notable differences can be found among evolutionary biologists who study animal, including occasionally human, behavior. Accordingly, it is not surprising to discover differences in approaches to the study of human social behavior among scientists and scholars whose work is framed in terms of theory of organic evolution by natural selection.

Though Tooby and Cosmides' characterization of sociobiology as an instance of what they call a "fitness-*teleological*" (emphasis ours) variant of evolutionary thought is subject to dispute, they are correct in their claim that efforts to identify evolved adaptations for social behavior are central to sociobiological thinking and research (2016: 14–16). As noted in the beginning of Chapter 7, Wilson defined sociobiology very broadly "as the systematic study of the biological basis of all social behavior" (1975: 4). More specifically, however, the theoretical thought and empirical research to which most practicing sociobiologists devote themselves represent efforts to determine: (1) if specific patterns of social behavior are evolved adaptations, and (2) if so, what specific adaptive problems have they evolved to solve (Alcock 2001: 10–16, 23–40). Thus, Tooby and Cosmides are correct in locating sociobiology within "the modern adaptationist revolution in theoretical evolutionary biology," exemplified by the work of George C. Williams in his now-classic volume, *Adaptation and Natural Selection: A Critique of Some Current Evolutionary Thought* (1966) (Tooby and Cosmides 2016). Furthermore, as discussed in Chapter 7, it is the focus on ultimate, not proximate, causes of social behavior to which sociobiologists primarily devote themselves. Thus, a sociobiologist who studied extreme efforts by husbands to try to control the behavior of their wives would likely be trying to determine if this effort at hyper-controlling behavior was an expression of mate guarding, which, in turn, is conceptualized by sociobiologists as an evolved adaptation in response to the anxiety induced by the threat of paternity uncertainty. The "adaptive problem" to be solved by the husband is the threat posed to him by his wife's possible sexual infidelity. The evolved adaptation for solving this problem with which males *may* have been equipped by natural (and/or sexual) selection is an evolved psychology and derivative behavior that maximizes male vigilance and behavioral control in order to inhibit sexual infidelity by his mate. Put simply, and in terms that will be familiar to sociologists, the evolutionary function of hyper-controlling behavior by a male is to prevent his mate's being fertilized by another male, thereby presenting a direct fitness threat. Mate-guarding behaviors evolve in response to the threat of cuckoldry. Assuming that such a behavioral complex is likely to have evolved in the archaic environments in which the male's ancestors lived, the sociobiologist may then pose the question, "Are male efforts at controlling their mate's behaviors adaptive in the current environments in which humans live?" Such an inquiry would likely be framed so as to try to conduct research that would look for evidence of a correlation between this form of mate guarding and the reproductive success of males that engaged in it.

Unlike sociobiologists, evolutionary psychologists are likely to be indifferent about whether such behavior is adaptive in contemporary environments. They may very well *assume* that such behavior was adaptive in the archaic environments in which ancestral humans lived, but they are likely to be indifferent to questions of whether such behavior remains adaptive in the contemporary world. Instead, having identified a widespread, recurrent, durable human behavior, evolutionary psychologists *assume* that it is likely to have evolved in ancestral human environments in which it was then adaptive, but they neither assume, nor try to determine, if the behavior is adaptive in the environments in which humans now live. Rather, they devote themselves to the task of trying to identify evolved mental "mechanisms" that constitute the proximate causes of the behaviors under consideration, and in so doing, they attempt to reconstruct the phylogenetic histories of these behaviors. Thus, when studying a phenomenon such as behavioral cues that signify mate desirability among humans, evolutionary psychologists commonly begin with the assumption that such cues, in ancestral environments, probably signaled adaptive value in the individuals that exhibited them. Then, however, most evolutionary psychologists organize their inquiries about these cues in efforts to identify the mechanisms that produce the behaviors under consideration. Their focus is on identifying "evolved behavioral mechanisms," not on trying to determine if behaviors produced by those mechanisms are, in fact, adaptive in contemporary environments.

Notes

1 In a personal communication with Richard Machalek (1986), Wilson commented that "Sociobiology is only the application of the theory of natural selection to the study of social behavior."
2 Suffering from *bioilliteracy* about basic aspects of evolutionary biology, too many sociologists and other social scientists have been too dependent on popular accounts and criticisms of sociobiology to enable themselves to reach well-informed, independent assessments of what sociobiological thinking actually entails as well as its potential value for their own understanding of human social behavior and societal life. According to Alcock (2015), perhaps the foremost authority to whom many who are lacking in first-hand knowledge of evolutionary biology turned to for "expert counsel" was Stephen Jay Gould, many of whose criticisms of sociobiology, in Alcock's view, amounted to little more than name-calling (2015: 158). A similar lamentation of sociologists' having abdicated personal responsibility for learning what sociobiology actually entails is found in Lopreato's (1984) criticism of Richard Lewontin as a self-appointed "Paladin" who set out to "rescue" hapless social scientists from the misadventure of sociobiology (1984).
3 In personal communications with A. H. Harcourt and K. J. Stewart, Jonathan H. Turner reports that these two primatologists observed that female gorillas form a social relationship with silverbacks for convenience and safety, but they are not sexually exclusive with the silverbacks.

9
Evolutionary Psychology and the Search for the Adapted Mind

Some evolutionary thinkers regard human sociobiology and evolutionary psychology as essentially the same enterprise, while others emphasize differences between the two. Persuaded that the label of "evolutionary psychology" is little more than a strategy for evading the antipathy of some critics toward sociobiology, E. O. Wilson observes the following: "Given our growing understanding of gene-culture coevolution, however, and in the interest of simplicity, clarity, and—on occasion—intellectual courage in the face of ideological hostility, evolutionary psychology is best regarded as identical to human sociobiology" (1998: 150). In contrast, John Tooby (by training an anthropologist) and Leda Cosmides (by training a psychologist), who regard themselves as evolutionary psychologists, distinguish between human sociobiology and evolutionary psychology: "Hence, one of the several reasons that evolutionary psychology is distinct from the fitness-teleological branch of human sociobiology and other similar approaches lies in its rejection of fitness maximization as an explanation for behavior" (Tooby and Cosmides 2016: 16, 18).

Both sociobiology and evolutionary psychology entail, at a basic level, the unitary effort to analyze human behavior and the human brain/mind in terms of Darwin's theory of evolution by natural selection. Even in biology, this is a wide-ranging enterprise, and notable differences can be found among evolutionary biologists who study animal behavior, including human behavior. Accordingly, it is not surprising to discover differences in approaches to the study of human social behavior among social and behavioral scientists whose work is framed in terms of theory of organic evolution by natural selection.

Though Tooby and Cosmides' characterization of sociobiology as an instance of what they call a "fitness-*teleological*" (emphasis ours) variant of evolutionary thought is subject to dispute, they are correct in their claim that efforts to identify evolved adaptations for social behavior are central to sociobiological thinking and research (2016: 14–16). As noted in the beginning of Chapter 7, Wilson defined sociobiology very broadly, "as the systematic study of the biological basis of all social behavior" (1975: 4).

More specifically, however, the theoretical thought and empirical research to which most practicing sociobiologists devote themselves represent efforts to determine (1) if specific patterns of social behavior are evolved adaptations, and (2) if so, what specific adaptive problems have they evolved to solve (Alcock 2001: 10–16; 23–40). Thus, Tooby and Cosmides are correct in locating sociobiology within "the modern adaptationist revolution in theoretical evolutionary biology". Furthermore, as discussed in Chapter 7, it is the focus on ultimate, not proximate, causes of social behavior to which sociobiologists primarily devote themselves. Both sociobiology and evolutionary psychology are grounded in the "adaptationist revolution," but sociobiologists attempt primarily to identify the ultimate causes of a behavioral adaptation and whether that behavior is adaptive in current environments. Evolutionary psychologists also begin with the premise that a behavior may express an evolved psychological response to an archaic adaptive problem, but they are generally less interested in trying to determine if a particular pattern of behavior is adaptive in current environments. Specifically, evolutionary psychologists are interested in identifying evolved psychological adaptations that shape human behavior, regardless of whether such psychological processes are adaptive in contemporary social contexts.

According to Buss, Donald Symons' book *The Evolution of Human Sexuality* (1979) can be regarded as the "first major treatise on evolutionary psychology proper, highlighting the centrality of psychological mechanisms as adaptations, and using human sexuality as a detailed vehicle for this more general argument" (2016b: 287). Central to the evolutionary analysis of human sexuality is the study of human mating systems, which include a complex of behaviors that evolutionary psychologists call "mating strategies" (Buss 2016a; Kenrick, Maner and Li 2016: 930–33). Evolutionary psychologists have been particularly interested in mate selection and retention behaviors as two aspects of the complex suite of behaviors that they call "sexual strategies" (Buss and Schmitt 1993). Because of their direct bearing on individuals' prospects of reproductive success (Darwinian fitness), and because they are central to the establishment and maintenance of a successful mating relationship, the phenomena of mate attraction and retention provide good examples of social phenomena that illustrate the logic and goals of evolutionary psychology. In addition, by the 1990s, human mating had become the "most studied domain of evolutionary psychology," so a consideration of mate attraction and retention promises to provide an instructive vantage point from which to develop a basic understanding of evolutionary psychology itself (Buss 2016b: 280).[1]

Mate Attraction and Retention: Two Adaptive Problems and Their Solutions

Mate Attraction

As first emphasized in Trivers' theory of parental investment and sexual selection (1972), both males and females derive the same genetic "dividends" by cooperatively "investing" in the production of offspring (50% of their genes gain representation in each offspring they help produce), but the investment that each sex makes in the reproductive partnership is often asymmetrical. Among some species featuring the internal fertilization of the female's ova, the male invests nothing beyond contributing his sperm to the fertilization, and all subsequent parental investment is provided by the female. In other species with internal fertilization, the male may form a social tie with his reproductive partner that lasts throughout her pregnancy and possibly for years beyond, perhaps even his entire lifetime. In this type of reproductive scenario, while absolute parity between reproductive partners may never occur, a considerable degree of symmetry may very well develop between them in terms of the parental investment that each provides.

Each reproductive partner represents a certain type and degree of "value" to the other in terms of the prospective fitness dividends that each can derive from their reproductive partnership (Sugiyama 2016: 324–31). Mate value is expressed by two types of resources that are brought to the reproductive partnership: *somatic* resources (e.g., labor, food, nests), which contribute to the survival and general health and well-being of each partner, and *reproductive* resources, including the quality of genes transmitted by the successful fertilization of an ovum. As discussed in Chapter 7, sociobiologists have done a great deal of research on sexual selection, including research on processes by means of which individuals display their mate value to prospective reproductive partners. When the study organisms are humans, evolutionary scientists, especially evolutionary psychologists, conduct much of this research under the rubrics of "mate preferences" and "physical attractiveness" (Buss 1989; Schmitt 2016; Sugiyama 2016). Much of this research has been devoted to identifying processes by means of which individuals choose particular mates over others. The qualities desired in prospective mates vary according to a number of criteria, and evolutionary psychologists characterize humans as a species that has evolved a "pluralistic mating repertoire," one which is "facultatively responsive to sex, temporal contexts, personal characteristics such as mate value and ovulatory status, and evocative of features of culture and local ecology" (Schmitt 2016: 294). Put simply, humans display diverse mating strategies ranging from lifelong monogamy to variants of polygamy including polygyny, polyandry, and promiscuity.

Evolutionary psychologists David Buss and David Schmitt have extended Trivers' theory of parental investment and sexual selection to develop "sexual strategies theory" (1993). A basic dimension along which human mating systems vary is the duration of a mating relationship, and evolutionary psychologists distinguish between "long-term" and "short-term" sexual strategies (Buss and Schmitt 1993; Buss 2016a). Short-term sexual strategies can be nearly ephemeral, lasting little more than the duration of interactions that lead up to and conclude with sexual intercourse. Long-term strategies can last for the lifetimes of each mate. Evolutionary psychologists have identified sex differences in patterns of long-term and short-term mating, including variability in the qualities that participants prefer in partners as well as the types of benefits that derive from these two types of mating strategies (Buss 1989; Schmitt 2016: 297–300).

Ceteris paribus, men risk much less and stand to gain much more in terms of fitness benefits provided by short-term mating relationships than do women. If a male achieves a mating that is injudicious (i.e., maladaptive in Darwinian terms), he has sacrificed only the time and energy required to achieve the mating. If, however, a female makes a maladaptive mating choice, becomes pregnant, and bears an offspring with low survival and reproductive prospects, she has incurred a much greater and long-term obligatory reproductive commitment that may yield poor fitness returns. The basic limiting constraint on lifetime reproductive success for a male is the number of fertilizations he can achieve. Daly and Wilson report that Moulay Ismail, one-time emperor of Morocco, sired 888 offspring (1988: 134). In contrast, the most children to have been born to one mother was 69 (Puts et al. 2016: 386). For females, lifetime reproductive success is limited basically by demands of obligatory parental (maternal) investment. Internal fertilization and gestation obligate a female to a 9-month month commitment which is followed by up to 4 years of lactation and nursing per offspring. Accordingly, the *potential* lifetime reproductive success of women is much lower than it is for men.

Though both men and women can benefit (in fitness terms) from both short-term and long-term mating strategies, the nature of the benefits varies between the sexes and by local circumstance. Nevertheless, both men and women express preferences for similar qualities in mates such as intelligence, being kind and understanding, and in good health. In fact, in a research program on thirty-seven cultures that has come to be regarded as something of a classic in evolutionary psychology, Buss and his colleagues (Buss 1989; Buss et al. 1990) identified attributes that members of each sex target in a desirable mate. Among eighteen such traits, males and females rank the top four identically: (1) mutual attraction-love, (2) dependable character, (3) emotional stability and maturity, and (4) pleasing disposition (in Hopcroft 2016: 35). Furthermore, though the rankings differ slightly, nine of the top ten traits identified as desirable by both sexes are identical. Evidence indicates that prospective mates also look for similarity in attitudes, personality traits, and religious beliefs (Buss 2003, 2016a: 136). It is not surprising to find such overlap between males and females in terms of the qualities they prefer in a mate, because such cues signal the likelihood that a reproductive partnership formed by individuals expressing such traits will produce healthy offspring as well as the requisite quality and quantity of parental investment to insure that the offspring will survive to reproductive age. In short, evolutionary psychologists have identified a number of traits common to both sexes that function as cues to good parenting.

However, natural selection also favors differences in female versus male preferences for mates, because males and females confront different adaptive problems relevant to mating and reproductive success. A brief review of these differences will illustrate what evolutionary psychologists have learned about evolved male-female differences in mate preference, specifically, what they have learned about physical and behavioral qualities that members of each sex find attractive in the other. And, as we shall see, evolutionary psychologists have emphasized that mate preference cues comprise suites of qualities, the salience of which varies between short-term and long-term mating behaviors, by cultural context, by local ecological circumstances, by sex ratios, and by other situational conditions and dynamics as well (Schmitt 2016: 304–309).

What Do Women Want in a Mate, and Why?

A simple thought experiment makes vivid why evolutionary theory leads to predictions that humans possess evolved psychological preferences for certain types of mates rather than others (Buss 2016a: 102–103). Assuming that genetic differences in prospective mates contribute to variability in the likelihood of offspring survival and healthy development, and assuming that observable physical and behavioral variation among individuals provides cues about such genetic differences, it is plausible to predict that individuals would evolve sensitivities to those cues and the fitness-relevant information encoded in them. Imagine two individuals, A and B, both of whom are seeking a mate. Imagine further that A lacks any ability to detect cues in prospective mates that might influence survival and developmental prospects of that prospective mate's offspring. Assume, in contrast, that B is able to detect in prospective mates cues that provide reliable information about the survival and developmental prospects of offspring produced by prospective mates. Sexual selection theory leads to the prediction, then, that B would be more likely to make mate choices that would be fitness-enhancing than would A. Put differently, B's alleles would be more likely to proliferate over generational time than would A's alleles, because B's alleles would equip B with the ability to detect and respond advantageously (from a fitness-enhancing perspective) to qualities in prospective mates that would signal their "mate value," a concept that refers to potential of an individual to contribute to the reproductive success of a mated pair (Sugiyama 2016).

Sugiyama uses the term "attractiveness" to designate adaptations in individuals that constitute "evolutionarily relevant cues to human social value across multiple domains of interaction," including cues that signify mate value (2016: 317). Further elaborating the thought experiment described above, imagine an individual in possession of an evolved psychology of utter indifference to physical and behavioral variation in prospective mates, a psychology that would make *all members of the opposite sex equally attractive as prospective mates* (Buss 2016a: 102). Assume further, however, that physical and behavioral variation among prospective mates is not "fitness neutral," that is, assume that some types and degrees of such variation do, in fact, signal variability in the ability of prospective mates to produce offspring whose survival and reproductive chances are not all equal. In this scenario, selection would favor an individual who is able to discern such variability and direct his/her mating effort toward prospective mates with the highest "mate value." Over time, the array of alleles possessed by such an individual would gain greater representation in descendant populations than those of an individual whose alleles made him/her utterly indifferent to cues of mate value. It is this logic, derived from Darwin's theory of sexual selection and Trivers' derivative theory of parental investment, which has guided evolutionary psychologists in their research on mating and mating systems.

In effect, evolutionary psychologists have reintroduced Freud's famous question, "What does a woman want?" But they have framed his question anew, in a Darwinian key: What do women want in a man, and why? Furthermore, they have supplemented Freud's question with a second: What do men want in a woman, and why? From an evolutionary perspective, one would predict that human females would be expected to have evolved a psychology that would express preferences for qualities in a mate that would increase their fitness prospects. And, as should be clear by this point in our deliberations, evolutionary thinking by *either* sociobiologists or evolutionary psychologists does not require that females conceptualize fitness as a conscious goal toward which they would be expected to strive, despite Tooby and Cosmides' curious, and in our view misplaced, concern about "fitness teleology" in sociobiological analysis (2016: 14). Instead, if females have evolved a psychology that causes them to view as more attractive those traits in a male that have the consequence, typically unintended, of enhancing their production of offspring that survive to reproductive age, then selection will favor both those male traits as well as female preferences for them. The same logic, of course, applies to males, but only some of the same traits are likely to be viewed as equally attractive in both females and males, given biological differences in the respective roles played by males and females in their reproductive partnerships.

This is not to say, however, that a heritable preference for certain sorts of traits necessarily confers better health or survival prospects on the bearers of those traits. For example, if females possess an allele that simply has the effect of making them prefer a certain quality in males, irrespective of the survival value conferred or not conferred by that trait, and if that allele predisposes them to mate preferentially with such males, then the female preference for that male trait can evolve purely by the dynamics of sexual selection. Accordingly, caution should be exercised in concluding that a male trait that is the target of female preference necessarily confers enhanced survival prospects for any offspring produced by that male. In non human species, biologists label such traits as "ornaments" (e.g., the peacock's tail), and the ornament may serve only to attract mates even while failing to provide survival or health benefits to the ornament's bearer or the bearer's offspring. If the trait, such as the peacock's ostentatious tail, does not produce maladaptive consequences (e.g., increasing risk of predation) for offspring, then it can proliferate simply as a result of female preference and choice, regardless of its non-adaptive consequences. Acknowledgement by sociobiologists and evolutionary psychologists of the process by which sexual selection can cause females to favor traits in males that are irrelevant to their health and survival illustrates the misplaced nature of the claim by critics such as Stephen Jay Gould and Richard Lewontin that both sociobiologists and evolutionary psychologists mindlessly favor an "adaptationist programme" that advocates the view that all traits are adaptive and that the task of evolutionary analysts is but to identify the putative adaptive value of a trait and construct a "just-so story" about how it evolved and what adaptive function it performs (1979). Rather, the existence and acknowledgement by evolutionary psychologists (and sociobiologists) of traits that are adaptively neutral in terms of survival benefits conferred but, rather, are the product of sexual selection makes clear the absence of an "adaptationist programme" among these behavioral scientists (Alcock 2001: 57–68).

What sorts of male traits have been identified by evolutionary psychological theory and research as among those toward which human females are drawn in their search for mates, and why? Stated slightly differently, what qualities in a male are females likely to find as attractive in a prospective mate, and why are these qualities the targets of female preferences? From the standpoint of a female's genetic interests, a prospective mate constitutes an array of two types of resources: (1) reproductive resources, primary among which are "good genes" that can enhance the survival and reproductive prospects of her offspring (e.g., genes that confer parasite resistance as explained by Hamilton and Zuk 1982), and (2) somatic resources in the form of food, shelter, protection, parental care, and other types of resources that contribute to the health, general well-being, and survival prospects of her offspring. In short, beyond providing "good genes" to her offspring, a male can provide "good parenting" to a mother's offspring. By this logic, females should possess an evolved psychology that directs them preferentially toward males that can provide both of these types of resources.

Epigenesis and the principle of gene-environment interaction in the expression of a genotype means that any evolved psychological adaptations for mate preference never operate in an environmental vacuum, that is to say, in the absence of various contextual and situational factors, including historical, social structural, and cultural contexts. Contextual effects exert their influence with regard to both short-term and long-term mating strategies, and they operate on both female and male decision-making. Contextual effects that can influence a woman's mate preferences include factors such as personal resources she controls (including economic resources and political power), the mate preferences exercised by other women (a form of cultural influence), the expected (or desired) duration of the mating relationship, and the mate value of the woman herself, which influences the degree of choice that she can exercise in selecting a mate (Buss 2016a: 122–25). Contextual factors that influence men's mate preferences include the positions they occupy in stratification systems, "contrast effects" created by comparing prospective mates to images of women presented in various media, physiological states (such as testosterone levels) created by a man's relationship status, and the mate value of the male pursing a mate (Buss 2016a: 152–56).

For both short-term and long-term mating opportunities, females are expected to possess specialized evolved psychological adaptations that express themselves as preferences based on their estimates of a male's mate value (Sugiyama 2016: 324–31). That is, evolutionary reasoning leads to the prediction that females will prefer as mates males of high mate value. Though both females and males can be expected to have preferences for healthy mates with prospects of producing healthy offspring, parental investment theory invites the additional prediction that a significant determinant of perceived mate value in males is any cue that indicates both the male's *ability* and *overt propensity* to behave as a reliable provider. Accordingly, females should be expected to be alert to and attracted by cues that indicate interpersonal compatibility, good health, good parenting skills, physical capabilities for providing protection to both the female and her offspring, and what biologists call high "resource holding potential" (RHP), the ability to acquire and provide somatic resources, as well as overt behavioral evidence of resource acquisition and reliable, long-term provision of the same (Buss 2016a: 106).

A large body of empirical research conducted by evolutionary psychologists, including cross-cultural studies, reveals clear female preferences for long-term mates that exhibit the following qualities: higher social status, the possession of economic resources and prospects for financial success, age and maturity, evidence of ambitiousness, and evidence of behavioral dependability and stability (Buss 2016a: 105–14; Schmitt 2016: 297–98). Male physical attributes that signal high potential parental investment include height and athletic ability, strength, bilateral symmetry (an indicator of developmental regularity), and physical cues signifying masculinity (Buss 2016a:114–18). These and related traits translate into high RHP, thereby qualifying the male as a *potentially* competent and reliable provider of somatic resources. Additional cues provide information about overt paternal behaviors that realize a male's RHP by converting it into actual provisioning and protection of the mother and her offspring. These cues indicate behavioral evidence of qualities such as a male's kindness and generosity, his emotional predisposition to nurturance, his expression of an ability to love and commit to others, and evidence of his willingness to devote time and other resources to invest in and care for children (Buss 2016a:118–22; Ellis 1992; Feingold 1992; Schmitt 2016: 297–98).

Until recently, before efforts to integrate neo-Darwinian theory and research into psychology, studies of human mating conducted by psychologists were "barely visible on the scientific map" and "woefully simplistic," and the phenomenon of short-term mating strategies, especially as exercised by women, was "largely ignored" (Buss 2016b: 289–90). Extending Symons' early explanations of the significant potential fitness benefits for men provided by short-term matings, Buss and Schmitt's sexual strategies theory revealed potential fitness benefits of short-term matings that could accrue to women as well (1993). For women, selective engagement in short-term matings can yield five categories of potential benefits: (1) immediate access to resources, especially resources controlled by high-status males; (2) high-quality genes, even for women in a monogamous, pair-bonded relationship; (3) the replacement of a current mate of lower mate value for one of higher mate value; (4) assessing a male's quality as a prospective long-term mate (what might whimsically be called the "try to buy plan"); and (5) a strategy for controlling/manipulating a mate by engaging in extra-pair copulations as a way of exercising revenge for his infidelity and threatening him with further infidelity, as well as providing "stark evidence" to her mate of *her* mate value to other males (Buss 2016a: 178–80). Thus, it is clear that short-term matings can confer fitness benefits either to a female without a mate or to a female in a pair-bonded mate relationship.

What Do Men Want in a Mate and Why?

The dramatic differences between a man's potential lifetime reproductive success versus that of a woman might lead to the prediction that human males should adopt but one mating strategy: promiscuity that is limited only by the availability of female sexual partners. The facts of human reproductive biology alone could be cited to support such a speculation. The maximum number of offspring sired by a man has been over 1,000 (Puts, Bailey, and Reno 2016: 386). If a man mates with 100 fertile women per year, he can produce as many as 100 offspring, but a female typically can produce only 1 baby per year (Schmitt 2016: 298). Buss (2016a: 103) reports that human males can produce 12 million sperm per hour, but a female produces only about 400 ovulated eggs over the course of her lifetime. Still, the production of sperm by males is not unlimited. According to Shackelford et al. (2016), sperm are costly to produce, and the frequency of ejaculation as well as the variable circumstances of ejaculation (copulation, masturbation, nocturnal emission) influence both the number and quality of sperm (e.g., motility) contained in the ejaculate. Consequently, a phenomenon called "prudent sperm allocation" has been discovered in number of species, including humans (Shackelford et al. 2016). Prudent sperm allocation refers to the (unconscious) ability of males to adjust the number of sperm delivered by the male "during each insemination in response to auditory, chemosensory, tactile, or visual *cues* of sperm competition (Shackelford et al. 2016: 428). If a male detects the likelihood of recent (within 5 days) multiple matings by his female partner, mechanisms of prudent sperm allocation can adjust the amount of sperm he delivers during copulation. Nevertheless, the extraordinary abundance of male gametes relative to those of females strongly implies the likelihood of the evolution of a male mating psychology that favors multiple matings with multiple females, and less concern by males with mate quality than that which would be expected from females.

All the same, the significant asymmetry between women and men in lifetime reproductive potential does not mean that males should always be expected to pursue a mating strategy of promiscuity. In that humans are a highly altricial species, and because a man's offspring can benefit significantly from his paternal investment, monogamy can be a reproductive strategy by means of which many, if not most, males can achieve the highest level of lifetime reproductive success in the context of constraints on mating opportunity, including sociocultural constraints, to which men are commonly subjected. As a result, natural selection can favor male mating strategies that are selective in terms of female reproductive partners. Though sexual selection theory commonly touts "choosiness" among females, the exercise of male choosiness can also be fitness-enhancing for his lifetime reproductive prospects. What specific qualities should a man prefer in a woman with whom he aspires to mate? And what sort of evolved psychology might we expect in a male whose mating efforts are guided by fitness-enhancing preferences?

As with females, male preferences in reproductive partners vary between their adoptions of short-term versus long-term mating strategies. The dominant criterion guiding male short-term mating strategies is the pursuit of the maximum number of partners available. In support of this approach, research has documented men's desire for maximum variety in mates, a willingness by males to engage in sex very soon after meeting a woman, and a much greater willingness to have sex with women described as displaying "average attractiveness" (Schmitt 2016: 298–300). By way of contrast, women are much less predisposed to try to maximize the number of men with whom they have sex, are much more reluctant to engage in sex soon after meeting a man, and are much more likely to require that the man be "highly attractive" if he is to be a short-term mating partner. But even then, women are very unlikely to have short-term sex with a man whom they have just met and who is essentially a stranger (Schmitt 2016: 300).

It is in the context of pursuing long-term mating strategies that men's preferences for mates best illustrates the adaptive problems with which they are confronted in expending mating effort. Only the failure to secure a mating partner at all presents a greater adaptive challenge to males than suffering the fate of being cuckolded. Some estimates of the incidence of babies born to "extra pair paternity" (EPP) have ranged from 10–30%, but recent research reveals that the incidence is much closer to 1–2% (Larmuseau, Matthijs, and Wenseleers 2016: 327). In fact, by using methods employing both genetic and genealogical information, researchers estimate that the incidence of EPP has been nearly constant at about 1% for several hundred years (Larmuseau, Matthijs, and Wenseleers 2016: 328). However, the male *fear* of being cuckolded need not be proportionate to the actual, objective threat to paternity posed by EPP. For example, Sugiyama reports that "A man who maintained exclusive mating access to a woman over her reproductive lifetime could, on average, sire five or six children with her" (2016: 331). Imagine that the number were five, and one of those five was the product of EPP. This would mean that, though the man was among a very small proportion of men who were cuckolded, 20% of his parental investment (PI) was provided to another man's child (assuming that the PI was distributed evenly among the five offspring). If the man's wife produced only two or three children and one was the product of EPP, then 33–50% of the man's PI was unknowingly allocated to another man's child. In Darwinian terms, these are not insignificant fitness costs. Interestingly, some evolutionary psychologists have employed an analogy derived from a hunting context to label "rivals who attempt to lure someone else's mate away either for a sexual encounter or for a long-term relationship," and they call such interlopers "poachers" (Schmitt and Buss 2001). The threat that a mate will be usurped by a rival will be discussed later, in relation to the topic of mate retention (or mate guarding, as sociobiologists call it), as will evolved psychological adaptations for coping with this fitness threat.

Thus, although the risk of being cuckolded is very small, the actual fitness costs in terms of "misallocated" paternal investment incurred by the cuckold can be extremely high. Consequently, it should not be surprising to discover that men often experience an incidence and degree of paternity anxiety that is very high, despite the low incidence of the threat itself. Accordingly, even in the face of a low incidence, the high cost of being cuckolded could explain high levels of evolved paternity anxiety among males. Furthermore, the threat of cuckoldry is often encoded in culture in the form of what could be seen as Simmelian social types. In the military, the mythical figure of "Jody" plays this role. Jody is the man "back home" with whom the soldier's wife is committing adultery, and Jody is a recurrent character in soldiers' conservations about their girlfriends and wives. In some Latino cultures, the figure of "Sancho" plays the same role. Sancho is the guy who vaults over the back fence when the husband returns home unexpectedly. The figure of the "milkman" who delivers milk to homes unoccupied by husbands was, in an earlier era, another cultural representation of the same threat. Thus, acting on an evolved emotion of male sexual jealousy, cultural forces can easily amplify paternity anxiety to a degree that is disproportionate to the actual incidence of EPP. The threat that a mate will be usurped by a rival will be discussed later in relation to the topic of mate retention (guarding) and evolved psychological adaptations for coping with this fitness threat.

In the context of both short-term and long-term matings, evolutionary theory suggests that men should have evolved preferences for cues that signal health and fertility in prospective mates. In fact, evolutionary psychologists routinely conceptualize beauty as a constellation of traits that are correlated with health, fertility, and promising fitness outcomes (Sugiyama 2016; Symons 1995). It is interesting to note that some of these traits, such as bilateral symmetry, allow conceptions of beauty to be calibrated by local cultural influences. Thus, variation in a phenotypic trait such as body weight can be subject to cultural constructions of ideal beauty, and these constructions vary both across cultures and sometimes, in a single culture over time. For example, in some cultures, or during certain historical periods, heavier people may be seen as more beautiful than thinner people (think of women in Rubens' paintings versus contemporary runway models), but regardless of weight, greater bilateral symmetry has been found to be correlated consistently with the perception that a person is attractive. Similarly, during the agrarian era of American history, very light skin color among Caucasians was seen signifying beauty, but by the mid-20th Century, a "good tan" had come to be viewed as attractive. During both historical periods, however, evolutionary psychologists would predict that people who are more symmetrical would have been viewed as more attractive than people with less symmetrical traits, regardless of their skin tone.

Though evolutionary psychology, as a distinct scientific discipline, is less than 40 years old, it has produced a surprisingly large literature of theoretical thought and empirical research about traits that comprise attractiveness and beauty in prospective mates (Sugiyama 2016). Evolutionary psychologists have documented the existence of widespread, cross-cultural evidence of mate preferences that are cues of health and phenotypic and genotypic quality in both males and females. Included among such traits are skin quality (color, texture, color homogeneity); hair quality (length, lustrousness); and fluctuating asymmetry, an indicator of developmental stability in response to environmentally induced stress (Sugiyama 2016: 338–50). In addition, evolutionary psychologists have adduced evidence that some traits which constitute cues of potential mate value vary between males and females, and they call these traits "sexually dimorphic cues to health and phenotypic and genotypic quality" (Sugiyama 2016: 353). Among the most widely reported and best documented traits that males seek in mates are youth, length and quality of women's hair, skin quality, facial symmetry, facial "averageness," overall body fat distribution as measured by weight to height (body mass index, or BMI), body shape (especially waist-to-hip ratio, or WHP), and "femininity" (Buss 2016a; Sugiyama 2016: 329–31).[2] Though considerable empirical research on these cues as targets of male preference in mates has yielded extensive findings, it is clear that traits such as fluctuating asymmetry feature a great deal of complexity, and the fitness-relevant information encoded in this cue is often context-dependent. Consider, for example, but one cue pertaining to body fat distribution in women: the deposition of gluteofemoral fat (GFF). Gluteofemoral fat differs from abdominal and visceral fat in that it is richer in long-chain polyunsaturated fatty acids (LCPUFAS), which are required for fetal and infant brain development (Sugiyama 2016: 361). Accordingly, fats deposited in the gluteofemoral region of females became targets for mate preference assessments by males. In fact, research by evolutionary psychologists indicates possible complex interrelatedness between female WHP and GFF in attracting men to some female phenotypes over others.

Similarly, fluctuating asymmetry (FA) as a preference cue exhibits considerable complexity, including sensitivity to context effects. For example, females with low FA fare better on measures of health and fitness, and their facial symmetry seems to be more important than their body symmetry. Nevertheless, it is possible that the relationship between FA and health may be more salient as a mate preference cue in populations inhabiting environments plagued by stressors such as disease, high levels of pathogens, and dietary deficiencies (Sugiyama 2016: 345–50). In less stressful environments, the salience of FA as a fitness cue may diminish. Thus, though evolutionary theory and much of the empirical research that it has inspired provides support for the notion that humans are likely to possess evolved psychological adaptations for mate selection, the complexity of any such mechanisms and their likely sensitivity to variation in the contexts in which they are expressed requires evolutionary scientists to exercise caution in the ways they invoke these putative adaptations to explain mating behaviors.

Finally, in addition to physical cues, evolutionary psychologists hypothesize that males may also possess evolved psychological adaptations that target female behaviors as cues of mate value, especially cues that might indicate sexual fidelity in female mates. As reported earlier, research conducted on thirty-seven cultures by Buss and his colleagues (Buss et al. 1990) revealed that the most desirable trait in a prospective mate, as ranked by both men and women, is "mutual attraction-love," and the next three traits are dependable character, emotional stability and maturity, and a pleasing disposition. All of these constitute cues that are essentially behavioral in nature, though "attraction" could include physical qualities as well. Love and being possessed of a "dependable character" almost certainly increase the prospects of sexual fidelity in a mate, and the high ranking of these two traits as qualities desired by both women and men is not at all surprising, because both of these traits provide solutions to the adaptive problem of mate retention and fidelity, the topic to which we now turn.

Mate Retention

By definition, mate retention is not an adaptive problem for individuals pursuing short-term matings. But it is a critical issue, for both males and females, who are in pursuit of long-term mating relationships. This is especially true when mate retention efforts are directed toward a partner with high mate value. The sociobiological and evolutionary psychological focus on mate retention is a topic that is easily subsumed under general phenomenon of "control." The sociologist Jack P. Gibbs contends that all scientific disciplines need a "central notion" that guides their thinking and research, and Gibbs proposes "control" as a candidate for sociology's "central notion" (1989). In most basic terms, the adaptive problem of mate retention among humans is the problem whereby both men and women need to be able to exercise control over the behavior of their mates so as to yield favorable fitness outcomes from the mating relationship. In that regard, we see a remarkable convergence between evolutionary and sociological theory, the full implications of which have yet to be specified and fully developed.

Mate retention refers not only to the basic problem of maintaining a stable, enduring relationship with a mate, it also includes any behavior by means of which one partner inhibits rivals from usurping mate value from one's partner as well as preventing one's mate from allocating mate value to mate "poachers." Among women, for example, this commonly means exercising control over the conduct of their male partners so as to make sure that they provide somatic resources to themselves and their offspring rather than to a female rival and any offspring she might have. Among men, this commonly entails efforts to inhibit any inclinations by their partners to mate with other men. Evolutionary psychologists have identified mate retention strategies employed by both men and women, and they have reported evidence from empirical inquiries designed to search for evolved psychological adaptations that enable mate retention efforts. We will review briefly some of these male and female strategies for mate retention.

From an evolutionary standpoint, it is arguable that an important precondition for men and women to be able to exercise control over each other's behavior is the ability of humans to form and maintain strong interpersonal social ties. Maryanski and Turner (1992), Turner (2000), and Turner and Maryanski (2008a) provide an evolutionary analysis of the selection forces and phylogeny of hominins that eventually made it possible for humans to form and maintain strong, long-term, stable social ties based on emotions. Like other apes, and unlike monkeys, early humans lacked the ability to form and maintain all but a few types of strong social ties. It was only when selection forces "remodeled" the hominin brain so as to enhance the "emotional palette" with which early humans became equipped that they became able to form strong, durable social ties that could become the foundation of enhanced group solidarity, including solidarity within the mated pair (Turner and Maryanski 2008a).

Consistent with Turner's and Maryanski's analysis, evolutionary psychologists have identified evolved psychological adaptations to which they attribute the ability of humans to form and maintain strong mating ties, and on the basis of which mates can exercise control of each other's behaviors. The fundamental emotion on the basis of which a stable mating bond can develop and be maintained is love (Fletcher et al. 2014; 2015). The evolutionary psychologists Campbell and Loving (2016) distinguish between "passionate love" and "companionate love" as two emotions that are foundational to pair-bonding mating systems. Both of these emotions are interpreted as "commitment devices," each of which supports mate retention strategies employed by both men and women (Campbell and Loving 2016: 492–94). Passionate love comprises the development of intense feelings between individuals that also commonly entails sexual intimacy. Strong, positive interpersonal feelings also characterize companionate love, but they are less intense than those characterizing passionate love, and they typically do not lead to sexual intimacy (Campbell and Loving 2016: 483–85). Romantic mating relationships feature elements of both passionate and companionate love, and strong friendship (companionate love) has been identified as an important component of stable, long-term mate relationships. Campbell and Loving note that, from the earliest days of its emergence, evolutionary thinking in psychology has interpreted romantic love as a "commitment device to maintain relational bonds between mothers and fathers and to facilitate mutual investment in offspring" (2016: 485). The formation of strong pair bonds promotes high levels of parental investment by both mates, and this commonly yields enhanced fitness (Geary 2000). Evolutionary psychologists engaged in the study of the biological foundations of love and mating systems have analyzed the manner in which various hormones (including cortisol, testosterone, and oxytocin) are implicated in either inhibiting or promoting the formation and maintenance of love-based mating relationships (Campbell and Loving 2016).

If love is the emotion upon which strong mating ties are formed and maintained, jealousy is the evolved emotional response to threats confronting mate relationships, and it is jealousy that commonly activates behavioral tactics that contribute to mate retention. Jealousy is a "negative emotional experience resulting from the potential loss of valued relationships to real or imagined rivals" (Campbell and Loving 2016: 493; Salovey 1991). Though psychologists have determined that women and men both experience jealousy at common frequencies and with equal intensity, the nature of jealousy that is precipitated in the context of a mate relationship differs between women and men. In that regard, evolutionary psychologists distinguish between jealously as a response to perceived sexual infidelity, versus jealousy as a response to perceived emotional infidelity. A substantial body of empirical research has established that men are more likely to be disturbed by the prospect of sexual infidelity committed by their mate, while women are more disturbed by the prospect of their mate's committing emotional jealousy (Buss 2000).

When viewed from the vantage point of evolutionary theory, particularly the theory of parental investment, these male-female differences in the nature of jealousy become clear. Infidelity comprises an adaptive problem for any individual, male or female, confronting it. However, the specific consequences of infidelity pose different threats to males than they do to females. Specifically, infidelity poses the threat of cuckoldry to males, the threat of providing paternal investment to another man's offspring. Because of the biology of internal fertilization, females do not confront the threat of cuckoldry, but infidelity by their mates can threaten them and their offspring with a "misallocation" of their mate's paternal investment to the offspring of another female. Thus, while the prospect of their mate's having sexual intercourse with another man is highly disturbing to men, the prospects of a man's forming a close emotional tie to a rival woman is highly disturbing to women. In short, men are most troubled by sexual infidelity, and women are most troubled by emotional infidelity. Thus, both types of infidelity pose fitness threats, but the nature of the threat differs between men and women, and as a result, the nature of the jealously experienced also differs. Buss concludes that over 100 empirical studies support the assertion that males and females possess sex-specific design features in the psychology of jealously, features that reflect the different adaptive threats that infidelity poses to males versus females (2016a: 333–34).

Both types of jealousy can activate mate retention tactics for coping with the fitness threat posed by infidelity, and we will review briefly tactics commonly employed by women for mate retention and tactics employed by men.

Female Tactics for Mate Retention

Although evolutionary psychologists do not routinely characterize it as such, an evolutionary sociologist is likely to conceptualize a mate relationship as an *exchange relationship*. Fundamentally, a mate relationship forms when a female and a male cooperate to provide both somatic and reproductive resources in the production of offspring. A stable mate relationship is a stable exchange relationship. In exchange theory terms, an exchange relationship is jeopardized when either or both parties to the exchange fails to meet the terms of the exchange in providing the resource(s) on which the relationship is based. From an exchange perspective, mate retention constitutes the adaptive challenge of assuring that one's mate remains in the exchange relationship and provides the resources on which her/his partner depends.

From the perspective of a woman's fitness interests, male mate value consists of two dimensions: (1) the quality of genes a male can provide and (2) the somatic resources a male can provide. Somatic resources include basic forms of paternal investment such as child care and protection, other forms of labor (energy), information, and material resources available to the male. Retaining a male means retaining access to these resources. Once secured, a female need not be concerned with the retention of "good genes" provided by the male, but the reliable provision of all other types of resources is contingent on effective mate retention. A male's mate value is evident in a number of ways. First, the qualities that females prefer in mates converge on traits that are relevant to resource provision, including his access to economic resources, the social status he occupies, his age, and physical and behavioral qualities that relate directly to his ability to procure and provide resources (e.g., health/strength, ambition and industriousness, dependability and stability, all of which have been documented by empirical research as being important criteria employed by women in their selection of a mate). The loss of a mate to a rival, then, means the loss of the resources he can provide in the exchange relationship. Second, the precedence of emotional jealousy over sexual jealousy among women indicates the threat of losing a mate to his forming a strong emotional tie to another woman, and thus, the implicit threat of his redirecting resources from the woman and her children to a rival and her offspring. For a woman, mate retention means resource retention, and emotional jealousy is an evolved psychological mechanism that motivates a woman to employ mate retention tactics in the face of a threat posed by a rival. If a woman can retain a mate, she is maintaining a stable exchange relationship from which she benefits by receiving somatic resources from the male and, in the case of subsequent pregnancies, possible high-value genetic resources as well.

According to considerable empirical research conducted by evolutionary psychologists, women have at their disposal a variety of mate retention tactics. First, they can employ behaviors designed to enhance their beauty and appearance, especially by making themselves appear younger and thereby displaying higher mate value. Second, they can behave so as to attract the attention of other males, thereby providing clear evidence of their mate value and the tenuousness of the pair bond between themselves and their mate. Deliberately inducing jealousy in a mate is a tactic employed more commonly by women than by men (Buss 2016: 337). Third, they can derogate the mate value of other women who might become rivals in their efforts at mate retention (Buss and Dedden 1990). Fourth, to the extent that they control somatic resources upon which their mate depends, they can exercise advantage in a "power-dependency" relationship with their mate (Emerson 1972). Women also employ some of the same mate retention tactics adopted by males, including efforts to maintain constant and close proximity to their mate, using emotional manipulation to control their mate, signaling compliance and subordination (recall discussion of Hopcroft's work on young females' expression of deference to males in Chapter 8), and threatening rival females (Buss 2016: 36). For the most part, however, female mate retention tactics entail efforts to maximize their perceived mate value to their mate, and this often entails efforts to enhance their beauty and a youthful appearance, both cues of fertility and high reproductive value. It is important to recall that these cues of female mate value have been documented in cross-cultural analyses such as the study conducted by Buss on mating systems in thirty-seven cultures. The male preference for youth and beauty is not restricted to contemporary, western contexts and very well may represent an evolved behavioral propensity universal among humans.

Male Tactics for Mate Retention

As discussed earlier, the greatest adaptive threat confronted by males with established mating relationships is female sexual infidelity. Accordingly, evolutionary reasoning invites the prediction that males are likely to be hyper-vigilant to this threat and are likely to employ multiple behavioral tactics in order to neutralize it. In fact, researchers have documented the existence of an "infidelity overperception bias" that reflects a hypersensitivity to the threat of sexual infidelity by a partner, and men display this bias more so than do women (Andrews et al. 2008; Buss 2016a; Goetz and

Causey 2009). Buss describes male tactics of mate retention as ranging from "vigilance to violence," and we will review briefly some of the tactics males employ in their efforts to cope with the adaptive problem of female sexual infidelity.

Though unlikely to be exhaustive, it is possible to identify at least six types of mate retention tactics commonly employed by males. These include: (1) sequestering the female from potential rivals, (2) magnifying the male's mate value to his mate, (3) emotional manipulation, (4) communicating compliance to the female, (5) threat signals and behavior, and (6) overt violence.[3] Though women also employ some of these mate retention tactics on occasion, men are more likely to try to conceal and sequester their mates from potential rivals. Though not framed in terms of an evolutionary perspective, an influential analysis of the effects of sex ratios on gender relations conducted by Guttentag and Secord (1983) provides vivid historical examples of the extremes to which men will go to isolate women, especially women of prime reproductive age, from male rivals. The extremes taken by men in classical Athenian society in order to control and subjugate women were nothing short of astounding, especially in a society that purported to advocate the advantages of a democratic polity. It is also not surprising that men will display conspicuously resources they control in an effort to maximize their perceived mate value to both their mates and to prospective mates. This is a propensity that has been documented and systematically analyzed by sociologists at least as early as Thorstein Veblen's classic, *The Theory of the Leisure Class* (1899). In his discussion of the phenomenon of conspicuous consumption, a clear example of resource display, Veblen contends that men use this behavior to "display prowess," an observation entirely consistent with current evolutionary thinking about mating and mate retention strategies. Conspicuous consumption advertises both status and resources, assets of prime value to males in mate competition. Somewhat surprisingly, Buss (2016a) reports that men are more likely than women to adopt submissive and self-abasing behaviors in order to try to retain a mate and that men are more likely than women to resort "groveling and saying they would do anything their partner wanted to stay in the relationship" (2016a: 337). This finding is inconsistent with characterizations of males commonly present in theories of "patriarchy" and male dominance, this illustrating the sorts of counter-intuitive findings that can derive from evolutionary theory and research. Finally, and unsurprisingly, men are clearly more predisposed than are women to resort to threats and the overt use of physical violence against both their mates and rivals as a mate-retention strategy, a finding that is *consistent* with many accounts of males found in theories of patriarchy. This is a pattern that was well documented and scrupulously analyzed in one of the early, now-classic volumes in evolutionary psychology, Martin Daly's and Margo Wilson's *Homicide* (1988). Additional work by Wilson and Daly has documented how men sometimes use violence and the threat of violence as efforts to try to deter infidelity by their mates (Wilson and Daly 1993, 1996). The proximate psychological mechanism commonly activating male violence against mates and partners is sexual jealousy (e.g., Cousins and Gangestad 2007; Kaighobadi and Shackelford 2009; Stieglitz et al. 2012). In short, Buss concludes that male sexual jealously appears to be the proximate psychological mechanism that motivates violence against mates so as to "keep a mate faithful, prevent future infidelity and prevent defection from a relationship" (2016: 342).

In summary, mate attraction and mate retention behaviors provide an excellent opportunity to peer into the window of work now being conducted by evolutionary psychologists. These two phenomena, both strongly related to the fitness prospects of both men and women, illustrate how evolutionary psychologists have adopted key explanatory principles derived from evolutionary theory, especially the theories of sexual selection and parental investment, and attempted to identify evolved behavioral predispositions that are implicated in human social relations and social interaction.

Searching for the Adapted Mind: A Cautionary Epilogue

Any social or behavioral scientist whose thinking has become informed and guided by neo-Darwinian evolutionary theory has crossed an explanatory river of no return. For such scholars and scientists, the tabula rasa model of the human brain/mind as a determinant of human behavior, including social behavior, is no longer tenable. Rather, a 21st Century understanding of the human brain/mind begins with the premise that it is instantiated with evolved psychological adaptations that bear the imprint of selection forces that operated during the phylogeny of the human species. The task lying before these scientists and scholars is how best to study and understand the properties of the adapted mind and how these properties influence human social behavior.

Recently, some sociologists who are predisposed to abandon the tabula rasa model of the human brain/mind and replace it with a conception of the adapted mind have begun integrating evolutionary psychology into their own work. One such thinker is Satoshi Kanazawa, a sociologist by training who has embraced the evolutionary psychology project. An example of his efforts in this regard is provided by what he calls the "Savanna-IQ

Interaction Hypothesis" (Kanazawa 2004: 279–80). Kanazawa subscribes to the view that the human mind comprises both specialized, evolved psychological adaptations for coping with specific adaptive problems (such as mate selection) as well as general, global thinking and reasoning abilities for coping with other challenges, especially those that are evolutionarily novel. All humans possess general intelligence (as measured by IQ tests), and IQ levels vary among individuals. Kanazawa contends that there is less variation among individuals in terms of their ability to solve basic adaptive problems that are species-specific and have been confronted by humans since ancestral times. In that regard, Kanazawa views natural selection as having equipped all humans with essentially the same basic capabilities for coping with the universal adaptive challenges that humans have faced their entire species-history. Among these are to be found evolved psychological mechanisms such as the evolved mate preferences we identified and discussed earlier in this chapter.

However, Kanazawa's "Savanna-IQ Interaction Hypothesis" enables him to offer new interpretations of a number of aspects of human behavior that are otherwise anomalous and perplexing. For example, he explains why predictions derived from microeconomic theories such as decision-making theory and game theory often fail (2004: 41). He also explains why the assumptions about the threat of free-riding featured in public choice theory do not apply to the ancestral conditions in which humans evolved (Kanazawa 2004: 46). On the other hand, given that the assumptions on which social network theory is based probably accurately characterize empirical conditions closely approximating those that existed in ancestral human environments, social network models better predict and explain social relations than do other theories of micro-level social interaction.

Kanazawa and his colleagues also adopt an evolutionary psychological approach to offer new explanatory approaches to other social phenomena, including friendship (Kanazawa 2010), the adoption of non-conformist social attitudes and behaviors (Kanazawa and Hellberg 2010), and the disproportionate representation of young males among violent crime and property crime offenders (Kanazawa and Still 2000). In short, Kanazwa's work provides a good illustration of how some evolutionary sociologists have begun to integrate theory and research produced in evolutionary psychology into their own analyses.

Both sociobiology and evolutionary psychology have made notable progress toward the development of an evolutionary science of social behavior, including human social behavior. However, it is useful to be reminded of a number of pitfalls that lie before anyone who would pursue this research program in all but the most cautious manner. Toward that end, we will introduce and review briefly a number of issues that require careful consideration by anyone so predisposed. These issues include: (1) the just-so story problem, (2) the nature of adaptations, and (3) the problem of emergent phenomena.

The Just-So Story Problem

Darwin himself famously stated that there is "grandeur" in viewing life as the product of evolution by natural selection. Once understood, the theory of natural selection can inspire an explanatory enthusiasm which, unfortunately on occasion, can inhibit rather than promote scientific understanding of the living world. One such pitfall to which overenthusiastic Darwinian novices occasionally succumb is what has come to be known as the "just-so story" problem. First made popular by an essay entitled "Sociobiology: The Art of Storytelling" written by the paleontologist and evolutionary biologist Stephen J. Gould (1978), the just-so story problem refers to an alleged propensity by sociobiologists (and later, evolutionary psychologists) to: (1) assume that all traits exhibited by organisms are evolved adaptations and (2) produce accounts of the adaptive value of these traits that are consistent with the logic of natural selection but (3) fail to put to empirical test the claim that a trait is, in fact, an evolved adaptation (Alcock 2001: 64–68). For example, in an effort to account for the bright, pink coloration of flamingoes, it was proposed by one enthusiastic adaptationist that the coloration served to camouflage the birds as they flew against a backdrop of pink hues created by sunrises and sunsets. This kind of thinking illustrates the extent to which some overly zealous adaptationists are willing to go in order to interpret *all* traits of organisms as adaptive products of natural selection. (Later research revealed that the pink coloration of flamingos is an incidental by-product of their diets. Born with gray plumage, flamingos acquire their pink coloration from carotenoids in the crustaceans they eat.)

As a cautionary tale, Gould's warning about the construction of just-so stories was not without value, especially during the early years (i.e., 1975–1985 or so) of the "second Darwinian revolution." As a useful criticism of the work currently done by almost all sociobiologists and evolutionary psychologists, it has very limited applicability (Alcock 2001: 57–80). Simply put, the body of research and theory produced by neo-Darwinian analysts of human social behavior over the past four decades contains vanishingly little, if any, evidence of just-so stories published as serious candidates for scientific explanations. Nevertheless, *if* adopted as a putatively legitimate component of evolutionary reasoning, the practice of producing just-so stories is ill-fated at the outset. Consequently, it is useful for us to consider in more detail the just-so story problem in order to produce a sufficient level of vigilance that will preclude any such accounts from being taken seriously as bona fide variants of evolutionary thought and inquiry.

Just-so stories fail to surmount the bar of scientific adequacy for several reasons. First, they are based on the assumption that *all* traits possessed by organisms are adaptive. Even a cursory understanding of current evolutionary analysis makes that assumption unsustainable. Second, the only criterion of explanatory adequacy to which just-so stories are held to account is their *plausibility* as determined by their *consistency* with key elements of evolutionary reasoning. More specifically, if a just-so story about the adaptive value of a trait is somehow viewed as plausible within an evolutionary interpretive framework, then it is seen by its advocates as constituting a bona fide explanation. ("Yes, flamingoes *must be* at great risk of predation during dusk and dawn; thus, natural selection equipped them with colors that cleverly camouflage them against the hues of morning and evening skies.") This protocol is entirely indefensible in terms of the standards to which all contemporary evolutionary scientists are held, including sociobiologists and evolutionary psychologists. This is not to say that, on occasion, someone who identifies him/herself as a sociobiologist or evolutionary psychologist might not advocate a just-so story as a putative explanation of one or another form of behavior. However, the chances are vanishingly small that any such account would ever see the light of day in a reputable venue in which sociobiological and/or evolutionary psychological research is published (e.g., scientific journals such as *Evolution and Human Behavior, Evolutionary Behavioral Sciences, Behavioral and Brain Sciences, Human Nature, Evolutionary Psychology*, as well as numerous other scientific journals dedicated to the evolutionary analysis of human biology and behavior). The flaws of just-so story thinking are so firmly ensconced in the current scientific culture on evolutionary analyses of human social behavior that any effort to insinuate just-so stories into that scientific literature are doomed at the outset (see especially Alcock 2001: 149–87; 2015: 158–60). Nevertheless, the recent, rapid growth of evolutionary thinking in the social and behavioral sciences warrants consideration of the just-so story problem, if for no other reason than to remind new "devotees" to evolutionary thinking of a serious pitfall to be avoided at all costs.

At some risk of oversimplification, it might be said that a just-so story about the adaptive value of a given trait is a hypothesis of sorts, perhaps quite logically deduced from well-established explanatory principles derived from evolutionary theory and research, but a just-so story is a hypothesis that has been accepted *without having been empirically tested*.

Instead, the sheer plausibility of the account and its fidelity to orthodox evolutionary reasoning is seen as sufficient to warrant its acceptance as an established scientific finding. However inventive, creative, and persuasive an idea about the adaptive significance of a given trait might be, it remains *nothing more* than either a just-so story or, more promisingly, an untested hypothesis until it has been framed so as to be *falsifiable by empirical evidence.*

It is important to be reminded of the rather extraordinary public debut that sociobiology made in the mid- to late 1970s when E. O. Wilson's *opus* was published. It attracted surprisingly widespread attention, even in some public media. For example, the August 1, 1977, cover of *Time* magazine carried the caption: "Why You Do What You Do: Sociobiology: A New Theory of Behavior," and it was illustrated with a robotic-like couple to whom puppet strings were attached, thereby suggesting a strongly deterministic explanation of behavior. The unusual publicity accompanying the publication of Wilson's book also occasioned the convening of various conferences and meetings to discuss the new field of sociobiology, and sessions of mainstream scientific associations were devoted to discussion and criticism of sociobiology. In this sort of environment of intellectual fervor that spilled over into public life, more than a few just-so stories were constructed and promoted as new "scientific" explanations of "why we do what we do." It is hardly surprising, then, that one year after the *Time* article appeared, Gould published his criticism of just-so story telling in sociobiology.

Yet, a defense can be mounted in support of the just-so story-telling impulse that is sometimes activated by the evolutionary imagination. Consider the logic of sexual selection theory and, more specifically, Trivers' derivative theory of parental investment in relation to the previous discussion of mate preferences exhibited by humans. Recall the notion of "mate value" as a concept for capturing variation in the value of prospective mates as potential reproductive partners. As we have seen, females are expected to be motivated (almost certainly unconsciously) by a predisposition to select as mates males that are likely to provide both "good genes" and paternal investment (care) for any offspring they sire. Accordingly, females are expected to be responsive to the sorts of physical and behavioral cues signifying high male mate value, including social status and economic resources. Males, on the other hand, are predicted to be selective for female traits that indicate high reproductive potential. Foremost among such cues are physical and behavioral traits that signify youth and health, both of which are proxies for female reproductive value, or fertility.

Having been led thus far by the theory of parental investment, it would be easy to conclude that males, "by nature," are adapted to be highly attracted to beautiful young women and that females are, "by nature," are adapted to be highly attracted to affluent males who also show some evidence of being nurturing. This kind of thinking is entirely consistent with the theory of organic evolution by natural selection, including the theories of sexual selection and parental investment. It is also consistent with many anecdotal observations. Old guys with Rolex watches and Mercedes rides are found not uncommonly in the close company of what the evolutionary sociologist Rosemary Hopcroft called beautiful, young (or at least youthful *appearing*) "foxy ladies," some of whom are, unsurprisingly, blondes (2016: 48–52). At this point, a highly zealous adaptationist might very well feel satisfied at having explained these male-female differences and then decide to close the book on the matter. Gould, on the other hand, would be entirely justified in using this scenario to illustrate the flaws of just-so stories and further indict both sociobiology and evolutionary psychology. Were consideration of the matter to end here, we would have nothing more than an example of a just-so story that illustrates the ill-fated nature of sociobiological and evolutionary psychological research.

However, even in its rudimentary form, the thinking derived from this view of sexual selection and parental investment theory has the *potential* to convert this narrative from a mere just-so story into an opportunity for legitimate scientific research. In fact, this is precisely what has occurred in much of the research previously discussed in this chapter on male-female similarities and differences in mate preference. Rather than remaining content to create just-so stories that posit the existence of evolved psychological adaptations for mate preferences and conclude inquiry at that point, researchers have stated formal, falsifiable hypotheses and adduced a considerable body of replicable empirical findings in relation to their inquiries of mate preference cues and mate selection behaviors. Consequently, numerous empirical studies have revealed that males do, in fact, focus preferentially on cues of female youth and beauty in prospective mates, while females, though attentive to signs of physical qualities like strength and health in males, focus much more sharply on social status and resources when sorting out prospective mates. And while the pattern might easily have been reversed due to cultural variability, studies such as Buss' analysis of mating in thirty-seven cultures failed to find evidence of such reversals. Thus, what might have remained only a just-so story has given rise to many empirical inquiries, each of which could have adduced information that falsified the stated hypotheses. In short, the journals that publish sociobiological and evolutionary psychological research are full of studies reporting empirical analyses and data, but conspicuously devoid of articles that constitute nothing but just-so stories.

Furthermore, researchers have adopted the sort of tentativeness about their findings that is the hallmark of good scientific research. For example, the theory of fluctuating asymmetry as a cue on which both males and females focus when assessing prospective mates generated a great deal of enthusiasm and subsequent research when it was first proposed and investigated. Subsequently, researchers have remained optimistic that fluctuating asymmetry, in some manner, constitutes a criterion in terms of which individuals assess prospective mates, but they have also introduced various qualifications that were unknown during the early stages of this research program. For example, while the early stages of research on fluctuating asymmetry might have tempted researchers to conclude, simplistically and dogmatically, that "the more symmetrical a person, the higher his/her mate value," subsequent research has revealed that the manner in which fluctuating asymmetry is related to mate preference decisions is complicated by other factors such as epigenetic effects of early life stress on hormonal states, certain kinds of infections, the incidence of oxidative stress, and a variety of other biological factors (Sugiyama 2016: 345–50). Nevertheless, the research on fluctuating asymmetry has gone far beyond being nothing more than a just-so story, leading the evolutionary psychologist Steven Pinker to conclude that, in light of the fact that

> most things that exist in the physical world are *not* symmetrical, (and that) among all possible arrangements of a volume of matter, only a tiny fraction are symmetrical. . . . Symmetry has *everything* to do with selection. . . . Symmetry is so improbable and difficult to achieve that any disease or defect can disrupt it, and many animals size up the health prospects of prospective mates by checking for minute asymmetries.
>
> (1997: 168)

In short, what might have begun and ended as nothing more than a just-so story about how fluctuating asymmetry is a cue of attractiveness and thus helps shape mate selection decisions has, instead, developed into an extensive and sophisticated research program that has yielded many empirical research findings about how this trait may shape mating behaviors in both humans and other animals. In this context, and despite Gould's invective, there is nothing wrong with some early just-so story-telling in the evolutionary behavioral and social sciences, as long as inquiry does not cease when the story ends, and the story-tellers do not try to equate their parables, however compelling, with fully developed and rigorously tested programs of scientific inquiry.

The Nature of Adaptations

The realization that an adaptation need not be restricted to an organism's morphological or physiological traits alone but might be extended to include its behaviors, including social behaviors, was foundational to the emergence and development of the second Darwinian revolution (e.g., Alexander 1979; Hamilton 1964; Trivers 1971; Williams 1966). Hamilton's notion of kin selection and Trivers' notion of reciprocal altruism first explained how it could be possible for the genotype of one individual to "manipulate" the behavior of another individual and thereby establish a genetic substrate for the incidence and conduct of social behavior. More simply put, it became possible to view, in genetic terms, social behaviors as adaptations that could evolve by natural selection. And in that animal (including human) behavior is, of course, always the product of brains and nervous systems, it followed that the behavioral outputs of those brains and nervous systems could be the products of specialized, evolved psychological adaptations. Thus, the stage was set for the development of evolutionary psychology, the study of the brain/mind as a complex of evolved adaptations produced by the forces of natural (and sexual) selection.

But it was not until George C. Williams published his now-classic monograph, *Adaption and Natural Selection* (1966) that the concept of "adaptation" received a rigorous and paradigm-changing scrutiny. Unbeknownst to some thinkers who regard themselves as enthusiastic neo-Darwinians, Williams warned that interpreting any of an organism's traits as an evolved adaptation should be a conclusion of last resort, because adaptation is "a special and onerous concept that should not be used unnecessarily" (1966). This was Williams' way of saying that viewing a trait as an adaptation, however tempting, is not something about which one should rush to judgment. A behavior, for example, might have *adaptive consequences* without that behavior's having been produced by an *adaptation* that evolved by natural selection *because it produced those adaptive consequences*. Accordingly, neo-Darwinian social and behavioral scientists, including evolutionary psychologists, must be cautious and restrained in concluding that any given behavior is the product of an evolved psychological adaptation for producing that behavior and bestowing whatever adaptive outcomes that might issue from it. In that regard, it is useful to be reminded of the criteria specified by Williams that must be met before one should begin to conclude that any behavior is the product of an evolved psychological adaptation.

Williams enumerated these criteria, and a brief consideration of each will illustrate why caution must always be exercised in interpreting a trait as an adaptation. First, adaptations are responses to problem that must be solved in order for an organism to survive and eventually, reproduce. Organisms that possess qualities that enable them to survive and reproduce better than organisms lacking those qualities will leave more descendants, and the information (in the case of organic evolution, genes) that produces those qualities will proliferate. Second, adaptations provide evidence of complex and highly improbable design, and that complexity is organized so as to enable the organism to solve a specific problem efficiently and effectively. As Steven Pinker cleverly explained, while a dead computer can be used as a paperweight, a dead paperweight cannot be used as a computer (1997: 171). The extraordinarily improbable complexity of a computer is compelling evidence for design that facilitates information processing. One might say that the computer is a complex of adaptations for processing information, and while the mass of a computer also enables it to be used as a paperweight, it would be absurd to claim that a computer is an adaptation to prevent paper from blowing away. Or, invoking a biological example, the shape of human ears provides compelling evidence that they are an adaptation for capturing and channeling *auditory* information, but they are not a biologically evolved adaptation for transmitting the *visual* information encoded in a pair of earrings. Nor is the cylindrical shape of a human finger an adaptation for displaying a metal band that announces mating status. Third, as mentioned earlier, a trait featuring complexity of design solves an adaptive problem efficiently and effectively. The greater the degree of efficiency and effectiveness with which the problem is solved, the more likely the trait is to be an evolved adaptation. Fourth, the trait under consideration as a possible adaptation solves the problem reliably across context and over time. It exhibits consistency in its ability to solve the problem except in extreme or entirely novel environments. Fifth, the trait is species-typical, that is, it develops reliably in all members of the species that feature it, and it fails to develop only in atypical or abnormal circumstances. The trait is not distributed variably and unpredictably among members of the species in which it is found, though variation in the ability of the trait to produce the outcomes for which it was designed by natural selection can, and does, occur. For example, all normally developing humans have eyes, but visual acuity varies from individual to individual. Finally, what Williams called "evidence of special design" exists in the service of a function (or functions) performed by the trait, functions that contribute either to the survival or reproductive prospects of the organism, and sometimes, to both. Human eyes provide information about distant objects that could be threats to survival (e.g., an approaching predator), or an opportunity for reproductive success (the existence of an attractive member of the opposite sex on the other side of a room). In the first case, the eye increases the chances that its bearer will not be killed and eaten, while in the second case, the eye increases the possibility that its bearer might become a parent.

Thus, while any of a number of psychological conditions and their behavioral outputs may be adaptive for individuals that possess them, they are not necessarily *evolved adaptations*. One of the most daunting, but not insurmountable, tasks confronting evolutionary psychologists who are in pursuit of a scientific understanding of evolved adaptations that comprise the human mind is the challenge of sorting out evolved psychological adaptations from mental processes and overt behaviors that happen to have adaptive consequences, but *lack evidence of special design for producing those consequences*.

Emergent Products of Evolved Adaptations

Long recognized as the appropriate subject matter of sociology, the structures of society and the cultural arrays that help assemble and regulate those structures have been understood to consist of qualities that are not reducible to the "components" from which they arise. This is commonly described as the problem of "emergence" or "emergent properties," and it has preoccupied sociologists at least since Emile Durkheim's claim that the unique calling of sociologists is the study of "social facts," which are irreducible properties of populations and societies, not individuals. The defining feature of emergent phenomena is that their qualities cannot be inferred from the qualities of the individual components that generate them. Rather, emergent properties are generated by the *relations* among components, not the traits of the individual components themselves. Thus, the explanation of emergent phenomena requires an analytical approach that acknowledges emergent complexity and the identification of processes by means of which that complexity develops and functions. This is well understood by biologists, including sociobiologists. And though he is an unapologetic advocate of *sophisticated* reductionist thinking in science, E. O. Wilson himself is emphatic that it is not possible to explain, in its totality, complexity in nature absent close attention to the phenomenon of emergence. Even when considering phenomena as "simple" as living cells, Wilson contends that

> At each level of organization, *especially* at the living cell and above, phenomena exist that require new laws and principles which still *cannot be predicted from those at more general levels*. Perhaps some of them will remain forever beyond our grasp.
> (Wilson 1998: 55, emphases ours)

Thus, it is axiomatic to sociobiologists like Wilson, that sociobiology alone (as well as evolutionary psychology) cannot traverse the entire explanatory distance from physics, to chemistry, to genetics, to whole organism biology, to psychology, to culture, and to human social behavior (1998: 204). For example, even if evolutionary psychologists succeed in establishing with compelling empirical evidence, virtually beyond a shadow of a doubt, that the evolved psychology of the human male is equipped with an adaptation that arouses high levels of anxiety when perceiving the threat of his mate's sexual infidelity, the discovery of this adaptation will not, in-and-of-itself, explain the complex processes that generate the interpersonal structures, institutional configurations, stratification systems, and cultural configurations that are widely labeled "patriarchy." Neither sociobiology nor evolutionary psychology advocate claims that extraordinarily oppressive systems of gender domination such that found in Athens during classical antiquity and described by Guttentag and Secord (1983) can be explained entirely by some sort of genetic substrate (and evolved adaptations) for "male dominance." There are no "genes for patriarchy." However, a comprehensive analysis of social systems that sequester, subordinate, exploit, and subjugate women might include, *as a starting point*, a consideration of evolved male mating preferences which express themselves in particular demographic circumstances; historical eras; sociocultural contexts (which, themselves, bear the imprint of their developmental histories); and technological environments. Reductionism is, as Wilson puts it, the "search strategy employed to find points of entry into otherwise impenetrably complex systems" (1998: 54). But it is *not* the single vantage point or exit portal from which complex systems like societies and their emergent properties can be grasped and understood fully in their entirety.

Sociobiology and evolutionary psychology, then, can offer *foundational knowledge* about evolved, species-typical, human behavioral *propensities* that contribute to the generation of the structures and cultures of patriarchy, but patriarchy as an emergent component of any human society defies any effort to be explained reductively by evolved psychological adaptations and behavioral propensities *alone*. Even when trying to explain a phenomenon as "simple" as cellular biology, Wilson cautions that "the explanations of the physical sciences are necessary but not sufficient" (Wilson 1998: 68). They are not sufficient because even "simple" levels of biological organization at the level of the cell feature stunning degrees of emergent complexity. In fact, Wilson expands his thesis to say, "Let me now indicate how bad the problem really is. It is not even possible to predict the three-dimensional structure of a protein from a complete knowledge of its constituent atoms" (1998: 83). This is not the declaration of a thinker who is about the task of trying to claim that either sociobiology or evolutionary psychology is capable of explaining the emergent complexity of even so "simple" a structure as the nuclear family in genetic or evolved psychological terms alone. Even the simplest, elementary forms of human sociality entail the generation of complex, emergent social phenomena which themselves are not reducible to the properties of the alleles borne by the actors who express these forms of sociality. Darwin was right in his intuition that particulate inheritance makes and shapes all living things, including humans, and Durkheim was right in his intuition that human social life is not reducible to particulate qualities alone.

And if, as Wilson says, "the explanations of the physical sciences are necessary but not sufficient" to explain the biology of the cell, then the explanations of evolutionary biology and evolutionary psychology are also necessary but, by themselves, insufficient to explain human social behavior and human society. Sociobiology and evolutionary psychology are developing into what almost certainly will become foundational disciplines on which the social sciences can build, but there is a point beyond which the concepts, theoretical principles, research methodologies, and empirical findings of these two evolutionary sciences must be succeeded by the evolutionary *social* sciences, including evolutionary sociology, a field that is best positioned to make intelligible the irreducible structures and processes comprising human sociocultural systems.

Notes

1 Evolutionary psychology is producing a large and rapidly growing literature of scientific studies. Two recent sources are very useful in helping orient readers to this field: (1) David M. Buss' textbook, *Evolutionary Psychology: The New Science of the Mind* (2016, 5th edition; Routledge), and David M. Buss (ed.), *The Handbook of Evolutionary Psychology*, 2 vols., (2016, 2nd edition; Wiley-Blackwell). Both of these volumes were helpful in providing current information for this chapter.
2 Facial "femininity" is operationally defined with "cues such as relatively large eyes, thinner jaws, small chin, high cheekbones, and a relatively short distance between mouth and jaw" (Buss 2016a: 140).
3 These categories were constructed from an inventory of mate retention tactics reported by Buss (1989).

10
The Limitations of Darwinian Analysis

The success of sociobiology and evolutionary psychology in penetrating some of the social sciences has led to a certain level of over-reach beyond what Darwinian-inspired analysis can explain. There are, of course, many who would disagree with this assertion, including many sociologists like Stephen K. Sanderson (1999, 2015), who sustains an emphasis on the unit of selection as the individual phenotype (and underlying genotype), with the population of individuals and/or their sociocultural formations as being the units that evolve. The vast majority of sociologists, however, have been somewhat hostile to this position, but often for the wrong reasons, such as concerns over reduction of sociology to biology or, god forbid, to psychology, and concerns about the implications of any use of biology in sociology in light of past abuses like Social Darwinism and eugenics. Unlike these more emotionally and often ideologically driven concerns, there are sound intellectual and explanatory reasons for being very skeptical that natural selection as conceived by Darwin and as codified into the Modern Synthesis on "the driving forces of evolution" (i.e., selection, genetic drift, gene flow, and mutations) are up to the task of explaining evolution of sociocultural formations. The evolution of biological organisms, as Herbert Spencer realized well over 140 years ago in his organismic analogy, has parallel properties and dynamics to those driving the evolution of superorganisms (i.e., the organization of organisms). More importantly, however, some of the properties and dynamics of organic and superorganic (social) evolution are dramatically different. If there is to be a *new* evolutionary sociology, it needs to embrace what the Modern Synthesis provides but, at the same time, recognize what it cannot provide: a complete explanation of superorganic evolution. Darwinian natural selection can take us only so far, and as we will outline in Chapter 11, there are other, sociocultural forms of natural selection that are needed to explain the evolution of societies, intersocietal systems, and the corporate units that serve as the building blocks of these large formations. In this chapter, we will outline the limitations of in emphasizing purely biologically based forces on sociocultural formations, which will help explain why we need to introduce new types of natural selection that are just as "natural" for superorganisms as Darwinian natural selection is for understanding the evolution of organisms.

Can the Behavior of Individuals Explain the Emergent Properties and Dynamics of Superorganisms?

Figure 10.1 outlines the model of explanation of sociobiology and evolutionary psychology, as well as all those who insist upon fidelity to the model presented by the Modern Synthesis. Selection is initiated by changes in the environment which affect organisms' access to resources that allow them to reproduce, setting off competition for resources and selection of those whose phenotypes (and underlying genotypes) enabling individual organisms to secure sufficient resources to survive and reproduce. Those organisms revealing variants of their phenotypes (including behavioral propensities) that do not allow them to secure sufficient resources are selected out of the population, thereby modifying the distribution of genes generating phenotypes in a population. And, if this process continues over time or is accelerated by intense selection, gene flow, genetic drift, and/or mutations, speciation may occur. At a minimum, and this is what Darwin emphasized, there will be descent with *modifications*. It should be

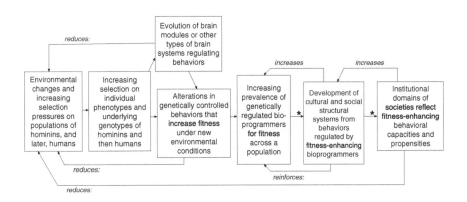

Note: *Almost all explanations ignore the sociology of how and why cognitive, emotional, and behavioral capacities and propensities become *institutionalized* in societies by specific processes of culture- and structure-building. There is an implicit assumption that this process of transforming neurological and behavioral propensities into social structures and institutions is automatic. Even with "just-so" stories or simulations employing agent-based modeling techniques are used to "explain" how behaviors become structured and regulated by culture, these are often rather ad hoc and rather speculative.

Figure 10.1 Limitations in the Models of Sociobiology and Evolutionary Psychology

emphasized that Darwin never used Spencer's phrase, "survival of the fittest," and its more recent incarnation when run through the conceptual mill of neoclassical economics, "maximization of fitness." Indeed, Darwin emphasized that selection produced "just enough" change to allow members of a species of organism to sustain themselves and reproduce. Nor did he argue for another unfortunate borrowing from neoclassical economics for an "evolutionary stable equilibrium" as if evolution outcomes were like markets. A given pattern descent with modification will, instead, be stable if nothing changes in the environment that affects members of a population's capacity to secure resources enabling them to reproduce.

Biologists have been reluctant, to say the least, to adopt the notion of group selection (e.g., Pinker 1997), proposed by Wynne-Edwards (1986) decades ago. Similarly, those in the social sciences adopting the ideas of the Modern Synthesis are similarly reluctant to argue for group or multi-level selection. For those in biology willing to consider any notion of "group selection," an allele must cause behavior that reduces fitness of individuals that bear that allele, while simultaneously, increasing the mean fitness of the group in which that individual lives and acts. Without meeting this criterion, group selection cannot exist in the evolutionary biology sense of the term. Whatever the merits of this argument, which some see as rather narrow while others the opposite, biology cannot seriously address what is obvious to any social scientists: Corporate units involving divisions of labor among conspccifics can act as survival machines; and in the case of humans or perhaps other highly intelligent animals that can use agency to construct such corporate units, selection can be on the group as much as the biological phenotype.

Thus, for biologists and many others selection is on phenotypes, including hard-wired and *genetically controlled behaviors* of individual organisms, rather than on corporate units like groups, communities; organizations that, in turn, are the building blocks of institutional systems (e.g., economy, polity, religion, kinship, etc.), societies, and intersocietal systems. If sociobiology and evolutionary psychology stopped with only trying to explain genetically controlled behaviors, as well as other phenotypic traits of organisms, there would be no conflict with sociology, which is the study *of emergent social structures and their cultures* that arise from behavior and interaction among individual people. Moreover, if they would not so fervently doubt that there is group or "multi-level" selection, then again there would not be much disagreement with sociologists. There are, of course, many fervent doubters of the notion of multi-level selection who would not even admit this much; and as a result, they cannot explain very much about complex, agency-driven social behaviors among humans, nor do they have the intellectual tools to explain the operation of such complex social forms as human societies. They are trapped by too much fidelity to a narrow view of evolution, which even Darwin did not share because he understood that organisms with capacities for agency are able to create new survivor machines (e.g., see Darwin's 1871 *The Descent of Man and Selection in Relation to Sex*).

Within sociobiology, for example, certain human behaviors are posited—e.g., kin selection (preference for those sharing genes), reciprocity (in exchanges of resources), altruism (support for those not sharing genes), and reciprocal altruism (reciprocity with non-kin with expectations for future assistance), and all of the behaviors are also emphasized by evolutionary psychologists as well. These universal behaviors are then viewed as the explanation of institutional systems from which societies are built. Sometimes explanations take the form of highly speculative "just-so" stories of how a behavioral propensity leads to its institutionalization, or sometimes simulations are performed showing collective outcomes of individual behaviors without specifying the mechanisms and processes by which such outcomes occur. Whatever the case, there is a lack of social science sophistication in these analyses, despite the obvious intellect of those who make this case. Often a rate (or rates) of this or that behavior is seen as explained by the nature of the behavior, when collectively iterated over time. These explanations in sociobiology and evolutionary psychology are more plausible, but in the end, they often fail to indicate how and through what sociocultural filters and constraints a behavior becomes a rate of behavior that can explain an institutional phenomenon. Whether it is rates of divorce, deviance, homicide, marriage, endogamy or exogamy, and the like, the explanation is seen as ultimately biologically driven. And, when performed by non-sociologists, there is virtually no mention of any sociological literatures. Such is not always the case, but their explanations rarely talk about the biasing effects of existing sociocultural formations on rates of any kind of behavior; and indeed, the power of social structure and culture to inhibit the expression of biologically driven behaviors is rarely discussed. Thus, the sociology is left out, and it is not surprising that most sociologists—certainly not all, to be sure, but most—remain unconvinced, if not hostile.

Evolutionary sociology thus cannot, therefore, be a simple and rote extension of sociobiology and evolutionary psychology, which seek to explain *behaviors*; and in so doing, these approaches are often assumed or even asserted to be able to explain the dynamics of social structures and their cultures. But they cannot, and particularly so since they often are locked into a biological view of evolution. As we will outline in detail in Chapter 11, there are other natural selection processes working on the properties of individuals honed by millions of years of Darwinian natural selection. And along with this line of emphasis, it become essential that the new evolutionary sociology embrace group selection or, more diplomatically, multi-level selection: not just multi-level Darwinian selection but *selection unique to human superorganisms* where selection can be simultaneously Darwinian and working on phenotypes and underlying genotypes, while also being more sociological working on sociocultural phenotypes (e.g., social structure and their cultures) that have been created and sustained and, hence, that can be changed by human capacities for agency. And once we are willing to take this analytical step, the nature of evolution and the units of evolution change. Without taking this step, one is locked into a view of Darwinian selection that is not well suited to explaining sociocultural phenomena and change in superorganisms.

Multi-Level Selection as Critical to Integrating the New Evolutionary Sociology With the Modern Synthesis

As emphasized, Darwinian selection is on individual variations among members of a population; and from this selection, the distribution of genes and alleles across a population evolves. Darwin himself in later editions of his *Descent of Man* (1871, 1873) recognized that "blind" natural selection working on phenotypes would be different for highly intelligent animals that have the capacity for agency and that can change the very environments to which they must adapt. Ironically, this simple idea has at times been lost or certainly underemphasized in much analysis of sociocultural evolution. Humans as organisms can create new social structures, or sociocultural variants, because they are teleological and can work toward goals and innovate. Humans and their sociocultural formations are built from corporate units (e.g., groups, organizations, communities) that used organize adaptive activities into even larger sociocultural formations like institutional and stratification systems, societies, and even intersocietal formations. Humans, then, do not have to "wait" for the forces of biological evolution to generate new variants on which selection can go to work; they can themselves *create then needed variants in sociocultural formations* and, in the not-too-distant brave new world, will increasingly be able to create genetic variants as well. Thus, sociocultural evolution has a heavy dose of Lamarckian evolution as humans and the social structures organizing their activities exercise their capacities for agency, inventing, borrowing, and otherwise acquiring new characteristics that are then passed down over time. Selection is not, as we will see in Chapter 11, working on genetically driven phenotypical features of human morphology and behavior but is now being supplemented by sociocultural types of selection working of sociocultural phenotypes and morphologies and social processes generated by these morphologies.

In the famous words of Richard Dawkins (1976), the *survival machines* protecting the precious cargo of organismic phenotypes (the genotype of an organism) are now more extensive. They include *all* of those corporate units building up institutional systems, societies, and intersocietal systems that protect individuals and thereby make humans more fit in their environments. The diverse types of groups, organizations, and communities that form the basis for institutions that, in turn, are the building blocks of societies and intersocietal systems are, themselves, also *superorganisms*. And, these superorganisms reveal many different types of social structural and cultural morphologies that, for the most part, *protect human biological phenotypes* and, hence, the human genome. As such, they are subject to selection pressures, which may be Darwinian in that they can kill individuals (e.g., a pandemic, a war, a natural disaster, etc.), but selection is also forcing the development by acts of agency of new sociocultural morphologies that reduce direct selection on the biological phenotypes of individuals. A pandemic, for example, represents a challenge to the genetically regulated immune system of individuals, to be sure, but it has a challenge to corporate units constituting the *medical care system* of a population. When religion and prayer are the only medical care systems of a population, then Darwinian selection will be more intense and will select on the phenotypes of individuals; when a population can create drugs to boost immune systems or to target specific pathogens through the institutionalization of science and medicine, then selection is also on the institutions of medicine and science, and perhaps polity as well, in a society or system of societies. To take another example of when two societies go to war, selection is on each society's respective organizational capacities for coercion (see Turchin's analysis in Chapter 4), relative size and level of organization as a society, varying types and levels of technology, productive and distributive systems, alliances with other societies, and many other sociocultural forces. All of these, of course, affect how many people die, but survival and descent with modification are determined by selection of the more "fit" *society* and its capacity to wage war. The outcome of the war can be to eliminate the other society, but far more common is some form of consolidation of societies under new geopolitical arrangements from coercive occupation through forced trade and exchange to cooptation and mixing of institutional and cultural systems. The descent with modification often involves changes to both the conquering and conquered population and their organization; and while the distribution of human phenotypes may be modified, far more important are modifications of sociocultural formations as "survivor machines" for individual phenotypes. The population's gene pool may have changed (e.g., losing many male genotypes, for example, or changing genotypes through coercive interbreeding of conquering males with females in a conquered society), and so, biological evolution may indeed have also occurred in warfare, but it is driven more by a very different set of selection pressures than by Darwinian selection on human phenotypes.

Equally significant is the fact that *selection is now multi-level*, potentially operating simultaneously on the phenotypes (and genotypes) of individual persons and many layers of sociocultural phenotypes organizing and protecting individual phenotypes. Also significant is that sociocultural phenotypes protecting the phenotypes of individual persons are *embedded in each other*, with the result that selection on one sociocultural formation will eventually become selection on all of the constituent social units from which this formation is constructed. Figure 10.2 represents this successive embedding of biological and sociocultural phenotypes. The cargo of biological reproduction—the genotype of an individual—is, of course, embedded in this phenotype, but human phenotypes include emotional, cognitive, behavioral, and organization capacities that lead humans to build up complex and layered defense systems, beginning with groups that are embedded in organizational systems that are embedded in communities. Many of these capacities are not, however, driven by the genome in any tightly regulated sense, thereby allowing humans to creatively construct new types of corporate units into ever-more elaborate sociocultural formations that protect their genomes.

The three basic types of corporate units—that is, groups, organizations, and communities—are embedded in each other; and moreover, they are the building blocks of institutional domains, societies, and intersocietal systems, which in turn are also embedded in each other. Selection can operate at each level, consecutively or sequentially, before it ever can have an effect on person-level phenotypes. And, even selection generated by extreme environmental changes—e.g., warfare, ecological disaster, environmental degradation, pandemic, etc.—will more often be on the embedded system of sociocultural formations and will, therefore, have to work its way down to the genome by altering the successive and interwoven layers and levels of sociocultural environments in which the phenotype of the individual are embedded.

Some appear to argue that this is still all Darwinian selection, but in making this claim, a great deal of sociological evidence to the contrary

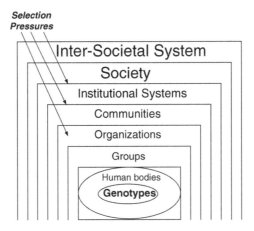

Note: While selection pressures can come from many sources, they must almost always have to pass through the sociocultural epidermis of communities, organizations, and groups. And indeed, they may emerge inside these structures. But the image of the genome as being only protected by the body is quite misleading, and increasingly so in a complex and highly differentiated societal and intersocietal system with many layers of embedding and interdependencies that are also under selection. The human body is inside a series of boxes that have boundaries and, more importantly, have the capacity to be agents of change on their structure, culture, and operation to defend the precious cargo of the human body.

Figure 10.2 Levels of Selection in the Sociocultural Universe

must be ignored, which is what most sociobiologists and evolutionary psychologists do as a matter of course. And for this reason, the vast majority of sociologists will not accept such arguments from sociobiologists and evolutionary psychologists. Economists and rational choice political scientists (and sociologists) may accept these arguments because they are blinded by neoclassical economics, which manages to ignore even Adam Smith (1759), who recognized that humans are creative moral animals, regulated by social structure and culture. Despite the development of behavioral and institutional economics, the discipline of economics is not very concerned with the economy as *an institutional system*, much less *all of the other institutional systems* in any differentiated society that make most of the predictions by behavioral economics exercises in bracketing out much of the real social universe in order to make the mathematics work. Even many sociologists—not just rational choice theorists—but also important evolutionists (e.g., Sanderson 2015) appear to operate with these blinders on, even when arguing that it is sociocultural formations that evolve!

Thus, as emphasized earlier, once selection no longer operates exclusively on individual phenotypes but on the social and cultural constructions of humans who can create a whole new universe—the social universe—Darwinian selection must be supplemented by more purely sociological analysis. And so, as one moves up the successive layers of embedding outlined in Figure 10.2, selection becomes ever-more sociocultural and ever-less Darwinian. For example, as we reviewed in Chapter 4, geopolitical systems are like any morphological structure subject to selection, but it is now *multi-level selection*; and trying to explain such complex entities as world systems—whether geoeconomic or geopolitical—by Darwinian selection alone will miss about all of the important dynamics of these system that cause their descent with modification.

What Is Evolving in Sociocultural Evolution?

In biological evolution, it is the distribution of genes in the gene pool of a population that is evolving by means of natural selection on phenotypes, the variation of which is determined by normal variance in traits (often on a bell curve), mutations, gene flow, and genetic drift. If we ask this same question about sociocultural evolution—that is, what is evolving?—the answer is not so clear. It depends upon the goals of analysis. For example, for early sociologists, it was societies as a whole that were evolving, generally from simple to ever-more complex forms (see Chapter 3); for world systems theorists, it is systems of societies operating in terms of the dynamics inhering in geoeconomics and geopolitics that are evolving. Yet, for a theorists of organizational ecology, it is populations of organizations that are evolving as some survive and others die out in market competition; but for a historian on a particular organization—say, General Motors—this particular organization is evolving (revealing descent with modification is our definition of evolution). Similarly, communities and even groups change over time and, hence, are evolving. In fact, rarely is sociological analysis concerned with biological evolution of gene pools describing the distribution of genes in a particular population or society (perhaps sociologists should pay more attention to this type of evolution, but it is not the main focus of sociology). So, a first point of difference with Darwinian views of evolution is that the unit of evolution can vary, from larger-scale sociocultural formations to the changes and modifications of their constituent corporate units.

This evolution is, as is outlined in Chapter 11, driven in part by selection on variations in various levels of sociocultural units but with a major difference: These variations are created, often in the absence of existing variants that can deal with adaptive problems. Hence, *the sources of variations* are very different in human superorganisms than in biological organisms. In the biological universe, selection is on variations in the distributions on phenotypical traits as these are modified by random mutations, gene flow, and genetic drift; and while one can generate crude parallels by seeing innovation as like a mutation, gene flow as like diffusion, and genetic drift as like migration or conquest of one population with a somewhat different culture into another. But, these are just analogies and, hence, not particularly useful in developing explanatory theory. The source of variation is, therefore, very different in superorganic evolution than in organic evolution, despite some parallels that are more evocative than explanatory.

If the mechanisms by which variations exist are different from organic in superorganic evolution, how do we conceptualize "inheritance" and "change" in the superorganic? If evolution is descent with modification, how is descent to be conceptualized? When persons are born, they live and die, and in between, they reproduce new offspring (in most cases). Descent is thus measured by the inheritance of genes and the phenotypes that they generate across generations; and with the ability to map the human genome and to compare phenotypes, it is possible to trace modifications and retentions in patterns of descent. But societies do not have babies, although corporate units can often engage in replication (in the obvious case, franchises of retail outlets), and here it is possible to record modifications over time with some fidelity because one can observe a deliberate effort to replicate a particular structure and culture, although even this can be adjusted to particular sociocultural environments. And over time, as competition and markets change, deliberate agentic/strategic changes are implemented, and these too can be recorded. Yet, there is nothing equivalent in sociocultural evolution to the notion of "generations" at which point it is possible to record precisely modifications carried on by the next generation. Even in specific types of corporate units—say, a big company like Walmart—there is no generational change; rather it is a rather ad hoc process, often sudden, in accordance with competitive pressures or other environmental pressures.

Thus, at every level of the human social universe—as roughly outlined in Figure 10.2—it is difficult to determine what is evolving, when evolution actually occurs, how to determine descent (of what?), and what has been modified during descent. This is why history is often highly interpretative. The best that is possible is to select a social unit from a group or organization, or even a population of organizations, to a larger-scale structure like an institutional domain (say, polity, kin system, or economy) or society or intersocietal system over time and see, first of all, how long it lasts even in modified form; secondly, if it is replaced by an entirely new formation (sociocultural speciation?); and thirdly, how it has been modified over time. Indeed, this is the kind of thing that early stage-model theorists sought to do: record patterns of changes in key institutional systems—economy, law, religion, polity, kinship, science, education, etc.—and see if there was a pattern within and among institutional systems at each demarcated stage (which might be considered a kind of "generation," but it was more of an analytical and abstracted generational stage than an actual empirical transformation during which the new generation could be observed). Thus, economies evolved when examined during the long-course of societal evolution through a combination of innovation, diffusion, warfare, and other social and, at times, ecological processes. But, again, this evolution of superorganisms is only roughly parallel to populations in organic evolution, as Spencer emphasized in his organismic analogy. Populations of organisms and sociocultural formations making up superorganisms are not isomorphic, nor are they even homologies because the source of evolution can come from any constituent unit (as occurs in a revolution or social movement, as corporate units are organized for change in a particular institution, such as law or polity) and because what actually evolves can be only a subset of units within a larger social formation. Thus, it is difficult to sort out the relevant morphologies in determining what units are evolving with what modifications over what periods of generational (if any) time.

The early and present-day sociological stage modelers of evolutionary change were and are still trying to stabilize the unit of change—whole societies—and record new types of societies that emerged from earlier, simpler types. There were, and still are, many problems with this kind of analysis, but stage modeling did one important thing: It sorted our syndromes or configurations of institutional systems and the corporate units from which they are built that appear to evolve together as a cluster of features. Moreover, Stage models also provided an explanation of how and why stratification emerged in human societies (as corporate units within institutional domains distributed resources with more or less inequality; see Lenski 1964, 2005; Turner 1984). Stage models thus made it possible see understand the emergence, development, and modification of the two building blocks of human societies: institutional domains and stratification systems. And, in being able to draw such generalizations, the analysis of what was evolving was greatly simplified but hardly simple. Moreover, the nature of the analysis is still very different than in studying populations of organisms and hence not in any clear way isomorphic or even parallel (beyond notions of size and increased differentiation of organic and superorganic in Spencer's analogy).

In the end, then, superorganic evolution involves descent with modification, in Darwin's terms, but (a) the selection dynamics involved go beyond Darwinian natural selection, the sources and origins of variation on which selection works are different, (b) the selection on these variations is different, (c) the units and subunits evolving are not regulated by a master set of instructions (the genome), and (d) the way that the units evolving interact, and become modified is very different in superorganic compared to organic evolution.

We can add to these differences yet another: Selection does not always lead to death of the less fit but, instead, their incorporation into a larger superorganism or their movement to a new niche within a superorganism. At times, corporate units die, institutions die from stagnation, societies disintegrate, and intersocietal systems collapse. But even under these most extreme outcomes, elements are retained, and often become reintegrated into new superorganisms. The result is that selection can produce apparent "sociocultural death" of corporate-unit phenotypes and their cultures, along with the larger systems built from them, but some corporate units or cultural systems can survive or re-emerge in ways not possible with organic life. To destroy an institutional system, such as the polity of a society, does not mean that the administrative structures from which this polity has been constructed also "dies." These structures and their human inhabitants can live on and be reorganized into a new type of political formations within a new societal-level superorganism; the same is true for almost all other institutional systems in human societies.

Thus, the units of evolution in superorganisms evidence different properties than most organisms, although regeneration of destroyed body parts is a common survival strategy among some species (but the difference with human superorganisms is that regeneration does not restore the superorganism back to its original form but typically generates a new superorganism). Such processes are even more evident when the humans of a conquered society live on and adapt to a new set of imposed institutional systems by a new polity, often by having to adjust their behavioral outputs in ways that violate their genetic programming. Thus, organic and superorganic evolution do not always occur in synchronization; indeed, just the opposite. From a biological lens, the population has not evolved (unless there has been a killing of a significant portion particular types of phenotypes, e.g., men warriors, or children and older persons by particular diseases brought by conquerors), and while coercion may change the way that individuals behave (say in violation of behavioral universals outlined by sociobiologists and evolutionary psychologists), no evolution has occurred in a biological sense, at least for the current generation. New generations may involve a new mixing of genes that occurs as conquerors and the conquered begin interbreeding as is often the case in coercive conquests, thus accelerating biological evolution but such evolution is now the direct outcome of superorganic evolution of, say, a geopolitical system. Thus, there can be evolution at all levels outlined in Figure 10.2, but this multi-level evolution only makes isolating what is evolving that much more difficult. But, one thing is clear, not all of the evolution involved is organic, and neither is it driven by the same mechanisms as organic evolution. The goal of the new evolutionary sociology is to isolate these different mechanisms in order to explain the relationship between organic and superorganic evolution.

Conclusion

Even though the units under selection, the units that are evolving, and the mechanisms by which evolution occurs are different for superorganic compared to organic forms, there can be some integration of more biological and sociological approaches. In Chapter 11, we outline different types of natural selection that occur "naturally" in superorganisms. We cannot ignore Darwinian natural selection in trying to understand the evolution of human phenotypes, including behavioral propensities hard-wired into the human genome. These do have large effects on human behavior and interaction, and they have significant effects on human motivations in sociocultural contexts. The new evolutionary sociology must always retain evolutionary biology. But, there are other types of non-Darwinian selection that work on sociocultural phenotypes of superorganisms, and we will need to recognize that they are just as natural a part of the social universe as is Darwinian selection in the biotic universe.

Fidelity with biology, then, is retained by the notion of selection: Selection on variants of both biological and sociocultural phenotypes is occurring, but the nature of selection itself, the way in which variants on which selection is produced, and the units undergoing evolution are *all* different. Simply transporting sociobiology and evolutionary psychology into sociology will not explain anything more than, at best, the origins of hard-wired behaviors, but such models of behavior cannot fully explain the complex layering of sociocultural formations into various types of superorganisms, nor can they explain very much about the dynamics of sociocultural formations, despite the efforts of highly accomplished scholars. The human organism, as a product of biological natural selection, creates and sustains superorganisms, and the processes by which superorganisms evolve are simply different than those by which populations of organisms evolve.

11
New Models of Natural Selection in Sociocultural Evolution

Darwinian Natural Selection

The Modern Synthesis in biology emphasizes four "forces of evolution"—natural selection, mutation, gene flow, and genetic drift—which drive evolution by affecting the distribution of genes in a population's gene pool (Mayr 2001). Mutations, gene flow, and genetic drift all have effects on variations in phenotypes of individuals on which natural selection goes to work, but particularly important (and often underemphasized) is *the existing distribution of traits* of a species, particularly those that reveal distributions on a normal bell curve. For example, the relative size of organisms among a species will often reveal a normal distribution; and as we will emphasize in the review of the new neurosociology in Chapter 14, selection works on *existing variations by selecting out those on one tail or the other of a bell curve* and preserves those traits (and underlying genes) that promote fitness. Hence, even without mutations, gene flow, or drift, selection on tails of existing distributions of traits can dramatically modify the distributions of alleles in the gene pool. And for a complex structure like the brain where mutations would be almost universally harmful (Fisher 1930) and where gene flow and genetic drift were not in play to any great degree, directional selection on tails of *existing distributions* of phenotypic variants is *the most important force of evolution*. Any change in the environment of a species will activate selection immediately, and the first targets of selection will be on existing pre-adaptations and the tails of trait distributions in the phenotypes of a species; mutations, drift, and flow may soon kick in, but for many of the Darwinian arguments about hominin and human evolution, it is still directional selection that has driven much of the long-term evolution of primates and hominins.

Table 11.1 summarizes the basic processes operating in Darwinian natural selection, while Figure 11.1 presents their dynamics in a process model. Environmental changes initiate selection dynamics, whatever the source of these changes. The changes can be the result of a decline in key resources, the invasion of a resource niche by new conspecifics or other species, population growth among members of a population that increases niche density and hence competition for resources, or any force that alters the availability

TABLE 11.1 Darwinian Selection Among Organisms

1. Organic life forms survive by securing resources from their environments, with those able to secure sufficient resources to reproduce themselves being the most fit.
2. Among organisms, fitness is the degree to which individual organisms can secure resources and reproduce themselves.
3. Environmental change, for any reason, changes the availability of resources and often sets into motion competition within and between species of organisms for resources, increasing selection on *variants* of the phenotypes of those organisms that, under conditions of competition, can secure resources and reproduce.
4. Environmental changes stem from such forces as:
   a. Ecological alterations in the distribution of physical and biotic resources in an environment
   b. Growth in the population of organisms of a given type in a resource niche
   c. Migrations of other types of organisms into a resource niche
5. Variations of phenotypes (and underlying genotypes) in a population of organisms can be found in pre-adaptations and existing bell curve-like distributions of traits, with additional sources of variations potentially coming from mutations, gene flow, and genetic drift.
6. Competition for available resources among variants of a given type of organisms or between different organisms increases the intensity of Darwinian selection and causes changes in the distribution of phenotypes and genes in the gene pool of a population of a species.
7. Thus, evolution is descent with modification in the distribution of variations in phenotypes and genotypes, with the distribution of alleles in a species' gene pool determined by those variations in phenotypes that have allowed organisms to secure resources, survive, and reproduce.

of resources to a given species of organisms. Environmental changes that generate selection revolve around the capacity of members of a population to gain access to life-sustaining resources and to thereby survive and reproduce (thereby passing on their genes to the next generation). Any disruption to this capacity will increase competition among conspecifics and/or between conspecifics and other life forms in a given resource niche. As noted, selection occurs on the phenotypes among individual members of a population, but emphasis in biology is on the evolution of the population, particularly the distribution of genotypes in the gene pool. The fundamental unit in Darwinian theory, then, is *the population* defined as a distribution of (a) phenotypes and (b) genotypes constituting a gene pool. In contrast, we should note, the unit of selection in sociocultural systems is *both* biological phenotypes and sociocultural phenotypes, as is outlined in Figure 10.2 on page 253. Both are subject to selection, but the nature of the selection shifts the more we move away from a focus on biological phenotypes to concern with modifications of sociocultural phenotypes.

Moreover, as we have emphasized in Chapter 10, cultural transmission does not work like genetic transmission, a point of emphasis that social scientists have emphasized for over a hundred years (e.g., Spencer 1874–1896, Durkheim 1893, Steward 1955, Runciman 1983–1897, 2009; Richerson and Boyd 2005; Turner and Maryanski 2008b; Turner 1995, 2010). The fidelity of cultural transmission over time (generations *cannot* be calculated in sociocultural evolution) is very loose compared to that of genetic inheritance, and the selection processes that affect the structures in which culture is embedded are very different than those outlined in Table 11.1 and Figure 11.1. Hence, "fitness" cannot be defined by something as fanciful as "cultural memes in a meme pool" (Dawkins 1976) because culture makes little sense when broken down into bits of information; the power of culture only comes by virtue of *the interconnectedness among symbols and systems of symbols and their embeddedness in social structures*. To conceptualize, a meme pool distorts what culture is and how it operates to provide informational controls on human actions as they are organized into social structures. The unit of selection is, as we emphasized in Chapter 10, the number, distribution, and modes of integration of corporate

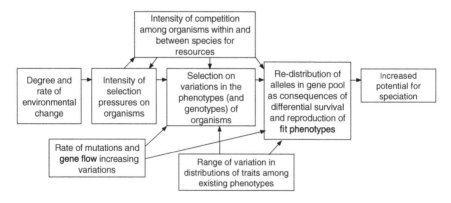

Figure 11.1 Darwinian Selection and the "Modern Synthesis" in Biology

units (revealing divisions of labor in pursuit of goals and the cultural systems (texts, technologies, ideologies, beliefs, stocks of knowledgeability, norms, and expectations) inhering in and, to much less precise degree, directing actions, interactions, and patterns of social organization.

In Darwinian evolution, there is a closer connection between genetic instructions and the phenotypes on which selection works, with the result that selection on phenotypes has more predictable effects on the distribution of genes and alleles in a population of organisms. However, Darwinian natural selection is a very important dynamic in the new evolutionary sociology because the social universe, as we know it today, could not have evolved without the anatomical and especially neuroanatomical modifications to species of primates forged by Darwinian natural selection. The human capacity for teleology and hence creativity evolved in those great ape-like hominins on the human clade and then during the transition from the last hominins (*Homo erectus*) to humans (*Homo sapiens*). Unlike much sociology, evolutionary sociology emphasizes that it is not possible to understand fully most of the topics of interest to sociologists, and social scientists more generally, without knowledge about how human anatomy and neuroanatomy evolved to generate an animal capable of building up complex structures and, then, deliberately changing these structures and their cultures in order to adapt to altered environmental conditions. This has been the great, though rather obvious, insight of sociobiology and evolutionary psychology; and rather than be threatened by this search, sociology should embrace inquiry into the cognitive, emotional, and behavioral capacities and propensities of humans as highly evolved great apes. In embracing these efforts, contemporary sociology will be doing what virtually all the early masters of sociology implicitly did: assumed that there is a "human nature" which undergirds the sociocultural systems making up the social universe of *Homo sapiens*. Whether Marx's analysis of alienation, Durkheim's views on anomie and egoism, Pareto's six instinctual drives, Mead's views on self, Cooley's need to avoid shame, and in more contemporary theorizing, exchange theory's emphasis on needs to gain profits in exchanges, symbolic interactionist's theorizing on the need to verify identities, ritual and dramaturgical theory's emphasis on the need to experience positive emotions from rituals, and so on. Sociological theorizing has always had implicit views of human nature that were highly speculative. With evolutionary sociology, however, it becomes possible to actually document this "nature" driving human behavior with the tools of evolutionary biology.

As we will argue, the thrust of Darwinian natural selection on the basic anatomy and neuroanatomy of animals like contemporary great apes—that is, chimpanzees, gorillas, and orangutans—created a big-brained, highly emotional animal capable of some remarkable capacities that are outlined in Part III of the book. The basic thrust of Darwinian selection was to convert animals—the great apes—that are not highly social nor group oriented into animals capable of being more social and group oriented. Sociologists do not typically realize that natural selection was working to overcome the hard-wired, genetically driven propensities of humans' primate ancestors to be weak-tie, low-sociality animals that did not form permanent groups. Sociologists generally assume that humans are *naturally* social and *naturally* group-forming animals, when in fact, the opposite is the case. And this is why it is important to discover how natural selection altered the hominin line over millions of years of biological evolution to become more social, more group oriented, and hence more human. Thus, evolutionary sociology should begin with understanding how Darwinian selection altered the nature of great apes to create human beings who became capable of stronger social ties and more cohesive group formations, from which they could built up social structures in the pattern implied by Figure 10.2 on page 253. This Darwinian story will be told in Chapters 12–17. For the present, let us turn to non-Darwinian forms of natural selection, which carry the names of the key sociological figures who inspired the study of these somewhat different types of sociocultural selection. We terms these: (1) *Spencerian selection*, Type-1 and Type-2; (2) *Durkheimian selection*; and (3) *Marxian selection* to honor the figures in sociology who first conceptualized these key selection dynamics (Turner and Maryanski 2008a; Turner 1995; Turner and Abrutyn 2017; Turner 2016; Turner et al. 2017). Evolutionary sociology begins with Darwinian selection as it has honed the cognitive, emotional, and behavior capacities and propensities of humans, but if we want to understand the dynamics of evolution on layers of sociocultural formations outlined in Figure 10.2 on page 253, we need to recognize that there are other types of non-Darwinian selection operating in the human social universe.

Spencerian Natural Selection

It is easy to forget that the idea of evolution was as prominent in early sociology as in early 19th biology and that the famous phrase "survival of the fittest" was never uttered by Darwin, except in the preface to *On the Origin of Species* (Darwin 1859) when complimenting Herbert Spencer for his early phrasing of what he would term *natural selection*. In Spencer's sociology, the notion of "survival of the fittest" generally denoted the process whereby societies fought over resources, with the more organized and hence "more fit" society winning out over the less fit society. Inhering in this analysis is a type of selection that J. Turner has labeled *Spencerian selection, Type-2*, to be discussed in more detail shortly. As outlined in Chapter 4 on intersocietal evolution, geopolitical analysis in sociology and the social sciences more generally can be considered a type of natural selection because societies and intersocietal systems are constantly modified over time by warfare or threats of warfare, as well as by competition in markets.

Spencer is most associated with the use of the organismic analogy, as we stressed in early chapters. Sociological functionalism was born in Spencer's analysis of evolution in which he argued that, as superorganisms evolve by becoming larger and more complexly structured and differentiated, they do so along four fundamental axes: (1) production, (2) distribution, (3) reproduction, and (4) regulation. That is, as societies grow in size, new fault lines posing adaptive problems develop in terms of how to produce enough to support the larger population; how to distribute information and resources across a population; how to reproduce members of societies and the corporate units organizing their activities; and how to regulate, coordinate, and control individuals and corporate units through the mobilization of power and use of cultural symbol systems (e.g., law, ideologies, values). In this analysis, which was never as functional as modern commentators have emphasized, is a type of non-Darwinian selection that J. H. Turner has termed *Spencerian selection, Type-1*, also to be examined shortly. This is a kind of selection that, in some ways, is the opposite of what Darwinian natural selection emphasizes; Type-1 Spencerian selection occurs when a population faces adaptive problems along one of the above fault lines—i.e., production, distribution, reproduction, and regulation—for which there are *no presently viable social structural variants* to address the problem. Under these conditions, there are Type-1 Spencerian selection pressures on individual and corporate actors to discover, invent, and/or borrow new types of sociocultural variants to deal with the problem; and if they cannot, then the society will become less fit, either disintegrating or being conquered by a more fit society (through *Type-2 Spencerian selection*, to be examined shortly). Now, let us turn to a more detailed review of these types of selection.

Type-1 Spencerian Selection

As was reviewed in Chapter 3, Spencer's sociology outlines theoretical principles that can explain the dynamics of societies as they evolve from simple to ever-more complex formations. For Spencer, evolution at all levels of reality, including the biological, physical, sociocultural, and even ethical, is a movement from simple-homogeneous masses to increasing complex-heterogeneous formations (Spencer 1862). For human societies, this evolution is set off by population growth which, in turn, increases selection pressures along the potential fault lines—i.e., production, reproduction, distribution, and regulation—of all human societies. Can a society produce and distribute resources necessary to sustain individuals, families, and corporate units organizing their activities? Can members of the society and the structures organizing their activities be reproduced? Can power be consolidated around power as well as around systems of values, ideologies, beliefs, and norms over which there is consensus and toward which individuals develop commitments? And, are distributive infrastructures and exchange structures sufficient in moving information, resources, and across territories and social strata? Any problem along these fault lines generates *Type-1 Spencerian selection*.

As organic and superorganic forms grow, they become more differentiated along these four fault lines or axes of differentiation; and in the case of superorganic evolution, there is no guarantee that members of a society or the corporate units organizing the activities of members can create a solution to these adaptive problems that escalate with population growth. And so, Spencer held out the real possibility that societies can disintegrate or dissolve because actors could not discover, invent, or borrow new variants that met these selection pressures. Spencer, in his organismic analogy, thought that organisms also revealed these same adaptive problems, and today, we would argue that these generate Darwinian selection pressures for organisms. Selection here must be on tail ends of distributions of relevant traits, on relevant pre-adaptations, on mutations if they occur with sufficient frequency across a large swath of a population, on gene flow, and on genetic drift. If the selection pressures are intense, it is likely that organisms will go extinct because, unlike humans, most organisms do not possess the same capacities for agency to remake rapidly their morphology, much less genotypes.

Yet, humans have had two episodes of near extinction over the last 200,000 years; and so, at times selection pressures can overwhelm a population, especially one with simple hunting and gathering technologies that do not allow a population to make dramatic changes in their social morphologies. The verdict is, of course, out on whether or not the high-technology societies organizing humans can address many of the Spencerian Type-1 problems of humans' own creation, such as global warming, environmental degradation, inequalities in resource distribution, and violence (war, terrorism, revolutions, coups, etc.) in societies where nuclear weapons now exist or, inevitably, will be available in international black markets.

Humans are a teleological organism, as are the superorganic corporate units that they create; and thus, when faced with adaptive problems they have the capacity to restructure themselves by creating new types of corporate units organized into new forms of institutional systems that can address and, hopefully, resolve or hold off adaptive problems. So, here is selection in which there is an absence of sociocultural variants available to manage adaptive problems; the selection pressures do not arise from competition among existing variants but from the *very lack of useful variants*, setting into motion human and corporate-unit agency to find solutions, if possible. The hope is that new variants can resolve productive, reproductive, distributive, or regulatory problems. These new variants are "acquired" through diffusion, invention, or even plain luck; and thus, Type-1 Spencerian selection also emphasizes the Lamarckian aspects of much sociocultural evolution. Indeed, in Spencerian selection, Lamarckian ideas are no longer the competitive loser, as they once were, to Darwin's portrayal of organic natural selection; they are now fundamental to any species that has the capacity for agency and that, hence, can reconstruct the survivor machines—corporate units organized into larger sociocultural formations—that protect the genetic legacy installed by Darwinian selection.

To some degree, of course, humans are constrained by their cognitive, emotional, and behavioral propensities inherited from the operation of Darwinian natural selection, and often, they are constrained by the inertia inhering in existing institutional systems and their cultures. So, although humans' cognitive, emotional, and behavioral propensities enable them to be teleological and to exert agency, existing structures and regulating ideologies, beliefs, and norms developed in the past to solve old adaptive problems can constrain what options are perceived to be available, possible, or desirable in the face of new selection pressures. In this case, as noted, a society may disintegrate or be subject to selection forces inhering in Type-2 Spencerian selection.

Table 11.2 and Figure 11.2 outline the basic dynamics of *Type-1 Spencerian selection*. Adaptive problems for which there are no fitness-enhancing variants in a population's sociocultural morphology, particularly corporate units within institutional domains, will generate selection pressures along the axes of societal differentiation or fault lines along which all superorganisms develop adaptive problems. Many environmental changes leading to adaptive problems are generated by the superorganism itself; indeed most are generated this way, as is the case today with environmental degradation, global warming, population growth, political instability, economic recessions, and all of the chronic and not fully resolved problems facing

TABLE 11.2 Selection in the Absence of Fitness-Enhancing Variants: Spencerian Type-1 Selection

1. Adaptive problems for which there are no fitness-enhancing variants in the sociocultural morphology (social phenotype) organizing members of a population are often generated by:

    a. Ecological changes (both biophysical and sociocultural) in a population's environment

    b. Population growth and diversification

    c. Internal pressures from existing sociocultural phenotypes, typically revolving around complexity of social morphology

    d. Increases in inequalities/stratification

2. These kinds of adaptive problems generate selection pressures that, in the absence of existing fitness-enhancing corporate units, push on individual and collective actors to develop new types of fitness-enhancing corporate units and modes of their integration into new or existing institutional systems.

3. All institutional systems in human societies have evolved under Spencerian more than Darwinian selection pressures.

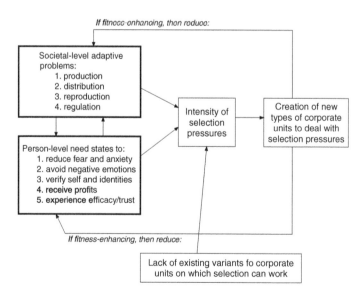

Figure 11.2 Type-1 Spencerian Selection Pressures

societies. Thus, as they get larger and more complex, superorganisms often create the very new environmental problems that generate Spencerian selection pressures.

In much the same vein, many adaptive problems arise from person-level needs, where fundamental need-states of all humans (as a result of Darwinian selection dynamics) are not adequately met; and the greater the number of people in a society whose needs go unmet, the more selection pressure they generate. These needs will be examined in Chapter 13 on human nature where we will emphasize such needs as verifying self and identities, experiencing profits and fairness in most exchange relations across diverse corporate units in differentiated institutional domains, feeling efficacious in social relations, experiencing a sense of trust in others, and sensing inclusion in the ongoing flow of interaction in important groups within key organizations within institutional domains. The more fundamental needs that go unmet, the greater is the intensity of the negative emotions experienced, and the more individuals will collectively feel a sense of deprivation and, hence, the more likely will they put pressure on key institutional systems to change. Most of the time, these need-states exert a quiet and persistent pressure on corporate units in institutional domains that distribute valued resources, but when people collectively experience deprivations over inequality and fail to meet key human need-states, mobilization for conflict often ensures and, occasionally, unleashes what can be seen as *Marxian selection* (to be discussed later).

Type-1 selection pressures arise, then, not only from social structural arrangements within a society and from changes in a society's external environmental conditions but also from the basic nature of humans as evolved great apes. Institutional change in societies generally occur when these pressures intensify, forcing individual and collective actors to find or create new sociocultural variants that can relieve these Type-1 selection pressures. If the institutional system is too rigid, traditional, and conservative to allow for new variants of structure and culture to be implemented, then a society is doomed to disintegration from Marxian selection and/or Type-2 Spencerian selection.

Type-1 Spencerian selection is derived from Spencer's weak functionalism (see Chapters 2 and 3) and avoids the criticism that such approaches are inherently conservative. True, as noted above, institutional systems can be resistant to change, and Spencer emphasized that a population that cannot reconstruct its institutional systems is doomed to disintegration and dissolution or, alternatively, is doomed to conquest by a society with a stronger set of institutional domains (in accordance with Type-2 Spencerian selection). Spencer held out that, over the long run of human evolutionary history, enough societies could create new institutional systems that then serve as successful adaptive templates for other societies or, equally likely, could allow the society finding a successful template to engage in conquest of other societies that could not do so. In either case, the overall level of complexity of societies has grown. Each institutional domain that successively evolved after kinship—religion, economy, polity, law, medicine, science, etc.—was created under Type-1 Spencerian selection pressures, or borrowed from other populations, or imposed upon a population by conquest.

Institutions, which are the structural backbone of all societies, did not just emerge; they were created by populations under intense Type-1 Spencerian selection and, at times, Type-2 Spencerian selection pressures where external threats from another society led to institutional change in the threatened society or was imposed by another society. War and conquest allowed more fit institutional systems to spread among conquered populations, obviously at the price of their sovereignty and perhaps subordination as well. As we have noted in several chapters, near the end of his life, Spencer argued that war was no longer necessary, and in fact, it was counterproductive because it concentrated power and stifled innovations in all spheres except war-making. With the advance of industrial capitalism, Spencer felt that markets and competition in markets could be the next engines of institutional change, setting off yet another kind of selection, Durkheimian selection, that we will examine shortly. Markets, Spencer felt, were innovation-generating machines because they create incentives for individual and collective actors to innovate to fill needs (both personal and societal, as generated by selection pressures). Innovation would now be directed toward domestic production and distribution, creating the wealth to increase the standards of living in all societies. While this was a bit optimistic, to say the least, Spencer's argument anticipated the commentary in the second half of the 20th Century about the effects of the military-industrial complex on domestic production.

Type-2 Spencerian Selection

In Table 11.3 and Figure 11.3, the elements and dynamics, respectively, of *Type-2 Spencerian selection* are delineated. Societies, Spencer emphasized, frequently engage in warfare in battles leading to the "survival of the fittest" society and, then, either the subordination of the conquered society in some pattern of institutional domination or, much more rarely, the complete destruction of a society and its population. As noted above, Spencer saw the evolution of societies as very much driven by warfare, which can

TABLE 11.3 Spencerian Selection, Type-2, From Geopolitics and Geoeconomics

1. All societies reveal some pattern of intersocietal relations.
2. Economic or political inequalities among societies in an intersocietal system can lead to (a) intersocietal warfare or (b) asymmetrical trade relations.
3. Inequalities in power and/or economic power generally cause changes in both the dominant and dominated societies, and particularly the dominated, as the institutional systems and culture of the dominant societies move into the dominated society.
4. If a coercive strategy of domination is pursued by a conquering society, then the institutions and culture of the dominate society will be imposed on the conquered society, thereby increasing inequalities as the culture and institutional systems of conquerors are imposed on those of the conquered. Such dynamics generally increase tensions, deny members of the conquered society the ability to meet fundamental need-states, and arouse negative emotions against conquerors.
5. These dynamics lead to selection that, in the shorter run, causes selection of culture and institutional systems of the dominant society, but they also increase the likelihood that Type-1 Spencerian pressures will increase, and indeed, Marxian selection pressures may begin to increase.
6. If, on the other hand, a cooptive strategy of domination is pursued, then the institutional systems and culture of the dominant society, particularly if domination is more economic than political, will diffuse into the dominated society and activate more Durkheimian selection (see Table 11.4) that leads to a gradual transition to a blended culture and set of institutional systems.
7. If, at any time, a coercive strategy is pursued to replace a cooptive strategy, then the dynamic outlined in (4) and (5) above will be activated, thereby increasing the likelihood of Marxian selection dynamics emerging.

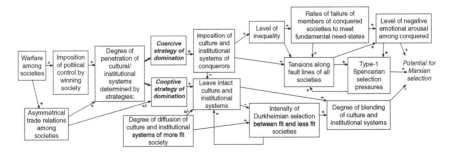

Figure 11.3 Type-2 Spencerian Selection From Geopolitics (and Geoeconomics)

be conceptualized as a kind of selection favoring the society with the strongest institutional system, especially a polity capable of mobilizing coercive force and an economy able to generate the resources to support a large and effective coercive force. Societies with larger populations, with consensus over values, ideologies, and beliefs; with higher levels of technology; with larger populations from which to draw military forces; with polity that is centralized and yet legitimated (often by religious beliefs and elites); with an economy that produces large economic surpluses, with superiority in military and technologies; and with other advantages such as a marchland situation (with no enemies behind its home base) or key alliances with other societies can typically win a war with a society revealing lower levels of all these resources. If the conquered population is not exterminated, then it is absorbed in some manner; and even with high domination, a larger swath of persons now lives in a "more fit" sociocultural formation, even if they are exploited by the military actions of a marcher polity (see Chapter 4 for more recent conceptualizations of these dynamics).

As one society conquers another, much of its culture (particularly its religion but also other cultural beliefs and ideologies) and many of its organizational structures as these build out institutional systems diffuse to the conquered population. The selection processes inhering in war thereby reconstruct the institutional systems of the conquered population as a larger and, for the time being, more fit superorganism. Thus, traveling along with war and conquest are the cultures and institutional systems of conquering societies. And, while these are often resisted by those conquered and, at times, not pushed on a population's conquerors who leave most of the existing institutional systems largely intact (e.g., the Roman Empire), new ideas, technologies, organizational templates, and at times opportunities become available to the conquered. In these various ways, then, the institutional systems of the conquered societies change.

Warfare and the associated dynamics unleashed by warfare have historically been one of the key forces driving "descent with modification" at the level of societies and intersocietal systems, as well as the internal cultures of even subordinated societies, in the new geopolitical formation that evolves. Geoeconomics can cause much descent with modification of societies and well as the intersocietal system in which they are embedded. Control of markets and imposition of asymmetrical trade relations generally leads to a coopting strategy of domination, as outlined in Figure 11.3, that sets into motion Durkheimian (see next section) selection among corporate units and ideological systems that, in turn, causes a blending of cultural and institutional systems of dominant and dominated societies, with a bias favoring the dominant society. And, should a coercive strategy be pursued at any point, then the dynamics described at the top half of Figure 11.3 are likely to be activated.

One force emphasized in Figure 11.3 is conquest which in the short run generally increases inequalities in the new superorganism composed of the conquered and their conquerors, especially when a coercive strategy of domination is pursued by the conquering polity. As a result, new types of Type-1 selection pressures can emerge in such new superorganisms, especially pressures for new forms of regulation, but also distribution, production, and reproduction of the new institutional systems under conditions of high inequality where fundamental needs of the conquered are consistently not being realized. Threat of revolts and other threats represent Type-1 Spencerian selection pressures or even Marxian selection pressures on the institutional systems—polity, law, economy, and even religion—in the new superorganism, often leading to adaptive response that may work in the short run (coercive repression) but that themselves create new levels of Type-1 selection pressures from those not receiving resources, not having opportunities, and not meeting fundamental human needs (installed by Darwinian selection). The stage is thus set for a round of Marxian selection in the midst of Type-1 and Type-2 Spencerian selection, often generated by the unfulfilled needs of the subordinated that are part of the legacy of Darwinian selection.

Durkheimian Selection

In his *The Division of Labor in Societies* (1893), Emile Durkheim outlined a casual explanation for the movement from mechanical to organic solidarity—a distinction that he eventually abandoned by 1895 in favor of only one kind of solidarity (emotion arousing rituals sustaining collective representations, as outlined in *The Elementary Forms of the Religious Life* [1912] and a series of papers and lectures that most sociologists have not read). As outlined in Chapter 5, Durkheim borrowed very explicitly from Darwin, arguing that material density (concentrations in space) and moral density (rates of interaction) lead to increased competition among individuals (and by implication, the corporate units organizing their activities), with those who are most fit surviving and reproducing in a niche, while those that are less fit migrating to new niches or using their capacities for agency to create a new resource niche. Actors do not appear to die in Durkheim's model; rather, they just specialize ("socially speciate") as they seek or create new niches in which they can sustain themselves. Despite this rather benign view of the social universe, Durkheim was the first to attempt to adopt Darwin's model to the social universe. Table 11.4 and Figure 11.4 summarize the key elements in Durkheim's argument.

TABLE 11.4 Durkheimian Selection on Corporate Units and Multi-Level Evolution

---

1. A society or any macro-level superorganism can be viewed as a set of resource niches in which corporate units seek resources to survive.
2. As corporate units enter and sustain themselves, additional corporate units will enter this niche.
3. As the population of corporate units seeking resources in a niche increases, so does the level of density among these units.
4. With increasing density comes increasing competition among corporate units (multi-level or group selection) in a niche that leads to a number of potential outcomes:
   a. Some organizations will die.
   b. Other organizations will move to another existing niche.
   c. Still other organizations will create a new resource niche.
5. With any of the outcomes under 4a, 4b, or 4c, density in a niche is reduced, thereby generating opportunities for new corporate units to enter this niche and survive, as long as density remains below the carrying capacity of the niche.
6. These Darwinian-like selection processes generally occur within an existing regulatory system that institutionalizes competition, typically through sociocultural formations that have evolved under Type-1 Spencerian selection pressures (see Table 11-2):
   a. Markets
   b. Political authority
   c. Legal regulation
7. Both the units subject to selection and the regulatory systems regulating competition have capacities for agency, innovation, and other teleological capacities for creating new variants in the morphology and culture of corporate units seeking resources or regulating resource-seeking activities of corporate units in a population.

We have added a somewhat more realistic view of what selection does because, clearly, organizations and other types of corporate units often "die" in the competitive struggle for resources. Moreover, Durkheimian selection also occurs under conditions of some regulation, often imposed by polity and law, and is most dynamic when a market mechanism exists to institutionalize competition for resources. Later ecological analyses by

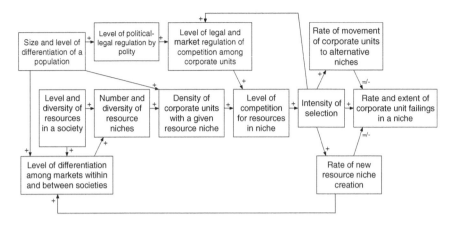

Figure 11.4 Durkheimian Selection Among Corporate Units Within Societies

sociologists emphasized the importance of markets, regulated by polity and law, as increasing the prevalence of what we are terming *Durkheimian selection* in differentiating societies. These ecological theories were analyzed in Chapter 5, but let us review them again to emphasize how important Durkheimian selection is as societies become more complex.

Urban ecology as initiated by the Chicago School and carried forth at the University of North Carolina, viewed communities much like ecologists did, and still do: as a series of resource niches in space, which organisms and, in the case of sociocultural systems, superorganisms like families, governmental agencies, schools, churches, businesses of many kinds, or any other type of corporate unit seek to occupy. Markets institutionalize this process by establishing a "price" for various ecological spaces, with the distribution of corporate units into urban districts reflecting varying abilities to pay the price for different urban spaces. Of course, there have always been other mechanisms of distribution, such as power and moral persuasion, that also affect where various types of corporate units occupy urban space. The underlying model of urban ecology was presented in Figure 5.3 on page 106 and represents an application of Durkheimian ideas borrowed from Darwin to understand the differentiation of space in sociocultural systems.

Also compatible with Durkheim's argument and also borrowed from more general ecological models is organizational ecology, which emerged in the 1970s from students of the last of the Chicago School urban ecologists, Amos Hawley (1944, 1986). Michael Hannan and John Freeman (1977, 1989) sought to examine the life and death of populations of organizations in which organizations seeking resources in a given niche were defined as a population. As density among organizations increases in a niche, so does competition that, in turn, leads to increased levels of selection. Since resource niches tend to become populated beyond the capacity of the niche, the death rate for organizations is initially high, revealing a sudden and dramatic drop in the number of organizations that can sustain themselves in the niche. The death rate tends to overshoot the carrying capacity, with the result that new organizations can begin to repopulate the niche but never at the same rate or extent as when the niche first became legitimated. Thus, after the initial founding of a niche, the volatility of life and death of organizations declines, but rarely is a true equilibrium ever reached. The basic model of organizational ecology was outlined in Figure 5.5 on page 109 (Hannan and Freeman 1977, 1989; Hannan et al. 2007) and can be used to guide the review below.

Early organizational ecology focused mostly on profit-making companies in capitalist societies, but the dynamics can be extended to all organizations in all types of societies, whatever the exact nature of the economy or, for that matter, all other institutional domains. Even when explicit markets do not exist to institutionalize the competition for resources, religious, familial, educational, scientific, legal, political, artistic, sport, and other types of corporate units serving as the building blocks of differentiated institutional domains can all be subject to the forces of Durkheimian selection because all must find resources—money, cultural symbols, members, customers, believers, political, and virtually any resource needed to sustain the organization. And, it is rare for there not to be competition for these resources; and as density of corporate units seeking resources of a given type, the level of competition and selection inevitably increase. The patterns of differentiation among corporate units and institutional domains in a society thus reflect the operation of Durkheimian selection which, Durkheim felt, is parallel to the differentiation of species in Darwinian selection.

Corporate units, particularly organizations, distribute resources to their incumbents which can vary, depending upon the nature of the institutional domains built up by corporate units and their modes of integration into a differentiated institutional system. Money is obviously one resource that is distributed by many organizations across domains, particularly in capitalist societies, but sociologists have often tended to ignore other types of resources. Power is, of course, a resource that sociologists have studied extensively, but often not conceptualized as something that is distributed as authority within many different types of corporate units in diverse domains. In essence, the polity in a society "franchises" power out to corporate units as authority to regulate the internal workings of corporate units in diverse institutional domains; and so, authority is yet another resource like money that is distributed in virtually all corporate units, from families through churches and schools to arts organizations.

Moreover, institutional domains tend to reveal *their own* generalized symbolic media, which is exchanged among individuals and corporate units within an institutional domain, or between corporate units in different domains. So, for example, polity gives *power* as authority to scientific organizations to regulate the search for *verified knowledge*, the generalized symbolic medium of science; and the reason that polity gives money is because it seeks verified knowledge, thereby setting up a stable system of exchange of money for verified knowledge between polity and science as differentiated domains. Thus, in science, verified knowledge becomes the symbolic media for talk, discussion, and discourse among scientists; it also becomes the goal marked by totems of its virtue that is sought by scientific corporate units; it also is converted into an ideology legitimating and valorizing the search for knowledge, per se; and it is the valued resource that scientists are able to secure in their work because it is value, in and of its own right, but also because it can be exchanged for power, money, prestige, and other valued resources. Table 11.5 outlines the various generalized symbolic media for various institutional domains; and while power as authority and money circulate within and between these domains, these media from, respectively, polity and economy, do not obviate the value of the generalized symbolic media unique in other differentiated domains (Turner 2015; Abrutyn and Turner 2011).

Most corporate units reveal some inequality within their divisions of labor, with some having more power than others and thus able to secure more money and greater shares of the generalized symbolic medium, which is valuable in its own right, within a domain. Stratification systems are built up from this unequal distribution of resources by corporate units using the generalized symbolic medium of differentiated domains. And, while money, power, and prestige have been studied the most by sociologists, other generalized symbolic media are also distributed unequally and can become another basis of stratification in their own right and by their effects on individuals' capacity to gain access to power, money, and prestige. For example, a person who has received *love and loyalty* within family and kinship has received a very valued resource, per se, but high levels of this resource often give individuals the confidence and security to obtain other valued resources like money and power (Turner 2010, 2015). The same can be true of other valued resources; those with high levels of *knowledge*, for example, have received a valued resource in its own right, but this resource can also be used to charge rents in the job markets and thereby gain access

TABLE 11.5 Generalized Symbolic Media of Institutional Domains

Kinship	**Love/loyalty,** or the use of intense positive affective states to forge and mark commitments to others and groups of others
Economy	**Money,** or the denotation of exchange value for objects, actions, and services by the metrics inhering in money
Polity	**Power,** or the capacity to control the actions of other actors
Law	**Influence,** or the capacity to adjudicate social relations and render judgments about justice, fairness, and appropriateness of actions
Religion	**Sacredness/piety,** or the commitment to beliefs about forces and entities inhabiting a non-observable supernatural realm and the propensity to explain events and conditions by references to these sacred forces and beings
Education	**Learning,** or the commitment to acquiring and passing on knowledge
Science	**Knowledge,** or the invocation of standards for gaining verified knowledge about all dimensions of the social, biotic, and physico-chemical universes
Medicine	**Health,** or the concern about and commitment to sustaining the normal functioning of the human body
Sport	**Competitiveness,** or the definition of games that produce winners and losers by virtue of the respective efforts of players
Arts	**Aesthetics,** or the commitment to make and evaluate objects and performances by standards of beauty and pleasure that they give observers

Note: These and other generalized symbolic media are employed in discourse among actors, in articulating themes, and in developing ideologies about what should and ought to transpire in an institutional domain. They tend to circulate within a domain, but all of the symbolic media can circulate in other domains, although some media are more likely to do so than others.

to money and often authority as well. Thus, the corporate units within institutional domains are the ultimate source of inequality and stratification systems in all societies. Social class location in this system, even when somewhat vague as in post-industrial systems, becomes an important marker of worth and value for individuals and families; indeed, it is a social category that often defines who persons and families are.

Thus, societies are not only organized around corporate units as they build out institutional domains but also around what can be termed *categoric units* (Hawley 1986; Turner 1995, 2010a), which are not only social distinctions that are made by virtue of the resources that people and families have been able to secure in institutional domains but also by the distinctions that mark people in terms of age, gender and sex, ethnicity, religious affiliation, place of birth, and the like. These two become *parameters* (Blau 1977) marking differences among people, leading to differential evaluation of persons in terms of the moral worth of their categoric-unit memberships (see discussion on pp. 110 to 112 in Chapter 5). Often, these types of categoric units are correlated or consolidated with particular locations in the stratification system, with the result that evaluations take on more power to define the moral worth of persons and how they will be treated in a society. For instance, an ethnic minority or majority in some cases can be over-represented in the lower social classes, thereby doubling up on the negative evaluations of these individuals by their ethnicity and class location.

As we emphasized in Chapter 5 and noted above, Peter Blau (1977, 1993) has conceptualized societies in terms of the distributions of individuals by what he termed "*parameters*," which are the yardsticks by which people are measured for membership in particular categoric units. People with high levels of money, age, education, power, and/or prestige are defined by *graduated* parameters that vary by degree (with people having high, medium, or low amounts of these being evaluated differently). In contrast, other parameters are *nominal* because they define people as either "in or out" of a categoric unit, such as gender, ethnicity/race, religious affiliation, sexual orientation, class, etc. Of course, people reveal a configuration of both types of categoric-unit membership, but for our purposes in understanding Durkheimian selection dynamics, a society can be considered as the sum total of the distribution of persons along any given parameter. Some of these intersect—African Americans can be rich or poor—and they can consolidate—African Americans are over-represented in poverty in American society. The more intersection that occurs, where there is little correlation among memberships in graduated or nominal categories, the more ambiguous the distribution becomes and, in fact, the more integrated is a society because there are no great fault lines, say, with respect to some ethnics over-represented in the lower (or upper) class that can generate conflict; instead, all ethnics are equally likely to be in the lower, middle, or higher classes in proportion to the relative numbers in the general population—a most unlikely occurrence in the real world but one to strive for.

Miller McPherson and colleagues (McPherson and Ranger-Moore 1991; McPherson and Rotolo 1996) have conceptualized the distribution of memberships, as defined by nominal and graduated parameters denoting various social categories or what we are terming categoric units as a *Blau-space*, in deference to Peter Blau's (1977, 1993) analysis. Any distribution can, they argue, become resource niches for corporate units seeking customers of a particular kind or location along graduated parameters; seeking members (in churches, social clubs, service organizations, political parties); or seeking recruits (to social movement organizations, armies, political parties). While money and other resources may also flow, organizations often recruit particular *types of individuals*, but if the number of organizations seeking members, recruits, or customers at particular points in Blau-space becomes too crowded, then this increased niche density will cause selection in much the same manner as with business corporate units in economic market niches, even without an explicit market. The result will be that some organizations will die because they cannot attract sufficient numbers of persons at this point in Blau-space or, as in Durkheim's analysis, they may have to shift to a different point in Blau-space—in other words, they must move to a new resource niche to sustain the organization. McPherson's (1983) analysis of the ecological dynamics of service organizations in communities in the United States (e.g., Lion's Club, Optimists, etc.) documents that the preferred membership in these clubs (white, male, middle- to upper-class persons involved in business and governance in a community) became too dense because many people in this particular resource niche, or set of Blau-space points, had lost interest in membership; and so the large number of clubs that had once occupied this niche in the 1940s and 1950s in the U.S. made the now-shrunken niche overpopulated with too many service clubs. To avoid extinctions, which still occur in many communities, many clubs shifted to new niches, or different points in Blau-space, by including women, non-white minorities, and working-class persons in order to survive.

In large complex societies, organizations seek many different kinds of resources; and the differentiation of populations by points in Blau-space marking categoric-unit memberships opens a large number of resource niches where organizations can attract customers, members, and recruits. There are, in essence, both explicit market processes using money involved but also what can be defined as *quasi-markets* that respond to supply (of resources in a given niche) and demand (by corporate units) that abides not so much by the principles of capitalism as first outlined by Adam Smith but by principles that have been derived by organizational ecology from Darwin, often via Durkheim's seminal insights. These dynamics revolving around the relationship between categoric units and corporate units are outlined in Figure 5.6 on page 111 and later in this chapter in Figure 11.5. These are important dynamics in building up institutional systems, as is the case when religious organizations seek members, when political parties seek voters, when the military seeks recruits, when service clubs seek members, when universities seek students, when social movement organizations seek followers, or when corporate units of any kind begin to define resources in terms of categories of persons.

Durkheim's (1893: 267) early application of Darwinian ideas to understanding differentiation—a kind of social speciation—and the various forms of urban and organizational ecological analysis that emerged in the 20th Century and persist to this day are as close as most sociological analysis gets to Darwinian theory, save for those sociologists who are committed to sociobiology or evolutionary psychology. But even here, the unit of analysis has changed from the phenotype of individual organisms to the morphology of corporate units that are teleological and that, hence, can remake themselves and acquire new characteristics by virtue of their capacities for agency. Still, much else is the same as in Darwin's analysis: Corporate units seek resources to survive and reproduce; the social universe can thus be viewed as a large number of resource niches that determine the sociocultural phenotype of corporate units in a population; they differentiate in terms of the kinds of resources that they seek and the niches in sociocultural space that they inhabit (although the biophysical environment can also be a critical set of niches); populations of corporate units in a niche are what evolve rather than the social structure and culture of particular corporate units; and selection increases with niche density, leading to the death of less fit corporate units or their movement to new niches as a different kind of corporate unit (sociocultural speciation). Such is the power of Darwin's ideas, but we should not forget the differences in the nature of the units being analyzed and their capacities for self-transformations, which dramatically change analysis even with its ecological- and biological-sounding vocabulary.

Marxian Selection

Competition for resources in societies often becomes intense, violent, and, unlike Durkheim selection, less regulated by existing institutional systems. Indeed, the conflict is often over existing institutions, particularly polity, law, and not infrequently, religion; and equally often, the conflict between subpopulations in a society is directed at eliminating existing institutional practices and/or changing them in fundamental ways. There is a vast literature in conflict sociology, much of it derived from Karl Marx's seminal ideas, as well as an almost equally large (and overlapping with Marxian scholarship) literature on social movements (which also overlaps with forms of Durkheimian selection). This large swath of social science theorizing and empirical work can also be viewed in selectionist terms, since competition between segments of a population involves mobilization of resources to prevail in conflicts over the fundamental structure and culture of a society. Such conflicts generally arise from sectors of a society that have been subordinate and on the short-end of resource distributions by corporate units in institutional domains. At times, mobilization can be by the more affluent classes in a society when their expected shares of resources begin to decline (Turner 2015).

The conflict always begins with an accumulating set of grievances that are articulated in everyday routines among individuals and families in locales where people interact, but eventually, leaders emerge and begin to articulate counter-ideologies against the legitimating ideologies of those sectors of the society that control institutional systems, generally in the economy, polity, and legal system but also often in religious systems if one religion or sect within a religion dominates over other religions. There emerges a kind of Durkheimian competition among various factions and their leaders, and eventually, some factions win out, or at other times, consolidation of factions occurs, with the result that leadership and the organizational base for conflict becomes more coherent. At any point in this early mobilization, sporadic conflict and riots can emerge because individuals' emotions are aroused but, often, without a clear target or focus.

Karl Marx's analysis of conflict and the implicit theory that he developed in *The German Ideology* and *The Communist Manifesto* (both with F. Engels in 1846 and 1848) and, later by Marx alone, in *Capital* (1867) best capture the fundamental conditions under which violent conflicts emerge. From an evolutionary standpoint, these can be viewed as yet another kind of selection dynamic arising from conditions producing economic inequalities and emotionally charged mobilization by the deprived. Marx goes wrong in many of his predictions, but he had an ecological view of how conflict emerges through subordinates in a system of inequality successively acquiring resources—leadership, counter-ideologies, emotionally aroused and committed adherents (demographic resources), organizational resources, material resources—like any other set of corporate units in a society. Over time, he felt that there would be a convergence of subordinates under a common leadership and organizational framework for a social class to go from being a less focused categoric unit to a large-scale corporate unit or affiliation of corporate units transforming a class "of itself" to one mobilized "for itself" and ready to take political and economic power. Unlike Durkheimian selection, Marxian selection is conflict over the very institutional systems—economy, markets, polity, law, and religion—that regulate

Durkheimian competition and prevent it from erupting into an internal war between factions in a society. Moreover, Marx even goes beyond Spencer who did postulate that conflict would increase with the consolidation of power and with the inevitable rise in inequality that comes from this consolidation, but Spencer never laid out the specific processes by which subordinates in a system of inequality would become mobilized. And so, by drawing inspiration from Marx and supplementing Marxian ideas with more recent theories of conflict and social movements, it is possible to isolate this important type of non-Darwinian selection.

Ironically, most conflicts in the world today and for much of history have not been so directly class-based as based on memberships in non-class categoric units, particularly religious affiliation and ethnicity, although these non-class categoric units are often consolidated or correlated with memberships in lower social classes. Still, such is not always the case since many terrorists, for example, are of middle-class origins; and in fact, they have served as leaders recruiting less affluent participants to ethnic and religious conflict. Still, the dynamics of the conflict, when supplemented by more contemporary theories, are very similar to what Marx argued for class conflict. Table 11.6 and Figure 11.5 outline the basic elements and processes of Marxian selection.

Marxist, conflict theorists, theories of organizational ecology, and social movements models all converge and offer a powerful model of selectionist dynamics in superorganisms. These literatures all begin with grievances of subpopulations against the existing institutional system and particular corporate units in key institutional domains (Snow and Soule 2010). These grievances are held by members of categoric units that are devalued, subject to discrimination, and often persecuted by members of other categoric units who dominate key institutional domains and who thereby are able to disproportionately influence the operation of these domains and the cultural symbols (ideologies) legitimating their operation. Unlike Marxists, however, class is only one of a number of types of categoric units that experience grievances; and while these other types of categoric units—particularly ethnicity, religious affiliation, and often country of origin—may be consolidated with class and thus cause economic deprivations, prejudicial beliefs are typically directed at the non-class parameters defining people as members of categoric units. As grievances intensify, these emotionally aroused members of devalued categoric units become resource niches for entrepreneurial leaders who are seeking to develop a social movement organization (SMO) to confront existing institutional systems; and since parameters like ethnicity and religious affiliation, more than class membership, often define people's personal identities,

TABLE 11.6 Marxian Selection and Institutional Change

1. In societies revealing high levels of inequality, particularly by ethnicity and religion attached to lower classes, social movement organizations (SMOs) mobilize politically and seek to change the distribution of resources within an institutional system.

2. The starting point for such SMOs is almost always dissatisfaction with, and negative emotional arousal against, an existing institutional system or set of institutional domains.

3. Mobilization for conflict is an ecological process, because it involves efforts by social movement organizations, and competing corporate units, to secure resources in a variety of resource niches, including:

    a. Demographic (members and adherents to a cause)
    b. Cultural (symbols organized into ideologies)
    c. Network (other corporate units, networks to other corporate units)
    d. Material (money)
    e. Political (power and networks of power)
    f. Organizational (models and templates for organizing people into action)
    g. Emotional (arousal of negative emotions against existing arrangements/enemies and positive emotions around ideologies of SMOs)
    h. Leadership (that can articulate ideologies, arouse emotions, and organize adherents to the goals of the SMO)

4. Because such movements can often challenge existing distributions of resources within and across institutional systems, they often encounter intense resistance that, in turn, leads to conflict, often violent.

5. Whatever the level of violence, such conflict is a selection mechanism determining which political agenda will prevail in modifications to institutional systems.

6. The sets of organizations that engage in conflict (extreme competition) for resources determine the degree to which an institutional system will be restructured or a set of institutional systems will be restructured (selection and descent with modifications in the institutional systems of a society).

7. The more resources an SMO can generate vis-à-vis the existing system of organizations within and across institutional domains, the more conflict will change the institutional domains organizing a population.

8. The more conflict changes institutional systems in one society, the more likely are movements to be copied or to spread to other societies, thereby creating trans-social change in institutional structures.

9. The fewer resources available to SMOs, the less likely are they to change institution domains by direct action but, instead, by the reactions of existing centers of power to their challenge. Thus, even when the corporate units organizing a domain prevail in a challenge to their hegemony, the culture and a structure of the domain and perhaps several domains changes as a result of the conflict and the effort to mobilize for potential conflict in the future.

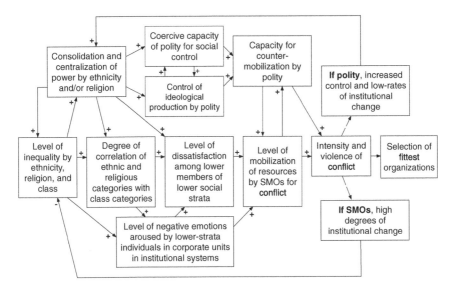

Figure 11.5 Marxian Selection and Institutional Change

the emotions attached to the devaluation of, and discrimination against, such identities arouse intense negative emotions, which emerging leaders exploit as yet one more resource niche composed of pools of negative emotion among particular members of devalued categoric units.

Typically, the emerging ideologies denote why these grievances have accumulated historically, who and what is responsible, and what must be done; and as this framing of the issues and emotions attached to these issues occurs, successful leaders arouse positive emotions in their followers for their willingness to address these issues, while demonizing those persons and those structural and cultural arrangements that are seen as responsible (Jasper and Owens 2014), and this polarity of more positive designations of self and negative emotions toward the targets of protest dramatically intensifies the emotional dynamics.

As this process of taking what Smelser (1963) termed "generalized beliefs" and reframing them into specific targets, while at the same time jacking up the positive emotions of the categoric members toward themselves as a person, as a collective force, and as a worthy category of persons, the coming conflict becomes highly moralized—something that is naturally done in religious conflict but that must be done in almost all successful revolts against sources of established power. This moralization is also what can make the conflict particularly violent because moral causes cannot broker comprises to morality.

In these dynamics, cultural and emotional resources must be secured in key resource niches, and these resources are as critical as the securing of actual armaments or tools used to effect a revolt. Yet, Marxian conflict is still very much an ecological process of seeking these cultural and emotional resources or creating these as resource niches through leadership and ideological mobilization that will sustain the coming conflict. Yet, other resources are necessary as Marxian, SMO theories, conflict theories, and ecological theories would all emphasize. These resources include, as noted briefly earlier: (1) material resources like money from patrons who may or may not be engaged in the social movement (indeed, they often come from outside a society); (2) organizational resources like churches, unions, and other associations that can give structure to collective action and that can provide the necessary bureaucratic base of any successful movement; (3) networks and alliances with populations experiencing similar grievances to those mobilizing or those sympathetic to the cause being pursued; (4) systemic liaisons with targeted communities, kin units, occupational groups, philanthropists, and other potential sources of recruits and money; (5) demographic resources like younger recruits more willing to take risks but also members of other categoric units sympathetic to the mobilization; and (6) technological resources to facilitate communication, transportation, and, potentially, warfare.

The success of an SMO or a revolutionary group, including terrorist groupings, is related to success in securing the kinds of resources listed above, their capacity to neutralize active resistance by other categoric units in a population, their ability to draw resources from outside of a society and thereby avoid domestic power-use by superordinates to close off subordinates' access to resources (whether money, organizational knowhow, and even recruits from the outside are not so easily controlled by polity that is under assault), and their ability to secure sufficient resources to sustain the conflict over time, if initially riots and other acts of collective behavior do not succeed. When the polity is weak (low legitimacy, in fiscal crisis, confronting enemies beyond its borders) and when actors in the military and judiciary cannot be relied upon by leaders of polity, then selection may favor those who are mobilizing for conflict. Conversely, when the coercive power of the state is high, fiscally sound, given legitimacy by large sectors of the population, secure from outside conflicts, and in control of the state apparatus and military, then it is very difficult for selection to favor those who are mobilizing. Yet, even when the polity prevails, it will have changed the institutional structure of a society and altered some of its key cultural beliefs and ideology; for, preparing for conflict and pulling its resources together for conflict almost always involves changes in key institutional systems, such as economy, law, education, and religion. These changes may prove effective in the short run, but if they escalate inequalities and create additional grievances among members of other categoric units, particularly the more affluent and previously valorized ethnics or members of religious sects, then the long-term legitimacy of the polity is in jeopardy because expectations and fundamental person-level needs of members in these categories are not being realized. Thus, as institutional systems are changed in response to episodes of Marxian selection, the costs of success in one conflict can set up conditions that weaken polity and make it less likely to be successful in future conflicts.

The more violent the conflict becomes, whether successful or not, the more likely will the polity have altered institutional systems in order to maintain social control. A number of conditions increase the likelihood of violence during Marxian selection: intensity of negative emotions aroused, especially emotions like vengeance and retribution; attributions for grievances are clearly defined and focused on demonized targets; emotional-arousing rituals are part of the organizational system being developed; ideologies justifying revolt are highly moralized and imbued with religious symbols and totems, backed up and reinforced by emotion-arousing rituals; movement success is critical to sustaining people's identities especially with respect to ethnicity and religious affiliation; younger age cohorts (a categoric unit) willing to take the risks of violent acts represent a high proportion of those recruited to a cause.

It is typically difficult for the state to match these emotion-arousing conditions since, in the end, it is a bureaucratic organization, many of whose members do not have the same stake in the outcome as the leaders of the polity. The same is often true of the military and police. But if incumbency in the state apparatus is consolidated with members of particular categoric units with long-term hostility to those engaged in revolt, then the state and military can often mobilize a high-solidarity military force quite willing to use violence against historical enemies. And, if both sides are mobilized emotionally and see the fate of their respective categoric-unit identities as on the line, then the selection may be particularly violent, involving selecting out (through genocide) of targeted categories of persons. But, if the two sides are relatively equal in their coercive capacity and their ability to sustain their organizational systems, then the violence will persist for a long time; and the longer it persists, the more polarized will members of the two sides become—thus setting up longer-term Marxian selection dynamics.

As a relevant aside, one of the reasons that religious conflicts are often so violent and long term is that both sides have well-established organizational systems, well-established networks for recruiting members, highly moralized beliefs, high levels of self-identification with religious beliefs, highly charged emotional symbols or totems toward which emotion-arousing rituals are to be directed, clear leadership structures that are typically hierarchical, and access to recruits and material resources outside the boundaries of a society. Marx dreamed the proletariat could become organized as a class "for itself." Yet, religion has, in essence, institutionalized in its corporate units what a social class would have trouble doing. And for this reason, leaders of conflicts seek to use or even hijack religious structures as a "ready-made" structure that already has institutionalized a membership core, a base of recruiting, a system of leadership, a network of alliances, a set of moralized beliefs, a totem marking belief, and a pattern of emotion-arousing rituals. And so, it should not be surprising that conflicts that have a basis in class inequalities are often transformed into religious conflicts because of the capacity of religious corporate units to provide what is difficult to mobilize on the basis of class issues, per se. Marx might be turning over in his grave on this issue because of the obfuscation that occurs when religion becomes the structure and cultural basis of revolt, probably because he overestimated the degree to which people in diverse and complex societies with market systems could ever come to perceive their common class interest. They can always, however, perceive their interests to religion, if they are religious.

Much societal evolution, then, is driven by Marxian selection among big-brained and emotional animals (the result of Darwinian selection) who are organized into categoric and corporate units. It is difficult to sustain a model of Darwinian natural selection when looking at what has been a very common process among individuals organized for conflict within corporate units built to realize the interests of members of devalued categoric units. The units of selection are no longer individual phenotypes (although some Darwinian selection will occur if deaths are biased on biological features, like sex or skin color) but, instead, corporate units mobilizing large portions of the total population; and it is no longer the population that evolves (though, this too can also occur) but the morphology and culture of a society as a superorganism. Moreover, while the behavioral, cognitive, and emotional capacities of humans are involved in Marxian selection (indeed they ultimately make it possible), they cannot explain these dynamics. A Darwinian approach can only tell us why humans are capable of the violence so evident in much of the social universe, and such an approach can inform analysts about the modification of the genome if violence cause shifts in the gene pool (by, for example, killing off a large proportion of young men), but Darwinian theory cannot explain why and how this capability gets mobilized to produce Marxian selection dynamics that can change not only societies but, in the case of extreme violence, the human genome as well (see Sanderson 2015, however, for an effort to develop a Darwinian theory of conflict).

Conclusion

In this chapter, we have tried to emphasize that selection is a much more widespread process than conceived by the Modern Synthesis in biology. Selection occurs at the level of human superorganisms through at least the four additional types of non-Darwinian selection dynamics outlined in this chapter—that is, Type-1 Spencerian selection, Type-2 Spencerian selection, Durkheimian selection, and Marxian selection. In trying to sustain fidelity, many existing efforts in using Darwinian ideas become incapable of understanding the structures and processes of human superorganisms. Certain parallels, even isomorphisms can be found, but they tend to be very narrow and unable to explain the complex and robust dynamics of large-scale superorganisms, where the unit of selection is no longer the population of phenotypes but the structure and cultures of sociocultural formations. If models of selection remain tied to a strictly Darwinian view of blind, non-teleological selection working only on a distribution of phenotypes and underlying genotypes, it can at best only explain the evolution of certain universal behaviors, cognitive biases and capacities, and emotional propensities of *individual* humans—which is as far as sociobiology and evolutionary psychology can go with any precision. Once such approaches try to explain *emergent social structures and cultures*, they lose precision and often become explanations by speculative just-so stories. Some of these stories can be useful explaining rates of certain behaviors because these are summations of individual behaviors statistically, but even here, these rates are circumscribed social structures and culture.

Yet, the goal in this chapter is to try to remain somewhat true to the underlying idea of selection but to put this idea into terms that sociologists might appreciate. For many, committed to high fidelity in biology, this chapter is probably a big disappointment, but less so, we hope, to sociologists who have been skeptical of how biological reasoning in a more general sense can be adapted to sociological models. If only selection as conceptualized by Darwin and the Modern Synthesis is acceptable, then only individual behaviors can be explained, and only partially at that. If this kind of effort to expand the notion of selection to different types of units beyond organismic phenotypes and to units that have capacities to remake their universe in more of a Lamarckian than Darwinian sense is not acceptable, then high-fidelity models of selection that remain true to the Modern Synthesis will not explain very much about the superorganismic world that humans have constructed and live in; and scholars should stop trying to do so. Such effort will be in vain because they fail to see the fundamental nature of the human social universe as more than just behavior.

From the other side, this chapter tries to review literatures that are well known by sociologists, in an effort to sensitize sociologists to the potential for developing evolutionary models and theories to explain the social universe of humans. We can selectively bring biological approaches into sociology modified to fit the realities of the social universe as sociologists see it; and in so doing, make sociology a more robust and explanatory social science.

Part III
New Darwinian Approaches Within Sociology

12
New Forms of Comparative Sociology
What Primates Can Tell Sociology About Humans

Humans are, in essence, evolved great apes. The great apes include two forms of chimpanzees (common and bonobo), two variants of gorillas (highland and lowland), and one species of orangutans. There are also several species of gibbons and siamangs, but these are tree-living, small Asian apes that are very far off the great-ape line. Humans share 99% of their genes with chimpanzees, 98% with gorillas, and 96–97% with orangutans, although these genes are arrayed on an extra pair of chromosomes among great apes. The important point is that humans and great apes are very closely related; and this close relationship signals that humans and species of present-day great apes had a common ancestor. Around 13 million years ago, present-day orangutans (the only Asian great apes) and humans' hominin ancestors shared a common ancestor; around 10 million years ago, gorillas and hominins had a common ancestor; and finally, around 6 million years ago, chimpanzees and hominins shared a common ancestor. Thus, with each splitting off from a common ancestor, the genes regulating phenotypes, including behavioral dispositions, of great apes became part of the hominin genome. And, as is evident today, humans and all great apes are genetically very similar, even though small differences in genes have produced wide variations in the phenotypes of humans and great apes.

This genetic closeness means that a great deal about humans and their nature (see Chapter 13) can be learned from studying the neuroanatomy of the brain, the morphology of the body, the behavioral phenotypes, and the organizational phenotypes of great apes. Moreover, since the basic habitat to which the great apes have had to adapt over the last 13 million years has not changed dramatically or fundamentally, the phenotypical characteristics of the great apes (and their underlying genotypes) have changed much less than those of humans' hominin ancestors that had to adapt to an entirely new habitat. Over the last 13 million years, the great apes remained in the forest habitats of Africa and Asia, while humans' hominin ancestors were eventually forced to adapt to the open-country savanna of Africa and eventually to diverse habitats in other parts of the globe.

And so, as we stare the great apes in the eye, we can see back in time to what our ancestors were like; and if we study the behaviors and organizational patterns of great apes, we can get a sense for the behavioral and organization propensities of humans' distant ancestors and, hence, humans today. Furthermore, because the habitat of great apes did not change dramatically (although specific niches certainly changed but not as much as those of hominins), while the habitat of hominins has changed dramatically, the differences between the biological, behavioral, and organizational characteristics of humans compared to great apes give us the opportunity to see what natural selection altered from the basic phenotypes of humans' distant ape ancestors. For, in having to adapt increasingly to savanna conditions and then diverse habitats outside of Africa, natural selection reworked the biological, behavioral, and organizational phenotypes of late hominins. We can see, therefore, not only the nature of humans' distant great-ape ancestors, but we can also see what natural selection did to them as hominins increasingly had to spend ever-more time on the African savanna.

Thus, because of the genetically close relationship to extant great apes, new possibilities for cross-species comparative analysis open up. In this chapter, we will review a methodology—termed *cladistic analysis* in biology—that can allow us to discern human nature as partly great-ape nature but also as an evolved nature that changed, to a certain degree, during hominins' forced adaptation to savanna conditions, and beyond. To perhaps state the argument too expansively, cladistic analysis becomes much like the Hubble telescope because it allows sociologists to look back millions of years in time and "see" those animals from which the hominin and, eventually, human line evolved. We no longer need highly speculative and philosophical portrayals of human nature; we can be much more specific and confident that the inferences made and conclusions drawn have a firm empirical base.

Cladistic Analysis Applied to Primates

What Is Cladistic Analysis?

Cladistic analysis is very much like historical reconstruction of texts and languages. When confronted with, for example, languages that can be seen as having a common root language, analysis begins by analyzing what present languages have in common. What is common to all of the languages will, it is assumed, have been key ingredients of the root language. Cladistic analysis in biology uses the same logic: To examine a set of species that are believed to have evolved from a common species, it is necessary to focus on what behaviors or other phenotypical traits they have in common. These *common features* are most likely the best picture of the biological or behavioral phenotypes of their last common ancestor.

Cladistic analysis makes two assumptions, sometimes termed "hypotheses." First is the *relatedness hypothesis* making the assumption that any similarities in a class of objects are not due to chance or random factors but, instead, are the outcome of "descent with modification" from a common ancestor. Second is the *regularity hypothesis* arguing that modifications or changes in present-day forms are not random but show a clear systematic bias that links descendants to each other and their common ancestor (Jeffers and Lehiste 1979). Added to these two assumptions is an effort to employ a "control group" or "out-group" population as a basis of further comparisons to be used in order to assure that changes are indeed unique to the species under investigation. If possible, "the-next-most-closely related" taxonomic group is selected (Andrews and Martin 1987) and used to determine similarities and differences between this group and the target population. If this out-group population reveals similarities to the set of species under study, then those similarities reflect traits from their common ancestors, whereas if they reveal different patterns or traits, these are the result of the adaptations to a somewhat different habitat or set of niches within a habitat. In performing cladistic analysis on great apes, then, chimpanzees, gorillas, and orangutans are considered to have descended from a common ancestor since they are so closely related to each other at the genetic and phenotypic levels; and since humans are closely related to great apes, one can include humans as part of the set of species to be studied. The control group or "out-group" population is Old World monkeys who are the mostly closely related taxonomic primates to the great apes. And so, if great apes reveal differences with monkeys that are systematic and definitive, then this furthers the assumptions built into the two hypotheses on relatedness and regularity.

Maryanski's Pioneering Cladistic Analysis

Most studies of primates and animals in general reveal a behavioral bias, but several decades ago, Alexandra Maryanski (1986, 1987, 1992, 1993, 1995, 1996) performed cladistic analysis on apes, using selected species of Old World monkeys as the control or out-group population. Rather than examine behavior, per se, as is done in most field studies on primates, Maryanski examined *social structures*, conceptualized as *the networks* among specific sex and age classes of apes and monkeys. If there were common patterns of network structure among apes that distinguished them from Old World monkeys, then these patterns could be seen as the social structure of the last common ancestor to great apes *and* the first humans. Thus, the telescope provided by cladistic analysis is, in Maryanski's study, focused on the distant social structures of the ancestor from which all great apes, hominins, and humans evolved.

The Basic Social Structure of Great-Ape Societies

All great apes reveal several common features in their respective social structures. The most prominent feature of these societies is male-female promiscuity. Great apes are highly sexual and generally receptive to sexual relations. Indeed, at times when females are receptive to sex, males will line up and wait for their turn. The result of this pattern of promiscuity is that paternity is *never known* among great apes. At times, friendships develop between adult males and females, but these are not known to be exclusive sexual partnerships, just favored males or females. The second important characteristic among great apes is that all females leave their natal community at puberty and migrate to another community, never to return to see their mothers. The same is true of males among gorilla and orangutan societies, but in chimpanzee societies, males remain in their natal community and maintain cordial relations with their respective mothers, but do not form any type of group relationship with their mothers. Instead, males occasionally visit their mothers, but as is the case with all great apes societies, group structures are not permanent. The most salient structure is the community or home range of the population; this home range can extend for many square miles, perhaps as much as 10 square miles, although the incursion of humans into the habitats of great apes has reduced this range, especially among mountain gorillas. The only very strong tie in great-ape societies is that between a mother and her young offspring, which is almost universal among mammals. But again, this tie is broken when females all leave their natal community and when gorilla and orangutan males do so as well. The result is the intergenerational continuity across generations is broken between mothers and their daughters and, for two of the three great apes, among mother and son gorillas and orangutans as well. It is very likely that such was also the case with chimpanzees at one time, but adaptation to their current niches may have altered this ancient pattern of transfer and its effect on severing of intergenerational ties. Of course, at no time are there strong ties with fathers because fathers are never known because of sexual promiscuity. Thus, kinship built from nuclear families does not exist among great apes, and thus kin selection is *not* a prominent mechanism of group formation and cooperation in great-ape societies.

Among great apes, *groups are not a natural formation*. Groups tend to be very temporary, fusing together for brief times, and then dispersing in a fusion-fission pattern. The most permanent groups are those of lead silverback male gorillas; and these can consist of a female with children attaching herself to a lead male for, in essence, baby-sitting services for a time. When her children leave the natal community, this tie is broken; and there is no suggestion that she and the lead male are a conjugal couple because females often wander off from the silverback, leaving him to baby-sit, in order for her to have sexual liaisons with other males who hang about the perimeter of group in a constant flow of individuals in, out, and around the quasi-group of the lead silverback. Among chimpanzees, temporary groups form to patrol the home range, and this group will attack any male who seeks to cross this boundary. In contrast, migrating females from other communities are welcomed as replacements for those who, at puberty, have left their natal community. Chimpanzees will also evidence friendship ties that periodically lead males to assemble for a short duration. These groups may also contain ties among brothers, but far more important than kin ties among chimpanzee are personal friendships that develop among non-kin males. Orangutans—the arboreal/terrestrial Asian great ape—reveal no permanent groups; indeed, orangutans are virtually solitary with, at best, a male courting a female for a short time, impregnating her, and then leaving her to raise her offspring until both male and female offspring move away from their natal community at puberty and immigrate to another community. Thus, in contrast to most mammals, great apes do not reckon kin beyond mother-offspring ties, do not form permanent groups, and reveal very little intergenerational continuity with the constant transfer of offspring at puberty to other communities. Moreover, for the most part, females entering a community at puberty are strangers to each other, unless they come from the same community. They often sit in propinquity to let their offspring play, but they do not appear to form strong social bonds with either males or other females.

The Cladistic Reconstruction

Thus, by the logic of cladistic analysis, ties that can form networks are mostly weak or non-existent among the great apes. There are no high-solidarity groups, although at times chimpanzees can engage in emotion-arousing carnival-like ritual activities—e.g., hooting, dancing, pounding logs—when larger numbers periodically gather. Such displays are also something that humans do as well. But, these are not permanent or regularly scheduled activities; they last for a short time, and then disband. The only permanent social structure among great apes, then, is the larger, more inclusive community, which appears to be their only permanent and stable social structure. Groups are fluid, and great apes are often isolated and alone as they move about a community, joining others for a time, then disbanding. Great apes are thus highly individualistic, mobile, and often autonomous; they do not form any permanent groups, beyond a mother and her young offspring; and they reckon the larger community, the boundaries to be protected, and the demography of who belongs and does not in the community. In Table 12.1, these descriptive features of great-ape societies are translated into ties among conspecifics in chimpanzee, gorilla, and orangutan communities. The most notable feature

TABLE 12.1 A Cladistic Analysis of Extant Great Apes

Species of Apes

	Gorillas (Gorilla)	Chimpanzees (Pan)	Orangutans (Pongo)	Last Common Ancestor
Adult-to-Adult Ties:				
Male-Male:	0	0/+	0	0*
Female-Female	0	0	0	0*
Male-Female	0/+	0	0	0*
Adult-to-Adult Offspring *Procreation Ties:*				
Mother-Daughter	0	0	0	0*
Father-Daughter	0	0	0	0*
Mother-Son	0	+	0	0*
Father-Son	0	0	0	0*
Adult-to-Pre-Adolescent *Offspring Ties:*				
Mother-Daughter	+	+	+	+*
Father-Daughter	0	0	0	0*
Mother-Son	+	+	+	+*
Father-Son	0	0	0	0*

Notes:
0 = no or very weak ties
0/+ = weak to moderate ties
+ = strong ties
* is used to denote a reconstructed social structure, in this case the likely structure of the last common ancestor to humans and extant great apes. As is evident, this structure is most like that of contemporary orangutans.

of Table 12.1 is the larger number of zeros (0's) marking non-existent to weak ties, the relatively small number of weak to moderate (+/0) ties, and the very small number of strong ties (+). One convention of cladistic analysis is to juxtapose the likely features of the common ancestor to this set of great-ape species; and this is done in the far right column with the (*) aside each hypothesized tie of the last common ancestor to great apes and, of course, hominins and humans as well. In this reconstruction, the only strong ties are those of mothers to their young sons and daughters, with this tie becoming non-existent when they both emigrate from their natal community. This absence of ties means that the last common ancestor revealed virtually *no social structures* beyond the regional community; they were perhaps most like the contemporary orangutan where individuals are isolates and loners within a larger regional community. Seemingly, through adaptations to new niches in the arboreal habitat, both gorillas and chimpanzees have developed a small set of stronger ties, although they reveal structures very similar to the last common ancestor.

Why Did Great Apes Become Weak-Tie, Low-Sociality Animals?

Why would the ancient ancestor of great apes and humans evidence so few even moderate ties, to say nothing of strong ties, and virtually no kinship ties beyond mother and her young offspring? The more detailed answer can be found in Maryanski's other, book-length works (Maryanski and Turner 1992; Turner and Maryanski 2005, 2008a), and thus, we will offer only a short answer. Thirty million years ago, apes and Old World monkeys were similar, but there were important differences. One is that, on average, apes were much larger than monkeys; and the other is what are termed "life history characteristics" were (and are) different: Apes mature much more slowly than monkeys. They spend a longer time in their mother's womb, breast feed much longer, and have longer infancy and juvenile periods of development than do monkeys. By 20 million years ago, monkeys and apes began to differentiate in terms of phenotypes and in their organizational structures. It cannot be known if great apes once had a more structured set of relations like those of monkeys today, but it is clear that monkeys and apes began to adapt to different niches in the arboreal habitat of Africa.

Monkeys gained the upper hand in the arboreal habitat, perhaps because they learned to eat unripe fruit, whereas apes did not and cannot to this day. As a result, monkeys were able to control the core and more verdant areas of trees where there was more food, room, and structural support for more permanent groupings. In contrast, apes were forced to the terminal feeding areas in the trees where there is less food, less room, and less structural support for large or permanent groupings. The result was something that natural selection rarely does: take away existing traits. Yet, it seems that the weak-tie, low-sociality, and mobile pattern of ape behavior evolved to replace any behavioral propensities to form permanent or stable groups for the simple reason that the terminal feeding areas could not support such social structures. Rather, apes could not accumulate and grow in numbers within the community; they had to leave as resources declined at one point in the treetops, a strategy that also assured a considerable amount of genetic mixing. Strong ties and loyalties would only make great apes less fit because these ties could push them to exhaust resources and overpopulate niches that could not support large numbers of individuals. And so, the reckoning of a larger inclusive community, the absence of permanent local groups structures, the promiscuity without attachment among adults, and the transfer of all offspring from their community increased chances of survival by not overtaxing resources in niches of the arboreal habitat.

The behavioral and structural strategy proved fitness-enhancing because at one time there were many species of apes compared to the few that exist today. Moreover, adaptation to this precarious niche differentiated ape anatomy and neuroanatomy from those of monkeys. Apes became much smarter than monkeys; they acquired the capacity to rotate their arms 360 degrees or brachiate (arm over arm) through the trees. They developed stronger hands, fingers, wrists, arms, and shoulder joints. Their arms are longer and stronger, and their fingerprints are more pronounced. All of these changes represent natural selection pushing the basic primate anatomy and neuroanatomy in a direction allowing great apes to survive and move about in the more precarious terminal feeding areas of the arboreal habitat. So, just as the anatomy and neuroanatomy of apes changed with adaptation to this highly specialized niche, so did the social phenotype of apes change to one built around low sociality and impermanence of groups.

We can complete the cladistic analysis by comparing ape social structures to those of Old World monkeys. In Maryanski's analysis, monkeys evidence almost the exact opposite pattern of social organization. Monkeys are group-oriented rather than community-oriented like great apes. Females never leave their natal community; instead, they form dense network ties or *matrilines* with their collateral and cross-generational female relatives. Males all leave their natal group, migrating to a new group where they often join in the competition producing male dominance hierarchies. Thus, males migrate into a group, compete for dominance, with a hierarchy of male dominance emerging in most monkey troops (in contrast, among apes, only gorillas reveal a consistent pattern of male dominance).

The dominant male monkey tries to hoard females and use them as a kind of harem but, typically, is not entirely successful because female matrilines are not so easily dominated; and indeed, some matrilines have hierarchies of female dominance. Moreover, other males are not disposed to let the dominant males control access to females, and so, a great deal of "cheating" by females on the dominant male inevitably occurs. By the logic of cladistic analysis, then, the relational patterns of Old World monkeys and the networks that they create *are very different* than those of great apes, confirming that the social structure of great apes societies is unique to this set of species because it is so different than that of Old World monkeys. We can, therefore, have some confidence that the organizational features of great ape societies were operating as the first hominins began to emerge and split off from their common ancestor with apes. Indeed, the great apes probably should belong in the human genus, *Homo*, although there is resistance to making such a dramatic change in the classification of primates. But the great apes are more closely related to humans than to monkeys; and moreover, chimpanzees are more closely related genetically to humans than to any other great ape. At the very least, then, it would make sense to put chimpanzees in the genus *Homo*.

The Implications of Cladistic Analysis for Evolutionary Sociology

The Rapid Decline of Apes

It is perhaps embarrassing to know that humans are descendants of a common ancestor to present-day great apes that lost out in competition in the arboreal habitat to monkeys. Moreover, over the last 13 million years, apes have declined relative to all other primates. In Table 11.2, the relative numbers for species of Prosimians (pre-monkeys), Ahthropoidea (Old and New World Monkeys), and Apes and Humans are delineated. There are sixty-two species of Prosimians, fifty-three species of Old World monkeys, seventy-eight species of New world monkeys, and thirteen species of Apes and Humans, eight of which are gibbons and siamangs (not great apes). There are only four species of great apes left on the planet from what was once hundreds of species, and of course, there are human great apes who have overpopulated the planet and are seemingly well adapted but obviously there are warnings from Malthus' four horsemen—war, pestilence, disease, and famine—plus a few more that will only aggravate Malthus' list—nuclear holocaust, global warming, and ecological decline. If we count species rather than total numbers, earth is the planet of the monkeys, which may make for less interesting movies but is a closer description to what has transpired over the last 10 million years. Indeed, overpopulation by

TABLE 12.2 Relative Numbers of Species of Primates in the Primate Order

Suborders	Number of Species*
1. *Prosimii*	62
2. *Anthropoidea*	
Superfamilies:	
1. *Ceboidea*	53
(New World Monkeys)	
2. Cercopithecoidea	78
(Old World Monkeys)	
3. Hominoidea	
(Apes and Humans)	13
Families:	
1. Hylogatidae	8
(Gibbons and Siamangs)	
2. Pongidae	4
(Great Apes)	
3. Hominidae	1
(Humans)	

* Of the 206 total species counted in Table 12.2, only 13 are apes, including humans as an evolved ape. There are 131 species of monkeys and, closer to humans, 78 species of Old World monkeys. The 8 species of gibbons and siamangs are very far from the great-ape and human lines, and so, it is clear that intelligent great apes constitute a very small percentage of the primate order—only 3%. Thus, great apes have been an evolutionary failure, except for humans (although the final verdict is still out on *Homo sapiens*).

humans now threatens the remaining species of great apes in what remains of their natural habitat. It is very likely that, in 50 years, *no* great ape will be able to live outside zoo-like enclosures, perhaps large-scale enclosures but zoos nonetheless. And human survival is not assured into the next century.

What, then, happened to apes? It is one thing to lose out in the arboreal habitat but still survive and even prosper in the terminal feeding areas of this habitat, but another to simply fall off the face of the earth. Why did the numbers of species of apes decline so dramatically at the very time that hominins were evolving along the human clade? The answer does not reside in ape intelligence because they are among the most intelligent animals to ever exist. The answer can be found in biological, behavioral, and organizational phenotypes of great apes. Phenotypical features that turned out to be a successful adaptation in the arboreal habitat were not well suited to new, more terrestrial habitats to which many arboreal primates had to adapt.

About 10 million years ago, the forests of Africa began to recede and, in their place, emerged the vast savannas of Africa. Forests still exist, of course, but they now constituted a much smaller habitat than was the case 30–20 million years ago, to say nothing of 63 million years ago when the first primates appeared after the destruction of most large reptiles and dinosaurs. As the forest receded, there was not enough room or resources for all existing arboreal primates; and so, many had to come to the ground for at least part of the time to secure food. For well-organized monkey troops, many species were able to adapt to the expanding savannas because they were so well organized. Today, a troop of terrestrial monkeys marches across the open-county grasslands in almost military formation with the lead male at the front and other males surrounding smaller females and their young. Most predators are reluctant to take on this phalanx of quasi-military precision because any threats cause males to converge to deal with the potential predators, whether alone or in packs. Thus, adaptation of monkeys to savanna conditions was much easier because they were already well organized in the manner described earlier.

In contrast, apes were not well organized because they revealed no permanent group structures, no consistent intergenerational structures, no nuclear families, and no band-like structures to protect them from predation. They were, in essence, sitting ducks in the open country; and so, the more the shrinking forest could not offer protection, the more vulnerable great apes became. It is not surprising, then, that most apes perished. Given that great apes had been evolving weak-tie, low-sociality, and non-group patterns of social organization, what strategies were available for natural selection on those species of great apes that had to spend ever-more time on the African savanna?

How Did Savanna-Dwelling Apes Survive?

STRATEGIES FOR SURVIVAL
One strategy would have been for selection to work on the relatively weak, though still evident, dominance patterns among the common ancestor of hominins with present-day chimpanzees. Chimps often form dominance hierarchies, but they are not enduring; brothers or male friends may form alliances for strategic reasons for a time that come and go but are not part of the ongoing structure of the community. So, there was a behavioral

propensity for at least episodic dominance on which selection could go to work, if dominance had fitness-enhancing value. But, without the matrilines typical of female monkeys, where females are organized into tight cliques of inter- and intragenerational female kin, the dominant males would have great trouble controlling female strangers in a strange new community, nor would individualistic chimpanzees in general be likely to fall into line; they would be more likely to move away from centers of dominance.

Another strategy that did work for some time was to make great apes very large and imposing. For example, *Gigantapethecus* was 8 feet tall and survived for considerable time on the African savanna. The individualism of great apes would work in favor of this strategy because a group of such large animals would have trouble finding sufficient food, but if they sustained the fusion (when resources were plentiful) and fission (when resources were not), this large animal would give predators caution, especially an animal that could pick up rocks and sticks to throw and beat on predators. And given that *Gigantapethecus* stood upright (and thus looked even more imposing to predators) and walked on two legs, this adaptation proved to be successful on the savanna. In the end, however, such large animals would have problems of overheating in the hot climate, but perhaps more fundamentally, they went extinct when hominins were beginning to get better organized, and a lone and weak-tie ape, no matter how large, could not compete for resources against organized groupings of smaller ape-like hominins on the human clade.

It is possible to gain some further insights on how a great ape can survive on the African savanna by looking at the organizational patterns of the few contemporary chimpanzee groupings that now spend considerable time on the savanna, although many retreat to the forest to sleep in safety (Baldwin 1979; Baldwin et. al 1982; McGrew 1981, 1983, 1992, 2010; McGrew et al. 1981). These chimpanzees try to do what early hominins did: Adjust the male (and occasionally with females) patrol activities of chimpanzees in the forest to a kind of hunting and scavenging band, very much like human hunter-gatherers probably did and still do in a few pockets around the world. They begin to form a more stable subgroup within the larger community, but chimpanzees probably have an advantage here that early apes on the savanna did not: Males stay in their natal communities and thus can serve as the backbone of more stable groups, whereas the last common ancestor to hominins and great apes reveals from the cladistic reconstruction both female and male transfer from their natal community, thus destroying this potential source of more stable groupings. Another clear adaptation of these savanna-dwelling chimpanzees is that they develop more technologies for hunting and gathering, and moreover, they begin to form a division of labor between males and females very much like human hunter-gatherers (i.e., males hunt, females gather). So, group formation begins with male solidarities, which are evident in forest-dwelling chimpanzees, that can be converted into more stable groups among other age-sex classes of individuals. The last common ancestor and most other apes did not have this propensity among chimpanzee male solidarities on which selection could go to work, but it probably became the first element of hominin adaptation to the savanna among those hominins that carried a chimpanzee-like community formation of males staying in their natal community and developing friendships. Most other apes did not have this chimpanzee-like structure; and the result was the extinction of species of great apes that were ill suited to open-country savanna conditions where tight-knit, group-level organization is necessary for survival.

Moreover, primates in general, but apes in particular, reveal other liabilities on the savanna, in addition to their lack of tight-knit group structures: They are slow because they are built for swinging in the trees rather than running on the ground; they do not have the normal olfactory senses of terrestrial mammals and must rely on sight rather than chemical smells to discern if predators are present (a large disadvantage since smells travel even when predators are hiding behind obstructions); and they are highly emotional and individualistic and, when danger appears, most apes become noisy and agitated running about in a frenzy (making them easy to find and pick off). Thus, the biological phenotype of apes on the ground does not promote fitness, although apes can make weapons and throw these at predators, but not typically in a very coordinated manner. But, the lack of a sociocultural phenotype revolving around tight-knit group structures was probably the biggest obstacle to survival; great apes are not group-oriented animals, and they do not form kinship systems or strong bonds, although friendships represent one potential source of increased bonding as is evident among those chimpanzees in Senegal that have ventured out for part of the day on the savanna (for relevant data, see Baldwin 1979; Baldwin et al 1982; McGrew 1981, 1983, 1992, 2010; McGrew et al. 1981; Tutin et al. 1982; Pruetz 2006; Pruetz and Bertolani 2007, 2009; Stanford 1990; Mitani and Watts 2001; Mitani and Rodman 1979; Moore et al. 2015).

How Were Increased Strength of Social Ties and Group Solidarities Ever Formed?

As will be outlined in Chapter 13, apes possess a great many behavioral propensities for increasing tie strength and forming groups revealing more solidarity, but apparently these were not sufficient by themselves to overcome the weak-tie, non-group organizational patterns of great apes. The missing ingredient, as will be argued in Chapter 13, was an expanded set of emotions that could be used to forge stronger bonds of solidarity. Apes are highly emotional; and while their range of emotions is greater than most other mammals, their lack of bioprogrammers for kin ties, for strong social ties in general, and for group formations may have exceeded most great apes' emotional capacities to overcome this obstacle. Even those apes that forage on the savanna cannot survive there if they must be on the savanna *full time*.

What we argue, then, is that, during hominin evolution, the emotional centers of the brain were growing as selection worked on existing emotional systems to make hominins ever-more emotional (Turner 2000); and with more emotions, the existing behavioral propensities that were once insufficient to overcome the lack of bioprogrammers for strong ties and group solidarities could be supercharged and made sufficient. For, if we look at humans today, solidarities are maintained by the arousal of positive emotions, but sustaining a relationship and a group is always difficult for humans because, at humans' ape core, they do not have strong-group or even strong-tie bioprogrammers. Strong ties and group solidarities are maintained by emotions attached to all of the diverse interpersonal capacities that all great apes possess and, hence, early hominins also possessed. These interpersonal capacities, per se, were not enough to overcome the lack of bioprogrammers, but with emotional enhancements, they were. Since the hominin brain did not grow dramatically until late *Homo erectus* some 1.8 to 3.5 million years ago, it was not culture or language that allowed hominins to forge stronger ties and sustain groups; it was the subcortical portions of the brain that grew first and allowed hominins to survive; and as emotions increased fitness, selection continued to expand this capacity giving late hominins sufficiently strong social ties and groups to survive and, indeed, to begin to move about the earth to new habitats.

Emotions, then, are the key to understanding why some great apes along the hominin-human clade survived, and so it is the subcortex of the brain more than the neocortex that is responsible for the survival of those few apes whose descendants would eventually allow for the emergence of *Homo sapiens*. Moreover, as we will explore in Chapter 14 on neurosociology, cladistic analysis can help us understand how the brain evolved during hominin evolution. The brain evolved in ways that made hominins more emotional and continued to do so up to late *Homo erectus* at around 1 million years ago when, suddenly, the hominin neocortex began to grow rapidly. Why was this so, and so late in hominin evolution? The answer, to be supplied in Chapter 14, is that cognitions cannot be remembered and decisions cannot be made without emotional tags on cognitions and options; and the more complex and nuanced the emotional capacities of a great ape, the greater will be its intelligence. Indeed, all intelligent mammals—dolphins, whales, elephants, and humans—are also highly emotional. The same is true to birds—intelligence depends upon emotions. And so, the emotions that allow low-sociality and non-group-forming hominids to survive by becoming more social, attached, and committed to groups would, as their complexity and nuance increased, provide the emotional substructure that is critical to intelligence in *all life forms on earth* (Damasio 1994; Turner 2000; Turner et al. 2017).

Conclusion

Cladistic analysis on ape behaviors and social structures allow us to understand the evolution of hominins, and they force social scientists and philosophers to alter some of their assumptions about humans, such as humans are "naturally" social and group oriented, and that kinship is the "natural group" for an evolved ape. There is little evidence to support these two assumptions when we look at great apes from a distant mirror in which we can see our remote ancestors reflected. The survival of animals without strong bioprogrammers for kinship, for group formations in general, and for dense networks of strong ties was somewhat of a miracle; and thus, it is also a miracle that humans ever evolved. But, natural selection working blindly and randomly hit upon the solution among some hominins: enhance emotions to overcome the lack of strong bioprogrammers for group formation; and as these allowed for stronger and more stable social ties and groups, fitness among these hominins was enhanced. And if fitness was enhanced, selection would continue to select on the tails of those subcortical structures in hominin brains enhancing emotions and increasing their variety, range of valences, and nuance. Eventually, a threshold was passed, and emotions could now provide the needed engine for greater intelligence through dramatic and rapid enlargement of the neocortex among late hominins like *Homo erectus* and perhaps *Homo naledi*.

Thus, the comparative analysis of primates opens new vistas for sociological analysis. We are no longer doomed to speculate blindly on "states of nature"; the accumulating data on primates, coupled with cladistic analysis of the behaviors and organizational structures, allow sociologists to look back millions of years to see humans' root ancestor and to appreciate the obstacle to hominin and, hence, human evolution. By chance, natural selection began to select on subcortical areas of the hominin brain to enhance emotions and thereby release all the unrealized potential of existing interpersonal capacities. And as emotions were built up, selection of the neocortex of the hominin brain would increase intelligence and allow for culture and spoken language. But these hallmarks of human beings were only possible by the work of natural selection on the neuroanatomy of hominins to make them more emotional; without this critical step in the evolution of hominins, humans would never have evolved. And, equally important, this step is not something that is in the past; rather, it is still the fundamental basis by which humans build up social relations and sociocultural formations.

13
In Search of Human Nature
Using the Tools of Cross-Species Comparative Analysis

Like any animal, humans reveal sets of cognitive, emotional, and behavioral capacities and predispositions that are, to some degree, under genetic control. Environmental conditions can, of course, have large effects on *which* capacities and predispositions get expressed, but even with this caveat, humans' evolved neuroanatomical phenotypes and behavioral phenotypes have large effects on human interactions and sociocultural formations. By the logic of cladistic analysis, comparing the cognitive, emotional, and behavioral features of all present-day great apes gives us a great deal of information about the genetically controlled behaviors of humans who share a last common ancestor with our closest primate relatives. In fact, using data on primates can be seen as a means for getting around the obfuscating effects of culture on humans and gaining insight into humans' biological nature.

For, in essence, human nature is an evolved great-ape nature, as emphasized in Chapter 12. The dramatic enhancement of subcortical areas of the human brain generating emotions and even more dramatic increases in the size of human neocortical areas allowing for language, complex and abstract thinking, and the production of culture make humans a very special kind of great ape, to be sure, but we still are, at our biological core, humans are evolved apes. As we saw in Chapter 12 through cladistic analysis on extant great apes, Darwinian natural selection rewired emotion and cognitive centers of the hominin and human brain to overcome the low-sociality, weak-tie, and non-group propensities of the last ancestor to great apes, hominins, and humans. As it did so, selection supercharged already in-place capacities and behavioral dispositions that all great apes, and humans' last common ancestor with the great apes, possessed. What a comparison of great-ape and human behaviors reveals is that much human social interaction *is very much like great-ape interaction* but enhanced by virtue of the supercharging effects of enhanced subcortical emotion centers and dramatically expanded neocortical capacities of the large human brain (three times the size of a chimpanzee's brain).

In doing a more general comparative analysis of great-ape emotional, cognitive, and behavioral capacities and predispositions, we can discover even more about human nature. Great apes evidence a large number of capacities and behavioral dispositions that are also part of the human genome as it affects a wide variety of neurological and anatomical systems. Some of these capacities and behavioral dispositions were probably enhanced through Darwinian natural selection during hominin evolution; others did not need to be enhanced to increase fitness because, by just expanding the emotional palette of hominins, enhancement of all great-ape behavioral propensities would occur. Most of these dimensions of what we can loosely call "human nature" would seem to make great apes highly social, but surprisingly, they did not, as is evident from the field studies on primates outlined in Chapter 12. As emphasized in Chapter 12, great apes possess a range and variety of interpersonal capacities and proclivities that would seemingly make them more social, but without their enhancement by emotions, they did not produce animals disposed to form strong ties that, in turn, could be used to build group structures. Instead, these capacities were available to monitor others and perhaps allow some degree of sociality and group formations when absolutely necessary, as is evident today among chimpanzees that now seek to survive by spending time on the open-country habitat in Senegal. But for most great apes living 6 million years ago, these interpersonal mechanisms *could not* overcome the weak-tie, non-group structures of all ape societies. The result was that there are very few species of great apes left on the planet, a fact that is distorted or obscured by the fact there are so many—some 7 billion—of one species: *Homo sapiens*. In Chapter 14, the neurology behind the comparison in this chapter of ape and human disposition to act in certain ways will be explored; for the present, the goal is simply to delineate *human nature as essentially as it follows from great-ape nature*. To achieve this goal, we will outline ape nature by, first, looking at what were once termed *pre-adaptations* in evolutionary biology (which is still a better term than the proposed alternatives that tend to connote teleology to what is a random/chance process); second, we will then delineate *behavioral propensities* pulled from the large literature on great-ape interactions; and third, we will make some reasonable speculations from the literatures on ape behavioral propensities and pre-adaptations about humans' biological nature.

Pre-Adaptations Among Apes

A *pre-adaptation* is a trait that evolved as a by-product of selection processes that generated another trait. As Darwinian natural selection works to select on variants in phenotypes that can increase fitness of a species, these very selection processes often produce additional traits that, at some subsequent point in time, become adaptive and subject to further selection. Natural selection is a blind process, without stated goals, that selects those variants in phenotypes and underlying genotypes that increase adaptation; and as it proceeds to alter the distribution of phenotypes and genotypes in the direction of increasing fitness, it can alter other aspects of phenotypes and genotypes among members of a population. These additional changes have no selective advantage or disadvantage *at the time they first emerged* but, as environmental conditions change and Darwinian selection picks up again, these collateral traits my come to have selective advantages or disadvantages. When they promote fitness and are enhanced through a new round of selection, they are conceptualized as a *pre-adaptation* or by another set of confusing terms in the current literature. But, the basic idea remains the same: Selection at an earlier time produces traits that have fitness-enhancing properties at a later point in time. Below are several pre-adaptations that are critical to understanding human behavior, interaction, and organization.

The Pre-Adaptation for Language

One of the earliest adaptations of the first primates moving to the arboreal habitat involved a shift from olfactory dominance of most mammals to visual dominance of those small rat- or mouse-like insectivores that first ascended into the forests of Africa some 63 million years ago and thereby initiated primate evolution. The sense modalities of the human brain—olfaction (smelling), vision (seeing), haptic (feeling with touch), and auditory (hearing)—must always have one sense that is dominant over the others in order to prevent sensory conflict and overload. Most mammals are olfactory dominant, meaning that the other senses—vision, haptic, and auditory—are subordinated to smell. Thus, when an animal senses something through any sense, it will seek to smell what it senses, subordinating visual, auditory, and haptic cues to smell to form a response to the sensory input. A few mammals are auditory dominant, bouncing sounds off objects to determine their shape and location. And relatively few are visually dominant.

Life in the trees represents an adaptation to a three-dimensional environment where one false step means death by gravity. Smelling, touching, and echolocation are not particularly efficient or safe means for moving about in a three-dimensional environment above the ground, and so, Darwinian natural selection began to enhance the vision centers of primates and give vision dominance over smell, touch, and sound. By rotating the eyes for overlap of visual fields among the small mammals that initiated the primate line in the arboreal habitat, depth perception became possible; and, later, color was added to enhance the ability to see texture. The result was a visually dominant mammal that, when smelling, hearing, or touching something that arouses its attention, will immediately turn to look at what it is sensing. Thus, while vision can be supplemented by olfactory, haptic, or auditory sensory inputs, the brain is wired so that vision will dominate and not lead to sensory conflict with other sense modalities (i.e., smell, touch, and sound).

As simply an artifact of rewiring the brain for visual dominance, the basic neurological capacity for language was created in some primates, *if* the primate possessed a sufficient level of intelligence. Prosimians, for the most part, are visually dominant, while all monkeys and apes are visually dominant, but only great apes pass the threshold of intelligence to take advantage of this pre-adaptation for language. It is in the associated cortices around the inferior parietal lobe in the brain, where the temporal (auditory), parietal (haptic), and occipital (vision) lobes meet, that this capacity for language is lodged (Geschwind 1965a, 1965b, 1985; Geschwind and Damasio 1984; Maryanski and Turner 1992; Ettlinger 1977; Jarvis and Ettlinger 1977; Passingham 1982: 51–55). The ability of great apes to use language—through the sign language of the deaf or through pictograms manipulated on computer keyboards (see Rumbaugh 2015; Schweller 2015)—is made possible by this pre-adaptation. Discovery of the genes producing muscles and vocal structures (mouth, tongue, lips, larynx) with capacity for finely articulate speech indicates that spoken language among humans probably evolved around 200,000 years ago (Enard, Khaitovich et al. 2002; Enard, Przeworski et al. 2002) and, thus, may be somewhat unique to humans.

As will be argued in Chapter 14, it seems unlikely that such an amazing neurological capacity would lie dormant for millions of years. J. H. Turner (2000) has argued that, under pressures to make low-sociality hominins more social, natural selection worked on this capacity for language to enhance the emotional capacities of hominins. Emotions are communicated by visual and at times auditory phonemes ordered by a syntax that produces a quasi-"language of emotions" which is more primal and primary than spoken language, having evolved millions of years before spoken language (Turner 2000). Indeed, when humans today seek to understand what another person is "feeling," they rely on their dominant visual sense modality to read the affective states signaled by "body language," particularly facial expressions, of others. Thus, in our view, the pre-adaptation for language was critical to making the enhancement of emotions so effective in creating social bonds and solidarities because, when ordered as a kind of visual language, the power of emotions is that much greater.

The Pre-Adaptations From Fuller Palette of Emotions

As noted in the Chapter 12 and to be more drawn out in Chapter 14, intelligent animals also have an expanded palette of emotions that tag cognitions for memory and for decision making over alternative lines of conduct. Great apes, as highly intelligent mammals, thus already have a large set of variants of primary emotions, such as anger, fear, sadness, and happiness, and perhaps even more complex emotions that combine these primary emotions like primary colors on a color wheel (Plutchik 1980; Turner 2000). If emotions—indeed, a quasi-language of emotions—were to be the key to increasing sociality and solidarity of groups among hominins, then the availability of this larger palette of emotions presented an avenue for Darwinian selection. For, the big take-home message of Chapter 12 is that the key to survival of hominins as they increasingly had to live in open-country savanna was that alternative mechanisms had to replace what had been lost by apes in the arboreal habitats of Africa: bioprogrammers for group formation. Most mammals have such bioprogrammers in their biologically driven propensity to form packs, prides, herds, troops, and other types of groupings for defense and foraging. Emotions may have, at first, hurt early savanna dwellers because they did not have neocortical control of subcortical emotional responses and, hence, attracted predators. And so, we can hypothesize that selection favored increased neocortical control of subcortically generated emotions so that slow primates without a strong sense of smell would not attract predators.

This output control over emotional arousal would increase the likelihood that something like the production of a language would be more likely to evolve. In fact, some species of monkeys that live on the savanna (because, unlike great apes, they have bioprogrammers for troop formation) move across the savanna almost silently but, if danger does appear, they are well organized for defense and counter-attacks against predators, even packs of predators. Once neurological control of emotion centers increased among evolving hominins, these neuro-nets could be further selected upon to enhance the range and varieties of emotions of hominins experienced and expressed and, in the long-term of hominin evolution, to make the production of not only emotional cues but spoken language more likely to evolve—as yet another critical pre-adaptation created by selection as worked on a previous pre-adaptation.

Natural selection thus worked on the existing palette of emotions of great apes, first expanding control on emotional outputs and, then, the range and variants of intensity of an increased variety of emotions that could be used to forge stronger bonds of solidarity. As this initial selection in this direction increased fitness, selection would continue to push toward ever-more complex and nuanced emotions that could be strung together in a language of emotions that carried common meaning among conspecifics. And, the more this language increased fitness, the more selection would continue to expand the repertoire of emotions, control over the expression of emotions, and thereby the grammars by which to combine them in sentence-like sequences that would carry common meanings. In turn, as we will emphasize later, this direction of selection would become the necessary pre-adaptation for growth of the neocortex and, ultimately, the evolution of spoken language.

Yet, for millions of years, the neocortex of *Australopithecines* and hominins only grew about 125 cc beyond that of the common chimpanzee; and so, clearly, the less visible part of the brain, or the subcortical centers where emotions are generated, was probably doubling in size, while the neocortex only grew by 25% as revealed by endocasts. And so, the somewhat expanded emotions of great apes over other primates were a critical pre-adaptation that set into motion the first language (of emotions) and began the subcortical build-up of emotional variants that eventually would make growth of the neocortex fitness-enhancing. But much of the work had already been done by the time the neocortex began to grow, as will be outlined in Chapter 14. A primal language *had already been wired into the brain*, thus providing yet another pre-adaptation for spoken language among *Homo sapiens*.

The neurological basis for culture had also been set with the capacity to read gestures signaling emotions and to develop common meanings. It is then but a short step to using spoken gestures to do the same thing as hominins gained increased neocortical control over their expressions of emotions, intent, and purposes. And, as the palette of emotions and their expression in a visual language of emotions (a language still used by humans when they want to communicate emotionally) became the key pre-adaptation for higher intelligence and spoken language that would come with growth of the neocortex and with key alternations in the auditory system of late hominins or, perhaps, only *Homo sapiens* (Enard, Khaitovich et al. 2002; Enard, Przeworski et al. 2002).

The Pre-Adaptation From Mother-Infant Bonding

All mammals evidence mother-offspring attachments—at times, for the life of offspring but almost always for the infant through juvenile stages of development. The *anterior cingulate gyrus* (see Figure 14.1 on page 339) is an area separating subcortical from full neocortical tissue in the human brain, and it is here that mother-offspring attachment, play, and infant cries when separated from mothers emanate. As a dedicated area, the *anterior cingulate gyrus* for these unique mammalian behaviors could be subject to further selection if increased mother-infant bonds would enhance fitness. Since chimpanzee mothers are very attached to their offspring and suckle them for as much as 5 years, they form strong social bonds—about the only really strong bonds among great apes. But, at some point, natural selection would have to forge a social formation very alien to great apes: the nuclear family and kin attachments more generally. Without the nuclear family, human societies could never have evolved, but the obstacle to be overcome in creating such a unit are very high: male-female promiscuity so that paternity is never known and offspring transfer from their natal community at puberty, never to return to their mothers. Thus, mother-infant bonding was perhaps one pre-adaptation that could be selected upon to begin to (a) prolong offspring attachments to mother and, perhaps, even to keep closer and in contact with their mothers and (b) somehow pull males (whether the actual father or not is not so critical) to bond with females and her offspring in the precursor to the nuclear family. Selection probably needed more hooks than just the behavioral propensities generated in the anterior cingulate gyrus, but it is very likely that selection did work on this structure as one path to increasing group stability not evident in great-ape societies.

The Pre-Adaptation for Non-Harem Pattern of Mating Among Apes

Most monkeys reveal dominance hierarchies among males, as well as networks of female matrilines. Dominant males seek, with only partial success, to use these female matrilines as a harem, in which the dominant males try to have exclusive sexual relations with females—again with incomplete success. But, male monkeys are disposed to engage in such behavior, and females are disposed to form cohesive matrilines. Great apes are just the opposite: Females are strangers to each other because they have migrated in at puberty from different natal communities and do not generally form strong bonds (rather, mutual tolerance so that offspring can play together); males and females are sexually promiscuous and do not normally develop attachments to particular partners. And while this ape pattern presented a problem for Darwinian selection to create the nuclear family, a hard-wired harem pattern of mating would be even more difficult to overcome. A nuclear family is built from sexual attraction between a particular male and a particular female, although most pre-literate societies and a few literate ones have allowed for multiple female partners for a male (polygamy) and, its converse, multiple male partners for a female (polyandry). And, in all human societies, promiscuity is common.

However, without females forming a matriline and without male needs to dominate this matriline, a major roadblock to a nuclear family of parents and offspring is removed. Selection could work on attaching males and females during the critical years of infant vulnerability, while creating the structure—the conjugal pair and nuclear family—that became the basis for the first human societies. Promiscuity may still have persisted (since humans are still evolved great apes), but if a stable set of relationships forming the nuclear family could be in place, then band-based societies of hunter-gatherers could evolve. *Homo erectus* was probably far along on this transformation because, otherwise, it is hard to see how this immediate hominin ancestor could have migrated around the globe.

As will be reviewed in Chapter 14 on comparative neurosociology, the subcortical area of the mammalian brain dedicated to the pleasurable sexual feelings in mammals—the *septum and septal area*—is over twice as big, controlling for body size, among humans compared to highly sexed and promiscuous chimpanzees. Why would this bilateral organ need to be twice as big? It cannot be to enhance sexual pleasure since chimpanzees clearly derive that from their smaller septum. The answer may be that with increased selection on the tail favoring larger size of the normal distribution of the septum across a population, new emotions associated with sex were activated in those with a larger septum—emotions such as attachment, even love, or other emotions that would increase the bonds between sexual partners. Otherwise, it is hard to see how selection could overcome the obstacle presented by promiscuity, which is still an obstacle in sustaining stable nuclear families among humans today. And so, without a harem pattern, selection was able to select on a key subcortical structure—the septal area—and begin to pull males and females together—a step that had to occur if human societies were to evolve. So, without the harem pattern of sexual mating, natural selection had a more open road to using the septal area that could encourage even more sexual drive (and promiscuity) but that, also, could push for more male-female bonding. For without strong bioprogrammers for such bonding—that seem to exist, as an aside, only among the small Asian apes (gibbons and siamangs) far off the great-ape clade—Darwinian selection would have to find another route—one revolving around new kinds of emotions. And perhaps the dramatic increase in the size of the septum is the "smoking gun" of how Darwinian selection pulled off this critical step in attaching males and females during late hominin evolution.

The Pre-Adaptation of 'Life History' Characteristics

As noted in Chapter 12, monkeys and apes were probably different for many millions of years in their life history characteristics, even as their body phenotypes seemed close (Turner and Maryanski 2008a). Apes are not only bigger and smarter, on average, than monkeys, they also take longer to develop at all phases of the life-cycle (gestation, nursing, infancy, and juvenile phases); apes live longer and space their births further apart than monkeys. And, these differences are dramatic. For example, a large monkey like a male baboon will be in the gestation phase for 175 days, nurse for 420 days, and remain an infant for 1.6 years, whereas a chimpanzee male will remain in the womb for 228 days, nurse for 1,460 days, and be an infant for 3 years. Overall, male baboons (a large monkey) will be in the nursing, infant, and juvenile phases for 4.4 years, while the male chimpanzee will be in these phases for 7 years. Baboons space babies 1.7 years compared to 5.6 years for chimpanzees.

This prolongation of all phases of the life-cycle can be seen as a pre-adaption for what eventually occurred among humans: dramatic growth in the neocortical portions to the human brain to three times the size of that among chimpanzees, forcing birth of very neurologically immature infants, and thereby necessitating a longer period of nursing and care of vulnerable offspring. A mammal that had offspring frequently would never have been able to grow the brain in the way that it did during the late phases of hominin evolution. But an animal like a great ape that already had bioprogrammers for prolonged pregnancy, long periods of nursing and offspring care, and over 5 years between births could allow the brain to grow in the womb to the maximal size to make it through the birth passages; and then, it could still give birth to a very immature infant in order to get the enlarged head through the female cervix and provide the infant and juvenile care required of a neurologically vulnerable offspring for at least 5 years. These characteristics would be unlikely to evolve to accommodate a sudden need for an early birth of big-brained offspring; for whatever reason, they were already part of the genome of great apes, thereby allowing for brain growth to the human measure.

Moreover, prolonged infant care encourages other social processes that would be important for the evolution of the nuclear family: kissing, hugging, infant and juvenile play, role-taking, bonding to adults and siblings, and eventually a father who stayed with the female (Eibl-Eibesfeldt 1996). Moreover, this process arousing positive emotions could also have served as yet another "hook" to pull males into an emerging proto-familial relations with females, especially as the enlarging septum was generating new kinds of emotions between males and females that are not experienced by great apes, although male and female great apes do, at times, form what appear to be attachments of some sort (perhaps, these are the great apes at one tail-end of the bell curve for septum size, which was available for natural selection to work on). And so, once there is some pull of males to females, the behaviors of females to their offspring could pull males into something like a nuclear family; and as selection began to push on all the relevant neurostructures, such as the anterior cingulate gyrus and septum, the nuclear family emerged with late *Homo erectus* (1 to 0.5 million years ago) or perhaps only with *Homo sapiens* (0.2 million years ago).

The Pre-Adaptation Provided by Mammalian Play

Young mammals universally play, another activity stimulated by the anterior cingulate gyrus. Many scholars now see play as involving a rather complex set of interpersonal skills that are critical to human interaction (Burghardt 2005). Play requires participants to assume complementary roles, say, pursuit and fleeing. It also involves understanding that such play is not true aggression and must be done without hurting the other. Aside from this rule, there may be other rules that various types of play require the young to learn. One of these is play reversal: The pursued becomes the "aggressor," and the aggressor suddenly becomes the pursued in a rapid shift in roles. And there may be particular gestural ways of communicating such shifts. Much of this activity appears to be hard-wired, but the existence of such bioprogrammers is something that could have been selected upon to enhance behaviors that are essential to human sociality and to creating solidarity: role-taking and role-making, ritual, mimicry, interpersonal attunement, and controlling negative emotions (Huizinga 1955; Beckoff and Pierce 2009; Bellah 2011b).

Others have argued that play does even more; it is a necessary precursor to the evolution of mind and cultural beliefs (Donald 1991, 2001; Bellah 2011b). Indeed, one of the features of human interaction that is rarely emphasized is that *it is very complex* (Turner 2002, 2007), involving a wide range of gesturing techniques, monitoring emotions of self and other, and coordinating both speech and body language in accordance with cultural codes applicable to situations. Only animals that, in their youth, engage in such play activities could learn the techniques necessary to carry out normal (but highly complex) interactions. Without the neurological propensity to engage in play, there would be no basis for early practice of adult interactions, nor would there be a neurological wiring or activation of this wiring on which other necessarily learned aspects of give-and-take during interaction could be built up in stocks of knowledge (Schutz 1932).

The Pre-Adaptation Provided by Low Levels of Grooming, Capacities for Cognitive Mapping, and Reckoning of Community

Robin Dunbar (1996) has argued that language evolved as a kind of verbal grooming that could replace physical grooming as groups became too large for direct and frequent physical contact among all members. His argument ignores that fact that apes do not groom that much compared to monkeys who use grooming to sustain solidarity; apes engage in greeting rituals and can become highly emotional in carnivals of effervescent emotions when gathered periodically in larger numbers, but *grooming is not a critical part of these behaviors*. Moreover, apes can reckon who belongs and who does not in a community of perhaps 150 individuals scattered and mobile across a community or home range that can be as large as 10 square miles. And so, apes *can already do* what Dunbar believes is the condition that pushed for language. Still, part of Dunbar's argument might be correct: Chimpanzee brains may be larger than those of monkeys because they have to reckon a much larger social unit: the community or regional population. The community is not only a larger space; it also has more members compared to monkey troops. Language did not emerge to replace grooming; rather, language itself is a pre-adaptation that was already present to be selected upon, if needed. Moreover, the ape brain was always larger than that of monkeys, and it was either a pre-adaptation for community formations or was selected for as larger community formations developed in the arboreal habitat.

In some ways, the very lack of high rates of grooming, coupled with the need to reckon who belongs and does not belong in communities, requires cognitive mapping of communities and its inhabitants. Language capacities as a pre-adaptation were, we would argue, usurped early in hominin evolution to make emotions a more powerful force for increasing solidarity visually in the language of emotions rather than in a tactile (haptic) way, as is the case in grooming. Of course, touching and grooming would be very effective enhancers of emotions used to forge social bonds, just as a handshake, hug, or pat on the back is for humans today—something that great apes already do as much as they ever groom. The subcortical portions of the brain grew and language emerged not so much to replace grooming but to operate as alternative means (among lower sociality apes) for creating social solidarity through signaling emotions; and eventually the language of emotions would dramatically enhance the power of emotions to forge social bonds. Then, as emotions become complex and varied, and indeed could even create common meanings among hominins, they provided the pre-adaptation for growth of the neocortex that would allow for spoken language that could be used to create culture composed of arbitrary signals communicating meanings. Indeed, it was the very lack of grooming and the already in-place capacity to mentally map the larger community that become a pre-adaptation not so much for solidarity but for what, we term in Chapters 16 and 17, *megasocieties* and *ultrasociality*.

A monkey could never create a macrosociety because they are programmed to form local troops. The *community is the natural unit of orientation for great apes* rather than the local groups, which are always temporary. Within communities, there can be some attachments, as with male friends among chimpanzees, but these are more the exception than the rule. Great apes do not have many strong ties and, hence, needs to groom; and yet, they must keep track of who is in and who should not come into a community. A monkey could not live in such a large, weak-tie system, but it is the system in which great apes evolved in the arboreal habitat and took with them to the African savanna—with disastrous consequences since tight-knit groups would be more fitness-enhancing in this new terrestrial habitat.

Yet, the capacity to see beyond the group, to be able to live among relative strangers, to avoid constant grooming and rituals of solidarity, and to form more temporary groups could be seen as a pre-adaptation for macrosocieties of great size, large populations, constant change, and interactions with strangers. Natural selection found a way to make hominins more social and group oriented, but it did not take away the cognitive capacity to reckon larger social structures beyond the group, to map out the ecology and demography of these larger communities, to move about these communities alone or with only temporary companions, and to remember who belongs and does not belong. Most mammals are oriented to kin and local groupings, whereas most apes are oriented to community more than to kin and local groupings. Kinship units like the nuclear family and groupings *are not* as "natural" to an ape, perhaps even an evolved ape like humans, as we might think. Humans must work very hard at forming and sustaining friendships and groups because they must do a great deal of interpersonal work and emotion management (Turner 2002). In contrast, humans rather naturally adapt to communities, often representing their totems in totem-like oval stickers on their back windshields or license plates proclaiming their pride in their hometowns or towns of residence. By extension, humans can rather easily identify with nation-states, feeling and expressing positive sentiments to their country and symbolizing these sentiments with totems like flags. Attachments to community and, with a bit more work, to nation are easier for an evolved ape to do than create and sustain interpersonal relations—which may seem shocking. But, face-to-face interpersonal behavior is quite tiring, both physically and emotionally, because of the need to sustain and control face-engagements.

This conclusion may seem absurd given the amount of time and energy devoted to texting and social media by persons around the world, but it can be argued that both these almost compulsive activities are means for maintaining relationships *without* all of the interpersonal work that face-to-face interaction requires. Hominins were rewired to be more social creatures and, as will be emphasized later, have needs for a sense of group inclusion; and texting and social media allow this sense to be achieved without doing all of the interpersonal work of actual face-to-face interaction in high-solidarity groups like families. And in the case of social media, it would seem natural for an evolved ape to orient to a larger community of so-called "friends" with whom one does not have to interact personally, just manage on their computers. It is more natural for an evolved ape like humans—despite all of the emotional enhancements, spoken language, and culture that all were necessary to make humans more social and group oriented—to orient to the more inclusive structures organizing people in societies. Without this orientation, macrosocieties would not have been possible. Humans would still be hunter-gatherers or perhaps simple horticulturalists; and while this may seem to be an extreme statement, it is one conclusion to be drawn from the cladistic analysis performed on extant great apes in Chapter 12.

Behavioral Propensities Among Apes

There is now a large literature from field observations of primates in captive research sites and even observations from experimental research designs on primate behaviors. Most of this research examines behavioral capacities and propensities. For example, studies of the language capacities of great apes raised by humans, as well as in controlled experiments documenting this capacity, challenge what was once thought a capacity exclusive to humans. Such can no longer be the case; and it is likely that dolphins, whales, and elephants have this same capacity to learn and use language. But, great apes do not develop this capacity in their natural habitats, but when exposed to humans and given the means via sign language or use of computer pictograms to express themselves, they can understand normally spoken language of humans and respond to these others using non-verbal communications channels.

In this section, however, the emphasis is on behaviors that all great apes are capable of performing; and when these are viewed as a whole, it is clear that so many of the behaviors of humans are not nearly as unique to *Homo sapiens* as was once thought. This finding should not be so surprising because of the genetic closeness of great apes to humans. What is surprising, however, is that these behavioral abilities were not sufficient to get apes better organized when selection from savanna conditions was intense. Something more was required: emotional enhancements.

Individualism and Mobility

From the cladistic analysis performed in Chapter 12 (see Table 12.1 on page 298), apes do not form permanent groups but orient to the larger community—as we emphasize also above. Moreover, what was not as much emphasized Chapter 12 is that apes are highly *individualistic* and *mobile*, moving about their larger community alone or in the short-term company of others. Sociologists generally have a more "collectivist bias" in all aspects of their support for various ideological positions, even if they are not concerned with human nature. But, an implicit assumption in much sociology that humans are biologically hard-wired to form groups and to be oriented to the collective. To the extent that the data on great apes can be used to speculate on human nature, this common assumption among sociologists and many social philosophers *needs to be heavily qualified*. Apes do orient to the larger community; and in fact, the collective community is the unit in which they do the most cognitive mapping; and so, this community orientation might be seen as confirming human collectivism. However, *apes do not form many strong ties with others*; they often wander around alone in their communities; and they form groups that soon disband, and these groups do not appear to have a permanent membership or structure. Some apes form friendships—mostly chimpanzee males—but these are not group-based friendships; they are dyadic and loose, and most male chimpanzee males tend to prefer unrelated males rather than their male kin as "friends." But, on the whole, even friendships are scarce across all great apes: Orangutans are virtual loners, wandering and living alone, except when males briefly court females to have sex (then depart) or when females care for their offspring until puberty; gorillas reveal tolerance among males that sometimes evolve into friendships, but the dominance of the lead silverback keeps most males out on the fringes of the troop or, if a member, only a temporary member. So, one behavioral propensity of great apes is individualism, mobility, and a certain level of interpersonal autonomy from conspecifics, with stronger ties occasionally emerging. And, even when apes like chimpanzees congregate occasionally in one place, a carnival of emotional contagion develops (see below) but soon dissipates and does not seem to have any permanence (although it may, in Durkheimian terms, provide ritual homage to the collective). The one time that chimpanzees form a strategic group is when males gather to patrol the boundaries of the community, but this group dissipates after its mission is completed.

Thus, we have to face the fact that, as part of humans' genetic heritage, there are *not* strong, direct bioprogrammers for collectivism, especially for local group solidarities. And, as emphasized, this lack of group orientation and strong-tie networks was the fatal weakness for virtually all species of great apes that ever lived, because there are only four types of great apes left on the planet, including humans. But still, the evolution of hominins occurred under intense selection pressures. The direction that natural selection took was more indirect than trying to install bioprogrammers for groupness and collectivism. By enhancing emotions, it became possible to forge social bonds revolving around positive emotional arousal that was highly rewarding to conspecifics. Yet, in using emotions to supercharge the interpersonal mechanisms to be discussed below makes interactions among people and the formation of groups a constant work in progress; it is not a natural process when the great-ape genome is considered but, rather, a process made possible by emotions as they increased the power of the many interpersonal capacities that apes possess, despite not forming strong ties or permanent groups.

Thus, laid over humans' great-ape propensity for individualistic behaviors and lack of group activity is an emotionally charged set of interpersonal mechanisms by which humans construct friendships, and groups, and the larger-scale structures and their cultures that typify human societies. But these are fragile structures because they are not direct outcomes of bioprogrammers; they need to be constructed and sustained by a great deal of interpersonal and emotion work. And, they are vulnerable to the dramatically enhanced emotional system that humans possess, as can be seen by individual collective violence that tears down structures.

The long-standing ideological conflict between collectivist and individualistic orientations to how societies should be structured is a conflict at the cultural level, but at the biological level, it is also a conflict between humans' great-ape genome, which has not gone away since we share so many genes with great apes but, instead, is a conflict with the genome of humans' common ancestor with great apes, on the one side, and supercharging with emotions of interpersonal mechanisms examined below, on the other. It is a neurological as much as an ideological conflict. Both sides in this ideological debate are, simultaneously, right and wrong. And this is where evolutionary sociology can perhaps clarify why this conflict exists; it exists because each human has a neurology wired to go either way toward autonomy and individualism or toward collective effervescence and solidarity. Ironically, it is not a conflict that can be resolved by going one way or the other because, as typically happens, individualism makes people lonely (and the emotions associated with this state), but subordinating this individualism to groups often produces resentment against too much control or creates a sense of emotional engulfment. Humans have behavioral propensities that are thus often in conflict, a conflict that was necessary if hominins were to survive on the African savanna and evolve into *Homo sapiens*; and thus it is a neurological and behavioral conflict with which humans must learn to live.

Reading Face and Eyes

Great apes can read and interpret gestures in the face and eyes of conspecifics (Osgood 1966; Menzel 1971; Stanford 1990; Mitani and Watts 2001; Turner and Maryanski 2008a); and, in fact, apes will almost always follow gaze and eye movements in order to ascertain what others are observing and thinking (Hare, Call and Tomasello 2001, 2006); Tomasello and Call 1997; Call and Tomasello 2008; Povinelli 2000; Povinelli and Eddy 1997; Itakura 1996; Baizer et al. 2007; Tomasello et al. 2001: Okamoto et al. 2002). Since emotions are more easily read by studying faces, these capacities of great apes were likely selected upon during the evolution of what Turner (2000) termed the "language of emotions." Since the dominant sense modality of great apes and humans is visual (relatively rare compared to olfaction), selection on emotional enhancement and attention to face and gaze became critical in forming the first language of hominins, perhaps millions of years before spoken language began to evolve with late hominins or, as some data suggest (Enard, Khaitovich et al. 2002; Enard, Przeworski et al. 2002), only with early humans.

Imitation of Facial Gestures Reveal Emotions

The above conclusion is supported by a propensity that both human and ape infants reveal: to learn facial and bodily gestures carrying meanings very early in life (Emde 1962; Ekman 1984; Sherwood et al. 2005; Tomonaga 1999; Subiaul 2007; Horowtiz 2003; Gergely and Csibra 2006). Among human infants, this capacity is dramatically evident when, within 2 weeks of birth, babies will imitate facial emotions emitted by caretakers.

A smile from a caretaker will be immediately imitated by a baby, as well as a frown, expression of surprise, and other facial states communicating emotions. It is clear that babies *are genetically programmed* to do so; and if we consider that they do not seek to imitate sounds at this age (they are like great apes, in a sense, that their vocal capacities require anatomical changes that only come with maturation); and in fact, babies "babble" for almost 2 years before they begin to "speak." Often, stages of maturation and development reflect evolutionary stages of development; and if such is the case in the almost immediate imitation by the newborn of facial gestures almost right out of the womb, this behavioral propensity suggests that a gesture-based language of emotions may have evolved first, especially since apes do not have the physical capacity to articulate speech in the human measure and, hence, most of their communication is gestural, although great apes can emit and understand sets of vocal calls that carry common meanings.

The capacity to articulate fine-grained vocalizations, however, involved many anatomical changes to the muscles of the face and mouth, the tongue, the larynx, vocal cords, and general structure of the wind passages of late hominin. And perhaps, it is for this reason that the genes regulating the formation of these speech-facilitating structures appear to have been under selection for only 200,000 years or the time frame for *Homo sapiens* (Enard, Khaitovich et al. 2002; Enard, Przeworski et al. 2002). It is most unlikely, if this genetic analysis by Enard and colleagues is correct, that a visual language did not evolve along the hominin line because, even today, chimpanzees can communicate instrumental coordination of action through facial gestures that are not easily read by researchers (Menzel 1971). Selection took the easier route of drawing on already existent capacities—that is, a larger palette of emotions and a clear propensity for primates to read emotions in faces—by selecting on these to unlock that pre-adaptation for language that all great apes and, hence, the last common ancestor of apes and hominins possessed. The conclusion that "body language" preceded spoken language is, therefore, not so far-fetched; and in fact, it may be that spoken language was *built on the neurological wiring for body language*, rather than the other way around. Yet, in one sense, the capacity of great apes to make auditory calls carrying meanings suggests that they have some control over auditory signals; and this capacity would be an important cognitive pre-adaptation for the evolution of more refined vocalizations that would eventually come with further alteration in the structures necessary for refined speech production that evolved with *Homo sapiens* or, perhaps, during late hominin evolution from 1 to 3.5 million years ago with *Homo erectus*.

Role-Taking and Empathy

In light of great apes' ability to read gestures of face for emotions and even more instrumental activities, it should not be surprising that great apes can role-take, in G. H. Mead's (1934) terms, and thereby achieve empathy with conspecifics and humans as well (de Waal 1996, 2009). Mead felt that role-taking—reading gestures to determine the behavioral dispositions of others—was unique to humans, but clearly it is not. We cannot even be sure that humans have a better capacity for this behavior than great apes, although it would be reasonable to assume that selection was working rapidly to make hominins more social and, hence, more willing and capable of role-taking and establishing empathy at an emotional level. But these abilities were not sudden nor a large evolutionary leap but, rather, a modest extension of what is already in the great-ape genome. Certainly the enhancement of emotions and, more significantly, the dramatic expansion of the neocortex in late hominin evolution made the stocks of knowledge (Schutz 1932) to be scanned and the cultural codes to be discerned in role-taking more complex but not fundamentally different, as a basic process, from what all low-sociality great apes can do today. But, the key point is that great apes and, hence, the last common ancestor of great apes and hominins on the human clade were not only disposed to role-take and establish empathy when needed, they must also have used these dispositions at critical times to sustain a sense of the larger community in which they lived. But, even with some emotional entrainment from empathy, great apes still *did not* develop widespread solidarities and strong ties. More was needed, and this extra punch to existing capacities and dispositions came from selection working on already enhanced emotional palettes to make affect *even more* powerful as the first and primal language of emotions of hominins and humans, thereby supercharging all their interpersonal processes.

Rhythmic Synchronization, Mimicry, and Ritual Behaviors

The discovery of the operation of mirror neurons (Rizzolatti and Sinigalia 2008; Rizzolatti et al. 1996, 2002, 2005; Rizzolatti and Craighero 2004) in monkeys and, then, their presence in both apes and humans has provided an underlying neurological explanation of many interaction processes, including imitation of facial gestures, following the gaze of conspecifics, role-taking, and empathy among great apes and, of course, humans as well. In fact, mirror neurons are involved in activating a series of behavioral propensities of great apes that are also evident among humans, including rhythmic synchronization of voice and bodies during interaction, collective emotionality and emotional effervescence (see below), and even rituals among collectively assembled apes. Mirror neurons not only cause mirroring of the responses and gestures of others, they also activate other brain systems that facilitate social bonding (Iacoboni et al. 2005; Iacoboni 2009) and adoption of others' emotional states (Ross et al. 2008). In turn, the release of neuroactive peptides and neurotransmitters (Barraza and Zak 2009) by mirror neuron activities increases the flow of positive emotions between conspecifics and thereby leads them to share emotional states, to develop common meanings, to understand each other's intended behaviors (Decety and Sommerville 2003; Gallese 2001), to increase attachment behaviors, to achieve a sense of trust, and to increase the level of group affiliations and solidarity (Campbell 2010). Mimesis is thus a key process affecting a wide variety of interactive processes among not only great apes, but also among humans. Human interactions are thus built around a series of focusing processes that are clearly incipient propensities in great apes and, from additional Darwinian selection, critical to human sociality and group solidarity. And, a most important point is that natural selection did not have to wait for mutations; rather, existing structures in primate and great-ape neurology were already present, with directional selection working to enhance these incipient propensities in hominins.

One propensity is, at noted above, mimesis. Another is what Randall Collins (2004) has labeled the "rhythmic synchronization" of vocalization and bodies. Chimpanzees will, when co-present and aroused, engage in collective acts of animated behaviors and screeching that fall in the collective rhythmic flow of bodies and vocalizations. Some have seen this kind of behavior as "musilanguage" or a proto-language revolving about singing and rhythm (Bellah 2003; Brown 2000; Mithen 2005) that early humans used to generate solidarity through the mirror neuron system (as this activates the brain systems generating neurotransmitters and neuroactive peptides in the brain). Another is a form of dance, involving a kind of collective jumping around in unison, which intensifies the action of mirror neurons (as these neurons activate brain systems generating positive emotions leading to attachment behaviors). Some see these mimetic behaviors as the basis for all rituals, large and small, that humans use to initiate and animate interactions (Alcorta and Sosis 2005). Chimpanzees will also often engage in what can only be described as rhythmic drumming, pounding on logs often with sticks, while jumping around, and operating much like drums in collective marches. There is a number of key brain systems involved here (see Aldecoa 2016 for a summary, and Chapter 14), but the end result is synchronization of the bodies and minds of chimpanzees who reveal empathy and even proto-common meanings with conspecifics (de

Waal 2008, 2012), especially since quasi-ritualized collective actions escalate emotions that, in turn, increase memory formation of events in the neocortex of chimpanzees.

Thus, the human capacity for synchronization, mimicry, and ritualized behaviors is only a small extension of what great apes can do; and so, natural selection could have targeted the mirror neuron system and its connection to both subcortical and neocortical system process among hominins. For as synchronization proceeds from mimicry and as mimicry activates a host of rhythmic and emotion-arousing behaviors, solidarity is achieved, at least for the duration of the interaction. Moreover, even as the emotion subsides, it will have tagged cognitions about collective events that are more likely to be remembered, thus furthering a sense of the community which, with additional selection on these capacities, could have led hominins to begin forming stable groups and group attachments.

Collective Emotional Effervescence

Another critical behavioral propensity evident among chimpanzees is what is sometimes called "carnival" by field researchers. When chimpanzees assemble, as described above, the mirror neuron system and mimicry kick off a rather animated (with quasi-dancing and music language) emotional effervescence, much like that at among humans during "raves" or festivals like Mardi Gras. Emile Durkheim (1912) emphasized the collective emotional "effervescence" of Aranda aborigines in Spencer and Gillin's (1899) description of aboriginals in central Australia, in and around Alice Springs. Durkheim (1912) was to see this collective effervescence and the rituals (directed to totems symbolizing the collective) as the fundamental basis of societal integration (after he had abandoned the notion of "mechanical" and "organic" solidarity by 1895). Erving Goffman's (1967) most critical insight in his portrayal of "interaction rituals" is the use of lower-key rituals to arouse less intense emotional effervescence in ways that open, close, structure, and repair encounters when breached; and it is this lower-key effervescence that sustains encounters and increases both social bonding and group solidarities among individuals. Thus, even at the micro level of the ordinary face-to-face encounter, less intense chimp-like "carnivals" arousing positive emotions become the foundation of all human behavior and, ultimately, of all patterns of social organization (Goffman 1967; Turner 2002). Again, it was not a giant neurological step from what chimpanzees do compared to what humans do each and every time they interact. The enhancing of emotions, the increased control of emotions, and the subsequent enlargement of the neocortex during late hominin evolution did not have to generate an entirely new set of behavioral capacities but, instead, simply provide additional neurology to enhance, regulate, and channel behavioral propensities clearly evident in the great apes, particularly humans' closest relative, chimpanzees.

Reciprocity

All higher primates, and even most advanced mammals, possess behavioral propensities to reciprocate favors of conspecifics (Cosmides 1989; de Waal 1989, 1991, 1996; de Waal and Brosnan 2006). On the one hand, reciprocity reinforces an existing exchange relationship and thus promotes social bonding; on the other hand, it can create new bonds among conspecifics by the arousal of positive emotions when exchanges are completed. There are different types of exchange relationships among humans: *reciprocal exchanges* where favors or reinforcements at one point in time are reciprocated at a subsequent point in time, *negotiated exchanges* involving active bargaining back and forth at one point in time about the distribution of resources, and *generalized exchanges* where resources flow across actors and circle back around to the starting point of a protracted chain of exchange. Reciprocal exchanges, such as gift-giving or trading favors, are the most likely to generate solidarities, and these are the dominant form of exchanges among primates. These are what sociobiologists termed acts of *reciprocal altruism* as hard-wired in humans, and since they are clearly evident among both higher monkeys and apes, they were part of the behavioral repertoire of the last common ancestor to great apes and hominins. So, once again, selection does not need to create anything new, but simply select on appropriate tail ends of distributions for exchange behaviors and thereby increase sociality and bonding among low-sociality hominins.

Calculations of Justice and Fairness

Sarah Brosnan and colleagues (Brosnan et al. 2005) have reported that capuchin monkeys exchanging behaviors desired by trainers for food resources would immediately stop exchanging if they observed another monkey getting more resources for the same behavior from a trainer. This behavior is rather complex because it involves a comparison of one's own payoffs for a given amount of work with the payoffs of others, and clearly the arousal of a negative emotion that revolved around a proto-sense of morality that the exchange is not fair or just. Similarly, Brosnan and de Waal's (2003) study of chimpanzees noted that a chimpanzee exchanging with a caretaker stopped exchanging when it was discovered that a relative was not receiving the same reward from the caretaker, clearly another act of pro-morality about the fairness in general but especially for those who are related. Thus, there can exist a kind of proto-morality, revolving around emotional reactions to non-reciprocity or unfairness in the rewards received for behavioral performances. This is not the morality of a legal or religious system of moral codes, but it is the neurology that gives these codes moral power. Thus, before emotions in the subcortex of the brain of evolving apes were enhanced among hominins, before the neocortex grew, and before language and culture emerged as result of this growth, the last common ancestor, by the logic of cladistic analysis, had much of the basic wiring in place for a sense of justice, giving natural selection something to select on. Morality did not come with just a big brain, culture, and language; it existed and still exists among many higher mammals as a hard-wired neurological response to perceive unfairness in exchanges of resources. Again, selection would select on tail ends of the distribution of this capacity to sense justice, or perhaps all that was necessary was expanding the palette of emotions and enlarging the neocortex of late hominins with no need to change the neurology producing justice reactions, just the emotions activating these reactions and the capacity of the neocortex to articulate and catalogue moral codes. Morality, then, is ultimately given "teeth" and power by emotions and by the capacity to make simple comparisons of exchange payoffs of one animal relative to another; it is not something wholly unique to humans but simply an extension of what all great apes and most higher monkeys and mammals can do.

Seeing Self as an Object in the Environment

George Herbert Mead (1934) believed that only humans could see themselves as an object in an environment, but such is now obviously not the case. The well-known studies using mirrors to see if an animal can recognize itself in a mirror indicate that a few highly intelligent animals have the neurological capacity to see themselves. Dolphins and elephants (Whitehead and Rendell 2015) recognize that what they are seeing in the mirror is a reflection of themselves, whereas dogs and cats cannot (Gallup 1970,1979, 1982). Seeing oneself in a mirror does not necessarily mean that animals have a self concept or identity of themselves in the way humans do, but it portends the basic wiring on which this capacity to form a self-conception and identity is ultimately built. Charles Horton Cooley (1902) used the mirror analogy when he argued that human selves are created by "the looking glass" or mirror, but in this case, the mirror is the gestures and responses of others to a person; and the person thus sees themselves reflected in these gestures causing an evaluation of self and the emotional experience of either shame or guilt when the responses of others are approving or disapproving.

Great apes, but not monkeys, immediately recognize their reflection in a mirror as an image of themselves, and they take great delight in moving about, dancing, touch parts of body, etc. to confirm that such is indeed the case. Great apes do not experience shame or pride in the way described by Cooley, but they have the neurology to recognize themselves reflected in the mirror and, then, test out this perception with actions designed to see self as an object in the larger environment. It is still not clear if they have Cooley's capacity for a looking-glass self consisting of the gestures of conspecifics or trainers, but clearly the neurological capacity to perceive of self as an object—to have self-awareness—is present, and perhaps only selecting on the emotional repertoire of all great apes and, later, the neocortex would be all that was necessary for Darwinian natural selection to create the behavioral capacity outlined by Mead and Cooley for humans. Yet, even chimpanzees can have some notion of themselves as a particular kind of object, as observations by those who have raised chimpanzees in their homes suggest. When, for example, asked to sort out pictures in two piles, as to whether or not the picture is of an ape or human, chimps raised in homes will place their own picture (which they immediately recognize) in the human pile. Again, the neurology for a wholly new behavior did not have to be created by natural selection working on mutations because its basic wiring was already in place for hominins; rather, selection needed only to enhance an already existing capacity, which may have meant nothing more than what selection was already doing: enhancing emotions that would lead to an enlarged neocortex in which more elaborated conceptions of self could develop.

Having a sense of self would be critical to social bonding and group solidarity because, when individuals can see themselves in the looking glass or mirror of others' gestures and experience positive or negative emotions in how others are evaluating their self-presentations, they become highly motivated to seek approval from others and, eventually, begin to evaluate self by cultural moral codes. As this transition occurs, social control becomes self-control; and with self-control, it becomes possible to form social bonds and to regulate self from the perspective of others and group norms as well as other cultural codes.

As natural selection was expanding the complexity and nuance of the emotional palette of hominins which, in turn, would allow the neocortex to grow and engage in more complex thinking and memory formation (because cognitions could be tagged with a wider variety of emotions).

this path of evolution by Darwinian natural selection would be sufficient to install the full capacity for a self-conception and the capacity to develop situational identities (Burke and Stets 2009; Turner 2002, 2007). And as this capacity of identity formation increased, it would feed back and encourage further selection on the hominin subcortex and neocortex because a sense of self dramatically increases social control and makes individuals dependent upon group approval to experience positive emotions about self. The result is that groups become more viable and can be used to build up social structures and their cultures.

Status Differences and Hierarchy

Monkeys generally form linear hierarchies among males and, at times, hierarchies in female matrilines. Hierarchies increase the level of structure in monkey societies and force monkeys to be troop- or group-oriented compared to apes who are community-oriented, with a fission-fusion pattern in groups that are only temporary. The only ape that forms a stable group are the species of small gibbons and siamangs living higher in the trees of some Asian forests, but these species of apes are very far off the great-ape line. Unlike great apes, these species form a conjugal pair where males and females often form a strong bonds for a lifetime; and when offspring are born, they comprise a nuclear family, although both female and male offspring at puberty leave their natal community forever. Orangutans are virtually solitary and, as emphasized in Chapter 12 with the cladistic portrayal, are very much like the last common ancestor of great apes and hominins, revealing no permanent ties beyond mother-young offspring ties that are broken at puberty when both male and female offspring leave the natal community. Gorillas evidence some hierarchy with the lead silverback, but the composition of the group that he supposedly "leads" is constantly changing. Chimpanzees form only temporary groups as well as longer-term male friendships that are sustained by frequent gatherings and interaction, and they also form less lineal dominance hierarchies, but these tend not to cut across the whole community and often disappear. Thus, there is relatively little structure to great-ape societies and only, at best, a medium amount of hierarchy, but still, there clearly are some tendencies to form hierarchies but nothing like those among monkeys.

Nomadic hunter-gatherers do not reveal inequalities by gender, nor by hierarchies of leadership; and yet, they are clearly working very hard to assure that inequalities in status do not form (Boehm 2013). Some persons by age or special skill may enjoy prestige, but this does not translate into power and authority. Hunter-gatherers probably learned early on that inequalities in power create tensions that can destroy the band, and so a normative culture evolved to sanction anyone who begins to consider himself or herself as "above others."

Yet, settled hunter-gatherers immediately evidence inequalities and leadership by a "Big Man" who controls resources but is also required to redistribute these in prestige-giving rituals to the rest of a community. But, nonetheless hierarchy appears with the Big Man and his allies controlling much activity in the communities that form among settled hunter-gatherers. And, subsequent societal evolution (see Chapter 3) involves differential evaluations of social categories of person; status locations in corporate units; and inequalities in power, prestige, material wealth, and other resources (Lenski 1964; Turner 1984, 2015).

Thus, hominins certainly evidenced differentiations by gender and age, and perhaps some hierarchy, but by the time of hunting-gathering among humans evolved, these had disappeared; or, at the very least, a normative culture developed to repress propensities for hierarchy or differential evaluation. This behavioral capacity to reckon status remained, however, but cultural norms did not let this capacity evolve into hierarchies of power and control. Still, the existence of some behavioral propensities among chimpanzees and gorillas clearly argues for their continuation in humans; and, when regulation and control are needed as societies and populations grow, hierarchies of power consistently form. Without power and authority, larger-scale sociocultural formations among individualistic evolved apes like humans would not be viable. Indeed, without the ability to build up divisions of labor in corporate units as the building blocks of institutional domains like polity, kinship, religion, law, etc., larger-scale human societies would not be possible. Moreover, as societies grew and as migration to and from different societies occurred, other differences beyond sex and age—differences like religious affiliation, ethnicity, homeland, and the like—would increasingly be reckoned as formerly isolated populations came into contact. But the pattern of status recognition was still relatively loose: Locations in corporate units in divisions of labor and social categories defining persons were not locked into the genome; rather, only the propensity to "notice difference" has a genetic basis, wired into visual dominance where all differences are noticed and interpreted. Just how these get consolidated into social structures was more pliable and loose, unlike the situation with monkeys who are always oriented to hierarchy.

There was, then, considerable flexibility in the behavioral disposition of humans in their assessment of status in divisions of labor and diffuse status characteristics by virtue of belonging to salient social categories. The result historically has been the capacity to develop new types of societies and to change existing societies, often by conflict, but to change them nonetheless. Apes are very individualistic and often quite autonomous and mobile about their communities. These behavioral propensities allowed humans to construct the many different types of societies outlined in Chapter 3 and what will surely be new types of societies in the future.

Most mammals do not have such flexibility; their genome locks them into particular ways of organizing differences. And while culture and technology allow construction and reconstruction of human societies, none of this could have occurred in the evolutionary history of human societies, if humans had not possessed an evolved behavioral predisposition to reckon status differences but to have flexibility in how these status differences are institutionalized into a society. Monkeys, for example, could not be this flexible; they are trapped by the hard-wired propensity of females to form matrilines (and at times, hierarchies arise in these matrilines) and males to compete for dominance, which constricts their options in troop formation. An evolved great ape is not so limited because of a lack of strong bioprogrammers for group formations and hierarchies within groups and by the existence of bioprogrammers for reckoning the larger community and potentially beyond are the only stable structure. There could never be a planet of the monkeys because they could not conceive of how to organize at a larger societal, much less, world-level, even if they had more intelligence, because of their powerful bioprogrammers for dense female networks and male hierarchy. In contrast, earth is—for better or worse—"the planet of the apes" because human great apes developed the capacity for language and culture over ancient behavioral propensities for loose hierarchies and flexible reckoning of status differences.

What Is Human Nature?

This exposition of pre-adaptations and behavioral propensities that are, in all likelihood, genetically controlled to some degree should inform any discussion of human nature. It is difficult to define the notion of human nature because it only suggests that humans have a "nature" that leads them to behave in certain ways. But the "nature" part is problematic because: Does "nature" mean a biological nature that is common to all humans, as is often implied? Or does it mean biologically based propensities interacting with sociocultural contexts? It is unlikely that these questions can be answered to everyone's satisfaction, and our goal is not to make pronouncements of what human nature is but instead to guide the search for those wishing to make such pronouncements. It is possible to posit universal need-states, which J. Turner has done (Turner 2002, 2007; 2010, 2015), but these are still speculative, although they are derived from earlier versions of the materials summarized in this chapter. The more fundamental issue is that any speculation about human nature should have an empirical base. The best empirical base is to try to discover the underlying biology of humans as they evolved, particularly the biology that has the most effect on how humans behave and interact. This is the best that we can do with the new evolutionary sociology. We can use cladistic analysis to look back in time and see the behavioral and organizational traits of the animals from which we all ultimately evolved. We can do comparative analysis of humans' closest living relatives to see how great apes are wired to behave and then examine the selection pressures that were working on this biology to create *Homo sapiens*. From this kind of analysis, some useful leads are outlined and can, we feel, inform speculation. In Chapter 14, we will add a bit more detail on the evolution of the neurology that humans now possess and that, certainly, is part of any informed speculation on human nature.

Conclusions

The history of sociological theorizing is full of both explicit and implicit assumptions about human nature. But once the value of studying such close relatives—the great apes and primates in general—became clear, cladistic analysis could reveal the characteristics of humans' distant ancestor millions of years ago. And coupled with the accumulated data on the behavioral propensities of these close relatives sharing common ancestor with humans, we have even more data on what the hard-wired behavioral dispositions of our distant ancestors and hominins were like. The pre-adaptations and behavioral propensities outlined in this chapter thus provide a much more rigorous and refined view of what is part of human nature. Evolution is a conservative process; and in the case of hominin evolution, it did not so much "invent" new structures but *modified existing ones* running along the great-ape line until the present. The evolution of hominins has been, as Darwin emphasized, "descent with modifications," but the modifications are more by degree than fundamentally new kinds of behavior propensities. What makes humans "human" is what made apes "apes"; selection has been on *existing structures* and then modifying them to solve the one big obstacle to hominin evolution on the African savanna: the problem of overcoming a lack of bioprogrammers to form strong ties among all age and sex classes and to form more permanent groups with higher levels of solidarity. Most apes of any type did not make it because they could not overcome this obstacle, but for those evolving great apes on the hominin line, natural selection randomly hit upon the solution: enhance with increased emotions all of the behavioral propensities among great apes along the human clade as a strategy to increase sociality and solidarity among hominins. The savanna was the graveyard for virtually all apes except, in the end, humans. All other apes, except for those few chimpanzees that scratch out an existence on the savanna today in Senegal, but even they, must sometimes retreat to the forest. So, what is really exceptional about human nature is how close it reflects ape nature, but with one very large difference: human emotionality, which is a double-edged sword because it was what made survival possible but, on the other side, negative emotions collectively experienced can destroy societies. And it is this emotionality that allowed the brain to grow to create yet another double-edged sword: civilizations with vast technologies that can support billions of people in mass societies and, on the other side of the sword, that can create weapons of mass destruction that those aroused by negative emotion are willing to use on their fellow conspecifics.

Sociology has historically focused on language and culture as the driving forces of humanity, but in fact, directional selection on existing phenotypical traits of great apes has been far more important in creating humans. To be sure, earlier enlarging of subcortical areas of the brain to set up the necessary neurological infrastructure for growing the neocortex to human proportions very late in hominin evolution made humans a very special kind of great ape, but the fundamental nature of this now much smarter animal that could employ spoken language and thereby create culture has really not been modified as much as we might think. Our nature as evolved apes continues to generate pressures to create sociocultural formations that are more compatible with this nature; and while this nature can be violated by these formations, at least for a while, humans' evolved nature is not linguistic or cultural as much as it is a modified biological heritage from the common ancestor that we all share with the great apes.

In Chapter 14, another line of the *new* evolutionary sociology is outlined: neurosociology. Our concern is not with neurology, *per se*, in this book, but with the evolution of the human brain. Thus, only part of what it is hoped will become a large and robust field—the study of the effects of neurology on humans, human behavior, and human social organization, and equally important, vice versa—will be addressed in this volume, with its focus on evolutionary analysis. Our concern will be what we consider a first step in a neurosociology: understanding why and how the brain evolved over the last 10 million years, resulting in a big-brained animal with too much emotional volatility. Once this evolution is understood, then specific studies on the relationship between neurology and society can push neurosociology forward. Neurosociology should become a much bigger field, extending far beyond evolutionary sociology; yet, evolutionary sociology can add a great deal to this field as it begins to grow.

14

The Evolution of the Human Brain
Applications of Neurosociology

A new mode of sociological inquiry in sociology has been labeled "neurosociology" (Franks 2010; Franks and Turner 2013). When viewed in an evolutionary context, emphasis is on how the brain evolved during hominin evolution from the last common ancestor of present-day great apes and humans, although we can push the analysis back to the evolution of primates and, even further, to the beginning of mammals. Thus far, we have examined many topics in the new evolutionary sociology that engage this nascent sub-discipline of neurosociology. In this chapter, we turn to what early pioneers in social science applications of neurology, like Michael Gazzaniga (1985, 2005), first emphasized: the *evolution* of the brain. In order to understand human behavior and patterns of social organization, it is very useful to have a picture of how and why the hominin and then human brain evolved over the last 6 million years. Evolutionary psychology took up this challenge as its signature calling (see Chapter 9) but began with the wrong view of how the neurology of the hominin brain evolved through mutations creating discrete special-function modules that resolved adaptive problems during the Pleistocene. Sociobiology implied, at the very least, a neurological explanation for behaviors such as kin selection, reciprocal altruism, reciprocity, and other behaviors considered to be universal among mammals and humans because they enhanced fitness, whereas evolutionary psychology started with an emphasis on exchange and reciprocity (e.g., Cosmides 1989; see also Chapter 9 and references therein).

While evolutionary psychology appears to have dropped the notion of modules and simply emphasized selection on the brain, and while sociobiology has also slowly been coming around to the view that group selection is a reality, we need not follow their early leads, nor should we *only* examine hard-wired behaviors because these alone cannot explain emergent sociocultural phenomena. Still, as has been examined in a number of chapters, there are hard-wired behavioral capacities that were inherited from mammals and, more recently, from primate ancestors of humans. Some of these, such as reciprocity, appear across a good portion of the primate line and even in the line of intelligent mammals, whereas other behavioral traits, such as kin selection, appear among most mammals and insects but not as direct bioprogrammers in great apes and, hence, humans. Thus, we need to be careful about overgeneralizing from the findings of sociobiology and evolutionary psychology; instead, we need to explain why the hominin brain evolved into the human brain under rather intense selection pressures.

The Organization of the Human Brain

The Archeology of the Brain

Some years ago, Paul MacLean (1990) proposed model of the "triune brain," which presented a graphic that appears to show the early mammalian brain as layered over the reptilian brain and, then, the large neocortex of humans layered on top of this early, and much smaller, mammalian brain. For a long time, researchers on emotions followed Paul MacLean's view that the mammalian brain was built over the reptilian brain, but it now appears that such is not quite the case. Rather, reptiles/birds evolved from a different, but closely related, line of vertebrate amphibians, and there probably was not much difference between the respective cortices of mammals and reptiles at these beginning stages of their respective evolution. Mammals did not have a neocortex and, in all likelihood, neither did reptiles at the very beginning of terrestrial life on the planet. They both probably had somewhat truncated versions of a primitive subcortex evident in both reptiles and mammals today (see Dugas-Ford and Ragsdale 2015). Moreover, in thinking about the imagery of MacLean's model of the triune brain, it is important to remember that the brain is spherical, and hence, its various layers as they evolved are *not* like those in a cake but more like those in a sphere or ball that has been built up from a core. So, the oldest part of the brain, built from the brain stem and diencephalon, penetrates up *into the center of the brain*, with new neocortical layers of tissues and structures wrapping around the brain that mammals inherited from early amphibians.

In Figure 14.1, we present several views of the human brain, one of its outside surface and another of its key structures. The subcortex is basically the brain inherited from early amphibians, but it has additional structures, and as we will emphasize, it is the place where emotions in mammals are generated. On top of the corpus callosum—the open passage where billions of neurons connect to two halves of the brain—is the cingulate cortex, which probably was the first layer of neocortical cells in the evolution of mammals that laid over the most primitive of vertebrae amphibian brain. For, in its anterior portions, the unique behaviors of mammals are generated—behaviors such as mother-infant bonding, play, and mother-offspring separation cries. Over and around the cingulate cortex are the lobes of the neocortex that follow—frontal, temporal, parietal,

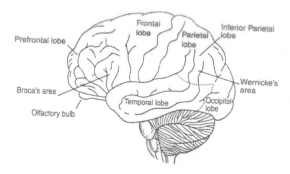

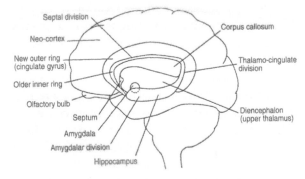

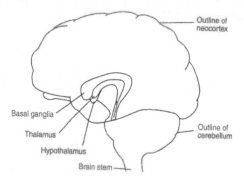

Figure 14.1 Key Areas of the Brain during Hominin and Human Evolution

and occipital. The frontal lobe is where longer-term memories are stored but not until the subcortical hippocampus has tagged them with emotions that are reactivated to cement the memory in, at which point it is shipped up to the frontal lobe for longer-term storage. Just below the frontal lobe is the pre-frontal cortex, which is the key structure in connecting neocortical and subcortical structures and in decision-making.

As was discussed in Chapter 13 and as will be elaborated upon shortly, the parietal, temporal, and occipital lobes meet toward the posterior of the neocortex and are association cortices around the inferior parietal lobe that are responsible for great-ape and human neurological capacities for language. Also important are two discrete areas, although these spill over across the entire left side of the temporal lobe: Broca's area which is what allows for speech production by downloading the brain's way of thinking (which is much faster than internalized speech) into sequences of words; and its location makes sense because the temporal lobe is the sense modality for auditory responses, and the location of Broca's area is next to the lower part of the fissure separating the frontal from parietal lobe, where the neurological (haptic) centers for the structures for fine-grained speech production are found. The proximity of Broca's area to the parietal lobe is important because control of the lips, tongue, larynx, and other structures responsible for human speech production are regulated by the parietal lobe, which is the lobe for haptic responses (touch and general sense of body). Broca's area is found in very rudimentary form as an asymmetrical area in chimpanzees and great apes more generally. However, the location of this asymmetry in the left temporal lobe is not precisely the same among chimpanzees and humans. And, the neurons in the parietal lobe allowing for fine-grained speech production are not exactly the same in chimpanzees (see Falk 2007 for a review of the literature). Still, by the logic of cladistic analysis, the area in chimpanzees is probably much as it was for the last common ancestor of hominins and chimpanzees; and when finely articulated speech could become fitness-enhancing, selection went to work to alter these asymmetries on the left temporal lobe into more specialized structural features of Broca's area in humans. The counterpart of Broca's area on the other side of the brain is involved in rhythm and singing in humans, and so it is clear that natural selection eventually usurped an existing module like that evident among chimpanzees and converted it to a more specialized speech-production module—note, it did not create a new module as evolutionary psychology might once have argued. Rather, natural selection took an *existing* module-like structure, sometimes termed "the cap" in primates and made it central to speech production—once speech production late in hominin evolution was fitness-enhancing; and it rewired portions of the parietal lobe to create the capacity for fine-grained enunciations that are critical to human speech production (Enard, Khaitovich et al. 2002; Enard, Przeworski et al. 2002).

Moving back toward the inferior parietal lobe is another area that great apes have in comparatively well-developed form: Wernicke's area, which is responsible for the uploading of speech sounds into the brain's ways of processing information. Among great apes, this area may have been used to upload both vocal and visual signals for processing by the brain. Unlike Broca's area, Wernicke's area in great apes is much more similar to this area in the human brain; and indeed, it appears to have been an early adaptation along the primate line because it is also found in macaque monkeys. The important point here is that the two key structures necessary for speech production and comprehension—Broca's and Wernicke's areas—*already existed* in the hominin line long before speech production and comprehension began to evolve in late hominins or, perhaps, only in early humans. Thus, Broca's area and the more fully developed Wernicke's area can be considered pre-adaptations for language in the human measure. And coupled with the hard-wired capacity of great apes for language facility in general (as a result of selection in the association cortices around the inferior lobe), Wernicke's area allows great apes to learn and comprehend human speech at the level of a young human child.

Moving downward in our archeological excavation of the brain into the subcortical areas, we encounter those structures responsible for the production of emotions, such as the amygdala which is the ancient area for fear and anger among the early vertebrate amphibians from which mammals evolved. The thalamus routes all sensory inputs to the appropriate lobe—parietal for touch, occipital for vision, temporal for sound, and olfactory bulb for smell (although smell operates somewhat independently because it is located in the subcortex, but is still very much directly connected to the thalamus and amygdala). At the same time, sensory inputs are also routed to emotion centers generating neurotransmitters, neuroactive peptides, and more general hormonal responses in ways that allow animals to respond behaviorally to environment conditions. The hippocampus and the associated transition cortices are involved in memory formation—from working memory during conversations with others to more enduring memory formation processes in which cognitions are tagged with relevant emotions. This tagging and then re-remembering the tagged cognition (and thereby activating the emotions associated with this cognition, typically in somewhat diluted form) allows memories to form and endure and, after about 2 years, a memory that has been repeated with its associated emotions will be shipped up from the hippocampus to the frontal lobe for longer-term storage.

Not visible in Figure 14.1 are the larger and more dense sets of neurons that travel back and forth from the pre-frontal cortex, through the amygdala which, in humans, has been partially usurped as a routing station for neurons connecting the neocortical and subcortical areas of the brain, mostly via the pre-frontal cortex, to the hippocampus where memories are first formed. Moreover, the amygdala is also very much involved in determining the place of an individual in a given context and is "at the ready" to arouse appropriate emotions in this context; and moreover, the amygdaloid body's lateral portions, which are unique to humans, are involved in role-taking and empathy.

Thus, rational thought and deliberation are only possible with emotional tags on all cognitions; and thus the old philosophical opposition of emotions and rationality is simply wrong, neurologically (Damasio 1994). And, as bears repeating from Chapter 13, it is the evolution of these subcortical areas in the hominin brain that was more responsible for hominin survival than a larger neocortex, spoken language, and culture in the human measure. Long before speech and culture using artificial symbols to denote meanings evolved, the emotion centers of the hominin brain had grown. And indeed, as will be emphasized shortly, without this prior growth of emotional capacities among hominins, a larger brain and articulated speech would have little fitness-enhancing value.

The Nature of Brain Evolution

The human brain is a larger, more complexly wired version of the basic mammalian brain, as the mammalian brain was modified during the evolution of the primate order, as we explore next. The brain did not evolve by mutations as a dominant force, once the basic architecture was set up by natural selection. As Fisher (1930) long ago demonstrated and as others have confirmed, most mutations are harmful; and mutations in a complex, interdependent system like the brain are very much like explosions destroying complex neuro-nets rather than building up new, fitness-enhancing brain structures. Rather, it is more from *directional selection* on *existing* modules—if we still want to call them this—that the brain evolved. By selecting on the tails of bell-shaped curves summarizing the distributions of brain components and neuro-nets, natural selection did a great deal of *rewiring* of the mammalian and primate brain to produce the human brain. Yet, the basic architecture remains much the same, although in humans certain structures like Broca's area and the amygdala have been selected on and altered functionality as a result of long-term directional selection. Other structures had been made larger and more enhanced in various ways by directional selection; and a good many neuro-nets have been added to the human brain, thus increasing its overall connectivity. And so, the brain has changed but not in dramatic ways; and it would be hard to say that any *new* special-function modules have emerged by virtue of mutations. Instead, directional selection usurping some existing modules for additional functions, enlarging existing modules to enhance or supplement their functions, and increasing the connectivity among all brain structures has been the primary route by which the brain was rewired during hominin evolution.

Moreover, certain changes in the brain had to precede other changes during this rewiring. The unique features of humans—their large and complex palette of emotions, their capacity for finely articulated speech, their ability to store vast amounts of information in a very large neocortex (relative to body size), their capacity for rational thought and deliberation in abstract terms, and their ability to talk—depended upon pre-adaptations that could be subject to directional selection. And, as we will document, the first big changes in the brains of hominins revolved around the enhancement of emotions in the subcortex. For without the initial enhancement of emotions, none of the other unique features of humans could ever have evolved.

Neurological Evolution Among Primates

Selection on Neurology for Visual Dominance During Early Primate Evolution

The human brain very much reflects early primate adaptation to the arboreal habitat. Around 63 million years ago, small rodent-like mammals began to leave the ground and sought to adapt to the forest habitats of the world. The extinction of dinosaurs greatly facilitated this movement of formerly terrestrial small mammals to the arboreal habitat, and over the next 20 million years, prosimians (pre-monkeys), monkeys, and apes evolved, with monkeys eventually being the most fit of all three branches of the primate line (the verdict is still out on humans who have been so fit that they may have altered their environments in ways that reduce their fitness). In monkeys and apes, the most significant neurological change came with the shift in the dominant sense modality of most mammals—olfaction—to visual dominance, which clearly would be fitness-enhancing in a three-dimensional environment. It is much easier to see one's way around the branches of the forest habitat than to smell one's way. The olfactory bulb of primates thus became smaller, particularly those of monkeys and apes that went the full measure to true visual dominance, subordinating all other sense modalities to vision. The olfactory bulb in mammals is subcortical, right in front of the amygdala (the center for fear and anger emotional responses in all mammals, and indeed, reptiles as well); and this combination would be very fitness-enhancing since signals from the olfactory bulb could, via the thalamus, almost immediately activate "flight or fight" responses in the face of danger. But, by being subcortical, olfaction cannot be controlled by the neocortex, with the result that we can often experience a flood of emotions associated with scents of past situations that were emotional.

At the neocortical level, haptic senses (touch and feel) are, as noted earlier, located in the parietal lobe, auditory senses (hearing and producing sounds) are arrayed along the temporal lobe, and visual sensory inputs eventually go to the occipital lobe. The rewiring of the primate brain to make vision dominant involved a series of association cortices in and around the *inferior parietal lobe*, where the temporal, parietal, and occipital lobes meet. The result is that, when primates and humans hear or touch something, they immediately move their eyes to determine what these inputs are indicating, and what is seen will direct the responses of an organism. Similarly, smells will move the eyes to the direction of the smells, if direction can be determined by a smaller nest of cells in the primate olfactory bulb. Visual dominance among mammals is comparatively rare; most mammals are olfactory dominant and will seek to smell sensory inputs and subordinate all other senses to smell, although many mammals also have very keen vision, especially predators that must also see their prey in order to attack effectively at vulnerable spots on the run. A few mammals like bats are auditory dominant and direct their movements through echolocation without actually "seeing" objects, while others like dolphins and whales use echolocation and supplement dominant auditory inputs with visual information.

With vision as the dominant sense modality, the way that a primate experiences the world is very different from the way that most other mammals experience their environment. Moreover, once vision is dominant, selection pressures will need to work through this dominant visual modality. Thus, while we tend to think of speech (auditory) and culture as humans' most distinctive feature, it is visual dominance that also makes humans very special in the mammalian world. And, as will become evident, the first languages were probably visual in nature, not auditory because there is so much extra work that natural selection had to do to make an evolving hominin able to engage in finely articulated speech. Indeed, as some have argued, fine-grained speech may be uniquely human because data on the genes regulating the structures needed for speech in the human measure—larynx, lips, tongue, facial muscles, etc.—have only been under selection for 200,000 years (Enard, Khaitovich et al. 2002; Enard, Przeworski et al. 2002). Still, great apes and other primates evidence call systems that communicate common meanings; and so, this system of calls can be considered a pre-adaptation for language production because it has made the first critical step to such production: voluntary control by the neocortex of auditory signals.

Yet, Turner (2000, 2007) has argued that the first language was more visual than auditory because of the limitations on the range and nuance of vocalizations among great apes and the last common ancestor to extant great apes and humans. Indeed, the fact that interpersonal relations among humans *still* rely primarily on the visual as much as the auditory sense modality, particularly when reading the emotional states of others, tells us that selection was creating a visually based quasi-language of emotions as it rewired the hominin brain.

Of special importance, then, is a pre-adaptation that came with rewiring the primate brain for visual dominance: the potential for language comprehension and production. The association cortices around the inferior parietal lobe that give primates visual dominance created, as an unselected by-product, the capacity of some primates to use language, *if a threshold of intelligence* was passed. Monkeys did not pass this threshold, nor did pre-monkeys (prosimians), but great apes—or the ancestors of present-day chimpanzees, gorillas, and orangutans—passed this threshold (Geschwind 1965a, 1965b, 1965c, 1985; Geschwind and Damasio 1984). Other extant apes—small arboreal gibbons and siamangs—do not pass the needed threshold of overall intelligence, and it is for this reason that they are not part of the great-ape family.

In addition to the association cortices (coupled with the needed intelligence) that allow for language, the existence of a homologous Wernicke's area assures that great apes can upload spoken language by humans into the way their brains process information; and so, together, the association cortices around the inferior parietal lobe and an intact and fully functional Wernicke's area represent pre-adaptations for language in humans and perhaps late hominins, although great apes also have some sort of visually based language communicated subtly (Menzell 1971) as well as a call-based language built around a series of discrete calls and cries that communicate common meanings. The result is that great apes have the neurological capacity to learn auditory languages of humans and understand naturally spoken verbal sentences, if *they are raised in a language* environment (Rumbaugh 2013, 2015). They cannot speak because, like humans' hominin ancestors, they do not have the necessary alternations in the structures (like the parietal lobe and the structures around the mouth, lips, larynx, and tongue) that make fine-grained speech possible. But they can learn the sign language of the deaf or use pictograms on computers to knock out sentences in response to human verbalizations (Rumbaugh and Savage-Rumbaugh 1990; Savage-Rumbaugh and Lewin 1994; Rumbaugh 2015). They can do this at the level of a 3-year old, but their responses, particularly on computer pictograms, are often far beyond those of a 3-year-old human child.

Thus, the fundamental capacity for speech did not arise because of selection *for* speech but simply as a by-product of selection working to make primates visually dominant, although the existence of a homologous Wernicke's area suggests that selection had already given primates some very early capacities for controlled symbolic communication, whether visual or call-based.

A simple thought experiment indicates why it would not be possible for language to have emerged because of a mutation or mutations for speech production. Imagine that a particular primate suddenly could speak (from a set of simultaneous mutations on all of the organs necessary for speech production) and then ask: With whom would this animal communicate? Thus, there had to be a set of pre-adaptations or *an existing hard-wired capacity already in place*, neurologically, for language to evolve *across the entire species* for something as complex as language to evolve; and it needed to be associated with something like the switch to visual dominance and thus be part of *all members of a species' behavioral repertoire*. Then, as selection favored enhancing language capacities across all members of species, directional selection on variations in the distribution of key structures could push a species over time toward actual language production. Given the complexity of changes needed for fine-grained speech, the first languages were visual since *no new structures* would be needed for great apes and, no doubt, hominins to see, upload, and interpret signals and signs from conspecifics.

As we will argue, this amazing capacity for language did not just "sit there" in the neurology of hominins; it was used early on as hominins evolved. And as was outlined argued in Chapter 13, this first language was based upon emotions, or what Turner (2000) has termed "the language of emotions." Moreover, as can also be argued—not without counter arguments, however—the language of emotions is the neurological platform on which spoken language evolved in the transition to *Homo sapiens*. The "language of emotions" has language-like qualities for ordering sequences of body and facial signals communicating emotional meanings that others understand and, via mirror neurons (see later discussion), can respond to and thereby coordinate appropriate actions. This quasi-language did not come after speech, but *before* speech and was much more than a simple call system. It is the reading of emotions that is humans' primal and primary language, with articulated speech a later refinement that perhaps only exists among humans, although dolphins, whales, elephants, and highly intelligent birds also seem to have some form of call or linguistic system that might even portend to a "cultural life" (Whitehead and Rendell 2015).

The Evolution of the Neurology of Sociality Among Hominins

The Evolution of the Neurology of Emotions

As is outlined in Chapters 12 and 13, most apes went extinct as the forests in African shrunk with global cooling and the consequent expansion of savanna conditions. As Table 12.1 on page 298 emphasizes, the last common ancestor of humans and great apes evidenced very low levels of sociality, tie formation, and, at best, only weak and temporary group structures. The only permanent structure was a sense of the larger community, with individuals moving constantly about this community alone or in very short-term groupings of conspecifics. The savanna, however, requires group organization for defense and foraging for food; and apes were singularly impaired on this score. Moreover, great apes do not have great control over their subcortically generated emotions and thus can be loud when aroused in the face of danger, a surefire way to attract more predators. Additionally, their lack of a strong olfactory sense, and heavy reliance on vision, makes detection of predators more difficult. And, apes on the savanna will be slow because they are built by tens of millions of years of selection for adaptation to arboreal habitats. Thus, they cannot outrun predators with knuckle walking or even with bipedal strides that allow for running. And so, it is not surprising that most apes went extinct in trying to adapt to the savanna. In contrast, monkeys, are organized by generations of female kin in dense networks, coupled with dominance hierarchies among males, hence, have been able to survive in savanna and, more generally, in open-country habitats for millions of years.

Selection pressures for increased sociality, for strong social bonds, and most significantly, for group forms of social structure were intense, but natural selection is a blind process and did not hit upon a solution for most apes trying to adapt to the savanna or to the forests to transition to the savanna. Among humans' hominin ancestors, however, blind selection hit upon what would be the solution: enhancing the already robust sets of emotions that great apes can experience and express by selecting on subcortical areas of the basic great-ape brain. Selection first increased the variants among primary emotions such as sadness, happiness, fear, and anger, and then over several million years selection began to mix these variants together into elaborations and combinations that dramatically expanded the emotional repertoire of hominins. Eventually, selection created complex emotions like shame and guilt to increase the self-control of late hominins and perhaps only humans in groups (see Turner 2000 and 2007 for more details on specific emotions and their combinations that evolved among hominins and humans).

As emotions enhanced sociality, and bonding and group formation that increased and allowed for increased fitness, blind natural selection would have continued to push for the language of emotions, in which something like phonemes became organized into syndromes of meanings that looked somewhat like morphemes and where morpheme-like constructions were strung into visually based "sentences" revealing a syntax and grammar of emotional meanings. We can see this language-like system everyday as we read people's facial and body gestures for meanings about their emotional states and likely courses of action. We can further appreciate how complex and sophisticated this system is if we turn off the sound of any movie or theatrical production and find ourselves able to follow the story line by just reading the sequences of facial and body gestures of the actors communicating emotions. If we can do this today, even with spoken language skills, hominins without such spoken language skills could do so as well. Indeed, all great apes can read the emotions of their conspecifics as well as the emotions among humans rather effortlessly and, indeed, achieve a sense of empathy with not only conspecifics but their human trainers as well. Great apes are highly empathic, and so it was not a large stretch for natural selection to enhance this capacity over millions of years to the human measure, thereby giving hominins the ability to forge strong bonds. As Table 14.1 outlines, the work of selection can be seen in the enlargement of subcortical areas of the brain when comparing extant apes as a proxy (by the logic of cladistic analysis, reviewed on pp. 294 to 298) for the last common ancestor of current great apes and humans. Human subcortical areas are, in general, twice the size of those among great apes, clearly indicating what natural selection was doing during early evolution of hominins. Moreover, there is much more connectivity within structures of the subcortex and between the subcortex and the neocortex of humans when compared to great apes.

TABLE 14.1 Relative Size of Brain Components of Apes and Humans, Compared to *Tenrecidae*

Brain Component	Apes (Pongids)	Humans (Homo)
Neocortex	61.88	196.41
Diencephalon thalamus hypothalamus	8.57	14.76
Amygdala	1.85	4.48
centromedial	1.06	2.52
basolateral	2.45	6.02
Septum	2.16	5.48
Hippocampus	2.99	4.87
Transition cortices	2.38	4.43

Source: Data from Stephan 1983; Stephan and Andy 1969, 1977; and Eccles 1989.
Note: Numbers represent how many times larger than *Tenrecidae* each area of the brain is, with *Tenrecidae* representing a base of 1.

During this period from 1 to 6 million years ago, the neocortices of *Australopithecines* and hominins did not grow significantly, perhaps by 125 cc over the modal size of great-ape Australopithecine brains that range from 375 to 425 cc of great apes. Spoken language and culture were not the key to survival, however. Rather, the language of emotions building on the pre-adaptations is evident in great apes today and certainly in the last common ancestor of great apes and humans—namely, the association cortices around the inferior parietal lobe and Wernicke's area, plus perhaps the asymmetries that allowed selection to mold Broca's area. Only with early hominins did the brain begin to grow beyond that of the last common ancestor to humans and great apes.

Selection on Late Hominins for a Larger Neocortex

The size of the brain among late hominins, such as *Homo erectus*, *Homo habilis* (who some see as an early *Homo erectus*), and yet-to-be definitively dated *Homo naledi*[1] (at this writing) reveal a great deal of variation in their overall size, which would reflect most on the varying size of the neocortex. This variation runs from around 500 cc to almost 1100 cc among fossils that can be roughly dated from 2 to 0.35 million years ago when *Homo sapiens* first emerged. Perhaps there was this much variation, but one reasonable hypothesis is that this variation reflects growth from a size of around 500 cc at 2 million years to 1 million years and, then, a very rapid growth from around 500 cc to over 1,000 cc, which is the lower range of the human brain, during the last 800,000 years of hominin evolution during the run-up to *Homo sapiens*. If this speculation is correct, we can ask: Why the sudden growth so late in hominin evolution? Why did it not come earlier? Or, alternatively, why did the neocortex hardly grow for several million years of hominin evolution? The answer is that hominins survived by the language of emotions rather than by complex culture or spoken language, which were very late arrivals in the hominin line or perhaps only fully evident and functional with the emergence of *Homo sapiens*.

One of the great discoveries of modern neurology is that, without emotions, humans and other mammals cannot remember a cognition, cannot make rational decisions, and indeed cannot even deliberate very effectively as cognitions slip away because they do not have emotional tags that give them meaning (see Damasio 1994; Le Doux 2002). There are "natural experiments" on humans where accidents have severed the neurons linking the pre-frontal cortex to subcortical areas of the brain where emotions are generated. There are also medical procedures that force surgeons to sever these links because of strokes and epileptic fits that cannot be controlled. There are also the devastating effects of neurological pathologies like Alzheimer's disease when it first attacks the hippocampus where shorter-term memories are formed and only later spreads and attacks the frontal lobe where long-term memories are stored. When the normal processes whereby memories are formed in the hippocampus are disrupted and/or where connections between the pre-frontal cortex and subcortical areas of the brain are severed, individuals have great difficulty holding onto memories in their immediate past, and they have even more difficulty making decisions, per se, and even more difficulty making rational or optimal decisions. What these data demonstrate is that intelligence as measured by memory and decision-making capacity is lost without the ability to connect and tag cognitions with emotions.

One observation, often made but not always fully drawn out, is that intelligent animals are *always emotional animals*. Why should this be so? The answer is that storing, remembering, retrieving, and deliberating over cognitions cannot occur without these cognitions being tagged with valenced emotions. And, the more complex the emotional repertoire of an animal, the more complex can its cognitions become, and the more intelligent it will seem by the measure of memory, bringing memories to bear on situations, and making fitness-enhancing decisions that facilitate adaptation. Because a large neocortex is incredibly expensive in terms of energy consumption for any animal, enlarging this part of the brain without a large repertoire of emotions and, indeed, without a language built around emotions would not be fitness-enhancing. Without a system for tagging and organizing cognitions in terms of emotional valences, the enlarged neocortex would be an empty warehouse, consuming energy but not giving any fitness-enhancing benefits. However, if there is a wide variety of emotional tags organized by a language of emotions, then the complexity, nuance, and subtly of cognitions would increase; and the result would be for memories to be retrieved rapidly by the pre-frontal cortex and used in deliberations that facilitate adjustment and adaptation.

The late big burst of growth in the hominin neocortex is probably a good indicator of *when* the language of emotions had reached a point of development where it could make growth of the neocortex of late *Homo erectus* and perhaps *Homo naledi* as well fitness-enhancing, allowing true human-like stores of culture and, for the first time, making selection on the structures needed for finely articulated speech built upon the platform provided by millions of years of evolution of the language of emotions which, in turn, was built upon the neurological platform provided by the pre-adaptations for language inhering in Wernicke's area and the association cortices around the inferior parietal lobe. It is probably at this point, that selection began to work on reformatting Broca's area for speech production, if the rest of the equipment needed for articulate speech could evolve. Increasing the size of the neocortex would allow for more intelligence, expanded memory, more rapid retrieval of stored memories, and dramatically more rapid decision making; and these changes would increase the fitness of a species. As selection was working on these, it would inevitably push intelligence and capacities for symbolic representations to new levels, thereby making late hominins and certainly the first humans true culture-using animals. Without the prior rewiring of the hominin brain to be emotional, then, what are often seen as humans' most distinctive traits—language and culture—would never have evolved.

Selection on Interpersonal Capacities of Hominins

Chapter 13 outlines how cladistic analysis and comparative neuroanatomy can be used to discover hard-wired pre-adaptations and behavioral propensities of the last common ancestor to present-day apes and humans. In Table 14.2, these are listed (see pp. 311 to 333 for a fuller discussion). In using cladistic analysis of the behavioral and organizational propensities of great apes, we can gain insight into how the brain of the last common ancestor was wired, although it is not possible at this point to isolate all of the specific neurological assemblages producing these traits. Still, they offer neurosociology something to look for; and from an evolutionary perspective, we can at least emphasize those pre-adaptations that became critical to overcoming the selection pressures facing low-sociality hominins that did not organize into permanent groups but, instead, only had a sense of community and a cognitive map of who belongs and does not belong in this community. We have already examined how language facility was a pre-adaptation revolving around the rewiring of the brain for visual dominance, the existence of Wernicke's area, and the asymmetry along the left temporary lobe (in Broadmann areas 44 and 45) that is labeled Broca's area in humans. We have outlined here and in Chapter 13 the importance of the pre-adaptation for a robust set of variants on primary emotions and then demonstrated how selection worked on these to enhance emotionality and thereby begin the process of allowing hominins to forge strong bonds and begin to possess the capacity to form groups. Yet, emotions alone were not all that was involved, as is evident by looking down the list in Table 14.2.

Emotions were not, by themselves, capable of increasing sociality and group formation among hominins. As was emphasized in Chapters 12 and 13, emotions enhanced *existing* behavioral and interpersonal capacities in ways that allowed for more sociality. For great apes today and certainly those that evolved along the hominin line *already had rather sophisticated and fine-tuned capacities* for interpersonal attunement when meeting up with conspecifics. Several clusters of these are neurologically important to understanding how and why hominins beat the odds and were able to survive on the African savanna, during a period when most apes went extinct.

Cluster #1: Pre-Adaptation to Reckon Community and See Self As an Object

Alexandra Maryanski (2017) has recently emphasized that the unusual pattern of reckoning community but not sustaining close social ties nor forming groups of high solidarity, on the one hand, and the capacity of all great apes to see themselves in a mirror and hence see themselves as an object in their environment have been critical in the evolution of hominins and humans. Animals that can (1) perceive a larger, more macro-level structure and the members who belong in it and who, at the same time, (2) have the capacity to see self as an object will neurologically be very different than animals that do not have these capacities. Most mammals are kin- and group-oriented and do not see the larger social environment in which they live, nor their place in this environment. But great apes can. They know who belongs in the community, and they see themselves vis-à-vis these others who are part of their community. While this may not seem like a large cognitive leap in perceiving reality, it actually is. Very few animals on earth, ever, have had these cognitive capacities. In one sense, as was outlined in Chapter 13, this cluster of capacities represents a pre-adaptation for macrosocieties because apes and humans can see outside the confines of kin groups and constantly reckon the larger social whole, recognize their place in this larger social formation, and do something that most mammals cannot do: interact with strangers on a daily basis in both focused and unfocused encounters. Humans are, by far, the largest animal that can form macrosocieties made of millions if not billions of persons; the social insects are the only other highly mobile life form that can also create macrosocieties, and of course, they are tiny in comparison to humans. (Note: some plant forms look very much like macrosocieties, spreading out over vast territories while remaining interconnected; for example, Pando, a Quaking Aspen located in Utah that is 80,000 years old, evidences 47,000 trunks spanning 107 acres, and weighs 6,615 tons is an example of a macro-plant society or organism.)

But, in addition to being a pre-adaptation to macrosocieties, cluster #1 puts pressures on great apes to have enhanced interpersonal capacities, even if these are not used to forge strong social bonds and groups. As evolving great apes, hominins also reckoned community and had a sense of self; and with these capacities, conspecifics have the ability to maintain "weak ties" within a community. Animals that wander alone or in and out of temporary groups within a defined home range or community need to be able to interact with others whom they may not have seen for months;

and they must pull off these encounters in ways that avoid breaches and potential conflict. Thus, cluster #1 puts selection pressures on the ancestors of great apes and humans to have a high level of *interpersonal skills* that is not dependent upon bioprogrammers. And, by looking down Table 14.2, it is clear that great apes are neurologically wired for interpersonal facilities that sustain weak ties, while at the same time, maintaining low-sociality and fusion-fission grouping patterns within a larger home range. The ability of all great apes to (a) role-take (to use Mead's [1934] terms) or have a Theory

TABLE 14.2 Hard-Wired Pre-Adaptations and Behavioral Propensities of the Last Common Ancestor to Humans and Great Apes

Pre-Adaptations:

1. Neurological capacity to learn and communicate using human language
2. Strong ties between mothers and offspring
3. Promiscuous mating system with paternity never known
4. Life history characteristics: (a) long gestation, infancy, and juvenile periods of development; (b) larger average size of bodies compared to monkeys; and (c) greater intelligence that all other primates except humans
5. Play activities among all young
6. Orientation to community rather than groups, with cognitive mapping of territory and who belongs and does not belong inside the boundaries of this territory

Behavioral Propensities:

1. High individualism and mobility around home range
2. Transfer of males and females at puberty from their natal community to another community, never to return (except chimpanzee males)
3. High levels of reading eyes and faces of conspecifics for meanings and dispositions to act
4. At birth, high rates of imitation of facial gestures signaling emotions
5. Rhythmic synchronization of bodies and voice, mimicry, and ritual when conspecifics assemble in larger numbers, mostly among chimpanzees
6. High levels of emotional effervescence during assemblies of conspecifics
7. Attention to reciprocity of others who have received resources
8. Calculations as to fairness and justice in exchanges of resources
9. Capacity of individuals to see themselves as objects in their environment, especially vis-à-vis others and the responses of others to self

of Mind (to use Premack and Woodruff's [1978] label) and (b) experience empathy in reading face, eyes, and body gestures for emotions, while also maintaining weaker social ties, were critical to ape societies where local densities had to be low (because of the lack of support and food in the arboreal habitat). But in stripping away bioprogrammers for strong and enduring kin ties, selection needed to replace these bioprogrammers with greater interpersonal techniques for sustaining weak ties within a larger community. In turn, these became critical pre-adaptations that could be enhanced and used to build stronger ties and more permanent groups, once natural selection hit upon emotion centers as a strategy to realize stronger ties and more permanent group formations as the habitat of hominins became increasingly the open-country habitat of the African savanna. These new ties and groups would, however, be more flexible than those of most other mammals that form packs, herds, pods, and other group formations; and building flexible ties increased the adaptability of late hominins in moving into new habitats and niches. And, once culture and language began to evolve, these flexible and adaptive mechanisms for social bonding and group formation would make late hominins and early humans even more adaptable to diverse niches in diverse habitats.

Cluster #1 also leads great apes and the last common ancestor to apes and humans to see self as an object of evaluation by others. When animals are not organized by strong bioprogrammers but, instead, must constantly construct and *re*construct social ties and relations as they move about their communities, they will—if their neocortex is sufficiently large and their emotion centers sufficiently developed—see themselves as objects of evaluation and will experience emotions signaling whether this evaluation by others is positive or negative. Morality cannot evolve to the human measure without this basic capacity hard-wired into an animal's neurology. The process of seeing self in relation to others and evaluating self by what is seen are the underlying mechanisms of all higher morality regulated by cultural codes—once the neocortex grows to the point of allowing moral codes to be articulated. And, for animals like humans as evolved great apes that are neurologically disposed to form mostly weak ties, morality becomes critical to maintaining groups and group ties. As Durkheim (1912) was the first to recognize, religion evolved early in human societies because, as evolved apes, humans could see themselves within a larger community—even a sacred community—and evaluate self on the basis of a morality, charged up by emotion-arousing rituals.

Cluster #2: Exchange, Calculations of Justice, and Morality

Higher mammals and intelligent birds appear to have a kind of proto-morality built around expectations for rewards from others. For example, B. F. Skinner's pigeons would become quite outraged over the failure to receive expected rewards in the infamous Skinner box, and while Skinner would caution reading "inside the mind," it is obvious that once expectations are established, their violation invites anger and other negative emotions. All exchange theories in sociology include a rule on justice, which simply builds upon this early insight from behaviorism. Indeed, anyone who has owned a pet realizes how "upset" they become, if their expectations (e.g., for food at a particular time) are not realized; they sanction those who were supposed to provide the expected payoff. Higher primates, including monkeys, all reveal a propensity to exchange resources, and they calculate whether or not the exchange has been fair or just in terms of resources given and received. And if they perceive injustice they will stop exchanging, and often emit negative sanctions.

Thus, the neurological basis for morality is built into the mammalian line, and among higher monkeys and all great apes, exchange and calculations of fairness and justice are universal. As natural selection pushed for increase emotionality in order to forge stronger social bonds and groups, it raised the stakes of failures to meet expectations and calculations of unfairness in resources exchanged. This seeming "outrage" is not morality in the human sense, where moral codes are held in stocks of knowledge in a larger neocortex, tagged with a variety of often intense emotions, but it is not a far leap to human-level morality from what higher mammals reveal. With language and a larger neocortex, morality could be articulated and standards of justice and fair exchange could be normatively established, thereby allowing humans to know the rules and abide by them. Indeed, morality in the form of moral codings is critical to social control among humans; and this morality depends upon a sense of self so that person can see that they have violated a moral code, or they can anticipate the responses of others to self when a moral code has been violated.

Social control is best when it involves self-control, in which persons evaluate themselves and experience pride or satisfaction with abiding by moral codes and shame (for failing to meet expectations of others) and/or guilt (for violating a moral code). These emotions are extremely painful, and often so painful that they are repressed (in the hippocampus where the pre-frontal cortex cannot gain complete access), setting off many of the dynamics described in the psychiatric literature or in some sociological literatures (e.g., Scheff 1988; Turner 2000, 2002, 2007).

Indeed, for animals without powerful bioprogrammers for sociality and groups, but with fine-tuned interpersonal capacities, morality increases capacities for self-control as individuals appraise self in relation to others' expectations and to moral codings in culture. And, this type of self-control became ever-more critical as societies began to grow. Indeed, morality without genetic codes (as is the case with insect societies) is, as Durkheim (1912) in his late work, realized a kind of pre-adaptation for macrosocieties among humans. Moral codings that invite sanctions from others but, more importantly, self-sanctioning are essential to sustaining order among individuals who are not in constant interaction and who move about sociocultural spaces and who must interact with strangers.

Still, while human morality is indeed a complex form of social control, it does not represent as dramatic a jump as is often assumed. Higher mammals, primates, and hominins all revealed a proto-morality; and with emotional enhancements, further growth on a widespread neurological platform already generating a proto-morality would be comparatively easy. This morality allowed for social control among the first groupings of humans, and it probably is behind the evolution of religion in human societies (Turner et al. 2018). And, as societies began to grow some 6,000 years ago, the integration of such societies would depend upon the propensity of humans to: (a) articulate moral codes and direct emotion-arousing rituals to totems symbolizing these codes, (b) sanction conspecifics for conformity or violation of moral codes, and (c) encourage self-sanctioning by persons for conformity to, and over violations of, moral codes. From these capacities, shame and guilt could evolve (Boehm 2013). Without the capacity for (a), (b), and (c), the scale of human societies would have been limited, but the ability for individuals to orient themselves collectively (even without being members of the same groups or in interaction) and to see themselves as an object within this collectivity (and thereby self-sanction) dramatically increases the likelihood that larger societies remain integrated and viable.

Cluster #3: The Pre-Adaptation for Play, Behavioral Capacities for Role-Taking and Empathy, and Propensities for Ritual

In the anterior cingulate gyrus is the neurology for play among young mammals. Play is a critical "training ground" for role-taking and empathy during which conspecifics mutually read each other's gestures to anticipate their dispositions and likely courses of action. Play involves a constant give and take, with one individual playing a role with sudden reversal of roles (e.g., pursuer and pursued). Larger-brained mammals that can store information about "roles" and enter the "minds" (e.g., Theory of Mind) of conspecifics can learn to do so in play activities when young are more likely to exhibit the suite of the interpersonal capacities listed in Table 14.2. These interpersonal capacities were essential for survival of great apes in weak-tie communities, but they became increasingly important to developing stronger ties and group affiliations when enhanced with emotions. The result is that humans today can use the same interpersonal capacities to (a) forge weak-tie *and* strong social bonds and (b) move through temporary groupings *and* become committed members of more permanent groupings. This ability to form flexible bonds and memberships in various types of groupings is possible because of the core weak-tie behavioral propensities of humans' primate ancestors and the enhancement, varieties, and nuances of emotions that can be experienced by humans. Depending upon the emotions or interpersonal practices (activated or not activated), social relations can be strong or weak, and group affiliations can be temporary/transitory or permanent and strong. And, add to these capacities for constant self-evaluation from the perspective of others in situations and from the normative and moral codings attached to situations (Mead's "generalized other" or Durkheim's "collective representations"); and when these capacities come together, they make humans able to move through complex social structures where the nature of ties, obligations, expectations, and moralities are constantly changing. Most mammals could never do what humans are able to do because their neurology imposes strong bioprogrammers for certain types of affiliations (e.g., kinship, herd, pack, pod, troop, etc.), whereas humans do not have such bioprogrammers. As a consequence, they can use (a) the interpersonal facilities evident in all great apes, (b) the large store of stocks of knowledge at hand (Schutz 1932) allowed by a large neocortex, and (c) the expanded repertoire of emotions to actively construct a wide variety of types of social relationship and to be members of many different types of groupings.

All of this is possible because of the neurology that was inherited from great apes, via the last common ancestor, and that selection enhanced with increased emotionality. And, with this emotionality, it eventually became possible for selection to enlarge the neocortex of late hominins and early humans to increase fitness, especially if the capacities for language that existed in the great-ape line could evolve rapidly during late hominin evolution into a spoken language on top of the platform provided by the "language of emotions" (Turner 2000, 2007).

The Evolution of Culture and Language Among Humans

With the evolution of a complex and nuanced repertoire of emotions, as well as a quasi-language system to order them into shared meanings, selection could produce (a) a larger neocortex; (b) a new sense modality of language via the auditory channel (i.e., spoken language); and (c) a rewiring of the neuro-nets within and between (i) subcortical emotion centers, (ii) pre-frontal cortex, and (iii) other neocortical centers. And all of this rewiring would dramatically increase fitness. Moreover, since selection along these lines would inevitably lead to a dramatically expanded capacity for culture, in which emotionally charged cognitions can be remembered, stored, retrieved, and most, importantly, talked about, a new form of culture could evolve. With only the visual sense modality, culture is very limited because it cannot be embellished, codified, and otherwise organized into sets of meanings that can orient conspecifics and regulate their actions and interactions. For example, chimpanzees are seen to have "culture" because they can learn a particularly useful behavior, such as using sticks to encourage termites to assemble themselves on the stick for easy, popsicle-like consumption; and then, they can pass this knowledge down across generations. This is "culture" in the limited sense because there are limitations as to how knowledge is developed, stored, and communicated. With a spoken language system, meanings can be produced in a much more precise way and, most importantly, elaborated, remembered, and easily communicated. Culture in the human measure, then, would be dependent upon spoken language which is more precise, denotative, and, most critically, conducive to building up cognitive complexity that, in turn, can be used to accumulate large stores of knowledge, to develop new technologies, and to codify regulatory symbol systems (e.g., norms, values, ideologies, law, etc.) that increase the adaptive capacities of populations of conspecifics and, in the case of humans, that would come to serve as pre-adaptations for macrosocieties. And once spoken language could be written down, all of the above effects are multiplied.

Early Social Science Efforts to Understand Culture, Language, Interaction, and Society

For descendants of low-sociality, non-group-forming animals, the ability to build up cultural systems of the type enumerated above provides alternatives to bioprogrammers for sociality and group formation. And, these alternatives will be more flexible and allow members of a population to adapt and adjust to changing and diverse habitats, and niches in these habitats. It is difficult to know just when the transition to this type of animal occurred, but at the earliest, it would by .5 million years ago with late *Homo erectus* (and perhaps *Homo naledi*) and, at the latest, with *Homo sapiens* at 0.35 million years ago. Within sociology, early conceptualizations of dynamics of culturally organized brains have been somewhat imprecise, but in many ways, some have captured the essence of what a big-brained animal can do with two language systems—the language of emotions and spoken language—to build up cultural meanings. Alfred Schutz (1932), for example, saved phenomenology from its self-reflective abyss by developing the notion of "stocks of knowledge at hand" to describe how humans interact. Humans store vast amounts of "knowledgeability," much of which can*not* be easily articulated but nonetheless rapidly (via the pre-frontal cortex) downloaded to specific situations and used implicity to mediate and regulate face-to-face interaction. We can add to this imagery a view of this knowledgeability as tagged with emotions so that it can be remembered and, moreover, organized by the language of emotions into meanings that can be brought to bear partially assembled but still capable of being reassembled to facilitate interaction in situations.

George Herbert Mead's (1934) conception of "mind" represents another early conception of these dynamics. Mind for Mead was a behavioral capacity that, following John Dewey (1922), involved the capacity to "imaginatively rehearse" alternative lines of conduct and select that line that best allows for adjustments in, and adaptations to, ongoing organized social contexts. Such minded processes involve the ability to role-take (e.g., Theory of Mind) with others who are present, others who are not present, and even generalized others (or communities of attitudes) in a situation. All of these capacities involve assessments of self as an object and the need to adjudicate and adjust lines of conduct to the expectations of generalized others and individuals' conceptions of themselves in a given situation. Interaction is a kind of cybernetic system in which each act of a person generates what Mead saw as "me" images on how actions are evaluated by others and how they are evaluated by reference to "generalized others," which in today's vocabulary can be seen as the symbol systems of culture as it applies to a given situation. Thus, action and interaction as these build up, change, or reproduce structural arrangements (what Mead termed "society") and culture (or generalized others) are always a succession of acts (what Mead terms "I" moments), followed by "me" images as feedback, and readjustments of conduct ("I") in light of feedback from others ("me") and perceptions of the expectations held by generalized others (or cultural systems).

The Neurology of Interaction, Culture, and Society

MEMORY FORMATION

As noted earlier, memories are formed by the hippocampus in the subcortex of the brain. Experiences are tagged with emotions, stored in the hippocampus; and if they are remembered periodically with the attendant emotions being aroused (often in diluted form), the cognitions will eventually be shipped up to the frontal lobe for longer-term storage. Stocks of knowledge are thus ordered mostly in the frontal lobe, while information being assembled for these stocks resides in the hippocampus to determine if the cognitions are sufficiently emotionally significant to a person to warrant longer-term storage.

What is not fully understood is how such stocks of knowledge are assembled and stored for retrieval by the pre-frontal cortex for use by persons in interaction. The process of potentiation of nerve bundles and memory are well known and, to a great extent, understood, but just how and in what ways the memories and cultural information needed for social relations is *ordered* or *catalogued* in memory is not so clear.

Ordering Memories

We can offer some speculations based upon how the brain evolved about how this ordering occurs, but these are speculations, rather than established facts. Moreover, these speculations are perhaps suspect because they draw from old literatures, although these are highly suggestive.

(1) Emotional Tags. Since the language of emotions evolved before auditory-based language, the valence of the emotions tagging cognitions is certainly one important ordering mechanism. The more negative or positive the emotions experienced and attached to a memory, the more likely it is to be remembered. However, this process is complicated by the dynamics of repression, where highly unpleasant, emotionally charged memories that cause devaluation of self (by guilt and shame) are pushed below the level of consciousness. They are kept in the hippocampus, somewhat out of reach of the pre-frontal cortex, but typically these emotions "leak" out but often in transmuted form (Turner 2002, 2007), with the result that the memory and valences of emotions are not "remembered." However, if memories are not repressed, then the valence of the emotions experienced will sort cognitions out. Those that are intensely negative or positive will be remembered and often pulled into a situation when the situation approximates that which generated the memory (in behaviorist terms, a "response generalization").

Less intensely felt emotions will, it can be argued, be less likely to be downloaded by the pre-frontal cortex unless they are closely related to the situation that produced them, or in fact, are a repeat of that situation. Thus, one of the important sorting mechanisms is the intensity and strength of emotional tags attached to cognition which, first of all, determines if cognitions will be remembered at all and, secondly, if and when cognitions will be easily retrieved and made salient to a particular situation. This process is somewhat complicated, however, by repression where a situation can generate intense emotions with the person not fully understanding why they are experiencing emotions.

(2) Gestalt Processes. While Gestalt Psychology is a very old perspective, as is its cousin, Field Theory, they offer concepts of brain activity that may still be useful in understanding memory formation (e.g., Lewin 1947; Heider 1946, 1958: Festinger 1957; Newcombe 1953). The most important of these gestalt processes include the following:

a. *Congruence and Consistency.* There is a large literature on the tendency of humans to seek cognitive consistency and congruence. Humans are motivated to maintain consistency among cognitions; and if they cannot, they will make behavioral adjustments to do so. Thus, one ordering principle will be consistency among cognitions, with those consistent with each other and constituting a coherent set of cognitions being remembered as a bundle of memories that can be easily retrieved by the pre-frontal cortex. Still, cognitions that remain inconsistent with other bundles of cognitions will also be remembered because of the negative emotions that they aroused. Indeed, the more inconsistent the cognitions relative to those cognitions ordered as consistent bundles of information, and the longer this inconstancy lasts and arouses negative emotions, the more likely are these inconstant cognitions to be at the forefront of persons' "minded deliberations," to use Mead's terms.

b. *Contrast-Conceptions.* Humans always notice differences, and the brain tends to store memories in terms of differences and opposites. And, the more emotions aroused over these differences, the more differences are remembered and brought to situations. Thus, the brain will remember people by their categories vis-à-vis other categories: young-old, white-black, male-female, prestigious-stigmatized, work-play, instrumental-ceremonial, etc. Thus, when individuals interact in situations, they note contrast-conceptions with respect to the social categories of others and self, their locations high or low in status hierarchies, the nature of the situation as work or ceremonial, the level of morality or practicality relevant, and many other distinctions. The more positive and negative emotions accompany these distinctions, the more likely are they to be remembered and the more salient they become in ordering interactions.

c. *Attributions.* Humans almost always make attributions for their experiences, particularly those that arouse emotions, whether negative or positive (Heider 1946, 1958; Piaget 1948; Weiner 1986). They will see self, others, situations, culture, or social structures as "responsible" for their experiences; and these attributions will not only affect the valences and intensity of the emotions experienced (e.g., shame for failures by self or anger for failures by others, to meet expectations), but also how memories are stored. And the more negative and intense are the emotions attached to attributions, the more likely are they to be remembered and retrieved in situations similar to those where the attributions were originally made.

Attributions have both distal and proximal biases, based upon the valence of the emotions experienced (Lawler 2001; Turner 2002). When experiences are positive, individuals exhibit a *proximal bias* and make causal attributions to self for actions leading to positive experiences, or sometimes they will also make attributions to immediate others. In contrast, negative emotions experienced will generally cause individuals to invoke a *distal bias* and thereby make external attributions to others, to situation, to social structure, to devalued categories of others, or to culture. The more others in a situation have power to sanction a person, the more the attributions will blame devalued categories of others, social structure, and culture for causing a negative outcome (Turner 2000, 2002, 2007; Lawler 2001). Thus, memories are ordered by attributions and perhaps divided into those that are positive and attributed to the qualities of self and those that are negative and the "fault" of safe and distal objects like categories of others (that cannot sanction a person).

Fundamental Categories

Philosophers, sociologists, and anthropologists have all pondered the question of whether or not there are fundamental categories inherent into the human brain.

(1) Causality. One fundamental category of the mind is assessing causality; and this is the driving force behind attribution dynamics, for individuals generally seek to understand and label experiences in terms of causality: *Who* caused *what* and *when* and *where*?
(2) Time. Another fundamental category is time, and while the conception of time can vary by culture, humans appear to reckon time: past, present, future; seasons; and perhaps even days and some metric of days. The brain often orders memories, then, by when they occurred at a given time, and coupled with causality and attributions, events are sorted for memory and retrieval by time, plus other intersecting categories.

(3) Place. People also sort memories by where they are formed, and the more emotional the experience, whether positive or negative, the more likely is the place where these emotions were aroused to be remembered—unless an extremely negative emotion like shame is repressed, but even then, subconscious memories will often generate transmuted emotions when a person occupies a place where a very negative experienced occurred. For example, a person who experienced humiliation but repressed this emotion may experience diffuse anxiety or even anger when in the same or similar place, but this person may be confused by the sudden onset of these emotions because they have been kept from consciousness in order to avoid the pain of an emotion like shame.

(4) Sacred vs. Profane. On the one hand, this dichotomy can be considered a contrast conception, but it appears that the human brain is wired to make this distinction as a by-product of the abilities to experience intense emotions, coupled with a large neocortex able to conceptualize "other worlds" beyond the mundane and profane. In fact, it could be argued that religion is a virtually universal property of human societies because the brain has the capacity to visualize sacred and special places, including the existence of a supernatural realm inhabited by forces and beings that are different from the normal, profane, and even mundane world of the "here and now." There was probably no selection for this basic category; rather it is the by-product of the emotional and cognitive capacities of the human brain that evolved under different kinds of selection pressures for increased sociality and group formation.

We should perhaps cut short this kind of highly speculative exercise and end this chapter by emphasizing the list of behavioral propensities and pre-adaptations in Table 14.2 and the discussion in Chapter 13. These behavioral capacities and propensities were inherited by hominins from the last common ancestor of humans and extant great apes, and they were the basis for overcoming the weak-tie and non-group propensities of hominins, once emotions were enhanced and could supercharge these behavioral propensities with an enhanced range of emotional valences. Each of them may order cognitions in ways that make them retrievable in interpersonal situations in groupings; and so, they might add yet another set of mechanisms for ordering memories. Add to these interpersonal mechanisms the speculations above, and perhaps some more, we have a large set of viable hypotheses on how the brain stores culture, making it ready for rapid retrieval.

Conclusion

An implicit neurosociology has been part of sociological theorizing since its inception. Spencer's *The Principles of Psychology* (1855), coupled with his *The Principles of Biology* (1864–1867); Emile Durkheim's (1912) turn to study of religion and increasing recognition that certain categories of the mind undergird religion (see his and Mauss' *Primitive Classification*); Alfred Schutz's *Phenomenology of the Social World* (1932); and George Herbert Mead's *Mind, Self and Society* (1934) all contain elements of neurosociology, albeit implicitly. Little was known about the brain and its evolution in their time, but they were addressing both evolution and mind; and it is but a short step to the brain. Today, neurosociology is in its infancy, having emerged only in the 21st Century, although there is a number of sociologists who, for 20 or so years, have tried to analyze brain functioning as it relates to human behavior, interaction, and social organization (e.g., TenHouton 1999, 2009). In this chapter, we have tried to demonstrate that evolutionary sociology has a great deal to add to neurology for the simple reason that the hominin brain evolved under selection pressures that were sociological in nature: the pressures to make hominins more social and group oriented, or go extinct like all other great apes trying to adapt to the African savanna.

A sociological analysis within an evolutionary sociology forces the recognition that emotions began to evolve long before the neocortex, that emotions were the key to the timing of ultimate growth of the neocortex, that selection pressures for sociality and groupness were driving most of how the brain became rewired, that language of emotions was more important to hominin survival than either spoken language and culture, and that cognitions cannot endure or be understood and explained without reference to emotional dynamics. These points of emphasis in evolutionary sociology represent a good beginning for neurosociology, because the goal of neurosociology is to explain the two-way relationship between the brain, on the one side, and human behavior and social organization, on the other. This relationship is what drove the evolution of the brain; and this is the kind of insight that evolutionary sociology can provide in contrast to sociobiology and evolutionary psychology.

Note

1 This fossil may have some surprises because estimates of its time frame vary enormously, from 2.5 million years ago to under a million years ago. Thus, whether *nadeli* is an early *Homo erectus* or a late one has yet to be definitively determined.

15
Cross-Species Comparative Sociology

Sociologists rarely use the expression "comparative sociology" to characterize analyses that venture beyond the study of human societies. However, the possibility and promise of extending the scope of sociological analysis to include animal as well as human societies is implicit in the work of one of sociology's early founders, George Simmel (Wolff 1950).[1][2] Simmel advocated what he called "formal sociology," which can be described as the study of "generic" social processes and forms of social organization (Wolff 1950: 21–23). He distinguished between the "form" and "content" of social organization. For example, as a generic social form, all triads share certain properties. Triads make possible the existence of coalitions (two members can cooperate to exert influence over the third), thus creating true social power rather than mere individual influence. However, the actual membership of a coalition comprises its content, and content matters. Thus, a triad consisting of a mother, a father, and a child will exhibit different dynamics from a triad consisting of a mother, a father, and the mother's lover or the father's mistress. The content of a triad cannot be ignored, but Simmel contended that, underlying all triads with variable empirical content, are certain universal, generic properties that shape the social dynamics observed in a triad. Simmel's logic suggests interesting questions: Are the properties of social forms sufficiently common so as to be evident in both human and animal societies? For example, are the properties of triads such that they impose the same constraints and enable the same possibilities when expressed either by humans or animals? Thus, is it possible to extend the scope of Simmel's formal sociology to encompass both human and animal sociality? If so, this alludes to the possibility of a "truly comparative" sociology, one that entails comparisons of social behavior and organization across species lines.

Though far from fully developed, hints of the contours of a truly comparative sociology are available in both conventional sociological analysis as well as in more recent studies that explicitly include animal social behaviors exhibited by a range of both invertebrate and vertebrate taxa.

Early Precedents of a Cross-Species Comparative Sociology

The very notion of a "science of human society" alludes to the nomothetic aspirations of sociology during its founding days. For example, Auguste

Comte proposed a two-pronged sociology, one prong of which would be devoted to studying the structures of group life ("social statics"), with the second prong focusing on social processes ("social dynamics"). Later, both Herbert Spencer (1851) and Emile Durkheim (1893) provided much more fully developed analytical schemes for systems for studying the universal structures and processes that comprise group life in any human society during any time in history. Their work was foundational to the development of the 20th Century functionalism (or structural-functional analysis) of Talcott Parsons, Robert Merton, and others. As in the work of Comte, Spencer, and Durkheim before them, the 20th Century functionalists attempted to map out and analyze the universal and generic features of any social *system*, thereby enabling them both to analyze social change within a society and to systematically compare similarities and differences among societies across the globe and over historical time. Eventually, this kind of thinking manifested itself in what came to be known as "systems theory," or "general systems theory," and was developed by social scientists in multiple disciplines (e.g., Bailey 1989; Boulding 1956, 1978; Buckley 1967; Luhmann 1982; Miller 1978, von Bertalanffy 1968).

This nomothetic impulse in attempting to identify and analyze the generic structures and processes of groups and societies is also evident in many other strains of sociological thought, including conflict theory, human ecology, exchange theory, and network analysis for example. The search for universal, generic structures and processes that comprise any human group and society implies not only that it may be possible to identify universal properties of any *human* social system, but rather, that it may very well be possible to identify and analyze universal properties that constitute the social systems manifested by any social species. Toward that end, we review recent sociological efforts to pursue cross-species analyses of social phenomena such as dominance hierarchies, vacancy chains, and systems of social exploitation ("social parasitism" or "expropriation").

Dominance Hierarchies in Comparative Perspective

A dominance hierarchy consists of a ranking of social statuses, and the occupants of higher-ranking statuses enjoy more "power, influence, and valued prerogatives than other members" (Mazur 2015: 474). Dominance hierarchies are found among many social species, including of course, humans. As early as the 1970s, Allan Mazur pioneered efforts to bring a biological perspective to sociological analyses of dominance structures and processes by comparing human and animal societies (Chase 1980: 908). Mazur noted that dominance hierarchies are common among numerous animal species, and he systematically compared features of human dominance hierarchies to those found in a series of other primates (1973). It is notable that one of Mazur's earliest such analyses appeared in the *American Sociological Review*, a leading outlet for sociological research that almost never publishes studies about non-human social behavior or societies. Mazur's 1973 article in this venue made clear the possibility of expanding conventional sociological thinking to include animal as well as human societies. Subsequently, Mazur and his colleagues published comprehensive analyses of dominance patterns and dynamics in face-to-face interactions among humans in which they adopted a "biosociological" approach (e.g., 1976, 1980, 1998, 2005, 2015).

About the same time, Ivan Chase launched a sustained program of analyzing patterns of hierarchy and dominance in both animal and human societies (Chase 1974, 1980). With the publication of *Sociobiology: The New Synthesis* (Wilson 1975), a discussion, often heated, commenced about the value of applying biological thinking to the study of human social behavior. Chase, however, pursued a line of inquiry that explored the possible value of bringing sociological thinking to bear on the study of animal societies. Chase noted that hierarchy in animals and humans is a "near universal phenomenon" (2016: 2), and he identified numerous species, ranging from some insects to humans, in which dominance hierarchies occur (Chase 1980, 2002, 2003, 2016). Prior to the experimental work conducted by Chase on animal dominance hierarchies, it was common for behavioral biologists to try to explain dominance hierarchies in animals in terms of variation in individual attributes displayed by members of those hierarchies. For example, it was common to try to identify individual traits such as an animal's weight, age, physiology, genotype, or other individual attributes as determinants of that animal's rank in a hierarchy. Intuitively, it made sense to researchers to hypothesize that older, larger, and more experienced individuals are more likely to be dominant over younger, smaller, and less experienced competitors. Furthermore, it was common to assume that, once established, a dominance hierarchy tended to be "static" and generally impervious to change.

Chase developed and executed a research program, much of which entailed the conduct of controlled experiments on various species, in an effort to determine if "individual attribute" explanations or "social interaction" approaches better explain the development and ongoing dynamics of animal dominance hierarchies. In so doing, he introduced thinking that is explicitly sociological to the empirical analysis of animal social systems. In our view, this approach represents a very promising line of inquiry, the full potential of which has yet to be realized by sociologists. The basic question that has guided much of Chase's research is this: "Why should species so diverse as animals are from one another, and as all the animals are from humans, form dominance hierarchies so similar in structure?" (Chase 1980: 905). By reviewing extant research literature on dominance hierarchies among animals, and by conducting experimental research himself on various taxa including chickens, cichlid fish, and sunfish, Chase set out to try to understand how dominance hierarchies develop and operate *across species lines*, thereby providing a highly instructive example of the kind of sociological inquiry that can be conducted by sociologists who are willing to venture beyond the biological "provincialism" that has restricted most sociological inquiry to humans alone.

Chase's research on dominance hierarchies can be summarized in response to two key questions: (1) Is the position of an individual in a hierarchy better predicted by that individual's personal attributes or by the dynamics of dominance competitions among individuals? And (2), does it matter if dominance contests occur between individuals in isolation from others, or does social context influence the outcomes of dyadic dominance competitions? Let us consider Chase's findings in relation to both of these questions.

Individual Attributes or Social Interaction?

Chase identifies a "standard approach" that has been used by biologists who study dominance hierarchies in animals, and it entails two hypotheses: Hypothesis 1 states that an animal's "prior attributes (e.g., age, weight, experience, genotype, etc.) contribute significantly to its rank in a hierarchy, and Hypothesis 2 states that an "individual's action" in a dominance contest contributes significantly to the rank it achieves, and in most cases, this means that a contest winner tends to win subsequent contests, while a contest loser tends to lose future contests (2016: 3–5). Furthermore, such individual "prior attributes" are said to result in the formation of dominance hierarchies that are basically static and largely impervious to change (2016: 1). Chase criticizes the standard approach for its failure to require the observation of actual behavioral dynamics that create dominance hierarchies. Instead, Chase contends that behavioral biologists have a tendency to observe hierarchies that have already been formed and then try to infer the processes that generated them rather than observe these processes directly. Chase calls this the "reverse engineering" approach, and he faults it for its inability to reveal dynamic processes of social interaction by means of which dominance hierarchies are actually generated (2016: 2). Though Chase acknowledges that individual attributes do influence the rank that an individual occupies in a hierarchy, he faults current sociobiological approaches for explaining dominance hierarchies as being too simple and overly concerned with individual differences (2002: 13). Toward that end, Chase attempts to identify actual social behaviors that yield dominance hierarchies among multiple species of animals, including possibly, humans.

Some of Chase's earliest work toward that end entailed observing the social dynamics of "real creatures forming social systems" in experimental conditions (1980). Specifically, Chase staged a series of dominance contexts in which three chickens (hens) were put in an experimental situation wherein they encountered each other for the first time. Chase observed the "agonistic" behaviors (both acts of aggression and acts of submission) that transpired in their interaction so as to determine how a dominance hierarchy forms (1980: 906). Chase observed four basic "attack sequences" by means of which the chickens established dominance: the "double attack" whereby A attacks B and then attacks C, the "double receive" whereby A attacks B and then C also attacks B, the "attack the attacker" sequence whereby A attacks B and then C attacks A, and finally, the "pass on" whereby A attacks B and then B attacks C (1980: 915). Though individual attributes of the competitors did influence the outcomes, they could not explain the final structure of the dominance hierarchy, which was the product of individual attributes, the attack sequences enacted, and the consequences of those sequences. One of the major findings produced by Chase's work was the discovery that dominance hierarchies tend toward transitivity (A dominates B, B dominates C, and A dominates C) versus intransitivity (A dominates B, B dominates C, and C dominates A). Furthermore, Chase was able to establish that the double attack sequence tends to produce transitivity and thus, linear hierarchies (1980: 917). Some attack sequences virtually guarantee transitivity in small groups (less than 10 members), and transitivity is common among species such as chickens, rhesus monkeys, Japanese macaques, cichlid fish, and some ants (Chase 2003: 1197–98). In fact, Chase established that the dynamics of social interaction can produce linearity in dominance hierarchies *independently* of the attributes and actions of individuals (2016: 9–10). In summary, Chase's work makes clear that only by thinking sociologically, in terms of the dynamics of social interaction networks, is it possible to explain the processes by means of which dominance hierarchies are constructed among multiple species of social organisms.

Does Social Context Influence the Outcomes of Dominance Contests?

If the standard approach of trying to explain dominance hierarchies only on the basis of differences in attributes between individual competitors were viable, the presence or absence of others during dyadic dominance competitions wouldn't matter. Chase and his colleagues set out to try to determine if the presence of others in close proximity to two individuals vying for dominance can affect the characteristics of the contest and eventually, the dominance hierarchy that emerges (Chase et al. 2003). If a dyadic contest that occurs in isolation of others affects the properties of the dominance hierarchy differently than a dyadic context that occurs in a socially embedded context, then evidence suggests that individual attributes alone do not determine the properties of dominance hierarchies. Rather, it is necessary to consider the social dynamics within which individual attributes are expressed in order to explain the development of a dominance hierarchy. Using cichlid fish as study organisms, Chase and his colleagues conducted controlled experiments in order to try to determine if social context shapes three key features of a dominance relationship: (1) stability, (2) replication, and (3) winner/loser effects. If a dominance relationship is *stable*, one contestant (e.g., A) delivers most of the attacks, and the other contestant (B) receives these attacks but does not deliver attacks to A. If a dominance relationship is *replicated*, A maintains dominance over B when the two individuals encounter each other repeatedly over time. Winner/loser effects are present if winning a specific dominance encounter increases the likelihood that the winner will win subsequent contests. The same logic applies to the effect of losing a contest on the likely outcomes of subsequent contests. That is, the effects of winning or losing can "carry over" to subsequent dominance interactions.

The results of the experiments conducted by Chase et al. (2003) provide persuasive evidence that the stability of dominance relationships is strongly influenced by social context. Specifically, dominance relationships formed in isolation from other individuals were highly stable, and over thirty-six trials, dominance relationship persisted for 24 hours without subordinate fish expressing any aggression toward their dominant counterparts (Chase et al. 2003: 1200–1201). However, when a dominance relationship formed between two fish in the context of groups consisting of three or four, from 20–35% of subordinates directed aggression toward dominant fish, and often dominance relationships were reversed (Chase et al. 2003: 1200). This experiment provided strong evidence that social contexts exert a de-stabilizing effect on dominance relationships formed between two individuals. Dominance relationships formed in isolation, however, were much more stable, and asymmetries in attributes (e.g., weight) between individuals were more influential in determining dominance outcomes (Chase et al. 2003: 1201–1202).

Social context also exerted a strong influence on the replication of dominance relationships. Among dominance relationships formed in isolation from other individuals, reversals of dominance occurred in only 7% of the experimental trials when the same individuals had multiple encounters with each other (Chase et al. 2003: 1201–1202). However, dominance reversals occurred in 24% of trials among dominance relationships that were formed in the context of groups comprising three to four individuals (Chase et al. 2003: 1201–1202). These findings occurred while controlling experimentally for weight differences among competitors.

An interest among behavioral biologists in winner/loser effects on the development of dominance relations pre-dates the work of Chase and his colleagues. Three broad approaches have typified the work of biologists studying the formation and maintenance of dominance relations: The first approach ignores the social context in which dominance relations form; the second approach regards social context as having "moderate importance," and the third approach treats social context as having "crucial importance" in dominance relations (Chase et al. 2003: 1194). Approaches to explaining dominance relations that largely ignore social context include those that focus on the differences in individual attributes among competitors and those that use game-theoretic models that feature interactions between two players absent the influence of third parties (Chase et al. 2003: 1195).

Some researchers take into account the experiences of dominance competitors themselves, specifically, whether one is a loser or a winner in such contests. This approach allows for the possibility that the minimal social experience of winning or losing a contest can carry over to subsequent contests and affect an individual's chances of becoming dominant or subordinate in encounters with others. Researchers have found evidence of both winner and loser effects in a number of species, but winner effects are both less common and less enduring than are loser effects (Chase et al. 2003: 1196). Until the work of Chase and his colleagues, no one had studied how winner/loser effects might be influenced by whether a dominance contest transpired in the absence of others, or it if occurred in a group context. Consequently, Chase and his colleagues conducted experiments on cichlid fish in an attempt to determine if social context has an influence on winner/loser effects. By conducting experiments on pumpkinseed sunfish (*Lepomis gibbosus*), Chase and his colleagues found that, if a winner effect exists, it is of limited duration (15 minutes or less) and is unlikely to last more than an hour (1994: 397). When winner/loser effects were studied among cichlid fish, loser effects could last up to a day or more (Chase et al. 2003: 1196). In these experiments on cichlids, being isolated versus being socially embedded did not influence the incidence of winner effects, but loser effects were much more pronounced when produced in dyadic competitions that occurred in isolation versus those that transpired in group contexts (Chase et al. 2003: 1207–1208).

Although the mechanisms responsible for producing winner/loser effects, when they occur, are not well known, Chase and his colleagues speculate that processes of "eavesdropping" or other "audience" mechanisms might provide information about contestants that could influence how observers react to them (2003: 1197). Chase and his colleagues also report that social context and information about win/loss outcomes of contestants can influence other categories of social behavior including "selfish herd" behavior (associating with others to reduce threats of predation), acquiring information about food sources, and coordinating cooperative efforts among individuals (2003: 1198).

The work of Chase and his colleagues does not lead to the conclusion that individual attributes or prior experiences of competitors are irrelevant in determining the outcomes of dominance contests. In fact, they state explicitly that both individual attributes and social interaction processes contribute to the development and operation of dominance hierarchies (Chase et al. 2002). But their research documents clearly that, even among acultural species with relatively simple cognitive abilities (e.g., fish, chickens), the traditional, standard biological model of trying to explain dominance hierarchies in terms of individual differences alone is inadequate. Instead, a sociological perspective that focuses attention on specific attack strategies and their outcomes and dynamic network analysis is needed to understand how dominance hierarchies develop and work. This means that standard biological efforts need to be supplemented with, or even replaced by, a sociological mode of analysis that focuses directly on the generative processes by means of which social interaction creates dominance hierarchies across species lines.

Resource Allocation in Comparative Perspective

Members of social species procure resources by a wide variety of means. Eusocial insects (ants, bees, wasps, termites) cooperate in foraging for and even cultivating food (honeybees, leafcutter ants). Wild canids (African cape hunting dogs, wolves) and African lions hunt cooperatively, as do orcas and predatory fish. Numerous species, both invertebrates and vertebrates, construct residences such as nests and subterranean burrows (e.g., naked mole rats, ants, termites, and wasps); dens (wolves); "lodges" (beavers); and so on. Once a resource has been procured and enters a social system, if it is not consumed it can be reallocated. Research on social processes of resource reallocation across species lines has identified and addressed two interesting, cross-species forms of resource reallocation: (1) vacancy chains and (2) social parasitism. Both of these areas of research illustrate the explanatory potential inherent in analyzing social behavior across species lines.

Vacancy Chains in Animal and Human Societies

Vacancy chains are social phenomena by means of which valued resources are distributed among members of a population. A vacancy chain is initiated when an actor (individual or group) abandons a resource that is reusable, discrete, and identifiable and can be used by only one individual or group at a time (Chase 2012: 135). A good example of such a resource is any residence vacated by an occupant, thereby making the residence available to a new inhabitant. Chase (1991, 2012) and Chase and his colleagues (1988a, 1988b) have studied vacancy chains among hermit crabs, crustaceans that must procure a snail shell in which they can live. As the crab grows, it outgrows its shell and must find another. A shell abandoned by a larger crab then becomes a vacant residence that can be appropriated by another smaller crab. That crab, in turns, abandons the shell in which it has been living, thereby creating a vacant residence for a third crab, and so on. Thus, the abandonment of a still-useful resource by one individual results in reallocation to another individual that can benefit from the abandoned resource. In human terms, a vacancy chain can be thought of casually as a sort of "hand-me-down" system, except that the prior "owner" of the resource probably does not designate its future recipient(s).

Vacancy chain analysis was first pursued by Frank Kristof, an urban planner and researcher in New York who discovered that vacancy chains develop when new apartments are constructed (Chase 2012). Subsequently, the sociologist Harrison White discovered the development of vacancy chains among ministers in Methodist, Presbyterian, and Episcopal congregations (1970). White, who coined the term "vacancy chains," analyzed them as mechanisms by means of which occupational mobility occur (Chase 1991: 148). White described how a vacancy chain was launched when a Methodist minister retired, leaving his pulpit available to a successor. When his successor moved to the retiree's vacant pulpit, his pulpit became available to a second successor. In this case, five ministers moved from the churches they occupied to other churches, thereby illustrating the role that vacancy chains can play in organizational social mobility (White 1970; Chase 1991). Subsequent investigations revealed that similar vacancy chain dynamics occur in other occupational arenas including football coaches, state police, military officers, and even drug syndicate operatives (Chase 2012).

Thinking in comparative, cross-species terms, Chase thought that vacancy chains may not be restricted to humans alone but rather, may occur among other species as well. Aware that hermit crabs (*Pagurus longicarpus*) have a soft abdomen that requires protection, thereby motivating them to find snail shells in which they can live, Chase launched a research program in which he observed and analyzed vacancy chain dynamics as social processes for the reallocation of snail shells (Chase and DeWitt 1988, 2012; Chase et al. 1988, 1991). Aware that vacancy chains are likely to be found not only among humans and hermit crabs but among other organisms such as limpets, lobsters, various fish, octopuses, and woodpeckers, Chase was persuaded that it should be possible to identify common, universal properties of vacancy chains whatever the species in which they occur, thereby making vacancy chains a suitable topic for cross-species comparative sociological analysis (2012). Toward that end, Chase developed a mode of structural analysis that enabled him to specify the properties of vacancy chains and how they function as mechanisms for resource reallocation among various social species.

Not all resources are candidates for reallocation by vacancy chain dynamics. Initially, White identified three key properties of resources that can be moved in vacancy chains. They (1) are scarce and valued, (2) are owned/occupied by one user at a time, and (3) can be vacated/abandoned by their user (White 1970; Chase 2012). Chase elaborated on White's conceptualization by saying that such resources are discrete, identifiable, and reusable (1991: 135). The snail shells occupied by hermit crabs fit the bill for qualifying as such a resource, as do apartments occupied by humans, or shoes that remain "serviceable." Like hermit crabs, human families can "outgrow" apartments, and growing children can literally outgrow shoes before they become unusable. Many other such resources can be identified, but few have yet to be subjected to vacancy chain analysis.

Like the resources they transmit, vacancy chains themselves have variable properties, and Chase has identified several including chain length, the number of individuals among whom resources move, variable attributes of those individuals, variable aggregate benefits that accrue to populations in which vacancy chains occur, variable effects on the "careers" (life chances) of individuals who participate in vacancy chains, the number of "moves" made by a resource before the chain ends, and so on (Chase 1991: 139–48). Among humans, empirical evidence exists that jobs, houses, and cars are routinely distributed by vacancy chain dynamics, though other resources almost certainly are similarly transmitted (Chase 1991: 151).

Chase and DeWitt have characterized vacancy chain dynamics as social processes comprising "non-reciprocal exchanges," because the recipient of a resource does not provide the donor with a resource in return for the one received from the donor (1988). The process can be viewed as a form of exchange because, as in the case of hermit crabs, a crab abandons the shell it was occupied "in exchange" for another unoccupied shell that better fits it. But it is not a form of exchange in that crab A provides a shell for crab B, which, in return, provides a shell (or perhaps even some other resource) to crab A as a form of "repayment." It is possible, however, to conceptualize a vacancy chain as a social process that closely resembles "serial reciprocity," a concept created by the economist Kenneth Boulding (1981) and developed more fully by the sociologist Michael Moody (2008). In serial reciprocity, the recipient of a benefit provided by a donor does not pay the donor back but, rather, transmits a benefit to a third party in return for the resource provided by the donor. According to Moody, the transaction can be understood as a form of reciprocity, because subjectively, the recipient understands his/her action as a form of "payback" to donor, though the third party is the actual recipient of the beneficiary's action. For example, A provides a resource to B who, eventually and in turn, provides a resource to C as a form of "payback" to A. C then provides a resource to D "in return" for the resource that s/he received from B, and so on. In popular culture, the basic dynamics of serial reciprocity are commonly referred to with the expression "pay it forward." Both Boulding and Moody suspect that serial reciprocity is both more common and sociologically significant than commonly recognized. Recently, Machalek and Martin (2012) used the concept of serial reciprocity to explain social mechanisms by means of which early Christianity might have grown in response to epidemics that activated chains of such reciprocity among those who benefited from the care of nurses.

Moody contends that the processes comprising serial reciprocity can be viewed as true reciprocity not because the original donor receives a return benefit from the beneficiary, but rather, because by transmitting a resource to a third party, the original beneficiary feels *subjectively* that s/he has paid back his/her donor. Subjectively, the original recipient of the resource provided by the original donor feels that his/her "debt" to the donor has been met by providing a resource to a third party. And though vacancy chains transmit a resource to a series of recipients, such behaviors need not be accompanied by the subjective sense that debts are being discharged or that "payback" is being enacted. At best, the transmission of a resource by a vacancy chain could be thought of as a form of "incidental" serial reciprocity in that A's abandonment of a resource enables B to seize the resource after having abandoned a resource that B controlled which now can become possessed by C, and so forth. In short, vacancy chains make resources available to others simply because they have been abandoned, not because one party has deliberately targeted another to be the recipient of the resource. And in order to take possession of the abandoned resource, another resource in possession of the recipient must be abandoned by the recipient. Thus, when a hermit crab A abandons a shell that it has outgrown to as to take occupancy of a better-fitting shell, the abandoned shell can be occupied by another crab B, but the acquisition of that shell by crab B was not the result of A's having somehow targeted B as the recipient of the abandoned shell. Similarly, if a person who has outgrown a pair of shoes simply leaves them in a public area where they can be discovered and appropriated by someone else who they will fit, then it is difficult to construe such a process of resource transmission as any form of reciprocity. If, however, the shoes are sold at a yard sale, then direct reciprocity has ensued. Or, if the abandoned shoes are donated to an agency that will find a needy person to whom they can be allocated, then either altruism has occurred, or perhaps a chain of serial reciprocity might be activated. In summary, it may not be useful to conceptualize vacancy chain dynamics as what Chase called "non-reciprocal exchange." More accurately, if less crisply, such dynamics might better be labeled "non-reciprocal resource transmission" or perhaps some other more elegant term.

Of greater importance is Chase's claim that vacancy chains may very well constitute generic social processes that are present in the social systems of multiple social species. Chase contends that "some social patterns are so fundamental that we share them even with primitive creatures" (2012: 5), and vacancy chains may be a good example of such patterns. Chase elaborates to say that

> the allocation of resources via vacancy chains in human and hermit crab populations (can reveal) unexpected similarities (and) that this kind of resource allocation has specific and analogous consequences for social organization in any population in which it occurs—whether animal or human.
>
> (1988: 84)

Chase's point goes directly to the notion of the value of a cross-species comparative sociology. By assuming that certain forms of social organization and processes of social interaction are generic to all social systems, regardless of the species that exhibit them, the door is opened to conducting research on fundamental and universal properties of social systems, a goal of sociologists that pre-dates contemporary systems theory, structural-functionalism, and appears as early as Spencer's work, still some of the most systematic in that vein of inquiry. By demonstrating the existence of common structures and processes in social phenomena such as dominance hierarchies and vacancy chains, Chase and his colleagues have illustrated the value and promise of developing a truly comparative sociology, one that crosses species lines.

Social Parasitism in Animal and Human Societies

Vacancy chains represent a social process of resource reallocation from which the resource provider derives neither a benefit nor suffers a cost, while the resource recipient derives a benefit. As noted earlier, biologists call this form of symbiosis "commensalism." In the case of hermit crabs, the crab abandoning a shell that it has outgrown neither derives a benefit nor incurs a cost from abandoning the shell, but another crab that acquires the abandoned shell derives a benefit. In social parasitism, however, a resource is acquired by one individual or group at the expense of another individual or group. That is, A derives a benefit and B suffers a cost. Various forms of social parasitism are common among social species, including humans. As with dominance hierarchies and vacancy chains, it is possible to identify and analyze generic social process and structures that constitute systems of social parasitism as they occur across species lines. Toward that end, Machalek has attempted to specify the basic contours of a general theoretical approach to the study of social parasitism as it manifests itself across species lines, including patterns of social parasitism in human societies (Machalek 1995, 1996; Cohen and Machalek 1988). We will review and summarize Machalek's approach to the study of "expropriative" behavior among humans and other animals as another example of cross-species comparative analysis of resource distribution in societies.

Machalek's analysis of "expropriative strategies" for resource acquisition (1995, 1996) and Cohen and Machalek's general theory of "expropriative crime" (1988) both employ a distinction between two types of behavior by means of which organisms acquire resources: production and expropriation. A productive behavioral strategy is one by means of which an individual acquires a resource by means of its own effort. A fox catches a rabbit, a digger wasp constructs a burrow, or a bower-bird constructs an arch made of twigs and other items and recruits a mate. All of the effort expended in securing each of these resources has been provided by the "producer" alone. An expropriative strategy, however, is one in which an individual expends effort in producing a resource which is then usurped by another individual before the producer can consume it. An example of such expropriative behavior in animals is provided by Hansen's work on bald eagles (1986). Bald eagles routinely catch fish which they then transport to their nests and eat or feed to their chicks. Not uncommonly, however, an eagle that has caught a fish finds itself beset upon by another eagle who attacks it until the first eagle releases the fish to defend itself, thereby creating an opportunity for its tormentor to seize the fish and usurp it from the producer. Behavioral biologists call this type of behavior "kleptoparasitism," or parasitism by "theft," sometimes also called "piracy" (e.g., Barnard 1984; Elgar 1986; Cangialosi 1990; Tershey et al. 1990; Forbes 1991). Hansen's research revealed that, of all fish consumed by eagles, 42% are acquired by fishing, and 58% are acquired by "stealing" fish caught by other eagles as they transport them (1986: 791). Kleptoparasitism among eagles is but one variant of social parasitism that has been documented and analyzed by behavioral biologists. A brief review of a few studies of social parasitism among animals provides a sense of how this process of resource allocation manifests itself in nature.

In addition to bald eagles, spiders are also vulnerable to kleptoparasitism. Spiders capture food by spinning webs and trapping prey which is sometimes usurped by others (Cangialosi 1990; Elgar 1989). Among mammals, hyenas have been observed to expropriate prey killed by other predators and even observed following these predators as they hunt, seizing prey once it is killed (Estes and Goddard 1967). Among invertebrates, the staphylinid beetle (*Atmeles pubicollis*) insinuates itself into ant colonies and uses a combination of chemical and tactile signals to misrepresent itself as a member of the colony and thus solicits a regurgitation of liquid food from its ant "hosts" (Hölldobler 1990; Wilson 1975: 375–77).

A number of species that construct residences such as nests or burrows occasionally fall victim to social parasites. Digger wasps and other wasp species construct burrows and nests that are sometimes usurped by others (Brockmann et al. 1979; Cervo et al. 1990). Birds such as juncos (Sullivan et al. 1989), snow geese (Lank et al. 1990), cliff swallows (Brown and Brown 1990), and other species (Rowher and Freeman 1989) can fall victim to social parasites that displace them from the nests or burrows they construct. Among ants, some take up residence in the nests of other ant species while the nest is still occupied by the ants that constructed it. In some cases, social parasites exploit the labor of their hosts. Among birds, a common form of such exploitation is called "brood parasitism," and birds that adopt brood parasitic strategies include cuckoos, cowbirds, zebra finches, and black-headed ducks (Mueller et al. 1990; Birkhead et al. 1990; Wilson 1975; Meyerriecks 1972; and Lack 1968). In such cases, the parasitic bird lays an egg in the nest of its host, and when the egg hatches, the host mother fails to recognize the chick as an alien and cares for it as if it were her own. The alien chicks sometimes extract a disproportionate share of the food provided by the mother, and her own chicks can starve as a result. In some cases, the alien, parasitic chick will kill the mother's own chicks or expel them from the nest. Brood parasitism is very common among some bird taxa, and Wilson has identified "at least 50 species of cuckoos" among which brood parasitism is an obligate (versus facultative) form of reproduction (1975: 364).

Another form of labor parasitism occurs when "satellite" strategists exploit labor that is expressed as information by a male attempting to recruit mates. Satellites have been observed among both vertebrate and invertebrate species including crickets, frogs, and toads. Males of these species will use loud acoustical signals (vocalizations among frogs and toads, stridulation among crickets) in an effort to attract a mate. Other males will position themselves in various "orbits" surrounding the calling male and attempt to intercept and mate with any female that approaches the vocalizing male. Attempting to intercept and mate with a female approaching a caller yields poor mating success in some species such as bullfrogs (Howard 1978), but among other species such as treefrogs, satellite males may achieve reproductive rates that approximate those of callers (Perrill et al. 1978).

It is possible to generalize about social parasitism and identify various *dimensions* and *forms* in terms of which patterns of social parasitism vary. The basic components of any act of expropriation (social parasitism) include a *resource* that can be usurped, a *producer* that makes the resource available, and an *expropriator* that attempts to usurp the resource. Among bald eagles, the resource is the fish, the producer is the eagle that catches the fish, and the expropriator is another eagle that attempts to wrest the fish away from the producer. The nature of the productive process also influences the probability that social parasitism will occur. For example, the spatial and/or temporal distance between production and consumption influences the likelihood that a producer will be exploited by a social parasitism. For a herbivore, production entails finding and grazing on forage. Because the act of grazing (e.g., biting a mouthful of grass) is also the first step of consumption, a prospective food parasite has virtually no opportunity to usurp this resource from the producer. Perhaps the only way in which social parasitism might occur in such a foraging context would be for the producer to locate the food source and then be displaced from it by a parasite that drives the forager away. By way of contrast, an eagle that swoops down on a river and catches a fish must transport the fish to its nest to consume it and feed it to its chick. The distance and time required to transport the resources creates a rich opportunity for expropriative effort by another eagle. In fact, other aspects of the context in which eagles forage for fish contribute to the likelihood that kleptoparasitism will occur. For example, fish are concentrated in space, often by a small body of water, or in both space and time, such as relatively small channels of water through which spawning fish must pass seasonally. The concentration of this food source attracts eagles which, in turn, are highly visible to each other as they forage. When a fish is seized by a producer, the act of production is highly visible to potential usurpers, and the process by means of which they transport the fish to its nest is also highly visible, thereby attracting social parasites. In contrast to a herbivore that is grazing on forbs and from whose mouth vegetation is highly unlikely to be seized, every fish that an eagle manages to catch is vulnerable to expropriation by other eagles in the area.

As mentioned earlier, another dimension in terms of which expropriation varies is the specific resource being usurped. The three basic types of resources that can be expropriated are objects (e.g., fish, nests); labor (energy expended by a bird mother foraging for her chicks); and information (the vocalizations of males recruiting mates). In the case of both brood parasitism and nest parasitism, both the objects (the food provided to a parasitic chick) and the labor of the mother (who foraged for the food and whose labor constructed the nest in which the parasitic chick resides) are parasitized. The "strategies," to use the term employed by behavioral ecologists and sociobiologists, that social parasites adopt in attempting to expropriate resources from producers vary, and that variation in strategy traits can be described as follows (Machalek 1996):

Degree of crypsis. A cryptic expropriative strategy is one that is not detected by its victim. Ants use xenobiosis, for example, to steal food from their hosts without being detected. Among humans, forms of theft such as embezzlement represent the execution of a cryptic expropriative strategy. The expropriative act is undetected.

Degree of deceptiveness. A deceptive expropriative strategy is detected by its victim, but the strategy and/or its executor is not recognized as expropriative in nature. Thus, the staphylinid beetle which uses olfactory and tactile cues to mimic its host is mistakenly identified as a member of the colony and thus, fed by actual colony members. Similarly, the cuckoo that deposits into the nest of a host an egg that mimics very closely the egg of the host herself is using deception to exploit the maternal care provided by the host.

Degree of boldness. A bold expropriative strategy is both detected by its victim and identified as a threat, and it is executed forcefully (coercively) in an effort to overwhelm the producer and usurp its product. Examples abound such as food kleptoparasitism among eagles; nest parasitism among swallows; prey parasitism by hyenas; and innumerable forms of coercive crime (e.g., armed robbery, extortion, hijacking) among humans. Bold expropriative strategies are predisposed by asymmetries of age, size, strength, experience, and other "resource holding potential" (RHP) traits between the producer and the expropriator (Machalek 1996: 6–7; Cohen and Machalek 1988: 471–72).

Degree of adaptability. Expropriative strategies vary in terms of how adaptable, or mutable, they are. As changes occur within the environments within which strategies are executed, some strategies change but others do not. For example, changes in the opportunity structure of expropriation, changes in the intensity of competition among expropriative strategies, or changes in the characteristics of those who adopt and execute strategies all can favor strategies that can adapt to such changes (Machalek 1996: 7–8). Especially relevant to strategy adaptability is the scenario in which counter-expropriative strategies evolve, thereby giving rise to arms races between expropriative strategies and counter-expropriative strategies.

Strategies can vary in terms of other properties as well, but the aforementioned discussion provides an illustration of what is meant by variability in the dimensions of expropriative strategies. Whatever variability exists in terms of the properties of specific expropriative strategies that are expressed in the context of producer-expropriator dynamics, at least five basic forms of expropriation can be identified. First, expropriative strategies can be executed either by individuals or by groups. Among animals, kleptoparasitism by eagles is often executed by single expropriators. Among social insects, however, entire colonies and castes of ants can usurp the labor of entire castes of other ants ("slaves") in what biologists call "dulosis," or "slavery" (Hölldobler and Wilson 1990: 445–46). In its extreme form, labor expropriation among ants is a permanent feature of the relationship between one species of ants and another. In such cases, it is known as "inquilinism" and can mean that the parasitic species is totally dependent on its hosts and is incapable of foraging for itself, caring for its brood, or repairing its nests (Hölldobler and Wilson 1990: 467).

A second type of variation in strategy form is the complexity of expropriative activity. An *opportunistic* expropriative strategy is one in which the availability of a resource to a potential expropriator is incidental to the behavior of the host, not the result of instrumental activity by the expropriator. In the event that an eagle catches a fish in the proximity of another eagle, the producer has made available a resource for expropriation incidentally, not because the expropriator somehow induced the producer to catch the fish. On the other hand, a *manipulative* expropriative act is one by means of which an expropriator behaves so as to influence the behavior of the producer so as to make available a resource that can be usurped. For example, a European cuckoo chick that opens its beak so as to induce the behavior of a warbler mother to feed it is exercising a manipulative expropriative strategy. Similarly, by inducing an ant to pick it up and carry it into the ant's nest, a staphylinid beetle is manipulating the behavior of its host so as to position it to be able to solicit food regurgitations from the ants into whose colony it was able to insinuate itself (Wilson 1975: 375–77). Almost certainly, no species rivals humans in terms of its ability to use complex systems of culture and symbolic communication in order to manipulate the behaviors of producers to make available resources that can be usurped by expropriators. A classic example of such dynamics is Karl Marx's analysis of the effectiveness with which the capitalist class can produce and use ideology to manipulate the behavior of host proletarians to produce and transfer surplus value in the form of profit to their capitalist parasites.

A third type of variation in strategy form is denoted with the terms *facultative* versus *obligate* strategies. Adopting and executing expropriative behavioral strategies is an option for members of some species, it is not a "necessity." Biologists call this *facultative* expropriation. Facultative expropriation may occur only sporadically, as suitable occasions for expropriation arrive. For example, an eagle is not, by virtue of some sort of biological necessity, forced to adopt and execute kleptoparasitic strategies for acquiring fish. Instead, it can, in principle, forage exclusively by catching and consuming its own fish. Many instances of social parasitism are facultative and often supplement the execution of producer strategies (fishing rather than stealing fish caught by others). Among a few species, however, expropriative behavior is not an option, it is necessitated by the biology of the organism itself. This is called *obligate* social parasitism, and what has been called the "ultimate" parasitic ant, *Teleutomyrmex schneideri*, perhaps best illustrates inquilinism, this example of obligate social parasitism. In fact, *T. schneideri* has evolved to be so dependent on a host, that its morphology has degenerated such that it has lost the ability to work at all and must depend on a host species (such as *Tetramorium caespitum*) whose workers it captures and "enslaves" as a labor force on which it depends.

Facultative or obligate strategies may vary in the duration during which they are executed. Some forms of expropriation are executed only on a *temporary* basis, while others are a *permanent* feature of the organism that relies upon them. Expropriation is not always a risk-free strategy for the prospective expropriator. Even a lion that attempts to expropriate an antelope from a hyena that killed it faces some risk of injury, sometimes serious injury that may, if followed by infection, lead to the death of the lion. Accordingly, if prey is abundant, it may pay a predator to forego efforts to expropriate a prey item from another hunter and, instead, hunt for itself, even if successful expropriation is a more economical way of acquiring food. If, however, prey is scarce, and starvation is the alternative to expending expropriative effort and incurring associated risks, then it may be prudent to adopt the temporary strategy of expropriation. However, even an obligate expropriative strategy may be adopted by an organism only temporarily, during certain stages of its life-cycle. For example, chicks that hatch as brood parasites in the nest of a host species only expropriate the labor of their "foster" mother until they fledge, at which time they become independent, self-sufficient foragers. Their brood parasitism is obligate when they are chicks, but it is temporary and specific to a stage in their life-cycle. When they become adults, the brood parasitism strategy (being fed by a host species mother) is abandoned. By way of contrast, however, the parasitism of slave-making ants is both obligate and permanent. They never "outgrow" the necessity of capturing and exploiting the labor of a "slave caste" (Hölldobler and Wilson 1990).

Finally, expropriation can assume either a *gross* or *subtle* form. The existence of either gross or subtle expropriation presupposes the existence of a system of cooperative exchange between at least two actors, a condition not required for the evolution of other forms of expropriation. Framing his discussion of gross and subtle expropriation in game-theoretic terms, the evolutionary biologist Trivers uses the term "gross cheating" to refer to a situation where reciprocity is expected but not forthcoming, and subtle cheating to refer to a situation where reciprocity occurs, but either the quality or quantity of the resource provided by the reciprocator does not match that of the resource originally provided by the other exchange partner (1971: 46–47). Among animals, opportunities for either gross or subtle cheating are not as common as they are among humans, because such forms of expropriation require the development of systems of reciprocity and exchange such as those represented by human economies. However, an example of a system of animal reciprocity that invites the incidence of gross or subtle cheating can be found in both invertebrate and vertebrate taxa. Among invertebrates, the ability of the staphylinid beetle to induce its ant hosts to provide a regurgitation of liquid food without ever "repaying" the host illustrates gross cheating among invertebrates. Among vertebrates, the system of reciprocity among vampire bats in which successful hunters provide blood regurgitations to unsuccessful hunters provides an example of a system of cooperation based on reciprocity that is vulnerable to invasion by either gross or subtle cheating, or both.

Comparative Sociological Analysis of Expropriation

Many scholars and scientists who are interested in expropriative behaviors are likely to focus primarily on questions such as the following: What type of individual is likely to adopt an expropriative strategy, and why? What kinds of individual traits either predispose or inhibit expropriative efforts among individuals that possess them? Among humans, what sorts of biographical experiences and psychological traits predispose individuals to try to execute expropriative behaviors in order to realize their interests? Why do some individuals employ expropriative behavioral strategies but others do not? How do individuals acquire expropriative strategies?

Although such questions offer promise for inspiring productive inquiries, other types of questions invite the development of a new form of analysis, that which integrates sociological thinking with that found in the evolutionary life sciences, including behavioral ecology. Rather than focusing on questions about individual causes and correlates of expropriative behavior, a new, cross-species variant of sociology invites inquiry about *properties of social systems and the environments in which they exist* in order to explain the emergence and development of expropriative behaviors in both animal and human social systems. We now provide a brief overview of how a cross-species sociology frames the study of social and environmental factors that either predispose or inhibit the incidence of expropriation (Machalek 1996: 13–26). In our view, such an analysis can be pursued most fruitfully by integrating elements of the branch of behavioral biology known as "behavioral ecology" with traditional sociological reasoning. Behavioral ecologists study the influence of environments, including both physical and social environments, on patterns of animal behavior and the effects of those patterns on the survival and reproductive chances of animals (Krebs and Davies 1997; Alcock 2013). And though behavioral ecologists take into consideration individual differences in explaining animal behavior, their primary focus is on the manner in which physical and social environments shape behavior. In that regard, behavioral ecology is the branch of behavioral biology most similar in its approach to sociology.

How can features of physical and social environments affect the emergence and incidence of expropriative behaviors? To answer this question, we focus attention on the following basic contexts of these environments: (1) the physical context, (2) the demographic context, (3) the social structural context, and, in the case of humans, (4) the cultural and historical context.

The Physical Context of Expropriation

The likelihood that expropriative behaviors will occur within a social system is affected by characteristics of the physical environment in which production occurs. The aforementioned discussion of kleptoparasitism among American bald eagles illustrates this influence (Hansen 1986). Fish, the prey items on which eagles prey, are not evenly or randomly dispersed over a wide geographic area. Rather, they are concentrated in bodies of water such as streams and lakes. And, in fact, some species such as salmon are also temporally concentrated when they spawn. The concentration of fish puts foraging eagles in close proximity of each other, and the foraging success or failure of each eagle is highly visible to others. Accordingly, the process of seizing a fish in such a highly "public" venue increases the likelihood that expropriative activity will occur among the foragers. In short, the physical context within which fishing occurs strongly predisposes the adoption of expropriative behaviors by eagles that can observe the foraging success of others in their vicinity. Kleptoparasitism also occurs among other birds that forage in open, aquatic environments, such as seagulls. Similar scenarios are observed in both terrestrial and marine contexts when humans have transported valued resources over highly visible routes, leading to forms of piracy on the high seas and banditry on overland routes.

Mammals that forage in highly visible, "public" environmental contexts can also suffer expropriation by competitors. For example, predators that hunt on savannas can fall victim to other predators that usurp the prey they kill. A classic example is found among lions who, observing hyenas killing a prey item, will drive the hyenas from their kill and usurp it for themselves (Schaller 1972).

Even climatic features of environments, such thermal conditions, can affect the incidence of expropriative behaviors. As Hölldobler and Wilson put it, "there exists the possibility that life in certain climates and environments actually does predispose ant species toward parasitism" (1990: 447). For example, they report that dulosis (ant slavery) is common "in the colder parts of Europe and Asia but rare in the warmer parts . . . and has never been reported from the tropical or south temperate zones" (Hölldobler and Wilson 1990: 447). Why would colder environments predispose the evolution of dulosis among ants? According to Hölldobler and Wilson, cooler temperatures dull the defensive responses of a prospective host colony when it is invaded by parasitic queens, thus enabling the parasites to insinuate themselves into the hosts' nest. Hölldobler and Wilson conducted experiments in which they chilled ant colonies and observed that ant queens were less likely to be attacked by soldiers defending host colonies (1990: 447).

The Demographic Context of Expropriation

The structures and processes of populations also can affect the incidence and nature of expropriative activity. For example, population size and density can predispose or inhibit expropriative behaviors. As populations increase in size and density, more resources become available to prospective expropriators, and the resources are more concentrated, making expropriation potentially more "profitable" than in smaller, less dense populations. Similarly, as more resources of greater value are transported through a population, a process that Spencer classified as part of the "distributive system" of a society (Turner 2013), more opportunities for expropriation are created as more potential targets become available to exploitation by various kleptoparasitic strategists.

Variation in the composition of populations can also affect the incidence of expropriation. Among humans, for example, criminologists have identified what they call the "age-graded crime curve" (Hirshi and Gottfredson 1983; Greenburg 1985; Cohen and Land 1987). Certain types of expropriative crimes, such as armed robbery and burglary, require executors that are healthy and strong, even when aided by modern technologies of expropriation such as firearms. As such physical competence in humans tends to peak at about age 20 and decline thereafter, expropriative strategies requiring physical prowess are less likely to be adopted as means of usurping resources from producers. Accordingly, as a population ages and the proportion of its members in its late teens and early 20s declines, the incidence of crimes such as armed robbery declines. On average, armed robbery is not a prudent occupational choice for middle-aged men and women. Alternatively, as people age and achieve positions of greater status and power within the work force, new kinds of opportunities for expropriation become available to them, and the incidence of white-collar crimes such as embezzlement and fraud can increase (Cohen and Machalek 1988: 481–84).

Among humans, an even clearer pattern of risky and violent behaviors often associated with expropriative crime can be observed when considering the age and sex ratios in a population. It is well known that young males are much more likely to engage in risky and violent behaviors than are young females. Thus, the proportion of young males within a population may predict the likelihood that violent, expropriative crimes are likely to occur within a society.

Population traits of a more nuanced nature can also influence the incidence of expropriative activity in a social system. Neo-Darwinian evolutionary theory suggests that the incidence of expropriative activity within a population would be expected to increase simply as the population grows larger. This is because the average degree of genetic relatedness among members of large populations is likely to be less than among members of small populations. In classic sociobiological theory based on the principles of kin selection and inclusive fitness, a close degree of genetic relatedness is predicted both to promote cooperation and to inhibit antisocial behavior among individuals. Accordingly, kin selection theory would predict a higher rate of intrapopulation expropriation as populations increase in size, because the intrapopulation genetic relatedness among population members declines. However, in populations where cohesion and cooperation is mediated primarily by reciprocity and exchange versus genetic relatedness, there is less reason to expect a correlation between large population size and the incidence of expropriation. Rather, other population attributes such as the age-sex ratios can be expected to have a stronger influence on the rate of expropriation.

The Social Structural Context of Expropriation

As noted earlier, both sociologists and behavioral ecologists consider social structures as environmental contexts that both constrain and potentiate the behaviors of social species. Sociologists (as well as other social scientists) and behavioral biologists often converge on studying various aspects of social structure as well as on approaches for conducting such inquiries. This convergence can be illustrated with respect to the study of patterns of expropriation. For example, by adopting the perspective of game theory (developed largely by social scientists and mathematicians and later adopted by biologists), evolutionary biologists have begun to analyze how "cheating" (defection, in game-theoretic terms), a form of expropriation, destabilizes systems of cooperation. Commonly relying on the "prisoner's dilemma" model in which two parties in the absence of a third-party "enforcer" interact by either cooperating with each other or by defecting, evolutionary game theorists such as Axelrod have identified features of dyadic interaction that either promote or inhibit expropriation (1984). For example, for an actor in a prisoner's dilemma, information about the other actor's prior conduct, or what game theorists call "reputation," is very valuable (Axelrod 1984: 150–54). In small groups and societies, such information is commonly available to individuals directly, based on their own interaction with others, or indirectly, based on information provided by others. As the size of groups and societies increases, anonymity among actors increases, thereby elevating the probability that individuals must, on occasion, interact with strangers about whom they possess little if any information. This makes participants in a prisoner's dilemma vulnerable to defection. This is particularly true when interaction between two actors occurs only on a one-time basis and is not iterated. As Mayer observed, "the greatest enforcer of morality in commerce is the continuing relationship" (1974: 280). Among humans in small group contexts, such as hunting-gathering bands, individuals interact repeatedly with the same individuals, thereby enjoying information about the trustworthiness of potential interaction partners. In societies with large populations whose members are largely strangers to each other, individuals do not enjoy the advantage of personal knowledge of potential interactive partners and are therefore more easily victimized by defectors.

Iterated interaction enables the victim of an act of defection to retaliate against an expropriator, thereby both punishing the other actor for his/her misconduct as well as reducing the likelihood of future defection with a threat of retaliation. Developing a reputation of retaliating effectively against defectors helps reduce the threat posed by future acts of exploitation. The evolutionary psychologists Martin Daly and Margo Wilson explain how this dynamic works among humans to help deter the threat of violence, including homicide (Daly and Wilson 1988: 221–51). Game-theoretical models have been developed and adopted by both evolutionary-minded social analysts and biologists in efforts to explicate how various forms of expropriation evolve in both animal and human social systems. Best suited for explaining social structure and interaction at the dyadic level, game theory provides an analytical vantage point from which the elementary dimensions of expropriative behaviors can be observed and specified.

The Cultural and Historical Context of Expropriation

Among humans, both culture and historical context significantly influence the nature and incidence of expropriation. Arguably the first theorist of social exploitation among humans, Marx demonstrated how class structures, cultural configurations (especially ideology), and historical era converged to account for the precise nature and sociological significance of economic expropriation and political subjugation in post-hunting-gathering societies. Similarly, Max Weber and Vilfredo Pareto made the topic of expropriation and domination central to their sociological projects, and both thinkers emphasized the importance of cultural and historical constraints on the development and nature of various patterns of expropriative behaviors.

The role of culture, especially ideology, is particularly significant in understanding the social relations of expropriation among humans, in large part, because it is ideology that generates meanings that influence the extent to which various forms of expropriation that are associated with systems of domination based on race, gender, class, religion, and other social attributes are tolerated or resisted by those who are targeted by expropriative strategies. In short, explaining any system of expropriation in human societies requires careful and thorough consideration of both the cultural environments and historical eras in which expropriation occurs. As the species whose social life is most heavily infused with and guided by culturally produced, organized, and transmitted meaning, any effort to understand patterns of expropriation among humans must devote particular attention to the cognitive lives and historical eras of *Homo sapiens*.

Structures of Ant Societies and the Incidence of Social Parasitism

As numerous game-theoretical analyses have demonstrated, dyadic interaction consists of social processes that invite the incidence of expropriative behavior, even though only two actors are engaged in interaction. As the size, scope, and complexity of social structures grow, the opportunity for the incidence of patterns of expropriation grow as well. This is true regardless of the species that produce the structures. Among social species, two taxa produce social systems that are unmatched by any others in terms of the opportunities they present for the development of patterns of expropriation. These taxa are humans and the eusocial insects. A brief review of social parasitism in ant societies illustrates the existence of the sorts of social structures and processes that enable the evolution of expropriation, and a consideration of some of the behavioral capabilities of the ants themselves illustrates how even a minimal behavioral repertoire can enable the emergence of very powerful and complex systems of expropriation.

Hölldobler and Wilson report the existence of interspecific symbioses among hundreds of species of ants, and they document the existence of at least 200 species of ants that are social parasites of other ant species (1990: 436; 438–45). Why is the incidence of social parasitism so high among ants? The simplest answer is that the social organization of ant behavior makes available for usurpation perhaps the greatest concentration of valuable resources among any group of organisms, with the possible exception of humans. Although the social insects (ants, bees, wasps, and termites) make up only 2% of the 900,000 known insect species, they account for half of the world's biomass (Hölldobler and Wilson 2009: 26). Ants and humans exhibit what Hölldobler and Wilson call an "odd parity," a situation whereby the 1 million billion to 10 million billion ants alive on earth roughly equal in biomass the 6.6 billion humans (at the time of their writing) alive at the same time (2009: 27). What makes humans the dominant terrestrial vertebrate on earth, and ants the dominant terrestrial invertebrate? According to biologists such as Hölldobler and Wilson, it is their common ability to assemble, live in, and cooperate in extremely large-scale, complex, and highly productive social systems. The very productivity of these social systems and the ways that they are organized and function, however, also explain the fact that they are commonly plagued by social parasitism, whether among ants or among humans. A brief overview of some key aspects of social parasitism among ants reveals how the structures and processes of ant social systems makes almost inevitable the existence and widespread proliferation of social parasitism among these creatures. It also provides valuable clues about how such social systems enable the existence of social parasitism among *any species of organisms* that manage to construct and execute such forms of sociality.

The contours of what Machalek calls a "megasociety" (originally labeled a "macrosociety") help explain the high incidence of social parasitism in ant societies (1992). A megasociety features a very large population (hundreds to millions of individuals) whose members are organized into a division of labor executed by subpopulations (in the case of ants, "castes") of specialists. It is the very structure of a megasociety such as an ant colony and the processes of social interaction found therein that occasion the incidence of expropriative behaviors. Megasocieties bring extraordinary *ergonomic force* to productive processes. The division of labor among ant castes enables them to produce nests and build food supplies that can support colonies ranging from tens to hundreds of millions of individuals (Wilson 1971; Hölldobler and Wilson 1990, 2009). Wilson has described aptly an ant colony as a "factory within a fortress," but it is simultaneously a factory, a warehouse, and a distribution center, all of which make resources highly concentrated and allocated in a manner that invites their usurpation by various strategies of expropriation. Three basic categories of resources are concentrated in an ant colony and, thus, are available for potential expropriation: nests (residences), food, and labor. Ant nests house not only members of the species that construct them, but often, members of other species as well. By evolving cryptic strategies, members of these alien species effectively usurp living space, which also provides close proximity to other resources they can expropriate from their hosts.

There are two types of nests comprising members of two different species: (1) *compound nests*, in which two species live in close proximity and even share nest galleries but keep their brood separate, and (2) *mixed nests (colonies)*, "in which the brood are mingled and cared for communally" (Hölldobler and Wilson 1990: 445). Four types of expropriation occur in compound nests: (1) *cleptobiosis*, in which the members of one species usurp food from host workers returning to their nest; (2) *lestobiosis*, in which members of one species actually take up residence in the walls of nests built by their hosts and enter the nest chambers to steal their hosts' food and on occasion even prey upon their hosts, transforming them from resident parasites to resident predators; (3) *parabiosis*, in which members of one species use the nests and foraging trails constructed by their hosts; and (4) *xenobiosis*, in which one species cohabits with its hosts and solicits food regurgitations from them (Hölldobler and Wilson 1990: 445–46).

True social parasitism in ants is most fully expressed in mixed colonies, and the parasitism assumes three forms: (1) *temporary social parasitism*, in which an impregnated queen of one species invades the nest of a host, kills the host queen, and usurps the labor of the host workers, which are eventually replaced by workers produced by the invading (parasitic) queen; (2) *dulosis* (slavery), in which members of one species raid the nest of another, typically closely related species, seize its pupae, and bring them back to their nest to become an "enslaved" work force. The enslaved worker ants perform tasks such as foraging, nest building, and brood care; and (3) *inquilinism* (permanent parasitism), in which the parasitic species spends its entire life in the hosts' nest and often loses its worker caste, exploiting instead the workers of its host caste. In extreme instances, the parasitic species undergoes physical degeneration that causes it to lose its ability even to forage and feed itself.

The very nature of ant nests and the characteristics of colonies that construct and occupy them create conditions that make their victimization by various expropriative strategies unsurprising. A type of social system comprising a population of hundreds to millions of highly productive workers, nests with complex and highly functional architectures, and large stores of food represents a rich concentration of resources that is highly susceptible to invasion by a range of expropriative behavioral strategies. In fact, over time, this complex configuration of both physical and social conditions can act as selection forces which, ironically, can help shape highly specialized and effective adaptations among the social parasites themselves. For example, the mandibles of some slave-making species are modified so as to make them superb weapons for conducting raids but useless for foraging; among other species, special "appeasement glands" evolve to release pheromones that dull the defensive reactions of soldiers in a nest that is being raided; "propaganda pheromones" evolve which, when released, cause the defending soldiers to become confused, fail to recognize their nestmates, and attack each other; among some slave-making species, soldiers that conduct raids have evolved special grooves along the sides of their heads into which their antennae can be folded, thereby protecting them against injury (Hölldobler and Wilson 1990: 454–64). In addition to evolved morphological adaptations, systems of social parasitism also favor the evolution of behavioral adaptations. For example, prospective parasitic queens of various species have evolved a range of behavioral strategies that enable them to insinuate themselves into host colonies and take control of them. Some invading queens lie down, curl up, and fold their legs to their bodies, thereby resembling pupae which are then taken into the host nest by host workers. Other parasitic queens "play dead" and are taken into the nest as food; some invading queens adopt gestures of conciliation which enable them to repress attacks by host soldiers, and other queens adopt highly stealthy behavior that enables them to elude detection until it is too late. Once an invading queen has successfully breached the defenses of the host colony, she routinely kills the resident, host queen, after which the host workers typically "adopt" their new, alien queen and support her survival and reproductive efforts.

And ants are parasitized not only by other species of ants, but by other arthropod species as well, species that entomologists call "myrmecophiles," obligate invertebrate symbionts that live with ants and often exploit them (Hölldobler and Wilson 1990: 471–529). These include, for example, beetles, mites, flies, wasps, collembolans, homopterans, and many other varieties of insects. In a colorful passage provided by the famous myrmecologist W. M. Wheeler, who was well known for his vivid prose, we are provided with an image of what social parasitism among humans would look like if we too were hosts of multiple alien species dining among us, at our expense:

> Were we to behave in an analogous manner we should live in a truly Alice-in-Wonderland society. We should delight in keeping porcupines, alligators, lobsters, etc. in our homes, insist on their sitting down to our table with us and feed them so solicitously with spoon victuals that our children would either perish of neglect or grow up as hopeless rhachitics.
>
> (Wilson 1975: 377)

From Ants to Humans

Studies of social parasitism by behavioral biologists illustrate how patterns of social organization and interaction can create opportunities for contests over resources and the invasion of systems of production by expropriative strategies. Among humans, some forms of expropriation are prohibited by law. Illegal forms of expropriation have been conceptualized as "expropriative crimes," and Cohen and Machalek have developed a framework, based on behavioral ecological studies of social parasitism, for analyzing such crimes (Cohen and Machalek 1988, 1994; Machalek and Cohen

1991). Although individuals, acting either alone or collectively, engage in expropriative behavior, the focus of Cohen's and Machalek's approach is the influence of *patterns of behavior* on other *patterns of behavior*. Specifically, Cohen and Machalek distinguish between two strategies for acquiring resources: "production" versus "expropriation." Among humans, production entails "the investment of labor, aided by technology, for the appropriation of natural resources that are modified for human use," and expropriative strategies are "patterns of behavior by which individuals or groups usurp labor, objects of symbolic or material value, or other such resources from other individuals or groups" (Cohen and Machalek 1988: 468; 479). By focusing on the social organization of production and how it enables the incidence and proliferation of expropriation, Cohen and Machalek offer an explanation of expropriative crime that derives from the naturalistic framework for studying social parasitism that has been developed by evolutionary biologists and behavioral ecologists.

Viewing expropriative crime in this manner is consistent with the notion that certain types of crimes are "normal" and do not require analysts to resort to attributions of either individual or collective pathology in order to explain such crime. The idea of the "normalcy of crime" originates in sociology with the work of Durkheim (Machalek and Cohen 1991). This is not to say, however, that individual traits are irrelevant to explanations of any expropriative behaviors. In fact, Cohen and Machalek adopt the behavioral ecological concept of "resource holding potential" (RHP) to address how individual traits contribute to the incidence of expropriation in human populations (1988).

As in studies of social parasitism in animal social systems, Cohen's and Machalek's analysis of expropriative crime is fundamentally *sociological* in nature. By conceptualizing social behaviors as strategies for resource acquisition, and by analyzing how the nature and frequency with which certain strategies influence the nature and incidence of other strategies, Cohen and Machalek, like behavioral ecologists before them, have developed a new method of explaining how and why certain kinds of expropriative behaviors arise, proliferate, and/or decline in human populations without having to invoke notions of psychological "pathology" or social "dysfunction." Furthermore, Cohen and Machalek have demonstrated the value of thinking about human behaviors such as expropriative crime in terms of cross-species, comparative sociological terms. By considering how behavioral ecologists approach and explain social parasitism among animals, Cohen and Machalek have been able to import key explanatory concepts and principles derived from behavioral ecology into a sociological explanation of expropriative crime.

It is important to realize, however, that this approach does not neglect or deny the unique, species-typical traits possessed by humans, traits that contribute directly to patterns of human expropriation. For example, the highly evolved cognitive capabilities of humans; the ability to produce and use symbols; the ability to encode, store, and transmit information with culture; and the extraordinary learning capabilities of humans all have direct and profound effects on the manner in which patterns of expropriation are manifested in human populations. This is particularly evident in the powerful and sophisticated manner in which humans develop and employ deception in order to execute expropriative strategies. The importance of deception in human sociality has been a fundamental theme in sociology dating back to Marx's analysis of the role of ideology in promoting false consciousness as well as Pareto's emphasis on the importance of derivations in obscuring the actual motivations that propel human conduct. In fact, because of behavioral capabilities that are uniquely human, it could be claimed that humans are the premier practitioners of expropriative behaviors.

Conclusion

Extending the analysis of forms of social organization and patterns of social interaction to include non-human as well as human actors takes sociology a step closer toward the development of a truly comparative sociology, one that subordinates the study of any particular species to the study of fundamental forms and processes of social behavior. Studies such as the aforementioned on phenomena such as dominance hierarchies, vacancy chains, and patterns of expropriation illustrate how adopting a cross-species approach to the study of sociality offers the promise of enabling sociologists to identify and explain the truly "elementary forms" of social behavior, forms that are not restricted to one or a few species alone. Toward that end, the pursuit and further development of a cross-species, comparative sociology offers promise of expanding the scope and domain of sociological inquiry far beyond the more provincial, single-species focus on humans that has characterized most of its history. There is no more reason to insist that sociology must remain a "one species social science" than there is to contend that geology, for example, must comprise a "one mineral physical science." By adopting a cross-species perspective on sociality, sociologists can make progress toward fulfilling Simmel's goal of developing a truly "formal sociology," one that transcends the boundaries of human social existence alone.

Notes

1 Humans are, of course, animals, but we will distinguish between human and animal societies in the interest of parsimonious expression.
2 Chapter 16 includes a discussion of megasocieties and how they evolve.

16
Cross-Species Analysis of Megasociality

In his outline of the useful methodologies for collecting data on the subject matter of the new science of sociology, Auguste Comte (1830–1842) emphasized a comparative method that included examining social organization among other species and then comparing these to human social organization. Herbert Spencer (1874–1896) later made much the same point in his (in)famous organismic analogy where societies and organisms were seen as revealing parallel lines of organization and where superorganisms (the organization of organisms) included all species that reveal a division of labor, which could then be compared to that in human societies. And Charles Darwin compared humans and other animals, particularly primates, in several works including *The Descent of Man* (1871) and *The Expression of the Emotions in Man and Animals* (1872). As evolutionary analysis in general declined in the early decades of the 20th Century, however, so did comparisons of humans with other life forms.

In the early 1990s, Richard Machalek (1992) revived this kind of species comparison by addressing the question of why macro or very large, complex societies—sometimes termed "ultrasociality" or "megasociety" today—are surprisingly rare.[1] Among those animals that have created megasocieties of up to hundreds of millions of conspecifics coordinating their actions in a complex division of labor are some of the smallest organisms—the social insects—and one of the larger organisms to now roam earth—humans. Humans weigh 1 to 2 million times more than ants, and the brain of an ant is about the size of a grain of salt, while that of a human is about 3.5 pounds. How can species that are so different from each other have evolved the same form of societal organization, and why did it happen?

In this chapter, we will review Machalek's analysis of megasociality and briefly compare ant and human megasocieties, or what others such as Peter Turchin (see Chapter 4) term "ultrasociality." The goal of such comparisons is not so much to focus on any particular species but on "sociality" as a fitness-enhancing strategy expressed by very different life forms, and in making this comparison, better explain human megasociality and why it evolved.

After reviewing Machalek's analysis, we will turn in Chapter 17 to the long research program by Alexandra Maryanski and Jonathan H. Turner, who have engaged in a variety of comparative approaches to compare humans with their closest genetic cousins, the great apes. In ways that are not intuitively obvious, both approaches to comparative cross-species analysis yield converging findings.

Megasociality in Ants

Emile Durkheim has become immortalized in sociology, in part, because of his success in having identified a distinct subject matter for the discipline, a subject matter that previously had not been specified and isolated as requiring the development of a new science for its analysis. The term Durkheim used for this new class of phenomena requiring the development of a new science was "social facts," and it referred to emergent properties of collective phenomena that are irreducible to the components from which they derive (1895). For Durkheim, social facts have a *sui generis* quality in that they are "greater than the sum of their parts," or as the complexity theorist John Holland puts it, they are an emergent reality in that "more comes out than was put in" (1998: 13). Though most contemporary sociologists have been persuaded by Durkheim's contention that social facts, under whatever label, are sociology's distinct subject matter, not so many are aware that social facts are far from unique to humans. Instead, evolutionary biologists (including both sociobiologists and behavioral ecologists) now routinely acknowledge and analyze the emergent properties of animal societies constructed by organisms as simple as ants (Hölldobler and Wilson 1990: 3). For example, even E. O. Wilson, widely regarded as the "father of sociobiology" and often criticized for advocating reductionism, typically in the form of "genetic determinism," unequivocally states that the study of all societies, whatever the species, requires *both* reductionist and holistic thinking and analysis (Wilson 1998; Hölldobler and Wilson 1990: 3). A good example of empirical research that confirms Wilson's insistence on the emergent nature of social phenomena even in animal societies is provided by the discussion of Chase's work on dominance hierarchies provided in Chapter 15.

However, an even better example of a system of social facts that illustrates the extraordinary complexity of emergent properties of some animal societies is available in the case of the megasocieties constructed and inhabited by the eusocial insects, especially the ants. The complexity of ant societies illustrates a basic principle derived from both sociological thinking and, more recently, from the growing field of complexity studies (e.g., Epstein and Axtell 1996; Holland 1995, 1998; Kauffman 1995; and Langton 1989). Even a very small number of algorithms, *when interacting*, can produce a disproportionate degree of complexity within a system. Though emergence is a much-touted phenomenon in the relatively new field of complexity studies, it is old news in sociology, thanks to the work of the likes of Spencer and Durkheim over a century ago. However, a review of how relatively simple organisms like ants can create societies of extraordinary complexity provides instruction on the potential value of analyzing social structures and processes across species lines. Toward that end, we provide a brief review of megasocieties among ants before proceeding to a consideration of human megasociality and, in Chapter 17, the evolved features of human nature that make human megasociality possible.

Although only a minority of sociologists may find the social organization of animal societies as inherently interesting as they find human societies, a careful consideration of ant societies reveals many structures and processes found in such societies that are clearly sociologically significant and invite sociologists' careful attention, should they seek genuinely to understand, in a truly Simmelian manner, elementary forms of sociality that are distributed among many social species on Earth. In fact, some forms of sociality such as megasociety are perhaps best studied in non-human species such as the eusocial insects, thereby providing support for the "Krogh principle" which states "for many problems there is an animal on which it can be most conveniently studied" (Krebs 1975: 221).

The Organism: A Short Primer on the Behavioral Biology of Ants

A basic principle on which any analysis of ant megasocieties depends is this: *The behavioral complexity of any individual ant alone is insufficient to explain the organizational complexity and dynamism of an ant colony.* Hölldobler and Wilson report that "the total behavioral repertory of an individual ant worker is relatively simple, consisting according to species of no more than 20–45 acts" (1990: 358). This range of behavioral complexity is very modest by vertebrate standards. However, extraordinary complexity can be generated in systems that are regulated by far simpler sets of rules. For example, in a game of traditional tic-tac-toe, the number of legal configuration exceeds 50,000, and in more complex games like chess, a 50-move sequence can generate more different ways of playing games than there are atoms in the planet Earth (Holland 1998: 23, 37). Thus, a population of even only several thousand ants, each of which is equipped with a capability to produce as few as 20 behaviors, interacting with each other can produce enormous behavioral complexity and variation at the colony level.

The key to understanding the behavior of an ant colony lies in systems of ant communication. The most important medium of communication among ants is chemical, in the form of "semiochemicals" which include pheromones. Ant communication organs are exocrine glands, and more than ten have been identified, enabling individual ants to send ten to twenty different signals. The "meaning" of the chemicals is context-dependent, illustrating how emergent social conditions shape ant communication. Ants also rely on acoustical and tactile signals, but to a much lower degree than chemicals. Ant dependence on visual signals is minimal or non-existent, in sharp contrast to many vertebrate species like primates.

Complexity theorists explain that learning is not required among agents to build complex behavioral systems. By vertebrate standards, ants possess minimal learning abilities. For example, it takes ants two to three times longer than rats to learn to navigate a six-point maze, but they have been shown to be able to remember up to four landmarks outside their nest over winter (Hölldobler and Wilson 1990: 366). A few learning capabilities among ants, however, are noteworthy. Ants have highly evolved capabilities for learning the odor of their colony, thereby being able to distinguish nestmates from other conspecifics. This process occurs by imprinting that takes place during sensitive learning periods. Even more interesting is the fact that, if deprived of social interaction during a critical learning period, ants fail to develop normal behavioral competences required of colony members. Most sociologists are aware that social interaction is required for normal development among humans, but most are likely to find surprising that ants also depend on exposure to social stimuli for normal development. Finally, ants exhibit what Hölldobler and Wilson call "temporal learning" (1990: 366). That is, they can learn that it is advantageous to forage only during specific 30-minute windows during the day so as to minimize competition with other ant foragers. This illustrates the abilities of ants to respond variably to local social situations, further documenting the emergent nature of an activity as basic as foraging. Interacting with other colony members enables a population of ants to assemble a "superorganism," perhaps the pinnacle of emergent social behavior in non-human species.

The Superorganism: How Tiny Lives Build Titanic Societies

Ascertaining what is an individual and what is a group is not self-evident when considering many invertebrate species. For example, to a biologically uninformed observer, a jellyfish such as the Portuguese man-of-war appears for all intents and purposes to be an individual. However, like other colonial hydrozoans of the order Siphonophora, the man-of-war is actually a colony of individuals called "zooids." A colony of eusocial insects inverts this reality. That is, though ant colonies seem indisputably to constitute a population of motile individuals, entomologists have made a persuasive case for contending that the colony is actually a "superorganism" and that individual ants are more closely akin to the cells in the body of a true individual, a metazoan animal (Wilson 1975: 383–86). And while the zooids that comprise a jellyfish colony are integrated by physical bonds, the individuals that comprise an ant colony are integrated into a superorganism by bonds of communication. Thinking of an ant colony as a superorganism becomes more plausible when one realizes that, unlike true individuals, ants, with the exception of the queen(s), have not evolved to reproduce *as individuals*. Rather, they reproduce "vicariously" by supporting the reproductive activity of the queen. This is not unlike the arrangement whereby the only cells directly involved in reproduction in sexually reproducing species are sperm and egg cells. The cells making up all of the remaining tissues of the body are not directly engaged in reproduction but rather, exist in a "support capacity" to the eggs and sperm. And while natural selection favors reproduction of individuals in most species, among ants (and other eusocial insects), reproductive success is measured at the colony level. That is, ants have evolved to maximize their inclusive fitness by founding new colonies, not by reproducing new individuals.

The notion of an ant colony as a superorganism gained currency in the early 1900s under the influence of William Morton Wheeler, one of the pre-eminent myrmecologists of the 20th Century (1911). By the mid-1960s, the idea had fallen into disrepute among biologists, but by the late 20th Century, entomologists were once again reviving the notion of the superorganism, and in 1990, Hölldobler and Wilson declared it to be a "venerable idea" (1990: 358–59). Specifically, myrmecologists concluded that, by developing a new, scientifically based analytical-holism that is compatible with the experimental, reductionist epistemology and methodology of conventional scientific research, the concept of the superorganism as an emergent reality merited scientific status. A brief overview of key features of the superorganism that is an ant colony illustrates the emergent nature of one of the most complex social systems found in nature among motile organisms:

- *Population size.* Ant societies have populations ranging from as few as 35 or so individuals to as many as 306,000,000.
- *Internal social organization.* Ant colonies are organized into clusters of "acts" (or behaviors) called "roles," and a colony subpopulation called a "caste" specializes in performing one or more of these roles for the

colony. Roles include such activities as foraging, grooming and feeding the queen, constructing and repairing nests, caring for brood, and colony defense. At least three kinds of castes can be identified: (1) physical castes which have distinct morphologies; (2) temporal castes, which represent changing role responsibilities of ants as they age through the life-cycle; and (3) physiological castes, which are distinguished by their physiological state, such as being inseminated. In some cases, physical castes exhibit dramatic differences, such as soldier ants of some species which are 300 times the weight of workers in their own colony. In other cases, the morphology of the worker ants does not vary significantly, nor does it change during the ant's adult lifetime. Instead, the individual ant's ergonomic responsibilities may follow a sequence such as serving as a brood nurse while it is young, a nest repairer as it becomes older, a forager while yet older, and a soldier in very late life. Interestingly, the sequence of this role succession seems to reflect a tendency to deploy ants to increasingly dangerous roles as they age, thereby enabling the colony to avoid unnecessary labor force mortality while an ant is young and much of its working life lies before it. (And the temptation is irresistible to observe that while humans send their young males to die in warfare, ants send their old females, because all "soldier" ants are female.)

- *Behavioral flexibility*. Despite having very small brains and limited learning capabilities, ant colonies exhibit a surprising degree of behavioral flexibility. Workers of some species are able to shift back and forth between performing specialized and generalized roles. This individual behavioral flexibility contributes significantly to the colony's ability to adjust colony-level behavioral patterns in response to changing external environmental conditions as well as changes that are internal to the colony, such as a sudden reduction in its population size due to conflict or predation.
- *Colony life-cycle*. As with individuals, ant colonies undergo a series of specific life-cycle changes. Three general stages can be specified: (1) the *founding stage* during which a queen leaves her natal nest, joins a "nuptial flight," is inseminated, establishes a new colony by laying eggs, and establishes a first-generation caste of workers; (2) the *ergonomic stage* during which the queen produces an increasingly large and specialized work force; and (3) the *reproductive stage* during which reproductive effort shifts from producing more members of worker castes to the production of virgin queens and males, which then disperse from their nest to participate in nuptial swarms and found new colonies.

Durkheim developed his concept of social facts in relation to human societies. At least two ways of thinking about social facts are provided in his writings. Early in his discussion, Durkheim stated "Here, then, are ways of acting, thinking, and feeling that present the noteworthy property of existing outside of individual consciousness" (1966: 2). The reference to "thinking," "feeling," and "consciousness" clearly refers to social facts as they exist in human societies. However, his second conception asserts that

> a social fact is every way of acting, fixed or not, capable of exercising on the individual an external constraint ... every way of acting which is general throughout a given society, while at the same time existing in its own right independent of its individual manifestations.
>
> (1966: 18)

By not requiring capacities for thought, feeling, or consciousness among actors, the second definition permits conceptualizing social facts as properties of animal societies, including ant societies. As in human societies, three basic categories of social facts are *population traits, social structure*, and *social processes*. We will discuss how ant societies exhibit all three types of social facts.

Population Traits

A fundamental population trait that exerts significant influence on patterns of social behavior in ant colonies is population size. For example, when ant colonies are young, their queens produce large numbers of small workers called "minims." Minims behave more "timidly" than do larger soldiers when confronted with threats. As worker caste numbers increase, the queen produces more larger workers as well as soldiers who behave in a bolder and more confrontational manner when encountering threats. When the worker population size is small, the colony cannot afford risky behavior that would reduce its numbers. Accordingly, worker aggressiveness is positively correlated with population size, the basic social fact exhibited by ant societies (Hölldobler and Wilson 1990: 295).

Using a concept called "adaptive demography," Wilson explains how demographic features of a colony change in adaptive response to both external, environmental changes as well as to changes internal to the colony itself (1971). As the population of a colony grows, the queen produces castes in different proportions. That is, when the population is small, the queen produces workers that are members of a "generalist" caste that are "Jacks (or, perhaps more accurately, 'Jills') of all trades" and can perform diverse types of labor for the colony. However, as the population grows, the queen begins to produce new castes that specialize in tasks such as brood tending, nest repair, and defense. Thus, caste proportions change in response to population size. This suggests an interesting question: What happens if a colony that is several years old suddenly loses a large proportion of its labor force? Does the colony "interpret" this labor force reduction to mean that the colony is "young" and that workers should be replaced in ratios one would find in a young colony, or does the colony "recognize" its true age and replace workers in proportions that reflect true colony age rather than population size? To bring empirical evidence to bear on this interesting question, Wilson conducted an experiment in which he significantly reduced the size of four colonies of leafcutter ants (*Atta sexdens*) from populations of about 10,000 workers each to 236 workers each, thereby making each colony resemble a small, newly founded colony rather than one which was actually 3 to 4 years old. When each colony began to replace its decimated labor force, it produced workers in caste ratios that typify young, newly founded colonies. That is, each colony exhibited sensitivity to population size, not actual population age in "deciding" how to restock its labor force. It is as if the small population size effectively "told" the queen, "This is a very young colony that needs generalists, not specialists, so produce generalists until the population size increases significantly."

Social Structure: The Dense Heterarchy

In human societies, dominance hierarchies and stratification systems are good examples of social facts that constrain the behaviors of individuals and exert a regulatory effect on members of the society as a whole. In the superorganism that is an ant colony, hierarchy in this sense is absent, and the "queen" is not literally a "ruler" who "administers" her six-legged "subjects." Instead, the behaviors of ants are subject to a social fact called a "dense heterarchy" (Wilson and Hölldobler 1988). While power and influence in hierarchies are exercised from "top down," in the dense heterarchies found in ant colonies, influence is "lateral," or "horizontal," among nestmates. A "dense" heterarchy refers to an interactive context in which the members of a population are perpetually subject to likely influence from any other member of the population. Higher levels of density mean increases in the probability that any two nestmates will encounter each other over a short time period. The behavioral constraints imposed by this type of social fact derive from the cumulative effect of behaviors executed by every individual which every member of the colony encounters and with which it interacts, and it is from innumerable such interactions that colony-level social organization derives.

Hölldobler and Wilson provide examples of three categories of ant behavior that are regulated by dense heterarchies: food sharing, food retrieval, and egg-laying (1990: 455–56). Ants share food by a process called "trophallaxis," the transmission of liquid food from one ant to another by regurgitation. An ant distributing food is not guided by its own physiological state and nutritional needs but, rather, by that of the nestmates in its colony to whom it is distributing food. How does the "feeder" know what sort of food (Honey? Vegetable oils? Egg yolk?) its nestmates need, and how much of each type of food is needed? The problem is solved by a behavioral feedback mechanism. The "feeder" approaches its nestmates and offers a certain type and volume of food. As long its nestmates accept the offering, the feeder continues to move among colony members distributing this food. However, as acceptance rates in the colony decline, the feeder reduces either the amount or type of food offered or the specific worker caste to whom the food is being provided. This process illustrates how the behavior of the individual feeder is regulated not by its own level of hunger or satiation but, rather, by the nutritional state of the colony as a whole. And since an ant colony, not an individual ant, is the unit (target) of selection, this mechanism assures that the nutritional needs of the colony as a whole are met.

Upon finding a food source, foragers have to recruit nestmates to help transport the food back to the nest. Again, dense heterarchies enable ants to perform that task. Having found a food source, the forager returns to its nest, turns around, and then returns once again to the food source, using its ovipositor ("stinger") to deposit a pheromone trail as it proceeds. Upon detecting the pheromone trail, its nestmates join it in route to the nest, depositing their own trails as they travel. More and more ants join the procession to retrieve food until the food supply is exhausted or the site becomes overcrowded with workers, at which point fewer workers are recruited and the "convoy" dissipates and ceases to operate.

Finally, dense heterarchies determine the rate at which the colony queen lays eggs. Should not enough eggs be laid, the colony will not grow at an optimal rate. Should more eggs be laid than can be cared for, colony growth may also be arrested. The mechanism by means of which the egg-laying rate is regulated is the number of fourth-instar larvae that are present in the colony. These larvae perform the task of transmitting food to the nurse workers which, in turn, transmit the food to the eggs. The amount of food so delivered regulates the rate of egg production. Thus, interaction among the larvae, the nurse workers, and the queen form a positive feedback loop that calibrates the rate of egg production in relation to labor force conditions and needs within the colony.

Series-Parallel Operations in the Division of Labor

Only the eusocial insects and humans organize large populations of individuals into a complex division of labor executed by subpopulations of specialists (Machalek 1992). Myrmecologists identify three types of task-processing operations: (1) *series operations* in which one individual performs one task at a time, (2) *parallel-series operations* in which multiple individuals are performing such sequences independently of each other, and (3) *series-parallel operations* in which two or more individuals are cooperating in the performance of a particular task and multiple such tasks are being performed simultaneously within the colony. Series-parallel operations are familiar to most sociologists as what social thinkers from Adam Smith, Durkheim, and others called simply "the division of labor." In order for series-parallel operations to function efficiently and effectively, the individuals involved must reach a threshold of competence for executing a task. For example, if two ants are cooperating to relocate a larva in a nest, they must not work at cross-purposes. One must not pull when it should be pushing, and vice versa. If each "knows" whether to push or pull, then series operations will be more effective. If each ant in the colony attains a threshold of competence for a task, then series-parallel operations create redundancy within the *components* of the system rather than creating redundant *systems*, and component redundancy provides more reliability (and efficiency and effectiveness) than if the system were to be divided into multiple, redundant "mini-systems" (Machalek 1999: 56–57).

Series-parallel operations illustrate emergent properties of the ant superorganism. They show how both reductionist and holistic thinking is needed to understand colony-level behavior. Reductionist thinking focuses on the individual and reveals how individual competence is required to perform tasks, and holistic thinking reveals that effectively coordinated cooperation among nestmates yields an emergent, effective, and efficient division of labor. In this case, the whole *is* "greater than the sum of its parts" *if* each part exhibits a requisite level of behavioral competence. The ergonomic efficiency and effectiveness of the division of labor in an ant colony can be explained only by integrating reductionist and holistic analyses.

Social Processes: Colony Homeostasis

Homeostasis refers to the ability of a system that has been perturbed to return to its pre-perturbed state. Homeostatic processes exist at multiple levels of biological organization from the cell up to and including the superorganism. The range of behavioral capabilities required to achieve and regain homeostasis when a system is perturbed does not have to be instantiated in any individual member of the superorganism's population.

Instead, the necessary range of behaviors, and the colony's derivative behavioral flexibility, can be distributed among the entire population of colony members.

Thus, the roughly twenty to forty-five distinct behaviors of which any given ant is capable of performing is sufficient to produce behaviors required by the colony to regain homeostasis when the system is perturbed. For ant colonies, perturbations are created by forces associated with events such as floods, predation, parasitism, raids by other colonies, or disease. Often, such crises result in the disruption of caste ratios. Ants possess a variety of behavioral mechanisms that enable the colony to regain homeostasis in caste composition. These mechanisms include, among others, variation in pheromone production and release; variable levels of care and nursing provided to eggs, pupae, and larvae; variable concentrations of members of one caste in relation to members of other castes; proximity of members of other castes during performance of tasks; and the volume of larvae present in a nest that must be fed (Machalek 1999: 59).

However, the existence of adaptive, emergent social processes that can produce homeostasis and re-establish it when it is disturbed should not invoke a Panglossian view of the emergent structures and processes comprising an ant superorganism. Rather, natural selection does not provide fail-safe assurances that "all will be well," whatever the circumstance encountered by a colony. Wilson provides an example of the failure of homeostatic mechanisms when, on occasion, ants of the species *Pheidole dentate* are raided by fire ants (*Solenopsis invicta*). Alarm pheromones are released by *Pheidole* workers when they are raided by *Solenopsis*. At a certain point, these pheromone concentrations can reach a level beyond which *Pheidole* workers no longer behave adaptively so as to repel the invaders and protect the nest but rather, suddenly all rush frantically away from the nest and become dispersed to the point they can no longer mount a capable defense. Essentially, the *Pheidole* workers have "routed" themselves by their overproduction of alarm pheromones. Wilson calls this behavior "absconding," and it is a maladaptive pattern that derives from interactions among members of the *Pheidole* worker caste that is under assault.

Even before Durkheim introduced the concept of social facts into sociological discourse, both Comte and Spencer explicitly described human societies as emergent realities. Spencer went so far as to characterize societies as "superorganic," a term used not much later by the myrmecologist Wheeler to describe an ant colony (1911). By analyzing both human and animal societies, it becomes clear that both types of social systems feature emergent properties. Emergence does not require high levels of individual intelligence among members of societies, nor does it require (though it clearly is enhanced by) complex cultural capabilities. Instead, even the simplest of organisms, by interacting with each other, can produce disproportionately complex patterns of behavior at the societal level. In short, in any society, social facts are *derivative of* but not *reducible to* traits of the individuals that produce them.

As noted earlier, megasociality occurs in nature among members of only two taxa, humans (and then only recently, over the past 5,000 years or so) and the eusocial insects. Arguably, the evolution of megasocieties has enabled humans to become the dominant terrestrial vertebrate on Earth, and ants the dominant invertebrate. Yet, as individual organisms, ants and humans are so phylogenetically distant from each other that it is implausible to suggest that something about their shared biology can explain the evolution of megasocieties among these two groups of organisms. How did megasociality evolve among both ants and humans?

Conclusion: Megasocieties Among Creatures Great and Small

The goal of cross-species analysis begins by defining the elementary forms and properties of those forms of organization shared by human and non-human organisms. Then, analysis should focus on the "design problems" that constrain the evolution of a particular form and the conditions that must be met for this form of organization to evolve. This type of analysis emphasizes the various kinds of constraints for the assembly of a particular form of organization, including organismic constraints, ecological constraints, cost-benefit constraints, and finally sociological constraints. This step involves a review of the prerequisites for a particular form of organization to come into existence.

Constraints on the Self-Assembly of Megasocieties

About 5,000 years ago humans assembled and began living in megasocieties after having lived in small, foraging societies for close to 200,000 years. As soon as hunter-gatherers began to settle in more permanent communities, their populations began to grow and, often, these populations were forced to adopt horticulture, which led to an increase in the size of a population. And eventually, agrarian societies evolved to support even larger populations; and finally, just a few hundred years ago, industrial and later post-industrial societies of enormous size began to evolve.

As noted above, megasocieties are rare because the evolution of this form of social organization requires developing solutions to a number of imposing constraints that inhibit the development of this societal form. These constraints include: (1) organismic constraints, (2) ecological constraints,

(3) cost-benefit constraints, and (4) sociological constraints. Each of these is briefly summarized below:

(1) *Organismic Constraints.* The morphology of a species can inhibit or facilitate evolution of macrosocieties. For example, whales are enormous animals that are very intelligent, appear to have a rudimentary language, and live in social communities, but they would always have trouble building macrosocieties because of their size and body plans and because of their enormous needs to consume large quantities of food. Their body plans would, moreover, not easily allow them to develop a division of labor whereby they could coordinate their behavior into respective specialties. Thus, for a megasociety to evolve, body plans must be smaller, capable of being altered for specialized activities, and able to coordinate specialized labor.

(2) *Ecological Constraints.* The ecosystem to which a species must adapt also sets limits on both population size and complexity. Ecosystems vary by their size, food resources, shelter, diversity of species, the size of their respective populations, incidence of predation, and prevalence of disease and other pathogens. For example, insects are very small organisms and are much more likely than whales to find a habitat that can accommodate a very large population. What is interesting is that humans are very large animals that require a high intake of nutrients to support not only a large body, but a large brain; and humans are susceptible to predation, diseases, and pathogens. Consequently, it is somewhat surprising that humans have been able to overcome ecological constraints, and at the same time, the size of the human population has grown to a point where it is facing ecological constraints of a species requiring so much energy and protein that ecological disruption on a world scale has inevitably increased, thereby presenting dangers to human survival and virtually every other species of life on earth.

(3) *Cost-Benefit Constraints.* Building a megasociety depends upon having an excess of benefits to costs in amassing a large population with a coordinated division of labor. Large and complex societies confront a number of costs, as is the case with insects that can become victims of parasitism by other species that expropriate labor and/or food; and these costs cannot exceed the benefits of coordinated labor among large numbers of conspecifics. In the case of insects, the large size of their populations and their coordination of labor compensate for their small size, allowing every member of the society, and the population as a whole, to secure food and protection. There is, then, strength in numbers, especially numbers where individuals engage in specialized,

coordinated labor. In the case of humans, it is only through divisions of labor that they can secure sufficient resources to survive and support very large populations of large-bodied mammals.

(4) *Sociological Constraints*. The evolution of megasocieties and ultrasociality requires a unique form of social interaction among members that is rare in nature and beyond the capacities of most animals. These unique forms of interaction include:

  a. Individuals must be able to engage in interpersonal cooperation with strangers.
  b. Individual members of society must be divided among distinct categories of conspecifics, each of which engages in a specialized activity.
  c. Individuals at each point in the division of labor must be integrated into a larger social whole that promotes the survival and well-being of the entire population.

Most mammals are organized by kinship, or genetic relatedness, which makes it very difficult to have large numbers of individuals in a society. The greater the degree of genetic relatedness among animals, the more likely are they to interact and organize into smaller kin-based groups. Thus, at the core of troops, groups, packs, pods, and other forms of grouping among mammals are kin ties, although subgroupings of kin can become part of a larger assembling of individuals, such as in herds. In contrast, ants and other species of insects are often organized into distinctive categories that are specialized (for foraging, defense, brood tending, nest repair, etc.) and recognized by conspecifics by olfactory cues, with the result that strangers can recognize each other's category (and, hence, function) and coordinate their respective activities. All of this differentiation is genetically based, and in many cases, a shortage of members in a particular category can activate genes that compensate for that shortage. Thus, insect societies are highly organized by genetic bioprogrammers; consequently they do not require large brains or culture to produce megasocieties.

In contrast, for most of their time on earth, humans survived by recognizing a few basic categories—age, sex, and gender—in kin units that divided coordinated labor by gender and, to some extent, age. But these were very small societies of several nuclear kinship units in a hunting and gathering band occupying a delimited territory. But, as horticultural and then agrarian societies evolved, the number of social categories within each society also expanded, and increasingly, individuals had to interact with some strangers and be organized by much larger units beyond kinship that coordinated labor. What has been evident over the last 5,000 years is that humans can form *both* close kin ties and yet interact with strangers in ever-larger units coordinating their labor. Humans, then, are a unique mammal, because they have two languages (the language of emotions read visually and the spoken language using the auditory sense modality), coupled with very large cognitive capacities that enable them to categorize others and situations, while remembering the relevant categories, status positions, roles, and norms appropriate for positions in complex divisions of labor. Thus, humans can overcome the liabilities of their body constraints, costs relative to the benefits of a divisions of labor that increase productivity and fitness, and sociological constraints revolving around the capacity to interact with strangers; to divide persons, situations, and labor into distinct categories; and to integrate complex divisions of labor among very large numbers of individuals.

Humans and Constraints on Megasociality

Humans can create megasocieties, then, through alternative mechanisms than those available to insects for overcoming basic constraints. However, as human populations grow, their impact on their ecosystems may create new and intensified constraints that cannot be overcome. Humans have been able, thus far, to do so because they are evolved great apes and equipped with language and culture, both of which enable the construction of megasocieties. And the biological legacy that humans have inherited from the last common ancestor is significant in enabling humans to overcome the organismic (large size), cost-benefit, and sociological constraints confronting any species that would evolve megasociality. By pursuing a cross-species, comparative sociology and using cladistic analysis (more specifically, data adduced about great apes and primates in general), archeology, paleontology, and comparative neurology, it is now possible to determine how humans have been able to overcome sociological constraints and evolve megasocieties.

Note

1 In his 1992 paper on this topic, Machalek used the term "macrosociety" to designate a society with a very large population whose members are organized into a complex division of labor that is executed by categories of specialists. Subsequently, Machalek uses the term "megasociety" to identify such social systems. The term "macro" typically refers to the scale of observation and analysis adopted by sociologists. For example, a "macro-level" analysis takes a "big picture" view of a social phenomenon, looking, perhaps, at the major contours of a society such as its stratification systems. A "micro-level" analysis "zooms in" to consider social phenomena at a much closer, more local level, such as that

of a small primary group of friends. By way of contrast, the notion of a megasociety refers to the size of the phenomena being analyzed. A modern, urban industrial society comprising hundreds of millions of people is a megasociety in comparison to a small hunting-gathering band consisting of a population of forty or fifty people. One could conduct either a macro-level or micro-level analysis of either a megasociety or a much smaller social system like a hunting-gathering society.

17
The Behavioral and Interpersonal Basis of Megasociality
Evidence From Primates

Maryanski's and Turner's Evolutionary Analysis of Human Societies

The Power of Cladistic Analysis

Homo sapiens are evolved great apes; and because of this fact, humans share a very high percentage of their genes with present-day great apes—one species of orangutan, two species of gorillas, and two species of chimpanzees. Great apes have their genes spread across an extra chromosome pair, but as noted in Chapters 12 and 13, the percentage of genes in common with great apes is roughly 96–97% with orangutans, 98% with both subspecies of gorillas, and 99.6% with common and bonobo chimpanzees. This very high percentage of shared genetic material allows for the application of what is known in biology as *cladistic analysis* (see Chapters 12–14 for a fuller explanation; see also Maryanski and Turner 1992; Turner and Maryanski 2008a; see also Jeffers and Lehiste 1979; Andrews and Martin 1987).

As outlined in previous chapters, the basic logic of cladistic analysis is that, when a set of species is believed to have a common ancestor, a comparison of key traits across these species allows for inferences about the traits of the common ancestor from which they all evolved. Alexandra Maryanski, as emphasized in Chapter 12, performed cladistic analysis on the behavioral and organizational features of great-ape societies, employing monkey societies as a control to assure that the shared characteristics of great apes are unique to apes and not common in all primates. As is reported in Chapters 12–14, the findings are rather startling: Great apes reveal rather low sociality as measured by the number of strong social relations that they have with conspecifics; apes do not form permanent groupings; apes do not form intergenerational ties because, for both orangutans and gorillas, males and females leave their natal communities at puberty (female chimpanzees do so as well, but males remain in their natal community). The only consistently strong tie among great apes is mother-young offspring bond, a tie which is broken at puberty except for chimpanzee males who maintain a moderate-to-strong tie with their mothers through periodic visits but for short periods of time. Chimpanzee males also form friendships, while lead silverbacks gorillas and females with offspring often form a temporary alliance until these offspring leave the community.

All great apes are promiscuous, and thus paternity is never known; and with male and female transfer at puberty, the tie with mothers (except chimpanzee mothers) is broken forever. Thus, there are virtually no ties that allow for intergenerational continuity among great apes, and hence, the last common ancestor to present-day great apes. There is the mother-son tie among chimpanzee that cuts across generations, but this tie does not lead to group formation but instead, as noted, periodic visits to their mothers. Otherwise, there is nothing on which to build intergenerational ties.

Since all females in a community are immigrants from other communities (replacing the females who have left at puberty) and since both orangutan and gorilla males also transfer at puberty, male gorillas and orangutans are also immigrants. They are, in essence, strangers to each other and generally do not form strong bonds.

By systematically recording the ties and networks from field studies on great apes, Maryanski was able to perform cladistic analysis, the results of which are outlined in Table 12.1 on page 298. As the far right column summarizes, there were virtually no strong ties among the last common ancestor to great apes and humans. The only strong tie was mother-young offspring, a universal tie among almost all mammals, but this tie is broken (except by chimpanzee males) at puberty.

This lack of social relations among conspecifics is also reflected in a complete lack of group formation, beyond the mother-young offspring ties that constitute a group until puberty, at which point offspring leave their mothers. Otherwise, the last common ancestor did not form stable or permanent groupings. Among orangutans, individuals are virtually solitary; and among chimpanzees, friendships form and male ties with mothers are sustained through visits, but no permanent groups exist in any great ape; and among gorillas, there is a temporary tie between a lead silverback and a mother with young offspring, which is broken when offspring leave their natal community forever.

The Implications of Sexual Promiscuity, Transfer Patterns, Weak Ties, and No Permanent Groups

Unlike most mammals, kin selection or the favoring of genetically close relatives as a basis for group organization is not operative among great apes because of promiscuity, offspring transfer (except chimpanzee males) at puberty, and their replacement by migrating males and/or females from other communities. Without strong ties among adult conspecifics across generations, groups of any sort are not a "natural" organizational pattern for great apes. And what is true of great apes today was very likely the case millions of years ago with the common ancestor that all great apes share with humans. Even if we move up in time to the common ancestor that humans share with chimpanzees 4–5 million years ago, ties are still predominately weak, and there are no permanent groupings among humans' closest primate cousins.

This lack of strong ties and permanent groups caused the extinction of most great apes that were forced to the edges of the forests and to the open-county African savanna, beginning about 10 million years ago. Without strong bonds and groups to defend against predators and to organize food collection, great apes were doomed to extinction. All species of great apes today require the protection of the forests to sustain their weak-tie systems of organization where groups are only temporary. Yet, while this form of organization was maladaptive for most great apes when forced to leave the shrinking forests to the open-country savannas of Africa, it can be seen as a pre-adaptation for macrosocieties—if such formations would eventually enhance fitness. Great apes are not trapped in tight-knit groups as a result of kin selection, nor do they automatically form strong ties; and they often live as relative strangers to each other because of the migration patterns in which the young of one community are exchanged by transfer patterns for the young from other communities. Thus, in terms of the sociological constraints on macrosocieties outlined in Chapter 16, the descendants of great apes are in a better position to overcome these because they can engage in interaction with relative strangers, because they are not tied to local groups by kin selection, and because they are not prone to forming stable groups at all. They live in a weak-tie, non-group world in which individuals move about alone or in temporary assemblages, and as a result, they are capable of moving in and out of weak-tie social relationships among members of their home range without difficulty. These features of great-ape behavior and organization still reside in humans, although as will be emphasized shortly, humans are capable of forming stronger bonds of solidarity in groups, but even as they do so, humans remain capable of being in less constraining situations and of interacting with strangers.

Implications of Community as the Basic Organizational Unit for Great Apes

Chimpanzees, particularly common chimpanzees, evidence expansive home ranges or communities from which female offspring transfer at puberty, forever, to be replaced by female strangers from other communities. Apes reckon who belongs and who does not belong in the community, and among chimpanzees, males will patrol in temporary group formations the perimeter of the community to keep males from other communities entering a home range. These communities can become quite large—easily 10 square miles—with the result that individuals move constantly about alone, in small and very temporary hookups, and occasionally in groups that form but soon break apart. And at times, larger numbers of chimpanzees will assemble and engage in emotion-arousing festivals or carnivals.

There is some evidence that orangutans and gorillas also organize by communities (Schaller 1963, 1964, 1972), but the data are hard to assess, especially since gorillas' habitats have been encroached by humans, thereby disrupting natural organizational patterns. Still, it is likely that the common ancestor of all present-day great apes lived in bounded communities where they would constantly move about alone or in temporary assemblies. Thus, the more inclusive community rather than local group is the more natural social unit for great apes and, in all likelihood, the last common ancestor to great apes and humans. The last common ancestor and even humans today are still very much oriented to larger communities; sustaining groups, for humans, involves a great deal of interpersonal work, whereas in contrast, humans easily identify with their communities. The result is that humans are cognitively hard-wired to look beyond local groups and kin units; and this orientation allows them to be mobile and able to interact with strangers, while at the same time having a sense of collective membership in a community. And, as hominins became ever more intelligent, this orientation to community could probably be extended to much larger units and thereby served as a pre-adaptation for the ability to identify with and, hence, feel part of a macrosociety composed of millions of individuals. Moreover, the fact that chimpanzees today can form emotion-arousing rituals, reminiscent of Emile Durkheim's (1912) portrayal of Australian aborigine emotional "effervescence" when gathering, suggest that humans also have a hard-wired propensity to develop commitments to larger-scale macrostructures as one basis for integration of such large units.

Thus, a community orientation as opposed to a hard-wired propensity to form groups around kindred, coupled with the capacity to engage in ritual homage to the community, were both pre-adaptations for macrosocieties. Unlike monkeys who form very tight-knit groups, where a macro-orientation is impossible, humans' common ancestor shared with great apes some very unique features that, once macrosocieties began to grow, made such growth less problematic than it would be for virtually all other mammals. Indeed, humans as evolved great apes possess some of the key attributes that would allow them to overcome the sociological, organismic, and cost-benefit constraints outlined at the end of Chapter 16 that make ultrasociality so rare among organisms.

The Implications of Existing Pre-Adaptations and Interpersonal Capacities for Macro Societies

The methodology summarized in Chapters 12–14, and briefly outlined above, can be used to discover the pre-adaptations and behavioral capacities of great apes and, hence, the last common ancestors to humans and apes. Table 14.2 on page 352 lists the (1) pre-adaptations, or traits wired into great-ape neurology as a by-product of selection for other traits, and (2) the behavioral propensities that all great apes exhibit are listed (see Chapters 12 and 13 for more details). The traits listed allow humans to adapt to macrosocieties and thereby overcome the sociological constraints reviewed in Chapter 16 (see pp. ___ to ___).

Pre-Adaptations

Among the pre-adaptations of apes, we can group these under two headings: community organization and emotionality.

1. Community Orientation. Great apes, when compared to monkeys, do not groom each other to a high degree. For most monkeys, mutual grooming is how troop solidarities are sustained in groups, but apes do not form long-term and stable groups, and hence, they do not need to groom to sustain what they do not form. Instead, great apes, as noted above, clearly have a cognitive orientation to the larger home range or community. This is known for sure among chimpanzees, and as mentioned earlier, there are suggestions of this same orientation among other great apes. Indeed, it may have been a cognitive ability of all great apes, but this cannot be known for sure. Still, humans' closest relative, chimpanzees, clearly have this orientation, and thus, it is part of our human genome. In this orientation, the boundaries of the community are understood and, moreover, the individuals belonging to the community are known, even if they are not seen for considerable periods of time. For most primates and mammals more generally, this a very unusual cognitive capacity because most primates and mammals are oriented to groups, although highly intelligent mammals like dolphins, whales, and elephants appear also to have to capacity to reckon a community of conspecifics.

The lack of grooming allows great apes to sustain weak-tie relationships and not be pulled into strong-tie relations—something that they are not prone to do anyway. But, as will be outlined shortly, selection would eventually push hominins to become more group oriented by enhancing their emotions, but in so doing, the propensity to sustain weak ties was not selected out. Rather, it was retained in the behavioral repertoire of those great apes on the hominin line, with the result that hominins could develop *both* stronger ties and, at the same time, retain the ability to interact with relative strangers. Emotions as the replacement for bioprogrammers for group attachments that were lost or, alternatively, never existed among great apes in the arboreal habitat would, therefore, increase the flexibility of humans when larger societies became adaptive some 5,000 years ago.

The pre-adaptation for play (among all mammals) is perhaps important in this context because, while adults among great apes do not form strong ties, infants and young juveniles play together. Play requires the ability to read the role that another infant is playing (say, pursuer) and then assume the complementary role (pursued), and then to suddenly shift or reverse roles, or even start playing other roles, even among juveniles who are only periodically seen. For macrosocieties to exist, individuals must learn to play and interpret the roles of many others who are strangers; and the innate capacity to play hones skill at this kind of behavior and, thus, serves as a pre-adaptation for relying upon interpersonal skills listed under "Behavioral Propensities" in Table 14.2.

The ability of great apes to learn naturally spoken human languages (Rumbaugh 2013, 2015) is also an important pre-adaptation for macrosocieties. When almost all others are unknown and strangers, coupled with both close and distant relations with specific others, the ability to communicate with something like emotional phonemes and syntax is essential to sustain such a society. Great apes have both visual and, to a lesser extent, auditory languages that they use in their natural habitats, and the fact that they can learn (by mere exposure when young) and use the languages of humans (if they can "speak" through the visual sense modalities such as hand signals or pictograms on computers) indicates that language was not as great a leap in evolutionary development, as is often thought. Coupled with a larger neocortex and emotional enhancements, the core capacity for language was an essential pre-adaptation for macrosocieties because it provides a common medium whereby individuals can communicate meanings and coordinate actions. Having to groom in order to get things done would impose a roadblock to macrosocieties; having language would facilitate interaction with many others, including strangers, in a wide variety of contexts.

2. *Emotionality*. Great apes are highly emotional and have a relatively large palette of primary emotions for a mammal. The existence of this repertoire of primary emotions was to become one of the most important pre-adaptations of the last common ancestor because natural selection began to work on subcortical areas of the brain long before the neocortex among hominins began to grow significantly. By enhancing emotions, low-sociality apes could become more social and eventually develop strong

emotional ties to each other that would allow for group formation, which was essential to the survival of hominin on the African savanna. By using this more indirect route to stronger ties of solidarity, natural selection was able to overcome the great liability of all great apes that went extinct on the savanna, but it set up as basis for supercharging, in essence, all of the behavioral propensities listed in Table 14.2 on page 353.

What has always been interesting is that the behavioral propensities of great apes were not enough to increase sociality, tie strength, and group formations for survival on the African savanna. Clearly, the list of capacities that make great apes very capable in interaction were not sufficient to increase tie-strength and to form more permanent groups. For, if these interpersonal skills were sufficient, more apes would have survived on the savanna. As selection hit upon the strategy of enhancing hominin emotions (Turner 2000, 2002, 2007), the power of the interpersonal mechanisms listed in second half of Table 14.2 was dramatically increased. Thus, without the enhancement of emotions, the behavioral propensities listed in Table 14.2 were not sufficient, alone, to increase the strength of weak ties that would, in turn, lead to more permanent groups of hominins.

Yet, as selection worked along these lines, it did not take away the community orientation or the capacities of hominins, and then humans, to interact with strangers and to have many weak-tie, temporary groupings with conspecifics. As a result, humans became capable of engaging in *both* strong- or weak-tie social relations and stable or temporary groupings. Indeed, humans are of two minds, capable of feeling lonely without some strong ties and often feeling engulfed by ties that are too constraining. And while this duality can make for personal problems for individuals if out of balance, this duality is essential for macrosocieties. Individuals have to be able to work in weak-tie groups within divisions of labor and not become engulfed in such groups to the point of losing the ability to interact with strangers or see beyond the boundaries of local groups. At the same time, community-oriented hominins and then humans needed to forge stronger ties and more permanent groups; and emotionally charged behavioral propensities allow stronger ties and commitments to groups to develop in kin units and groupings within the division of labors that are critical to population-level fitness. This flexibility in calibrating the strength of social ties required and the varying levels of commitment to group structures is necessary in complex, differentiated societies where individuals move through different types of roles in varying types of social structures on a daily basis. Macro societies would not be possible without this flexibility.

Behavioral Propensities

All of the behavioral propensities of humans existed in great apes, as can be seen by the list in the second portion of Table 14.2 on page 353. Even language capacity, as noted above, was already present, although this language was originally visually based and, in all likelihood, was a "language of emotions" that would order emotional signals into a "body language" carrying common meanings (Turner 2000, 2007). It is this language that would enhance the interpersonal capacities of hominins to the point where the weak-tie and non-group propensities of great apes could be overcome by a complex set of interpersonal mechanisms listed in Table 14.2 and discussed below and in more detail in Chapters 12 and 13. The data are clear that selection was working on subcortical areas of the brain to increase the palette of emotions that humans could activate during interactions (Turner 2000; Barger et al. 2006, 2012, 2014).

1. *Role-Taking and Related Capacities.* All great apes can read the gestures of conspecifics (and humans as well), experience their dispositions emotionally, and determine the likely courses of action of conspecifics. They can do this visually by reading eyes and face, and they are particularly attuned, as are humans, to the emotions that are revealed. As a result, they can experience empathy with conspecifics and with humans as well. Auditory language only increases all of these interpersonal skills, but the ability to read emotions is perhaps as important as spoken language. And, great apes and hence hominins and eventually humans could do so with relative strangers. While knowing a conspecific certainly increases the ability to role-take, the fact that the dispositions and likely courses of action from relative strangers can also be read represents a very important pre-adaptation to macrosociety. If only close friends can be subject to role-taking, such a limited capacity would impose another barrier to macrosociety. But, animals that can read the gestures of strangers, and even those of another species (e.g., humans), are able to extend the range of contacts well beyond local groups and kin units.

2. *Emotions, Rhythmic Synchronization, Mimicry, and Ritual.* We know that humans, when they interact, open their encounters with rituals, fall into rhythmic synchronization of talk and bodies, mimic others' gestures, experience heightened emotions or what Emile Durkheim (1912) termed "effervescence." Much contemporary theorizing on interpersonal processes among humans emphasizes these interpersonal capacities (e.g., Goffman 1967; Collins 1975, 2004; Turner 2002, 2007). Humans inherited these behavioral capacities from the last common ancestor of hominins and great apes. What they accomplish are short-term solidarities that smooth

encounters out, and if repeated in chains of encounters, these interpersonal propensities can generate more enduring solidarities (Collins 2004). Human groups and virtually all other social structures in macrosocieties are, ultimately, created by these interpersonal practices during the course of interaction. And they are activated *anytime* humans interact; the same is true among great apes, and thus we can see these propensities of our hominin ancestors as a pre-adaptation for macrosociety. They allow humans to immediately develop lower-key, local solidarities when interacting, even with strangers.

In fact, macrosocieties are not possible without this set of interpersonal propensities that all normal human beings can execute, and while great apes did not form such societies, humans nonetheless inherited the basic capacity to interact with all others at almost any time from the great apes. Great apes reveal these capacities because selection installed them so that apes in their movements within home ranges would encounter conspecifics that they had not seen for a while, and without bioprogrammers for groupness, selection increased interpersonal skills so that conspecifics could interact and form lower-key and temporary solidarities that reinforced memberships in a community, while also sustaining weak ties.

Not only do these propensities facilitate interaction and social relationships with wide varieties of others in diverse situations, they are also one of the key mechanisms by which macrosocieties among humans become integrated. Durkheim in the second half of his career increasingly recognized that complex societies are held together by collective representations (culture) symbolized in totems, with rituals directed at these totems arousing collective emotions that bind individuals together. Most importantly, individuals at very different locations in a society's division of labor can focus on common symbols (totems) representing common cultural values and beliefs; and, then, by dramatically escalating their emotions through ritual activity, a society of strangers can become integrated. It is for this reason that Durkheim dropped completely, after 1895, his earlier notion of "mechanical vs. organic" solidarity, and the idea of a "collective conscience," in favor an emphasis on "rituals" directed by "totems" symbolizing "collective representations" as the primary mode societal integration (Durkheim 1912). This same mode is what allows chimpanzees, for example, to sustain a general sense of solidarity, without strong ties, with conspecifics in their communities. When larger numbers gather in one place, they engage in rituals, mimicry, and synchronization of bodies and vocal gestures and thereby arouse more intense emotions or experience Durkheim's "emotional effervescence" that reaffirms their membership in the larger community. Without this more generally affective attachment to larger social structures, a key condition of the sociological constraints outlined in the conclusions to Chapter 16 could not be overcome; and with it, evolved apes like humans would become capable of constructing societies that rival those of insects—even with our very large and expensive-to-maintain body plans.

3. *Reciprocity, Fairness, and Justice in Exchanges.* All great apes and higher monkeys, as well as higher mammals, reckon the fairness of exchanges in resources (Brosnan and de Waal 2014); and moreover, they are prepared to reciprocate now or in the future the receipt of resources from another. There is a kind of proto-morality built into this behavioral propensity that strengthens relationships and constrains free-riding and failure at reciprocity and fairness in the exchange of resources. When expectations of reciprocity and/or for fair exchanges are not realized, higher mammals react negatively and are prepared to sanction those who have violated these expectations. Ultimately, as humans built up moral codes with their larger neocortices and facility with spoken language, this culture-based morality was built on the neurological platform inherited by humans' hominin ancestors. As emphasized macrosocieties develop collective representations, many of which involve statements of morality, and it is the collective commitment to these moral codes, reinforced through emotion-arousing rituals, that is a pre-condition for macrosocieties. While macrosocieties can become integrated by the exchanges of resources inherent in a complex division of labor, there is almost always an underlying morality to these exchanges, and among humans, this morality is codified values, beliefs, and normative expectations that all or most in a society accept. Thus, the propensities for (a) expectations around exchanges to develop and (b) calculations of justice and fairness in exchanges to occur have existed for many millions of years in higher mammals, and particularly higher primates. And, these propensities can be seen as pre-adaptations for viable macrosocieties in which strangers in diverse social categories could exchange resources with complex divisions of labor and, at the same time, sustain a common morality—a capacity that overcomes all three of the sociological constraints enumerated in the end of Chapter 16.

4. *Individualism, Mobility, and Self.* Great apes are highly individualistic and disposed to be mobile around their larger home range. Without this propensity, a macrosociety cannot be built because individuals would be tied to local group solidarities. Macro societies are built from individuals playing specific roles in complex divisions of labor and from their willingness, even the genetically driven propensity, to move as individuals rather than groups to new positions in this division of labor. Thus, individualism is a pre-adaptation for a needed flexibility among individuals to move from

old to new status/roles and to be willing to move across space in order to do so. Markets in macrosocieties would not be very dynamic, for example, if all decisions were group-based rather than made by individuals.

A few higher mammals—humans, great apes, dolphins, probably whales, and elephants—can all do an amazing thing: They can see themselves as an object in their environment, to use G. H. Mead's (1934) phrase, vis-à-vis others in this environment (Gallup 1970, 1979, 1982). Along with this capacity comes a sense of self as an entity, perhaps helped by the individualism that some community-oriented, higher mammals possess. With a sense of self, the entire relationship among conspecifics is altered. Individuals seek to have this sense of themselves affirmed and reaffirmed by others; and behaviors are more orchestrated so as to present a self to conspecifics in ways that are likely to be positively sanctioned. And the more intelligent the animal that can have this sense of self, the more powerful is self as a mediator between self and others. Role-taking now becomes oriented to determining the self that is being presented to others, and behaviors become more orchestrated, both consciously and unconsciously, in presenting self to others.

Moreover, once a sense of self began to evolve along the hominin line, it could become the fulcrum around which social control in societies would operate. When individuals evaluate self from the perspective of moral codes as well as from the reactions of others to their self-presentation, a powerful force of social control is introduced in a society. Individuals engage in self-control in order to avoid painful emotions like humiliation, shame, embarrassment, and guilt; and this kind of self-control is a powerful integrative mechanism in societies revealing differences among individuals coordinated by a division of labor. With each person at each location in the division of labor seeking to have the self affirmed by others and by moral codings, social control moves beyond just interpersonal reactions of others toward more collective control through culture; and control of this nature has a capacity to integrate large, complex societies where individuals live and work in somewhat partitioned locations in divisions of labor but, at the same time, seek the same thing: to have the self verified.

In quickly reviewing the implications and consequences of the pre-adaptations and behavioral propensities of great apes, it is possible by the logic of cladistic analysis to not only learn a great deal about human nature as it evolved from hominin and great-ape nature, but to understand why it is that a very large animal like humans could create macrosocieties and overcome organismic constraints of very large animals and, hence, the sociological constraints of creating macrosocieties. The ecological constraints are just beginning to loom in a threatening way to any congratulatory mood that humans might have about the long-term survival of human ultrasociality. Still, we trust that the utility of studying primates and using methodological techniques such as cladistic analysis can inform sociology about why and how humans were able to create and live in macrosocieties.

Conclusion

In this chapter, we hope to have demonstrated the utility of making cross-species comparisons with an eye to what they tell us about humans and their societies. Comparisons of humans to insect societies, as was done in Chapters 15 and 16, to and great-ape societies in this chapter can provide very useful information that allows us to understand human societies. The analysis Chapter 16 on insect societies raises the question of constraints on animals if they are to organize large, complex societies that reveal a division of labor and some degree of integration. Turner and Maryanski's (2008a) analysis of primate societies provides needed information about *how humans were able to overcome these constraint*s by virtue of the legacy of pre-adaptations and behavioral propensities inherited from the last common ancestor to present-day apes and humans.

It would seem that other kinds of comparisons could be as fruitful as the two outlined in this chapter. One area of interesting comparative research would be with very intelligent birds who, with their modified reptilian brain, nonetheless reveal high levels of emotions, strong attachments to conspecifics and humans, some kind of language system, and patterns of species organization that could be very useful in understanding the biological basis of human behavior, interaction, and social organization. Another type of comparative analysis would be with aquatic mammals like dolphins/killer whales (who are not actually whales) and whales who appear to be very intelligent, who have a sense of self, and who are organized in communities. The same kind of analysis focusing on elephant societies could yield additional insights into the biology of human social organization. There is, then, a lot of potential comparative work that could be done by a *new* evolutionary sociology.

Epilogue
Prospect for a New Evolutionary Sociology

Evolutionary analysis has been part of sociology from its very beginnings; and indeed, the discipline has as long a provenance with evolutionary analysis as does biology. Yet, at the end of sociology's first hundred years after Auguste Comte gave the discipline its name, evolutionary analysis was virtually abandoned for several decades until the mid-1960s. The early stage models of societal evolution were ethnocentric, viewing western European society as the pinnacle of societal development and pre-literate societies as "primitive" by comparison, even as they inspired much sociological thinking about the evolution of societal formations. The rediscovery of Gregor Mendel's insights about the genetic basis of evolution, coupled with the eugenics movement and notions of selective breeding, killed off the sociological analysis of evolution by 1925. The result has been a very suspicious, if not hostile, reaction by many sociologists to efforts by some to bring biology and evolutionary analysis back into the discipline and, in particular, any view that biology has effects on human behavior and the organization of sociocultural formations. The rise of sociobiology in biology and the early proclamations that a science of society can be subsumed as a subfield into biology in a "new synthesis" certainly did not help efforts to bring evolutionary analysis back into sociology. Indeed, it fueled long-standing fears stemming from sociology's collective insecurities about reducing sociology to another discipline—whether biology, psychology, or economics.

We assembled the chapters in this book as one attempt to overcome these biases and fears about bringing evolutionary analysis back into sociology and, most importantly, about bringing biology into the discipline. Labeling an evolutionary sociology as racist, sexist, ethnocentric, reductionist, etc. seeks only to make sociology seem overly insecure and mired in debates that ended decades ago. Our feeling is that sociology should embrace evolutionary analysis in all of its manifestations and that it should no longer fear biology. Concern with evolution and biology can only make sociology a more robust science. Moreover, Comte's proclamations that sociology would eventually contribute to biology (as the "queen science" in his hierarchy of sciences) is no longer so fanciful in the 21st Century. Current models from biology and psychology *could use a heavy dose of sociology* to overcome their limitations, even weaknesses.

We, as the authors of this book, do not always fully agree on some of the issues, as has been apparent, but our disagreements do not lead us to reject biology, neurology, cross-species analysis, and evolutionary psychology but, instead, to embrace them for what they can add to more purely sociological explanations. Indeed, this is the rationale for writing this book: *to demonstrate that sociology can be dramatically enriched by incorporating all forms of evolutionary analysis into its canon.* Of course, evolutionary analysis, no matter how broadly conceived, cannot explain everything of interest to sociologists. Rather, the *new* evolutionary sociology, as we term the matter, should simply be seen as one set of theoretical approaches and methods that can increase the power of many, but certainly not all, sociological explanations of social phenomena.

We began in the first section with a review of the original ways that sociologists employed evolutionary analysis, with a view that these approaches have enjoyed a new hearing beginning in the 1960s. Indeed, they have been revised and revitalized in new, creative ways; and so, even as sociologists embrace new theoretical and methodological approaches, we should not forget where sociology began, and we should embrace the continued utility of stage models of societal evolution, of intersocietal analysis as it has been modified with world systems theorizing, and even a new form of functionalism. And, coupled with new forms of ecological analysis and the new methods that we introduce in Part II of this book, evolutionary sociology offers a great deal to mainstream sociology. Indeed, all of these new and revitalized approaches borrow at least some key ideas from more biological/ecological analysis: population growth, population density, competition for resources, conflict, and selection. Yet, these cannot be used in exactly the same manner as in biology/ecology because the units involved, the units under selection, and the units evolving are sociocultural formations more than populations of biological individuals (although these are also evolving as well); and once this step is taken, evolutionary sociology becomes more purely sociological and less concerned with biological models and more concerned with developing sociological models of evolutionary processes.

Part II of the book deals with the challenges posed by biology, sociobiology, and evolutionary psychology to evolutionary analysis in sociology. Our view is that the challenge is more apparent than real because the new evolutionary sociology must address Darwinian selection and the evolution of humans and populations of humans. Yet, in many respects, sociobiological approaches and evolutionary psychology have not adequately addressed the social universe as studied by sociologists. These approaches have, for example, done relatively little actual research on the evolution of primates, with specific generalizations drawn from even biological methodologies like cladistics analysis. There has been a great deal of speculation by sociobiology and evolutionary psychology on bioprogrammers in the human species and the neurological basis of these, but much of this work involves some questionable assumptions, such as kin selection, as a driving force on hominins that only very late in their evolution revealed anything like a kinship system. Other analytical approaches in sociobiology and evolutionary psychology, such as the emphasis on reciprocity and reciprocal altruism, have more merit, but here, the issues and dynamics are not conceptualized in quite the same way as in sociology. Still, the goals of both sociobiology and evolutionary psychology should be one of, but not the only, goal of the new evolutionary sociology: to discover the biological and neurological bases of innate human behaviors, as honed by natural selection during the course of hominin evolution. Indeed, Part III of the book presents some of our best suggestions for how this goal can be best realized.

As sociologists, we should resist viewing sociocultural formations as direct manifestations of evolved behavioral propensities; rather, human behaviors are always a mix of evolved biological traits *and* evolved sociocultural formations. Thus, for sociologists, individual behaviors, no matter how fundamentally embedded in the human genome, cannot explain social structure and culture in a manner that would satisfy most sociologists. There are emergent properties to sociocultural formations that operate independently of biological dynamics and forces, and they reveal complex interaction effects with the behaviors of individuals. Even something like a rate of a particular behavior (which is, in essence, aggregated individual behaviors) is also influenced by the varying social experiences of persons in many diverse kinds of sociocultural formations. Thus, the new evolutionary sociology should assiduously avoid proposing "just-so stories" and, instead, seek to tease out what is biologically based as an evolved trait and what is socioculturally based as an evolved sociologically based trait. And only then should we engage in analysis of the interaction effects of what is biologically and socioculturally based. Explanations will be more complex, to be sure, but they will be more robust. The notion of co-evolution was invented to emphasize this point, but it often has been subverted to quick extrapolations from presumed behaviors, giving short shrift to analyses of cultural and social structural forces.

As we emphasized in Chapters 10 and 11, Darwinian/biological analysis can only take us so far. Biology cannot explain all that is of interest to sociologists, although biologists and evolutionary psychologists can, within the purview of their respective disciplines, be content with such explanations in terms of evolved individual traits directing behavior. As the study of social behavior *and* social organization, *and* the cultural constraints on behavior and organization, sociology cannot stop where biology and evolutionary psychology should stop (but often do not). Sociology is not just the study of alleles and their effects on human behaviors; it is the study of the dynamics of sociocultural formations, and as a result of this emphasis, a great deal changes in the way evolutionary analysis is conducted. The units of selection change, the types of selection change, and the nature of selection become multi-level. Selection works on groups and other corporate units built into institutional domains, societies, and systems of societies. Thus, a sociologically oriented evolutionary analysis is about the dynamics of culture and social structure rather than just individual behaviors. Of course, most of what sociology tries to study is, to be sure, influenced by natural selection, and perhaps even group selection in the biological sense, but the subject matter of sociology is even more influenced by the emergent properties and inherent dynamics of social structure and culture. And the nature of biological evolution also changes once the genome is embedded in more than a biological phenotype and, instead, in multiple layers of sociocultural formations that have been created by humans by virtue of their capacities for agency.

It is probably true that early efforts in sociobiology and evolutionary psychology over-reached in their explanations, but such is much less the case today; and it is time that sociologists engaged their colleagues in biology, ecology, and evolutionary psychology. Sociology need not fear its "reduction" to another science; in fact, just the opposite should be the case. As we explained in relation to our discussions of comparative sociology, behavioral biologists now take into account emergent properties of non-human animal societies, an analytical approach that rejects simplistic reductionistic explanations of animal social behavior. Sociologists well trained in biological analysis should perhaps challenge some of the orthodox assumptions in biology and psychology, and out of such debates all fields can benefit.

The last part of the book—Part III—reviews some of the approaches that have appealed to the authors. Certainly the Machalek side of the authorship is far more sympathetic to taking sociobiology and evolutionary psychology as far as it can be taken in sociology; the Turner side of authorship sees this tendency as often over-reaching and ignoring the vast literature on sociocultural dynamics that has accumulated in sociology's 200 years as an explicit discipline with a name: sociology. Still, the authors are in complete agreement on the importance of comparative analysis, in number of forms. For Turner and his frequent co-author, Alexandra Maryanski, the comparative analysis should focus on studying humans closest living relatives—great apes—and performing cladistic analysis and then evolutionary analysis on hominins to address the very questions that sociobiologists and evolutionary psychologists also seek to answer. But, as is evident in Chapters 12, 13, 14, and 17, Turner and Maryanski's analyses look very different from those developed in sociobiology and evolutionary psychology, even though we are using biological methods to try to understand how the brain of hominins was rewired to produce genetically driven capacities and behavior propensities that affect patterns of human social organization. Why should this be so? The obvious but not trivial answer is that *we are sociologists* and remain aware of sociological literatures that are all too often ignored by biologists and evolutionary psychologists.

The Machalek side of this co-authorship develops another type of comparative analysis, emphasizing comparisons across species to see what insights their behavioral and organizational patterns can offer sociological analysis of human behaviors and organizational patterns. The emphasis on megasociality is an important one because one of the most amazing feats of humans is the creation of very large societies organizing a very large animal. Comparisons with other, much smaller life forms like insects, and perhaps even plant life, can be informative because, as is outlined in Chapters 15 and 16, great insight can be achieved by examining design problems and solutions to these problems that are only possible by undertaking true cross-species analysis.

In a very real way, both Comte and Spencer advocated this kind of cross-species analysis; indeed, Spencer defined sociology as the study of superorganisms, or the organization of organisms into societies. The study of superorganisms is, therefore, inherently sociological in nature; and Machalek's and Turner's respective efforts in Chapters 16 and 17 represent different cross-species comparative approaches that can produce insights not only about non-human forms of megasociality, but about large-scale human societies as well.

This book has been written with a dual purpose. One purpose has been to convince our fellow sociologists that they should not fear evolutionary analysis, even when it is Darwinian and biological (including neurological). Such analyses is not about to gobble up sociology; indeed, just the opposite. A biologically informed sociology can extend its reach and influence to other life sciences, including behavioral biology. Another goal of the book has been to juxtapose evolutionary approaches—revitalized ones in Part I and more recent ones in Part III. Thus, Parts I and III can be seen as book ends that make the approaches offered in biology and psychology in Part II more sociologically relevant. As noted, the authors do not fully agree on the value of sociobiology and evolutionary psychology for the new evolutionary sociology, and Turner is more critical of these two disciplines than is Machalek. However, the critique provided should, at minimum, encourage devotees of other disciplines to learn some sociology. Sociology does have something positive to add to biology and psychology, just as biology and evolutionary psychology have very useful ideas to offer sociology, but *the basic subject matters of these disciplines are different*. And these differences are profound because they change the way in which sociologists do evolutionary analysis—from the very beginnings of the discipline with Comte and Spencer right up to the present day. E. O. Wilson's early work on human sociobiology appeared to many sociologists as a naïve over-reach. Subsequently, however, his work, especially in volumes such as *The Social Conquest of Earth*, attempts to draw upon information available from the social sciences. At the very least, Wilson's *Sociobiology* was also a call to sociology to embrace its roots in evolutionary analysis, to begin learning some biology, and to use such knowledge in sociology.

Evolutionary analysis cannot explain everything in sociology; it is just one of many approaches and angles by which we can gain insight into sociocultural phenomena. We should use it where appropriate, and use alternative modes of explanation when they seem more appropriate. But, we should not reject our heritage as a discipline born at a time when evolutionary analysis in biology made great strides; the sense of many early sociologists was that evolution is a fundamental property of the sociocultural universe. Now, just as those who seek to explain sociological phenomena in evolutionary terms should learn some sociology, so sociologists should begin to learn some evolutionary biology and psychology.

Bibliography

Abrutyn, Seth, and Jonathan H. Turner. 2011. "The Old Institutionalism Meets the New Institutionalism." *Sociological Perspectives* 54: 283–306.
Alcock, John. 2001. *The Triumph of Sociobiology*. Oxford: Oxford University Press.
———. 2013. *Animal Behavior: An Evolutionary Approach*. Sunderland, MA: Sinauer Associates.
———. 2015. "Where Do We Stand with Respect to Evolutionary Studies of Human Behavior?" In *Handbook on Evolution and Society: Toward an Evolutionary Social Science*, edited by Jonathan H. Turner, Richard Machalek, and Alexandra Maryanski, 157–76. New York, NY: Paradigm/Routledge.
Alcorta, Candace S., and Richard Sosis. 2005. "Ritual, Emotion, and Sacred Symbols." *Human Nature* 16 (4): 323–59.
Aldecoa, John. 2016. "Integration or Social Control: A Neurosociological Analysis of Religious Rituals in Human Evolution." M.A thesis, Department of Sociology, University of California, Riverside.
Alexander, Richard D. 1979. *Darwinism and Human Affairs*. Seattle, WA: University of Washington Press.
Andrews, P. A. 1981. "Species Diversity and Diet in Monkeys and Apes During the Miocene." In *Aspects of Human Evolution*, edited by C. B. Stringer. London: Taylor and Francis.
———. 1989. "Palaeoecology and Laetoli." *Journal of Human Evolution* 18: 173–81.
———. 1996. "Palaeoecology and Hominoid Palaeoenvironments." *Biological Review* 71: 257–300.
Andrews, P. A., S. W. Gangestad, G. F. Miller, M. G. Haselton, R. Thornhill, and M. C. Neale. 2008. "Sex Differences in Detecting Sexual Infidelity: Results of a Maximum Likelihood Method for Analyzing the Sensitivity to Sex Differences to Underreporting." *Human Nature* 19: 347–73.
Andrews, P. A., and J. Kelley. 2007. "Species Diversity and Diet in Monkeys and Apes During the Miocene." In *Aspects of Human Evolution*, edited by C. B. Stringer. London: Taylor & Francis.
Andrews, P. A., and L. Martin. 1987. Cladistic Relationships of Extant and Fossil Hominoids. *Journal of Human Evolution* 16: 101–18.
Ardrey, Robert. 1961. *African Genesis: A Personal Investigation Into the Animal Origins and Nature of Man*. New York, NY: Collins.
———. 1966. *The Territorial Imperative*. New York, NY: Dell.
Arrighi, Giovanni. 1994. *The Long Twentieth Century*. London: Verso.
Axelrod, Robert. 1984. *The Evolution of Cooperation*. New York, NY: Basic Books.
Bailey, Kenneth E. 1989. *Social Entropy Theory*. Albany, NY: SUNY Press.
Baizer, J. S., J. F. Baker, K. Haas, and R. Lima. 2007. "Neurochemical Organization of the Nucleus *Paramedinaus Dorsalis* in the Human." *Brain Research* 1176: 45–52.

Baker, R. Robin, and Mark A. Bellis. 1995. *Human Sperm Competition*. London: Chapman & Hall.

Baldwin, P. J. 1979. *The Natural History of the Chimpanzee (pan troglodytes verus) at mt. assirik, Senegal*. Ph.D. Thesis, University of Stirling, Scotland.

Baldwin, P. W., C. McGrew, and C. Tutin. 1982. "Wide-Ranging Chimpanzees at Mt. Assirik, Senegal." *International Journal of Primatology* 3: 367–85.

Barger, Nicole, Kari L. Hanson, Kate Teffer, Natalie M. Schenker-Ahmed, and Katerina Semendeferi. 2014. "Evidence for Evolutionary Specialization in the Human Limbic Structures." *Frontiers in Human Neuroscience* 8 (Article 277).

Barger, Nicole., L. Stefanacci, C. M. Schumann, C. C. Sherwood, J. Anneses, J. M. Allman, J. A. Buckwalter, P. R. Hof, and K. Semendeferi. 2012. "Neuronal Populations in the Basolateral Nuclei of the Amygdala Increases in Humans Compared to Apes: A Stereological Study." *The Journal Comparative Neurology* 520: 3035–54.

Barger, Nicole, L. Stefanacci, and K. Semendeferi. 2006. "Comparative Volumetric Analysis of the Amygdaloid Complex and Basolateral Division of the Human and Ape Brain." *American Journal of Physical Anthropology* 134: 392–403.

Barnard, C. J. ed. 1984. *Producers and Scroungers: Strategies of Exploitation and Parasitism*. New York, NY: Chapman and Hall.

Baron, D. N. 1995. "Credit Unions." In *Organizations in Industry*, edited by G. Carroll and M. T. Hannan, 137–61. New York, NY: Oxford University Press.

Barraza, Jorge A., and Paul J. Zak. 2009. "Empathy Toward Strangers Triggers Oxytocin Release and Subsequent Generosity." *Annals of the New York Academy of Sciences* 1167 (1): 182–89.

Beckoff, Marc, and Jessica Pierce. 2009. *Wild Justice: The Moral Lives of Animals*. Chicago, IL: University of Chicago Press.

Bellah, R. N. 2011a. "Nothing is Ever Lost." An Interview with Robert Bellah. Interview by Nathan Schneider posted on the *Immanent Frame: Secularism, Religion, and the Public Sphere* 14.09.2011 (seen 21.01.2016).

———. 2011b. *Religion in Human Evolution: From the Paleolithic to the Axial Age*. Cambridge, MA: Harvard University Press.

Bickerton, D. 2003. "Symbol and Structure: A Comprehensive Framework for Language Evolution." In *Language Evolution: The States of the Art*, edited by M. S. Christiansen and S. Kirby, 77–93. Oxford: Oxford University Press.

Birkhead, T. R., T. Burke, R. Zann, F. M. Hunter, and A. P. Krupa. 1990. "Extra-Pair Paternity and Intraspecific Brood Parasitism in Wild Zebra Finches *Taeniopygi guttata*, Revealed by DNA Fingerprinting." *Behavioral Ecology and Sociobiology* 27: 315–24.

Blau, Peter M. 1964. *Exchange and Power in Social Life*. New York, NY: Wiley-Blackwell.

———. 1977. *Inequality and Heterogeneity: A Primitive Theory of Social Structure*. New York, NY: The Free Press.

———. 1993. *Structural Context of Opportunities*. Chicago, IL: University of Chicago Press.

Boehm, C. 2013. *Moral Origins: The Evolution of Virtue, Altruism, and Shame*. New York, NY: Basic Books.

Booth, A., A. Mazur, and K. Kivlighan. 2006. "Testosterone and Social Behavior." *Social Forces* 85: 167–91.

Boulding, Kenneth. 1956. *The Image*. Ann Arbor, MI: University of Michigan Press.

———. 1978. *Ecodynamics: A New Theory of Societal Evolution*. Beverly Hills, CA: Sage.

———. 1981. *A Preface to Grants Economics: The Economy of Love and Fear*. Westport, CT: Praeger Publisher.

Boyd, Robert, and Peter Richerson. 1985. *Culture and the Evolutionary Process*. Chicago, IL: University of Chicago Press.
Boyer, Pl. 2001. *Religion Explained: The Evolutionary Origins of Religious Thought*. New York, NY: Basic Books.
Bradley, B. 2008. "Reconstructing Phylogenies and Phenotypes: A Molecular View of Human Evolution." *Journal of Anatomy* 212: 337–53.
Bradley, B., M. Robbins, E. Williamson, H. Steklis, N. Steklis, N. Eckhardt, C. Boesch, and L. Vigilant. 2005. "Mountain Gorilla Tug-of-War: Silverbacks Have Limited Control Over Reproduction in Multimale Groups." *PNAS* 102: 9418–23.
Braudel, Fernand. 1972. *The Mediterranean and the Mediterranean World in the Age of Philip II*, two volumes. New York, NY: Harper and Row.
———. 1975. *Capitalism and Material Life, 1400–1800*. New York, NY: Harper and Row.
———. 1977. *Afterthoughts on Material Civilization and Capitalism*. Baltimore, MD: Johns Hopkins University Press.
———. 1979 [1982]. *Wheels of Commerce: Civilization and Capitalism, 15th–18th Century*. New York, NY: Harper-Collins.
Brockmann, H. J., A. Grafen, and R. Dawkins. 1979. "Evolutionary Stable Nesting Strategy in a Digger Wasp." *Journal of Theoretical Biology* 77: 473–96.
Brosnan, Sarah F., and Frans B. M. de Waal. 2003. "Fair Refusal by Capuchin Monkeys." *Nature* 128–40.
———. 2014. "Evolution of Responses to (Un)Fairness." *Science* 346 (6207): 125776–1–5.
Brosnan, Sarah F., Hillary C. Schiff, and Frans B. M. de Waal. 2005. "Tolerance for Inequity May Increase With Social Closeness in Chimpanzees." *Proceedings of the Royal Society of London* 272: 253–58.
Brown, C. R., and M. B. Brown. 1990. "Behavioral Dynamics of Intraspecific Brood Parasitism in Colonial Cliff Swallows." *Animal Behavior* 37: 777–96.
Brown, Steven. 2000. "The 'Musilanguage' Model of Music Evolution." In *The Origins of Music*, edited by N. Wallins, 271–300. Cambridge, MA: MIT Press.
Buckley, Walter. 1967. *Sociology and Modern Systems Theory*. Englewood Cliffs, NJ: Prentice Hall.
Burghardt, Gordon. 2005. *The Genesis of Animal Play: Testing the Limits*. Cambridge, MA: MIT Press.
Burke, Peter J., and Jan E. Stets. 2009. *Identity Theory*. New York, NY: Oxford University Press.
Buss, David M. 1989. "Sex Differences in Human Mate Preferences: Evolutionary Hypotheses Testing in 37 Cultures." *Behavioral and Brain Sciences* 12: 1–49.
———. 2000. *The Dangerous Passion: Why Jealousy Is as Necessary as Love and Sex*. New York, NY: Guilford Press.
———. 2003. *The Evolution of Desire: Strategies of Human Mating* (Revised Edition). New York, NY: Free Press.
———. 2016a. *Evolutionary Psychology: The New Science of the Mind* (Fifth Edition). New York, NY: Routledge.
———. ed. 2016b. *The Handbook of Evolutionary Psychology, Second Edition, Volume 1 Foundations. Volume 2 Integrations*. Hoboken, NJ: John Wiley & Sons.
Buss, David M., M. Abbott, A. Angleitner, A. Asherian, A. Biaggio, and 45 other Co-Authors. 1990. "International Preferences in Selecting Mates: A Study of 37 Cultures." *Journal of Cross-Cultural Psychology* 21: 5–47.
Buss, David M., and L. A. Dedden. 1990. "Derogation of Competitors." *Journal of Social and Personal Relationships* 7: 395–422.

Buss, David M., and David P. Schmitt. 1993. "Sexual Strategies Theory: An Evolutionary Perspective on Human Mating." *Psychological Review* 100: 204–32.
Call, Josep, and Michael Tomasello. 2007. *The Gestural Communication of Apes and Monkeys*. Mahwah, NJ: Lawrence Erlbaum Associates.
———. 2008. "Do Chimpanzees Have a Theory of Mind: 30 Years Later." *Trends in Cognitive Science* 12: 187–92.
Campbell, Anne. 2010. "Oxytocin and Human Social Behavior." *Personality and Social Psychology Review* 20 (10): 1–15.
Campbell, C., A. Fuentes, K. Mackinnon, S. Bearder, and R. Stumpf. 2011. *Primates in Perspective*. Oxford: Oxford University Press.
Campbell, Lorne and Timothy J. Loving. 2016. "Love and Commitment in Romantic Relationships." In *The Handbook of Evolutionary Psychology, Second Edition, Volume 1 Foundations*, edited by David M. Buss, 482–98. Hoboken, NJ: John Wiley & Sons.
Cangialosi, K. R. 1990. "Social Spider Defense Against Kleptoparasitism." *Behavioral Ecology and Sociobiology* 27: 49–54.
Carey, A. D., and J. Lopreato. 1995. "The Evolutionary Demography of the Fertility-Mortality Quasi-Equilibrium." *Population and Development Review* 21: 726–36.
Carroll, G. R. 1983. "Organizational Ecology." *Annual Review of Sociology* 10: 71–93.
———. 1988. *Ecological Models of Organizations*. Cambridge, MA: Ballinger.
———. 1994. "Dynamics of Publisher Succession in the Newspaper Industry." *Administrative Science Quarterly* 29: 93–113.
———. 1997. "Long-Term Evolutionary Change in Organizational Populations." *Industrial and Corporate Change* 6: 119–43.
Carroll, G. R., and J. Delacroix. 1982. "Organizational Mortality in the Newspaper Industry of Argentina and Ireland: An Ecological Approach." *Administrative Science Quarterly* 27: 169–98.
Carter, Gerald G., and Gerald S. Wilkinson. 2013. "Food Sharing in Vampire Bats: Reciprocal Help Predicts Donations More Than Relatedness or Harassment." *Proceedings of the Royal Society* 280: 20122573.
Caspi, A., J. McClay, T. E. Moffitt, J. Mill, J. Martin, I. W. Craig, A. Taylor, and R. Poulton. 2002. "Role of Genotype in the Cycle of Violence in Maltreated Children." *Science* 297: 851–54.
Cervo, R., M. C. Lorenzi, and S. Turillazzi. 1990. "Nonaggressive Usurpation of the Nest of *Polistes bigulmis bimaculatus* by the Social Parasite *Sulcopolistes atrimandibularis* (Hymenoptera Vespidae)." *Insectes Sociaus/Social Insects* 37: 333–47.
Chagnon, Napoleon A. 1988. "Life Histories, Blood Revenge, and Warfare in a Tribal Population." *Science* 239: 985–92.
Chapais, B. 2008. *Primeval Kinship: How Pair-Bonding Gave Birth to Human Society*. Cambridge, MA: Harvard University Books.
Chase, Ivan D. 1974. "Models of Hierarchy Formation in Animal Societies." *Behavioral Science* 19: 374–82.
———. 1980. "Social Process and Hierarchy Formation in Small Groups: A Comparative Perspective." *American Sociological Review* 45: 905–24.
———. 1991. "Vacancy Chains." *Annual Review of Sociology* 17: 133–54.
———. 2012. "Life is a Shell Game." *Scientific American* 306: 76–79.
Chase, Ivan D., Costanza Bartolomeo, and Lee A. Dugatkins. 1994. "Aggressive Interactions and Inter-Contest Interval: How Long Do Winners Keep Winning?" *Animal Behavior* 48: 393–400.

Chase, Ivan D., and W. Brent Lindquist. 2016. "The Fragility of Individual-Based Explanations of Social Hierarchies: A Test Using Animal Pecking Orders." *PLoS ONE* 11 (7): e0158900. doi:10.1331/journal.pone.0158900

Chase, Ivan. D., and Theodore H. DeWitt. 1988a. "Vacancy Chains: A Process of Mobility to New Resources in Humans and Other Animals." *Social Science Information* 27: 83–98.

Chase, Ivan D., Craig Tovey, and Peter Murch. 2003. "Two's Company, Three's a Crowd: Differences in Dominance Relationships in Isolated Versus Socially Embedded Pairs of Fish." *Behaviour* 140: 1193–217.

Chase, Ivan D., Craig Tovey, Debra Spangler-Martin, and Michael Manfredonia. 2002. "Individual Differences Versus Social Dynamics in the Formation of Animal Dominance Hierarchies." *Proceedings of the National Academy of Sciences* 99 (8): 5744–49.

Chase, Ivan D., M. Weissburg, and Theodore H. DeWitt. 1988b. "The Vacancy Chain Process: A New Mechanism of Resource Allocation in Animals With Application to Hermit Crabs." *Animal Behavior* 36: 1265–74.

Chase-Dunn, Christopher. 1998. *Global Formation: Structures of the World Economy*. Lanham, MD: Rowman & Littlefield.

———. 2001. "World Systems Analysis." In *The Handbook of Theoretical Sociology*, edited by J. H. Turner, 589–612. New York, NY: Plenum.

Chase-Dunn, Christopher, and Thomas D. Hall. eds. 1991. *Core/Periphery Relations in Precapitalist Worlds*. Boulder, CO: Westview Press.

———. 1992. "Comparing World-Systems: Concepts and Working Hypotheses." *Social Forces* 71 (4): 851–86.

———. 1997. *Rise and Demise: Comparing World-Systems*. Boulder, CO: Westview Press.

Chase Dunn, Christopher, and Hiroki Inoue. 2016. "Spirals of Sociocultural Evolution Within Polities and Inter-Polity Systems." Working paper, Institute for World Systems Research, UC Riverside.

Chase-Dunn, Christopher, and Bruce Lerro. 2014. *Social Change: Globalization From the Stone Age to the Present*. New York, NY: Paradigm/Routledge.

Chase-Dunn, Christopher, and Kelly M. Mann. 1998. *The Wintu and Their Neighbors: A Very Small World-System in Northern California*. Tucson: University of Arizona Press.

Chase-Dunn, Christopher, Susan Manning, and Thomas D. Hall. 1998. "Rise and Fall: East-West Synchrony and Indic Exceptionalism Reexamined." *Social Science History* 24 (4): 727–54.

Chase-Dunn, Christopher, and Alice Willard. 1993. "Systems of Cities and World-Systems: Settlement Size, Hierarchy, and Cycles of Political Centralization, 2000–1998 AD." Paper presented at International Studies Association meetings, March 24.

———. 1994. "Cities in the Central Political-Military Network Since CE 1200." *Comparative Civilizations Review* 30: 104–32.

Chatterjee, H., S. Ho, Ian Barnes, and Colin Groves. 2009. "Estimating the Phylogeny and Divergence Times of Primates Using a Supermatrix Approach." *BMC Evolutionary Biology* 9: 259–78.

Clark, C. 1987. "Sympathy Biography and Sympathy Margin." *American Journal of Sociology* 93: 290–321.

———. 1990. *Misery Loves Company: Sympathy in Everyday Life*. Chicago, IL: University of Chicago Press.

Clutton-Brock, T. 2009. "Cooperation Between Non-Kin in Animal Societies." *Nature* 462: 51–57.

Cohen, Lawrence E., and Kenneth C. Land. 1987. "Age Structure and Crime: Symmetry Versus Asymmetry and the Projection of Crime Rates Through 1990." *American Sociological Review* 52: 170–83.

Cohen, Lawrence E., and Richard Machalek. 1988. "A General Theory of Expropriative Crime: An Evolutionary Ecological Approach." *American Journal of Sociology* 94 (3): 465–501.

———. 1994. "The Normalcy of Crime: From Durkheim to Evolutionary Ecology." *Rationality and Society* 6: 286–308.

Coleman, James S. 1990. *Foundations of Social Theory*. Cambridge, MA: Belknap.

Collins, Randall. 1975. *Conflict Sociology: Toward an Explanatory Science*. New York, NY: Academic Press.

———. 1981. *Sociology Since Midcentury*. New York, NY: Academic Press.

———. 1986. *Weberian Sociological Theory*. Cambridge and New York, NY: Cambridge University Press.

———. 2004. *Interaction Ritual Chains*. Princeton, NJ: Princeton University Press.

———. 2008. *Violence: A Micro-Sociological Theory*. Princeton, NJ: Princeton University Press.

Comte, Auguste. 1830–1942 [1986]. *The Positive Philosophy of Auguste Comte*, 3 volumes, condensed and translated by H. Maritineau. London: George Bell.

———. 1851 [1875] *System of Positive Polity or Treatise on Sociology*. London: Burt Franklin.

Cooley, Charles Horton. 1902. *Human Nature and the Social Order*. New York, NY: Scribner.

Coser, Lewis A. 1956. *The Functions of Social Conflict*. London: Free Press.

Cosmides, Leda. 1989. "The Logic of Social Exchange: Has Natural Selection Shaped How Humans Reason?" *Cognition* 31: 187–276.

Cosmides, Leda, and John Tooby. 1992. "Cognitive Adaptations for Social Exchange." In *The Adapted Mind: Evolutionary Psychology and the Generation of Culture*, edited by J. H. Barkow, L. Cosmides, and J. Tooby, 163–228. New York, NY: Oxford University Press.

Cousins, A. J. and S. W. Gangestad. 2007. "Perceived Threats of Female Infidelity, Male Proprietariness, and Violence in Dating Couples." *Violence and Victims* 22: 651–68.

Crippen, Timothy. 2015. "The Evolution of Tenuous Pair-Bonding in Humans: A Plausible Pathway." In *Handbook on Evolution and Society: Toward an Evolutionary Social Science*, edited by Jonathan H. Turner, Richard Machalek, and Alexandra Maryanski, 402–21. New York, NY: Paradigm/Routledge.

Dahrendorf, Ralf. 1959. *Class and Class Conflict in Industrial Society*. Stanford, CA: Stanford University Press.

Daly, Martin, and Margo Wilson. 1988. *Homicide*. Hawthorne, NY: Aldine de Gruyter.

Damasio, Antonio. 1994. *Descartes' Error: Emotion, Reason, and the Human Brain*. New York, NY: G. P. Putman.

Damasio, Antonio, and Norman Geschwind. 1984. "The Neural Basis of Language." *Annual Review of Neuroscience* 7: 127–47.

Darwin, Charles. 1859 [1958]. *On the Origin of Species, By Means of Natural Selection*. New York, NY: New American Library.

———. [1875] 1871. *The Descent of Man and Selection in Relation to Sex*. New York, NY: D. Appleton and Co.

———. 1872. *The Expression of Emotions in Man and Animals*. London: John Murray.

Dawkins, Richard. 1976. *The Selfish Gene*. Oxford: Oxford University Press.

———. 1982. *The Extended Phenotype: The Gene as the Unit of Selection*. Oxford: W. H. Freeman and Company.

———. 1989. *The Selfish Gene*. (New Edition). Oxford: Oxford University Press.

———. 2015. *Brief Candle in the Dark: My Life in Science*. New York, NY: HarperCollins Publishers.
Deacon, T. W. 1997. "What Makes the Human Brain Different?" *Annual Review of Anthropology* 26: 189–93.
Decety, Jean, and Jessica A. Sommerville. 2003. "Shared Representations Between Self and Other: A Social Cognitive Neuroscience View." *Trends in Cognitive Sciences* 7 (12): 527–33.
Dennett, Daniel C. 2003. *Freedom Evolves*. New York, NY: Viking.
Dewey, John. 1922. *Human Nature and Social Conduct*. New York, NY: Henry Holt.
Dickinson, Janis. L., and Ronald L. Rutowski. 1989. "The Function of the Mating Plug in the Chalcedon Checkerspot Butterfly." *Animal Behaviour* 38 (1): 154–62.
Disotell, T. 2012. "Archaic Human Genomics." *Yearbook of Physical Anthropology* 55: 24–39.
Dobrev, S. D., T. Y. Kim, and G. R. Carroll. 2003. "Shifting Gears, Shifting Niches: Organizational Inertia and Change in the Evolution of the Automobile Industry, 1885–1981." *Organizational Science* 22: 264–82.
Donald, Merlin. 1991. *Origins of the Modern Mind: Three Stages in the Evolution of Culture and Cognition*. Cambridge, MA: Harvard University Press.
———. 2001. *A Mind So Rare: The Evolution of Human Consciousness*. New York, NY: Norton.
Drea, Christine M. 2005. "Bateman Revisited: The Reproductive Tactics of Female Primates." *Integrative & Comparative Biology* 45 (5): 915–23.
Duchin, Linda. 1990. "The Evolution of Articulate Speech: Comparative Anatomy of the Oral Cavity in Pan and Homo." *Journal of Human Evolution* 19: 687–97.
Dugas-Ford, Jennifer, and Clifton W. Ragsdale. 2015. "Levels of Homology and the Problem of Neocortex." *Annual Review of Neuroscience* 38: 351–68. Neuro.annualreviews.org.
Dunbar, Robin. 1996. *Grooming, Gossip and the Evolution of Language*. London: Faber and Faber.
Dunn, Mathew. 2016. "Reviving the Organismic Analogy in Sociology: Human Society as a Social Organism." Ph.D. dissertation, UC Riverside.
Durkheim, Emile. 1893 [1933]. *The Division of Labor in Society*. New York, NY: The Free Press.
———. 1895 [1966]. *The Rules of the Sociological Method*. New York, NY: The Free Press.
———. 1897 [1951]. *Suicide*. New York, NY: The Free Press.
———. 1912 [1965]. *The Elementary Forms of the Religious Life*. New York, NY: The Free Press.
Durkheim, Emile, and M. Mauss. 1903 [1963]. *Primitive Classification*. Chicago, IL: University of Chicago Press.
Eibl-Eibesfeldt, Iranaus. 1996. *Love and Hate: The Natural History of Behavior Patterns*. New York, NY: Aldine de Gruyter.
Eccles, J. C. 1989. *Evolution of the Brain: Creation of Self*. London: Routledge.
Ekeh, Peter. 1974. *Social Exchange Theory: The Two Traditions*. Cambridge, MA: Harvard University Press.
Ekman, Paul. 1984. "Expression and The Nature of Emotion." In *Approaches to Emotion*, edited by K. Scherer and P. Edman, 319–43. Hillsdale, NJ: Lawrence Erlbaum.
Elgar, M. A. 1989. "Kleptoparasitism: A Cost of Aggregating for an Orb-Weaving Spider." *Animal Behavior* 37: 1052–55.
Ellis, B. J. 1992. "The Evolution of Sexual Attraction: Evaluative Mechanisms in Women." In *The Adapted Mind: Evolutionary Psychology and the Generation of Culture*, edited by

Jerome H. Barkow, Leda Cosmides, and John Tooby, 267–88. New York, NY: Oxford University Press.
Emde, Robert N. 1962. "Level of Meaning for Infant Emotions: A Biosocial View." In *Development of Cognition, Affect and Social Relations*, edited by W. A. Collins, 1–37. Hillsdale, NJ: Lawrence Erlbaum.
Emerson, Richard M. 1972. "Exchange Theory, Part I: A Psychological Basis for Social Exchange; Exchange Theory, Part II: Exchange Relations and Network Structures." In *Sociological Theories in Progress*, edited by J. Berger, M. Zelditch, and B. Anderson, 38–87. New York, NY: Houghton-Mifflin.
Enard, W. 1978. "Myths About Hunter-Gatherers." *Ethnology* 17: 439–48.
Enard, W., P. Khaitovich, J. Klose, S. Zollner, F. Heissig, P. Giavalisco, K. Nieselt-Struwe, E. Muchmore, A. Varki, R. Ravid, G. M. Doxiadis, R. E. Bonttrop, and S. Paabo. 2002. "Intra-and Interspecific Variation in Primate Gene Expression Patterns." *Science* 296: 340–42.
Enard, W., M. Przeworski, M. S. Fisher, L. Lai, C.S.L. Wiebe, V. Takashi Kitano, A. P. Monaco, and S. Paabo. 2002. "Molecular Revolution of FOXP2, A Gene Involved in Speech and Language." *Nature* 418: 869–72.
Epstein, Joshua M., and Robert Axtell. 1996. *Growing Artificial Societies: Social Science from the Bottom Up*. Washington, DC: Brookings Institution Press.
Estes, Richard D. and John Goddard. 1967. "Prey Selection and Hunting Behavior of the African Wild Dog." *The Journal of Wildlife Management* 31 (1): 52–70.
Ettlinger, G. 1977. "Cross-Modal Equivalence in Non-Human Primates." In *Behavioral Primatology, Volume 1*, edited by A. M. Schriver. Hillsdale, NJ: Erlbaum.
Falk, Dean. 2000. *Primate Diversity*. New York, NY: W. W. Norton.
———. 2007. "The Evolution of Broca's Area, IBRO History of Neuroscience." www.ibro.info/Pub/Pub_Main_Display.asp?LC_Docs_ID=3145.
———. 2010. *The Fossil Chronicles: How Two Controversial Discoveries Changed Our Views of Human Evolution*. Berkeley, CA: University of California Press.
———. 2016. "Evolution of the Primate Brain." In *Handbook of Paleoanthropology*, edited by W. Henke and I. Tattersall, 1495–525. New York, NY: Springer.
Fashing, Peter. 2011. "African Colobine Monkeys." In *Primates in Perspective*, edited by C. Campbell, A. Fuentes, K. Mackinnon, S. Bearder, and R. Stumpf. New York, NY: Oxford University Press.
Faught, J. 1986. "The Concept of Competition in Robert Park's Sociology." *Sociological Quarterly* 27: 140–48.
Feingold, A. 1992. "Gender Differences in Mate Selection Preferences: A Test of the Parental Investment Model." *Psychological Bulletin* 112: 125–39.
Festinger, Leon. 1957. *A Theory of Cognitive Dissonance*. Evanston, IL: Northwestern University Press.
Fisher, Helen E. 1992. *Anatomy of Love: The Natural History of Monogamy, Adultery, and Divorce*. New York, NY: W. W. Norton and Company.
———. 2004. *Why We Love: The Nature and Chemistry of Romantic Love*. New York, NY: Henry Holt Company.
Fisher, R. A. 1930. *The Genetical Theory of Natural Selection*. Oxford: Clarendon.
Fiske, A. P. 1991. *Structures of Social Life*. New York, NY: The Free Press.
Fletcher, David J. C., and Charles D. Michener. eds. 1987. *Kin Recognition in Animals*. New York, NY: John Wiley & Sons.
Fletcher, G. J. O., J. A. Simpson, L. Campbell, and N. C. Overall. 2014. *The Science of Intimate Relationships*. Malden, MA: Wiley-Blackwell.

———. 2015. "Pair-bonding, Romantic Love, and Evolution: The Curious Case of *Homo sapiens*." *Perspectives on Psychological Science* 10: 20–36.
Forbes, C. S. 1991. "Intraspecific Piracy in Ospreys." *The Wilson Bulletin* 103: 111–12.
Fox, Robin. 2015. "Marry in or Die Out: Optimal Inbreeding and the Meaning of Mediogamy." In *Handbook on Evolution and Society: Toward an Evolutionary Social Science*, edited by Jonathan H. Turner, Richard Machalek, and Alexandra Maryanski, 350–82. New York, NY: Paradigm/Routledge.
Frank, Andre Gunder. 1969. *Latin America: Underdevelopment or Revolution?* New York, NY: Monthly Review Press.
———. 1978. *World Accumulation, 1492–1789*. New York, NY: Monthly Review Press.
———. 1979. *Dependent Accumulation and Underdevelopment*. New York, NY: Monthly Review Press.
———. 1998. *Reorient: Global Economy in the Asian Age*. Berkeley, CA: University of California Press.
Franks, David D. 2010. *Neurosociology: The Nexus Between Neuroscience and Social Psychology*. New York, NY: Springer.
Franks, David. D., and Jonathan. H. Turner. 2013. *Handbook of Neurosociology*. New York, NY: Springer.
Fukuyama, Francis. 1999. *The End of History and the Last Man*. New York, NY: Palgrave Macmillan, 1992.
Gallese, Vittorio. 1999. "From Grasping to Language: Mirror Neurons and the Origin of Social Communication." In *Towards a Science of Consciousness*, edited by S. Hameroff, A. Kazniak, and D. Chalmers, 165–78. Cambridge, MA: MIT Press.
———. 2001. "The 'Shared Manifold' Hypothesis: From Mirror Neurons to Empathy." *Journal of Consciousness Studies* 8 (5–7): 33–50.
Gallup, G. G., Jr. 1970. "Chimpanzees: Self-Recognition." *Science* 167: 88–87.
———. 1979. *Self-Recognition in Chimpanzees and Man: A Developmental and Comparative Perspective*. New York, NY: Plenum Press.
———. 1982. "Self-Awareness and the Emergence of Mind in Primates." *American Journal of Primatology* 2: 237–48.
Gangestad, S. W., and R. Thornhill. 1997. "The Evolutionary Psychology of Extra-Pair Sex: The Role of Fluctuating Asymmetry." *Evolution and Human Behavior* 18: 69.
Gasiano, E. 1996. "Ecological Metaphors as Boundary Work." *American Sociological Review* 101: 874–907.
Gazzaniga, Michael S. 1985. *The Social Brain: Discovering the Networks of the Mind*. New York, NY: Basic Books.
———. 1992. *Nature's Mind: The Biological Roots of Thinking, Emotions, Sexuality, Language and Intelligence*. New York, NY: Basic Books.
———. 2000. *The Mind's Past*. Berkeley, CA: University of California Press.
———. 2005. *The Ethical Brain: The Science of Our Moral Dilemmas*. New York, NY: Dana Press.
Gazzaniga, Michael S., and J. E. LeDoux. 1978. *The Integrated Mind*. New York, NY: Plenum Press.
Gazzaniga, Michael S., and Charlotte S. Smylie. 1990. "Hemisphere Mechanisms Controlling Voluntary and Spontaneous Mechanisms." *Annual Review of Neurology* 13: 536–40.
Geary, D. C. 2000. "Evolution and Proximate Expression of Human Parental Investment." *Psychological Bulletin* 126: 55–77.
Gergely, G., and G. Csibra. 2006. "Sylvia's Recipe: The Role of Imitation and Pedagogy." In *The Transmission of Cultural Knowledge*, edited by N. J. Enfield and S. C. Levinson, 229–55. Oxford: Berg Press.

Geschwind, Norman. 1965a. "Disconnection Syndromes in Animals and Man, Part I." *Brain* 88: 237–94.
———. 1965b. "Disconnection Syndromes in Animals and Man, Part II." *Brain* 88: 585–644.
———. 1965c. "Disconnection Syndromes in Animals and Man." *Brain* 88: 237–85.
———. 1985. "Implications for Evolution, Genetics, and Clinical Syndromes." In *Cerebral Lateralization in Non-Human Species*, edited by Stanley Glick. New York, NY: Academic.
Geschwind, Norman, and Antonio Damasio, 1984. "The Neural Basis of Language." *Annual Review of Neuroscience* 7: 127–47.
Gibbs, Jack P. 1989. *Control: Sociology's Central Notion*. Chicago, IL: University of Illinois Press.
Giddens, A. 1996. *Introduction to Sociology*. New York, NY: W.W. Norton.
Goetz, A. T., and K. Causey. 2009. "Sex Differences in Perceptions of Infidelity: Men Often Assume the Worst." *Evolutionary Psychology* 7: 253–62.
Goffman, Erving. 1959. *The Presentation of Self in Everyday Life*. New York, NY: Penguin.
———. 1963. *Behavior in Public Places*. New York, NY: The Free Press.
———. 1967. *Interaction Ritual*. Garden City, NY: Anchor Books.
———. 1971. *Relations in Public*. New York, NY: Basic Books.
———. 1974. *Frame Analysis: An Essay on the Organization of Experience*. New York, NY: Harper and Row.
———. 1981. *Forms of Talk*. Philadelphia: University of Pennsylvania Press.
———. 1983. "The Interaction Order." *American Sociological Review* 48: 1–17.
Goldstone, Jack. 1990. *Revolution and Rebellion in the Early Modern World, 1640–1848*. Berkeley, CA: University of California Press.
Gothhard, K. M., and K. L. Hoffman. 2010. "Circuits of Emotion in the Human Brain." In *Primate Neurology*, edited by M. L. Platt and A. A. Ghazanfar, 292–315. Oxford: Oxford University Press.
Gould, Stephen J. 1978. "Sociobiology: The Art of Storytelling." *New Scientist* 80: 530–33.
———. 2002. *The Structure of Evolutionary Theory*. Cambridge, MA: Harvard University Press.
Gould, Stephen J., and Richard C. Lewontin. 1979. "The Spandrels of San Marco and the Panglossian Paradigm: A Critique of the Adaptationist Programme." *Proceedings of the Royal Society B: Biological Sciences* 205: 581–98.
Gouldner, Alvin W. 1960. "The Norm of Reciprocity: A Preliminary Statement." *American Sociological Review* 25 (2): 161–78.
Greenburg, D. F. 1985. "Age, Crime, and Social Explanation." *American Journal of Sociology* 91: 1–21.
Gross, M. 1999. "Human Geography and Ecological Sociology: The Unfolding of Human Ecology, 1890–1930—and Beyond." *Social Science History* 28: 575–605.
Guttentag, Marcia, and Paul F. Secord. 1983. *Too Many Women? The Sex Ratio Question*. Newbury Park, CA: Sage.
Haldane, John B. S. 1932. *The Causes of Evolution*. London: Longmans, Green, 1932; paperback reprint, Ithaca, NY: Cornell University Press, 1966.
Hall, Thomas D. 2000. *The World-System Reader*. Lanham, MD: Rowman & Littlefield.
Hames, Raymond. 2016. "Kin Recognition." In *The Handbook of Evolutionary Psychology, Second Edition, Volume 1 Foundations*, edited by David M. Buss, 505–23. Hoboken, NJ: John Wiley & Sons.
Hamilton, William D. 1964. "The Genetical Theory of Social Behavior, I, II." *Journal of Theoretical Biology* 7 (1): 1–52.
———. 2001. *Narrow Roads of Gene Land: The Collected Papers of W. D. Hamilton. Volume 2: The Evolution of Sex*. Oxford: Oxford University Press.

Hamilton, William D., and Marlene Zuk. 1982. "Heritable True Fitness and Bright Birds: A Role for Parasites?" *Science* 218: 384–87.
Hammer, D. *The God Gene: How Faith Is Hardwired Into Our Genes*. New York, NY: Doubleday, 2004.
Hannan, Michael T. 2005. "Ecologies of Organizations: Diversity and Identity." *Journal of Economic Perspectives* 19: 51–70.
Hannan, Michael T., and John Freeman. 1977. "The Population Ecology of Organizations." *American Journal of Sociology* 82: 929–64.
———. 1985. "The Organizational Ecology of American Labor Unions, 1836–1985." *American Journal of Sociology* 92: 929–64.
———. 1989. *Organizational Ecology*. Cambridge, MA: Harvard University Press.
Hannan, Michael T., L. Polos, and G. R. Carroll. 2007. *Logics of Organization Theory: Audiences, Code, and Ecologies*. Princeton, NJ: Princeton University Press.
Hansen, A. J. 1986. "Fighting Behavior in Bald Eagles: A Test of Game Theory." *Ecology* 67: 787–97.
Hare, B., J. Call, and M. Tomasello. 2001. "Do Chimpanzees Know What Conspecifics Know?" *Animal Behavior* 61: 139–59.
———. 2006. "Chimpanzees Deceive a Human Competitor by Hiding." *Cognition* 101: 495–514.
Harris, Chauncey, and Edward Ullman. 1945. "The Nature of Cities." *The Annals of the American Academy of Political and Social Science* 242: 7–17.
Harris, Marvin. 1979. *Cultural Materialism: The Struggle for a Science of Culture*. New York, NY: Random House.
Hawkes, K. 1991. "Showing Off: Tests of a Hypothesis About Men's Foraging Goals." *Ethology and Sociobiology* 12: 29–54.
Hawley, Amos. H. 1944. "Ecology and Human Ecology." *Social Forces* 22: 398–405.
———. 1986. *Human Ecology: A Theoretical Essay*. Chicago, IL: University of Chicago Press.
Hechter, Michael. 1987. *Principles of Group Solidarity*. Berkeley, CA: University of California Press.
Heider, Fritz. 1946. "Attitudes and Cognitive Organization." *Journal of Psychology* 21: 107–12.
———. 1958. *The Psychology of Interpersonal Relations*. New York, NY: Wiley-Blackwell.
Henslin, James M. 1997. *Sociology: A Down-to-Earth Approach*. Boston, MA: Allyn and Bacon.
———. 2009. *Essentials of Sociology: A Down-to-Earth Approach* (Eighth edition). Boston, MA: Allyn & Bacon.
Hepper, Peter G. ed. 1991. *Kin Recognition*. New York, NY: Cambridge University Press.
Hess, B. B., E. W. Markson, and P. J. Stein. 1996. *Sociology*. Boston, MA: Allyn and Bacon.
Hirschi, T., and M. Gottfredson. 1983. "Age and Explanation of Crime." *American Journal of Sociology* 89: 552–84.
Hobson, John Atkinson. 1900. *Capitalism and Imperialism in South Africa*. London: Tucker Publishing Co.
———. 1902a. *The Evolution of Modern Capitalism*. London: Scott Publishing Co.
———. 1902b. *Imperialism: A Study*. London: Unwin Hyman.
———. 1938. *Imperialism*. London: George Allen and Unwin.
Hochschild, Arlie. 1979. "Emotion Work, Feeling Rules and Social Structure." *American Journal of Sociology* 85: 551–75.
———. 1983. *The Managed Heart: Commercialization of Human Feeling*. Berkeley, CA: University of California Press.

Holland, John H. 1995. *Hidden Order: How Adaptation Builds Complexity*. Reading, MA: Addison-Wesley.
———. 1998. *Emergence: From Chaos to Order*. Reading, MA: Perseus Books.
Hölldobler, Bert, and Edward O. Wilson. 1990. *The Ants*. Cambridge, MA: The Belknap Press of Harvard University Press.
———. 2009. *The Superorganism: The Beauty, Elegance, and Strangeness of Insect Societies*. New York, NY: W. W. Norton and Company.
Homans, George C. 1958. "Social Behavior as Exchange." *American Journal of Sociology* 63 (6): 597–606.
———. 1961. *Social Behavior: Its Elementary Forms*. New York, NY: Harcourt Brace Jovanovich.
Hopcroft, Rosemary L. 2002. "The Evolution of Sex Discrimination." *Psychology, Evolution, and Gender* 4 (1): 43–67.
———. 2006. "Sex, Status, and Reproductive Success in the Contemporary United States." *Evolution and Human Behavior* 27: 104–20.
———. 2009a. "Gender Inequality in Interaction—An Evolutionary Account." *Social Forces* 87: 1845–71.
———. 2009b. "The Evolved Actor in Sociology." *Sociological Theory* 27: 390–406.
———. 2015. "Sociobiology at Work in Modern Populations." In *Handbook of Evolution and Society: Toward an Evolutionary Social Science*, edited by Jonathan H. Turner, Richard Machalek, and Alexandra Maryanski, 122–35, Boulder, CO: Paradigm Press/Routledge.
———. 2016. *Evolution and Gender: Why It Matters for Contemporary Life*. New York, NY: Routledge Taylor & Francis Group.
Horowitz, A. C. 2003. "Do Chimps Ape? Or Apes Human? Imitation and Intention in Humans (*Homo Sapiens*) and Other Animals." *Journal of Comparative Psychology* 117: 325–36.
Howard, R. D. 1978. "The Evolution of Mating Strategies in Bullfrogs, *Rana catesbiana*." *Evolution* 32: 850–71.
Hoyt, Homer. 1939. *The Structure and Growth of Residential Neighborhoods in American Cities*. Washington, DC: U.S. Government Printing Office.
Huber, Joan. 2007. *On the Origins of Gender Inequality*. Boulder, CO: Paradigm.
Huizinga, Johan. 1955 [1938]. *Homo Ludens: A Study of the Play-Element in Culture*. Boston, MA: Beacon Press.
Iacoboni, Marco. 2009. "Imitation, Empathy, and Mirror Neurons." *Annual Review of Psychology* 60: 653–70.
Iacoboni, Marco, Istvan Molnar-Szakacs, Vittorio Gallese, Giovanni Buccino, John C. Mazziotta, and Giacomo Rizzolatti. 2005. "Grasping the Intentions of Others With One's Own Mirror Neuron System." *PLoS Biol* 3 (3): 529–35.
Inoue, Hiroko, Alexis Alvarez, Eugene N. Anderson, Kirk Lawrence, Teresa Neal, Dmytro Khutkyy, Sandor Nagy, Walter De Winter, and Christopher Chase-Dunn. 2016. "Comparing World Systems: Empire Upsweeps and Non-core Marcher States Since the Bronze Age." Working Paper #56, Institute for World Systems Research, UC Riverside.
Irwin, Michael D. 2015. "Evolving Communities: Evolutionary Analysis in Classical and Neoclassical Human Ecology." In *Handbook of Evolutionary Sociology*, edited by J. H. Turner, R. Machalek, and A. Maryanski, 316–32. New York, NY: Routledge/Paradigm.
Itakura, S. 1996. "An Exploratory Study of Gaze-Monitoring in Non-Human Primates." *Japanese Psychological Research* 38: 174–80.

Izard, Carroll E. 1992/1977. *Human Emotions*. New York, NY: Plenum Press.
Jarvis, M. J., and G. Ettlinger. 1977. "Cross-modal Recognition in Chimpanzees and Monkeys." *Neuropsychologia* 15: 499–506.
Jasper, James M., and Lynn Owens. 2014. "Social Movements and Emotions." In *Handbook of the Sociology of Emotions*, edited by Jan E. Stets and Jonathan H. Turner, 495–510. New York, NY: Springer.
Jeffers, R., and I. Lehiste. 1979. *Principles and Methods for Historical Linguistics*. Cambridge, MA: MIT Press.
Kaighobadi, F. and T. K. Shackelford. 2009. "Suspicions of Female Infidelity Predict Men's Partner-Directed Violence." *Behavioral and Brain Sciences* 32: 281–82.
Kanazawa, S. 2004. "The Savanna Principle." *Managerial and Decision Economics* 25: 41–54.
———. 2010. "Evolutionary Psychology and Intelligence Research." *American Psychologist* 65 (4): 279–89.
Kanazawa, S., and J. Hellberg. 2010. "Intelligence and Substance Use." *Review of General Psychology* 14 (4): 382–96.
Kanazawa, S., and M. Still. 2000. "Why Men Commit Crimes (and Why They Desist)." *Sociological Theory* 18 (3): 434–47.
Kauffman, Stuart. 1995. *At Home in the Universe: The Search for Laws of Self-Organization and Complexity*. Oxford: Oxford University Press.
Kay. R., and P. Ungar. 1997. "Dental Evidence for Diet in Some Miocene Catarrhines with Comments on the Effects of Phylogeny on the Interpretation of Adaptation." In *Function, Phylogeny, and Fossils: Miocene Hominoid Evolution and Adaptations*, edited by D. Begun, C. Ward, and M. Rose. New York, NY: Plenum.
Kemper, T. D., and R. Collins. 1990. "Dimensions of Microinteraction." *American Journal of Sociology* 96: 32–68.
Kenneth, R., Scott H. Johnson-Frey, and Scott T. Grafton. 2004. "Functional Imaging of Face and Hand Imitation: Towards a Motor Theory of Empathy." *NeuroImage* 21: 601–607.
Kenrick, Douglas T., Jon K. Maner, and Norman P. Li. 2016. "Evolutionary Social Psychology." In *The Handbook of Evolutionary Psychology, Second Edition, Volume 1 Foundations*, edited by David M. Buss, 925–42. Hoboken, NJ: John Wiley & Sons.
Keyes, Charles F. 1981. "The Dialectics of Ethnic Change." In *Ethnic Change*, edited by Charles F. Keyes, 4–30. Seattle, WA: University of Washington Press.
Kosfeld, Michael, Markus Heinrichs, and Paul J. Zak, Urs Fischbacher, and Ernst Fehr. 2005. "Oxytocin Increases Trust in Humans." *Nature* 435: 673–76.
Krebs, Hans A. 1975. "The August Krogh Principle: 'For Many Problems There Is an Animal on Which It Can Be Most Conveniently Studied'." *Journal of Experimental Zoology* 194 (1): 221–26.
Krebs, John. R., and Nicholas B. Davies. eds. 1997. *Behavioral Ecology: An Evolutionary Perspective* (Fourth edition). London: Blackwell Science.
Kummer, Hans. 1971. *Primate Societies*. Chicago, IL: Aldine & Atherton.
Lambert, C. A., and S. A. Tishkoff. 2009. "Genetic Structure in African Populations: Implications for Human Demographic History." *Cold Spring Harbor Symposia on Quantitative Biology* lxxiv: 395–402.
Langton, Christopher G. ed. 1989. *Artificial Life*. Redwood City, CA: Addison-Wesley.
Lank, D. B., P. Mineau, R. F. Rockwell, and F. Cook. 1990. "Frequency-Dependent Fitness Consequences of Intraspecific Nest Parasitism in Snow Geese." *Evolution* 44: 1436–53.
Larmuseau, Maarten H. D., Koen Matthijs, and Tom Wenseleers. 2016. "Cuckolded Fathers Rare in Human Populations." *Trends in Ecology and Evolution* 31 (5): 327–29.

Lawler, Edward J. 2001. "An Affect Theory of Social Exchange." *American Journal of Sociology* 107: 321–52.
Lawler, Edward J., and Jeongkoo Yoon. 1996. "Commitment in Exchange Relations: A Test of a Theory of Relational Cohesion." *American Sociological Review* 61: 89–108.
Le Doux, Joseph E. 2002. *Synaptic Self: How Our Brains Become Who We Are*. New York, NY: Viking.
Lenski, Gerhard. 1964. *Power and Privilege: A Theory of Stratification*. New York, NY: McGraw-Hill.
———. 2005. *Ecological-Evolutionary Theory: Principles and Applications*. New York, NY: Routledge/Paradigm.
Lenski, Gerhard, Jean Lenski, and Patrick Nolan. 1995. *Human Societies: An Introduction to Macrosociology* (Sixth edition). New York, NY: McGraw-Hill.
Lewin, Kurt. 1947. "Frontiers in Group Dynamics, I." *Human Relations* 1: 143–53.
Loewenstein, G., S. Rick, and J. Cohen. 2008. "Neuroeconomics." *Annual Reviews* 59: 647–72.
Lopreato, Joseph. 1984. *Human Nature & Biocultural Evolution*. Boston, MA: Allen & Unwin.
———. 2001. "Sociobiological Theorizing: Evolutionary Sociology." In *Handbook of Sociological Theory*, edited by Jonathan H. Turner, 405–33. New York, NY: Kluwer Academic.
Lopreato, Joseph, and Timothy Crippen. 1999. *Crisis in Sociology: The Need for Darwin*. London: Transaction.
Lorenz, Konrad. 1966. *On Aggression*. New York, NY: Routledge.
Luhmann, Niklas. 1982. *Systems Theory and the Differentiation of Society*. Translated by S. Holmes and C. Larmore. New York, NY: Columbia University Press.
———. 1984. *Social Systems*. Translated by J. Bednarz, Jr. and D. Baecker. Stanford, CA: Stanford University Press.
Lumsden, C. J., and E. O. Wilson. 1981. *Genes, Mind and Culture: The Coevolutionary Process*. Cambridge, MA: Harvard University Press.
Machalek, Richard. 1992. "The Evolution of Macrosociety: Why Are Large Societies Rare?" *Advances in Human Ecology* 1: 33–64.
———. 1995. "Basic Dimensions and Forms of Social Exploitation: A Comparative Analysis." *Advances in Human Ecology* 4: 35–68.
———. 1996. "The Evolution of Social Exploitation." *Advances in Human Ecology* 5: 1–32.
———. 1999. "Elementary Social Facts: Emergence in Nonhuman Societies." *Advances in Human Ecology* 8: 33–64.
Machalek, Richard, and Lawrence E. Cohen. 1991. "The Nature of Crime: Is Cheating Necessary for Cooperation?" *Human Nature: An Interdisciplinary Biosocial Perspective* 2: 215–33.
Machalek, Richard, and Michael W. Martin. 2004. "Sociology and the Second Darwinian revolution: A Metatheoretical Analysis." *Sociological Theory* 22: 455–76.
———. 2010. "Evolution, Biology, and Society: A Conversation for the 21st Century Classroom." *Teaching Sociology* 38 (1): 33–45.
———. 2012. "Sacrifice, Gratitude, and Obligation: Serial Reciprocity in Early Christianity." In *Biosociology and Neurosociology: Advances in Group Processes* Vol. 29, edited by Will Kalkhoff, Shane R. Thye, and Edward J. Lawler, 39–75. Bingley, UK: Emerald.
———. 2015. "Neo-Darwinian Evolutionary Theory and Sociology." In *Handbook of Evolution and Society: Toward an Evolutionary Social Science*, edited by Jonathan H. Turner, Richard Machalek, and Alexandra Maryanski, 1–52. Boulder, CO: Paradigm Press/Routledge.

MacLean, Paul D. 1990. *The Triunne Brain in Evolution: Role of Paleocerebral Functions*. New York, NY: Plenum Press.
Malinowski, Branislow. 1936. "Anthropology." In *Encyclopedia Britannica*, 1st Supplementary Volume. New York, NY.
———. 1939 "The Group and the Individual in Functional Analysis." *American Journal of Sociology* XLIV (6): 938–64.
———. 1941. "Man's Culture and Man's Behavior." *American Scientist* October: 198–207.
———. 1944. *A Scientific Theory of Culture and Other Essays*. Chapel Hill, NC: University of North Carolina Press.
Maryanski, Alexandra. 1986. "African Ape Social Structure: A Comparative Analysis." Ph.D. dissertation, University of California.
———. 1987. "African Ape Social Structure: Is There Strength in Weak Ties?" *Social Networks* 9: 191–215.
———. 1992. "The Last Ancestor: An Ecological-Network Model on the Origins of Human Sociality." *Advances in Human Ecology* 2: 1–32.
———. 1993. "The Elementary Forms of the First Proto-Human Society: An Ecological/Social Network Approach." *Advances in Human Evolution* 2: 215–41.
———. 1995. "African Ape Social Networks: A Blueprint for Reconstructing Early Hominid Social Structure." In *Archaeology of Human Ancestry*, edited by J. Steele and S. Shennan, 67–90. London: Routledge.
———. 1996. "Was Speech an Evolutionary Afterthought?" In *Communicating Meaning: The Evolution and Development of Language*, edited by B. Velichikovsky and D. Rumbaugh. Mahwah, NJ: Erlbaum.
———. 2018. *Emile Durkheim and The Birth of the Gods*. New York and London: Routledge.
Maryanski, Alexandra, P. Molnar, U. Segerstrale, and B. Velichikovsky. 1997. "The Social and Biological Foundations of Human Communication." In *Human by Nature*, edited by P. Weingart, S. Mitchell, P. Richerson, and S. Maasen. Mahwah, NJ: Erlbaum.
Maryanski, Alexander, and J. H. Turner. 1992. *The Social Cage: Human Nature and the Evolution of Society*. Stanford, CA: Stanford University Press.
Marx, Karl. 1867 [1967]. *Capital: Volume 1*. New York, NY: International Publishers.
Marx, Karl, and Frederick Engels. 1846 [1947]. *The German Ideology*. New York, NY: International Publishers.
———. 1847 [1971]. *The Communist Manifesto*. New York, NY: International Publishers.
Massey, Douglas. 2002. "A Brief History of Human Society: The Origin and Role of Emotion in Social Life." *American Sociological Review* 67: 1–29.
Mayer, M. 1974. *The Bankers*. New York, NY: Ballantine Books.
Maynard Smith, John. 1964. "Group Selection and Kin Selection." *Nature* 201: 1145–47.
———. 1982. *Evolution and the Theory of Games*. Cambridge: Cambridge University Press.
Mayr, Ernst. 2001. *What Evolution Is*. New York, NY: Basic Books.
Mazur, Allan. 1973. "A Cross-Species Comparison of Status in Small Established Groups." *American Sociological Review* 38: 513–50.
———. 1976. "Effects of Testosterone on Status in Primate Groups." *Folia Primatologica* 26: 214–26.
———. 2005. *Biosociology of Dominance and Deference*. New York, NY: Rowman & Littlefield.

———. 2015. "Biosociology of Dominance and Deference." In *Handbook on Evolution and Society: Toward an Evolutionary Social Science*, edited by Jonathan H. Turner, Richard Machalek, and Alexandra Maryanski, 474–92. New York, NY: Paradigm/Routledge.
Mazur, Allan, and A. Booth. 1998. "Testosterone and Dominance in Men." *Behavioral and Brain Sciences* 21: 553–63.
Mazur, Allan, E. Rosa, M. Faupel, J. Heller, R. Leen, and B. Thurman. 1980. "Physiological Aspects of Communication via Mutual Gaze." *American Journal of Sociology* 90: 125–50.
McGrew, W. C. 1981. "The Female Chimpanzee as a Human Evolutionary Prototype." In *Woman the Gatherer*, edited by F. Dahlberg. New Haven, NJ: Yale University Press.
———. 1983. "Animal Foods in the Diets of Wild Chimpanzees (Pan Troglodytes): Why Cross Cultural Variation?" *Journal of Ethology* 1: 46–61.
———. 1992. *Chimpanzee Material Culture: Implications for Human Evolution*. Cambridge: Cambridge University Press.
———. 2010. "In Search of the Last Common Ancestor: New Findings on Wild Chimpanzees." *Philosophical Transaction of the Royal Society* 365: 3265–67.
McGrew, W. C., P. J. Baldwin, and G.E.G. Tutin. 1981. "Chimpanzees in Hot, Dry, and Open Habitat: Mt. Assirik, Senegal, West Africa." *Journal of Human Evolution* 10: 227–44.
McKenzie, Roderick. 1933. *The Metropolitan Community*. New York, NY: McGraw-Hill.
McPherson, J. Miller. 1983. "An Ecology of Affiliation." *American Sociological Review* 48: 519–32.
———. 1988. "A Theory of Voluntary Organization." In *Community Organizations*, edited by C. Milofsky, 42–76. New York, NY: Oxford.
McPherson, J. Miller, and J. Ranger-Moore. 1991. "Evolution on a Dancing Landscape: Organizations and Networks in Dynamic Blau Space." *Social Forces* 70 (1): 19–42.
McPherson, Miller, and T. Rotolo. 1996. "Testing a Dynamic Model of Social Composition: Diversity and Change in Voluntary Groups." *American Sociological Review* 61: 179–202.
Mead, George Herbert. 1934. *Mind, Self, and Society*. Chicago, IL: University of Chicago Press.
———. 1938. *Philosophy of the Act*. Chicago, IL: University of Chicago Press.
Meldrum. J. 2006. *Sasquatch: Legend Meets Science*. New York, NY: Forge.
Meltzoff, A. N. 2002. "Imitation as a Mechanism of Social Cognition: Origins of Empathy, Theory of Mind, and the Representation of Action." In *Handbook of Childhood Cognitive Development*, edited by U. Goswami, 6–25. Oxford: Wiley-Blackwell.
Menzel, E. W. 1971. "Communication About the Environment in a Group of Young Chimpanzees." *Folia Primatologica* 15: 220–32.
Meyerriecks, A. J. 1972. *Man and Birds: Evolution and Behavior*. Indianapolis, IN: Pegasus, Bobbs-Merrill.
Miller, James G. 1978. *Living Systems*. New York, NY: McGraw-Hill.
Mills, C. Wright. 1956. *The Power Elite*. Oxford: Oxford University Press.
Mitani, John. C., and P. S. Rodman. 1979. "Territoriality: The Relation of Ranging Patterns and Home Range Size to Defendability, With an Analysis of Territoriality Among Primate Species." *Behavioral Ecology and Sociobiology* 5: 541–51.
Mitani, John, and David Watts. 2001. "Why Do Chimpanzees Hunt and Share Meat?" *Animal Behaviour* 61: 915–24.
Mithen, Steven J. 2005. *The Singing Neanderthals: The Origins of Music, Language, Mind, and Body*. Cambridge, MA: Harvard University Press.
Molm, Linda D., Jessica L. Collett, and David R. Schaefer. 2007. "Building Solidarity Through Generalized Exchange: A Theory of Reciprocity." *American Journal of Sociology* 113: 205–42.

Moody, Michael. 2008. "Serial Reciprocity: A Preliminary Statement." *Sociological Theory* 26: 130–51.
Moore, Deborah L., Kevin E. Bangergraber, and Linda Vigilant. 2015. "Genetic Analyses Suggest Male Philopatry and Territoriality in Savanna-Woodland Chimpanzees (*Pan troglodytes schweinfurthii*) of Ugalla, Tanzania." *International Journal of Primatology* 36: 377–97.
Morris, Desmond. 1969. *The Naked Ape: A Zoologist's Study of the Human Animal*. New York, NY: Dell.
Mueller, J. K., A. K. Eggert, and J. Dressel. 1990. "Intraspecific Brood Parasitism in the Burying Beetle, *Necrophorus vespilloides* (Coleoptera: Silphidae)." *Animal Behavior* 40: 491–99.
Murdock, George P. 1949. *Social Structure*. New York, NY: Palgrave MacMillan.
Newcombe, Theodore M. 1953. "An Approach to the Study of Communicative Acts." *Psychological Review* 60: 393–404.
Nolan, Patrick. 2014. *Studying Human Societies*. New York: Oxford University Press.
Nolan, Patrick, and Gerhard Lenski. 2014. *Human Societies: An Introduction to Macrosociology*. New York, NY: Oxford University Press.
Norenzayan, Ara. 2013. *Big Gods: How Religion Changed Conflict and Cooperation*. Princeton, NJ: Princeton University Press.
Nowak, Martin A., Corina E. Tarnita, and Edward O. Wilson. 2010. "The Evolution of Eusociality." *Nature* 466: 1057–62.
Okamoto, S., M. Tomonaga, K. Ishii, N. Kawai, M. Tanaka, and T. Matsuzawa. 2002. "An Infant Chimpanzee (Pan Troglodytes) Follows Human Gaze." *Animal Cognition* 5: 107–14.
Olsen, Mancur. 1971/1967. *The Logic of Collective Action*. Cambridge, MA: Harvard University Press.
Osgood, Charles E. 1966. "Dimensionality of the Semantic Space for Communication via Facial Expressions." *Scandinavian Journal of Psychology* 7: 1–30.
Panksepp, Jaak. 1982. "Toward a General Psychobiological Theory of Emotions." *Behavioral and Brain Sciences* 5: 407–67.
Pareto, Vilfredo. 1916. *Trattato Di Sociologia Generale* (4 vols.). Roma: G. Barbéra.
———. 1935 [1963]. *The Mind and Society: A Treatise on General Sociology. Volume Two: Theory of Residues*. Translated by A. Bongiorno and A. Livingston. New York, NY: Dover Publications, Inc.
Park, Robert E. 1936a. "Human Ecology." *American Journal of Sociology* 42: 1–15.
———. 1936b. "Succession, an Ecological Concept." *American Sociological Review* 2: 171–79.
Park, Robert E., and Ernest W. Burgess. eds. 1921. *An Introduction to the Science of Sociology*. Chicago, IL: University of Chicago Press.
Parker, G. A. 1970. "Sperm Competition and Its Evolutionary Consequences in the Insects." *Biological Reviews* 45: 525–67.
Parsons, Talcott. 1937. *Toward a General Theory of Action*. New York, NY: McGraw-Hill.
———. 1951. *The Social System*. New York, NY: The Free Press.
———. 1964. "Evolutionary Universals in Society." *American Sociological Review* 29: 339–57.
———. 1966. *Societies: Evolutionary and Comparative Perspectives*. Englewood Cliffs, NJ: Prentice-Hall.
———. 1971. *The System of Modern Societies*. Englewood Cliffs, NJ: Prentice-Hall.
Parsons, Talcott, Robert F. Bales, and Edward A. Shils. 1953. *Working Papers in the Theory of Action*. Glencoe: Free Press.
Passingham, R. E. 1973. "Anatomical Differences Between the Neo-cortex of Man and the Other Primates." *Brain Behavioral Evolution* 7: 337–59.

———. 1975. "Changes in the Size and Organization of the Brain in Man and His Ancestors." *Brain and Behavior Evolution* 11: 73–90.

———. 1982. *The Human Primate*. Oxford: Freeman.

Perrill, S. A., H. C. Gerhardt, and R. Daniel. 1978. "Sexual Parasitism in the Green Tree Frog, *Hyla cinerea*." *Science* 200: 1179–80.

Piaget, J. 1948. *The Moral Judgment of the Child*. New York, NY: Free Press.

Pinker, Steven. 1997. *How the Mind Works*. New York, NY: W. W. Norton.

Platnick, N., and H. D. Camerson. 1977. "Cladistic Methods in Textual, Linguistic and Phylogenetic Analysis." *Systematic Zoology* 26: 380–85.

Plutchik, Robert. 1980. *Emotion: A Psycho Evolutionary Synthesis*. New York, NY: Harper and Row.

Polak, Michal, Larry L. Wolf, William T. Starmer, and J.S.F. Barker. 2001. "Function of the Mating Plug in *Drosophila hibisci* Bock." *Behavioral Ecology and Sociobiology* 49 (2–3): 196–205.

Potts, R. 2004. "Paleoenvironmental Basis of Cognitive Evolution in Great Apes." *American Journal of Primatology* 62: 209–28.

Povinelli, D. J. 2000. *Folk Physics for Apes: The Chimpanzee's Theory of How the World Works*. Oxford: Oxford University Press.

Povinelli, D. J., and T. J. Eddy. 1997. "Specificity of Gaze-Following in Young Chimpanzees." *British Journal of Developmental Psychology* 15: 213–22.

Premack, D., and G. Woodruff. 1978. "Does the Chimpanzee Have a Theory of Mind." *Behavior and Brain Science* 1: 515–26.

Pruetz, Jill. 2006. "Feeding Ecology of Savanna Chimpanzees (*Pan troglodytes Verus*)." In *Feeding Ecology of Great Apes and Other Primates*, edited by G. Boesch, G. Hohmann, and M. Robbins, 161–82. Cambridge: Cambridge University Press.

Pruetz, Jill D., and P. Bertolani. 2007. "Savanna chimpanzees, (*Pan troglodytes Verus*), Hunt With Tools." *Current Biology* 17: 412–17.

———. 2009. "Chimpanzee (*Pan Troglodytes Verus*) Behavioral Responses to Stresses Associated With Living in a Savanna-mosaic Environment: Implications for Hominin Adaptations to Open Habitats." *Paleo Anthropology*: 252–62.

Puts, David A., Drew H. Bailey, and Philip L. Reno. 2016. "Contest Competition in Men." In *The Handbook of Evolutionary Psychology, Second Edition, Volume 1 Foundations*, edited by David M. Buss, 385–402. Hoboken, NJ: John Wiley & Sons.

Raaum, R., L. Kirstin, N. Sterner, C. Noviello, C. Stewart, and T. Disotell. 2005. "Catarrhine Primate Divergence Dates Estimated from Complete Mitochondrial Genomes: Concordance With Fossil and Nuclear DNA Evidence." *Journal of Human Evolution* 48: 237–57.

Rachman, S. J., and Martin P. Seligman. 1976. "Unprepared Phobias: Be Prepared." *Behaviour Research and Therapy* 14: 333–38.

Radcliffe-Brown, A. R. 1924. "The Mother's Brother in South Africa." *South African Journal of Science* XXI: 124–36.

———. 1935. "On the Concept of Function in the Social Sciences." *American Anthropologist* XXXVII: 392–97.

———. 1948. *A Natural Science of Society*. New York, NY: Free Press.

———. 1952. *Structure and Function in Primitive Societies*. London: Cohen and West.

Raghanti, M. A., C. D. Stmpson, J. L. Marchiewicz, et al. 2008. "Differences in Cortical Serotonergic Innervation Among Humans, Chimpanzees, and Macaque Monkeys: A Comparative Study." *Cerebral Cortex* 18: 584–97.

Ranger-Moore, J. 1997. "Bigger May Be Better, but Is Older Wiser/: Organizational Age and Size in the New York Life Insurance Industry." *American Sociological Review* 62: 903–20.
Rao, H., and E. H. Nielsen. 1992. "An Ecology of Agency Arrangements: Mortality of Savings and Loan Associations." *Administrative Science Quarterly* 37: 448–70.
Reuf, M., and W. R. Scott. 1998. "A Multidimensional Model of Organizational Legitimacy: Hospital Survival in Changing Institutional Environments." *Administrative Science Quarterly* 43: 877–904.
Richerson, Peter J. 1977. "Ecology and Human Ecology: A Comparison of Theories in the Biological and Social Sciences." *American Ethnologist* 4: 1–26.
Richerson, Peter J., and Robert Boyd. 2005. *Not by Genes Alone: How Culture Transformed Human Evolution*. Chicago, IL: Chicago University Press.
Rizzolatti, Giacomo, and Liala Craighero. 2004. "The Mirror-Neuron System." *Annual Review of Neuroscience* 27: 169–92.
Rizzolattti, Giacomo, L. Fadiga, L. Fogassi, and V. Gallese. 2002. "From Mirror Neurons to Imitation: Facts and Speculations." In *The Imitative Mind: Development, Evolution and Brain Bases*, edited by W. Prinz and A. N. Meltzoff, 247–66. Cambridge: Cambridge University Press.
Rizzolatti, Giacomo, Luciano Fadiga, Vittorio Gallese, and Leonardo Fogassi. 1996. "Premotor Cortex and the Recognition of Motor Actions." *Cognitive Brain Research* 3 (2): 131–41.
Rizzolattti, Giacomo, Marco Iacoboni, Istvan Molnar-Szakacs, Vittorio Gallese, Giovanni Buccino, John C. Mazziotta, and Giacomo Rizzolatti. 2005. "Grasping the Intentions of Others With One's Own Mirror Neuron System." *PLoS Biology* 3 (3): 529–35.
Rizzolatti, Giacomo, and Gorrado Sinigalia. 2008. *Mirrors in the Brain: How Our Minds Share Actions, Emotions, and Experience*. Oxford: Oxford University Press.
Ross, Marina Davila, Susanne Menzler, and Elke Zimmermann. 2008. "Rapid Facial Mimicry in Orangutan Play." *Biology Letters* 4 (1): 27–30.
Rowher, F. C., and S. Freeman. 1989. "The Distribution of Conspecific Nest Parasitism in Birds." *Canadian Journal of Zoology* 67: 239–53.
Rumbaugh, M. D. 2013. *With Apes in Mind: Emergents, Communication and Competence*. Distributed by Amazon.com.
———. 2015. "A Salience Theory of Learning and Behavior and Rights of Apes." In *Handbook on Evolution and Society: Toward an Evolutionary Social Science*, edited by J. H. Turner, R. Machalek, and A. Maryanski, 514–36. New York, NY: Routledge/Paradigm.
Rumbaugh, Duane, and E. Sue Savage-Rumbaugh. 1990. "Chimpanzees: Competencies for Language and Numbers." In *Comparative Perception*, vol. 2, edited by William Stebbins and Mark Berkley. New York, NY: Wiley and Sons.
Runciman, W. G. 1983–1897. *A Treatise on Social Theory, Volume 1–3*. Cambridge: Cambridge University Press.
———. 2009. *The Theory of Cultural and Social Selection*. Cambridge: Cambridge University Press.
Salovey, P. ed. 1991. *The Psychology of Jealously and Envy*. New York, NY: Guilford Press.
Sanderson, Stephen K. 1995/1999. *Social Transformations*. London: Basil Blackwell/Rowan & Littlefield.
———. 2001. "Explaining Monogamy and Polygyny in Human Societies." *Social Forces* 80: 329–36.
———. 2014. *Human Nature and the Evolution of Society*. Boulder, CO: Westview Press.

———. 2015. "Darwinian Conflict Theory: A Unified Evolutionary Research Program." In *Handbook on Evolution and Society: Toward an Evolutionary Social Science*, edited by Jonathan H. Turner, Richard Machalek, and Alexandra Maryanski, 228–66. New York, NY: Paradigm/Routledge.

Savage-Rumbaugh, Sue, and Roger Lewin. 1994. *Kanzi: The Ape at the Brink of the Human Mind*. New York, NY: John Wiley and Sons, Inc.

Savage-Rumbaugh, Sue, J. Murphy, J. Seveik, K. Brakke, S. L. Williams, and D. Rumbaugh. 1993. "Language Comprehension in the Ape and Child." In *Monographs of the Society for Research in Child Development*, 58. Chicago, IL: University of Chicago Press.

Savage-Rumbaugh, S., R. Seveik, and W. Hopkins. 1988. "Symbolic Cross-Model Transfer in Two Species." *Child Development* 59: 617–25.

Saxe, Rebecca, and J. Kanwisher. 2003. "People Thinking About Thinking People: The Role of the Temporo-Parietal Junction in 'Theory of Mind'." *NeuroImage* 19: 1835–42.

Saxe, Rebecca et al. 2006. "Reading Minds Versus Following Rules: Dissociating Theory of Mind and Executive Control in the Brain." *Social Neuroscience* 1: 284–98.

Schaller, George B. 1963. *The Mountain Gorilla—Ecology and Behavior*. Chicago, IL: University of Chicago Press.

———. 1964. *The Year of the Gorilla*. Chicago, IL: University of Chicago Press.

———. 1972. *The Serengeti Lion: A Study of Predator-Prey Relations*. Chicago, IL: University of Chicago Press.

Scheff, Thomas. 1988. "Shame and Conformity: The Deference-Emotion System." *American Sociological Review* 53: 395–406.

Schmitt, David P. 2016. "Fundamentals of Human Mating Strategies." In *The Handbook of Evolutionary Psychology, Second Edition, Volume 1 Foundations*, edited by David M. Buss, 294–316. Hoboken, NJ: John Wiley & Sons.

Schmitt, David P., and David M. Buss. 2001. "Human Mate Poaching: Tactics and Temptations for Infiltrating Existing Relationships." *Journal of Personality and Social Psychology* 80: 894–917.

Schutz, Alfred. 1932 [1967]. *The Phenomenology of the Social World*. Evanston, IL: Northwestern University Press.

Schwella, Ken. 2015. "Language Use Among Apes." In *Handbook of Evolution and Society*, edited by J. H. Turner, R. Machalek, and A. Maryanski. 537–45. New York: Routledge/Athem.

Segerstråle, U. 2000. *Defenders of the Truth: The Battle for Science in the Sociobiology Debate and Beyond*. Oxford: Oxford University Press.

Seligman, M.E.P. 1971. "Preparedness and Phobias." *Behavior Therapy* 2: 307–20.

———. 1993. *What You Can Change and What You Can't*. New York, NY: Fawcett Columbine.

Shackelford, Todd K., Aaron T. Goetz, Craig W. LaMunyon, Michael N. Pham, and Nicholas Pound. 2016. "Human Sperm Competition." In *The Handbook of Evolutionary Psychology, Second Edition, Volume 1 Foundations*, edited by David M. Buss, 427–43. Hoboken, NJ: John Wiley & Sons.

Shaw, R. Paul, and Yuwa Wong. 1989. *Genetic Seeds of Warfare: Evolution, Nationalism, and Patriotism*. Boston, MA: Unwin Hyman.

Sherwood, Chet C. 2007. "The Evolution of Neuron Types and Cortical Histology in Apes and Humans." In *Evolution of Nervous Systems 4: The Evolution of Primate Nervous Systems*, edited by T. M. Preuss and J. H. Kaas, 355–78. Oxford: Academic Press.

Sherwood, Chet C., R. L. Holloway, K. Semendeferi, and P. R. Hoff. 2005. "Is Prefrontal White Matter Enlargement a Human Evolutionary Specialization?" *Nature Neuroscience* 8: 537–38.
Sherwood, Chet C., F. Subiaul, H. Tadeusz, and W. Zawidzki. 2008. "A Natural History of the Human Mind: Tracing Evolutionary Changes in Brain and Cognition." *Journal of Anatomy* 212: 426–54.
Simons, Ronald L., Steven R. H. Beach, and Ashley B. Barr. 2012. "Differential Susceptibility to Context: A Promising Model of the Interplay of Genes and the Social Environment." In *Advances in Group Processes: Biosociology and Neurosociology*, edited by Will Kalkhoff, S. Thye, and E. Lawler, 139–63. Bingley: Emerald.
Simmel, Georg. 1906 [1990]. *The Philosophy of Money*. Translated by T. Bottomore and D. Frisby. Boston, MA: Routledge.
Skocpol, Theda. 1979. *States and Social Revolutions*. New York, NY: Cambridge University Press.
Smelser, Neil J. 1963. *Theory of Collective Behavior*. New York, NY: Free Press.
Smith, Adam. 1759 [1982]. *The Theory of Moral Sentiments*. Indianapolis, IN: Liberty Press.
Smuts, Barbara B. 1985. *Sex and Friendship in Baboons*. Piscataway, NJ: Aldine/Transaction.
Snow, David A., and Sarah A. Soule. 2010. *A Primer on Social Movements*. New York, NY: W. W. Horton & Company.
Sosis, Richard, and Candace Alcorta. 2003. "Signaling, Solidarity, and the Sacred: The Evolution of Religious Behavior." *Evolutionary Anthropology* 12: 264–74.
Spencer, Baldwin, and Francis Gillen. 1899. *The Nature Tribes of Central Australia*. New York, NY: Macmillan and Co.
Spencer, Herbert. 1851 [1988]. *Social Statics: Or, the Conditions Essential to Human Happiness Specified, and the First of Them Developed*. New York, NY: Appleton-Century-Crofts.
———. 1862 [1880]. *First Principles*. New York, NY: A. L. Burt.
———. 1864 [1968]. *Reasons for Dissenting From the Philosophy of M. Comte and Other Essays*. Berkeley, CA: Glendessary Press.
———. 1864–1867 [1898]. *The Principles of Biology*. New York, NY: Appleton-Century-Crofts.
———. 1873–1935. *Descriptive Sociology, or Groups of Sociological Facts*. 16 volumes, published by various publishers.
———. 1874–1896 [1899]. *The Principles of Sociology*. New York, NY: Appleton-Century-Crofts.
———. 1879–1892 [1897]. *The Principles of Ethics*, two volumes. New York, NY: Appleton-Century; see also Liberty Press.
Stanford, C. B. 1990. *The Hunting Apes: Meat Rating and the Origins of Human Behavior*. Princeton, NJ: Princeton University Press.
Stebbins, G. Ledyard. 1969. *The Basis of Progressive Evolution*. Chapel Hill, NC: University of North Carolina Press.
Steiglitz, J., M. Gurven, H. Kaplan, and J. Winking. 2012. "Infidelity, Jealousy, and Wife Abuse Among Tsimane Forager-Farmers: Testing Evolutionary Hypotheses of Marital Conflict." *Evolution and Human Behavior* 33 (5): 438–48.
Stel, Mariëlle, and Roos Vonk. 2010. "Mimicry in Social Interaction: Benefits for Mimickers, Mimickees, and Their Interaction." *British Journal of Psychology* 101: 311–23.
Stephan, H. 1983. "Evolutionary Trends in Limbic Structures." *Neuroscience and Biobehavioral Review* 7: 367–74.

Stephan, H., and O. J. Andy. 1969. "Quantitative Comparative Neuroanatomy of Primates: An Attempt at Phylogenetic Interpretation." *Annals of the New York Academy of Science* 167: 370–87.

———. 1977. "Quantitative Comparison of the Amygdala in Insectivores and Primates." *Acta Antomica* 98: 130–53.

Stephan, H., G. Baron, and H. Frahm. 1988. "Comparative Size of Brains and Brain Components." In *Neurosciences*. Vol. 4, edited by H. Steklis, and J. Erwin. New York, NY: Alan Liss.

Stephen, H., H. Frahm, and G. Baron. 1981. "New and Revised Data on Volumes of Brain Structures in Insectivores and Primates." *Folia Primatoligica* 35: 1–29.

Sterck, E. 2012. "The Behavioral Ecology of Colobine Monkeys." In *The Evolution of Primate Societies*, edited by J. Mitani, J. Call, P. Kappeler, R. Palomit, and J. Silk. Chicago, IL: University of Chicago Press.

Steward, Julian H. 1955. *The Theory of Culture Change: The Methodology of Multilinear Evolution*. Urbana, IL: University of Illinois Press.

Stuart, Robin. 1983. "A Note on Terminology in Animal Behavior, With Special Reference to Slavery in Ants." *Animal Behavior* 31 (4): 1259–60.

Subiaul, F. 2007. "The Imitation Faculty in Monkeys: Evaluating Its Features, Distribution, and Evolution." *Journal of Anthropological Science* 85: 35–62.

Sugiyama, Lawrence S. 2016. "Physical Attractiveness: An Adaptationist Perspective." In *The Handbook of Evolutionary Psychology, Second Edition, Volume 1 Foundations*, edited by David M. Buss, 317–84. Hoboken, NJ: John Wiley & Sons.

Sullivan, K. A., J. Cole, and E. M. Villalobos. 1989. "Intraspecific Nest Usurpation by a Yellow-Eyed Junco." *The Wilson Bulletin* 101: 645–55.

Swanson, Guy E. 1960. *The Birth of the Gods: The Origins of Primitive Beliefs*. Ann Arbor, MI: University of Michigan Press.

Symons, Donald. 1979. *The Evolution of Human Sexuality*. New York, NY: Oxford University Press.

———. 1995. "Beauty Is in the Adaptations of the Beholder: The Evolutionary Psychology of Human Female Sexual Attractiveness." In *Sexual Nature, Sexual Culture*, edited by P. R. Abramson and S. D. Pinkerton, 80–118. Chicago, IL: University of Chicago Press.

Temerin, A., and J. Cant. 1983. "The Evolutionary Divergence of Old World Monkeys and Apes." *American Naturalist* 122: 335–51.

TenHouten, Warren D. 1999. "The Four Elementary Forms of Sociality, Their Biological Bases, and Their Implications for Affect and Cognition." In *Advances in Human Ecology*, Vol. 8, edited by Lee Freese. Greenwich, CT: JAI Press.

———. 2007. *A General Theory of Emotions and Social Life*. London and New York, NY: Routledge.

Tershey, B. R., D. Breese, and G. M. Meyer. 1990. "Kleptoparasitism of Adult and Immature Brown Pelicans by Heermann's Gulls." *The Condor* 92: 1076–77.

Tiger, Lionel, and Robin Fox. 1966. "The Zoological Perspective in Social Science." *Man* 1: 75–81.

———. 1971. *The Imperial Animal*. New York, NY: Reinhart and Winston.

Tomasello, Michael, and J. Call. 1997. *Primate Cognition*. Oxford: Oxford University Press.

Tomasello, Michael, B. Hare, and T. Fogleman. 2001. "The Ontegeny of Gaze Following in Chimpanzees, *Pan Troglodytes*, and Rhesus Macaques, *Macaca mulatta*." *Animal Behavior* 61: 335–43.

Tomonaga, Michael. 1999. "Attending to the Others' Attention in Macaques: Joint Attention or Not?" *Primate Research* 15: 425.

Tooby, John, and Leda Cosmides. 2016. "The Theoretical Foundations of Evolutionary Psychology." In *The Handbook of Evolutionary Psychology, Second Edition, Volume 1 Foundations*, edited by David M. Buss, 3–87. Hoboken, NJ: John Wiley & Sons.
Trivers, Robert L. 1971. "The Evolution of Reciprocal Altruism." *Quarterly Review of Biology* 46 (4): 35–57.
———. 1972. "Parental Investment and Sexual Selection." In *Sexual Selection and the Descent of Man*, edited by B. G. Campbell, 136–79. Chicago, IL: Aldine Publishing Co.
———. 1974. "Parent-Offspring Conflict." *American Zoologist* 14 (1): 249–64.
———. 2005. "Reciprocal Altruism: 30 Years Later." In *Cooperation in Primates and Humans: Mechanisms and Evolution*, edited by P. M. Kappeler and C. P. van Schaik, 67–83. New York, NY: Springer.
Turchin, Peter. 2003. *Historical Dynamics: Why States Rise and Fall*. Princeton, NJ: Princeton University Press.
———. 2006. *War and Peace and War: The Life Cycles of Imperial Nations*. New York, NY: Pi Press.
———. 2013. "Modeling Social Pressures Toward Instability." *Cliodynamics* 4: 24–280.
———. 2016. *Ultra Society: How 10,000 Years of War Made Humans the Greatest Cooperators on Earth*. Chaplin, CT: Beresta Books.
Turchin, Peter, and Thomas D. Hall. 2003. "Spatial Synchrony Among and Within World Systems: Insights From Theoretical Ecology." *Journal of World-Systems Research* 9 (1): 37–64.
Turchin, Peter, Thomas E. Currie, Edward A. L. Turner, and Sergey Gavrilets. 2013. "War, Space, and the Evolution of Old World Complex Societies." *PNAS* 110 (41): 16384–89.
Turchin, Peter, and Sergey A. Nefadov. 2009. *Secular Cycles*. Princeton, NJ: Princeton University Press.
Turner, Jonathan H. 1972. *Patterns of Social Organization: A Survey of Social Institutions*. New York, NY: McGraw-Hill.
———. 1984. *Societal Stratification: A Theoretical Analysis*. New York, NY: Columbia University Press.
———. 1988. *A Theory of Social Interaction*. Stanford, CA: Stanford University Press.
———. 1990. "Emile Durkheim's Theory of Social Organization." *Social Forces* 68 (3): 1–15.
———. 1995. *Macro Dynamics: Toward Theory on the Organization of Human Populations*. New Brunswick, NJ: Rutgers University Press.
———. 1996a. "The Evolution of Emotions in Humans: A Darwinian-Durkheimian Analysis." *Journal for the Theory of Social Behavior* 26: 1–34.
———. 1996b. "Cognition, Emotion, and Interaction in the Big-Brained Primate." In *Social Processes and Interpersonal Relations*, edited by K. M. Kwan. Greenwich, CT: JAI Press.
———. 1996c. "Toward a General Sociological Theory of Emotions." *Journal for the Theory of Social Behavior* 29: 132–62.
———. 1997a. *The Institutional Order*. London: Longman.
———. 1997b. "The Evolution of Emotions: The Nonverbal Basis of Human Social Organization." In *Nonverbal Communication: Where Nature Meets Culture*, edited by U. Segerstrale and P. Molnar. Hillsdale, NJ: Erlbaum.
———. 1998. "The Evolution of Moral Systems." *Critical Review* 11: 211–32.
———. 1999. "The Neurology of Emotions: Implications for Sociological Theories of Interpersonal Behavior." In *The Sociology of Emotions*, edited by D. Franks. Greenwich, CT: JAI Press.
———. 2000. *On the Origins of Human Emotions: A Sociological Inquiry Into the Evolution of Human Affect*. Stanford, CA: Stanford University Press.

———. 2002. *Face to Face: Toward a Theory of Interpersonal Behavior*. Palo Alto, CA: Stanford University Press.

———. 2003. *Human Institutions: A New Theory of Societal Evolution*. Boulder, CO: Rowman & Littlefield.

———. 2007. *Human Emotions: A Sociological Theory*. Oxford: Routledge.

———. 2010. *Theoretical Principles of Sociology, Volume 1 on Macro Dynamics*. New York, NY: Springer.

———. 2013. *Theoretical Sociology: 1830 to the Present*. Los Angeles, CA: Sage.

———. 2015. *Revolt From the Middle: Emotional Stratification and Change in Post-Industrial Societies*. New York, NY: Routledge/Transaction Publishers.

Turner, Jonathan H., and Seth Abrutyn. 2017. "Returning the 'Social' to Evolutionary Sociology: Reconsidering Spencer, Durkheim, and Marx's Models of Natural Selection." *Sociological Perspectives* 60: 529–56.

Turner, Jonathan H., and Richard Machalek. 2017. *The New Evolutionary Sociology*. New York, NY: Routledge.

Turner, Jonathan H., Richard Machalek, and Alexandra Maryanski. 2015. *Handbook of Evolution and Society: Toward an Evolutionary Social Science*. New York, NY: Paradigm/Routledge.

Turner, Jonathan H., and Alexandra Maryanski. 1979. *Functionalism*. Menlo Park, CA: Benjamin-Cummings.

———. 2005. *Incest: Origins of the Taboo*. Boulder, CO: Paradigm/Routledge.

———. 2008a. *On the Origins of Societies by Natural Selection*. New York, NY: Paradigm / Routledge.

———. 2008b. "The Limitations of Evolutionary Theory From Biology in Explaining Socio-Cultural Evolution." *Sociologica* 3: 1–38.

———. 2015. "The Prospects and Limitations of Evolutionary Theorizing in the Social Sciences." In *Handbook on Evolution and Society: Toward an Evolutionary Social Science*, edited by Jonathan H. Turner, Richard Machalek, and Alexandra Maryanski, 92–111. New York, NY: Paradigm/Routledge.

Turner, Jonathan H., Alexandra Maryanski, Anders Klostergaard Petersen, and Armin Geertz. 2018. *The Emergence and Evolution of Religion: By Means of Natural Selection*. New York, NY and London: Routledge.

Turner, Jonathan H., and Jan E. Stets. 2005. *The Sociology of Emotions*. New York, NY: Cambridge University Press.

Turner, Ralph H. 1962. "Role-Taking: Processes Versus Conformity." In *Human Behavior and Social Processes*, edited by A. Rose, 20–40. Boston, MA: Houghton Mifflin.

Tutin, W., W. C. McGrew, and P. J. Baldwin. 1982. "Responses of Wild Chimpanzees to Potential Predators." In *Primate Behavior and Sociobiology*, edited by B. Chiarelli and R. Corruccini, 136–41. Berlin: Springer-Verlag.

Ulinski, Philip S. 1990. "The Cerebral Cortex of Reptiles." In *Cerebral Cortex, Vol. 8A: Comparative Structure and Evolution of Cerebral Cortex, Part I,* edited by Edward G. Jones and Alan Peters, 129–216. New York, NY: Plenum.

van den Berghe, Pierre. 1973. *Age and Sex in Human Societies: A Biosocial Perspective*. Belmont, CA: Wadsworth.

———. 1974. "Bringing Beasts Back in: Toward a Biosocial Theory of Aggression." *American Sociological Review*, 39: 777–88.

———. 1981. *The Ethnic Phenomenon*. New York, NY: Elsevier.

Veblen, Thorstein. 1899. *The Theory of the Leisure Class*. New York, NY: Palgrave Macmillan.

———. 1914. *The Instinct of Workmanship and the State of the Industrial Arts*. New York, NY: Palgrave Macmillan.

von Bertalanffy, Ludwig. 1968. *General Systems Theory*. New York, NY: Braziller.

Waage, Jon K. 1979. "Dual Function of the Damselfly Penis: Sperm Removal and Transfer." *Science* 203: 916–18.

Waal, Frans B. M. de. 1986. "The Integration of Dominance and Social Bonding in Primates." *The Quarterly Review of Biology* 61 (4): 459–79.

———. 1989. "Food Sharing and Reciprocal Obligations Among Chimpanzees." *Journal of Human Evolution* 18: 433–59.

———. 1991. "The Chimpanzee's Sense of Social Regularity and Its Relation to the Human Sense of Justice." *American Behavioral Scientist* 34: 335–49.

———. 1996. *Good Natured: The Origins of Right and Wrong in Humans and Other Animals*, Cambridge, MA: Harvard University Press.

———. 2008. "Putting the Altruism Back Into Altruism: The Evolution of Empathy." *Annual Review of Psychology* 59: 279–300.

———. 2009. *The Age of Empathy: Nature's Lessons for a Kinder Society*. New York, NY: Three Rivers Press.

———. 2012. "A Bottom-up View of Empathy." In *The Primate Mind: Built to Connect With Other Minds*, edited by F. B. de Waal and P. F. Ferrari, 121–38. Cambridge, MA: Harvard University Press.

———. 2016. "Apes Know What Others Believe." *Science* 354 (issue 6308): 39–40.

Waal, Frans B. M. de, and Sarah F. Brosnan. 2006. "Simple and Complex Reciprocity in Primates." In *Cooperation in Primates and Humans: Mechanisms and Evolution*, edited by P. Kappeler and C. P. van Schaik, 85–106. Berlin: Springer-Verlag.

Wallerstein, Immanuel. 1974. *The Modern World System, Volume 1 on Capitalist Agriculture and the Origins of the European World Economy in the Sixteenth Century*. New York, NY: Academic Press.

———. 1979. *The Modern World System, Volume 2 on The Capitalist World Economy*. Cambridge: Cambridge University Press.

———. 1984. "The Three Instances of Hegemony in the History of the Capitalist World-Economy." In *Current Issues and Research in Macrosociology*, edited by Gerhard Lenski, 100–108. International Studies in Sociology and Social Anthropology, Vol. 37. Leiden: E.J. Brill.

———. 1989. *The Modern World System, Volume 3 on The Second Era of Great Expansion of the Capitalist World Economy, 1730–1840*. New York, NY: Academic Press, republished in 2011 by University of California Press.

———. 2004. *World-System Analysis*. Durham, NC: Duke University Press.

Watts, D. P., and J. C. Mitani. 2001. "Boundary Patrols and Intergroup Encounters in Wild Chimpanzees." *Behaviour* 138: 299–327.

Weber, Max. 1922 [1968]. *Economy and Society*. Berkeley, CA: University of California Press.

Weiner, B. 1986. *An Attribution Theory of Motivation and Emotion*. New York, NY: Springer.

West, Stuart A., Claire El Moulden, and Andy Gardner. 2011. "Sixteen Common Misconceptions About the Evolution of Cooperation in Humans." *Evolution and Human Behavior* 32: 231–62.

Wheeler, William M. 1911. "The Ant-Colony as an Organism." *The Journal of Morphology* 22 (2): 307–25.

White, Harrison C. 1970. *Chains of Opportunity: System Models of Mobility in Organizations*. Cambridge, MA: Harvard University Press.
White, Leslie. 1943. "Energy and the Evolution of Culture." *American Anthropologist* 45: 353–56
———. 1959. *The Evolution of Culture*. Ann Arbor, MI: University of Michigan Press.
Whitehead, Hal, and Luke Rendell. 2015. *The Cultural Lives of Whales and Dolphins*. Chicago, IL: University of Chicago Press.
Whitmeyer, J. M. 1997. "Endogamy as a Basis for Ethnic Behavior." *Sociological Theory* 15 (2): 162–78.
Wilkinson, Gerald S. 1984. "Reciprocal Food Sharing in the Vampire Bat." *Nature* 308: 181–84.
Williams, George C. 1966. *Adaptation and Natural Selection: A Critique of Some Current Thought*. Princeton, NJ: Princeton University Press.
Wilson, Margo and Martin Daly. 1993. "An Evolutionary Psychological Perspective on Male Sexual Proprietariness and Violence Against Wives." *Violence and Victims* 8: 271–94.
———. 1996. "Male Sexual Properitariness and Violence Against Wives." *Current Directions in Psychological Science* 5: 2–7.
Wilson, Edward O. 1971. *The Insect Societies*. Cambridge, MA: The Belknap Press of Harvard University Press.
———. 1975. *Sociobiology: The New Synthesis*. Cambridge, MA: The Belknap Press of Harvard University Press.
———. 1998. *Consilience: The Unity of Knowledge*. New York, NY: Alfred A. Knopf.
———. 2012. *The Social Conquest of Earth*. New York, NY: Liveright.
Wilson, David Sloan, and Edward O. Wilson. 2007. "Rethinking the Theoretical Foundations of Sociobiology." *Quarterly Review of Biology* 82 (4): 327–48.
Wilson, Edward O., and Bert Hölldobler. 1988. "Dense Heterarchies and Mass Communication as the Basis of Organization in Ant Colonies." *Trends in Ecology and Evolution* 3 (3): 65–68.
Wirth, Louis. 1938. "Urbanism as a Way of Life." *American Journal of Sociology* 44: 8–20.
Wolff, Kurt H. 1950. Translated and ed. *The Sociology of Georg Simmel*. Glencoe, IL: Free Press of Glencoe.
Wolpoff, M. 1999. *Paleoanthropology*. Boston, MA: McGraw-Hill.
Wright, Robert. 1994. *The Moral Animal: The New Science of Evolutionary Psychology*. New York, NY: Pantheon.
Wright, Sewall. 1945. "Tempo and Mode in Evolution: A Critical Review." *Ecology* 26 (4): 415–19.
Wu, Chi-Chi, Pamela K. Diggle, and William E. Friedman. 2013. "Kin Recognition Within a Seed and the Effect of Genetic Relatedness of an Endosperm to Its Compatriot Embryo on Maize Seed Development." *Proceedings of the National Academy of Science* 110 (6): 2217–22.
Wynne-Edwards, Vero Copner. 1962. *Animal Dispersion in Relation to Social Behavior*. Edinburgh, Scotland: Oliver and Boyd.
———. 1986. *Evolution Through Group Selection*. Oxford: Blackwell Scientific.

Index

Note: Italicized page numbers indicate a figure on the corresponding page. Page numbers in bold indicate a table on the corresponding page.

adaptation: adapted mind 178; adaptive upgrading 53; defined 125; in evolution 121–2; evolved adaptations 243–5; in functionalism 25; social behavior and 164; value of traits 220
Adaptation and Natural Selection: A Critique of Some Current Evolutionary Thought (Williams) 122
adapted mind: evolved adaptations 243–5; just-so story problem 236–40; nature of 241–3; neo-Darwinian evolutionary theory 234; overview of 234–45
Adaption and Natural Selection (Williams) 241
adaptive demography 402–3
adaptively relevant 174
adaptive problems 267
adaptive upgrading 53
advanced intermediate societies 57
advanced primitive stage 55
age-graded crime curve 386
aging infrastructures 109
agrarian societies 49
alleles 125, 168–9, 248, 260
altricial birth 153
altruistic behavior 129–34, 136–42, 189, 249
Alzheimer's disease 349–50
American Sociological Review 367
American Sociological Society 104
animistic impulse 146
anisogamy (gamete asymmetry) 150, 193
anterior cingulate gyrus 315, 356
anthropological functionalism 22–4, *23*
ant societies and social parasitism 389–94
apes *see* primates
apparently altruistic behavior 138
arboreal habitat 300, 343
archaic stage 55–6

archeology of brain 338–42, *339*
asabiya solidarity 86–7
assortative mating 189
attachment hormones 197
attractiveness interactions 219
attributions in memory 361–2
auditory information 242
Australopithecines 314
autonomy in humans 324
Axial (pivotal) Age 95–7

baseline relatedness 137
basic organizational unit for great apes 414–15
behavioral adaptation 126
behavioral algorithms 178–9
behavioral biology of ants 398–9
behavioral ecology 126, 164
behavioral flexibility in megasociality 401
behavioral predispositions 186
behavioral propensities among apes: collective emotional effervescence 328–9; facial gestures and emotion 324–5; individualism and mobility 322–4; introduction to 321–2; justice and fairness 329–30; mirror neurons 326–8; reading faces and eyes 324; reciprocity 329; role-taking and empathy 326; self as object in environment 330–2; status differences and hierarchy 332–4; summary of 419–23
biased learning 173
Big Man systems 94
bilateral symmetry 178, 226
biodata 200
bio-ecology 103–4
biological evolution 264
biological foundations of love 229

457

biological infrastructure 210
biological paradigm 63
biological reductionism 175–7
biology and social life 121–4
biophysical environment 281
birth rates 89
Blau, Peter 110, 280
Blau-Space 110–12, *111*
body language 325, 419
bold expropriative strategy 380–1
Boulding, Kenneth 375
brain *see* human brain evolution
brain size among late hominins 349–51
Braudel, Fernand 74
Britton, Crane 24
Broca's area of the brain 340–1, 349, 350
brood parasitism 155, 378–9
Brosnan, Sarah 329
brute causation 146
Burgess, Ernest 102
Buss, David 217
Butler, Samuel 122

capitalism 3–4, 44, 74, 76, 77
Carey, Arlen 203
Cartesian reductionism 176
categoric units 114, 278–9
central notion in scientific disciplines 228
ceteris paribus 217
Chase, Ivan 367–9
Chase-Dunn, Christopher 77–84, *79*
cheating-detection cognitive algorithm 182
Chicago School of Urban Ecology 5, 102–5
chimpanzee studies *see* primates
cladistic analysis 294–301, **298**, 309, 412–13
clannish brain 186–9
classical Athenian society 233
Classical Period (1820–1920) evolutionary theorizing 37–51, *38*, *42*
coefficient of relatedness 133
Cold War 20, 84
collective action 139
collective conscience 43
collective effervescence in humans 324
collective emotional effervescence 328–9
collective representations 43, 420
collectivism 323
Collins, Randall 74, 84–6, 209, 326–8
colony homeostasis 405–7
colony life-cycle in megasociality 401
coloration in birds 156–7
communism 3, 19, 44–6
Communist Manifesto, The (Marx, Engels) 282
community organization of primates 416–17

comparative sociology *see* cross-species comparative sociology
complex-heterogeneous formations 266
Comte, Auguste 1, 4, 17, *38*, 38–39, 365–6, 396, 424
conflict-oriented approach 51
conflict-producing tensions 27
conflict theory 19, 60, 205–10, 283, 286–7
Confucianism 96
congruence in memory 361
consistency in memory 361
conspecific, defined 139
conspicuous consumption 233
construction of human societies 334
contrast-conceptions in memory 361
controllability 198–9
Cooley, Charles Horton 6–7, 330–1
co-progenitors 191–2
corporate-unit phenotypes 114, 252, 257, 274–6, 281
corpus callosum 338
Coser, Lewis 208
Cosmides, Leda 211–12, 214–15
cost-benefit constraints of megasociality 408–9
Course in Positive Philosophy (Comte) 1
credible threat of violence 180
Crippen, Timothy 186–9, 193–7
Crisis in Sociology: The Need for Darwin (Crippen) 186–7
critical sociology 2, 7
cross-species comparative analysis: behavioral propensities among apes 321–34; introduction to 294, 309–10; overview of 145; pre-adaptations among apes 310–21
cross-species comparative sociology: dominance hierarchies 366–72; early precedents 365–6; expropriative behaviors 383–9; introduction to 365; resource allocation in 372–83; social parasitism 377–83, 389–94
cryptic expropriative strategy 380
cultural context of expropriation 388–9
cultural group selection 134–5
cultural ideologies 92, 183
cultural kinship 189
cultural materialism 209–10
cultural memes 262
cultural transmission 262
cultural *vs.* genetic variation 170–2
culture of human brain evolution 357–63

Dahrendorf, Ralf 208
Daly, Martin 234, 388

Darwin, Charles: bio-ecology 103–4; challenge of Darwinian ideas 8–11; fitness benefits of mates 191, 194; functionalism 115–16; human animal comparisons 396; introduction to 1, 2; neo-Darwinian evolutionary theory 135–6, 184–5; organizational ecology 107–12, *108*, *109*, *111*; science of biology 18; second Darwinian revolution 236, 241; sexual selection 155–7, 183, 197, 219; specialization within a society 29; urban ecology *105*, 105–7, *106*; *see also* natural selection models

Darwinian analysis, limitations: individual behavior *vs.* dynamics of superorganisms *247*, 247–50; introduction to 246; multi-level selection with Modern Synthesis 250–4, *253*; sociocultural evolution 254–8; summary of 258–9, 428–9

Darwinian conflict theory (DCT) 206, 209

Darwinian natural selection: basic concepts and principles 124–8; biology and social life 121–4; evolutionary psychology 214; of fitness and kin 132–6; future predictions 180; gender differences 155–6; overview of 30–1, 38, 42, 70–1, 99, 260–4, **261**, *262*; pair bonding 196; reciprocal altruism 136–42; selection dynamics and 257; sociobiology and 128–42

Dawkins, Richard 122, 146–7, 251

deceptive expropriative strategy 380

delayed reciprocity 136–7, 138–9

deme, defined 128–9

demographic context of expropriation 385–7

demographic patterns 202–5

"demographic-structural" model 88

demographic transition 203

Dennett, Daniel 167

depression stage in population 92

Descent of Man and Selection in Relation to Sex, The (Darwin) 249, 250

Descriptive Sociology (Spencer) 40–1, 48

designated reproducer 130

differentiation-integration theory 42–4

directed learning 173

directional selection 342

distribution, defined 39

distributive system of society 386

Division of Labor in Society, The (Durkheim) 2, 5, 20–1, 42–3, 101, 273

domestic productivity 72

dominance hierarchies 366–72

dulosis (slavery) parasitism 391

Durkheim, Emile: collective emotional effervescence 328–9; differentiation-integration theory 42–4; ecological model *101*, 101–2; emotional "effervescence" 415; explanation of religion 181; functional analysis of 20–2; impact of 397; introduction to 3, 5–6; social conflict 208; social evolutionism 210; social facts concept 402, 406; specialization within a society 29, 366

Durkheimian natural selection 33, 273–81, **274**, *275*, **278**

ecological analysis 2, 6, 12–13, 29, 106, 281, 425

ecological approach to evolutionary sociology *101*, 101–2

ecological constraints of megasociality 408

ecological-evolutionary approach 62–7, *63*–5

Ecological-Evolutionary Theory: Principles and Applications (Lenski) 59, 62, 68

ecological theorizing: Blau-Space 110–12, *111*; Chicago School of Urban Ecology 102–5; geopolitical approach 99–100; macro-level of social organization 112–16, *113*, *114*; organizational ecology 107–12, *108*, *109*, *111*; origins of 99–105; summary of 116–17; urban ecology *105*, 105–7, *106*

economic surplus 59

economy as institutional system 253

egoism 6, 43

Elementary Forms of the Religious Life, The (Durkheim) 273

emergent features of human social life 165

emergent reality 175, 397, 400. 406

emergent social structures 248, 289

emotional "effervescence" 415, 419–20

emotional palette 313–14

emotional tags in memory 360–1

emotion-arousing rituals 288

emotions/emotionality: gesture-based language of emotions 324–5, 348; gestures among apes 324–5; neurology of 346–9, **348**; of primates 417–18

empathy 326, 356–7

"end of history" argument 77

epigamic display 152

epigenesis 167, 182, 240

ethnicity in sociobiology and human behavior 188–92

ethnicity/race parameters 279
ethnic parochialism 189
ethnic solidarity 82
ethnocentric biases 3
ethnocentrism 4, 190
eugenics 4, 51, 99, 246
Eurasian pastoralists 96
eusocial insects 121
evolution: adaptation in 121–2; biological evolution 264; driving forces of 246; intersocietal evolution 72; theorizing during Classical Period 37–51, *38*, *42*; universal processes of 146; variations in 255; *see also* cross-species comparative analysis; human brain evolution; intersocietal models of societal evolution; societal evolution
evolutionary biology 121–4, 142
evolutionary dynamics 28–34
evolutionary psychology: adapted mind 234–45; dynamics of superorganisms *247*, 247–50; introduction to 10–11, 214–15; mating attraction and retention 216–34; sociobiology and human behavior 210–13; traits and 226–7
evolutionary sociology: Darwinian ideas 8–11, 135–6; emergence of 1–8; evolutionary psychology 10–11; functionalism 2, 3; human nature 2, 6–8; new evolutionary sociology 424–9; overview of 11–14; social ecology 5–6; societal evolution, stage models 3–5; sociobiological inquiry 187–8; sociobiology 8–10, 249–50
evolutionary stable equilibrium 248
evolution of human brain *see* human brain evolution
Evolution of Human Sexuality, The (Symons) 215
evolved actor 177–83
evolved adaptations 243–5
exchange theory 141, 231, 263, 366
expropriative behavior in animals/humans 377
expropriative strategies 380–9
extra pair paternity (EPP) 224–5
extrinsic cultural information 179
eye expressions among apes 324

facial expressions among apes 324–6
facultative expropriative strategy 382
fairness among apes 421
female preferences for mates 218–23

female *versus* male preferences for mates 218
fertility patterns 202
fertility rates 204
feudalism 3
fictive kinship 189
Field Theory 361
Fischer, Helen 196
Fisher, R. A. 103
fishing communities 48
fitness benefits of mates 191, 194
fitness in natural selection 132–6
fitness maximization 147–8, 203, 211, 214
fitness-teleological variant 214–15
fluctuating asymmetry (FA) 227
forced division of labor 43
formal sociology, defined 365
foundational knowledge 244
Fox, Robin 183–4
Frank, Andre Gunder 74
Freeman, John 108–10, 275
free markets 77, 100
frontal lobe 340
functionalism: apparent death in sociology 21–2; appeal of 28–9; Darwin's functionalism 115–16; Durkheim's functional analysis 20–2, 112, 366; evolutionary dynamics 28–34; Hawley's functionalism 112–15, *113*, *114*; introduction to 2, 3; organismic analogy and 17–20; Parsonian functionalism 25–8; rebirth in sociology 24–8; rise in anthropology 22–4, *23*; sociological conflict theory 208–9; Spencer's functionalism 29–34, 112, 366
functions, defined 112
fundamental categories of human brain 362–3

gender inequality 200
gender relations success factors 192–202
gene-environment interaction 221
gene flow 247
gene pool 262
generalized beliefs 285
genes for patriarchy 244
genetically controlled behaviors 248
genetic determinism 165, 167–9, 397
genetic drift 247
genetic interests 130
genetics: alleles 125, 168–9; cultural *vs.* genetic variation 170–2; development of senses 177; function of 166–7; introduction to 165–6; MAOA

(monoamine oxidase A) gene 168; one gene, one disease (OGOD) model 172; polygenes 172; selfish behavior 138; social behavior 165–77, 325; traits and 226–7
geoeconomics 99, 272
geopolitics 84–6, 99–100
German Ideology, The (Marx, Engels) 282
Gestalt Processes in memory 361–2
gesture-based language of emotions 324–5, 348
Gibbs, Jack P. 228
global warming 266, 267, 301
gluteofemoral fat (GFF) 227
goal attainment in functionalism 25
goal-oriented beings 206–7
Goffman, Erving 328
"golden age" for elites 89–90
Goldstone, Jack 88
good of the group 122–3
good of the individual 123
good of the species 122
Gould, Stephen J. 167, 184, 236, 238–40
Gouldner, Alvin 137
graduated parameters 279–80
great-ape studies *see* cross-species comparative analysis; primates
Great Eurasian Steppe 96
group-based friendships 322
group impermanence of primates 413–14
group-level aggression 9
groupness 323
group selection model 105, 128, 135–6

Haldane, J.B.S. 134
Hall, Thomas 81
Hannan, Michael 108–10, 275
Hannan-Freeman Model of Organizational Ecology 108–10, *109*
haplodiploidy 129–31, 134
Harris, Chauncy 102
Harris, Marvin 209–10
Hawley, Amos 104–5, 106–7, 112–15, *113*, *114*
hegemonic sequences 76
herding communities 48
high-solidarity populations 95
hippocampus 341, 359
historical context of expropriation 388–9
Historical Dynamics (Turchin) 86
Hobson, J. A. 73–4
holistic thinking 177
Homicide (Daly, Wilson) 234
Homo erectus: capacity for teleology 263; culturally organized brains 358–9; neocortex of 307, 350; nuclear family 316, 318; speech production 325
homogamy 189
Homo naledi 307, 350
Homo sapiens: behaviors of humans 322; brain size 349; capacity for teleology 263; culturally organized brains 358–9; human nature, defined 335; neocortex of 307, 314, 350; nuclear family 318; pre-adaptations 310; speech production 325
Hopcroft, Rosemary 193, 197–202, 239
horticultural communities 48–9
HPCP principle 192
Huber, Joan 200–1
Human Area Relations Files 59
human biological phenotypes 251
human brain evolution: archeology of brain 338–42, *339*; brain size among late hominins 349–51; culture and language 357–63; evolved actor and 177–81; fundamental categories 362–3; interpersonal capacities of hominins 351–7, **353**; introduction to 337–8; memory formation 359–62; nature of 342–3; neurological evolution among hominins 346–57, **348**, **353**; neurological evolution among primates 343–6; neurology of emotions 346–9, **348**; organic evolution of 211; organization of 338–43; pre-adaptation and 318; summary of 364
Human Genome Project 170
human-like agency 146
human nature: defined 334–5; introduction to 2, 6–8; nature of 66–7, 309, 310; speculation of 8; summary of 335–6
Human Nature and Biocultural Evolution (Lopreato) 186
human reproductive biology 223
humans and constraints of megasociality 410
human social universe 255–6
Humboldt, Alexander 70
hunter gatherer societies 48, 60, 332–3
Hymenoptera 131

illegitimate teleology 19
inclusive fitness 132–4, 206
income gap 89
individualism: aggression 9; of apes 421–3; attributes 368–9; behaviors *247*, 247–50; mobility and 322–4

industrial capitalism 6
industrialization 100
industrial societies 49, *56*
inertia 69
infant mortality 204
inferior parietal lobe in the brain 312
infidelity as adaptive problem 230
infidelity over perception bias 232
innovation-generating machines 270
input-output analysis 26
inquilinism (permanent parasitism) 391
institutionalization of behaviors 249
institutionalization of competition 106, 276
institutional system of law 51
institutions 270
intelligence quotient (IQ) 235
interaction principle 167, 169
interdemic selection 128–9
interdependencies 69
internal fertilization 216
internal social organization in megasociality 400–1
international black markets 266
interpersonal capacities of hominins 351–7, **353**
interpersonal compatibility 222
intersexual selection 155, 157–9, 187
intersocietal models of societal evolution: Axial (pivotal) Age 95–7; Chase-Dunn, Christopher 77–84, *79*; directional nature of 83–4; early analysis of 72–3; geopolitical approach 100; geopolitics 84–6; phases within cycle *90*, 90–3; scaling up societies for war 93–5; summary of 97–8; theory of political cycles 86–8; ultrasocieties 93–7; Wallerstein, Immanuel 74–7; world systems 73–84, *79*
intersocietal warfare 50
intrasexual competition 187, 195
Irwin, Michael D. 103
iterated interaction 388

jealously and retention 230–2
Juglar cycles 76, 83
justice among apes 421
justice and fairness 329–30
just-so story problem 236–40

Kanazawa, Satoshi 234–5
Keller, Albert Galloway 59
key functions, defined 112
Khaldun, Ibn 86–8

killing instinct 8
kin recognition 189
kin selection 128, 132–7, 183, 191, 206
kinship system 50, 320
kleptoparasitism 378, 384–5
Kondratieff waves (K-waves) 75, 83
Kristof, Frank 373
Kuznet cycle 76

labor exploitation 45
Lamarckian ideas 267
language: body language 325, 419; of emotions 419; gesture-based language of emotions 324–5, 348; human brain evolution 357–63; musilanguage 327; pre-adaptations among apes 311–13; proto-language 327–8; quasi-language of emotions 313; quasi-language system 313, 357; spoken language system 358
latency in functionalism 25
law of evolution 18–19
learning *vs.* instinct 172–5
legitimacy/legitimating ideology 19, 108–9
Lenski, Gerhard 51, *54*, *56*, 58–71, *63*–5
Lewontin, Richard 184
life history characteristics 317–18
life-sustaining resources 261
lifetime reproductive success of women 218
long-chain polyunsaturated fatty acids (LCPUFAS) 227
looking-glass self 330–1
Lopreato, Joseph 150–1, 184–9, 203
Lorez, Konrad 9
low primitive stage 53–4
low-quality genes 152
Lumsden, Charles 173, 177

Machalek, Richard 396, 427–9
MacLean, Paul 338
macro-level of social organization 112–16, *113*, *114*
macrosociality 137, 320, 416–23
maladaptive consequences 125, 220
male dominance 244
male-female behavioral differences 149–55, 155–7, 180
male-female pair bond 193
male-male competition 155, 157–9, 195
male providers 222
male sexual jealousy 225–6
Malinowski, Bronislaw 22–4, *23*, 35
mammalian play 318–19
manipulative expropriative strategy 381–2
MAOA (monoamine oxidase A) gene 168

market system 50
Marx, Karl: alienation analysis 263; introduction to 3–4; societal evolution theory stage models 44–6; sociological conflict theory 208; species being 121
Marxian selection 269, 273, 281–9, **284**, *285*
Maryanski, Alexandra 295–9, 352, 396–7, 428
mate guarding 154
mate value 219, 238
mating attraction and retention: evolutionary psychology 216–34; female preferences 218–23; female retention 231–2; female *versus* male preferences 218; introduction to 216–18; male preferences 223–8; male retention 228–31, 232–4; selection 187; strategies 193; success factors 192–202, 216–34
matrilines 300–1, 316, 332
Matthew Principle 94
Mazur, Allan 366–7
McPherson, J. Miller 110–11, *111*, 279–80
Mead, George Herbert 4, 6–7, 330, 359
mechanical societal integration 20
mechanical solidarity 42–3
medical care system 251
megasociality in ants: behavioral biology 398–9; colony homeostasis 405–7; introduction to 396, 397–407; population traits 402–3; self-assembly constraints on 407–10; series-parallel operations 405; social parasitism and 390; social structure of 403–4; summary of 407–10; superorganisms and 399–407
megasociality in primates: behavioral propensities 419–23; cladistic analysis of 412–13; community implications 414–15; group organization 413–14; macrosociality 137, 416–23; pre-adaptation and 320; summary of 423
meme pool 262
memory formation 359–62
Mendel, Gregor 424
Merton, Robert K. 208
meso-level ecological analysis 112
microeconomic theories 235
mimicry 326–8, 419–21
minimum endogamous set (MES) 191–2
mirror neurons 326–8
mischief-making activities 190

mobility among apes 322–4, 421–3
mobility costs 113
model of geopolitics 73
modernity, transition to 57–8
modern societies 53, *58*
Modern Synthesis: in biology 67, 142; Darwinian natural selection 246–8, *262*, 289–90; forces of evolution 260; introduction to 28–30, 33; multi-level selection 250–4, *253*
monopolies 76
Moody, Michael 375
moralistic aggression 140–1
morality in mammals 330
morality of humans 354–6
morals in cultural codes 69
morphemes 347–8
morphological adaptation 125
mother-infant bonding 314–15, 338, 412
multiharem groups 194
multi-level selection 34, 134, 248, 250–4, *253*
Muquaddimah: An Introduction to History, The (Khaldun) 86
Murdock, George P. 40, 59
musilanguage 327
mutations 247, 342
mutual attraction-love 227–8
mutual influence 185
myrmecophiles 392

natural selection models: Darwinian model of 260–4, **261**, *262*; Durkheimian natural selection 33, 273–81, **274**, *275*, *278*; Marxian selection 269, 273, 281–9, **284**, *285*; Spencerian natural selection 264–73, **268**, *268*, **271**, *271*; summary of 289–90, 427; *see also* Darwin, Charles; Darwinian natural selection
neoclassical equilibrium model in economics 87
neocortex 330–1, 349–51
neo-Darwinian evolutionary theory 135–6, 184–5, 222, 234, 386
nepotism 190
neuroactive peptides 341
neurological evolution among hominins 346–57, **348**, **353**
neurological evolution among primates 343–6
neurology of emotions 346–9, **348**
neurosociology *see* human brain evolution
neurotransmitters 341
new evolutionary sociology 424–9

Newtonian physics 1
niche market cultures 109–10
Nolan, Patrick 67
nominal parameters 279–80
non-human social behavior 367
non-reciprocal exchanges 374–5
normative legitimacy 108–9
norm of reaction 170
novel environments 180–1
nuclear family 316, 318

obligate expropriative strategy 382
occipital lobe in the brain 312
Old World monkeys 295–9, **298**
olfactory dominance 311
oligopolies 76
one gene, one disease (OGOD) model 172
one species science 121
On the Origins of Species (Darwin) 5, 17, 128, 209, 264
open-country habitat 310, 414
opportunistic expropriative strategy 381
opportunity costs 200
oral traditions 24
ordering memories 360–2
organic evolution 124–6
organic societal integration 20
organic solidarity 42–3
organismic analogy: constraints of megasociality 408; evolution of superorganisms 256; functionalism and 17–20; introduction to 1–2; phenotypes 251
organisms, defined 40
organizational ecology 107–12, *108, 109, 111*
organization systems 27–8
oscillations 75
out-group population 295
out-of-date distribution systems 109

pair bonding 196, 229
palette of emotions 313–14
parameters, defined 279–80
parasitism (social) in animal/human societies 377–83
parental collaboration hypothesis 193–4
parental confidence 193
parental investment (PI) 123, 150, 192–3, 216, 225
parental uncertainty 154
parenting strategies 187, 193
parenting success factors 192–202
parent-offspring conflict 159–61

Pareto, Vilfredo 7, 186, 388
parietal lobe in the brain 312
Park, Robert 102, 104
Parsonian functionalism 25–8
Parsons, Talcott 51–7, 208, 210
passionate love 229
pastoral communities 48
paternity uncertainty 154, 197
pattern maintenance in functionalism 25
peripheral states 75
phenotypes/phenotypic traits: altruistic behavior 138; cladistic analysis 294–5, 303; classification of categories 125–6; corporate-unit phenotypes 114, 257, 274–6, 281; environmental variation 171–2; human biological phenotypes 251; organismic phenotypes 251; population-to-population phenotype transfer 63; sociocultural phenotypes 135; species-typical trait preferences 178, 226–7
physical attractiveness 216
physical context of expropriation 384–7
physical violence against mates 233–4
physiographic features 88
physiological adaptation 126
Pinker, Steven 240, 242
Pleistocene era 337
pluralistic mating repertoire 216
political democracy 77
political-military networks (PMNs) 81, 83
polity system 50
polyandry 161, 216, 217, 316
polygamy 216–17, 316
polygenes 172
polygyny 161, 194–5, 216, 217
population systems: density 89–92; growth 80; introduction to 31–2; size in megasociality 400; traits 402–3
population-to-population phenotype transfer 63
post-industrial period 61
Power and Privilege: A Theory of Stratification (Lenski) 58, 61, 65
power-dependency relationship 232
power elite 208
pre-adaptations among apes: among language 311–13; human nature, defined 334–5; introduction to 310–11; life history characteristics 317–18; macrosociality 416–18; mammalian play 318–19; mother-infant bonding 314–15; palette of emotions 313–14
precocial birth 153

predisposition patterns 187
primates: cladistic analysis 294–301, **298**; community organization of primates 416–17; emotionality of primates 417–18; evolution and visual dominance 343–6; great ape social structures 295–9, **298**; implications for evolutionary sociology 301–7, **302**; introduction to 293–4; mating of 195–6; neurological evolution among 343–6; rapid decline of 301–3, **302**; savanna-dwelling apes 303–7; sexual promiscuity of 413–14; summary of 307–8; transfer patterns of 413–14; visual dominance in early primate evolution 343–6; weak ties of 413–14; *see also* behavioral propensities among apes; megasociality in primates
primitive communism 3
primitive societies 53, *54*
Principles of Biology, The (Spencer) 18, 31
Principles of Sociology, The (Spencer) 1, 18, 20, 30, 35, 40–1, 48
production, defined 39
promiscuity 216–17, 223–4, 296, 300, 315–16, 413–14
proto-language 327–8
proto-morality 354–6, 421
proximate causation 144
putative kinship 189

quasi-language system 313, 357
quasi-markets 110, 280

racism 4
Radcliffe-Brown, A. R. 22, 27
rational choice theory 141
rational conflict theory 206–8
rationalism 46
reciprocal altruism 136–42, 189, 249
reciprocity among apes 329, 421
reckoning of community 352–4, **353**
reconstruction of human societies 334
reductionism 165, 397
reductionistic thinking 177, 243–4
regularity hypothesis 295
regulation, defined 39
related hypothesis 295
religion and warfare 95–6
religious beliefs/systems 50, 279, 288
reproduction, defined 39
reproductive resources 216
reproductive success 123, 192–202
residues, defined 186

resource advantages 84
resource allocation in comparative sociology 372–83
resource collection 207
resource holding potential (RHP) 222
rhythmic synchronization 326–8, 419–21
Richerson, Peter J. 103
ritual behaviors 326–8, 419–21
role-taking 326, 356–7, 419
Rules of the Sociological Method, The (Durkheim) 21

Sanderson, Stephen K. 206, 246
sauce béarnaise effect 173
savanna-dwelling apes 303–7
Savanna-IQ Interaction Hypothesis 235
scaling up societies for war 93–5
Schmidt, David 217
science of human society 365–6
second Darwinian revolution 236, 241
secular cycles *90*, 90–3
Secular Cycles (Turchin, Nefedov) 88
selectionist dynamics in superorganisms 283
self as object in environment 330–2
self-assembly constraints of megasociality 407–10
self-esteem 198–9
self-identification with religious beliefs 288
semiochemicals 399
semi-peripheral states 75
sense of self among apes 421–3
sentiments, defined 186
serial reciprocity 375
series-parallel operations 405
sex ratios 202
sex-specific behaviors 187
sexual feelings in mammals 316
sexual orientation parameters 279
sexual promiscuity of primates 413–14
sexual selection 155–7, 183, 197, 219
sexual strategies theory 215, 217
Simmel, Georg 4, 47–8, 208, 365
Simmelian social types 225
simple-homogeneous masses 266
Skinner, B. F. 355
social behavior 145
social commensalism 139
social conflict 205–10, 282
social context of dominance hierarchies 369–72
social control 355
Social Darwinism: eugenics movement and 51, 99; introduction to 4, 5,

246; overview of 8–11; rise of 165; ultrasocieties 93
social ecology 5–6
social environment 126, 164
social evolutionism 210
social facts concept 402, 406
socialization of individuals 68
social life 121–4
social movement organization (SMO) 283, 286
social mutualism 139
social parasitism 139, 377–83, 389–94
social speciation 101
social structures: context of expropriation 387–8; in Great-Ape societies 295–9, *298*; on macro-level 112–16, *113*, *114*; of megasociality 403–4; in Old World monkeys 295–9, **298**
social symbioses 139
societal community 58
societal evolution: additional theorizing 41–8, *42*; advanced intermediate societies 57; advanced primitive stage 55; archaic stage 55–6; in Classical Period 37–51, *38*, *42*; Comte, Auguste *38*, 38–9; in contemporary era 51–70, *54*, *56*, *63*–5; Durkheim, Emile 42–4; early theory of *38*, 38–9, 59–62, *54*, *56*; ecological-evolutionary approach 62–7, *63*–5; geopolitical approach 100; introduction to 3–5, 37; legacy of 48–51; Lenski, Gerhard 58–71, *54*, *56*, *63*–5; low primitive stage 53–4; Marx, Karl 44–6; Parsons, Talcott 51–7; Simmel, Georg 47–8; societal macrostructures 67–70; Spencer, Herbert 39–41, *42*; summary of 70–1, 288, 425; transition to modernity 57–8; Weber, Max 46–7
societal integration 20
societal-level cohesion 190
societal macrostructures 67–70
societal solidarity 82
Societies: An Introduction to Macrosociology (Nolan, Lenski) 59
Societies: Evolutionary and Comparative Perspectives (Parsons) 51–2
sociobiology: adapted mind 235–6; intersexual selection 155, 157–9; introduction to 8–10, 144–46; natural selection and 128–42; other social behavior 161–2; overview of 146–9; parent-offspring conflict 159–61; reproductive partners 149–55; sex and reproduction 149–61; sexual selection and gender behavior 155–7
Sociobiology: The New Synthesis (Wilson) 8, 124, 173, 183, 202, 367
sociobiology and human behavior: analysis of 183–6; basic contours of 186–8; biological reductionism 175–7; cultural *vs.* genetic variation 170–2; demographic patterns 202–5; ethnicity in 188–92; evolutionary psychology 210–13; evolved actor and 177–83; genetic determinism *vs.* 165, 167–9; genetics and 165–77; introduction 164–5; learning *vs.* instinct 172–5; social conflict 205–10; survival and reproductive success factors 192–202
sociocultural death 257
sociocultural evolution 126, 135, 254–8
sociocultural formations 250, 252–3, *253*
sociocultural phenotypes 135
sociological conflict theory 208–9
sociological constraints on megasociality 409
sociologically obvious 142
sociology, defined 1
solidarity in humans 324
somatic resources 216, 231
sophisticated reductionist thinking 243
Soviet Union 20, 85
speciation 5–6, 21, 42, 67, 115, 247
species being 121
species-typical trait preferences 178, 181
Spencer, Herbert: functionalism and 29–34, 112; geopolitical approach to ecological theorizing 99–100; intersocietal evolution 72; introduction to 1, 5, 17–18; law of evolution 18–19; Modern Synthesis 28–30, 33, 246; organismic analogy 17–18, 396; social evolutionism 210; societal evolution theory 39–41, *42*, 86, 366; world system evolution 80
Spencerian natural selection 33, 35, 264–73, **268**, *268*, **271**, *271*
sperm competition 195–6
sperm production 223
spoken language system 358
status groups 190
stratification systems 256
structural-functionalism 208
substructural systems 44
superorganisms: defined 40; dynamics of *247*, 247–50; evolution of 256; human biological phenotypes and 251;

introduction to 1, 3, 17; megasociality and 399–407; overview of 1, 3, 17, 31, 35; selectionist dynamics in 283; sociocultural evolution of 135
superstructural systems 44
survival machines 135, 251, 252
survival of the fittest 30, 99, 248, 264
survival success factors 192–202
Symons, Donald 215
System of Modern Societies (Parsons) 52

Taoism 96
target of selection 127
tautological problems 19
technology impact on production 113–14
teleological organism 267
temporal lobe in the brain 312
temporary social parasitism 391
tension management in functionalism 25
territoriality 190
Theory of Mind 353–4
theory of political cycles 86–8
Theory of the Leisure Class, The (Veblen) 233
three-dimensional environment 311
Tiger, Lionel 183–4
Tooby, John 211–12, 214–15
trans-familial forms of social organization 189
transfer patterns of primates 413–14
trophallaxis, defined 139
trophobiosis, defined 140
Turchin, Peter 85–97, 396
Turner, Jonathan H. 33, 71, 265, 312, 396–7, 428–9
two-child psychology 205
Type-1 Spencerian Selection 265–70, **268**, *268*, 289
Type-2 Spencerian selection 270–3, **271**, *271*, 289

ultrasociality 93–7, 320, 396
Ultra Society (Turchin) 93
unilateral reciprocity 136
unit of heredity 127
universal processes of evolution 146
urban ecology *105*, 105–7, *106*
urbanization 4, 89, 91–2, 203

vacancy chains in animal/human societies 373–83
vampire bats, reciprocal altruism 141
van den Berghe, Pierre 184, 188
variable environmental contexts 170
variations in evolution 255
Veblen, Thorstein 146–7, 233
verified knowledge 277
vertebrae amphibian brain 338
vigilance to violence 233
visual dominance 312, 343–6

waist-to-hip ratio (WHP) 227
Wallerstein, Immanuel 74–7
warfare in Axial (pivotal) Age 95–7
weak ties of primates 413–14
Weber, Max: expropriation studies 388; intersocietal evolution 72; introduction to 4; model of geopolitics 73; societal evolution theory stage models 46–7; sociological conflict theory 208, 209; status groups 190
Wernicke's area of the brain 341, 350
Wheeler, William Morton 400
Whitmeyer, Joseph 188, 190–1
Williams, George C. 122, 212, 241–2
Wilson, D. S. 134
Wilson, E. O. 8, 124, 134, 173–7, 206, 211, 214, 243–5, 397
Wilson, Margo 234, 388
Wirth, Louis 102
world economies 74
world empires 74
world systems: dynamics of growth 81–3; key properties of 78–81, *79*; overview of 74–7; rise of 73–7
Wynne-Edwards, V. C. 128–9